# A HANDBOOK TO LITERATURE

# A HANDBOOK TO
# LITERATURE

*With an Outline of Literary History*
*English and American*

BY

## WILLIAM FLINT THRALL

*Professor of English*
*University of North Carolina*

AND

## ADDISON HIBBARD

*Professor of English and*
*Dean of the College of Liberal Arts*
*Northwestern University*

## DOUBLEDAY, DORAN & COMPANY, INC.
*Garden City, New York*

PRINTED AT THE *Country Life Press*, GARDEN CITY, N. Y., U. S. A.

# PREFACE

Neither is a dictionary a bad book to read. There is no cant in it, no excess of explanation, and it is full of suggestion,—the raw material of possible poems and histories. Nothing is wanting but a little shuffling, sorting, ligature, and cartilage.

—Ralph Waldo Emerson

In preparing this volume the authors have had one major object in mind: to make readily clear to those engaged in the study of English and American literature the most important items in the framework of their study.

Their object has been to set the student or the general reader free for appreciation, for study of the different masterpieces, for a knowledge of authors and literary cultures, for, in fact, the more legitimate purposes of literary study, by placing before him for ready reference such factual information as he may want as a basis for the actual study of literature itself. The authors have, as no doubt have many teachers of English, too often felt the limitation on effective teaching which comes from interrupting the study of a piece of writing in order to discuss terms and mechanical matters of form and history. This handbook should minimize these interruptions.

This has been the chief purpose of their work. In this handbook are included brief explanations of the various rhetorical terms; somewhat more complete discussions of historical periods, and the various literary types and the forms of poetry; and chronological material systematically arranged to make clear the progress of the literature of England and America throughout the centuries. The book is, then, a presentation of the skeleton of literature rather than of the flesh, blood, mind, and spirit of literature itself.

The authors of the volume believe that in this book they have done something new. They know of scores of handbooks of composition but of no handbook to literature designed to meet the same purpose or attempting the exact features of this volume. But in claiming this distinction for their work, they realize, too, that they must assume the responsibilities which go with pioneer work. The enthusiasm which they have found in their work has been tempered always by a deep sense of their presumption in the attempt. Once they were fairly launched on the book, they learned only too well why this thing had not been done before. They were constantly aware of certain difficulties: Which items should be included and which omitted? How can one say in the space available all that should be said about romance or realism, about poetry or the essay, about Puritanism or the Renaissance? How can one dogmatize in a few hundred words on an aspect of literature as general as "imagery" or as comprehensive as "Arthurian romance"?

The only answer they can give to such questions as these is that they think the effort to be worth making, impossible of perfect accomplishment as it is. One of the chief charges students bring against English instruction is its nebulousness—the failure of instructors to be definite and specific. And, while the authors know that this unwillingness to dogmatize is often one of the chief virtues of instruction in English, they know, too, that definiteness is no crime when it can be secured in such matters as form and literary history. In keeping before them this ideal of definiteness, they recall, nevertheless, that they are not writing primarily for scholars who are specialists in a particular field; they make no plea of this fact, however, to excuse anything that might be downright misinformation. In a book attempting as many different facets of the study as this one does, errors and mistakes in emphasis are bound to creep in.

A word of explanation regarding the preparation of the items defined is perhaps justified. The authors have attempted, in each of the more important discussions, to attain four objectives: to explain briefly the meaning and use of the term itself; to give something of the history of the form discussed; to present, when possible, illustrations and examples which will make concrete the significance of the term; and, in some cases, to cite references for the further study of the subject. The question of scale has

# PREFACE

been a constant problem. The writers of this handbook have wanted to present discussions more fully than they are set forth in a dictionary and much more succinctly than they are developed in a special volume given to one subject. They have not attempted to be exhaustive. Again they have given little attention to significances other than the literary in such terms as bear importance in other fields as well as in the study of literature. They have, in short, tried to focus always on what the general reader or the college undergraduate may reasonably be expected to know on any *one* subject.

And finally, a word regarding indebtedness to sources. Teachers who have presented their material for many years draw their ideas and convictions from many directions which are not, in retrospect, always easy to fix. Old notes from scattered reading, discussions with colleagues, special lectures attended, theses and dissertations of students which have passed through their hands, as well as conscious study of sources and originals—all these somehow become the miscellaneous furniture of teachers' minds. This the authors admit. Furthermore, such general references as the Cambridge histories of English and American literature, Garnett and Gosse's *English Literature*, and the special articles in the *Encyclopædia Brittanica* have been frequently consulted. In particular fields they are often indebted to special books, such as Helen Louise Cohen's *Lyric Forms from France*, R. M. Alden's *English Verse*, Frederick Ryland's *Chronological Outlines of English Literature*, Professor Allardyce Nicoll's several books on the drama, and the Manly-Rickert volumes on contemporary British and American literature—an indebtedness which they have tried consistently to acknowledge either in the discussion of the particular items or elsewhere. The references frequently cited either refer to sources used by the authors or are to be taken as suggestions to the student for further study of the special topic.

For particular assistance in the preparation of this volume the writers take real pleasure in acknowledging the valuable help given by Miss Leonora Watts, Mrs. Helen Drynan Cameron, and Mrs. Rosalie Thrall Carmichael. For valuable criticism of the contents, they are indebted to Dr. John Webster Spargo of Northwestern University, and to Dr. George Raleigh Coffman,

# PREFACE

Dr. Richmond P. Bond, Dr. E. E. Ericson, Dr. Dougald MacMillan, and Dr. R. B. Sharpe of the University of North Carolina, who have read various parts of the manuscript. Others of their colleagues also have assisted generously in various ways. For the final form which the material assumes, however, the authors alone are to be held responsible.

WILLIAM FLINT THRALL
ADDISON HIBBARD

January, 1936

# CONTENTS

# A HANDBOOK TO LITERATURE

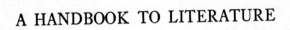

*Dictionaries are like watches; the worst is better than none, and the best cannot be expected to go quite true.*

—Doctor Johnson

# HANDBOOK TO LITERATURE

NOTE: Although the authors do not claim to have achieved complete logical consistency in their selection of terms for inclusion in this handbook, they have meant in the main to *exclude* mere allusion items, mythological terms, titles of books, names of authors, characters in fiction, and "literary curiosities"; and to *include* words and phrases useful to the student of literature as found in criticism, rhetoric, literary history, and versification, including terminology reflecting efforts to classify literature by types, forms, and traditions. Some items, including terms drawn from history and philosophy, have been included because of their "background" value, whether placeable in these categories or not. But no effort has been made to give a complete or even a balanced list of terms drawn from such allied fields, since expansion in these directions would add unreasonably to the bulk of matter and would run counter to the central objective of this handbook —the explanation of *literary* terms. Some terms logically admissible, too, have been omitted because they are treated adequately in general dictionaries or because they were regarded as of distinctly minor importance.

**Abstract Words:** Words which represent ideas or generalities as opposed to concrete or specific words representing particular objects or qualities. Abstract terms, such as "function," "legislation," "veracity," arouse little emotional or imaginative response in the reader; specific or concrete words by their very connotative qualities awake the imagination and create vivid mental pictures. "Darkness" is an abstraction; "gloaming," since it is a particular kind of darkness at a particular time of day and carries with it for the reader certain experiences associated with this time, is a specific or particular word. An experiment which will throw much light on the difference between abstract and specific words is looking up such a general word as "pain" in a good dictionary and pondering the specific varieties of pain there listed, such as "ache," "smart," "twinge," "gripe." Generally speaking, writing is likely to be classed as interesting when the number of abstract words in relation to specific words is few, and as dull when their number is many. However, as philosophical writing necessarily is largely abstract in nature whereas an account telling how to build a gas-engine is pretty likely to be specific—allowances must be made to avoid a too rigid application of this principle. See CONCRETE TERMS.

**Academic Drama:** One of the most important traditions contributing to the development of Elizabethan drama was the practice of writing and performing plays at schools. Little is known of the history, extent, or character of dramatic activities in universities before the Renaissance, though there is some evidence that student plays existed throughout the late Middle Ages. Records of school plays from the fifteenth century possibly refer to such medieval forms as "disguisings" (see MASQUE). The interest in Latin drama aroused by the Italian Renaissance (Petrarch wrote a Terentian comedy about 1331) led to translations and imitations of Plautus and Terence in other countries, such as Germany and Holland (where school plays of the "Prodigal Son" formula flourished), and eventually England (early sixteenth century). Boys in grammar schools (St. Paul's, Eton) acted both classical and original plays in the 1520's. By 1560 both Latin and English plays were produced at Eton, and in Spenser's time (1560's) Richard Mulcaster's boys at the Merchant Taylors School performed plays annually before the queen. Nicholas Udall's *Ralph Roister Doister*, probably written before 1553 for performance by the boys of Westminster School, is regarded as the first regular English comedy.

However important the production of plays in the grammar schools may have been, of still greater significance in the development of the drama was the practice, common in the sixteenth century, of writing and performing plays at the universities. Plays of Terence were acted by undergraduates in Cambridge as early as 1510. In 1546 at Trinity College, Cambridge, refusal of a student to take part in a play was punishable by expulsion. Though the primary purpose of the plays was educational, entertainment for its own sake was more and more recognized, and the use of English became more and more common. When Queen Elizabeth visited Cambridge in 1564 and Oxford in 1566 she was entertained with series of plays

4

of various types, foreshadowing later forms on the Elizabethan stage. The earliest extant university play in English is *Gammer Gurton's Needle* (written perhaps *ca.*1560). Some university pieces were connected with later Elizabethan plays, such as Thomas Legge's Senecan tragedy on Richard III, which may have contributed features to Shakespeare's play.

The full influence of academic drama upon the professional stage can only be estimated, but it is to be remembered that the "University Wits" (*q.v.*) left the universities at a time when academic plays were flourishing and went to London to play important rôles during the formative period of Elizabethan drama. In the main the academic drama transmitted to the professional drama the classical forms and techniques represented by Seneca in tragedy and by Plautus and Terence in comedy, though Italian sources were also employed. One interesting group of university plays had to do with problems of student life, such as town *vs.* college quarrels, an important instance being the trilogy of "Parnassus" plays at Cambridge about 1600, which incidentally reflect also the close connection then existing between dramatic interests in London and the universities. The plays were most commonly performed at night in the college hall before a restricted audience. The actors were costumed. (References: F. S. Boas, *University Drama in the Tudor Age* and Chap. xiv of *Camb. Hist. of Eng. Lit.*, Vol. VI; T. H. Vail Motter, *The School Drama in England*.)

**Academies:** Associations of literary, artistic, or scientific men brought together for the advancement of culture and learning within their special fields of interests. The term is derived from "the olive grove of Academe" where Plato taught at Athens. Though there are thousands of academies of one sort or another bringing together men of similar interests, there are in each country a few prominent organizations usually with some sort of official or national responsibility. The Royal Society of England, for example, has agreed to render such service as it can to the British government in the realm of science, and the governmental authorities have often called upon it for the solution of scientific problems. One general purpose of the literary academies has been, to quote the expressed purpose of *l'Académie*

5

*française* (originated *ca*.1629),"to labor with all care and diligence to give certain rules to our language and to render it pure, eloquent, and capable of treating the arts and sciences." A secondary objective has often been that of immortalizing great writers, though the success with which great writers have been recognized by such organizations is definitely a moot point. In addition to the French Academy and the Royal Society— already mentioned—the following ought to be cited: The Royal Academy of Arts founded in 1768 (England); the *Real Academia Española* founded in 1713 (Spain); and the American Academy of Arts and Letters (*q.v.*) founded in 1904 (United States). More like the original academy of Plato was the famous "Platonic Academy" led by Marsilio Ficino, which flourished at Florence, Italy, in the late fifteenth century and from which were disseminated the doctrines of Neo-Platonism (see PLATONISM) which colored much Renaissance English literature.

**Acatalectic:** See CATALEXIS.

**Accent:** In literary usage the most important application of the term is in reference to versification, where the orderly repetition of accent at stated intervals in the verse goes far towards determining the poetic quality of the writing and fixes the rhythm of the line. The Greeks and Romans measured poetic feet by the quantity of the syllables; in English verse, accent is the dominant determining influence. The English *accented* syllable is roughly equivalent to the Greek *long* syllable and the *unaccented* syllable to the Greek *short* syllable. The relation of accent to meter and versification is clear from the following example:

Ĭ come | frŏm haunts | ŏf coot | ănd hern

The whole question of accent and its relation to quantity is one of the most difficult of all problems of English versification. Certainly the quantity of a word or a syllable, even in English prosody, plays an important part in determining accent. For our purposes accent may be thought of as stress (emphasis in pronunciation) and quantity (*q.v.*) as that quality inherent in the sound of a syllable which, if it is long, makes it likely that the syllable will receive the accent or, if it is short, that it will be unaccented. In English verse, however, the quantity of a syllable is not the only factor which decides accent, since the rhetorical importance of a word, the place of the word in the grammatical structure of the line, or even etymological reasons may dictate that accent be accorded a word normally short. Thus *din* (short) might be unaccented and *dawn* (long) would usually be accented, but the other factors mentioned immediately above may demand that in a given line the accent fall on *din*, a quantitatively short syllable. Perhaps the best brief explanation of the inter-relationship existing between accent and quantity is to say that the accent pattern of a verse helps to fix the stress of a syllable, and that the quantity of a syllable often helps to determine the accent pattern. Accent is emphasis in pronunciation given certain syllables according to some dominant metrical pattern; quantity is one means by which words and syllables are adjusted to this pattern, one means even of determining the pattern. For a concise yet adequate introductory treatment of the problems of accent and quantity, see R. M. Alden, *Introduction to Poetry*, pp. 155–221. See QUANTITY, ICTUS, SCANSION.

**Acrostic:** Usually verse, though sometimes a piece of prose composition, arranged in such a way as to present names or phrases or sentences when certain letters selected according to an orderly sequence are brought together. The most simple acrostic forms use the first or last letter of each line; there are other more complicated types such as that which uses the first letter of the first line, the second letter of the second line, etc. The form is very old, having been used by early Greek and Latin writers as well as by the monks of the Middle Ages. Though some creditable verse has appeared in this form, acrostics are likely to be little more than tricks of versifying. An example of acrostic form presented through a conundrum follows: 1. By Apollo was my first made. 2. A shoemaker's tool. 3. An Italian patriot. 4. A tropical fruit. Answer: *Lamb* and *Elia* as shown in the wording:

| | | | |
|---|---|---|---|
| 1. | L | yr | E |
| 2. | A | w | L |
| 3. | M | azzin | I |
| 4. | B | anan | A |

**Acts** (of a Drama): The major parts of a Greek drama were distinguished from each other by the appearance of the Chorus. The Latin tragedies of Seneca were divided into five acts, a plan followed by English and other modern European dramatists. Though the division into five acts, in some cases and to some degree, may correspond to the five main divisions of the action (see DRAMATIC STRUCTURE), Freytag even going so far as to speak of the "act of the introduction," the "act of the ascent," the "act of the climax," the "act of the descent," and the "act of the catastrophe," it is certain that this correspondence, especially in Elizabethan plays, is not always present. The climax, for example, may come in the fourth act. Miss Woodbridge notes that the division into acts is partly a matter of stage convenience: "It gives the audience time to relax, and the actors time for rest or for change of costume; it furnishes opportunity for extensive scene-shifting."[1] It also allows the author greater freedom in assuming the passage of time. It must be remembered that the early texts of Elizabethan plays do not always indicate act-divisions, and that the lack of a curtain on the Elizabethan stage tended to make the change of acts unemphatic. Some authorities insist that the internal structure of the act should follow in general the pyramidal five-part form of the play itself, but such unity and structural plan cannot always be found. The acts in Shakespeare's dramas, for example, vary widely in this respect. In the nineteenth century the use of the act as a structural unit came to be less and less insisted upon. After 1880 the conventional five-act play gave way to plays of fewer acts. While plays of two acts and plays of four acts are not unknown, the three-act play is most common on the present-day stage. Late in the nineteenth century the "one-act play" (*q.v.*) developed and is now recognized as a separate *genre*. (Reference: see under DRAMATIC STRUCTURE.)

**Adage:** A proverb or wise saying made familiar by long use. Example: "No bees, no honey" (Erasmus, *Adagia*). See PROVERB.

---

[1]Elisabeth Woodbridge (Morris), *The Drama, Its Law and Its Technique*, Allyn and Bacon, 1898, p. 94. Reprinted by permission of the publishers.

**Adonic Verse:** A verse form associated with Greek and Latin prosody and denoting that meter which consists of a dactyl and a spondee, as ― ◡ ◡ | ― ―.

**Alcaics:** Verses written according to the manner of the odes of Alcaeus; that is, a four-strophe poem, each strophe composed of four lines, each line having four stresses. Since the pattern is a classical one based on quantitative measures, the type can only be imitated in English; exact English Alcaics are practically impossible.

**Alexandrine:** A verse line with six iambic feet (iambic hexameter). The form, that of heroic verse in France, received its name possibly from the fact that it was much used in Old French romances of the twelfth and thirteenth centuries describing the adventures of Alexander the Great, possibly from the name of Alexandre Paris, a French poet who used this meter. Its appearance in English verse has been credited to Wyatt and Surrey. Perhaps the most conspicuous instance of its successful use in English is by Spenser, who, in his Spenserian stanza, after eight pentameter lines employed a hexameter (Alexandrine) in the ninth line. An example of Alexandrine lines in recent English verse is found in Browning's *Fifine at the Fair:*

> If hunger, proverbs say, allures the wolf from wood,
> Much more the bird must dare a dash at something good.

**Allegory:** The treatment of a subject, an action, or a description in which the objects or incidents or people are presented through personification or symbolism. Rhetorically, the term signifies almost any extended metaphor, the chief requirement in this loose usage being simply that the passage convey a meaning other than, and above, the actual. Fables and parables are frequent forms of allegory. Medieval literature is particularly full of allegory and, in England at least, the form is very likely to be moral in purport. Conspicuous examples of sustained allegory are: *Everyman, The Vision of Piers Plowman, The Faerie Queene,* and *Pilgrim's Progress.*

**Alliteration:** The repetition of the initial letter or sound in two or more closely associated words or stressed syllables. An example of alliteration through the repetition of initial letters is found in Young's

> When *f*ortitude has lost its *f*ire,
> And *f*reezes into *f*ear—

The use of similar sounds for alliterative effect is evident in Tennyson's often quoted lines:

> The *m*oan of doves in i*mm*emorial el*m*s,
> And *m*ur*m*uring of innu*m*erable bees.

In modern English largely an ornament of poetry, alliteration in the primitive writing of many races was a vital structural element. Old English, Icelandic, and Middle English poets made much of the form and gave it an importance which has made its influence felt from that time through Langland, Chaucer, Spenser, Milton, and Coleridge, to Swinburne and Poe, and well into modern poetry. The device, however, is not restricted to poetry; Ruskin and others have practiced it frequently in prose, and in popular speech we have such frequent examples as: *bag and baggage, fire and flood, might and main, thick and thin.*

**Alliterative Romance:** A metrical romance (*q.v.*) written in alliterative verse, especially one produced during the revival of interest in alliterative poetry in the fourteenth century, e.g., *William of Palerne* (unrimed long lines similar to the alliterative verse of the Old English period), *Sir Gawain and the Green Knight* (in stanzas made up of varying numbers of long lines followed by five short rimed lines), and the "alliterative" *Morte Arthure.* See MEDIEVAL ROMANCE.

**Alliterative Verse:** A term used to characterize those old verseforms, usually Germanic in origin, in which the division of the lines and, in fact, metrical structure generally were based on periodic and regular repetition of certain initial letters or sounds within the lines. The intricacies of the form in different literatures and times are too involved for discussion here; the student who wishes to acquaint himself thoroughly with the subject should consult Klaeber's edition of *Beowulf* or Oakton's

*Alliterative Verse in Middle English.* A characteristic example of alliterative verse, taken from *Piers the Plowman*, follows:

And *Peers* was *proud* there-of    and *putte* hern alle to swynke,
And yaf hem *mete* and *monye*    as they *myght* deseruen.

Here alliterative verse disregards the number of syllables to the line but insists on uniformity in the number of the accents in each half-line (two) and prescribes that the first three of these accented syllables should be alliterative. (Reference: R. M. Alden, *English Verse* pp. 116 ff.)

**Allusion:** A rhetorical term applied to that figure of speech making casual reference to a famous historical or literary figure or event.

> I know not where is that *Promethean heat*
> That can thy light relume.
>         —Shakespeare

**Almanac:** In medieval times an almanac was a permanent table showing the movements of the heavenly bodies, from which calculations for any year could be made. Almanacs date from as early as the twelfth century. Later, almanacs or calendars for short spans of years and, finally, for single years were prepared. A further step in the evolution of the form came with the inclusion of useful information, especially for farmers. This use of the almanac as a storehouse of general information led ultimately to such modern works as the *World Almanac*, a compendium of historical and statistical data not limited to the single year. As early as the sixteenth century, forecasts, first of the weather and later of such human fortunes as plagues and wars, were important features of almanacs. Other names for almanacs in the sixteenth century were "prognostications," "calendars," and "*ephemerides*." At this time almanacs took on some features drawn from the ecclesiastical calendars and martyrologies, such as the noting of saints' days and church anniversaries.

The almanac figures but slightly in literature. Spenser's *Shepheardes Calender* (1579) takes its title from a French "Kalendar of Shepards" and consists of twelve poems, under the titles of the twelve months, with some attention paid to the seasonal implications. By the latter part of the seventeenth century almanacs contained efforts at humor, consisting usually of coarse jokes. This feature was elaborated somewhat later, with some refinements, as in Franklin's *Poor Richard's Almanac* (1732–1758), itself partly inspired by the English comic almanac, *Poor Robin*. In Germany in the eighteenth and nineteenth centuries almanacs included printed poetry of a high order. (Reference: G. L. Kittredge, *The Old Farmer and his Almanack*.)

**Ambiguity:** The expression of an idea in language of such a nature as to give more than one meaning and to leave uncertainty as to the true significance of the statement. Ambiguity may be intentional, as when one wishes to evade a direct reply (see Juliet's replies to her mother in Act III, Scene 5, of Shakespeare's *Romeo and Juliet*). The chief causes of ambiguity are undue brevity and compression of statement, "cloudy" reference of pronoun, faulty or inverted (poetical) sequence, and the use of a word with two or more meanings.

**American Academy of Arts and Letters:** An organization parallel in purpose to certain European societies was brought into being in 1904 to recognize distinguished accomplishment in literature, art, or music. Historically, the American Academy owes its origin to the activity of the American Social Science Association, which, in 1898, realized the need for a society devoted entirely to the interests of letters and the fine arts, and organized the National Institute of Arts and Letters with a membership limited to 250. Six years later it was deemed necessary to create a smaller society composed of the most distinguished members of the Institute; accordingly, in 1904, was organized the American Academy of Arts and Letters with a membership limited to fifty. Though both men and women are eligible, only members of the Institute may be elected to the Academy. The society was incorporated by act of the American Congress, April 17, 1916. The seven men first elected to membership were: William Dean Howells, Augustus Saint-Gaudens, Edmund Clarence Stedman, John LaFarge, Samuel Langhorne Clemens, John Hay, and Edward MacDowell. "The actual work of the Academy is to promote American literature and art by giving the stamp of its approval of the best that both the past and the present have to offer." This is done through public addresses and by bringing to the United States representatives of other academies. Annually the National Institute awards its gold medal for distinguished work in literature and the arts; every five years is conferred the William Dean Howells medal for the best American fiction; and annually another gold medal is awarded for good diction on the stage. Almost continuous art exhibitions are held in the Academy building, 633 West 155th Street, New York City.

**American Language:** A term used to designate certain idioms and forms peculiar to English speech in America. As is pointed out in the *Encyclopædia Americana,* these differences usually arise in one of three ways: some forms originate in America independent of English speech ("gerrymander" is an example); some expressions which were once native to England have been brought here and have lived after they had died out in England ("fall" for "autumn"); and certain English forms have taken on modified meanings in America (as we use "store" for "shop"). Besides these matters of vocabulary, H. L. Mencken points out six other respects in which American expression differs from English: syntax, intonation, slang, idiom, grammar, and pronunciation. For many years the sensitiveness of Americans made them deny the existence of anything like an "American language," but recently its existence has been generally recognized. (References: H. L. Mencken, *The American Language;* J. R. Bartlett, *Dictionary of Americanisms;* G. P. Krapp, *The English Language in America.* See also issues of the magazine *American Speech.*)

**American Literature, Periods of:** As in the case of the division of English literature into periods (see pp. 153–154), literary historians are not agreed upon a period-scheme for American literary history. Names for the earlier periods are commonly drawn from political or historical conditions, while later periods are given titles suggestive of prevailing literary movements or attitudes. Thus the first period is rather generally called the "Colonial period," the next the "Revolutionary period," and the next the "National period." Sometimes (M. C. Tyler)

13

the colonial period is subdivided into "First Colonial Period, 1607–1676," and "Second Colonial Period, 1676–1765." Though nineteenth- and twentieth-century literature is sometimes labeled "Golden period," "Age of Conscious Culture," etc., it is more likely to be described in terms of prevailing tendencies such as romanticism and realism, especially by recent writers. The arrangements by three American scholars may be quoted as indicating recent tendencies. H. S. Canby: Colonial America, 1607–1765; The New Nation, 1765–1800; The Romantic Revolution, 1815–1870; The Change to Realism, 1870–1900. F. L. Pattee: 1607–1787, Colonial and Revolutionary Period; 1787–1830, New York Period; 1830–1860, New England Period; 1860–1870, Period of Transition; 1870–1914, National Period. Norman Foerster: The Colonial Mind, The Romantic Movement, The Realistic Movement (Foerster does not supply dates). The headings employed in the "American" column of the "Outline of Literary History" elsewhere in this handbook may also be consulted, though they do not represent an independent effort to arrange the literature into periods, since they were determined partly by the necessity of correlating the material with that in the parallel "English" column, and partly by a desire to reflect some of the captions made familiar by their appearance in the commonly used literary histories and anthologies.

**Amerind Literature:** That body of writing and oral tradition developed by the various aboriginal tribes of America. The term is a combination of syllables from *American* and *Indian*. Originally transmitted almost entirely by word of mouth, the literature was at first such as could easily be memorized, the rituals of annual festivals, tribal traditions, narrative accounts of gods and heroes. Since much of this literature grew up about the rhythmic accents of the ceremonial drum, it took on a regularity of metric pattern which gave it the quality of poetry; another part, perhaps less associated with ceremonials, was more simply natural in its recounting of events and took the form of prose. A characteristic quality of this Amerind language is its building of many ideas into one term. ("Hither-whiteness-comes-walking" being, according to Mary Austin, the

Algonquin parallel for "dawn.") Most of this literature known to us today is confined to a few types: the epic, the folk-tale, the drama, ritualistic and ceremonial exercises, and narratives of adventure.

**Amphibrach:** A metrical foot in verse consisting of three syllables, the first and last unaccented, the second accented. Example: *ăr ránge mĕnt.*

**Amplification:** A figure of speech by which bare expressions, likely to be ignored or misunderstood by a hearer or reader because of their bluntness, are emphasized through restatement with additional detail. The device is used in music, oratory, and poetry quite commonly. The chief danger accompanying the use of amplification is that prolix writers will so elaborate a statement as to rob it even of its original meaning. Holofernes, in Shakespeare's *Love's Labour's Lost,* affords a perfect example of the evils of over-amplification:

He draweth out the thread of his verbosity finer than the staple of his argument. I abhor such fanatical phantasimes, such insociable and point-devise companions; such rackers of orthography, as to speak dout, fine, when he should say doubt; det, when he should pronounce debt,—d,e,b,t, not d,e,t; he clepeth a calf, cauf; half, hauf; neighbour *vocatur* nebour, neigh, abbreviated ne. This is abhominable, which he would call abominable,—it insinuateth me of insanie: *anne intelligis, domine?* To make frantic, lunatic.

**Ana:** Scraps of information relating to people or places or events. The seventeenth century in England was much devoted to this type of writing and to the collecting of anecdote. *The Table Talk of John Selden,* published in 1689, is a typical collection of these curiosities of literature. The term also exists as a suffix, as in Goldsmith*iana,* where it denotes a collection of miscellaneous information regarding Goldsmith.

**Anachronism:** False assignment of an event, a person, a scene, language—in fact anything—to a time when that event or thing or person was not in existence. Shakespeare is guilty of sundry anachronisms such as his placing cannon in *King John,* a play dealing with a time many years before cannon came into use in England. The anachronism, however, is a greater sin to the

15

realist than to the romanticist, and may or may not be important according to its effect on the literary structure as a whole. Humorists sometimes use anachronisms as a comic device.

**Anacoluthon:** The failure, accidental or deliberate, to complete a sentence according to the structural plan on which it was started. Used accidentally, anacoluthic writing is, of course, a vice; used deliberately for emotional or rhetorical effect it is a recognized figure of speech, effective especially in oratory. The term is also applied to units of composition larger than the sentence when there is within the unit an obvious incoherency among the parts. Browning is very much given to this sort of construction; the following stanza from *A Toccata of Galuppi's* will serve as an illustration:

> Ay, because the sea's the street there; and
> 'tis arched by . . . what you call
> . . . Shylock's bridge with houses on it,
> where they kept the carnival:
> I was never out of England—it's as if I
> saw it all.

**Anacreontic Poetry:** Verse in the mood and manner of the lyrics of the Greek poet Anacreon; that is, poems characterized by an erotic, amatory, or Bacchanalian spirit. The characteristic Anacreontic stanza consists of four lines rhyming *abab*, each line composed of three trochaic feet with one long syllable added at the end of the line: $\underline{\phantom{x}}\ \smile\ |\ \underline{\phantom{x}}\ \smile\ |\ \underline{\phantom{x}}\ \smile\ |\ \underline{\phantom{x}}$.

**Anacrusis:** A term denoting one or more extra unaccented syllables at the beginning of a verse before the regular rhythm of the line makes its appearance. Literally an upward or back beat. Alden cites the third verse of the following stanza from Shelley as an example:

> What thou art we know not;
> What is most like thee?
> *From* rainbow clouds there flow not
> Drops so bright to see
> As from thy presence showers a rain of melody.

**Anagram:** A word or phrase made by transposing the letters of another word or phrase, as "cask" is an anagram of "sack."

Anagrams have usually been employed simply as an exercise of one's ingenuity, but deserve mention here since writers have sometimes used them in verses and other work to conceal proper names or veiled messages. It is said, too, that some of the astronomers of the seventeenth century used anagrams to conceal certain of their discoveries until such time as it was convenient to announce their findings. Anagrams have been used rather frequently as a means of coining pseudonyms, as "Calvinus" became "Alcuinus", "Bryan Waller Procter" became "Barry Cornwall, poet", and "Arouet, l.j." (*le jeune*) is said to have given the name "Voltaire" to the world. *Erewhon* is an instance of an anagram as a book title. A variety of the anagram, the *palindrome*, is an arrangement of letters which gives the same meaning whether read forward or backward and is illustrated in the remark by which Adam is alleged to have introduced himself to his wife upon her first appearance before him: "Madam, I'm Adam."

**Analecta (Analects):** Excerpts from long pieces of writing; selections or fragments, literary gleanings, e.g., *Analects from Confucius*.

**Analogue:** This word, meaning something that is analogous to or like another given thing, has two special uses of interest to the student of literature: (1) philologically, an analogue may mean a cognate or word in one language corresponding with one in another, as the English word "mother" is an analogue of the Latin word *mater*—kinship or common origin is usually implied; (2) in literary history two versions of the same story may be called analogues, especially if no direct relationship can be established though a remote one is probable. Thus the story of the pound of flesh in *Gesta Romanorum* may be called an analogue of the similar plot in *The Merchant of Venice*.

**Analogy:** A comparison of two things, alike in certain respects; particularly a method of exposition by which one unfamiliar object or idea is explained by comparing it in certain of its similarities with other objects or ideas more familiar. In argumentation and logic analogy is also frequently used to establish contentions, it being argued, for instance, that since

A works certain results, B, which is like A in vital respects, will also accomplish the same results. Analogy, however, is often a treacherous weapon since few *different* objects or ideas are essentially the *same* to more than a superficial observer or thinker.

**Anapest:** A three-syllable poetic measure comprising two short or unaccented syllables followed by a long or accented one (⌣⌣—). The following lines from Shelley's *Cloud* are anapestic:

> Like a child from the womb, like a ghost from the tomb,
> I arise and unbuild it again.

**Anastrophe:** A rhetorical term signifying inversion of the usual, normal, or logical order of the parts of a sentence. Anastrophe is deliberate rather than accidental and is used, as in verse, to secure rhythm or to gain emphasis or euphony.

> Not fierce Othello in so loud a strain
> Roar'd for the handkerchief that caus'd his pain.
> —Pope

**Anathema:** A formal and solemn denunciation or imprecation, particularly as pronounced by the Greek or Roman Catholic Church against an individual, an institution, or a doctrine. The form conventionally reads: *Si quis dixerit*, etc., *anathema sit*, "If any one should say (so and so) let him be anathema."

**Anatomy:** Used even as early as Aristotle in the figurative sense of logical dissection or analysis, this term, which originally meant "dissection" in a medical sense, came into common use in England late in the sixteenth century in the meaning thus explained by Robert Burton in his *Anatomy of Melancholy* (1621): "What it is, with all the kinds, causes, symptoms, prognostickes, and severall cures of it." There are several pieces in English literature preceding Burton in which the medical sense of "anatomy" is still less evident, such as Thomas Nash's *Anatomy of Absurdity*, and John Lyly's *Euphues, the Anatomy of Wit*. The "anatomies" anticipated to some degree the characteristics of the essay and philosophical and scientific treatises of the seventeenth century.

**Ancients and Moderns, Quarrel of the:** In a broad sense, every age has its battle of the "ancients" and the "moderns" in the conflict between old ideas and standards of taste and new ones. Specifically, the phrase is used in literary history to designate the complicated controversy which took place in France and England in the late seventeenth and early eighteenth centuries over the relative merits of classical and contemporary thinkers, writers, and artists. Some of the forces which stimulated the dispute were the Renaissance in Western Europe, which produced both a reverence for classical authority and a desire to emulate classical writers; the growth of the new science in the seventeenth century; and the interest in such philosophical ideas as the doctrine of progress.

The dispute in France centered about the vigorous advocacy of the cause of the moderns by Charles Perrault, whose position received support from Fontenelle, Thomas Corneille, P. Perrault, and others. These moderns were opposed by Boileau, Racine, La Fontaine, La Bruyère, and others. Perrault in his poem (1687) lauding the age of Louis XIV and in his famous *Parallèles des anciens et des modernes* (1688–1697) and Fontenelle in his *Digression sur les anciens et des modernes* (1688) held that in art and poetry the efforts of the moderns showed superior taste and greater polish of form as compared with those of the ancients. The moderns were said to profit from improved methods of reasoning, scientific inventions, and Christianity. The philosophical doctrines of Descartes (1596–1650), who had rejected Aristotle, lent support to the moderns. The long-established assumption of the superiority of classical thought and art was thus vigorously challenged (see HUMANISM, CLASSICISM).

In England, the "battle of the books" began with the publication of Sir William Temple's *An Essay upon the Ancient and Modern Learning* (1690). Temple, who rejected the doctrine of progress and criticized the "pretensions" and "visions" of the members of the Royal Society, upheld the claims of the ancients in many fields and could not see that they were inferior to the moderns in knowledge or genius. The new inventions had not led to practical improvements. Modern students are not agreed as to whether Temple's work was an outgrowth of the French quarrel or was a natural result of the opposition which had existed in England for some forty years to the "advanced" thinkers who, under the inspiration of Bacon's writings and the ardent leadership of the Royal Society, had broken with the past and were espousing the new philosophy and the new science (Richard Boyle, Joseph Glanvil, Thomas Sprat, and others).   Temple was answered in 1694 by William Wotton in an ambitious treatise, *Reflections upon Ancient and Modern Learning*, in which he gave the palm to the moderns in most, though not all, branches of learning.   The scientific as opposed to the literary aspects of the quarrel were particularly stressed in England, the English moderns generally being willing to admit the superiority of the ancients in such fields as poetry, oratory, and art.

An episode which aroused much interest arose over the *Letters of Phalaris*, which Temple listed as a praiseworthy ancient work.   Soon thereafter, Charles Boyle, an Oxford man, published a new edition of the "Phalaris" letters, taking occasion to attack the Cambridge classical scholar Dr. Thomas Bentley for an alleged slight.   When Wotton published a second edition of his essay (1697), Bentley included in it an appendix which not only criticized Boyle's edition, but presented evidence, later elaborated in his famous *Dissertation* (1699), for believing that the Phalaris letters were spurious.   Thus a classical scholar appeared as a champion of the moderns; in fact, Bentley employed the methods of the new science in the field of classical literature itself, and his study went far toward initiating modern historical scholarship.   Jonathan Swift, in the "digressions" of the *Tale of a Tub* (written *ca.*1696) and in his famous *Battle of the Books* (written *ca.*1697, pub. 1704)—the most important literary document produced by the controversy in England— undertook the defense of his patron Temple, though Swift's satire is not altogether one-sided.   Perhaps the most significant result of the whole dispute lies in the impetus it gave to the liberalizing forces which were attempting to stimulate progress through the emancipation of the human spirit from the depressing effect of a too unyielding devotion to established tradition. (References: J. B. Bury, *The Idea of Progress;* R. F. Jones, "Ancients and Moderns: a Study of the Background of the

Battle of the Books," *Washington University Studies*, 1936; H. Gillot, *La Querelle des anciens et des modernes en France;* A. E. Burlingame, *The Battle of the Books;* W. A. Nitze and E. P. Dargan, *History of French Literature.*)

**Anecdote:** A short narrative detailing particulars of an interesting episode or event. In careful usage the term most frequently refers to a narrated incident in the life of an important person and should lay claim to an element of truth. Though anecdotes are often used by writers as the basis for short stories, an anecdote definitely differs from a short story in that it lacks complicated plot and is unified in its presentation of time and place elements and in its relation of a single episode. At one time the term connoted secret and private details of a man's career given forth in the spirit of gossip, though now it is used generally to cover any brief narrative of particulars. Anecdotic literature has a long heritage extending from ancient through modern times and comprising books as different as the *Dipnosophistai* of Athenaeus, the *Lives* of Plutarch, the *Anecdotes* of Percy, and the joke-books of Irvin Shrewsbury Cobb.

**Anglicism:** A peculiarity of expression or idiom characteristic of the English language and distinguishing it from other languages. The term is also given to foreign expressions when taken over into English and forced to conform to English usage and syntax. Any form of expression peculiar to the English.

**Anglo-Catholic Revival:** See OXFORD MOVEMENT.

**Anglo-French (Anglo-Norman):** Applied to the French language as used in England in the period following the Norman Conquest (*ca.*1100–*ca.*1350) and to the literature written in Anglo-French. As this period, especially the twelfth century, was a veritable cultural Renaissance and as the vast bulk of imaginative literature written in England at the time was in French, Anglo-French literature holds a place of real importance in English literary history. In general, it follows the lines of the contemporary literature of France itself and embraces (to follow Professor Schofield's list) romances, tales, historical works, political poems and satires, legends and saints' lives, didactic works, lyrics and debates, as well as religious drama. Much of this literature is in "Central French" rather than Norman French. Anglo-French literature flourished under the patronage of the Norman and early Plantagenet kings, particularly Henry II.

The relations of France and England were so close at the time that it is difficult now to be certain in all cases whether a given writer or work is to be classed as "Anglo-Norman" ("Anglo-French") or merely French. Many pieces of Middle English literature (such as *Havelok the Dane*) are merely English versions of Anglo-French pieces. Although the terms "Anglo-French" and "Anglo-Norman" are commonly used interchangeably, certain writers employ distinctions which have given each term special meanings. Thus "Anglo-French" is sometimes used to designate such French as shows definite influence of English idioms. Likewise "Anglo-Norman" is often restricted to the early period of Norman times (1066 *et seq.*), and sometimes is used to denote pieces written in England by persons of Norman descent employing the Norman dialect of French. "Franco-Norman" is also employed in this latter connection. (Reference: W. H. Schofield, *English Literature from the Norman Conquest to Chaucer*, Chap. iii.)

**Anglo-Irish Literature:** Literature produced in English by Irish writers, especially those living in Ireland and actuated by a conscious purpose to utilize Celtic materials, often employing an English style flavored by Irish idioms, called "Hibernian English" or "Anglo-Irish." See CELTIC RENAISSANCE. (Reference: A. P. Graves, *Camb. Hist. of Eng. Lit.*, Vol. XIV, Chap. ix.)

**Anglo-Latin:** A term applied to the learned literature produced in Latin by Englishmen or others dwelling in England during the Middle English period. It is largely in prose and includes chronicles, serious treatises on theology, philosophy, law, history, and science, though satire (like Walter Map's *De Nugis Curialium*) and light verse (like the Goliardic songs) were also written, as well as hymns and prayers and religious plays. (Reference: W. H. Schofield, *English Literature from the Norman Conquest to Chaucer*, Chap. i.)

**Anglo-Norman:** See ANGLO-FRENCH.

**Anglo-Saxon:** A Teutonic tribal group resident in England in post-Roman times. In the fifth and sixth centuries the Angles and Saxons from the neighborhood of what is now known as Schleswig-Holstein, together with the Jutes, invaded and conquered Britain. From the Angles came the name England (Angle-land). After Alfred (ninth century), king of the West Saxons, conquered the Danish-English people of the Anglian territory, the official name for his subjects was, in Latin, *Angli et Saxones* (the English themselves were inclined to use the term *Engle* and call their language *Englisc*). In later times the term "Anglo-Saxons" came to be used to distinguish the residents of England from the Saxons still resident in Europe proper. The term is now broadly used to distinguish the English peoples whether resident in England, America, or the various possessions. See OLD ENGLISH, ENGLISH LANGUAGE.

**Animal Epic:** See BEAST EPIC.

**Annals:** Narratives of historical events recorded year by year. Such records in Rome in Cicero's time were known as *annales maximi* because they were kept by the pontifex maximus. Anglo-Saxon monks in the seventh century developed another sort of "annals" by recording in ecclesiastical calendars after given dates important events of the year. This practice developed into such records as the Anglo-Saxon chronicles. Both "annals" (as in Ireland) and "chronicles" (as in England) were frequently written long after the events recorded had taken place, the dating being sometimes more or less speculative, especially when efforts were being made to "synchronize" events in secular and in Biblical or ecclesiastical history. The term "annals" in modern times is sometimes used rather loosely for historical narrative not recorded by years and for digests and records of deliberative bodies and of scientific and artistic organizations, like *Annals of Congress*, *Annals of Music*, *Annals of Mathematics*.

**Annuals:** Books appearing in successive numbers at intervals of one year and usually reviewing the events of the year within specified fields of interest, as college annuals. The term is sometimes applied also to such compendiums as the *World Almanac*, embracing historical data and miscellaneous statistics covering a long range of years. In the first quarter of the nineteenth century illustrated gift-books (*q.v.*) called "annuals" were popular, such as *Friendship's Offering*.

**Antagonist:** The character in fiction or drama who stands directly opposed to the protagonist. A rival or opponent of the protagonist (*q.v.*).

**Anthem:** In its popular use refers to any song of praise, rejoicing, or reverence. These emotions when related to one's country find expression in national anthems; when in praise of one's deity, in religious anthems. More restrictedly, an anthem is an arrangement of words from the Bible, usually from the Psalms, planned for church worship. Formerly it was essential that the music for an anthem be arranged for responsive singing, either by two choirs, a priest and a choir, or in another of various similar combinations.

**Anthology:** Literally a collection of "the flowers of verse" and originally signifying a collection from the Greek, has come now to mean simply a group of selections or extracts, either prose or verse, from the writing in any language of one or more authors. Of the hundreds of anthologies published some few have won permanent places in our literature. Palgrave's *Golden Treasury* is a standard anthology of English poetry.

**Anticlimax:** A sudden or gradual decrease in interest or importance in the items of a series of two or more statements. The opposite of climactic order. Anticlimax is both a weakness and a strength in writing; when effectively and intentionally used it greatly increases emphasis through its humorous effect; when unintentionally employed its result is bathetic (see BATHOS). An example of its deliberate use is found in Pope's *Rape of the Lock:*

> Not youthful kings in battle seiz'd alive,
> Not scornful virgins who their charms survive,
> Not ardent lovers robb'd of all their bliss,
> Not ancient ladies when refus'd a kiss,

> Not tyrants fierce that unrepenting die,
> *Not Cynthia when her manteau's pinn'd awry,*
> E'er felt such rage, resentment and despair,
> As thou, sad virgin! for thy ravish'd hair.

Unintentional anticlimax may be illustrated by this sentence (if it *is* unintentional): "The duty of a sailor in the navy is to protect his country and to peel potatoes."

**Antimasque:** A grotesque, usually humorous dance interspersed among the beautiful and serious actions and dances of a masque. It was often performed by professional actors and dancers and served as a foil to the masque proper, performed by courtly amateurs. The development and possibly the origin of the antimasque are due to Ben Jonson. See MASQUE.

**Antiphrasis:** Irony, the satirical or humorous use of a word or phrase to convey an idea exactly opposite to its real significance. Thus in Shakespeare's *Julius Caesar* Antony ironically refers to Caesar's murderers as "honorable men."

**Antiquarianism:** The study of old times through any available relics, especially literary and artistic. The antiquarian impulse is associated with history, folklore, social customs, patriotism, religion, and other interests. It is widespread in its manifestations and has existed among all nations, even in their primitive periods. The medieval "chronicles" and saints' lives reflect it, as does such a specific movement as the revival of the native English alliterative verse in the fourteenth century. Antiquarianism as an organized effort in England, however, is associated with the sixteenth century. In 1533 Henry VIII appointed John Leland the "King's Antiquary" and sent him throughout England to examine and collect old documents from libraries, cathedrals, colleges, abbeys, and monasteries. Leland's notes were of much use to later writers like Holinshed, and his work formed the basis for the Society of Antiquaries (1572–1605), of which Sir Walter Raleigh, John Donne, and other literary men were members. Much of the literature of the Renaissance, such as the chronicles, history-plays, topographical poems (like Drayton's *Polyolbion*), and patriotic epics (like Spenser's *Faerie*

25

*Queene*), reflects the antiquarian movement. William Camden was one of the greatest of Elizabethan antiquarians.

In the seventeenth century Fuller's *Worthies*, John Aubrey's *Lives*, Sir Thomas Browne's *Vulgar Errors*, and the books of Anthony à Wood (historian of Oxford University) are antiquarian in spirit. In the eighteenth century antiquarianism was largely motivated by the philosophical interest in primitive man, and explains in part Bishop Percy's *Reliques of Ancient English Poetry* (a collection of old ballads), the Celtic Revival (*q.v.*), and the literary forgeries (*q.v.*) of Chatterton and Macpherson. Indeed, the antiquarian interest formed an important phase of the Romantic Movement. The Gothic romances and the historical novels and metrical romances of Scott reflect it, and even Wordsworth's famous theories about the relation of poetry to the emotions and language of simple men are sometimes traced partly to the effect of the antiquarian impulse. In the eighteenth century the movement became even more widespread, as illustrated in the activities of Gray, Bishop Percy, and Thomas Warton. (References: *Camb. Hist. of Eng. Lit.*, Vols. I and IX; H. R. Steeves, *Learned Societies and English Literary History*.)

**Antistrophe:** A term associated with classical literature as one—the strophe being the other—of the two alternating divisions of the ode. As the Greek chorus sang the strophe, it moved from right to left in an imaginary circle; during the antistrophe the movement was reversed. Thus the term which originally implied direction of movement has, by association, come to refer to a division of the ode itself.

**Antithesis:** A figure of speech characterized by strongly contrasting words, clauses, sentences, or ideas. A balancing of one term against another for impressiveness and emphasis. An attractive device when used within reason, antithetical expression with some authors becomes a vice. Certain writers make a mannerism of it. Pope, in the *Rape of the Lock* for example, relies on this figure so frequently that its significance, which lies in the quality of surprise afforded by the sudden contrast, is likely to be lost in the regularity of its recurrence. "Man

26

proposes, God disposes" is an example of antithesis, as is the second line of the following characteristic Pope couplet:

> The hungry judges soon the sentence sign,
> *And wretches hang that jury-men may dine.*

True antithetical structure demands that there be not only an opposition of idea, but that the opposition in different parts be manifested through similar grammatical structure,—the noun "wretches" being opposed by the noun "jury-men" and the verb "hang" by the verb "dine" in the above example.

**Aphorism:** A brief statement, usually expressed in a single effectively phrased sentence, of some important truth. Strictly speaking an aphorism is based on a personal experience, but loosely the term has been used interchangeably with proverb, apothegm, precept, maxim, epigram, etc. An aphorism, however, differs from a proverb in that it is of individual authorship, whereas a proverb is likely to be the anonymous wisdom of a race or people; an aphorism differs from a maxim in that it is not necessarily directed towards a betterment of moral conduct. Barbed wit, an essential of the epigram, is not a vital quality of an aphorism. If there is any difference between aphorism and apothegm it is that an aphorism is a statement of a more abstract, general truth than an apothegm, which is likely to be more practical in nature. Polonius spoke maxims in giving his formal advice to Laertes; Hamlet uttered an aphorism, from his own experience, when he set down in his tables that "one may smile, and smile, and be a villain." See PROVERB.

**Apocryphal:** Now commonly means "spurious," because "apocrypha," which originally meant hidden or secret things, became the term used to denote Biblical books not regarded as inspired, and hence excluded from the sacred canon. Saint Jerome (A.D. 331–420) applied the term to certain books, such as Zoroaster, found in the Greek but not in the Hebrew Bible. Apocryphal books connected with both the Old and the New Testament circulated in great numbers in the early Middle Ages. Almost all literary types found in the Bible are represented by apocryphal compositions. Examples of Old Testament apocrypha include: The Book of Enoch (vision), Life of Adam and

Eve (legend), The Wisdom of Solomon (wisdom book), The Testament of Abraham (testament), and the Psalter of Solomon (hymns). New Testament types include: Acts of Matthew (apostolic "acts"), Third Epistle to the Corinthians (epistle), Apocalypse of Peter (vision), and Gospel of Peter (gospel). These books abound in miracles, accounts of the boyhood of Jesus, reported wise sayings of sacred character, and martyrdoms. Influence of apocryphal literature, blended with authentic Biblical influence, was exerted on such medieval literary types as saints' legends, visions, sermons, and even romances. Certain books accepted by the medieval church but rejected by Protestants became "apocryphal" in the sixteenth century, such as Ecclesiasticus, Baruch, and Maccabees, though they were usually printed in Protestant Bibles as useful for edification but not authoritative in determining doctrine. See CANON.

**Apology:** Two special uses of the word may be noted. It often appears in literature, especially in literary titles, in its older sense of "defense," as in Stevenson's *Apology for Idlers* and Sidney's *Apologie for Poetrie*. The Latin form *apologia* is also used in this sense, as in Cardinal Newman's *Apologia pro Vita Sua*. No admission of wrong-doing or expression of regret is involved. "Apology" is also an old spelling for "apologue," a fable.

**Apophasis:** A rhetorical figure denoting that convention in speech or writing wherein one makes an assertion even while he seems or pretends to suppress or deny it. "Were I not aware of your high reputation for honesty, I should say that I believe you connived at the fraud yourself."

**Aposiopesis:** The deliberate failure to complete a sentence. As a figure of speech the form is frequently used to convey an impression of extreme exasperation or to imply a threat, as, "If you do that, why, I'll ——." Aposiopesis differs from anacoluthon (*q.v.*) in that the latter completes a sentence in irregular structural arrangement; the former leaves the sentence incomplete.

**Apostrophe:** A figure of speech in which someone (usually absent), some abstract quality, or a non-existent personage is directly addressed as though present. Characteristic instances of apostrophe are found in the invocations to the muses in poetry—

> And chiefly Thou, O Spirit, that dost prefer
> Before all temples the upright heart and pure,
> Instruct me, for Thou know'st;

Or, to quote Milton again:

> Hail, Holy Light, offspring of Heaven firstborn!

The form is frequently used in patriotic oratory, the speaker addressing some glorious leader of the past and invoking his aid in the present. Since apostrophe is chiefly associated with deep emotional expression, the form is readily adopted by humorists for purposes of parody and satire.

**Apothegm:** See APHORISM.

**Arcadian:** Arcadia, a picturesque plateau region in Greece, the reputed home of pastoral poetry, was pictured by pastoral poets as a land of ideal rural peace and contentment. "Arcadian" suggests an idealized rural simplicity and contentment such as shepherds in conventional pastoral poetry exhibited. It is sometimes used as synonymous with bucolic or pastoral. Sir Philip Sidney, following Italian precedent, uses "Arcadia" as the title of his pastoral romance. See ECLOGUE, PASTORAL, IDYL.

**Archaism:** Obsolete diction, phrasing, idiom, or syntax. Used intentionally and effectively an archaic style is valuable in recreating the atmosphere and spirit of the past, as in Spenser's *The Faerie Queene;* unless carefully controlled, however, archaisms result in an artificial and affected style so absurd as to defeat the purpose of the writer.

**Architectonics:** A critical term which expresses collectively those structural qualities of proportion, unity, emphasis, and scale which make a piece of writing proceed logically and smoothly from beginning to end with no waste effort, no faulty omissions. The requirements of architectonics, a term borrowed from architecture, are felt to have been fulfilled when a piece of literature impresses a reader as a building, carefully planned and constructed, impresses the spectator. In his essay on "Style," Walter Pater writes of "that architectural conception of work, which foresees the end in the beginning and never loses sight of it,"—a statement which well expresses the quality implied in the word. The novels of Thomas Hardy and Walter Scott are noteworthy in their regard for "architectonics."

**Areopagus:** The "hill of Ares (Mars)," the seat of the highest judicial court in ancient Athens. By association the name has come to represent any court of final authority. In this sense Milton used the term in his *Areopagitica*, addressed to the British parliament on the question of censorship and the licensing of books.

"The Areopagus" is the name used for what some literary historians believe was a sort of literary club existing in London shortly before 1580, supposed to be analogous with the *Pléiade* group in France. Whether there was a formal club or not is doubtful, but it is true that certain writers and critics, including Gabriel Harvey, Sir Philip Sidney, Edmund Spenser, and Sir Edward Dyer were engaged in a "movement" to reform English versification on the principles of classical prosody. In their best work, however, Sidney and Spenser abandoned these experiments in classical measures in favor of Italian, French, and native English forms.

**Argumentation:** One of the four chief "forms of discourse" (compare "Exposition," "Narration," and "Description"). Its purpose is to convince a reader or hearer by establishing the truth or falsity of a proposition. It is often combined with exposition. It differs from exposition technically in its aim, exposition being content with simply making an explanation.

**Arminianism:** See CALVINISM.

**Arsis:** In prosody indicates both (1) the stressed syllable and (2) the emphasis itself given to the syllable. In the following verse the second, fourth, sixth, eighth, and tenth syllables may be said, under the first meaning, to be the "arses."

The Cūr | few tōlls | thĕ knell | ŏf part | ĭng dāy

Under the second meaning these same syllables may be said to receive the *arsis*. See ICTUS.

**Art Ballad:** A term occasionally used to distinguish the modern or literary ballad of known authorship from the early ballads of unknown authorship. Some successful art ballads are *La Belle Dame sans Merci* by Keats, *Rosabelle* by Scott, and *Sister Helen* by Rossetti. Possibly the most famous of all poems imitating the ballad manner is the *Rime of the Ancient Mariner* by Coleridge.

**Art Epic:** A term sometimes employed to distinguish such an epic as Milton's *Paradise Lost* or Virgil's *Aeneid* from so-called "folk epics" such as *Beowulf*, *Nibelungenlied*, and the *Iliad* and *Odyssey*. The folk epic is so named because it deals with tradition closely associated with the people or "folk" for whom it was written and whose credulity it commanded. The art epic is supposed to be more sophisticated, more highly idealized, and more consciously moral in purpose than is the folk epic, which it imitates. The author takes greater liberties with the popular materials he is treating and exhibits and expects less credulity. The events he narrates are in the more remote past. The present-day tendency to discredit the theories of epic origins advanced by the romantic critics of the eighteenth century is resulting in a breaking down of the assumed distinction between the two kinds, as the folk epics are now viewed as the work of single poets who worked according to traditional artistic technique. See EPIC.

**Art Lyric:** This is not so much an individual lyric type or form as it is a particular *manner*. The art lyric is characterized by a minuteness of subject, great delicacy of touch, careful perfection in phrasing, artificiality of sentiment, and formality. For its subject this kind of lyric avoids the passionate outbursts of a Burns, harking back, rather, to the sort of thing Horace and Petrarch wrote about, the tilt of a lady's eyebrow, the glow of a cheek. With Herrick and Lovelace and Jonson and Herbert, Elizabethan and seventeenth-century English writers made much of the manner, polishing and perfecting their songs to gem-like brightness; with Shelley and Keats the art lyric began to carry abstract ideas. In brief, it may be said that the art lyric differs from the ordinary lyric in the degree to which the poet's self-conscious struggle for perfection of form dominates the spontaneity of his emotion. Certain French lyric forms, the triolet, ballade, rondeau, and rondel, are instances of this highly polished manner of the art lyric.

**Art Theatre:** See LITTLE THEATRE MOVEMENT.

**Arthurian Legend:** The question often asked, "Is King Arthur a historical person?" cannot be answered by a plain yes or no. It is probable that the legend of Arthur grew up out of the deeds of some historical person. He was probably not a king and it is more than doubtful whether his name was Arthur. He was presumably a Welsh or Roman military leader of the Celts in Wales against the German invaders who overran Britain in the fifth century. Just as stories in later time grew up about Robin Hood or George Washington, the stories of the great deeds of this Welsh hero gradually grew into a great body of romantic story. He provided a glorious past for the Britons to look back upon, and there is some evidence that his glorification in twelfth-century writings was due to the desire of the Norman kings to strengthen the national background by treating Arthur as an illustrious predecessor on the throne of Britain. When Arthur had developed into a great king, he yielded his position as a personal hero to a great group of knights who surrounded him. These knights of the Round Table came to be representative of all that was best in the age of chivalry, and the stories of their deeds make up the most popular group ("Matter of Britain") of the great cycles of "medieval romance" (*q.v.*).

There is no mention of Arthur in contemporary accounts of the Germanic invasion, but a Roman citizen named Gildas who lived in Wales mentions in his *De Excidio et Conquestu Britanniae* (written between 500 and 550) the Battle of Mt. Badon, with which later accounts connect Arthur, and a valiant Roman leader of a Welsh rally, named Ambrosius Aurelianus. About 800, Nennius, a Welsh chronicler, in his *Historia Britonum* uses the name Arthur in referring to a leader (*dux bellorum*) against the Saxons. About a century later an addition to Nennius' history called *Mirabilia* gives further evidences of Arthur's development as a hero, including an allusion to a boar-hunt of Arthur's which is told in detail in the later Welsh story of Kulwch and Olwen (in the *Mabinogion*). There are other references to Arthur in the annals of the tenth and eleventh centuries, and William of Malmesbury in his *Gesta Regum Anglorum* (1125) who treats Arthur as an historical figure, identifies him with the Arthur whom the Welsh "rave wildly about" in their "idle tales." A typical British Celt at this time was ready to fight for his belief that Arthur was not really dead but would return.

About 1136 Geoffrey of Monmouth wrote his *Historia Regum Britanniae*, professedly based upon an old Welsh book. Geoffrey adds a wealth of matter to the Arthurian legend—how much of it he invented can not now be determined—such as the stories of Arthur's supernatural birth, his weird "Passing" to Avalon to be healed of his wounds, and the abduction of Guinevere by Modred. Arthur figures as a world-conqueror who exacts tribute of even the Romans. It is probable that Geoffrey was attempting to create for the Norman kings in England a glorious historical background. He traces the history of the Britons from Brut, a descendant of Aeneas, to the great Arthur. Soon after Geoffrey's time additions to the story were made by the French poet Wace in his *Roman de Brut*, and a little later appear the famous romances of Chrétien de Troyes, in Old French, in which Arthurian themes are given their first known highly literary treatment. About 1205 the English poet Layamon added some details in his *Brut*. By this time Arthurian legend had taken its place as one of the great themes of medieval romance.

The great popularity of Arthurian tradition continued through the Middle Ages, reaching its climax in medieval English literature in Malory's *Le Morte d'Arthur* (printed 1485), a book destined to transmit Arthurian stories to many later English writers, notably Tennyson. Spenser professedly used an Arthurian background for his great romantic epic *The Faerie Queene* (1590), and in the next century Milton contemplated a national epic on Arthur. Interest in Arthur decreased in the eighteenth century, but Arthurian topics were particularly popular in the nineteenth century, the best known treatment appearing in Tennyson's *Idylls of the King*. Tennyson's version, as well as E. A.

Robinson's *Tristram*, shows how different generations have modified the Arthurian stories to make them express contemporary modes of thought and individual artistic ends. Arthurian themes received powerful and sympathetic musical treatment in Richard Wagner's operas, *Lohengrin* (1850), *Tristan* (1861–1865), *Parsifal* (1877–1882). The burlesquing treatment of chivalry in Mark Twain's *Connecticut Yankee at King Arthur's Court* and the modernization in John Erskine's *Galahad* contrast strongly with the usual note of reverence and romantic idealization accorded to Arthurian tradition in English and American literature. (References: E. K. Chambers, *Arthur of Britain;* G. H. Maynadier, *The Arthur of the English Poets;* J. D. Bruce, *The Evolution of Arthurian Romance;* M. W. MacCallum, *Tennyson's Idylls of the King and Arthurian Story*.)

**Artificial Comedy:** A term sometimes used (as by Lamb) for comedy reflecting an artificial society, like the "comedy of manners" (*q.v.*).

**Artificiality:** In criticism a term characterizing writing which is consciously and deliberately artistic as opposed to natural. Just what constitutes artificiality is impossible to say since the expression is usually relative, but, in general, writing which is highly conventional, elaborate, ornate, courtly, affected, self-conscious is called artificial. Such writers as John Lyly and John Donne will generally be accepted as "artificial" in comparison with, say, such other writers as Henry Fielding and Robert Burns.

**Assonance:** Resemblance or similarity in sound between vowels in two or more syllables. Related to rime, assonance nevertheless differs from it in that rime is the exact correspondence of sound whereas assonance is only an approximate or suggested resemblance. Strictly speaking, assonance demands that the similarity lie within the vowels, not the consonants, and occur only in accented syllables. "Love" and "dove," though recent poets fortunately scorn the rime, are "full" or perfect rimes; "lake" and "fate" are instances of assonance. In certain Romance languages, notably in Old Spanish and Old French, assonance plays an important rôle, frequently being used in place of rime in line endings. English poets, too, have employed assonance at the close of lines and, perhaps more commonly, have employed it internally to enrich sound and melody. Poe and Swinburne are notable examples of poets relying largely on both rime and assonance for their musical effects. The so-called "modern" poets in their desire to free verse from many of its conventionalities and to impart variety to rime have twisted both rime and assonance into such clumsy combinations as "body" and "study," "little" and "beetle," and "flash" and "wash," words which present neither proper rime nor assonance though they bear some resemblance to both. Assonance is also used effectively in prose, particularly in prose which is poetic in quality.

**Atmosphere:** Refers to the mood or feeling in which a piece of writing is pitched. Atmosphere differs from setting and local color in that these latter elements are largely physical and geographic, whereas atmosphere is that intangible, subjective, mental and spiritual quality which represents the tone of the work, the effect which the writing has on the reader. We speak, for instance, of the "weird" atmosphere of a Dunsany story, the "romantic" atmosphere of a Stevenson novel.

**Attic:** Writing characterized by a clear, simple, polished, and witty style. Attica, a province of Greece today, was formerly one of the ancient Greek states. With Athens as its capital city, Attica arose to such fame for its culture and art as to survive in the term "attic," an adjective denoting grace and culture and the classic in art. Joseph Addison is a favorite example of an English author who may be said to have written "attic" prose.

**Attic Salt:** "Salt," in this sense, means simply "wit." Attic salt, then, is writing distinguished by its classic refinement of wit. See ATTIC.

**Augustan:** Specifically refers to the age of the Emperor Augustus of Rome (ruled 27 B.C. to A.D. 14), but since the time of Augustus was notable for the perfection of letters and learning, the term has, by analogy, been applied to other epochs in world history when literary culture was high. As Virgil and Horace made the Augustan age of Rome, so Addison and Steele, Swift

35

and Pope, are sometimes said to have made the Augustan age of English letters. The term now applies rather loosely to any period noted for the polish and refinement of its literature.

**Augustinianism:** See CALVINISM.

**Autobiography:** An account of one's life written by oneself. As a division of literature, the field is usually so loosely defined as to include memoirs, diaries, and even letters, as well as the more formal narrative life chronicles. Some of the more famous autobiographies are those by Benvenuto Cellini, Benjamin Franklin, John Stuart Mill, Anthony Trollope, Thomas Henry Huxley, and Henry Adams. See BIOGRAPHY.

**Awakening, The Great:** A phrase applied to a great revival of emotional religion in America which took place about 1735–1750, the movement being at its height about 1740–1745 under the leadership of Jonathan Edwards. It arose as an effort to reform religion and morals. Religion, under the "Puritan hierarchy" led by the Mathers, had become rather formal and cold, and the clergy somewhat arrogant. The low morals and the lack of religious zeal which prevailed were traceable in part to the general anti-Puritan reaction in England after 1660, the increasingly diverse character of the population in the colonies, the hard conditions of pioneer life, and the general reaction against the horror of the Salem Witchcraft. The revival meetings began as early as 1720 in New Jersey. In 1734 Edwards held his first great revival at Northampton, Mass. In 1738 the famous English evangelist George Whitefield began his meetings in Georgia and in 1739–1740 made a spectacular evangelistic tour of the colonies, reaching New England in 1740. Whitefield's meetings were marked by great emotional manifestations, such as trances, shoutings, tearing of garments, faintings. In 1740–1742 Edwards conducted a long "revival" at Northampton, preached in other cities, published many sermons, including *Sinners in the Hands of an Angry God* (1741). The conservatives or "Old Lights," representing the stricter Calvinists, led by the faculties of Harvard and Yale, protested against the emotional excesses of the movement; they were answered by Edwards in his *Treatise on the Religious Affections* (1746). Yet

Edwards himself opposed the more extreme exhibitions of emotionalism and by 1750 a reaction against the movement was under way. See CALVINISM, DEISM, PURITANISM.

**Background:** A term, like many others used in literary discussion, borrowed from the kindred art of painting, where it signifies those parts of the painting against which the principal objects are portrayed. In literature the term is rather loosely used to specify either the setting of a piece of writing or the tradition and point of view from which an author presents his ideas. Thus one might speak either (1) of the Russian "background" (setting) of *Anna Karenina* or (2) of the "background" of education, philosophy, and convictions from which Tolstoy wrote the novel.

**Balance:** In rhetoric refers to that structure in which parts of a sentence—as words, phrases, or clauses—are set off against each other in position so as to emphasize a contrast in meaning.

The memory of other authors is kept alive by their works; but the memory of Johnson keeps many of his works alive.
—Macaulay

As a critical term "balance" is often used to characterize nicety of proportion among the various elements of a given piece of writing. A story, for example, wherein setting, characterization, and action are carefully planned, with no element securing undue emphasis, might be said to have fine "balance."

**Ballad:** A form of verse adapted for singing or recitation and primarily characterized by its presentation in simple narrative form of a dramatic or exciting episode. A famous definition is that of F. B. Gummere who describes the ballad as "a poem meant for singing, quite impersonal in material, probably connected in its origins with the communal dance, but submitted to a process of oral tradition among people who are free from literary influences and fairly homogeneous in character." Though the ballad is a form still much written, the so-called "popular ballad" in most literatures properly belongs to the early periods before written literature was highly developed. The usual explanation of the origin of the ballad—or the explanation usual at least until Miss Louise Pound wrote her

37

*Poetic Origins and the Ballad*—indicated that primitive social groups, moved by some deep experience or some tragic incident, gathered to express their emotion through the dance and that this dance was accompanied by a recited narrative recounting the particular experience. Gradually tune and narrative took shape together and from this blending emerged the popular ballad. Scholars who hold to this theory deny individual authorship for the earliest ballads and hold for communal authorship. Miss Pound, however, scouts this explanation and holds for the primitive artist as the creator, arguing that it is absurd to assume "that individuals have choral utterance before they are lyrically articulate as individuals." Whatever the origin, it is true that the folk ballad is, in almost every country, one of the earliest forms of literature. Certain common characteristics of these early ballads should be noted: the supernatural is likely to play an important part in events, physical courage and love are frequent themes, the incidents are usually such as happen to common people (as opposed to the nobility) and often have to do with domestic episodes; slight attention is paid to characterization or description, transitions are abrupt, action is largely developed through dialogue, tragic situations are presented with the utmost simplicity, "incremental repetition" (*q.v.*) is common, imagination though not so common as in the "art ballad" (*q.v.*) nevertheless appears in brief flashes, a single episode of highly dramatic nature is presented, and, often enough, the ballad is brought to a close with some sort of summary stanza. The greatest impetus to the study of ballad literature was given by the publication in 1765 of Bishop Percy's *Reliques of Ancient English Poetry*. The standard modern collection is *The English and Scottish Popular Ballads* edited by Francis James Child. A workable one-volume collection is *The Oxford Book of Ballads* edited by Sir Arthur Quiller-Couch. (Reference: G. H. Gerould, *The Ballad of Tradition*, 1932.)

**Ballad-Opera:** A name given to a sort of burlesque opera which flourished on the English stage for several years following the appearance of John Gay's *The Beggar's Opera* (1728), the best known example of the type. Modeled on Italian opera, which it burlesqued, it told its story in songs set to old tunes and appropriated various elements from farce and comedy. See OPERA, COMIC OPERA.

**Ballad Stanza:** A stanza form characterized by four lines, the first and third lines having eight syllables each and the second and fourth six each. The rhyme scheme is *abcb*. The meter is most frequently iambic.

> Whare will I get a bonny boy
> Will tak thir sails in hand,
> That will gang up to the top-mast,
> See an he ken dry land?
> —From *Sir Patrick Spens*

**Ballade:** One of the most popular of the artificial French verse forms. The *ballade* should not, however, be confused with the *ballad*, which is commonly folk-poetry, since the *ballade* is essentially sophisticated.

For a fixed conventional verse-type the ballade form has been rather liberally interpreted. Perhaps early usage most frequently demanded three stanzas and an envoy, though the number of lines to the stanza and of syllables to the line seems to have varied. Typical earmarks of the ballade have been: (1) the refrain (uniform as to wording) carrying the motif of the poem and recurring regularly at the end of each stanza and of the envoy; and (2) the envoy, by nature a peroration of climactic importance and likely to be addressed to a high member of the court or to the poet's patron. A frequent rime-scheme has been *ababbcbc* for the stanza and *bcbc* for the envoy. Modern ballade form most commonly presents three-, eight-, or ten-verse stanzas with an envoy of four or five lines. Rimes in all stanzas must be the same for corresponding lines, but the rime-words should not be repeated. A good example of early use of English ballade form is Chaucer's "Balade de bon conseyl" while one of the best known modern ballades is Rossetti's rendering of François Villon's *Ballad of Dead Ladies*. (Reference: Helen Louise Cohen, *The Ballade*, 1915.)

**Barbarism:** See SOLECISM.

**Bard:** Commonly, in modern use, simply a "poet." Historically, however, the term refers to those poets who recited verses usually glorifying the deeds of heroes and leaders, to the accompaniment of a musical instrument such as the harp. "Bard" technically refers to the early poets of the Celts, as *trouvère* (*q.v.*) refers to those of Normandy, *skald* (*q.v.*) to those of Scandinavia, and *troubadour* (*q.v.*) to those of Provence. See WELSH LITERATURE.

**Baroque:** A term of uncertain origin applied first to the architectural style which succeeded the classic style of the Renaissance and flourished, in varied forms in different parts of Europe, from the late sixteenth century until well into the eighteenth century. One writer (Geoffrey Scott) has explained the baroque style as a blending of the "picturesque" elements (the unexpected, the wild, the fantastic, the accidental) with the more ordered, formal, idealistic, and logical style of the "high Renaissance." The baroque stressed movement, energy, and realistic treatment. Scott points out that although the baroque is bold and startling, even fantastic, it is not truly wild or accidental, since its "discords and suspensions" are consciously and logically employed. Another writer (Croll) describes the change to the baroque as "a radical effort to adapt the traditional modes and forms of expression to the uses of a self-conscious modernism." In its considered efforts to avoid the effects of repose, tranquillity, and complacency, it sought to startle by the use of the unusual and unexpected. This led sometimes to grotesqueness, obscurity, and contortion. Indeed, the student will often come upon the term in its older or "popular" sense of the highly fantastic, the whimsical, the bizarre, the decadent.

The realization that the baroque arose naturally from existing conditions and is a serious and sincere style, resting upon a sober intellectual basis and designed to express the newer attitudes of its period, has had the effect not only of causing the baroque to be regarded with more sympathy and seriousness than formerly, but also of extending the use of the term to literature as well as to painting and sculpture. The student of literature may encounter the term (in its older English sense) applied unfavorably to a writer's literary style; or he may read of the baroque period or "age of baroque" (late sixteenth, seventeenth, and early eighteenth centuries); or he may find it applied descriptively and respectfully to certain stylistic features of the baroque period. Thus the broken rhythms of Donne's verse and the verbal subtleties of the English "metaphysical poets" have been called baroque elements. Richard Crashaw is said to have expressed the baroque spirit supremely in verse. Perhaps the most influential recent student of the baroque style is the German art critic Heinrich Wölfflin, some of whose followers have made ambitious efforts to explain literature on the basis of his theories. Wölfflin's works and those of Sacheverell Sitwell may be consulted, as well as Geoffrey Scott's *The Architecture of Humanism.* An example of the use of the term in literary criticism may be found in M. W. Croll's essay on "The Baroque Style in Prose," in *Studies in English Philology in Honor of Frederick Klaeber.* See ROCOCO, CONCEIT, META-PHYSICAL VERSE.

**Bathos:** The effect resulting from an unsuccessful effort to achieve dignity or pathos or elevation of style; an unintentional anticlimactic dropping from the sublime to the ridiculous; the depth of stupidity. The term gained currency from Pope's treatment of it in one of the "Martin Scriblerus" papers in which he ironically defended the commonplace effects of the English "poetasters" on the ground that depth (*bathos*) was a literary virtue of the moderns, as contrasted with the height (*hypsos*) of the ancients. Two examples of bathos given by Pope may be quoted:

> Advance the fringed curtains of thy eyes,
> And tell me who comes yonder.

Here the author (Temple) is felt to fail because of the (unintentional) anticlimax resulting from the effort to treat poetically a commonplace, prosaic idea. Richard Blackmore, in his *Job*, thus describes a great crowd gathering about Job:

> A waving sea of heads was round me spread,
> And still fresh streams the gazing deluge fed.

Here again the extravagant or inept imagery, though seriously intended, defeats its own purpose, and bathos results. The "pathetic fallacy" (*q.v.*) is sometimes responsible for a "bathetic" effect. If a novel or a play or a cinema tries to make the

41

reader or spectator weep and succeeds only in making him laugh, the result is bathos. The term is sometimes, though less accurately, applied to the deliberate use of anticlimax for satiric or humorous effect.

**Battle of the Books, The:** See Ancients and Moderns, Quarrel of the.

**Beast Epic:** A favorite medieval literary form consisting of a series of linked stories grouped about animal characters and often presenting satirical comment on contemporary life of church or court by means of human qualities attributed to beast characters. Scholars still find a nice quarrel in trying to decide the exact origin of the beast epic, some holding that the stories developed from popular tradition and were later given literary form by monastic scholars and *trouvères* who molded the material at hand, others finding the origin in the writing of Latin scholastics. The oldest example known seems to be that of Paulus Diaconus, a cleric at the court of Charlemagne, who wrote about 782–786. Whether the form first developed in Germany or France is still question for scholarly combat, though there is no doubt that in the twelfth and thirteenth centuries the beast epics were very popular in North France, West Germany, and Flanders. The various forms of the beast epic agreed in having one episode generally treated as the nucleus for the story: the healing of the sick lion by the fox's prescription that he wrap himself in the wolf's skin. Some of the other animals common to the form, besides Reynard the Fox, the lion, and the wolf, are the cock (Chanticler), the cat, the hare, the camel, the ant, the bear, the badger, and the stag. The best known of the beast epics—and the most influential—is the *Roman de Renard*, a poem of 30,000 lines comprising twenty-seven sets or "branches" of stories growing up in France between 1130 and 1250, the composition of which is probably to be credited to the influence of the Latin beast epic, modified in turn by the ecclesiastics and the French *trouvères*. Two other important forms of the beast epic are: the German *Reinhart Fuchs*, the work of Heinrich der Glichezare about 1180, a poem of 2,266 lines, and the Flemish form, *Van den vos Reinaerde*, the work of two men, Arnout and Willem, a poem of 3,476 lines.

This last version, which contained rather more than the usual amount of satire, was published in translation by Caxton in 1481, a fact which made the Flemish form of the beast epic perhaps the most significant in England. For evidences of the influence in English literature, see Spenser's *Mother Hubberds Tale* and Chaucer's *Nun's Priest's Tale*. A full discussion of the beast epic and its probable history is given in Lucien Foulet's *Le Roman de Renard*.

**Beast Fable:** See FABLE.

**Beginning Rime:** See RIME.

**Belles-Lettres:** Literature, more especially that body of writing, comprising drama, poetry, fiction, criticism, and essays which lives because of inherent imaginative and artistic rather than scientific or intellectual qualities. Lewis Carroll's *Alice in Wonderland*, for example, belongs definitely to the province of belles-lettres, while the mathematical works of the same man, Charles Lutwidge Dodgson, do not. Now sometimes used to characterize light or artificial writing.

**Bestiary:** A type of literature, particularly popular during the medieval centuries, in which the habits of beasts, birds, and reptiles were made the text for allegorical and mystical Christian teachings. These bestiaries often ascribed human attributes to animals and were designed to moralize and to expound church doctrine. The natural history employed is fabulous rather than scientific and has helped to make popular in literature such abnormalities as the phoenix, the siren, and the unicorn. Many of the qualities literature familiarly attributes to animals owe their origin to the bestiaries. The development of the type is first attributed to Physiologus, a Greek sermonizer of about A.D. 150, but the form was rapidly taken over by Christian preachers and homilists throughout Europe. The bestiary in one form or another has been current in various world literatures: Anglo-Saxon, Arabic, Armenian, English, Ethiopic, French, German, Icelandic, Provençal, Spanish.

**Bible:** Derived from a Greek term meaning "little books," "Bible" is now applied to the collection of writings known as the

43

Holy Scriptures, the sacred writings of the Christian religion. Of the two chief parts, the Old Testament consists of the sacred writings of the ancient Hebrews, and the New Testament of writings of the early Christian period. The Jewish Scriptures include three collections—The Law, The Prophets, and Writings —written in ancient Hebrew at various dates in the pre-Christian era. The New Testament books were written in the Greek dialect employed in Mediterranean countries about the time of Christ. An important Greek form of the Hebrew Bible is the Septuagint, dating from the Alexandrian period (third century B.C.). Latin versions were made in very early times, both of the Old and New Testament books, including many of the "Apocrypha" (see APOCHRYPHAL), the most important being that made by St. Jerome about A.D. 400, known as the Vulgate —the Bible of the Middle Ages. See next three topics.

**Bible as Literature:** The high literary value of many parts of the Bible has been almost universally recognized. Such English authors as Milton, Wordsworth, Scott, Carlyle, and many others have paid tribute to Biblical literature, Coleridge even rating the style of Isaiah and the Epistle to the Hebrews as far superior to that of Homer or Virgil or Milton. The literary qualities of the Bible are accounted for partly by the themes treated, partly by the poetic character of the Hebrew tongue, and partly by the literary skill exhibited by Biblical writers. Professor Cook calls the themes of Biblical literature "the greatest that literature can treat": God, man, the physical universe, and their interrelations. Such problems as human morality, man's relation to the unseen world, and ultimate human destinies are treated with a simplicity, sincerity, intensity, and vigor seldom matched in world literature. The character of the Hebrew language, abounding in words and phrases of concrete sensuous appeal and lacking the store of abstract words characteristic of the Greek, imparted an emotional and imaginative richness to Hebrew writings of a sort which lends itself readily to translation (the idea of pride, for example, is expressed by "puffed up"). The Bible is partly in prose and partly in verse, the principles of Hebrew verse being accent and parallelism rather than meter. The literary types found in the Bible have been variously classi-

44

fied. A few examples may be given: the short story, Ruth, Jonah, Esther; biographical narrative, the story of Abraham in Genesis; love lyric, Song of Solomon; the battle ode, the song of Deborah (Judges, v); epigram, in Proverbs and elsewhere; devotional lyric, Psalms; dramatic philosophical poem, Job; elegy, lament of David for Saul and Jonathan (II Samuel, i, 19–27); letters, the epistles of Paul; etc. The study of the Bible as literature is in a state of undeserved neglect in America. See BIBLE, INFLUENCE on LITERATURE. (References: R. G. Moulton, *The Literary Study of the Bible;* I. F. Wood and E. Grant, *The Bible as Literature;* J. H. Gardiner, *The Bible as Literature;* C. A. Dinsmore, *The English Bible as Literature.*)

**Bible, English Translations of:** From Caedmon (seventh century) to Wycliffe (fourteenth century) there were from time to time translations and paraphrases in Old English and in Middle English of various parts of the Bible. They were all based upon the Latin Vulgate edition. Some were in prose and some in verse. The parts most frequently translated were the Gospels, the Psalms, and the Pentateuch. The Caedmonian paraphrases (seventh century) are extant, but Bede's prose translation of a portion of the gospel of St. John (seventh century) is not preserved. From the ninth century come some "glosses" of the Book of Psalms and prose translations by King Alfred. The West Saxon Gospels and the glosses in the Lindisfarne Gospels date from the tenth century, while Aelfric's incomplete translations of the Old Testament date from the late tenth and early eleventh centuries. The subordinate position occupied by the English language for some time after the eleventh century perhaps accounts for the lack of translations in Middle English times until the fourteenth century, when there was some renewed activity in preparing English versions and commentaries, notably by Richard Rolle of Hampole. In 1382 came the first edition of the Wycliffe Bible, largely the work of Wycliffe himself. A revision of this work, chiefly the work of John Purvey, 1388, though interdicted by the Church from 1408 to 1534, circulated freely in manuscript form for the next 150 years.

Printed English Bibles first appeared in the sixteenth century, products of the new learning of the humanists and the zeal of the Protestant Reformation. They were mainly based upon Greek and Hebrew manuscripts, or recent translations of such manuscripts. A list of important English translations follows: (1) William Tyndale—the New Testament (1525–26), the Pentateuch (1530), Jonah (1531). Tyndale is credited with the creation of much of the picturesque phraseology which characterizes his and later English translations. (2) Miles Coverdale, first complete printed English Bible (1535), based upon Tyndale and a Swiss-German translation. (3) "Matthew's" Bible (1537), probably done by John Rogers, based upon Tyndale and Coverdale, is important as a source for later translations. (4) Taverner's Bible (1539), based on "Matthew's" Bible, but revealing a tendency to greater use of native English words. Not influential. (5) The Great Bible (1539), sometimes called Cranmer's Bible, because Cranmer sponsored it and wrote a preface for the second edition (1540)—a very large volume designed to be chained to its position in the churches for the use of the public. Coverdale superintended its preparation. It is based largely on "Matthew's" Bible. (6) The Geneva Bible (1560), the joint work of English Protestant exiles in Geneva, including Coverdale and William Whittington, who had published in 1557 in Geneva an English New Testament which was the first version in English divided into the familiar chapters and verses. The Geneva Bible was dedicated to Queen Elizabeth and included woodcuts, maps, tables, and marginal notes. It became the great Bible of the Puritans and ran through sixty editions between 1560 and 1611. The phraseology was colored by Calvinistic tendencies. (7) Bishops' Bible (1568), prepared by eight bishops and others and issued to combat the Calvinistic, anti-episcopal tendencies of the Geneva Bible. (8) The Rheims-Douai Bible (1582), a Catholic translation based upon the Vulgate, issued to counteract the Puritan Geneva Bible and the Episcopal Bishops' Bible. The Old Testament section was not actually printed till 1609.

By far the most important and influential of English Bibles is the "Authorized" or King James Version (1611). It is a revision of the Bishops' Bible and was sponsored by King James I. The translators, about fifty of the leading Biblical scholars of the time, including Puritans, made use of Greek and Hebrew manuscripts. This version is still the most widely read English Bible and it exerted a most profound influence upon the language and literature of the English and American peoples through the seventeenth, eighteenth, and nineteenth centuries.

The Revised Version (1885) and the standard American edition of the Revised Version (1901), the joint work of English and American scholars, are modern versions which aim chiefly at scholarly accuracy. Although both forms of this revised version are thought by many to be inferior from a literary point of view to the King James Version, their greater authority is generally recognized, and they seem gradually to be replacing the older version for pulpit use and public service. (References: John Brown, *The History of the English Bible;* A. W. Pollard, *Records of the English Bible.*)

**Bible, Influence on Literature:** The unparalleled influence of the Bible upon English literature, though widely recognized, is so subtly pervasive that it can merely be suggested, not closely traced. Much of its influence has been indirect—through its effect upon language and upon the mental and moral interests of the English and American people. J. R. Green (*Short History of the English People*, Ch. viii) notes the fact that the first English Bibles of the sixteenth century brought to the common people a new world by the revival of ancient Hebrew literature: "Legend and annal, war-song and psalm, state-roll and biography, the mighty voices of the prophets, the parables of the evangelists, stories of mission journeys, of perils by the sea and among the heathen, philosophic arguments, apocalyptic visions, all were flung broadcast over minds unoccupied for the most part by any rival learning." The picturesque imagery and phraseology were an enriching element in the lives of the people, and profoundly affected not only their conduct but their language and literary tastes. "As a mere literary monument, the English version of the Bible remains the noblest example of the English tongue, while its perpetual use made it from the instant of its appearance the standard of our language."

Great authors commonly show a familiarity with the Bible, and few great English and American writers of the seventeenth,

47

eighteenth, and nineteenth centuries can be read with satisfaction by one ignorant of Biblical literature. Professor Cook suggests the various ways in which the Authorized Version of the Bible has affected subsequent English literature: use of Scriptural themes (Milton's *Paradise Lost*, Bunyan's *Pilgrim's Progress*, Byron's *Cain*); use of Scriptural phraseology; allusions or modified quotations (as "selling birthright" for a "mess of pottage"); incorporation, conscious or unconscious, of Biblical phraseology into common speech ("highways and hedges," "thorn in the flesh," "a soft answer," etc., etc.). The Bible is thought to have been highly influential in substituting pure English words for Latin words (Tyndale's vocabulary is 97 per cent English, that of the Authorized Version, 93 per cent). The style of many writers has been directly affected by study of the Bible, as Bunyan's and Lincoln's—even Whitman's style is sometimes accounted for on the basis of Biblical influence. (References: A. S. Cook, *Camb. Hist. of Eng. Lit.*, Vol. IV, Chap ii; E. W. Work, *The Bible in English Literature*.)

**Bibliography:** Used in several senses. The term may be applied to a "subject bibliography"; this is a list of books or other printed (or manuscript) material on any chosen subject. A subject-bibliography may aim at comprehensiveness, even completeness; or it may be selective, intended to list only such works as are most important, or most easily available, or most closely related with a book or article to which it may be attached. Bibliographies following a serious essay, for example, may be merely a list of sources used by the writer of the essay, or they may be meant to point out to the reader sources of additional information on the subject. In a related use, the word designates a list of works of a particular country, author, or printer ("national" and "trade" bibliography). Bibliographies of these kinds are sometimes called "enumerative bibliographies." The process of making such lists either by students or by professional bibliographers is also referred to as "bibliography."

In the historical sense, as used by book collectors, bibliophiles, and scholars, bibliography means the history of book production, history of writing, printing, binding, illustrating, and publishing. It involves a consideration of the details of book-making.

Bibliography in this sense is sometimes used by scholars in textual criticism—the employing of bibliographical evidence to help "settle such questions as that of the order and relative value of different editions of a book; whether certain sections of a book were originally intended to form part of it or were added afterwards; whether a later edition was printed from an earlier one, and from which . ₒ . and a number of other problems of a similar kind, which may often have a highly important literary bearing."[1]  This sort of bibliographical work has been much stressed in the twentieth century, especially by members of the London Bibliographical Society, one striking result being the discovery of the forged dates on certain quartos of Shakespeare's plays, actually printed in 1619 but assigned earlier dates on the title pages.

Another use of the term bibliography is to denote the methods of work of student and author: reading, research, taking of notes, compilation of bibliography, preparation of manuscript for the press, publication, etc.  These last two uses of the word are of especial interest to advanced students who take university courses in "bibliography."

"A bibliography of bibliographies" means a list of lists of works dealing with a given subject or subjects.  An "annotated bibliography" is one in which some or all of the items listed are followed by brief descriptive or critical comment.

A few reference books and bibliographies of special use to students of literature may be noted.  H. B. Van Hoesen and F. K. Walter's *Bibliography* and A. Esdaile's *A Student's Manual of Bibliography* are useful general introductions to the subject of bibliography.  R. B. McKerrow's *An Introduction to Bibliography for Literary Students* is particularly valuable to advanced students of sixteenth-, seventeenth-, and eighteenth-century literature and to professional bibliographers.  Of great practical value to students in search of reference material on authors and literary topics are Isadore G. Mudge's *Guide to Reference Books,* John Minto's *Reference Books*, and C. S. Northup's *A Register of Bibliographies of English Language and Literature*.  T. P. Cross's *Bibliography and Methods of English Literary History* contains a

[1]Ronald B. McKerrow, "Notes on Bibliographical Evidence," etc., *Transactions of the Bibliographical Society*, Vol. XII, 1914.

49

classified list of important bibliographical titles. Advanced students interested in following recent research in language and literature may consult certain annual lists: *Annual Bibliography of English Language and Literature* of the Modern Humanities Research Association (comprehensive); *The Year's Work in English Studies* (selective, critical); the "American Bibliography" in *Publications of the Modern Language Association* (American research); "Recent Literature of the English Renaissance," in *Studies in Philology;* "English Literature, 1660–1800: a Current Bibliography," in the *Philological Quarterly;* and "Victorian Bibliography" in *Modern Philology.* Of bibliographies for special periods of English literature the notable work of J. E. Wells, *A Manual of the Writings in Middle English 1050–1400* (with supplements) deserves special mention. See BOOK SIZES.

**Billingsgate:** Coarse, vulgar, violent, abusive language. The term is derived from the fact that the fish-wives in Billingsgate fish market in London achieved a certain distinction from the scurrility of their language.

**Biography:** For over a thousand years biography has held a place of varying importance in the annals of English literature. It is natural that this should be, since biography, as a literary form, satisfies three inherent promptings of man: the commemorative instinct, the didactic or moralizing instinct, and, perhaps most important of all, the instinct of curiosity. From these three motives biography derives its impetus.

*Biography Distinguished from Allied Forms.*—With biography have come several related forms—letters, memoirs, diaries and journals, autobiography—which, though they spring from these same desires of men, must be distinguished from biography proper. Memoirs, diaries, journals, and autobiography are closely related to each other in that each is recollection written down by the subject himself. The writer tells those items of his career which he is willing to share with others and recalls those enthusiasms which seem to him to have dictated his activity. Letters afford a different angle to the subject's life. Usually collected by a literary executor after the decease of the subject, they are likely to be colored by various prejudices and purposes.

The subject himself may or may not have been spontaneous in his correspondence. The editor may or may not be completely honest in his printing of the letters. Delightful as this kind of thing often is, it falls short of biography in that the reader sees the subject only at certain times and under special conditions. Nearer the biography than any of these forms—and yet not an exact parallel—is the "life and times" book. In this kind of writing the author is concerned with two points: the life of his central figure and the period in which this figure lived. The writer may do a very fascinating book, one both interesting and instructive, but pure biography, in the more modern sense, does not look two ways; it centers its whole attention on the character and career of its subject.

*What Is Biography?*—Since biography, then, is not to be confused with these other forms, it is well to see exactly what it is. In England the word *biography*, as a term denoting a form of writing, first came into use with Dryden, who, in 1683, defined it as "the history of particular men's lives." But the matter is hardly so simple as this. Since its earliest appearance as a written form—and it existed long before Dryden—biography has meant different things to different people. A definition of biography in the eighteenth century would not fit the conception held in, say, the sixteenth. And during the first quarter of the twentieth century very different qualities have been insisted upon. A "history of particular men's lives" may serve, perhaps, as a unifying principle for the numerous theories of biography, but it falls short of a definition of the term in the twentieth century.

Today the term carries with it certain definite demands. It must be a history, but an accurate history; one which paints not only one aspect of the man but all important aspects. It must be the life of a "particular" man focused clearly on that man with more casual reference to the background of the social and political institutions of his time. It must present the facts accurately and must make some effort to interpret these facts in such a way as to present character and habits of mind. It must avoid panegyric and the didactic as the man himself might have avoided the plague. But, on the other hand, it must emphasize personality. And this personality must be the central thesis of the book. If the biographer looks at the times, it must be only with the purpose of presenting a well-constructed and unified impression of the personality of his subject; if he introduces letters and anecdotes (as he surely will) it will be only such anecdotes and letters as reflect this central conception of personality. Biography today, then, may be defined as the accurate presentation of the life history from birth to death of an individual, this presentation being secured through an honest effort to interpret the facts of the life in such a way as to offer a unified impression of the character, mind, and personality of the subject.

*The Development of English Biography: The Commemorative Purpose.*—Just how this modern attitude differs from past conceptions may best be appreciated after a brief survey of the history of the biography as a literary type. Harold Nicolson, in his *Development of English Biography*, states that "we can trace the ancestry of English biography to the ancient runic inscriptions which celebrated the lives of heroes and recorded the exploits of deceased and legendary warriors." He reports it again as an element in such early Anglo-Saxon verse as *Beowulf* and the *Widsith* fragment. And in these early manifestations we find what was, probably, the first conception of biography—the commemorative instinct, the "cenotaph-urge." These accounts were written to glorify, and glorification, in far too many biographies, has remained as a prominent intent of the biographer. It has taken years to shake that conception off; indeed even now it is often present.

*The Didactic Purpose.*—This desire to commemorate greatness was, later on, united with a second purpose—the encouragement of morality. This purpose accounts for hagiography, records of saints. The church took a hand. Great men and women were commemorated for their virtue, their vices being conveniently overlooked. The lives of the saints occupied the attention of scholars in the monasteries. One list of early English historical material reports 1,277 writings, almost all of which were devoted to the glorification of one or another Irish or British saint. Even Bede (who died in 735) was little more than a hagiographer. It was not until Bishop Asser (893) wrote his *Life of Alfred the Great* that anything appears which very closely resembles biography. Here was the life narrative of a layman told in

Latin; but here, too, were the two early purposes of the biographer—commemoration and didactic moralizing.

*The Beginnings of Pure Biography.*—With Monk Eadmer of the twelfth century English biography reached another milestone. Eadmer, in his *Vita Anselmi*, somehow managed to humanize his subject beyond the capacity of former biographers. He introduced letters into his narrative to make his points; he reported anecdotes and conversation in a way which definitely brightened his pages. He wrote, in short, what Nicolson considers the first pure biography in England. This same century, the twelfth, saw the dying out—though not the disappearance—of the hagiographer and moralizing motive. Romance was coming to the front. Living began to take on some joy. And with this lighter mood of the fourteenth and fifteenth centuries biography gradually became somewhat less serious, less commemorative, less didactic.

*Biography Definitely "Arrives."*—For the purposes of this brief survey, however, this summary need not pause again until the middle of the sixteenth century when William Roper (1496–1578), More's son-in-law, wrote what is now most often referred to as the first English biography, his *Life of Sir Thomas More*, and George Cavendish (1500–1561) wrote his *Life of Wolsey*. With these two books, English biography had most certainly arrived as a recognized form of literature. The didactic purpose was still obvious, the commemorative spirit was still present. But both books make a greater effort to avoid prejudice than had before manifested itself in English biography. Both books resorted to episode and anecdote and fairly vivid dialogue. Both books devoted their space to the life of one man, the *Wolsey* beginning with the birth of the subject and ending with the death. But most important of all, both books made an avowed declaration to follow the truth. Hagiography and commemoration are present, but no writer before these two had made such general efforts to strike a fair balance, to write adversely of their subjects when adverse comment was necessary. And with this gesture toward the truth biography came more definitely into its own as a field of literature.

*The Seventeenth Century: Biographic Brevities.*—The next century, the seventeenth, did little to advance biography. It was, in general, a time of brevities. The character sketch, the ana, flourished. People were interested in ethical motives of one sort or another. The "character" (*q.v.*) was the contemporary enthusiasm. John Aubrey wrote his frank, gossipy *Minutes of Lives* as brief estimates of his contemporaries. Thomas Fuller wrote his *Worthies*. Diaries, letters, and memoirs were plentiful;—the *Memoirs of Lady Fanshawe* and the *Memoirs of Colonel Hutchinson* serve as examples. The first worth-while autobiography, perhaps, is that of Lord Herbert. But were it not for Izaak Walton's *Lives* the century would be almost a complete loss so far as biography is concerned. Walton, who wrote his *Lives* from 1640 to 1678, has been considered by some the first English professional biographer since he attempted the form deliberately and sustained it over a long period. Walton, too, contributed breeziness to the form, reverting to the manner of Monk Eadmer in his use of letters and adding for himself supposititious conversations between his subject and others. Opposed to Walton and his biographical manner there was Thomas Sprat, whose *Life of Cowley* appeared in 1668. Sprat is important to our purpose for his manner. To him it is that the Victorian demand for "decency" in biography seems largely due, for Sprat wrote a life that was a cold and dignified thing, formal and proper, emasculated and virtuous. "The tradition of 'discreet' biography," writes one critic, "owes its wretched origin to him."

*The Eighteenth Century: Biography at Its Best.*—If biography almost stood still during the seventeenth century, the eighteenth saw it march forward to the greatest accomplishment it has enjoyed. Boswell's Life of Dr. Johnson stands, probably for all time, at the head of any list of biographies. Two lesser luminaries were Roger North and William Mason—North (*Lives of the Norths*), who insisted that panegyric be avoided and wrote brightly and colloquially, and Mason (*Life and Writings of Gray*), who carried further the use of letters and pretty largely left his reader to deduce the sort of man his subject was by a simple placing before the reader of a wide range of illustrative material. Dr. Johnson himself dignified biography by developing a philosophy for the writing of the form and by his insistence that to a real biographer truth was much more important than respect for a dead man or his relatives. To Dr. Johnson probably more than to any other critic of the form goes the credit of having raised biography to the rank of literature and art. In his *Lives of the Poets* he himself practiced his doctrines. The writing of the supreme English biography was, however, reserved for Johnson's biographer—James Boswell. This is no place to estimate anew that frequently praised book. What is important is the new twist which Boswell gave to biographic method. He used most of the methods developed by earlier writers, but he wrought of them a new combination. Humor of a sort was here; here was introduced a great wealth of petty detail from which the reader might make for himself his deductive analysis; here, too, were the anecdote and ana elements of the seventeenth century; and, greatest of all, here were intimacy and personal comment. To Boswell was given the privilege of making biography actual, real, convincing. Here at last were the commemorative elements subordinated; the didactic qualities minimized. In the work of James Boswell biography painted a living, breathing human being.

*Victorian Biography Becomes Discreet.*—The Boswell tradition was in a fair way of being accepted when Victorianism, with its tedious studiousness, its two-volume "life and letters" biography, its "authorized" biographers more or less controlled by the family and relatives of the hero, blurred the picture. True enough, in the nineteenth century before Victorianism stultified biography, there had been Tom Moore's *Life of Sheridan* and *Letters and Journals of Lord Byron;* as well as Lockhart's *Life of Scott.* But on the whole the freedom which Boswell had brought to this writing was restricted and confined by the Victorians. Religious orthodoxy, piety, and moral judgments again were in the saddle. Tennyson spoke for the epoch when he thundered, "What business has the public to know about Byron's wildnesses? He has given them fine work and they ought to be satisfied." Hagiography had returned.

*The Twentieth Century Becomes Objective.*—The first quarter of the twentieth century saw biography shake off again this mantle of scrupulous morality. With the current century appeared an awakened intelligence and a more scientific spirit. Psychology, particularly, has brought with its rapid development new attitudes toward human nature, new efforts to understand and appreciate. And the scientific attitude brings with it less surety as to moral judgments. The time has gone further from hagiography than any former period. It no longer worships myths and legends because they are sacred myths and legends. Readers today are, in short, more anxious to arrive at the truth of life and existence. With Giles Lytton Strachey's *Eminent Victorians* and *Queen Victoria* this new spirit came suddenly. And in the light of this new spirit the twentieth century in both England and America for a while rewrote the biography of great men, estimating anew recent and contemporary heroes.

The pendulum, we have seen, swings back and forth many times. The best is reflected in the worst. Giles Lytton Strachey, André Maurois, Gamaliel Bradford have brought somewhat new emphasis; other biographers, who shall here be nameless, have distorted and confused the best of these recent methods until at times modern biography seems intent on nothing so much as showing the stains on the cloaks of the great. It will not be strange if ultimately bad biographers, like bad coinage, destroy that which is best in the recent attitudes. (References: D. A. Stauffer, *English Biography Before 1700;* Mark Longaker, *English Biography in the Eighteenth Century;* Harold Nicolson, *Development of English Biography;* Waldo H. Dunn, *English Biography.*)

**Blank Verse:** Blank verse may be said to consist of unrimed lines of ten syllables each, the second, fourth, sixth, eighth, and tenth syllables bearing the accents (iambic pentameter). This form has generally been accepted as that best adapted to dramatic verse in English and is commonly used for long poems whether dramatic, philosophic, or narrative. Because of its freedom it appears easy to write, but good blank verse probably demands more artistry and genius than any other verse form. The freedom gained through lack of rime is offset by the demands for richness to be secured through its privileges. This richness may be obtained by the skillful poet through a variety of means: the shifting of the caesura, or pause, from place to place within the line; the shifting of the stress among syllables; the use of the run-on line, which permits of thought-grouping in large or small blocks (these thought-groups being variously termed verse "paragraphs" or verse "stanzas"); variation in tonal qualities by changing diction from passage to passage; and, finally, the adaptation of the form to reproduction of differences in the speech of characters in dramatic and narrative verse and to differences of emotional expression.

Alden attributes the development of blank verse as an English form to the influence of classical humanism "the representatives of which grew skeptical as to the use of rime, on the ground that it was not found in classical poetry." It appears to have first found general favor in England as a medium for dramatic expression, but with Milton it was turned to epic use and since then has been employed in the writing of idylls and lyrics. The distinction of the first use of blank verse in English, though the claims are not quite clear, is generally given to Surrey, who used the form in his translation of parts of the *Aeneid* (made prior to 1547). The earliest dramatic use of blank verse in English was in Sackville and Norton's *Gorboduc*, 1565; the earliest use in didactic verse was in Gascoigne's *Steel Glass*, 1576; but it was only with Marlowe (prior to 1593) that the form first reached the hands of a master capable of using its range of possibilities and passing it on for Shakespeare and Milton to develop to its ultimate perfection. In more recent times some critics have manifested a willingness to extend the meaning of the term to include almost any metrical unrimed form, and not to restrict its use to verses of ten syllables and five accents. (References: J. A. Symonds, *Blank Verse;* R. M. Alden, *An Introduction to Poetry.*)

**Blues:** An Afro-American folk-song of recent development among the Negroes of the southern United States. A blues is characteristically short (three-line stanza), melancholy in tone, and marked by frequent repetition. Probably each blues was originally the composition of one person, but so readily are blues appropriated and changed that in practice they are a branch of folk literature. The following is an example:

> Gwine lay my head right on de railroad track,
> Gwine lay my head right on de railroad track,
> 'Cause my baby, she won't take me back.

For a full discussion of the subject, see *Blues*, by W. C. Handy.

**Bluestockings:** A term which suggests women of the intellectual type. It gained currency about 1782 as a result of its application (for reasons not now easy to establish beyond dispute) to a group of women of literary and intellectual tastes who held in London assemblies or "conversations" to which "literary and ingenious men" were invited. It was the English equivalent of the French *salon*. There was no formal organization and the personnel of the group changed from time to time, so that no "membership" list can be given with assurance or completeness. Among the women "bluestockings" were Mrs. Elizabeth Montagu (the "Queen of the Blues"), Hannah More, Fanny Burney, and Mrs. Hester Chapone. Horace Walpole was one of the male "members," and Dr. Samuel Johnson, Edmund Burke, and David Garrick were at times frequent visitors. The activities of the group were directed toward encouraging an interest in literature and fostering the recognition of literary genius (see PRIMITIVISM), and hence helped remove the odium which had attached to earlier "learned ladies." (Reference: C. B. Tinker, *The Salon and English Letters*.)

**Bombast:** Ranting, insincere, extravagant language. Grandiloquence. Elizabethan tragedy, especially early Senecan plays, contains much bombastic style, marked by extravagant imagery. An example may be quoted from Shakespeare's *Hamlet* (Act II, Sc. 2):

> Roasted in wrath and fire,
> And thus o'er-sized with coagulate gore,
> With eyes like carbuncles, the hellish Pyrrhus
> Old grandsire Priam seeks.

**Bon mot:** A witty repartee or statement. A clever saying. The art of the *bon mot* in America today is perhaps most definitely kept alive by some of the better columnists.

> Among our literary scenes,
> Saddest this sight to me,
> The graves of little Magazines
> That died to make verse free.[1]

---

[1]Keith Preston, *Pot Shots from Pegasus*, published by Covici-Friede, Inc. Reprinted by permission of the publishers.

**Book Sizes:** To understand the terms, quarto, octavo, and the rest, used in describing book sizes, it is first of all necessary to know the principle determining these sizes. This principle is best understood by imagining before one a sheet of paper, "foolscap" size, 17 inches by $13\frac{1}{2}$ inches.

When this paper is folded along 1–2, 3–4, and 5–6, the resulting folds mark off the sizes of book pages cut from the large foolscap sheet. Thus 1–2–7–8 represents one of two leaves cut from the original foolscap and is, therefore, a "folio" (Latin for *leaf*) sheet or page; 2–3–4–7 represents one fourth of the original sheet and, therefore, gives us a "quarto" page; 2–3–5–6 constitutes one eighth of the original and gives us an "octavo" page. A book size, then, is determined by the number of book leaves cut from a single large sheet.

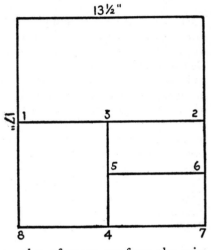

To determine the number of pages cut from the original sheet count the number of pages to a "signature"; this may often be done by noting the occurrence of the signature marks (themselves sometimes called "signatures") which appear at regular intervals at the foot of a page. These symbols are usually numerals or letters and may be found regularly in early printed books and sometimes in recently printed ones. They indicate the beginning of new signatures. *The number of leaves (not pages) in a single signature shows the number of leaves cut from the original sheet and is, therefore, the indication of the book size.* When there are two leaves to the signature, the book is a folio; when there are four leaves, it is a quarto; and so on. The table at the top of the following page shows in convenient outline form the principle explained above as it manifests itself in the more frequently used book sizes.

| No. of Leaves | Pages to Signature | Name |
|---|---|---|
| 2 | 4 | Folio |
| 4 | 8 | Quarto(4to) |
| 8 | 16 | Octavo(8vo) |
| 12 | 24 | duodecimo(12mo) |
| 16 | 32 | sixteenmo(16mo) |
| 32 | 64 | thirty-twomo(32mo) |
| 64 | 128 | sixty-fourmo(64mo) |

This would all be very simple but for the fact that in modern printing there is a variety of sizes of original stock. In addition to the "foolscap 8vo" in our example, we may have Post 8vo, Demy 8vo, Crown 8vo, Royal 8vo, etc., the terms Demy, Crown, and the others referring to varying sizes of original sheets which, in turn, give varying sizes of book pages even when the number of leaves cut from the sheets is the same. So complicated has the whole question of book sizes become that expert bibliographers urge more attention to the position of the watermark on the page (a guide to book measurements too complicated to discuss here) and even then frequently give up the question in despair. Publishers arbitrarily use 12mo., octavo, etc., for books of certain sizes regardless of the number of pages to the signature. For a full discussion of the subject see *An Introduction to Bibliography*, Ronald B. McKerrow, p. 164.

**Bourgeois Drama:** A loose term applied to plays in which the life of the common folk rather than that of the courtly or the rich is depicted. Such widely differing kinds of plays as Heywood's *Interludes*, *Gammer Gurton's Needle*, Dekker's *Shoemaker's Holiday* (realistic comedy), and Lillo's *The London Merchant* (domestic tragedy) are embraced in the term.

**Bourgeois Literature:** Literature produced primarily to appeal to the middle-class reader. Compare "bourgeois drama," where "bourgeois" does not denote the class of readers but the social sphere of the action of the play.

**Bowdlerize:** To expurgate a book or piece of writing by omitting all offensive, indecorous passages. "Bowdlerize" derives its significance from the fact that Thomas Bowdler, an

English physician, published (in 1818) an expurgated edition of Shakespeare.

**Brief:** A condensed statement, a résumé, of the main arguments or ideas presented in a speech or piece of writing. In legal practice, a formal summary of laws and authorities bearing on the main points of a case; in church history, a papal letter less formal than a bull.

**British Museum:** Of importance to students of literature since it houses probably the most important library in the world. The collection, founded in 1753 through a bequest from Sir Hans Sloane, now embraces over 5,000,000 items. It is located, in Great Russell Street, in Bloomsbury, London. The British Museum is particularly wealthy in its collection of valuable manuscripts including, besides the famous Harleian and Cottonian MSS., a series of documents from the third century to the present. Particularly noteworthy are its collections comprising English historical chronicles, Anglo-Saxon materials, charters, Arthurian romances, the Burney Collection of classical MSS., Greek papyri, Irish, French, and Italian MSS., and the genealogical records of English families. From time to time it has been given by bequest special libraries such as Archbishop Cranmer's Collection, the Thomas Collection, the C. M. Cracherode Collection, and the Sir Joseph Banks Collection. Other important features are its assortment of items from American, Chinese and Oriental, Hebrew, and Slavonic literatures. Some four thousand newspapers are filed and bound. According to the British copyright law the Museum is to secure copies of every publication entered at Stationers' Hall. The result of all this is an astonishing grouping together in one place of the learning and literatures of the world, so important a grouping that every advanced student of English and world literatures hopes for an opportunity to work in its archives.

**Broadside Ballad:** Soon after the development of printing in England ballads were prepared for circulation on folio sheets, printed on one side only, two pages to the sheet, and two columns to the page. Because of their manner of publication these were termed "broadsides." In quality these ballads ranged from reproductions of old popular ballads of real literary distinction to semi-illiterate screeds with little poetic quality. The subjects of these broadsides were of wide variety: accidents, dying speeches of criminals, miraculous events of one sort or another, religious and political harangues. They were often satirical in nature and frequently personal in their invective. In the sixteenth century, the heyday of their popularity, they served, as one critic states, as a "people's yellow journal." A few of the many modern collections of broadside ballads may be cited: *Roxburghe Ballads*, 9 vols.; *A Pepysian Garland* and *The Pack of Antolycus*, both edited by H. E. Rollins.

**Brook Farm:** A communal experiment growing out of certain aspects of New England transcendental thought. The farm, located at West Roxbury, Massachusetts, nine miles from Boston, was taken over in 1841 by a joint stock company, headed by George Ripley. The full name of the organization was "The Brook Farm Institute of Agriculture and Education." The basic reasons for the scheme were efforts to provide for the residents opportunity for cultural pursuits and leisure at little cost, the farm being supposed, through the rotation of labor of the members, to support the residents who, in most of their time, were to be free to attend lectures, read, write, and discuss intellectual problems. No doubt the project was much influenced by the doctrines of François Fourier and Robert Owen. It should be noted that while many transcendentalists manifested an active interest in the enterprise, the movement was in no proper sense the outgrowth of a general activity on the part of all transcendentalists. Hawthorne (see the *Blithedale Romance*) was there for a period as were other prominent leaders, but such people as Emerson, Alcott, and Margaret Fuller never actively took part. Dissension among the members, the discovery that the soil was not fertile enough to bring the necessary return from the labor expended, and the burning of a new and uninsured "phalanstery," were some of the reasons which in 1846 brought about the failure of the project. See TRANSCENDENTALISM. (Reference: Lindsay Swift, *Brook Farm*.)

**Bucolic:** A term used to characterize pastoral writing, particularly poetry, concerned with shepherds and rural life. The treatment is usually rather formal and fanciful. In the plural, "Bucolics," the term refers collectively to the pastoral literature of such writers as Theocritus and Virgil. In the present loose usage the expression connotes simply poetry of rustic background and is not necessarily restricted to verse with the conventional pastoral elements.

**Burlesque:** A form of comic art characterized by ridiculous exaggeration. This distortion is secured in a variety of ways: the sublime may be made absurd, honest emotions may be turned to sentimentality, a serious subject may be treated frivolously or a frivolous subject seriously. Perhaps the essential quality which makes for burlesque is the discrepancy between subject-matter and style. That is, a style ordinarily dignified may be used for nonsensical matter, or a style very nonsensical may be used to ridicule a weighty subject. Burlesque, as a form of art, manifests itself in sculpture, painting, and even architecture, as well as in literature. This type of writing has an ancient lineage in world literature: an author of uncertain identity used it in the *Battle of the Frogs and Mice,* to travesty Homer. Aristophanes made burlesque popular, and in France, under Louis XIV, nothing was sacred to the satirist. Chaucer in *Sir Thopas* burlesqued medieval romance as did Cervantes in *Don Quixote.* One of the best known uses of burlesque in drama is Gay's *Beggar's Opera.* In recent use the term—already broad —has been broadened to include musical plays light in nature though not essentially burlesque in tone or manner. (References: Richmond P. Bond, *English Burlesque Poetry, 1700–1750;* George Kitchen, *A Survey of Burlesque and Parody in English.*)

**Burletta:** A term used in the late eighteenth century for a variety of musical dramatic forms, somewhat like the ballad-opera (*q.v.*), the extravaganza (*q.v.*), and the pantomime (*q.v.*). One of its sponsors (George Colman, the younger) asserted that the proper use of the word was for "a drama in rhyme, entirely musical—a short comick piece consisting of *recitative* and *singing*, wholly accompanied, more or less, by the orchestra."

**Buskin:** A boot, thick-soled and reaching halfway to the knee, worn by Greek tragedians with the purpose of increasing their stature, even as comedians wore socks for the opposite purpose. By association "buskin" has come to mean tragedy. Milton used "the buskin'd stage" and "Jonson's learned sock" to characterize tragedy and comedy respectively.

**Cacophony:** The opposite of euphony; a term used to characterize a harsh, unpleasant combination of sounds or tones. Though most specifically a term used in the criticism of poetry, the word is also employed to indicate any disagreeable sound effect in other forms of writing.

**Cadence:** Measured, rhythmical movement either in prose or verse. The recurrence of emphasis or accent often accompanied by rising and falling modulations of the voice. Cadence is related to rhythm, but exists usually in larger and looser units of syllables than the formal, metrical movement of regular verses. Properly used, cadence can be made one of the most subtle and pleasing of stylistic qualities. See FREE VERSE.

**Cæsura:** A pause or break in the metrical or rhythmical progress of a line of verse. Originally, in classical literature, the cæsura characteristically divided a foot between two words. Usually the cæsura had been placed near the middle of a verse. Some poets, however, have sought diversity of rhythmical effect by placing the cæsura anywhere from near the beginning of a line to near the end. Examples of variously placed cæsuras follow:

> Sleepst thou, Companion dear, || what sleep can close
> Thy eye-lids? || and remembrest what Decree
> Of yesterday, || so late hath past the lips
> Of Heav'ns Almightie. || Thou to me thy thoughts
> Was wont, etc.
>
> —Milton

**Calendar:** See ALMANAC.

**Calligraphy:** The art of beautiful writing. In literature the significance of the term springs from the development of the art during the Middle Ages when the monks so generally gave their attention to the copying of ancient manuscripts. Much literature was preserved through their skillful penmanship.

**Calvinism:** Throughout the whole course of Western European Christian culture (and American culture as well), religious ideas and systems have profoundly affected, both directly and indirectly, literature and literary history. The great conflict of medieval times was between "Augustinianism," which would exalt the glory of God at the expense of the dignity of man (stressing original sin and the necessity of divine grace), and "Pelagianism," which asserted man's original innocence and his ability to develop moral and spiritual power through his own efforts. "Arminianism" was somewhat of a compromise between these positions, insisting upon the part both God and man must play in human redemption. ("Calvinism" was a Renaissance representative of the Augustinian point of view. At no time in the last four hundred years has the literature of England or America been free from reflections of Calvinistic thought and conduct. Though neither Milton nor Bunyan was a full-fledged Calvinist, *Paradise Lost* may be cited as an epic poem intended in the main to justify the Calvinistic theology, and *Pilgrim's Progress* as an allegory which reflects the effects upon human personality of the practical religion based upon Calvinism. Hawthorne's *Scarlet Letter* is a protest against the effects of the Calvinistic system upon the human mind and heart.)

Some understanding of the teachings of Calvinism—the charter of which is John Calvin's famous *Institutes of the Christian Religion* (1536)—is therefore important to the student of literature. Calvinistic doctrines have been summarized as follows (not all "Calvinists," of course, accepted unequivocally *all* of them): 1. God is a God of power, conceived as a king or ruler. 2. Hence the chief duty of man is to aid in making the will of God prevail. 3. This will of God can be discovered through the study of the Bible. 4. But this involves much mental work—hence the emphasis upon logical processes. The Bible furnishes the premises: man must reason from them. 5. Human nature was corrupted by Adam's sin and man therefore inherits a totally depraved nature, even infants being wholly sinful and subject to damnation. 6. Man can be saved only through God's grace by means of the Atonement. But this salvation is effective only for certain chosen ones. 7. Hence the famous doctrine of election or predestination. God must determine beforehand

65

which individuals are to be saved, which condemned. The "elect" discover their good fortune through the inner voice or witness of the spirit. Those not chosen develop their evil natures through the agency of Satan and thus merit their hard fate. 8. Though the church and state are theoretically separate, the Church might advise the state (in New England this came to mean that only the elect might enjoy the rights of citizenship). This system developed both zeal and intolerance on the part of the elect. It fostered education, however, which in early New England was regarded as a religious duty, and thereby profoundly affected the development of American culture. To this attitude of the Calvinistic Puritans may be traced much of the inspiration for such things as: the founding of many colleges and universities, the creation of a system of public schools, and the great activity of early printing presses in America—as well as the development of religious sects. Historically, especially in Europe, it is probably true that the political effects of Calvinism have been in the main calculated to encourage freedom and popular government. (Reference: G. P. Fisher, *History of Christian Doctrine*.)

**Canon:** (1) A standard of judgment; a criterion; (2) the authorized or accepted list of books belonging in the Christian Bible. "Apocryphal" books are uncanonical. The term is often extended to mean the accepted list of books of any author, such as Shakespeare. Thus *Macbeth* belongs without doubt in the "canon" of Shakespeare's work, while *Sir John Oldcastle*, though printed as Shakespeare's soon after his death, is not "canonical," because the evidence of Shakespeare's authorship is unconvincing. A similar use of the word is illustrated in the phrase "the Saints' Canon," the list of Saints actually authorized or "canonized" by the Church.

**Cant:** Insincere, specious language calculated to give the impression of piety and religious fervor. In critical writing the term is also used to signify the special language and phraseology characteristic of a profession or art, as "the pedagogue's cant," "the artist's cant." In this sense of a special language, the term indicates any technical or special vocabulary or dialect, as "thieves' cant," "beggars' cant," etc. More loosely still, the word signifies any insincere, superficial display of language, planned to convey an impression of conviction, but devoid of genuine emotion or feeling; that is, language used chiefly for display or effect.

**Canto:** A section or division of a long poem.   Derived from the Latin *cantus* (song) the word originally signified a section of a narrative poem of such length as to be sung by a minstrel in one singing.   Byron's *Childe Harold's Pilgrimage* is divided into cantos.

*Canzone:* A lyrical poem, a song or ballad.   In several ways the *canzone* is similar to the madrigal (*q.v.*).   The *canzone* is a short poem consisting of equal stanzas and an envoy of fewer lines than the stanza.   It is impossible to be specific as to the mechanics of the verse form since different writers have wrought rather wide variations in structure.   The number of lines to the stanza ranges from seven to twenty, and the envoy from three to ten.   Petrarch's *canzoni* usually consisted of five or six stanzas and the envoy.   In general it may be said that the *canzone* form is not unlike the *chant royal* (*q.v.*) though its conventions are less fixed.   The *canzone* is generally conceded to have first developed in Provence during the Middle Ages and Giraud de Borneil is credited with having first evolved the pattern which has proved very popular in Italy.   Others than Petrarch who have written *canzoni* are Dante, Tasso, Leopardi, Chiabrera, and Marchetti.   Frequent subjects used were love, nature, and the wide range of emotional reactions to life, particularly if sad, which poets commonly present.

**Caricature:** Descriptive writing which seizes upon certain individual qualities of a person and through exaggeration or distortion produces a burlesque, ridiculous effect.   Caricature more frequently is associated with drawing (cartoons) than with writing, since for writing the related types—satire, burlesque, and parody—are more generally used.   Caricature, unlike the highest satire, is likely to treat *personal* qualities, though, like satire, it lends itself to the ridicule of political, religious, and social foibles.   See T. Wright's *History of Caricature and Grotesque in Literature and Art.*

67

**Carol (Carole):** In medieval times in France a "carole" was a dance, the term later being applied to the song which accompanied the dance. The leader sang the stanzas, the other dancers singing the refrain. The "carole" became very popular, and in the twelfth and thirteenth centuries spread through other European countries and was instrumental in extending the influence of the French lyric. Later, "carol" was used to mean any joyous song, then a hymn of religious joy, and finally was used to designate Christmas hymns in particular. Some carols, such as "Joseph was an old man," were definitely popular, belonging to the culture of the folk, while later ones, such as Charles Wesley's "Hark, the Herald Angels Sing," are the product of more conscious and sophisticated literary effort. The Christmas hymn is called a *noël* in France. (References: R. L. Greene, *The Early English Carols;* E. B. Reed, ed., *Christmas Carols Printed in the Sixteenth Century.*)

**Caroline:** Applied to whatever belonged to or was typical of the age of Charles I of England (1625–1642), but more particularly to the spirit of the court of Charles. Thus "Caroline literature" might mean all the literature of the time, both Cavalier and Puritan, or it might be used more specifically to suggest that of the royalist group, such as the Cavalier Lyrists (*q.v.*). Caroline literature was in some senses a decadent carry-over from the Elizabethan and Jacobean periods. Melancholy not only characterized the work of the "metaphysical poets" (*q.v.*) but permeated the writings of both the conflicting groups, Puritan and Cavalier. Drama was decadent; romanticism was in decline; classicism was advancing; the scientific spirit was growing in spite of the absorption of the people in violent religious controversies. It was in Caroline times that the Puritan migration to America was heaviest. See BAROQUE, JACOBEAN; also "Outline of Literary History" (pp. 496–499).

***Carpe diem:*** "Seize the day." The phrase was used by Horace and has come to be applied generally to literature, especially to lyric poems, which exemplify the spirit of "Let us eat and drink, for tomorrow we shall die." The theme was a very common one in sixteenth- and seventeenth-century English love poetry; lover-poets continually were exhorting their mistresses to yield to love while they still had their youth and beauty, as in Robert Herrick's famous

> Gather ye rosebuds while ye may,
> Old Time is still a-flying;
> And this same flower that smiles today,
> Tomorrow will be dying.

**Catalexis** (adj.—**Catalectic**): Incompleteness of the last foot at the end of a verse; truncation at the close of a line of poetry by omission of one or two final syllables; the opposite of anacrusis. Catalexis is one of the many ways in which the poet secures variety of metrical effects. The term "acatalectic" is used to designate particular lines where catalexis is *not* employed. In the following lines written in dactylic dimeter, the second and fourth are "catalectic" because the second foot of each lacks the two unaccented syllables which would normally complete the dactyl. The first and third lines, in which the unaccented syllables are *not* cut off and which therefore are metrically complete, are "acatalectic."

> One more unfortunate,
> Weary of breath,
> Rashly importunate,
> Gone to her death!
>                   —Thomas Hood

**Catastrophe:** The final stage in the falling action of a tragedy. It ends the dramatic struggle and usually involves the death of the hero and others. By analogy the term is sometimes used to designate a tragic ending in non-dramatic fiction. See DÉNOUEMENT, DRAMATIC STRUCTURE.

**Catharsis:** Aristotle described the effect of tragedy as a *katharsis* (lit., "purging") of the spectator's emotions: the pity and fear excited by the tragic action "purge" by modifying or repelling passion. Though it is not certain just what Aristotle meant, the term now commonly denotes the "purging" or "purification" of the emotions through "imaginative participation" in the sufferings of others; or the "mood of emotional release and intellectual serenity" induced by tragic literature or art. (References: Ingram Bywater, *Aristotle on the Art of Poetry;* items listed under TRAGEDY and CRITICISM, HISTORICAL SKETCH.)

**Cavalier Lyric:** The sort of light-hearted poem characteristic of the Cavalier Lyrists (*q.v.*), or a poem intended to illustrate the spirit or the times of the Cavaliers, such as Browning's "Boot, Saddle, to Horse and Away."

**Cavalier Lyrists:** A group of court poets of the time of Charles I, especially Thomas Carew, Richard Lovelace, and Sir John Suckling. These men were soldiers and courtiers first, poets incidentally. Their verse was light-hearted in spirit; graceful, melodious, and polished in form; sometimes licentious and sometimes cynical. At times it breathed the careless braggadocio of the military swashbuckler, at times the aristocratic ease of the peaceful courtier. Many of the poems were "occasional" in character, as Suckling's charming if doggerel-like *Ballad upon a Wedding* or Lovelace's pensive *To Althea from Prison.* The themes were love and war and chivalry and loyalty to the king. Robert Herrick, except for Milton perhaps the most gifted poet of the Caroline period, is sometimes classed with the Cavalier Lyrists, though he was a country parson, not a courtier. His poems included in the group-title *Hesperides* are, many of them, quite in the vein of the Cavalier Lyrists.

**Celtic Literature:** Literature produced by a people speaking any one of the Celtic dialects. Linguistically, the Celts are divided into two main groups. The "Brythonic" Celts include the Ancient Britons, the Welsh, the Cornish (Cornwall), and the Bretons (Brittany); while the Goidelic (Gaelic) Celts include the Irish, the Manx (Isle of Man), and the Scottish Gaels. At one time the Celts, an important branch of the Indo-European family, dominated Central and Western Europe. The Continental Celts (including the Bretons, who came from Britain) have left no literatures. The Celts of Great Britain and Ireland, however, have produced much literature of interest to students of English and American literature. See IRISH LITERATURE, WELSH LITERATURE, SCOTTISH LITERATURE, CELTIC RENAISSANCE.

**Celtic Renaissance:** A general term for the great movement of the late nineteenth and early twentieth centuries which in its various phases and sometimes conflicting "movements" aimed at the preservation of the Gaelic language (the Gaelic Movement, *q.v.*), the reconstruction of early Celtic history and literature, and the stimulation of a new literature authentically Celtic (esp. Irish) in spirit.  From before the middle of the nineteenth century there had been a growing interest in Celtic, especially Irish, antiquities, and much work was done in the collection and study, and later in printing and translation, of early Irish manuscripts embodying the history and literature of ancient Ireland. Along with this was developed the practice of collecting and printing folk-tales still preserved in oral tradition.  In the 1890's came the Gaelic Movement, which stressed the use of the Gaelic language itself.  More fruitful was the contemporaneous Anglo-Irish movement, which stimulated the production of a new literature in English (or "Anglo-Irish") by Irish writers on Irish themes and in the Irish spirit.  Standish Hayes O'Grady's imaginative treatment of Irish history (1880) provided much impetus to the movement, and themes drawn from ancient Irish tradition were exploited in verse and drama.  Fortunately, some genuine poetic geniuses were at hand to further the project, such as W. B. Yeats, George W. Russell ("A.E."), George Moore, J. M. Synge, and (later) James Stephens, Lord Dunsany, and Padraic Colum.  From the beginning Lady Gregory was an enthusiastic worker—as collector, popularizer, essayist, and playwright.  A striking phase of the renaissance was its dramatic manifestation.  In 1899 under the leadership of Yeats, Moore, Edward Martyn, Lady Gregory, and others the Irish Literary Theatre was founded in Dublin.  Though this theatre was inspired by the more or less cosmopolitan "Little Theatre Movement" (*q.v.*), Yeats and Martyn did write for it some plays employing Irish folk-materials.  Later Yeats joined another group more devoted to the exploitation of native elements, The Irish National Theatre Society, to which he attracted J. M. Synge, the most gifted playwright of the movement, whose *Playboy of the Western World* (1907) and *Deirdre of the Sorrows* (1910) attracted wide recognition.  Later exemplars of dramatic activity are Lord Dunsany and Sean O'Casey.  The Celtic

71

Renaissance movement produced little of importance in Wales. In Scotland it is perhaps best represented by the work of "Fiona Macleod" (William Sharp). (References: Douglas Hyde, *Literary History of Ireland;* Ernest Boyd, *Ireland's Literary Renaissance.*)

**Celtic Revival:** A term sometimes used for Gaelic Movement (*q.v.*) or for Irish Literary Movement (*q.v.*) as well as for the eighteenth-century movement noticed below.

**Celtic Revival, The (Eighteenth Century):** A literary movement of the last half of the eighteenth century which stressed the use of the historical, literary, and mythological traditions of the ancient Celts, particularly the Welsh. Through confusion Norse mythology was included in "Celtic." The movement was a part of the Romantic Movement, since it stressed the primitive, the remote, the strange and mysterious, and since it aided the revolt against pseudo-classicism by supplying a new mythology for the overworked classical myths and figures. Specifically it was characterized by an intense interest in the druids and early Welsh bards, numerous translations and imitations of early Celtic poetry appearing in the wake of the discovery of some genuine examples of early Welsh verse. The most influential and gifted poet in the group was Thomas Gray, whose *The Bard* (1757) and *The Progress of Poesy* (1757) reflect early phases of the movement. The most spectacular figure in the group of "Celticists" was James Macpherson, whose long poems, *Fingal* (1762) and *Temora* (1763)—chiefly his own invention but partly English renderings of genuine Gaelic pieces preserved in the Scottish Highlands—he published as translations of the poems of a great Celtic poet of primitive times, Ossian. Both Gray's and Macpherson's work influenced a host of minor poets, who were especially numerous and active in the last two decades of the century. There was also a considerable reflection of the movement in the drama, e.g., Home's *The Fatal Discovery* (acted 1769) and Brooke's *Cymbeline* (1778). Late in the century the gloomy sentimentalism of Macpherson was less influential. (Reference: E. D. Snyder, *The Celtic Revival in English Literature.*)

**Chanson:** A song. Originally composed of two-lined stanzas of equal length (couplets), each stanza ending in a refrain, the chanson is now more broadly interpreted to include almost any poem intended to be sung, and written in a simple style.

**Chanson de geste:** A "song of great deeds." A term applied to the early French epic. There is some uncertainty as to the ultimate origin of the form. The earliest and best existing example, the *Chanson de Roland*, dates probably from *ca.*1100. The early *chansons de geste* are written in ten-syllable lines marked by assonance and grouped in stanzas of varying length. Cycles developed, such as that of Charlemagne (*geste du roi*); that of William of Orange, which reflects the efforts of Christian heroes against the invading Saracens; and that dealing with the strife among the rebellious Northern barons. The stories generally reflect chivalric ideals with little use of love as a theme. The form flourished for several centuries, a total of about eighty examples being extant. These epic tales supplied material ("Matter of France") for medieval romance, including English romances. See MEDIEVAL ROMANCE. An English translation of the *Chanson de Roland* appears in the 49th volume of the Harvard Classics. (References: W. P. Ker, *Epic and Romance;* George Saintsbury, *The Flourishing of Romance;* histories of French literature.)

**Chant:** Loosely used to mean a "song," but more particularly the term signifies the intoning of words to a monotonous musical measure of few notes. The words of the chants in the English Church are drawn from such Biblical sources as the Psalms. Cadence is an important element, and usually one note (the "reciting note") is used for a series of successive words or syllables. Dirges are often chanted. Repetition of a few varying musical phrases is a characteristic, and the intonation of the voice plays an important rôle. Chants are generally considered less melodious than songs.

**Chant royal:** One of the more complex, and therefore less used, French verse forms. The tradition for this verse form demands a dignified, heroic subject such as can best be expressed in rich diction and courtly formalities of speech. The *chant royal*

73

consists of sixty lines arranged in five stanzas of eleven verses each and an envoy of five verses, the envoy ordinarily starting with an invocation in the manner of the ballade. The rime scheme usually followed is ababccddede for the stanza and ddede (as in the last five lines of the stanza) for the envoy. The italicized e above indicates the recurrence of a complete line as a refrain at the end of each stanza and at the close of the envoy. All stanzas must be the same in all details and no rime-word may appear twice.

**Chantey (Shanty):** A sailors' song marked by strong rhythm and, in the good old days of sail, used to accompany certain forms of hard labor (such as weighing anchor) performed by seamen working in a group. The leader of the singing was referred to as the "chantey man," his responsibility being to sing a line or two introductory to a refrain joined in by the whole group.

**Chapbook:** A small book or pamphlet such as was sold to the common people in the sixteenth and following centuries by peddlers or "chapmen." Chapbooks dealt with all sorts of topics and incidents: travel tales, murder cases, prodigies, strange occurrences, witchcraft, biographies, religious legends and tracts, stories of all sorts. They are of interest to the literary historian because of their reflection of contemporary attitudes toward themes and situations treated in literature.

**Character:** A literary form which flourished in England and France in the seventeenth and eighteenth centuries. It is a brief descriptive sketch of a personage who typifies some definite quality. The person is described not as an individualized personality but as an example of some vice or virtue or type, such as a busybody, a superstitious fellow, a fop, a country bumpkin, a garrulous old man, a happy milkmaid, etc. Similar treatments of institutions and inanimate things, such as "the character of a coffee house," also employed the term, and late in the seventeenth century, by a natural extension of the tradition, "character" was applied to longer compositions, sometimes historical, as Viscount Halifax's *Character of Charles II*. The vogue of character-writing followed the publication in 1592 of a

Latin translation of Theophrastus, an ancient Greek writer of similar sketches. Though the "character" may have influenced Ben Jonson in his treatment of the man of "humours" in comedy, the first English writer to cultivate the form as such was Bishop Joseph Hall in his *Characters of Virtues and Vices* (1608). Two of his successors were Sir Thomas Overbury (1614) and John Earle (1628). Later, under the influence of the French writer La Bruyère, "characters" became more individualized and were combined with the essay, as in the periodical essays of Addison and Steele. Subjects of "characters" were given fanciful proper names, often Latin or Greek, such as "Croesus." Good modern collections of "characters" are Gwendolen Murphy's *A Cabinet of Characters* and Richard Aldington's *A Book of 'Characters.'* See ESSAY. (Reference: E. N. S. Thompson, *Literary Bypaths of the Renaissance.*)

**Characterization:** The depicting, in writing, of clear images of a person, his actions and manners of thought and life. A man's nature, environment, habits, emotions, desires, instincts: all these go to make people what they are, and the skillful writer makes his important people clear to us through a portrayal of these elements.

There are, perhaps, a hundred ways in which an artist may express his capacities, and most people, at different times, give different values to such elements as style, narrative power, poetic charm, plot, etc.; but of all these major qualities none is more important than characterization—the ability to create on the printed page living beings who somehow speak for the whole human race. Most writers, if given a wish by some good fairy, would choose the ability to portray truthfully the people of their imagination. This power, in the hands of a real artist, is far too subtle a thing to be successfully analyzed and made mechanical. There is no prescription which makes a writer a great portrayer of character. But some of the means adopted by writers in presenting clear characterization are: a formal analysis of the character, in which the author lists one quality after another; a narration of an action, in which the character takes part, since, in seeing the character act, we learn something of what he is; a cumulative method, by which the writer giving a touch here and

75

a touch there suggests ultimately a rounded presentation of the character.   See DEVELOPING CHARACTERS.

**Chartism:** A definite political movement in England just before the middle of the nineteenth century, the object of which was to secure for the lower classes more social recognition and improved material conditions.   The Chartists advocated universal suffrage, vote by ballot, annual parliaments, and other reforms. This platform is given in the *People's Charter* (1838).   Carlyle's *Chartism* (1839) is an attack upon the movement.   The chartist agitation is favorably reflected in some of Kingsley's novels. See INDUSTRIAL REVOLUTION.   (Reference: Mark Hovell, *The Chartist Movement*.)

**Chivalric Romance:** Medieval romance reflecting the customs and ideals of chivalry.   See MEDIEVAL ROMANCE, ARTHURIAN LEGEND, COURTLY LOVE, CHIVALRY IN ENGLISH LITERATURE.

✓   **Chivalry in English Literature:** The system of manners and morals known as chivalry, chiefly a fruit of the feudal system of the Middle Ages, because it had been presented in medieval romance in a highly idealized form amounting almost to a religious system for the upper classes, has furnished so much color and atmosphere and inspiration for later literature that some knowledge of its characteristics is essential to the student.   The medieval knight, seen in the more brilliant light of literary idealization (as a matter of fact the typical medieval knight had many unlovely characteristics), has been portrayed not only by the many writers, known and unknown, of medieval romance, but by later poets like Chaucer, with his "parfit, gentle knight" and Spenser, who fills the forests and plains of his *Faerie Queene* with a brilliant procession of courteous and heroic Guyons and Scudamores and Calidores.   Knights whose high oaths bind them to fidelity to God and king, truth to their lady-loves, and ready service for all ladies in distress or other victims of unjust tyrants, cruel giants, or fiendish monsters, have become commonplaces of romantic literature.

Their sketchily drawn but noble personalities impart a vigor and glow to the action of such historical novels as Scott's *Ivanhoe* and find a somewhat unreal but earnestly sympathetic treatment in the *Idylls of the King* of Tennyson. Tennyson's poem *Guinevere*, indeed, includes the following poetic statement of the ideals of knighthood (King Arthur is speaking):

> I made them lay their hands in mine and swear
> To reverence the King, as if he were
> Their conscience, and their conscience as their King,
> To break the heathen and uphold the Christ,
> To ride abroad redressing human wrongs,
> To speak no slander, no, nor listen to it,
> To honor his own word as if his God's,
> To lead sweet lives in purest chastity,
> To love one maiden only, cleave to her,
> And worship her by years of noble deeds,
> Until they won her.

A more faithful picture may perhaps be found in the pages of Malory's *Le Morte d'Arthur*, where the romantic glamour of knighthood, with all the effort to idealize Lancelot and Arthur and find in the "good old days" a perfect pattern for later times, is not allowed to obscure some of the less pleasing realities of medieval knighthood. So glorious a thing as chivalry has not, of course, gone unnoticed by the satirists. The early seventeenth century not only produced the immortal *Don Quixote* in Spain but Beaumont and Fletcher's dramatic burlesque *The Knight of the Burning Pestle* in England, while modern America has brought forth not only its broadly comic *Connecticut Yankee at King Arthur's Court* (Mark Twain) but its more subtly mocking *Galahad* (John Erskine). Some pieces of English literature which make use of chivalric elements are described in W. H. Schofield's *Chivalry in English Literature*.

**Chorus:** In ancient Greece, the groups of dancers and singers who participated in religious festivals and dramatic performances. Also the songs sung by the chorus. At first the choral songs made up the bulk of the play, the spoken monologue and dialogue being interpolated. Later, however, the chorus became subordinate, offering inter-act comments. Finally, it became a mere lyric used to take up the time between acts. In Elizabethan drama the rôle of the chorus was often taken by a single actor, who recited prologue and epilogue and gave inter-act comments which linked the acts and foreshadowed coming events. So in Sackville and Norton's *Gorboduc*, the "first" English tragedy, the chorus consists of a few stanzas accompanied by a dumb show, the latter foreshadowing the coming action. In Kyd's *Spanish Tragedy* the part of the chorus is played by a ghost and the figure Revenge, the ghost urging Revenge to inspire the actors to hasten the vengeance demanded by the action. Shakespeare sometimes employed the chorus, as in *Pericles*, where the old poet Gower, accompanied by a dumb show, provides prologue and inter-act comment, and in *King Henry the Fifth*, where the chorus comments on the action, explains change of scene, and prologue-like begs for a sympathetic attitude on the part of the spectators. Sometimes, within the play proper, one of the characters, like the Fool in *King Lear*, is said to play a "chorus-like" rôle when he comments on the action.

**Christianity, Established in England:** Although evidence for dating the introduction of Christianity into England is lacking, it is certain that there were Christians in Roman Britain as early as the third century, and it is probable that there was an organized church as early as A.D. 314, when the bishops of London and York are said to have attended a church council in Gaul. After the lapse into barbarism which followed the Germanic invasions of the fifth century, Christianity was reintroduced directly from Rome by St. Augustine, who landed in Kent in A.D. 597. It flourished in southeastern England under Ethelbert, spread northward, and gained a foothold in Northumbria under Edwin (d. 633), who had married a Kentish princess. Another group of missionaries soon came into Northumbria from the celebrated Celtic monastery of Iona, an island off the west coast of Scotland. Iona had been established in A.D. 563 by St. Columba, a missionary from Ireland, where a form of Christianity reflecting the monastic ideals of Bishop Martin of Tours (flourished *ca.*371-*ca.*400) had been introduced from Gaul in the fourth or early fifth century. The Celtic and Roman churches thus brought into contact differed in certain doctrines and customs (such as the date for Easter, the form of baptism, and style of tonsure for priests). The resulting disputes were settled at the famous Synod of Whitby in 664 in favor of the Roman party.

The establishment of Christianity in England of course had powerful and far-reaching effects upon literature, since the Church was for centuries the chief fosterer of learning. The pagan literature which survived from early Germanic times passed through the medium of Christian authors and copyists, who gave a Christian coloring to such literature as they did not wholly reject. For centuries most of the new writings owed both their inspiration and direction to Christian zeal and to the learning fostered by the Church. The Christianization in the thirteenth century of the great body of Arthurian romances is an outstanding example of the dominance of Christianity over medieval literary activity.

**Chronicle Play:** A type of drama flourishing in the latter part of Elizabeth's reign which drew its English historical materials from the sixteenth century "chronicles" (*q.v.*), such as Holinshed's, and which stressed the nationalistic spirit of the times. It enjoyed increasing popularity with the outburst of patriotic feeling which resulted from the defeat of the Spanish Armada (1588) and served as a medium for teaching English history to the uneducated portions of the London populace. The structure of the earlier chronicle plays was very loose, "unity" consisting mainly in the inclusion of the events of a single king's reign. The number of characters was large. Much use was made of pageantry (coronations, funerals) and other spectacular elements, such as battles on the stage. The serious action was often relieved by comic scenes or sub-plots, as in Shakespeare's famous Falstaff plays (*Henry IV*, 1, 2; *Henry V*). The tendency to merge with romantic comedies appeared as early as Greene's *James IV* (*ca.*1590); in Shakespeare's *Cymbeline* (*ca.*1610) the chronicle material is completely subordinated to the demands of romantic comedy. The relation of the chronicle play to tragedy is still more important, Shakespeare's *Richard III* (*ca.*1593) being an early example of the tendency of the chronicle play to develop into tragedy of character, a movement which culminates in such plays as *King Lear* (1606) and *Macbeth* (1606). The term "history play" is sometimes applied to a restricted group of chronicle plays like Shakespeare's *Henry V*, which are unified but are neither comedy nor tragedy. The earliest true chronicle play is perhaps *The Famous Victories of Henry V* (*ca.*1586). Peele's *Edward I* (1590–91) and Marlowe's *Edward II* (1592) are among the best pre-Shakespearean chronicle plays. (Reference: F. E. Schelling, *The English Chronicle Play*.)

**Chronicles:** A name given to certain forms of historical writing. One authority has said that chronicles differ from "annals" in their comprehensive or universal character—their concern with world history. Though there were prototypes in Hebrew, Greek, Latin, and French, it is the medieval chronicles in English and their Renaissance successors that are of chief interest to the student of English literature. The *Anglo-Saxon Chronicle*, begun under King Alfred late in the ninth century and carried on by various writers in a number of monasteries in succeeding centuries, has been called the "first great book in English prose." The record begins with 60 B.C. and closes with 1154 ("Peterborough" version). Alfred and his helpers revised older minor chronicles and records and wrote first-hand accounts of their own times. The work as a whole is a sort of historical miscellany, sometimes sketchy in detail and detached in attitude, at other times spirited, partisan, and detailed. An important Old English poem preserved through its inclusion in the *Anglo-Saxon Chronicle* is the spirited *Battle of Brunanburh*. A famous Latin prose chronicle is Geoffrey of Monmouth's *History of the Kings of Britain* (*ca.*1136), which not only records legendary British history but also romantic accounts of King Arthur. The earliest important verse chronicle in Middle English is Layamon's *Brut* (*ca.*1205), based upon Wace's French poetic version of Geoffrey. Layamon's book illustrates the literary interest of the medieval chronicle. It is a long poem composed in an imaginative, often dramatic, vein, and exhibits a picturesque style that is sometimes reminiscent of the best Old English poetry.

Later Middle English chronicles include those of Robert of Gloucester (late thirteenth century), Robert Manning of Brunne (1338), Andrew of Wyntoun (*Original Chronicle of Scotland*, early fifteenth century), John Hardyng (late fifteenth century), and John Capgrave (fifteenth century). With the rise of the

Tudor dynasty came a long-sustained wave of patriotic national-ism, one result of which was the production in the sixteenth century of innumerable "chronicles"—some in Latin prose, some in English verse; some mere abstracts, some very volumi-nous; some new compositions, some retellings of older ones. Some of the more important chronicles of Elizabeth's time, be-sides the famous *Mirror for Magistrates*, a series of "tragedies" (for this special meaning of "tragedy" see p. 440) embodying chronicle material, are Richard Grafton's (1563), John Stowe's (1565, 1580, 1592), and Ralph Holinshed's (1578). Not only are portions of this mass of chronicle-writing themselves of genuine literary value, full of lively anecdote and description, but some of them were important as sources for Shakespeare and other dramatists. See CHRONICLE PLAYS.

**Chronique scandaleuse:** A type of writing presenting in-trigues, love affairs, and petty gossip, and usually associated with life at court. As a rule these writings give the impression of having being written by an eye-witness. The personal ele-ment is important, and scandal is the food upon which such chronicles thrive. *The History of Louis XI* (1460–1483) of France, a *chronique scandaleuse* credited to Jean de Troyes, is an example. This same interest in gossip about the intimate, per-sonal life of the great and of the near-great survives today in the tabloids and in the stories, for instance, which are told of the life of moving-picture stars in Hollywood.

**"Ciceronians"** (Latin stylists): See PURIST.

**Classic** (noun): In the singular usually used for a piece of literature which by common consent has achieved a recognized position in literary history for its superior qualities; also an author of like standing. Thus, *Paradise Lost* is a "classic" in English literature. The plural is used in the same sense, as in the phrase "the study of English classics"; it is also used col-lectively to designate the literary productions of Greece and Rome, as in the phrase "a study of the classics is an excellent preparation for the study of modern literature."

**Classic, Classical** (adjectives): Used in senses parallel with those given under CLASSIC (noun); hence, of recognized excellence or belonging to established tradition, as a classical piece of music or such as bids fair to win such recognition, as "a classic pronouncement"; used specifically to designate the literature or culture of Greece and Rome or later literature which partakes of its qualities. "Classical literature" may mean Greek and Roman literature, or it may mean literature that has gained a lasting recognition, or it may mean literature that exhibits the qualities of Classicism (q.v.).

**Classical Tragedy:** This term may refer to the tragedy of the ancient Greeks and Romans, as Sophocles' *Antigone;* or to tragedies based upon Greek or Roman subjects, as Shakespeare's *Coriolanus;* or to modern tragedies modeled upon Greek or Roman tragedy or written under the influence of the critical doctrines of Classicism (q.v.). The earliest extant English tragedy, Sackville and Norton's *Gorboduc* (acted 1562), is sometimes called "classical" because it is written in the manner of the Senecan tragedies. Ben Jonson's tragedies *Catiline* and *Sejanus* not only are based upon Roman themes but are "classical" in their conscious effort to apply most of the "rules" of tragic composition derived from Aristotle and Horace. In the Restoration period John Dryden, under the influence of the French classical tragedies of Racine, advocated classical rules and applied them in part to his *All for Love*, which contrasts with Shakespeare's romantic treatment of the same story in *Antony and Cleopatra*. In the next century Joseph Addison's *Cato* has been referred to as "the triumph of classical tragedy." See CLASSICISM, TRAGEDY, SENECAN TRAGEDY, UNITIES, ROMANTIC TRAGEDY, and references following these topics.

**Classicism:** As a critical term, a body of doctrine which is thought to be derived from or to reflect the qualities of ancient Greek and Roman culture, particularly literature, philosophy, art, or criticism. It is commonly opposed to romanticism (q.v.) and realism (q.v.), although it is important to remember that these terms overlap in their "characteristics" and are not, strictly speaking, mutually exclusive. It is particularly dangerous to classify writers or types as perfect exponents of classicism. Ben Jonson, for example, was a self-proclaimed advocate of classicism as a critic and dramatist, yet his "classical" tragedies contain some definitely non-classical elements, such as comic relief and violation of one or more of the unities. Likewise some of the "romanticists" of the eighteenth century cultivated classical qualities, just as such a "neo-classicist" as Pope exhibited some "romantic" traits.

It is true, however, that classicism does stand for certain definite ideas and attitudes, mainly drawn from the critical utterances of the Greeks and Romans or developed through an imitation of ancient art and literature. Some of them may be suggested by the following words and phrases: restraint; restricted scope; dominance of reason; sense of form; unity of design and aim; clarity; simplicity; balance; attention to structure and logical organization; chasteness in style; severity of outline; moderation; self-control; intellectualism; decorum (*q.v.*); respect for tradition; imitation (*q.v.*); conservatism; "good sense."

Classicism in English literature has been an important force, often an "issue," since Renaissance times. The humanists became conscious advocates of classical doctrine, and even such an essentially romantic artist as the poet Spenser fell strongly under its influence, not only drawing freely upon classical materials but definitely espousing classical doctrines and endeavoring to "imitate" such classical masters as Virgil and Homer. Shakespeare, though he has left no formal statement of his critical attitude and though he is essentially a "romantic" dramatist, undoubtedly reflects classical influence. Sir Philip Sidney, though he wrote pastoral romances, speaks mainly as a classicist in his critical essay, *The Defence of Poesie*. Ben Jonson stands as the stoutest Renaissance advocate of classicism, both in dramatic criticism and in his influence upon English poetry. Milton has been said to show a perfect balance of romanticism and classicism. The classical attitude, largely under French inspiration, triumphed in the Restoration and Augustan periods, and John Dryden, Joseph Addison, and Alexander Pope, together with Doctor Samuel Johnson of the next generation, stand in English literary history as exemplars of the classical (or "neo-classic") spirit in literature and criticism. Though nineteenth-century literature was largely romantic (or in its later phases realistic), the vitality of the classical attitude is shown by the critical writings of such men as Francis Jeffrey, Matthew Arnold, and Walter Pater. See HUMANISM, NEO-CLASSICISM, CLASSICAL TRAGEDY, ROMANTICISM, REALISM. (References: Irving Babbitt, *The New Laokoön;* W. J. Courthope, *Life in Poetry, Law in Taste;* Sherard Vines, *The Course of English Classicism.*)

**Cliché:** From the French word for a stereotype plate; a block for printing. Hence any expression so often used that its freshness and clearness have worn off is called a *cliché*, a stereotyped form. Some examples are: "bigger and better," "loomed on the horizon," "the light fantastic," "stood like a sentinel," "sadder but wiser."

**Climax:** The highest point of interest in narrative fiction. Also in rhetoric the term is used to indicate the arrangement of words, phrases, and clauses in sentences in such a way as to form a rising order of importance in the ideas expressed. Such an arrangement is climactic and the item of greatest importance, necessarily at or near the close, is called the climax. Similarly in larger pieces of composition, the essay, short story, drama, or novel, events may be so ordered as to progress towards a highest point of interest and the idea or incident occupying this distinctive position is, again, the climax. As applied to the *structure* of a tragedy the term commonly means the turning point of the action. The murder of Banquo, along with the escape of Fleance and the appearance of Banquo's ghost at the emotionally climactic banquet scene—events which shake the spirit of the hitherto successful protagonist—may be regarded as the climax of *Macbeth.* See CRISIS, SHORT STORY, DRAMATIC STRUCTURE.

**Cloak-and-Sword Romance:** A play or novel characterized by much action and presenting gallant heroes in love with fair ladies, a glamorous color thrown over all. Settings and characters are often, though not necessarily, Spanish, Italian, or French, the manners are courtly and gracious, the plot full of intrigue resulting most commonly in duels. Anthony Hope's *Prisoner of Zenda*, George Barr McCutcheon's *Graustark*, and Booth Tarkington's *Monsieur Beaucaire* are three modern examples.

**Closed Couplet:** Two successive verses riming *aa* and containing within the two lines a complete, independent statement. It is "closed" in the sense that its meaning is complete within the two verses and does not depend on what goes before or follows for its grammatical structure or thought. Example:

> One prospect lost, another still we gain;
> And not a vanity is giv'n in vain;
> —Pope

**Closet Drama:** "A play not intended to be played. It is a poem in dialogue, conceived with no thought of the actual stage, not contaminated by any subservience to the playhouse, the players, or the playgoers. It is wrought solely for the reader in the library."[1] Browning's *Pippa Passes* is a closet drama in this sense. Giving the term a broader meaning, some writers include in it such dramatic poems as Swinburne's *Atalanta in Calydon* and other products of the effort to write a literary drama by imitating the style of an earlier age, such as Greek drama. T. H. Dickinson indeed says that the closet drama "arises from the application of the standards of one day to the art of a later day"—an effort to continue the tradition of Shakespeare or the tradition of the Greeks after the stage itself had lost both the traditions. Such poetic dramas as Tennyson's *Becket* and Browning's *Strafford* are not infrequently called closet dramas because, though their authors meant them to be acted, they actually are more successful as literature than acted drama. In English literature the nineteenth century was noted for the production of closet drama, perhaps because the actual stage was so monopolized by burlesque, melodrama, operetta, and such light forms that literary men were stimulated either to attempt to provide more worthy dramas for the contemporary stage or at least to preserve the tradition of literary drama by imitating earlier masterpieces. See DRAMATIC POETRY, POETIC DRAMA, PASTICHE. (References: Brander Matthews, *A Study of the Drama*, Chap. xii; T. H. Dickinson, *Contemporary Drama of England*.)

**Cockney School:** A derogatory title applied by *Blackwood's Magazine* to a group of nineteenth-century writers including

---

[1] Brander Matthews, *A Study of the Drama*, Houghton Mifflin Company, 1910, p. 252. Reprinted by permission of and arrangement with the publishers.

Hazlitt, Leigh Hunt, Keats, and Shelley, because of their alleged poor taste in such matters as diction and rime. Some offending rimes were *name* and *time*, *vista* and *sister*, words which, the suggestion was, could rime only to a cockney ear. One sentence from the denouncement printed in *Blackwood's Magazine* must serve as illustrative of the whole spirit of his attack: "They (the writers above) are by far the vilest vermin that ever dared to creep upon the hem of the majestic garment of the English muse."

**Coherence:** A fundamental principle of composition demanding that the parts of any piece of writing be so arranged and bear such a relationship one to the other that the meaning of the whole may be immediately clear and intelligible. Words, phrases, clauses, within the sentence; and sentences, paragraphs, and chapters in larger pieces of writing are the units which, by their progressive and logical arrangement, make for coherence or, contrariwise, by an illogical arrangement, result in incoherence.

**Coined Words:** Words consciously and arbitrarily manufactured "out of whole cloth," as opposed to those which enter the language as a result of one of the more natural processes of language development. Many words which were originally "coined words" (such as *telephone*, *airplane*, and *kodak*) have become accepted terms. Constantly occurring examples of such words are those fabricated by commercial firms for advertising purposes: "Nabisco" (National Biscuit Company), "Socony" (Standard Oil Company of New York). Frowned upon as a literary practice, word coining is nevertheless constantly affecting our language. See NEOLOGISM.

**Collaboration:** The association of two or more people in a given piece of literary work. Beaumont and Fletcher afford one of the most famous instances of collaboration in the field of English literature.

**Colloquialism:** An expression used in informal conversation but not accepted as good usage in formal speech or writing. A colloquialism lies between the upper speech level of dignified, formal, or "literary" language and the lower level of slang. It may differ from more formal language in pronunciation, grammar, vocabulary, imagery, or connotative quality. As in the case of slang, a colloquial expression eventually may be accepted as "standard" usage. "I'll be right over," is a permissible colloquial expression in an intimate telephone conversation, though formal style might call for a more dignified and "correct" phrase. *Fix* may be used as a colloquialism for "mend." See SLANG, PROVINCIALISM, DIALECTS.

**Colloquy:** A word for "dialogue" or "conference" occasionally employed in literary titles, as Erasmus' *Colloquies.* See DIALOGUE.

✓ **Colophon:** A publisher's symbol or device formerly placed at the end of a book but now more generally used on the title page or elsewhere near the beginning. The function of colophons is to identify the publisher. Colophons at different times and with different publishers have incorporated one or more of these items: title and author of book, the printer, the date and place of manufacture. The earliest known use of colophons was in the fifteenth century, at which time they were likely to be complete paragraphs wherein the author addressed the reader in a spirit of reverence—now that he had completed his work. Sir Thomas Malory, for example, closed his *Le Morte d'Arthur* with the statement that it "was ended in the ix yere of the reygne of Kyng Edward the fourth," and asks that his readers "praye for me whyle I am on lyue that God sende me good delyuerance, and whan I am deed I praye you all praye for my soule."

**Columns and Columnists:** Many metropolitan newspapers in recent years have turned over columns, usually on their editorial pages, to writers who are given an almost free rein to express themselves humorously, critically, and satirically on the political and social aspects of the day's events. These columns and their writers—"colyums" and "colyumists" as they are often called—sometimes rise to real literary significance and are among the most often quoted sources of contemporary writing. Some of the most famous recent writers in this class are Franklin P. Adams, Don Marquis, Christopher Morley, Bert L. Taylor, and Keith Preston. The influence of such writers on the thought of the day, as well as the scholarly and classical training of some of them, their humor, and their keen social satire, invite a comparison between their work and the journalism of Addison and Steele in the early eighteenth century.

**Comedy:** As compared with tragedy, comedy is a lighter form of drama which aims primarily to amuse and which ends happily. It differs from farce and burlesque by having a more sustained plot, more weighty and subtle dialogue, more natural characters, and less boisterous behavior. The border-line, however, between comedy and other dramatic forms cannot be sharply defined, as there is much overlapping of technique, and different "kinds" are frequently combined. Even the difference between comedy and tragedy tends to disappear, as Allardyce Nicoll points out, in their more idealistic forms. High comedy and low comedy may be further apart from each other in nature than are tragedy and some serious comedy. Psychologists have shown the close relation between laughter and tears, and comedy and tragedy alike sprang, both in ancient Greece and in medieval Europe, from diverging treatments of ceremonial performances.

Since comedy strives to provoke smiles and laughter, both wit and humor are utilized. In general the comic effect arises from a recognition of some incongruity of speech, action, or character revelation. The incongruity may be merely verbal as in the case of a play on words, exaggerated assertion, etc.; or physical, as when stilts are used to make a man's legs seem disproportionately long; or satirical, as when the effect depends upon the beholder's ability to perceive the incongruity between fact and pretense exhibited by a braggart. The range of appeal here is wide, varying from the crudest effects of low comedy to the most subtle and idealistic reactions aroused by some "high" comedy. The "kinds" of comedy and, in part, the relation between comedy and tragedy are thus accounted for. As one writer says: "We have seen that comic effects have a common basis in incongruity, contrast; that the incongruity may lie principally in the realm of events, and we have comic intrigue, or in the realm of appearances, and we have comic character; while usually both these are found in conjunction, but with preponderating emphasis on one or the other, which gives us farce or intrigue comedy on the one hand and character comedy on the other. . . . Comedy itself varies according to the attitude of the author or recipient, tending, where it becomes judicial, toward satire; where it becomes sympathetic, toward pathos and tragedy."[1]

English comedy developed from native dramatic forms growing out of the religious drama, the morality plays and interludes, and possibly folk games and plays and the performances of wandering entertainers, such as dancers and jugglers. In the Renaissance the rediscovery of Latin comedy and the effort to apply the rules of classical criticism to drama profoundly affected the course of English comedy. Foreign influences also have at times been important, as the French influence on Restoration comedy or the Italian influence upon Jacobean pastoral drama. The more ambitious comedy of the earlier Elizabethans was romantic, while the comedy of the seventeenth century, both Jacobean and Restoration, was prevailingly realistic (though the Fletcherian tragi-comedy flourished early in the century). Sentimental comedy was dominant in the eighteenth century, but was opposed late in the period by a revival of the realistic comedy of manners. In the early nineteenth century such light forms as burlesque and operetta were popular, serious comedy again appearing late in the century. Some of the more prominent authors of English comedy are: John Lyly, Robert Greene, George Peele, William Shakespeare, Ben Jonson, George Chapman, Thomas Middleton, Thomas Heywood, John Fletcher, Philip Massinger (Elizabethans and Jacobeans); Sir George Etheredge, William Congreve, and Thomas Shadwell (Restoration); Richard Steele, Richard B. Sheridan, Oliver Goldsmith (eighteenth century); T. W. Robertson (mid-nineteenth century); H. A. Jones, Oscar Wilde, A. W. Pinero, G. B. Shaw, J. M. Barrie (late nineteenth and twentieth centuries).

Attention may be called to a special use of the word "comedy" in medieval times, when it was applied to non-dramatic literary compositions marked by a happy ending and by a less exalted

---

[1] E. Woodbridge (Morris), *The Drama, Its Law and Its Technique*, Allyn and Bacon, 1898, p. 67. Reprinted by permission of the publishers.

style than was found in tragedy. Dante's *Divine Comedy*, for example, was so named by its author because of its "prosperous, pleasant, and desirable" conclusion, and because it was written in the vernacular (Italian) "in which women and children speak." The nomenclature employed in describing different kinds of comedy is somewhat confused, and it is impossible in this handbook to include all the terms employed by the many writers on the subject. An effort has been made to include the most important ones, however. See HIGH COMEDY, LOW COMEDY, REALISTIC COMEDY, ROMANTIC COMEDY, COURT COMEDY, TRAGI-COMEDY, SENTIMENTAL COMEDY, COMEDY OF MANNERS, INTERLUDE, TRAGEDY, DRAMA, WIT AND HUMOR. (References: A. H. Thorndike, *English Comedy;* Allardyce Nicoll, *The Theory of Drama;* George Meredith, *An Essay on Comedy;* H. Bergson, *Laughter;* Lane Cooper, *An Aristotelian Theory of Comedy;* Bonamy Dobrée, *Restoration Comedy,* 1660–1720.)

**Comedy of Humours:** A term applied to the special type of realistic comedy which was developed in the closing years of the sixteenth century by Ben Jonson and George Chapman and which derives its comic interest largely from the exhibition of "humorous" characters; that is, persons whose conduct is controlled by some one characteristic or whim or "humour" (see HUMOURS). Some single humour or exaggerated trait of character gave each important figure in the action a definite bias of disposition and supplied the chief motive for his actions. Thus in Jonson's *Every Man in his Humour* (acted 1598), which made this type of play popular, all the words and acts of Kitely are controlled by an overpowering suspicion that his wife was unfaithful; George Downright, a country squire, must be "frank" above all things; the country gull in town determines his every decision by his desire to "catch on" to the manners of the city gallant. In his "Induction" to this play Jonson explains his character-formula thus:

> Some one peculiar quality
> Doth so possess a man, that it doth draw
> All his affects, his spirits, and his powers,
> In their confluctions, all to run one way.

The comedy of humours owes something to earlier vernacular comedy, but more to a desire to imitate the classical comedy of Plautus and Terence and to combat the vogue of romantic comedy. Its satiric purpose and realistic method are emphasized and lead later into more serious character studies, as in Jonson's *The Alchemist*. It affected Shakespeare's art to some degree—the "humorous" man appearing now and again in his plays (Leontes in *Winter's Tale* is a good example)—and it is perhaps worth mentioning that most of Shakespeare's tragic heroes are such because they allow some one trait of character (ambition, jealousy, contemplation, etc.) to be overdeveloped and thus to destroy the balance necessary to a poised, well-rounded, and effective personality. The comedy of humours was closely related to the contemporary comedy of manners and exerted an important influence upon the comedy of the Restoration period. See COMEDY OF MANNERS.

**Comedy of Intrigue:** See COMEDY OF SITUATION.

**Comedy of Manners:** A term most commonly used to designate the realistic, often satirical, comedy of the Restoration period, as practised by Congreve and others. It is also used for the revival, in modified form, of this comedy a hundred years later by Goldsmith and Sheridan, as well as for a revival late in the nineteenth century. Likewise the realistic comedy of Elizabethan and Jacobean times is sometimes called "comedy of manners." In the stricter sense of the term, the type is concerned with the manners and conventions of an artificial, highly sophisticated society. The fashions, manners, and outlook on life of this social group are reflected. The characters are more likely to be types than individualized personalities. Plot, though often involving a clever handling of situation and intrigue, is less important than atmosphere and dialogue and satire. The prose dialogue is witty and finished, often brilliant. According to Allardyce Nicoll "the invariable elements of the comedy of manners are the presence of at least one pair of witty lovers, the woman as emancipated as the man, their dialogue free and graceful, an air of refined cynicism over the whole production, the plot of less consequence than the wit, an absence of crude realism, a total lack of any emotion whatsoever."[1] The appeal is intellectual but not imaginative or idealistic. Satire is directed in the main against the follies and deficiencies of typical characters, such as fops, would-be wits, jealous husbands, coxcombs and others who fail somehow to conform to the conventional attitudes and manners of the elegant society of the time. As this satire is directed against the aberrations of social behavior rather than of human conduct in its larger aspects, true humor can hardly be said to be present. A distinguishing characteristic of the comedy of manners, too, is its coarseness and immorality, a fact partly explained by the manners of the time and social groups concerned, and partly by the special satirical purpose of the comedy itself. As some one has said, the interest of the Restoration audience in the success of an adulterous intrigue may have resided less in an unwholesome interest in illicit love itself than in a desire to see the discomfiture of a husband who was so ill-bred as to be jealous of his wife. In its satire and realism and employment of "humours" the comedy of manners was somewhat indebted to Elizabethan and Jacobean comedy. It owed something, of course, to the French comedy of manners as practised by Molière.

The reaction against the obscenity and the immorality of the plays and a growing sentimentalism brought about the downfall of this type of comedy near the close of the seventeenth century and it was largely supplanted through most of the eighteenth century by "sentimental comedy" (*q.v.*). Purged of its objectionable features, however, the comedy of manners was revived by Goldsmith and Sheridan late in the eighteenth century, and in a somewhat new garb by Oscar Wilde late in the nineteenth century. A few typical comedies of manners are: Etheredge, *The Man of Mode* (1676); Wycherley, *The Plain Dealer* (1674); Congreve, *The Way of the World* (1700); Goldsmith, *She Stoops to Conquer* (1773); Sheridan, *The Rivals* (1775) and *The School for Scandal* (1777); Wilde, *The Importance of Being Earnest* (1895). See HIGH COMEDY, REALISTIC COMEDY, COMEDY OF HUMOURS. (References: John Palmer, *The Comedy of Manners*; A. Nicoll, *A History of Restoration Drama*.)

[1]From Allardyce Nicoll's *A History of Restoration Drama*, Cambridge University Press, 1923, p. 185. Reprinted by permission of The Macmillan Company.

**Comedy of Situation:** A comedy which depends for its interest chiefly upon ingenuity of plot rather than upon character interest; "comedy of intrigue." Background, too, is relatively unimportant. There is much reliance upon ridiculous and incongruous situations, a heaping up of mistakes, plots within plots, disguises, mistaken identity, unexpected meetings, etc. A capital example is Shakespeare's *The Comedy of Errors*, a play in which the possibilities for confusion are multiplied by the use of twin brothers who have twins as servants. In each case the twins look so much alike that at times they doubt their own identity. A comedy of this sort sometimes approaches farce (*q.v.*). Ben Jonson's *Epicene* and Middleton's *A Trick to Catch the Old One* are later Elizabethan comedies of situation or intrigue. A modern example is Shaw's *You Never Can Tell*. The phrase "comedy of situation" is sometimes used also to refer merely to an incident, such as Falstaff's description of his fight with the robbers in Shakespeare's *King Henry IV*, Part I. See FARCE-COMEDY.

**Comic Opera:** An operetta, or comedy opera, stressing spectacle and music but employing spoken dialogue. An early example is Sheridan's *The Duenna* (1775). The best known comic operas are those of Gilbert and Sullivan produced in London, chiefly at the Savoy (constructed for the purpose) in the 1870's and 1880's, e.g., *The Mikado* (1885). See BALLAD-OPERA.

***Commedia dell' arte:*** Improvised comedy; a form of Italian low comedy dating from very early times, in which the actors, who usually performed conventional or stock parts, such as the "pantaloon" (Venetian merchant), improvised their dialogue, though a plot or scenario was provided them. A "harlequin" interrupted the action at times with low buffoonery. A parallel or later form of the *commedia dell' arte* was the "masked comedy," in which conventional figures (usually in masks) each spoke his particular dialect (as the Pulcinella, the rogue from Naples). There is some evidence that the *commedia dell' arte* colored English low comedy from early times, but its chief influence on the English stage came in the eighteenth century in connection with the development of such spectacular forms as the pantomime (*q.v.*). (References: Winifred Smith, *The Commedia Dell' Arte;* A. Nicoll, *Masks, Mimes, and Pantomimes.*)

**Common Meter:** A stanza form consisting of four lines, the first and third being iambic tetrameter (eight syllables, ◡— ◡— ◡— ◡—) and the second and fourth iambic trimeter (six syllables, ◡—◡—◡—). An example:

> He either fears his fate too much,
> Or his deserts are small,
> That dares not put it to the touch
> To gain or lose it all.
> —Marquis of Montrose.

**Commonplace Book:** A classified collection of quotations or arguments prepared for reference purposes. Thus, a reader interested in moral philosophy might collect thoughts and quotations under such heads as truth, virtue, or friendship. Commonplace books were utilized by authors of essays, theological arguments, and other serious treatises. The commonplace book of John Milton is still in existence. The term is also sometimes applied to private collections of favorite pieces of literature such as the poetical miscellanies of Elizabethan times.

**Complaint:** A "plaintive" poem, such as Chaucer's *The Complaint Unto Pity*, *A Complaint to His Lady*, and the humorous *The Complaint of Chaucer to his Empty Purse*, written in the manner of the "complaints" of lovers to their unresponsive mistresses. In a "complaint," which usually takes the form of a lyric monologue, the poet commonly explains his sad mood, describes the causes of it, discusses possible remedies, or appeals to some lady or divinity for help "out of his distress." A somewhat wider sense of the term appears in the volume of Spenser's miscellaneous minor poems published in 1591 under the title *Complaints*. The printer, Ponsonby, justifies the title by saying they are all "complaints and meditations of the worlds vanitie; verie grave and profitable."

**Complication:** That part of a dramatic or narrative plot in which the entanglement of affairs caused by the conflict of opposing forces is developed. It is the tying of the knot to be untied in the "resolution." See DRAMATIC STRUCTURE.

**Conceit:** A term now commonly applied, with derogatory implications, to striking, strained, or affected modes of expression such as characterized Elizabethan love poetry and "metaphysical" verse. John Lyly, for example, calls love the "marrow of the mind," and Sidney prognosticates his future by the stars in Stella's face (Sonnet 26). "Metaphysical" conceits are bolder. Preachers are "God's conduits," and a philosopher "Nature's secretary" in one of Donne's poems, while in another the souls of two lovers are as "stiff twin compasses." George Herbert calls Spring a "box where sweets compacted lie." The conceits of the Elizabethan sonnets followed the vogue of the Italian and French imitators of Petrarch, while those of the next generation (the metaphysicals) were in part a development of the earlier style and in part a product of a new spirit. The Elizabethan conceits are commonly in the nature of ornamentation, superimposed upon an idea, while the better metaphysical figures are more organic, arising from the intellectual process of thinking in figures. Both, like euphuism (*q.v.*), are aspects of the general European tendency toward novelty and experimentation in language which developed in late Renaissance times.

Because of the difficulty of drawing a clear line of distinction between the successful and the unsuccessful use of metaphor and simile, and the feeling of many readers that some "conceits" are poetically felicitous, it is not wise to insist upon a hard-and-fast definition of the conceit. Professor Schelling described it as the poet's effort "to deck out his thought in striking, apt, and original figures of speech and illustration," and noted that such an attempt "easily degenerates into ingenuity, far-fetched metaphor, extravagance, and want of taste." Professor Alden's careful analysis led him to regard the intellectual interruption of a swift imaginative process as a distinguishing characteristic. His definition is: "A conceit is the elaboration of a verbal or imaginative figure, or the substitution of a logical for an imaginative figure, with so considerable a use of an intellectual process as to take precedence, at least for the moment, of the normal poetic process." Alden found three main classes: the verbal conceit (see PUN); the imaginative conceit (metaphor-simile type, personification type, and myth type); and logical conceits (paradox type and logical-metaphysical type). The last of these classes was especially cultivated by the metaphysicals, under the influence of Donne, who regarded the conceit less as a plaything than as an "appropriate means to the expression of his philosophy of love." In the poetry of the period the intellectual was superseding the "romantic-chivalric" view of life, and love, as well as religion, was subjected to unflinching intellectual analysis.

The Elizabethan conceit may offend by its triteness, the metaphysical by its strangeness. The style easily lent itself to excess, especially in the hands of imitators and poets of little genius. The conceit was unable to survive strict neo-classic standards of taste, but has been used by various modern poets—Browning, Emily Dickinson, T. S. Eliot, John Crowe Ransom, and many others. Not infrequently a conceit is elaborated through a whole stanza or even poem. This device is rather unhappily employed in the following "holy" sonnet of Donne in which the metaphor of the crown degenerates into labored word-play and gives way finally to a series of plays on the word *end:*

> Deign at my hands *this crown* of prayer and praise,
> *Weaved* in my lone devout melancholy,
> Thou which of good hast, yea, art treasury,
> All changing unchanged Ancient of days.
> But do not with a *vile crown* of frail *bays*
> Reward my Muse's white sincerity;
> But what *thy thorny crown* gain'd, that give me,
> A *crown of glory*, which doth flower always.
> The *ends crown* our works, but *Thou crown'st* our *ends*,
> For at *our ends* begins our *endless* rest.
> The first *last end*, now zealously possess'd,
> With a strong sober thirst my soul attends.
> 'Tis time that heart and voice be lifted high;
> Salvation to all that will is nigh.

See MARINISM, GONGORISM, BAROQUE, METAPHYSICAL VERSE. (References: R. M. Alden's two essays in the 1917 and the 1920 volumes of *Studies in Philology;* F. E. Schelling, *English Literature in the Lifetime of Shakespeare;* Lu Emily Pearson, *Elizabethan Love Conventions;* titles listed under METAPHYSICAL VERSE.)

**Concrete Terms:** Words or phrases which are specific rather than general; as "blackbird" is more concrete than "bird," and "bass" than "fish." In literature the proper use of concrete terms makes for vividness, clarity, and interest, whereas too much use of the general makes for vagueness and dullness. There is, for instance, considerably more picture-quality in asking Job where he was when "The morning stars sang together, and all the sons of God shouted for joy" than in merely asking him where he was when God created the world. See ABSTRACT WORDS.

✓ **Conflict:** The struggle which grows out of the interplay of the two opposing forces in a plot (*q.v.*). It is conflict which provides the elements of interest and suspense in any form of fiction, whether it be a drama, a novel, or a short story. There are at least three major types of conflict: (1) those which grow from the simple opposition of two physical forces and which find expression in a sprightly series of intense actions (as in many Dumas novels), (2) those which spring from the play of one quality of character upon another quality of character in a second person (as the "innate evil" of Iago plays upon the quality of jealousy in Othello), and (3) the internal or spiritual struggle of one trait with another trait within the same character (as Hamlet's inability to bring himself to the point of action struggles with Hamlet's desire to act).

**Connotation:** The implications words or phrases carry with them; what a word or phrase suggests as distinguished from what it says specifically. The connotative value of language increases with the number of specific terms used. See CONCRETE TERMS.

✓ **Contrast:** A rhetorical device by which one element (idea or object) is thrown into opposition to another for the sake of emphasis or clearness. The effect of the device is to make both contrasted ideas clearer than either would have been if described by itself. The principle of contrast, however, is useful for other purposes than to make definitions or to secure clearness. Skillfully used by an artist, contrast may become, like colors to the painter or chords to the musician, a means of arousing emotional impressions of deep artistic significance.

**Convention:** A literary "convention" is any device or style which has become, in its time and by reason of its habitual use, a recognized means of literary expression, an accepted element in technique. The use of alliterative verse among the Anglo-Saxons and of the heroic couplet in the time of Dryden or Pope are conventions in this sense. The personified virtues of the morality plays, the braggart soldier of the Elizabethan stage, and the fainting heroine of sentimental fiction are examples of conventional "stock characters" (*q.v.*). Features which later become conventions usually arise from freshness of appeal, acquire a pleasing familiarity at the hands of good writers, and eventually, through excessive or unskillful use, become distasteful and fall into disuse. Sometimes, however, discarded conventions are revived when apparently dead, as when the French poet Villon revived successfully the ballade. Poetic imagery tends to become conventional, as when a "code" of epithets, adjectives, metaphors, and similes came to be regarded by the Augustans as "poetic." Not infrequently conventions depart so far from the realities and probabilities of life that literature could not employ them if custom had not made them acceptable, as in the case of the soliloquy in drama. In real life men do not talk to themselves in long, rhetorical monologues in which they analyze their thoughts and motives. Yet the device has become so conventional in drama that Shakespeare could rely upon it as a medium for some of his finest effects, and such a modern playwright as Eugene O'Neill can have his characters speak their thoughts in the presence of other characters who are supposed to hear nothing, an illustration of how an impossibility in real life can become accepted in literature because of its conventional character. For an illuminating discussion of some aspects of the subject see J. L. Lowes, *Convention and Revolt in Poetry*. See TRADITION, STOCK CHARACTERS, MOTIF.

**Coronach:** A song of lamentation; a funeral dirge. A Gaelic word reflecting a custom in Ireland (where "keening" is the more commonly used term) and in the Scottish Highlands. The word means a "wailing together," and judging from Sir Walter Scott's presentation a typical coronach was sung by the

Celtic women. In one of his novels he says, "Their wives and daughters came, clapping their hands, and crying the coronach, and shrieking." In *The Lady of the Lake* (Stanza xvi of Canto III) appears a coronach of Scott's own composition:

> He is gone on the mountain,
> He is lost to the forest,
> Like a summer-dried fountain,
> When our need was the sorest, . . .

**Corpus Christi Plays:** See MYSTERY PLAY.

**Counterplayers:** The characters in a drama who plot against the hero or heroine, e.g., Claudius, Polonius, Laertes, and their associates in *Hamlet*. See ANTAGONIST.

**Couplet:** Two lines of verse with similar end-rimes. Formally, the couplet is a two-line stanza form with both grammatical structure and idea complete within itself, but the form has gone through numerous adaptations, the most famous of which is "heroic verse" (*q.v.*). In French literature "couplet" is sometimes used in the sense of "stanza." See CLOSED COUPLET.

**Court Comedy:** The characteristics of this type of comedy are explained by the fact that it was written to be performed at the royal court. *Love's Labour's Lost* is a court comedy belonging to Shakespeare's early period. Some years before Shakespeare came to London, the Elizabethan court comedy had been developed to a high degree of effectiveness by John Lyly in such plays as *Endimion* and *Campaspe*. Characteristics include: artificial plot; little action; much use of mythology; pageantry; elaborate costuming and scenery; prominence of music, especially songs; lightness of tone; characters numerous and often balanced (arranged in contrasting pairs); structure artificial; style marked by wit, grace, verbal cleverness, quaint imagery, puns; prose dialogue; pages prominent, being witty and saucy; eccentric characters such as braggarts, witches, and alchemists often employed; much farcical action; allegorical meanings sometimes embodied in the characters and action. Though some of these traits of the Lylian court comedy dropped out later, court comedy in the seventeenth century retained many of them and was always operatic in tone and spectacular in presentation. See Masque.

**Courtesy Books:** A name given to a class of books which flourished in late Renaissance times and which dealt with the ideals and training of the "courtly" person. Often in dialogue form, the courtesy book discussed such questions as the qualities of a gentleman or court lady, what constituted a gentleman, the etiquette of courtly love, the education of the future courtier or prince, and the duties of the courtier as a state counsellor. The courtesy book originated in Italy, the most famous example being Castiglione's *Il Cortegiano*, "The Courtier" (1528), which exerted great influence on English writers, especially after its translation into English by Sir Thomas Hoby in 1561. The earliest English courtesy book is Sir Thomas Elyot's *Book of the Governour* (1531).

Somewhat similar to the courtesy books, but not to be confused with them, were the numerous etiquette books written not to explain the character of the noble or royal person but to deal with the problems of conduct confronting the well-bred citizen as well as the "gentleman." One of the best is *Galateo* by the Italian Della Casa. Early English examples of this type are *The Babees Book* and Caxton's *Book of Courtesy*.

Many books of the seventeenth century carried on the tradition established by the Renaissance books of courtesy and etiquette, such as: John Cleland's *Institution of a Young Nobleman*, 1607 (Puritan); Henry Peacham's *Compleat Gentleman*, 1622 (courtly); Richard Brathwaite's *The English Gentleman*, 1630 (Puritan); and Francis Osborne's *Advice to a Son*, 1658 (a precursor of Lord Chesterfield's *Letters*). (References: E. N. S. Thompson, *Literary Bypaths of the Renaissance;* Ruth Kelso, *The Doctrine of the English Gentleman in the Sixteenth Century;* John E. Mason, *Gentlefolk in the Making*.)

**Courtly Love:** A philosophy of love and a code of love-making which flourished in chivalric times, first in France and later in other countries, especially in England. The exact origins of the system can not now be completely traced, but fashions set by the Provençal troubadours and ideas drawn from the Orient and especially from Ovid were probably the chief sources. The conditions of feudal society and the worship of the Virgin Mary, both of which tended to give a new dignity and independence to woman, also affected it. The method of debate or soliloquy by which the doctrines of courtly love are given expression in literature was probably indebted to current scholastic philosophy.

According to the system, falling in love is accompanied by great emotional disturbances; the lover is bewildered, helpless, tortured by mental and physical pain, and exhibits certain "symptoms," such as pallor, trembling, loss of appetite, sleeplessness, sighing, weeping, etc. He agonizes over his condition and indulges in endless self-questioning and reflections on the nature of love and his own wretched state. His condition improves when he is accepted, and he is inspired by his love to great deeds. He and his lady pledge each other to secrecy, and they must remain faithful in spite of all obstacles. Andreas Capellanus wrote a treatise late in the twelfth century in which he summarized prevailing notions of courtly love through imaginary conversations and through his thirty-one "rules." According to the strictest code, true love was held to be impossible in the married state. Hence some authorities distinguish between true "courtly love" as it is illustrated in the story of Lancelot and Guinevere in Chrétien's "The Knight of the Cart," and Ovidian love. Basically, courtly love was illicit and sensual, but a sort of Platonic idealism soon appeared and is found in the usual literary presentation, this modification being doubtless due to the softening influences of Christianity and polite society.

Courtly love ideas abound in medieval romance and are perhaps not unconnected with the later (Renaissance) Petrarchan and Platonic love doctrines as found, for example, in Elizabethan sonnet-sequences. The system of courtly love largely controls the behavior of the characters in Chaucer's *Troilus and Criseyde*. (References: W. G. Dodd, *Courtly Love in Gower and Chaucer;* H. O. Taylor, *The Medieval Mind*, Vol. I; T. P. Cross and W. A. Nitze, *Lancelot and Guenevere, A Study on the Origins of Courtly Love;* Sarah F. Barrow, *Medieval Society Romances*.)

**"Courtly Makers":** A phrase applied to the court poets in the reign of Henry VIII who introduced the "new poetry" from Italy and France into England. "Maker" was used in the sixteenth century, both in Scotland and England, for poet, the use of the term arising from the concept of the poet as a creator (the word "poet" itself comes from a Greek word meaning "maker" or "do-er"). The "courtly makers" were given credit by the Elizabethans for "reforming" or polishing the "rude and homely manner" of earlier English poetry. Their work was imitative and experimental, based upon forms and fashions already developed by the Italians. They were most successful perhaps in poetic translations or paraphrases and in songs, even Henry VIII himself being credited with the authorship of both words and music of several graceful songs. The introduction of the sonnet and of blank verse into English is due to the efforts of the two most important poets of the group, Sir Thomas Wyatt and the Earl of Surrey. Other "courtly makers" were William Cornish, Lord Vaux, Lord Rochford (George Boleyn), Sir Anthony St. Leger, Lord Morley (Henry Parker), Sir Francis Bryan, Sir Thomas Chaloner, John Heywood, Robert Fairfax, and Robert Cooper. Most of the work of these men has probably perished, as their ideas of "gentlemanly" conduct did not lead them to publish their work, poetry being cultivated as an incidental grace. Manuscript collections were made for private libraries, however, one of which, now commonly known as *Tottel's Miscellany*, was published in 1557 and exerted a powerful influence on Elizabethan poetry. In fact, the chief importance of the "courtly makers" lies in the pioneer character of their work, as their efforts were brought to a perfect flowering by the poetic generations which followed them. Sometimes the term "courtly maker" is applied to any court poet.

**Courts of Love:** A phrase applied to supposed tribunals for settling questions involved in the system of "courtly love" (*q.v.*). The judge, a court lady or Venus herself, would hear debate on such questions as: "Can a lover love two ladies at once?" "Are lovers or married couples more affectionate?" Though it was once generally believed that such courts were actually held in high society in chivalric times, modern scholarship is inclined to regard the courts of love as mere literary conventions. The term "court of love" is also sometimes extended to include allegorical and processional pageants such as the Masque of Cupid passage in Spenser's *Faerie Queene* (Book III, Cantos xi-xii). The phrase, too, is sometimes used loosely as a synonym for "courtly love."

**Crisis:** That part of the plot in a story, play, or novel which presents the critical stage in the dramatic action; the episode or incident wherein the situation in which the protagonist finds himself is sure either to improve or to grow worse. Sometimes it is loosely spoken of as the "highest point" of interest which the story attains, but this need not be true since the crisis is essentially a structural element of plot rather than the emotional appeal which a given event may have for the reader. In its strict usage "crisis" differs from "climax" (*q.v.*) in that the crisis frequently precedes the climax in point of time; yet it is related to the climax in that the decision made by a character at the point of crisis largely determines the nature of the climax.

**Critic:** One who estimates and passes judgment on the value and quality of the work of others. Literary critics are of all varieties: from sincere to maudlin, from honest to corrupt, and from intelligent to foolish. They range from the journalistic reviewers discussing three or four books a day to the dignified, careful critic who, with a background of culture and learning, passes judgment on movements and tendencies in the large. The first type gave cause for Disraeli's charge: "You know who critics are?—the men who have failed in literature and art." The second type, on the other hand, have wielded sufficient influence in letters actually to check tendencies and to create movements. To just what extent the personal element dictates the nature of criticism may be estimated by the recital of a few names in American criticism: Margaret Fuller, Edgar Allan Poe, James Russell Lowell, Stuart Sherman, H. L. Mencken, Paul Elmer More, and George Jean Nathan. The student who, even among such names as these, hopes to find an agreement and synthesis as to the nature of criticism—hopes, in short, to find the truth—is lost. There are no standards to which all critics subscribe, a fact which may seem discouraging to the beginner, but which is, after all, the very life of criticism itself. See CRITICISM.

**Criticism, Historical Sketch:** *Classical Criticism.*—The first important critical treatise, the *Poetics* of Aristotle (fourth century B.C.), has proved to be the most influential. This Greek philosopher defined "poetry" as an idealized representation of human action, and tragedy as a serious, dramatic representation or "imitation" (*q.v.*) of some magnitude, arousing pity and fear wherewith to accomplish a catharsis (*q.v.*) of such emotions; tragedies should have unity (see UNITIES) and completeness of plot, with beginning, middle, and end. The *Poetics* also treats the element of character in tragedy and the relation of tragedy to epic poetry as well as the relation of imaginative literature to such other forms as history and philosophy. Aristotle's treatise on the Homeric epic has not survived. The great attention given by the ancients to "rhetoric" is also important critically, though developed largely because of the interest in oratory. The great influence of the *Poetics* began in the Renaissance. Aristotle's criticism has been much debated by modern students and not infrequently misunderstood. It may be studied conveniently with the aid of a commentary such as that of Butcher.

Another Greek document of primary significance is the treatise of Longinus, *On the Sublime* (date uncertain, perhaps third century after Christ). Very different from the *Poetics* of Aristotle in content and spirit, this work acclaims sublimity, height, and imagination in a style that is itself enthusiastic and eloquent. Longinus finds the sources of the Sublime in great conceptions, noble passions, and elevated diction.

The foremost Latin critic was Horace, whose *Art of Poetry*, written as an informal epistle in verse, has exercised considerable power. It discusses types of poetry and of character, stresses the importance of Greek models, emphasizes the importance of decorum (*q.v.*), and advises the prospective poet to write both for entertainment and instruction. Many of Horace's phrases have entered into the common language of criticism, such as *ut pictura poesis*, "poetry is like painting,"; *labor limae*, "the labor of the file" (i.e., revision); and *aut prodesse aut delectare*, "either to profit or to please." The influence of Horace's criticism was especially great in England in the sixteenth and seventeenth centuries. Quintilian's *Institutes of Oratory* is, after Horace's epistle, perhaps the most important Latin critical treatise. Other ancient critics include Plato, Dionysius of Halicarnassus, Plutarch, and Lucian among the Greeks; and Cicero, the Senecas, Petronius, and Macrobius among the Latin writers. The art of rhetoric constituted an integral part of this literary criticism.

*The Middle Ages.*—So far as known, there was little interest in criticism in the Middle Ages. Much of what there was dealt perfunctorily with Latin versification, rhetoric, and grammar. The ecclesiastical theologians who dominated the intellectual life were inclined to regard literature as a servant of theology and philosophy, and there was consequently a reduced interest in imaginative literature as such. Classical pagan literature was generally neglected or little known, and there was not much contemporary literature of a sort to arouse critical interest. The rhetoricians dealt in great detail with technical matters of vital interest to the creative writer: the use and nature of figurative language; organization; beginnings; endings; development (amplification, condensation); style—especially the adaptation of style to type of composition; ornamentation, etc. The very great influence of such teachings upon the early work of Chaucer has been demonstrated in detail. Certain passages in Chaucer's poetry, too, show that he was conscious of the principles controlling literary composition.

The influence of St. Augustine (*d.* 430), who condemned the poets because they pictured the gods as vicious, doubtless contributed to the general distrust of literature on moral and religious grounds which persisted through the Middle Ages into modern times. It must be noted, however, that St. Augustine's attack on imaginative writing produced replies which anticipate later critical attitudes and arguments: the literary and the moral points of view should not be confused; the ancients should be followed, etc. Isidore of Seville (sixth and seventh centuries) listed the types and kinds of literature (based on Biblical forms).

But it was not until the end of the medieval period that a really great critic appeared in the person of the Italian poet Dante, whose *De Vulgari Eloquentia* (early fourteenth century) discusses the problems of vernacular literature. Dante reflects classical ideas on decorum, imitation, and the nature of the poet. He discusses diction, sentence-structure, style, versification, and dialects. Petrarch and Boccaccio, great Italian scholars and writers of the fourteenth century, produced critical works which belong in part to the medieval period and in part to the Renaissance which they helped to usher in. Boccaccio's famous defence of poetry in Books XIV and XV of his *Genealogia Deorum Gentilium* is particularly important to students of later criticism.

*The Renaissance: Italy and France.*—The Renaissance reacted against the theological interpretation of poetry current in the Middle Ages and attempted a justification of it as an independent art, along lines suggested by humanistic ideals. In Italy, Vida, Robortelli, Daniello, Minturno, Giraldi Cinthio, J. C. Scaliger, Castelvetro, and many others were concerned with such topics as: poetry as a form of philosophy and an imitation of life; the doctrine of verisimilitude (reproduction of actual conditions of life); pleasurable instruction as the object of poetry; the theory of drama, especially tragedy—the tragic hero and the unities were much debated; and the theory of the epic poem. The causes for the growth of classicism (*q.v.*) have been assigned (by Spingarn) to humanism (*q.v.*), Aristotelianism, and rationalism (*q.v.*)—with Platonism (*q.v.*), medievalism, and nationalism acting as romantic forces. These tendencies toward classicism actuated Italian criticism of the sixteenth century and French criticism of the seventeenth. The first French critical works were rhetorical and metrical, the most important being Sibilet's *Art of Poetry* (1548); but the first highly significant French criticism centered around the *Pléiade*, a group interested in refining the French language and literature by borrowings and imitations of the classics, Ronsard being its most famous writer and Du Bellay being the author of its manifesto, his epochal *Defence and Illustration of the French Language* (1549). Among the prominent seventeenth-century French critics were Malherbe, who reacted strongly against the *Pléiade*,

Chapelain, Corneille, Saint-Evremond, d'Aubignac, Rapin, Le Bossu, and Boileau, whose influence was especially powerful. These writers illustrate the course of French criticism in the direction of classicism, a rational crystallizing of poetic theory, and a codification of the principles of literary structure.

*The English Renaissance.*—In Renaissance England the earliest critical utterances were directed toward matters of rhetoric and diction, as in the "prefaces" of the printer William Caxton (late fifteenth century) and the rhetorics of Leonard Cox (*ca.* 1530) and Thomas Wilson (1553). As early as Sir Thomas Elyot's *Book of the Governour* (1531) the claims of English as a vehicle for literature were being urged against the extreme humanist opposition to the vernacular as crude and not permanent. The actual development of a native literature was accompanied by discussions of how best to build up the English vocabulary, the extreme humanists and "inkhornists," who favored the introduction of heavy Latin and Greek words, being opposed by those who stressed native words (see PURIST). Much attention was given to the requirements of decorum and imitation. The first technical treatise on English versification was Gascoigne's *Certain Notes of Instruction* (1575). Verse forms already developed in English, including rime, were perfected in the face of the critical impulse to insist upon such classical verse forms as the unrimed hexameter. Practice ran ahead of theory in this matter, as may be seen by comparing the actual practices of Sidney and Campion with their serious critical condemnation of rime. Campion's essay, *Observations in the Art of English Poesie* (1602), was promptly and effectively answered by Samuel Daniel in his *A Defence of Rime.* Similarly, Shakespearean romantic tragedy developed in spite of the prevailing critical insistence upon the unities.

But perhaps the most vital critical issue centered about the effort to justify literature in the face of the Puritan attack based upon moral grounds, a movement which attacked the drama in particular, as in Stephen Gosson's *The School of Abuse* (1579). Many of these critical questions were treated in Sidney's *Defence of Poesie* (pub. 1595), the most significant piece of criticism of the period. Sidney stressed the high function of the poet, exalted poetry above philosophy and history, answered the objections to poetic art, examined the types of poetry, and assigned praise and blame among the writers of the preceding generation on the basis of their conformity to classical principles as expressed by the Italian critics. Important critical expressions came from Francis Bacon (*Advancement of Learning*, 1605) and Ben Jonson (*Timber: or Discoveries*). In Jonson, a man of vast learning and uncommon common sense, we may see the definite tendency toward the neo-classicism (*q.v.*) that was to become the center of English criticism for more than a century.

*The Restoration: Dryden.*—The next master was John Dryden, with his numerous prefaces and essays, the greatest of which is the *Essay of Dramatick Poesie* (1668). This treatise, written in dialogue form with ease and vigor, fairly presents the claims of "ancients and moderns" (*q.v.*), of French and English dramatists; rime, tragi-comedy, and the unities receive consideration; the influence of Corneille is apparent; while much applied criticism keeps the essay from being entirely theoretical. In his *Preface to the Fables* (1700) Dryden gives a noteworthy estimate of the genius of Chaucer. Other Restoration critics include: Sir Robert Howard, Thomas Rymer, the Earls of Mulgrave and Roscommon, and Sir William Temple. The foreign influence was predominantly French.

*The Eighteenth Century: Pope, Addison, Johnson.*—Alexander Pope was not merely the first poet of his generation, but also its most significant critic, what with the prefaces to his translation of Homer and his edition of Shakespeare, and his *Essay on Criticism* (1711), by far the leading piece of verse criticism in the language. In this work Pope set forth the neo-classic principles of following nature and the ancients, outlined the causes of bad criticism, described the good critic, and concluded with a short history of criticism. Addison's critical papers in the *Spectator* (1711–1712) on tragedy, wit, ballads, *Paradise Lost*, and the pleasures of the imagination were designed for a popular audience, but they exerted a strong influence upon formal criticism and aesthetic theory. The neo-classical critics in general devoted themselves to such topics as reason, correctness, wit, taste, *genres*, rules, imitation, the classics, the function of the imagination, the status of emotion, and the dangers of enthusiasm. Rationalism and classicism and the "school of taste" were held in a balance that often proved precarious. Gradually, however, the sway of authority was weakened; the historical point of view gained in general acceptance; textual criticism became more scientific. But Samuel Johnson remained the defender of the older order; his large body of critical expression may be gleaned from his periodical essays, the preface to his edition of Shakespeare, and his *Lives of the Poets*. The personality of Doctor Johnson stimulated orthodoxy as much as did his writings.

*Early Romantic Tendencies.*—But there were dissenters who were foreshadowing the romantic ideals of the coming era—the Wartons, Edward Young, Bishop Hurd, and others. Joseph Warton (*Essay on the Genius and Writings of Pope*, 1756, 1782) refused Pope the highest rank among poets because of insufficient emotion and imagination; Thomas Warton (*Observations on the Faerie Queene of Spenser*, 1754) emphasized the emotional quality of the great Elizabethan poet; Young (*Conjectures on Original Composition*, 1759) spoke in favor of independence and against the imitation of other writers; Hurd (*Letters on Chivalry and Romance*, 1762) justified Gothic manners and design, Spenser's poetry, and the Italian poets; and attacked some of the main tenets of the Augustans (*q.v.*). Other eighteenth-century critics of note were John Hughes, John Dennis, Henry Fielding, Edmund Burke, Goldsmith, Lord Kames, Hugh Blair, and Sir Joshua Reynolds.

*Romanticism: Wordsworth, Coleridge, Shelley, Lamb.*—The volume of poems by Wordsworth and Coleridge entitled *Lyrical Ballads* (1798) is frequently cited as formally ushering in the Romantic Movement. For the second edition (1800) Wordsworth wrote a preface that acted as a manifesto for the new school and set forth his own critical creed. It was his object to "choose incidents and situations from common life," to use "language really used by men." Wordsworth was reacting from what he considered the artificial poetic practice of the preceding era; he condemned the use of personification and "poetic diction." There could be "no essential difference between the language of prose and metrical composition." Wordsworth defined the poet as a "man speaking to men" and poetry as "the breath and finer spirit of all knowledge," "the spontaneous overflow of powerful feelings" which takes its origin from emotion "recollected in tranquillity." Though not ideally equipped for the rôle of critic, Wordsworth here produced a document, free from inherited critical jargon and replete with illustrious passages. It is of prime importance in the history of English literature and criticism. His own poetic practice is not always consistent with his theory.

Coleridge, with his superior philosophical training and profundity of thought, became one of England's greatest critics, despite his digressiveness and verbosity. The *Biographia Literaria* (1817) is both autobiographical and critical. Therein he explained the division of labor in the *Lyrical Ballads:* his own endeavors "should be directed to persons and characters supernatural, or at least romantic; yet so as to transfer from our inward nature a human interest and a semblance of truth sufficient to procure for these shadows of imagination that willing suspension of disbelief for the moment, which constitutes poetic faith"; while Wordsworth was "to propose to himself as his object, to give the charm of novelty to things of every day, and to excite a feeling analogous to the supernatural, by awakening the mind's attention to the lethargy of custom, and directing it to the loveliness and the wonders of the world before us; an inexhaustible treasure, but for which, in consequence of the film of familiarity and selfish solicitude, we have eyes, yet see not, ears that hear not, and hearts that neither feel nor understand." These two fundamental romantic points of view were applied to *The Rime of the Ancient Mariner* of Coleridge and *Lucy Gray* of Wordsworth. Coleridge disagreed, however, with Wordsworth's statements about the principles of meter and poetic diction: rustic life is not favorable to the formation of a human diction; poetry is essentially ideal and generic; the language of Milton is as much that of real life as is that of the cottager; art strives to give pleasure through beauty. Coleridge subtly expounded the nature of beauty and the conditions for its existence. His discussion of the imagination and the fancy (*q.v.*) is penetrating. In his lectures on Shakespeare Coleridge did much to spread the romantic worship of the Bard's genius in all its aspects, though, like Lamb and Hazlitt, he contributed little new to Shakespearean criticism. The English romanticism of

Coleridge and others found considerable support in the philosophy, aesthetics, and literature of German romanticism.

Other critics of importance in the first half of the nineteenth century were Lamb, Hazlitt, and Leigh Hunt. Lamb's criticism was charming and enthusiastic but eccentric, capricious, and unorganized; it showed good taste, great originality of thought as well as keenness of phrase; and it stimulated the appreciation of earlier English literature. Hazlitt is more remarkable for many happy phrases, sound judgment, and an infectious spirit than for any systematic philosophy. Hunt is a most catholic and readable critic. The poet Shelley's *Defence of Poetry* (1821) is an abstract *apologia* reminiscent of Renaissance treatises. Other critics of this period are: William Blake, Cardinal Newman, Carlyle, De Quincey, Landor, Henry Hallam, and Macaulay. The review journals, the Whig *Edinburgh Review* (ed. Francis Jeffrey) and the Tory *Quarterly Review* (ed. William Gifford), voiced fundamentally conservative opinions and dominated periodical criticism.

*The Nineteenth Century: Arnold, Pater; Realism.*—Matthew Arnold was the leading critic of the last half of the nineteenth century. He thought of poetry as a "criticism of life" and of criticism itself as the effort to "know the best that is known and thought in the world and by in its turn making this known, to create a current of true and fresh ideas." Criticism should seek absolute truth. Form, order, and measure constituted the classical qualities which Arnold admired. He sought to judge literature by high standards; he used specimens (or "touchstones") of great poetry as well as his own sensitive taste in forming judgments. "The grand style," he said, "arises in poetry, when a noble nature, poetically gifted, treats with simplicity or with severity a serious subject." The greatness of a poet "lies in his powerful and beautiful application of ideas to life." Arnold was primarily interested in the true and the great; he subordinated the historical method. His vigorous and lucid style and his high ideals of life and literature have made him an extremely powerful figure in the history of criticism. Three of his better known critical essays are *The Function of Criticism* (1865), *The Study of Poetry* (1888), and *On Translating Homer* (1861).

In the later nineteenth century we find the tenets of romanticism still in the field and the principles of realism (*q.v.*) and of impressionism (*q.v.*) gaining ground. The expansion of natural science helped the progress of realistic and naturalistic criticism (see NATURALISM), which was a reaction against both classicism and romanticism. Historical criticism, the attempt to understand a work in the light of "the man and the *milieu*," had been in process of development for at least two centuries and at last was crystallized in the writings of the Frenchmen Sainte-Beuve and Taine. Impressionism grew out of romanticism and obtained an eloquent advocate in Walter Pater. Victorian critics discussed such topics as the function and nature of art and literature, the rôle of morality, the place of the imagination, the problems of style, the province of the novel, and the theory of the comic. Though there were no real schools of critics, the tendency of criticism was away from the application of standards toward the use of impressionistic methods. The German influence yielded ground to the French. Significant contributions were made by Thackeray on the English humorists; John Stuart Mill on the nature of poetry; Walter Bagehot on pure, ornate, and grotesque art in poetry; Pater on style and on hedonism in art; George Meredith on the comic spirit; Leslie Stephen on the eighteenth century; and Swinburne on the Elizabethan and Jacobean dramatists.

*American Criticism.*—Criticism in America, besides reflecting, sometimes tardily, European attitudes, has been concerned with questions peculiar to a literature growing out of a transplanted culture. To what extent is American literature derivative and imitative? How can American literature develop a purely American spirit? What is this spirit? What of the effect of Puritan ethical conceptions upon American literature? How has the frontier affected it?

Early nineteenth-century criticism, as evidenced by the earlier numbers of the *North American Review* (estab. 1815), was conservative and neo-classic. Pope reigned. Later, the romantic attitude triumphed, and Byron, Scott, Wordsworth, and eventually Shelley, Keats, Coleridge, Carlyle, and Tennyson were exalted. In the latter part of the century realism became a powerful force, as critical interest shifted from poetry to fiction, and there developed more interest in theory, in establishing fundamental critical tenets. The earlier writer-critics were in the main romantic, Poe, Lowell, and Emerson. Poe, however, stressed workmanship, technique, structure, the divorce of art and morality; was highly rational; and enunciated independent theories of the lyric and the short story. Emerson believed art should serve moral ends; asserted that all American literature was derivative; and assumed the romantic attitude toward nature and individualism. Lowell is first impressionistic and romantic; at times professedly realistic; and eventually classical and ethical, after his revolt against sentimentalism. Among the realists Henry James and William Dean Howells were greatly influential.

The course of criticism in the twentieth century, either in England or America, can not yet be charted. Certainly the revolutionary movements of the second and third decades have advanced the cause of realism and naturalism and some forms of extreme aestheticism. In America the group called by one writer "Radical Anarchists" has stimulated a vigorous protest from the "New Humanists" (see HUMANISM, THE NEW). Among the many writers who have played a part in this critical battle a few may be mentioned: W. C. Brownell, Paul Elmer More, Irving Babbitt, Stuart Sherman, Carl Van Doren, H. L. Mencken, John Macy. See ANCIENTS AND MODERNS, CLASSICISM, CRITIC, DECORUM, DIDACTICISM, EXPRESSIONISM, HUMANISM, IMAGINATION AND FANCY, IMITATION, IMPRESSIONISM, NATURALISM, NEO-CLASSICISM, PURITANISM, RATIONALISM, REALISM, ROMANTIC CRITICISM, ROMANTICISM, SENTIMENTALISM, STYLE, TRANSCENDENTALISM, UNITIES, VICTORIAN, and the various types, such as ESSAY, NOVEL, TRAGEDY. (References: S. H. Butcher, *Aristotle's Theory of Poetry and Fine Art;* J. F. D'Alton, *Roman Literary Theory and Criticism;* George Saintsbury, *History of Criticism,* 3 vols.; J. E. Spingarn, *History of Literary Criticism in the Renaissance* and [ed.] *Critical Essays of the Seventeenth Century;* Gregory Smith [ed.], *Elizabethan Critical Essays,* 2 vols.; W. H. Durham [ed.], *Critical Essays of the Eighteenth Century, 1700–1725;* A. Bosker, *Literary Criticism in the Age of Johnson;* J. H. Smith and E. W. Parks [eds.], *The Great Critics;* Norman Foerster, *American Criticism* and [ed.]

*American Critical Essays XIX and XX Centuries;* G. E. De Mille, *Literary Criticism in America.* E. B. Burgum [ed.], *The New Criticism.*)

**Cycle:** A word, originally meaning circle, which came to be applied to a collection of poems or romances centering about some outstanding event or character. Cyclic narratives are commonly accumulations of tradition given literary form by a succession of authors rather than by a single writer. "Cyclic" was first applied to a series of epic poems intended to supplement Homer's account of the Trojan War and written by a group of late Greek poets known as the Cyclic Poets. Other examples of cyclic narrative are the Charlemagne epics and Arthurian romance, like the "Cycle of Lancelot," etc. The medieval religious drama presents a cyclic treatment of Biblical themes.

**Cyclic Drama:** The great "cycles" of medieval religious drama. See MYSTERY PLAY.

**Cynicism:** Doubt of the generally accepted standards and of the innate goodness of human action. In literature the term is important as one used from time to time to characterize groups of writers or movements distinguished by dissatisfaction with contemporary conditions. Originally the expression came into being with a group of ancient Greek philosophers, a group led by Antisthenes and including such others as Diogenes and Crates. The major tenets of the cynics were belief in the moral responsibility of the individual for his own acts and the dominance of the will in its right to control human action. Reason, mind, will, individualism were, then, of greater importance than the social or political conduct so likely to be worshiped by the multitudes. This exaltation of the individual over society it is which makes most unthinking people contemptuous of the cynical attitude. Any highly individualistic writer, scornful of the commonly accepted social standards and ideals, is, for this reason, called cynical. Almost every literature has had its schools of cynics. In America the writing in the decade following the World War is strongly marked by cynicism. It is important to remember that cynicism is not necessarily a weakness or a vice, and that the cynics have done much for civilization. Samuel Butler's *Way of All Flesh* and W. Somerset Maugham's *Of Human Bondage* are two examples of the cynical novel.

✓ **Dactyl:** A metrical foot consisting of one accented syllable followed by two unaccented syllables, as in the word *mannikin*. See METER and VERSIFICATION.

**Dadaism:** A freakish, tongue-in-cheek, "literary" movement fostered by young journalists in Paris shortly after the World War. The dadaists argued that literature should at once be everything and nothing. And the dadaist movement was broad enough to include drums and cymbals, to hold its meetings in theatres as well as much less conventional places, and narrow enough to welcome anything which was obviously not literature. It was, in the words of one critic, "a campaign against literature." According to popular statement its name was derived from a belief on the part of its adherents that literature had been too effeminate, had too long acted from the conviction that the first word uttered by the baby was "mama" when it really should be "dada." To give literature this masculine purpose they organized and called themselves "dadaists."

Edmund Wilson points out that dadaism stems directly from the symbolists and holds that Isidore Ducasse of the earlier group was their patron saint. The movement, which for a few days and months created a mild furore in Paris, lived long enough to foster at least three journals (*Litterature, Proverbe*, and *391*, the last so called from the 391 presidents the group at one time boasted). During the time dadaism was attracting attention, kindred movements sprang up in Germany, Holland, Italy, Russia, and Spain. For an account of dadaism see Edmund Wilson's *Axel's Castle*, Appendix II.

**Dark Ages:** A phrase sometimes loosely used as a synonym for the medieval period of European history. Its use is vigorously objected to by most modern students of the Middle Ages, since the phrase reflects the old, discredited view that the period in question was characterized by intellectual darkness, an idea that arose from lack of information about medieval life. The studies of modern scholars have made it certain that "dark ages" is a phrase that completely misrepresents the medieval period, which, as a matter of fact, was characterized by intellectual, artistic, and even scientific activity which led to high cultural attainments. Most present-day writers, therefore, avoid the phrase altogether. Some who do use it restrict it to the earlier part of the Middle Ages (fifth to eleventh centuries). (Reference: W. P. Ker, *The Dark Ages*.)

**Decadence:** A term used in literary history and criticism to denote the decline or deterioration which commonly marks the end of a great period. Arthur Symons listed as decadent qualities "an intense self-consciousness, a restless curiosity in research, an oversubtilizing refinement upon refinement, a spiritual and moral perversity." It is best to remember, however, that the term is relative and can not always suggest the same qualities to the same writers and that no two periods of decadence can be just alike. In English dramatic history the period following Shakespeare was marked by such decadent qualities as a relaxing of critical standards, a breaking down of types (comedy and tragedy merging), a lowered moral tone, sensationalism, over-emphasis upon some single interest (like plot-construction or "prettiness" of style), a decreased seriousness of purpose, and a loss of poetic power. The late years of the nineteenth century are sometimes called decadent because of the decline from Victorian standards. Individual writers, as Oscar Wilde, are sometimes called decadent. The "silver age" of Latin literature (reign of Trajan), including such writers as Tacitus, Juvenal and Martial (satirists), Lucan, and the Plinys, is called decadent in relation to the preceding "golden age" of Augustus made illustrious by Virgil, Horace, Ovid, and Livy.

**Decorum:** A critical term describing that which is proper to a character, subject, or setting in a literary work. According to classical standards, the unity and harmony of a composition could be maintained by the observance of dramatic propriety. The style should be appropriate to the speaker, the occasion, and the subject matter. So Renaissance authors were careful to have kings speak in a "high" style (such as majestic blank verse), old men in a "grave" style, clowns in prose, and shepherds in a "rustic" style. Puttenham (1589) cites as an ex-

116

ample of the lack of decorum the case of the English translator of Virgil who said that Aeneas was fain to "trudge" out of Troy (a beggar might "trudge," but not a great hero). Beginning in the Renaissance the type to which a character belonged was regarded as a most important element in determining his qualities; age, rank, and social status were often held as fundamental in the art of characterization. Thus a too rigid adherence to such distinctions led to a hardening of character. But on the use of decorum in the *Iliad* Pope said: "The *Speeches* are to be considered as they flow from the characters, being perfect or defective as they agree or disagree with the manners of those who utter them. As there is more variety of characters in *The Iliad*, so there is of speeches, than in any other poem," and "Homer is in nothing more excellent than in that distinction of characters which he maintains through his whole poem. What Andromache here says can be spoken properly by none but Andromache."

**Definition:** A brief exposition of a term calculated to explain its meaning. Formal definitions consist of two elements: (1) the general class (*genus*) to which the object belongs, and (2) the specific ways (*differentiae*) in which the object differs from other objects within the same general class. For instance, in the first sentence above "brief exposition" lists the general class to which "definition" belongs and "calculated to explain its meaning" shows the way in which "definition" differs from other expositions which may be intended, for instance, to make clear the location of a site, the operation of a machine or any one of the various other functions which expositions in general may perform. The following examples should help to make this clear:

| Term defined | General class to which it belongs | Specific ways in which it differs from other objects in the same general class |
| --- | --- | --- |
| A canoe is a | boat | pointed at both ends and propelled by paddling. |
| A radio is an | instrument | for receiving or transmitting wireless messages. |

Rarely are single-sentence definitions satisfactory in themselves. But the principle above stated guides in forming longer expositions in which both the second and third elements of the definition may be extended almost indefinitely.

✓ **Deism:** The religion of those believing in a God who rules the world by established laws but not believing in the divinity of Christ or the inspiration of the Bible; "natural" religion, based on reason and a study of nature, as opposed to "revealed" religion. The scientific movement which grew out of the new knowledge of the world and the universe following upon the discoveries and theories of Columbus, Copernicus, Galileo, Francis Bacon, and later the members of the Royal Society, furthered the development of a rationalistic point of view which more and more tended to rely upon reason instead of upon revelation in the consideration of man's relation to God and the Universe. The fact that the conceptions of the physical world found in the Old Testament seemed inconsistent with the newer knowledge shook the faith of many in the doctrine of the special inspiration of the Bible. Deism was a product of this general point of view. It absorbed also something from the theological movements of Arianism (opposition to the doctrine of the Trinity) and Arminianism (which stressed moral conduct as a sign of religion and opposed the doctrine of election; see CALVINISM). The somewhat prevalent notion that the deists believed in an "absentee" God, who, having created the world and set in motion machinery for its operation, took no further interest either in the world or in man is perhaps unfair, as it is certainly not applicable to all eighteenth-century deists, some of whom even believed in God's pardoning of the sins of a repentant individual.

The reputed "father" of the deists was Lord Herbert of Cherbury (1583–1648); later philosophical representatives of the movement included the third earl of Shaftesbury (1671–1713) and Lord Bolingbroke (1678–1751). From Shaftesbury deistic views passed to Voltaire and other French philosophers, who in turn powerfully influenced later English (and American) thought. John Toland (1670–1722), Anthony Collins (1676–1729), and Matthew Tindal (d. 1733) wrote important deistic treatises. The fact that there were groups of theological deists as well as philosophical ones, some deists not agreeing with other deists, makes it difficult to give any accurate summary of the tenets of deism, but the following statements perhaps fairly represent the point of view of the English deists: 1. The Bible is not the inspired word of God; it is good so far as it reflects "natural" religion and bad so far as it contains "additions" made by superstitious or designing persons. 2. Certain Christian theological doctrines are the product of superstition or the invention of priests and must be rejected; e.g., the deity of Christ, the doctrine of the Trinity, and the theory of the atonement for sins. 3. God is perfect, is the creator and governor of the Universe, and works not capriciously but through unchangeable laws (hence "miracles" are to be rejected as impossible). 4. Human beings are free agents, whose minds work as they themselves choose; even God cannot control man's thoughts. 5. Since man is a rational creature, like God, he is capable of understanding the laws of the universe; and as God is perfect, so can man become perfect through the process of education. Man may learn of God through a study of nature, which shows design and must therefore be an expression of God. 6. Practical religion for the individual consists in achieving virtue through the rational guidance of conduct (as exemplified in the scheme for developing the moral virtues recorded by Franklin in his *Autobiography*). The deistic system is in some ways more optimistic than Calvinism, with which it came into conflict. Some of the "moderate" deists attempted to reconcile deism with Christianity on the ground that reason and revelation never disagreed and were but two different methods of discovering the same body of truth. Cushman says that deism was founded on three principles: (1) the origin and truth of religion may be scientifically investigated; (2) the origin of religion is the conscience; (3) positive religions are degenerate forms of natural religion.

The effects of deistic thinking upon literature were very great and cannot be briefly traced. The deism of Pope's *Essay on Man* (partly inspired by Bolingbroke) illustrates the effect on the "classical" school, while the doctrine of man's perfection in Shelley's poetry and much of the Wordsworthian worship of nature are examples of deistic influences on the "romantic" school. The poet James Thomson was an acknowledged deist.

Gibbon's *Decline and Fall of the Roman Empire* (1776–1788) excited much controversy because of its deistic treatment of Christianity. Tom Paine's *Age of Reason* is more deistic than atheistic. In America deism affected the writing of many writers of the Revolutionary period, notably Franklin and Jefferson. (References: Leslie Stephen, *English Thought in the Eighteenth Century*, Vol. I; H. E. Cushman, *Beginner's History of Philosophy*, Vol. II; N. L. Torrey, *Voltaire and the English Deists;* G. P. Fisher, *History of Christian Doctrine*, Chap. ix; J. H. Randall, *The Making of the Modern Mind*.)

**Dénouement:** The final unraveling of the plot in drama or fiction; the solution of the mystery; the explanation or outcome. Dénouement implies an ingenious untying of the knot of an intrigue, involving not only a satisfactory outcome of the main situation but an explanation of all the secrets and misunderstandings connected with the plot complication. In drama dénouement may be applied to both tragedy and comedy, though the special term for a tragic dénouement is "catastrophe." The final scene of Shakespeare's *Cymbeline* is a striking example of how clever and involved a dramatic dénouement may be: exposure of villain, clearing up of mistaken identities and disguises, reuniting of father and children, of husband and wife, etc., etc. By some writers dénouement is used as a synonym for "falling action" (*q.v.*). See also CATASTROPHE, DRAMATIC STRUCTURE, SHORT STORY.

**Description:** That one of the four chief types of composition (see ARGUMENTATION, EXPOSITION, and NARRATION) which has as its purpose the picturing of a scene or setting. Though often used apart for its own sake (as in Poe's *Landor's Cottage*) it more frequently is subordinated to one of the other types of writing; especially to narration, with which it most frequently goes hand in hand. Descriptive writing is most successful when its details are carefully selected according to some purpose and to a definite point of view, when its images are concrete and clear, and when it makes discreet use of words of color, sound, and motion.

***Deus ex machina:*** The employment of some unexpected and improbable incident in a story or play in order to make things turn out right. In the ancient Greek theatre when gods appeared in plays they were lowered to the stage from the "machine" or stage structure above. The abrupt but timely appearance of a god in this fashion, when used to extricate the mortal characters of the drama from a situation so perplexing that the solution seemed beyond mortal powers, was referred to in Latin as the *deus ex machina* ("god from the machine"). The term is now employed to characterize any device whereby an author solves a difficult situation by a forced invention. A villain may fail to kill a hero because he has forgotten to load his revolver. A long-lost brother, given up for dead, suddenly appears on the scene provided with a fortune he has won in foreign parts, just in time to save the family from disgrace or a sister from an unwelcome marriage. The employment of the *deus ex machina* is commonly recognized as evidence of deficient skill in plot-making or an uncritical willingness to disregard the probabilities. Though it is sometimes employed by good authors, it is found most frequently in melodrama, "movie" plots, and "cheap" fiction. See Plot.

**Developing Characters:** When a character in a play or story changes during the progress of the action, he is said to be a "developing character." He may deteriorate, like Meredith's Richard Feverel or Shakespeare's Macbeth; he may develop strength as a result of conscious moral struggle, like Eliot's Adam Bede; or he may alter his philosophy and habits under the stress of changed social environment, like Howells' Silas Lapham. A character who is uninfluenced by the action is called a "stationary" or "static" character. Scott's chief characters are often static, as are minor characters generally in drama and fiction. The type of story or play has much to do with whether the characters develop or not. Tragedies and novels of character demand developing characters, while comedies and many forms of the short story, such as the mystery story, whose interest depends chiefly on plot, have less need for them. See Characterization.

***Dial, The:*** A periodical published in Boston from 1840 to 1844 as the mouthpiece of the New England transcendentalists. Margaret Fuller was its first editor (1840–42) and Emerson its second (1842–44). Among the most famous contributors to *The Dial* were Alcott, the two Channings (William H. and William Ellery), Dana, Emerson, Margaret Fuller, Lowell, Thoreau, and Jones Very.

**Dialects, English:** When the speech of two groups or of two persons representing two groups both speaking the same "language" exhibits very marked differences, the groups or persons are said to speak different "dialects" of the language. If the differences are very slight, they may be said to represent "sub-dialects" rather than dialects. If the differences are so great that the two groups or persons cannot understand each other, especially if they come from separate political units or "countries," they are said to speak different languages. Yet the gradations are so narrow that no scientific method has been devised which will make it possible in all cases to distinguish between a language and a dialect. The chief cause of the development of dialects is isolation or separation due to lack of ease of communication. Natural barriers such as mountain ranges and social barriers caused by hostile relations tend to keep groups from frequent contact with each other with a resultant development of habitual differences in speech-habits, leading toward the formation of dialects or even languages. Likewise among neighboring groups the dialect of one group commonly becomes dominant, as did West Saxon in early England.

When the Teutonic tribes which form the basis of the English "race" (Angles, Saxons, etc.) came to England from the Continent in the fifth century, they spoke separate dialects of West Germanic. In Old English times (fifth to eleventh centuries) there were four main dialects: (1) Northumbrian (north of the Humber River) and (2) Mercian (between the Thames and the Humber), both being branches or sub-dialects of the original Anglian dialect; (3) the Kentish (southeastern England), based upon the language of the Jutes, and (4) the Saxon (southern England). The early literature produced in the Northern districts (seventh to ninth centuries) is preserved chiefly in Southern (West Saxon) versions of the tenth and eleventh centuries. In Middle English times the old dialects appear under different names and with new sub-dialects. Northumbrian is called

Northern; Saxon and Kentish are called Southern; the Northern English spoken in Scotland becomes Lowland Scotch; Mercian becomes Midland, and is broken into two main sub-dialects, West Midland and East Midland. The latter was destined to become the immediate parent of modern English. Middle English literature, therefore, exists in a variety of dialects, more or less clearly differentiated. Layamon's *Brut* and the *Owl and the Nightingale*, for example, are in the Southern dialect; *Cursor Mundi* and *Sir Tristrem* are in Northern; the *Ormulum* is early Midland, while *Havelok the Dane*, *Piers Plowman*, and the poetry of Chaucer are in later Midland. The Middle English dialects differed in vocabulary, sounds, and inflections, so that Northerners and Southerners had difficulty in understanding each other. A few examples of the differences may be given: In Northern, "they sing" would be "they singes"; in Midland, "they singen"; in Southern, "they singeth." Northern "kirk" is Southern "church." The present participle in Northern ended in *-ande;* in Southern, in *-inde* or *-inge;* in Midland, in *-ende* or *-inge.* Though the literary language in modern times has been standardized, it must not be supposed that dialects no longer exist, especially in oral speech. Skeat lists nine modern dialects in Scotland; in England proper he finds three groups of Northern, ten groups of Midland, five groups of Eastern, two groups of Western, and ten groups of Southern.

American dialects are less marked than English dialects, though dialectal differences are easily discernible. Besides such special cases as "Pennsylvania Dutch" (Elsie Singmaster) or Yiddish (Milt Gross), which are really examples of "mangled English," there are examples of dialects proper (partly inherited from the mother country, partly the result of regional circumstances). There are four main regional types or dialects of American English—those of New England, the South, the Central West, and the Far West. (References: W. W. Skeat, *English Dialects;* Joseph Wright, *English Dialect Dictionary.*)

✓ **Dialogue:** Conversation of two or more people as reproduced in writing. Most common in fiction, particularly in dramas, novels, and short stories, dialogue is nevertheless used in general expository and philosophical writing (Plato). An analysis of dialogue as it has been employed by great writers shows that it embodies certain literary and stylistic values: (1) It advances the action in a definite way and is not used as mere ornamentation. (2) It is consistent with the character of the speakers, their social positions and special interests. It varies in tone and expression according to the nationalities, dialects, occupations, and social levels of the speakers. (3) It gives the *impression* of naturalness without being an actual, *verbatim* record of what may have been said, since fiction, as someone has explained, is concerned with "the semblance of reality," not with reality itself. (4) It presents the interplay of ideas and personalities among the people conversing; it sets forth a conversational give and take—not simply a series of remarks of alternating speakers. (5) It varies in diction, rhythm, phrasing, sentence length, etc., according to the various speakers participating. The best writers of dialogue know that rarely do two or more people of exactly the same cultural and character background meet and converse, and the dialogue they write notes these differences. (6) It serves, at the hands of some writers, to give relief from, and lightness of effect to, passages which are essentially serious or expository in nature.

There is, of course, much writing making excellent use of dialogue: Anthony Hope's *Dolly Dialogues* may stand as an example from modern literature. Writers who have made much use of the dialogue form are Plato, Lucian, Tasso, Fénelon, Galileo, Berkeley, and Landor.

**Diary:** A day-by-day chronicle of events, a journal. Usually a personal and more or less intimate record of events and thoughts kept by an individual. Not avowedly intended for publication —though it is difficult to insist on this point since many diarists have certainly kept their tongues in their cheeks—most diaries, when published, have appeared posthumously. Far and away the most famous diary in English is that of Samuel Pepys, which details events between January 1, 1660, and May 29, 1669. Other important diaries are those of John Evelyn, Bulstrode Whitelocke, George Fox, Jonathan Swift, John Wesley, and Fanny Burney. The diary has, in late years, become a conscious literary form used particularly by travelers, statesmen, politicians, etc., as a convenient method of presenting the run of daily events in which they have had a hand. See BIOGRAPHY. (References: Arthur Ponsonby, *British Diarists* and *More English Diaries*.)

**Diatribe:** Writing or discourse characterized by bitter invective, abusive argument. A harangue.

**Diction:** The use of words in oral or written discourse. A simple list of words makes up a vocabulary; the accurate, careful *use* of these words in discourse makes good diction. The qualities of proper diction as illustrated by the work of standard authors are: (1) the apt selection of the word for the particular meaning to be conveyed, (2) the use of legitimate words accepted as good usage (excluding all solecisms, barbarisms, and improprieties) and (3) the use of words which are clear-cut and specific. The manner in which words are combined constitutes style (*q.v.*) rather than diction since diction refers only to the selection of words employed in the discourse. There are at least four grades of diction: *good usage* (which is literary and more or less formal diction), *colloquial* diction (which is free and easy and suitable for discourse among intimates and acquaintances), *journalistic* diction (which is affected in greater or lesser degree by various newspapers), and *slang*. The criterion by which "good diction" is established is simply that of what constitutes common usage among intelligent, educated people and in the writing of our most worthy authors.

**Dictionaries (English):** At different times during their five hundred years of development, English dictionaries have emphasized different elements and have passed through an evolution as great as any of our literary forms or tools. In their modern form dictionaries arrange their words alphabetically, give explanations of the meanings, the derivations, the pronunciations, illustrative quotations and idioms, synonyms, and antonyms. Sometimes, however, the "dictionary" is restricted to word-lists of a special significance as dictionaries of law, of medicine, of art, etc. The best American dictionaries today are *The Century* (1889), *The New Standard* (1893), and *The New International* (1898); but the most complete dictionary on the market is from England, the Oxford *New English Dictionary* (1884–1928).

"English lexicography began," says a writer in the *Encyclopædia Britannica*, "with attempts to explain Latin words by giving English equivalents" and cites the *Promptorium Parvulorum* (1440) of Galfridus Grammaticus, a Dominican monk of Norfolk, printed by Pynson in 1499 as an early example. Just which publication deserves the distinction of being called the first English dictionary it is difficult to say because the evolution was so gradual that the conception of what constituted a good word-book differed from year to year. Vizetelly gives credit to Richard Huloet's *Abecedarium* (1552) as the first dictionary; the *Britannica* article credits "the first approach to success in collecting and defining all words in good usage in the English language" to Nathan Bailey, whose work was not published until 1730; *The Dictionary of Syr T. Eliot, Knyght* (1538), appears to have been the work first to establish the term "dictionary."

The evolution of the English dictionary is a study interesting enough to warrant the serious attention of scholars. Here only an outline can be suggested. The early word-books started off listing simply the "hard words" which people might not be expected to know; the classification was sometimes alphabetical, sometimes by subject matter. Later, the lexicographers looked upon themselves as literary guardians of national speech and listed only such words as were dignified enough to be of "good usage"; the function of these compilers was to standardize, to "fix" the national language. Illustrative of this point of view were the collections of such scholarly academies as those of Italy and France; and, indeed, Dr. Samuel Johnson, a whole academy in himself, attempted this same sort of ideal in his famous dictionary (see list below). Archbishop Trench, a British scholar, declared roundly in 1857 that a proper dictionary was really an "inventory of language" including colloquial uses as well as literary uses and Trench's insistence on the philological attitude for the lexicographer probably did more to develop the modern word-book than any other single influence.

A list of some of the titles important in the evolution of the dictionary, exclusive of those given above, includes:

John Florio (1598), *Queen Anna's New World of Words.*

Robert Cawdrey (1604) (who used English words only), *A Table Alphabeticall Contyning and Teaching the True Writing and Understanding of Hard Usuall English Wordes.*

Randle Cotgrave (1611), *A Bundle of Words.*

John Bullokar (1616), *An English Expositor.*

Henry Cockeram (1623), *The English Dictionarie* (in which "idiote" was defined as "an unlearned asse").

Thomas Blount (1656), *Glossographia.*

Edward Phillips (1658), *The New World of English Words.*

Nathaniel Bailey (1721), *Universal Etymological Dictionary.*

Samuel Johnson (1755), *Dictionary of the English Language* (in which 50,000 words were explained. The most pretentious volume published up to that time. The personal element injected into definitions gives us such famous explanations as that for *oats:* "a grain which in England is generally given to horses, but in Scotland supports the people," and, further, that *Whig* was "the name of a faction" while *Tory* signified "one who adhered to the antient constitution of the state and the apostolical hierarchy of the Church of England, opposed to a Whig").

Thomas Sheridan (1780), *Complete Dictionary of the English Language* (which gave special emphasis to the pronunciation of the words).

Samuel Johnson (1798?), *A School Dictionary.* The first American dictionary. This Johnson was not related to the earlier Dr. Samuel. This first American dictionary simplified some of the English spellings and began the use of phonetic marks as aids to pronunciation.

Noah Webster (1828), *American Dictionary;* the most famous name in American lexicography.

Joseph Emerson Worcester (1846), *Universal and Critical Dictionary of the English Language.*

In 1884 was begun in England the great work *A New English Dictionary on Historical Principles*, founded mainly on material accumulated by the Philological Society, and edited by James A. H. Murray, Henry Bradley, and W. A. Craigie. From Murray's part in the editing of the first volume, the work is sometimes called *Murray's Dictionary*, though it is more commonly called the *New English Dictionary* or the *Oxford English Dictionary*. It was completed in 1928. Though issued in "parts" the full work is now printed in ten large volumes or twenty "half-volumes." It is easily the greatest of all English dictionaries in the fullness of its illustrative examples and in its elaborate analysis of the meanings and etymologies. The citations are drawn from English writings ranging in date from the years 1200 to 1928. It is particularly valuable for its dated quotations of actual sentences showing the meanings of a word at various periods. It contains 240,165 "main words," of which 177,970 are in current use. With the addition of subordinate words, combinations, and a small number of foreign words, the total number of words entered for definition runs to 414,825. See LEXICOGRAPHY.

**Didactic Poetry:** Verses which are essentially designed to teach a lesson. The term is rather vague and loose; since it is based on purpose rather than on form, different people will have differing convictions as to the degree of didacticism present in a given poem. All significant poetry presents one or more ideas and is concerned to some extent with truth. It is not, then, the mere presence of thought which makes a poem didactic. Bryant's *To a Waterfowl*, for instance, is obviously concerned with an idea, yet is probably not held by most people to be didactic; on the other hand the closing lines of the same poet's *Thanatopsis* are obviously didactic in spirit. Pope's *Essay on Criticism* is a clear instance of didactic poetry.

**Didacticism:** That quality of writing which manifests a desire on the part of the author to instruct and improve the reader. A very general term, it is impossible to block out its limits in a definite way acceptable to all since different people have different impressions of what constitutes a didactic manner. The term is often used contemptuously, but if all didactic writing were destroyed all literatures would be greatly impoverished. The truth probably is that we all accept didactic writing up to the point where it impresses us as self-righteous; then it becomes offensive and we hurl the charge of didacticism.

**Dilettante:** One who follows an art for the love of it rather than as a serious profession. In literature, as with the other arts, the term has taken on a derogatory meaning, however, and is more usually employed to indicate one who reads and talks books and writers from hearsay and a careless reading, perhaps of reviews, as opposed to the student who makes a careful and critical study of a writer, period, movement, or book. Originally a dilettante meant an amateur; now it usually means a dabbler.

**Dimeter:** A line of verse consisting of two feet. See SCANSION.

**Dirge:** A wailing song sung at a funeral or in commemoration of death. A short lyric of lamentation. See CORONACH, ELEGY, MONODY, PASTORAL ELEGY, THRENODY.

**"Disguisings":** See MASQUE.

**Dissertation:** A formal, involved exposition written to clarify some scholarly problem. "Dissertation" is sometimes used interchangeably with "thesis" (*q.v.*) but the usual practice, at least in college and university circles, is to reserve "dissertation" for the more elaborate essays and papers written "in partial fulfillment of the requirements for the doctor's degree" and to limit the use of "thesis" to smaller problems, less perplexing, less involved, submitted for the bachelor's or master's degree. Of course these words as employed in academic circles are part of the cant of college language since both "thesis" and "dissertation" are commonly used off college campuses simply to signify careful, thoughtful discussions, in writing or speech, on almost any serious problem.

**Distich:** A couplet. Any two consecutive lines in similar form and riming. An epigram or maxim completely expressed in couplet form. Example:

> Hope springs eternal in the human breast;
> Man never is, but always to be, blest.
> —Pope

**Dithyramb:** Literary expression characterized by wild, excited, passionate language. Its lyric power relates it most nearly to verse though its unordered sequence and development, its seemingly improvised quality, give it often the form of prose. Dithyrambic verse was probably originally meant to be accompanied by music and was historically associated with Greek ceremonial worship of Bacchus or Pan. It formed the original for the choral element in Greek verse, later developing into the finer quality which we know as Greek tragedy. Rather rare in English, dithyrambic verse is most closely related to the ode; it finds its best expression in Dryden's *Alexander's Feast*.

**Ditty:** A song, a refrain. The term is somewhat vaguely and loosely used for almost any short, popular, simple melody. It implies something familiar and is perhaps most often applied to songs of the sailor. The term is also used, in the sense of *theme*, to refer to any short, apt saying or idea which runs through a composition.

**Divine Afflatus, The:** A phrase used to mean poetic inspiration, particularly the exalted state immediately preceding creative composition, when the poet is felt to be receiving his inspiration directly from a divine source. The doctrine of divine inspiration for poets was advocated by Plato. Although the phrase and doctrine have been used in a serious and sincere sense by such a poet as Shelley, it is perhaps more often used nowadays in a somewhat contemptuous sense, to imply a sort of pretentious over-valuation in a would-be poet or a bombastic spirit in an orator, whose fervid style or manner is felt not to be justified by the actual substance of the poem or oration.

**Doctrinaire:** One whose attitude is controlled by a preconceived theory or group of theories and who is inclined to disregard other points of view as well as practical considerations. His view is likely to be theoretical, narrow, and one-sided, as compared with practical and broad-minded. Criticism like Dr. Samuel Johnson's may be "doctrinaire" because controlled by a definite code of critical doctrines. Literature itself may be called "doctrinaire" when written, like some of Carlyle's books, to demonstrate such a doctrine as "hero-worship" or the "gospel of work"; or like a novel of William Godwin's, to preach a social doctrine. Politically, the word was applied to the constitutional royalists in France after 1815.

**Doggerel:** Jerky, rude composition in verse. Any poorly executed attempt at poetry. Characteristics of doggerel verse are monotony of rime and rhythm, cheap sentiment, and trivial, trite subject matter. Some doggerel does, however, because of certain humorous and burlesque qualities it attains, become amusing and earns a place on one of the lower shelves of literature. Doctor Johnson's parody on Percy's "Hermit of Warkworth" is an example:

> As with my hat upon my head
> I walk'd along the Strand,
> I there did meet another man
> With his hat in his hand.

**Domestic Tragedy:** In spite of the authority of Aristotle and the examples of the great classical and romantic tragedies of Jonson, Shakespeare, and others, the English stage at various periods has produced tragedies based not upon the lives of historical personages of high rank (see TRAGEDY) but upon the lives of everyday contemporary folk. Running contrary to the prevailing critical conceptions of the proper sphere of tragedy, domestic tragedy was long in winning critical recognition. Indeed, Allardyce Nicoll notes that the earlier domestic tragedy of the eighteenth century was a purely English form, as only in England were dramatists bold enough to believe that a serious play could be contemporary and topical. In Elizabethan times were produced such powerful domestic tragedies as the anonymous *Arden of Feversham* (late sixteenth century), Thomas Heywood's *A Woman Killed With Kindness* (acted 1603), and *The Yorkshire Tragedy* (1608, anon.). The type failed, however, to hold its popularity in competition with other forms, and disappeared from the stage. This early Elizabethan domestic tragedy specialized in murder stories taken from contemporary bourgeois life. In the eighteenth century domestic tragedy reappeared, tinged this time with the sentimentalism of the age, as in George Lillo's *The London Merchant* (1731) and Edward Moore's *The Gamester* (1753), in the latter of which plays the tragic hero is a gambler who, falsely accused of murder, takes poison and dies just after hearing that a large amount of money has been left to him. The eighteenth-century domestic tragedy, however, was crowded out by other forms, though the idea was taken over by foreign playwrights and later in the nineteenth century reintroduced from abroad, especially under the influence of Ibsen, since whose time the old conception of tragedy as possible only with heroes of high rank has definitely given way to plays which present fate at work among the lowly. No catalogue of these modern plays can here be attempted, though John Masefield's *Tragedy of Nan* (1909) may be noted as an important twentieth-century example of the form. (References: A. H. Thorndike, *Tragedy;* A. Nicoll, *British Drama* and *A History of Early Eighteenth Century Drama;* Ernest Bernbaum, *The Drama of Sensibility;* R. M. Smith, ed., *Types of Domestic Tragedy.*)

**Doric:** The Doric dialect in ancient Greece was thought of as lacking in refinement, and Doric architecture was marked by simplicity and strength rather than by beauty of detail. So a rustic or "broad" dialect may be referred to as "Doric," and such simple idyllic pieces of literature as Tennyson's *Dora* or Wordsworth's *Michael* may be said to exhibit "Doric" qualities. It is often applied to pastorals. Perhaps the best single synonym is "simple."

**Double Rime:** See FEMININE RIME.

**Drama:** Aristotle called drama "imitated human action." But since his meaning of "imitation" (*q.v.*) is in doubt, this phrase is not so simple or clear as it seems. Professor J. M. Manly sees three necessary elements in drama: (1) a story (2) told in action (3) by actors who impersonate the characters of the story. This admits such forms as pantomime (*q.v.*). Yet many writers insist that dialogue must be present, e.g., Professor Schelling, who calls drama "a picture or representation of human life in that succession and change of events that we call story, told by means of dialogue and presenting in action the successive emotions involved." Dramatic elements have been combined and emphasized so differently in dramatic history as to make theoretical definition difficult.

*Origins: Greek and Roman Drama.*—Some account of how drama originated and how it has developed will perhaps throw more light upon its nature. Drama arose from religious ceremonial. Greek comedy developed from those phases of the Dionysian rites which dealt with the theme of fertility; Greek tragedy came from the Dionysian rites dealing with life and death; and medieval drama arose out of rites commemorating the birth and the resurrection of Christ. These three origins seem independent of each other. The word "comedy" is based upon a word meaning "revel," and early Greek comedy preserved in the actors' costumes evidences of the ancient phallic ceremonies. Gradually comedy developed away from this primitive display of sex interest in the direction of greater decorum and seriousness, though the "Old Comedy" was gross in character. Satire became an element of comedy as early as the sixth century B.C. Menander (342–291 B.C.) is a representative of the "New Comedy"—a more conventionalized form which was imitated by the great Roman writers of comedy, Plautus and Terence, through whose plays classical comedy was transmitted to the Elizabethan dramatists.

The word "tragedy" seems to mean a "goat-song," and may reflect Dionysian death and resurrection ceremonies in which the goat was the sacrificial animal. The dithyrambic chant used in these festivals is perhaps the starting point of tragedy. The possible process of development has been thus stated by Professor Nicoll: "From a common chant the ceremonial song developed into a primitive duologue between a leader, dressed probably in the robes of the god, and the chorus. The song became elaborated; it developed narrative elements, and soon reached a stage in which the duologue told in primitive wise some story of the deity. Further forward movements were introduced. Two leaders instead of one made their appearance. The chorus gradually sank into the background, no longer taking the place of a protagonist."[1] The great Greek authors of tragedies were Aeschylus (525–456 B.C.), Sophocles (496–406 B.C.), and Euripides (480–406 B.C.). Modeled on these were the Latin "closet-dramas" of Seneca (4? B.C.–A.D. 65) which exercised a profound influence upon Renaissance tragedy (see SENECAN TRAGEDY).

*Rebirth of Drama in Middle Ages.*—The decline of Rome witnessed the disappearance of acted classical drama. The mime (*q.v.*) survived for an uncertain period and perhaps aided in preserving the tradition of acting through wandering entertainers

[1]Allardyce Nicoll, *British Drama*, Thomas Y. Crowell Company, 1925, p. 15. Reprinted by permission of the publishers.

(see Jongleur, Minstrel). Likewise, dramatic ceremonies and customs, some of them perhaps related to the ancient Dionysian rites themselves, played an uncertain part in keeping alive in medieval times a sort of substratum of dramatic consciousness. Scholars are virtually agreed, however, that the great institution of medieval drama in Western Europe, leading as it did to modern drama, was a new form which developed, about the ninth and following centuries, from the ritual of the Christian Church (see Medieval Drama). The dramatic forms resulting from this development, mystery or cyclic plays, miracle plays, moralities, flourishing especially in the fourteenth and fifteenth centuries, lived on into the Renaissance.

*Renaissance English Drama.*—The new interests of the Renaissance included translations and imitations of classical drama, partly through the medium of school and university plays (see Academic Drama), partly through the work of university-trained professionals engaged in supplying dramas for the public stage or the court or such institutions as the Inns of Court (*q.v.*), and partly through the influence of classical dramatic criticism, much of which reached England through Italian scholars. Thus a revived knowledge of ancient drama united with the native dramatic traditions developed from medieval forms and technique to produce in the later years of the sixteenth century the vigorous and many-sided phenomenon known as Elizabethan drama, with its spectacular and patriotic chronicle plays, its tragedies of blood, its light-hearted court comedies, its dreamy and delightful romantic comedies, its pastoral plays, satirical plays, and realistic presentations of London life. These dramas were written by playwrights who made up collectively an illustrious group of able dramatists, led by the immortal Shakespeare. All English drama shared the decadent tendencies of Jacobean and Caroline times and in 1642 the Puritans officially closed the theatres.

*Restoration and Eighteenth-century Drama.*—The stout efforts of Ben Jonson in Elizabethan times to curb the romantic tendencies which had made possible the masterpieces of Shakespeare and to insist upon the observance of classical rules of drama bore late fruit when in Restoration times, under the added influence of French drama and theory, English drama was officially revived under court auspices. Neo-classic tendencies now held sway. Shakespeare was "rewritten" for the stage. The heroic play and the new comedy of manners flourished, followed in the eighteenth century first by the "sentimental" comedy and "domestic tragedies" and in the latter part of the century by a chastened comedy of manners under Goldsmith and Sheridan.

*Nineteenth-century Drama.*—Melodrama and spectacle reigned through the early nineteenth century, occasional efforts to produce an actable literary drama proving futile. The late nineteenth century witnessed an important revival of serious drama, with, however, a tendency away from the established traditions of poetic tragedy and comedy in favor of shorter plays stressing ideas or problems or situations and depending much upon dialogue.

*American Drama.*—In America theatrical performances, at first produced by amateurs, appeared very early in the eighteenth century in such cities as Boston, New York, and Charleston, S. C., though no drama was written by an American till about the middle of the century, at which time important groups of professional actors also appeared. The early drama was imitative and dependent upon English originals or models. The Revolutionary War produced some political plays. The first native tragedy was Thomas Godfrey's *Prince of Parthia* (acted 1767), and the first comedy professionally produced was Royall Tyler's *The Contrast* (1787). The early nineteenth century witnessed a growing interest in the theatre, William Dunlap and John Howard Payne (author of "Home, Sweet Home") being prolific playwrights. Increased use was made of American themes. In the middle of the century George Henry Boker produced notable romantic tragedies, and literary drama received some attention. American dramatic art advanced in the period following the Civil War with such writers as Bronson Howard, though it was restricted greatly by the triumph of commercial theatrical management. The early twentieth century has produced several dramatists of note (William Vaughn Moody, Percy MacKaye, Josephine Peabody, Eugene O'Neill) and has witnessed a remarkable growth of the "Little Theatre Movement" (*q.v.*).

Whether one enjoys drama as a reader or as a spectator, or

approaches it as a student who would penetrate the secret of its appeal or would attempt to contribute to a study of its artistry or history, it is desirable that one know something of the conventions one is called upon to accept. He must, in the first place, accept the fact of impersonation or representation. The actors on the stage must be taken as the persons of the story (though this acceptance by no means precludes a degree of detachment sufficient to enable the spectator to appraise the art of the actor). The stage must be regarded as the actual scene or geographical setting of the action. The intervals between acts or scenes must be expanded imaginatively to correspond with the needs of the story. Moreover, one must accept special conventions, not inherent in drama as such but no less integral because of their traditional use, such as the soliloquy, the "asides," the fact that ordinary people are made spontaneously to speak in highly poetic language and that actors always speak louder than would be natural, actually pitching their voices to reach the most distant auditor rather than the persons in the group on the stage, etc. Similarly one must be prepared at times to accept costuming that is conventional or symbolic rather than realistic. One advantage in the "historical" study of drama is the familiarity thus gained with conventions peculiar to a particular age.

Some additional details on dramatic history may be found in the "Outline of Literary History," *passim*. Other terms related to the study of drama included in this handbook are:

| | | |
|---|---|---|
| Academic Drama | Catharsis | Complication |
| Acts (of a Drama) | Celtic Renaissance | Conflict |
| Antagonist | Characterization | Convention |
| Antimasque | Chronicle Play | Counterplayers |
| Artificial Comedy | Classical Tragedy | Court Comedy |
| Ballad-Opera | Climax | Cyclic Drama |
| Blank Verse | Closet Drama | Decadence |
| Bombast | Comedy | Decorum |
| Bourgeois Drama | Comedy of Humours | Dénouement |
| Burlesque | Comedy of Manners | *Deus ex machina* |
| Burletta | Comedy of Situation | Developing Characters |
| Buskin | Comic Opera | |
| Catastrophe | *Commedia dell' arte* | Dialogue |

Domestic Tragedy
Dramatic Irony
Dramatic Monologue
Dramatic Poetry
Dramatic Structure
*Drame*
Droll
Elizabethan Drama
Epilogue
Exciting Force
Extravaganza
Falling Action
Farce
Final Suspense, Moment of
Folk Drama
Genteel Comedy
Hero and Heroine
Heroic Couplet
Heroic Drama
High Comedy
Imitation
Induction
Inns of Court
Interlude
Jig
Light Opera
Little Theatre Movement
Liturgical Drama
Low Comedy

Lyrical Drama
Masque
Medieval Drama
Melodrama
*Miles gloriosus*
Mime
*Mise en scène*
Morality Play
Motivation
Movement
Mummery
Musical Comedy
Mystery Play
One-Act Play
Opera
*Opéra bouffe*
Pageant
Pantomime
Patent Theatres
Plot
Poetic Justice
Private Theatres
Problem Play
Prologue
Proscenium
Protagonist
Pseudo-Shakespearean Plays
Public Theatres
Realistic Comedy
Restraint

Revenge Tragedy
Revue
Rising Action
Romantic Comedy
Romantic Criticism
Romantic Tragedy
Scenario
Scenes (of a Drama)
Senecan Tragedy
Sentimental Comedy
Setting
Shakespeare, Editors and Editions
Situation
Sock
Soliloquy
Stock Characters
Stichomythia
Structure
Sub-plot
Tragedy
Tragedy of Blood
Tragic Force
Tragic Irony
Tragi-comedy
Trope
Unities
University Wits
Vaudeville
War of the Theatres
Women as Actors

(References: Allardyce Nicoll, *The Theory of Drama;* F. E. Schelling, *English Drama;* Walter P. Eaton, *The Drama in English;* J. Brander Matthews, *The Development of the Drama;* Allardyce Nicoll, *British Drama;* A. W. Ward, *A History of English Dramatic Literature;* Karl Young, *The Drama of the Medieval Church;* E. K. Chambers, *The Mediaeval Stage,* 2 vols.; C. F. Tucker Brooke, *The Tudor Drama;* F. E. Schelling, *Elizabethan Drama,* 2 vols.; E. K. Chambers, *The Elizabethan Stage,* 4 vols.; Allardyce Nicoll's series of dramatic histories—Restoration, Early Eighteenth Century, Late Eighteenth Century,

Early Nineteenth Century, 2 vols.; T. H. Dickinson, *Outline of Contemporary Drama;* B. H. Clark, *A Study of Modern Drama* and *European Theories of the Drama;* William Archer, *The Old Drama and the New;* J. Brander Matthews, *Study of the Drama; Camb. Hist. of Eng. Lit.,* Vols. V, VI, and separate chapters in Vols. VIII, X, XI, XIII; A. H. Quinn, *History of the American Drama,* 3 vols. under 2 titles; Blanch M. Baker, *Dramatic Bibliography.*)

**Dramatic Irony:** The words or acts of a character in a play may carry a meaning unperceived by himself but understood by the audience. Usually the character's own interests are involved in a way he cannot understand. The irony resides in the contrast between the meaning intended by the speaker and the added significance seen by others. The term is occasionally applied also to non-dramatic narrative, and is sometimes extended to include any situation (such as mistaken identity) in which some of the actors on the stage or some of the characters in a story are "blind" to facts known to the spectator or reader. So understood, dramatic irony is responsible for much of the interest in fiction and drama, because the reader or spectator enjoys being in on the secret. For an example see TRAGIC IRONY. (Reference: "Introduction" to Germaine Dempster's *Dramatic Irony in Chaucer.*)

**Dramatic Monologue:** A lyric poem revealing "a soul in action" through the conversation of one character. The credit for developing this type is generally given to Browning who used it in such poems as *Andrea del Sarto.* Tennyson also used the dramatic monologue (*Ulysses, Rizpah*). Contemporary American poets find it a congenial form, as witness the writing of Robert Frost, E. A. Robinson, Amy Lowell, and Carl Sandburg. Three characteristics mark the type: it presents a dramatic moment in the life of the character; it reveals the character of the speaker; and a second person, a listener, is present and though he does not speak nevertheless plays a part in the development of the poem.

**Dramatic Poetry:** A term that, logically, should be restricted to poetry which employs dramatic form or some element or elements of dramatic technique as a means of achieving poetic ends. The "dramatic monologue" (*q.v.*) is an example. The dramatic quality may result from the use of dialogue, monologue, vigorous diction, blank verse, or the stressing of tense situation and emotional conflict. Because of the presence of dramatic elements in the poems to be included in the volume, Browning used the phrase "Dramatic Lyrics" as the subtitle of *Bells and Pomegranates*, No. III (1842). It must be recorded, however, that the phrase "dramatic poetry" is not infrequently employed broadly so as to include compositions which, like Shakespeare's *The Tempest*, may be more properly classed as "poetic drama" (*q.v.*), or which, like Browning's *Pippa Passes*, are more commonly called "closet dramas" (see CLOSET DRAMA).

**Dramatic Structure:** The ancients compared the plot of a drama to the tying and untying of a knot. The principle of dramatic conflict, though not mentioned as such in Aristotle's definition of drama, is implied in this figure. The technical structure of a serious play is determined by the necessities of developing this dramatic conflict. Thus a well-built tragedy will commonly show the following divisions, each of which represents a phase of the dramatic conflict: introduction, rising action, climax or crisis (turning point), falling action, and catastrophe. The relation of these parts is sometimes represented graphically by the figure of a pyramid, the rising slope suggesting the rising action or tying of the knot, the falling slope the falling action or resolution, the apex representing the climax.

The *introduction* (or *exposition*) creates the tone, gives the setting, introduces some of the characters, and supplies other facts necessary to the understanding of the play, such as events in the story supposed to have taken place before the part of the action included in the play, since a play, like an epic, is likely to plunge *in medias res*, "into the middle of things." In *Hamlet*, the bleak midnight scene on the castle platform, with the appearance of the ghost, sets the keynote of the tragedy, while the conversation of the watchers, especially the words of Horatio, supply antecedent facts, such as the quarrel between the dead King Hamlet and the King of Norway.

The *rising action*, or *complication*, is set in motion by the "exciting force" (in *Hamlet* the ghost's revelation to Hamlet of the murder) and continues through successive stages of conflict between the hero and the counterplayers up to the *climax* or turning point (in *Hamlet* the hesitating failure of the hero to kill Claudius at prayer).

The downward or *falling action* stresses the activity of the forces opposing the hero and while some suspense must be maintained, the trend of the action must lead logically to the disaster with which the tragedy is to close. The falling action is often set in movement by a single event called the "tragic force," closely related to the climax and bearing the same relation to the falling action as the exciting force does to the rising action. In *Macbeth* the tragic force is the escape of Fleance following the murder of Banquo. In *Hamlet* it is the "blind" stabbing of Polonius, which sends Hamlet away from the court just as he appears about to succeed in his plans. The latter part of the falling action is sometimes marked by an event which delays the catastrophe and seems to offer a way of escape for the hero (the apparent reconciliation of Hamlet and Laertes). This is called the "moment of final suspense" and aids in maintaining interest. The falling action is usually shorter than the rising action and often is attended by some lowering of interest (as in the case of the long conversation between Malcolm and MacDuff in *Macbeth*), since new forces must be introduced and an apparently inevitable end made to seem uncertain. Relief scenes are often resorted to in the falling action, partly to mark the passage of time, partly to provide emotional relaxation for the audience. The famous scene of the grave diggers in *Hamlet* is an example of how this relief scene may be justified through its inherent dramatic qualities and through its relation to the serious action.

The *catastrophe*, marking the tragic failure, usually the death, of the hero (and often of his opponents as well) comes as a natural outgrowth of the action. It satisfies, not by a gratification of the emotional sympathies of the spectator but by its logical conformity, and by a final presentation of the nobility of the succumbing hero. A "glimpse of restored order" often follows the catastrophe proper in a Shakespearean tragedy, as when Hamlet gives his dying vote to Fortinbras as the new king.

During the nineteenth century conventional structure gave way to a newer technique. First, comedy, under the influence of French bourgeois comedy, the "well-made play" of Eugène Scribe and others, developed a set of technical conventions all its own; and as a result of the liberal movement led by Ibsen, serious drama cast off the restrictions of five-act tragedy and freed itself from conventional formality. By the end of the century the traditional five-act structure was to be found only in poetic or consciously archaic tragedy, whose connection with the stage was artificial and generally unsuccessful. (References: G. Freytag, *The Technique of the Drama;* E. Woodbridge, *The Drama, Its Law and Its Technique;* G. P. Baker, *Dramatic Technique;* William Archer, *Play-Making.*)

**Drame:** A form of play between tragedy and comedy developed by the French in the eighteenth century and later introduced into England, where it is often called a "drama." It is a serious play, of which the modern problem play is an example.

**Droll:** A short dramatic piece (also known as "drollery" or "droll humour") cultivated on the Commonwealth stage in England as a substitute for full-length or serious plays not permitted by the government. A droll was likely to be a "short, racy, comic" scene selected from some popular play (as a Launcelot Gobbo scene from *The Merchant of Venice*) and completed by dancing somewhat in the manner of the earlier "jig" (*q.v.*). (Reference: Leslie Hotson, *The Commonwealth and Restoration Stage.*)

**Dumb Show:** A pantomimic performance used as a part of a play. The term is applied particularly to such specimens of silent acting as appeared in Elizabethan drama. The dumb show provided a spectacular element and was often accompanied by music. Sometimes it employed allegorical figures like those in the morality play and the masque. Sometimes it foreshadowed coming events in the action and sometimes it provided comment like that of the Chorus (*q.v.*). Sometimes it appeared as prologue or between acts and sometimes it was an integral part of the action, being performed by the characters of the play proper. Whatever its origin, it seems to have appeared first in the third quarter of the sixteenth century in the Senecan plays (see SENECAN TRAGEDY). It continued in use well into the seventeenth century. More than fifty extant Elizabethan plays contain dumb shows. The one appearing in Shakespeare's *Hamlet* (Act III, Scene ii) is unusual in that it is preliminary to a show which is itself a "play within a play." Other well-known Elizabethan plays containing dumb shows are Sackville and Norton's *Gorboduc* (1562), Robert Greene's *James the Fourth* (1591), John Marston's *Malcontent* (1604), John Webster's *Duchess of Malfi* (1614), and Thomas Middleton's *The Changeling* (1623). See DISGUISINGS, MASQUE, PAGEANT, PANTOMIME. (The origin of the dumb show is discussed by J. W. Cunliffe in *Early English Classical Tragedies*, "Introduction." An excellent general account is that of B. R. Pearn in *The Review of English Studies* for 1935.)

**Eclogue:** Literally, "eclogue" in Greek meant "selection" and was applied to various kinds of poems. From its application to Virgil's pastoral poems, however, "eclogue" came to have its present restricted meaning of a formal pastoral poem following the traditional technique derived from the "idylls" of Theocritus (third century B.C.). Conventional eclogue types include: (1) the singing match: two shepherds have a singing contest on a wager or for a prize, a third shepherd acting as judge; (2) the rustic dialogue: two "rude swains" engage in banter, perhaps over a mistress, perhaps over their flocks; (3) the dirge or lament for a dead shepherd (see PASTORAL ELEGY); (4) the love-lay: a shepherd may sing a song of courtship or a shepherd or shepherdess may complain of disappointment in love; (5) the eulogy. In Renaissance times, following Mantuan's Latin eclogues (fifteenth century) the eclogue was used for veiled satire, particularly satire against the corruptions of the clergy, against political factions, and against those responsible for the neglect of poetry. The earliest and most famous collection of conventional eclogues in English literature is Spenser's *Shepheardes Calender* (1579), made up of one eclogue for each month. See PASTORAL.

**Edinburgh Review:** A quarterly journal of criticism founded in 1802 by Francis Jeffrey, Sydney Smith, and Henry Brougham. The first issue, consisting of 252 pages, appeared October 10,

1802, under the editorship of Sydney Smith though Jeffrey was subsequently the editor for twenty-seven years. The state of criticism and book reviewing at the time was so low that the founders determined on a vigorous, outspoken policy which not only made a successful publication (10,000 circulation after ten years), but also stirred up the whole English-reading world. Among the contributors to the *Review* were some of the most brilliant writers of the time, the list including in addition to the editors such men as Walter Scott, Henry Hallam, and Francis Horner. The motto of the publication—*Judex damnatur, cum nocens absolvitur,* "the judge is condemned when the guilty man is acquitted"—indicates clearly the rigorous policy of the founders, and, if the ire which the magazine aroused in many quarters is a criterion, it appears that not only were few guilty men acquitted, but that many innocent men were condemned. After seven years of being browbeaten, the Tories started a rival journal, the *Quarterly Review* (1809), the two publications riding literary and political prejudices hard and enlivening British criticism while giving to journalism one of its most brilliant and erratic epochs.

One of the abhorrences of the *Edinburgh Review* was the "lakers" (Lake School of writers), more particularly Southey and Wordsworth. An article by Henry Brougham called *Hours of Idleness* (reviewing an early volume by Byron) provoked Byron's famous satire, *English Bards and Scotch Reviewers.*

**Edition:** "In modern times we can define 'edition' as the whole number of copies of a book printed at any time or times from one setting-up of type, and 'impression' as the whole number of copies printed at one time (in ordinary circumstances, the total number of copies printed without removing the type or plates from the press). By 'issue' is generally meant some special form of the book in which, for the most part, the original printed sheets are used but which differs from the earlier or normal form by the addition of new matter or by some difference in arrangement. Parts of an impression printed on different paper are also sometimes referred to as different 'issues.' The word is, however, very loosely used, and a cheap 'reissue' may merely mean the old book quite unchanged, except perhaps for the substitution of a cheaper binding, but at a reduced price."[1] As applied to old books, "edition" and "impression" are practically synonymous, because of the practice of distributing type after a printing. Other uses of the term "edition" appear in such phrases as "a ten-volume edition of Kipling" (referring to the form of publication) and "Grosart's edition of Spenser" (reflecting the fact of editing).

**Editorial:** A short essay, expository or argumentative in character, used in newspapers or magazines. The purpose of the editorial is usually to discuss current news events, and the subjects treated may range from matters of purely local importance through county, state, national, and international affairs. The usual editorial form falls naturally into three divisions: a statement of the event or situation to be discussed, a clarification of this situation through elaboration of the points concerned, and an expression of the opinion of the editorial office as to the significance, justice, or purpose inherent in the situation. Some publications print as editorials pleasant little essays on insignificant or minor situations, frankly admitting such bits to publication simply for the charm of their style or the grace of their humor.

**Effect:** Writers sometimes set themselves to create in a particular composition a particular impression (effect) in the mind of the reader. The effect striven for may be one of horror, mystery, beauty, or whatever the writer's mood dictates, but once the effect is hit upon, everything in the story—incident, character, setting—must work toward this controlling purpose. Poe is the arch-type of the writer who strives for effect. One of the paragraphs in his criticism of Hawthorne's *Twice-Told Tales* stands out as the best explanation of this principle of effect:

A skilful literary artist has constructed a tale. If wise, he has not fashioned his thoughts to accommodate his incidents; but having conceived, with deliberate care, a certain unique or single *effect* to be wrought out, he then invents such incidents—he then combines such events as may best aid him in establishing his preconceived effect. If his very initial sentence tend not to the outbringing of this effect, then

[1]R. B. McKerrow, *An Introduction to Bibliography for Literary Students*, p. 175. Oxford University Press. Reprinted by permission of the publishers.

he has failed in his first step. In the whole composition there should be no word written, of which the tendency, direct or indirect, is not to the one preëstablished design. And by such means, with such care and skill, a picture is at length painted which leaves in the mind of him who contemplates it with a kindred art, a sense of the fullest satisfaction. . . .

**Elaboration:** A rhetorical method for developing a theme or picture in such a way as to give the reader a completed impression. This may be done in various ways: by repetition of the statement or idea, by a change of words and phrases, by supplying additional details, etc. The bare statement that the "sea-water is salty" means something, of course, but this statement under certain conditions may need the elaboration which would come from (1) a chemical analysis showing the per cent of the solution, (2) a statement showing the impression of sea-water on the taste, (3) an incident narrating what happens to wrecked sailors who drink sea-water, etc. All this is elaboration of the central idea and, when used with restraint, makes for clearness. Over-elaboration, however, immediately becomes a fault since it results in Polonius-like diffuseness, wordiness, and stupidity. "Elaboration" is also used as a critical term characterizing a literary, rhetorical style which is rather ornate. One might say, for instance, "Oscar Wilde's style was elaborate."

**Elegy:** In modern use simply a lyric poem setting forth the poet's meditations upon death. The type, however, is not so much characterized by lyric expression of passionate sorrow as by conventional language expressing with dignity and decorum a formal grief. A classical form, common to both Latin and Greek literatures, the elegy originally signified almost any type of serious, subjective meditation on the part of the poet whether this reflective element was concerned with death, love, or war, or merely the presentation of information. In classic writing the elegy was more distinguishable by its form, that of a couplet in dactylic hexameter and pentameter, than by its subject matter. The Elizabethan poets used the term freely for love lyrics of various kinds, particularly love "plaints." Gray's *Elegy in a Country Churchyard* is probably the most famous English elegy. Here the grief expressed springs not so much from personal loss as from sadness at the general ineffectiveness of human life. Milton's *Lycidas* is perhaps the best-known personal elegy in our literature. See PASTORAL ELEGY. (References: Gayley and Kurtz, *Methods and Materials of Literary Criticism*, pp. 28, 392; J. C. Bailey, *English Elegies*, "Introduction.")

**Elision:** The omission of a part of a word for ease of pronunciation, for euphony, or to secure a desired rhythmic effect. This is most often accomplished by the omission of a final vowel preceding an initial vowel as "th'orient" for "the orient," but elision also occurs between syllables of a single word as "ne'er" for "never."

**Elizabethan Drama:** This phrase is commonly used for the entire body of Renaissance English drama produced in the century preceding the closing of the theatres in 1642, although it is sometimes employed in a narrower sense to designate the drama of the later years of Elizabeth's reign and the few years following it. Thus, Shakespeare is an Elizabethan dramatist, although more than one third of his active career lies in the reign of James I. Modern English drama not only came into being in Elizabethan times but developed so rapidly and brilliantly that the Elizabethan era is the golden age of English drama.

Lack of adequate records makes it impossible to trace the steps by which Elizabethan drama developed, though the chief elements which contributed to it can be listed. From "medieval drama" (*q.v.*) came the tradition of acting and certain conventions approved by the populace. From the "morality plays" (*q.v.*) and the "interludes" (*q.v.*) in particular came comic elements. With this medieval heritage was combined the classical tradition of drama, partly drawn from a study of the Roman dramatists, Seneca (tragedy) and Plautus and Terence (comedy), and partly from humanistic criticism based upon Aristotle and transmitted through Italian Renaissance scholarship. This classical influence appeared first in the school drama (see ACADEMIC DRAMA). Later it affected the drama written under the auspices of the royal court and of the Inns of Court (*q.v.*). Eventually it influenced the plays of the university-trained playwrights connected with the public stage. Indeed, the part played by the "University Wits" (*q.v.*) in adapting classical dramatic materials to the demands of the popular stage seems to have advanced dramatic technique to a point where it was ready for the perfecting touch of the master dramatist himself. The modern theatre arose with Elizabethan drama (see PUBLIC THEATRES, PRIVATE THEATRES). For types of Elizabethan drama and names of dramatists see "Outline of Literary History" (pp. 485–499) and the terms listed at the close of the account of DRAMA, especially TRAGEDY, ROMANTIC TRAGEDY, CLASSICAL TRAGEDY, TRAGEDY OF BLOOD, COMEDY, COMEDY OF HUMOURS, COMEDY OF MANNERS, COMEDY OF SITUATION, COURT COMEDY, REALISTIC COMEDY, CHRONICLE PLAY, and MASQUE. Authoritative books on Elizabethan drama include: E. K. Chambers, *The Elizabethan Stage*, 4 vols.; F. E. Schelling, *Elizabethan Drama*, 2 vols.; Tucker Brooke, *The Tudor Drama*.

**Elizabethan Literature:** A phrase sometimes broadly employed for English literature of the period from *ca.* 1550 to 1660, but sometimes narrowly for that of the reign of Elizabeth (1558–1603). See RENAISSANCE, JACOBEAN, CAROLINE; also "Outline of Literary History," pp. 485–500.

**Elizabethan Miscellanies:** See MISCELLANIES, POETICAL.

**Elizabethan Theatres:** See PUBLIC THEATRES, PRIVATE THEATRES.

**Ellipsis:** A figure of speech characterized by the omission of one or more words which, while essential to the grammatic structure of the sentence, are easily supplied by the reader. The effect of ellipsis is rhetorical; it makes for emphasis of statement. The device often traps the unwary user into difficulties, since carelessness will result in impossible constructions. The safe rule is to be sure that the words to be supplied occur in the proper grammatic form not too remote from the place the ellipsis occurs. In the following quotations the brackets indicate ellipsis:

Where wigs [strive] with wigs, [where] with sword-knots
sword-knots strive,
[Where] Beaus banish beaus, and [where] coaches coaches drive.
—Pope

147

**Emblem Books:** An "emblem" consisted of a motto expressing some moral idea and accompanied by a picture and a short poem illustrating the idea. The poem was always short—sonnets, epigrams, madrigals, and various stanza forms being employed. The picture (originally itself the "emblem") was symbolic. A collection of emblems was known as an emblem book. Emblems and emblem books, which owed their popularity partly to the newly developed art of engraving, were very popular in all Western European languages in the fifteenth, sixteenth, and seventeenth centuries. Examples of emblems: The motto *Divesque miserque*, "both rich and poor," illustrated by a picture of King Midas sitting at a table where everything was gold and by a verse or "posie" explaining how Midas, though rich, could not eat his gold; *Parler peu et venir au poinct*, "speak little and come to the point," illustrated by a quatrain and a picture of a man shooting at a target with a cross-bow. Edmund Spenser's earliest known literary work consisted of translations of sonnets of Du Bellay and Petrarch for *A Theatre of Worldlings* (1569), a translation of a Dutch emblem book. Several of Spenser's poems, such as *The Shepheardes Calender* and *Muiopotmos*, show the influence of emblems. Shakespeare seems to have made much use of emblem literature, as in the casket scene in *The Merchant of Venice*. Francis Quarles is the author of an interesting seventeenth-century emblem book. (References: E. N. S. Thompson, *Literary Bypaths of the Renaissance;* Henry Green, *Shakespeare and the Emblem Writers*.)

**Emotional Element in Literature:** The deliberate, conscious actions of man arise from one of two promptings: his reason or his emotion. This is not the place to argue which is the more frequently used: with everyone the two play their unequal parts. We act sometimes as reasoning animals; we act sometimes as creatures prompted by one or another of the emotions. In the human comedy in which we all act, our rôles are controlled largely by the brain or the heart. Literature knows this. Its stuff is woven from this conflict between reason and emotion; its warp is humanity and its woof is hate, love, fear, anger, joy, despair, sorrow, shame—any of the flashing moods which give color and texture to our daily lives. Reason has its place in the literature of argument, of persuasion, of logic; but emotion motivates most of our imaginative literature and gives us lyric poetry, tragedy, the novel of human nobility and the drama of human frailty. The emotions of pity and fear accompanying tragedy bring man to a catharsis; with the emotion of religion he explores divine provinces; moved by the emotion of the aesthetic he forms a conception of new beauties and new ideals.

All this indicates that emotion in literature has a double significance for the reader. He follows the story of *Othello*, for instance, noting how hate and jealousy and love deepen the intrigue. This faithful portrayal of the human emotions serves first the purpose of interesting him simply in the story. But with the passion of the final scenes comes a second and greater interest: the reader is moved deeply within himself, he draws conclusions about life, determines what his own conduct would be under similar conditions. His own life is somewhat different because of what he has read of Iago, Othello, and Desdemona. And this "purging," this application of the experience of others to his own situation, is perhaps the greatest significance of the emotional element in literature—its effect on the reader. And what is true of *Othello* is true to greater or lesser extent, with these same or other emotions, in *The Canterbury Tales*, the ballad of *Sir Patrick Spens*, *Dr. Faustus*, a lyric of Robert Herrick or of Robert Burns, a *Christabel*, or an *Ode to a Grecian Urn*. The presence of this emotional experience of the race it is which distinguishes literature from history and from science. Science records man's past as a reasoning animal; history records man's past actions; literature very largely records man's past emotions either realistically or imaginatively.

**Emphasis:** A principle of rhetoric dictating that important elements be given important positions and adequate development whether in the sentence, the paragraph, or the whole composition. The more important positions are, naturally, at the beginning and end. But emphasis may also be secured (1) by repetition of important ideas, (2) by development of important ideas through supplying plenty of specific detail, (3) by simply giving more space to the more important phases of the composition,

(4) by contrasting one element with another since such contrasts focus the reader's attention on the point in question, (5) by careful selection of details so chosen that subjects related to the main idea are included and all irrelevant material excluded.

**Empiricism:** In philosophy, the practice of drawing rules of practice not from theory but from experience. Hence an empirical method is sometimes equivalent to an "experimental" method. In medicine, however, an "empiric" usually means a quack. The term is sometimes borrowed by literary critics and used in a derogatory sense, an empiric judgment being an untrained one.

**End-rime:** See RIME.

**End-stopped Lines:** Lines of verse in which both the grammatical structure and the sense reach completion at the end of the line. The absence of *enjambement* (*q.v.*), or "run-on" lines.

> All are but parts of one stupendous whole,
> Whose body Nature is, and God the soul:
> —Pope

**English Language:** The English language developed from the West Germanic dialects spoken by the Angles, Saxons, and other Teutonic tribes which participated in the gradual invasion and occupation of England in the fifth and sixth centuries, a movement which resulted in the obliteration of the earlier Celtic and Roman cultures in the island. The word "English" applied to the language reflects the fact that Anglo-Saxon literature first flourished in the North and was written in the Anglian dialects (hence *Englisc*, "English") spoken in Northumbria and Mercia. Later, under King Alfred, the West Saxon region became the cultural center. The word *Englisc* was still employed as its name, however, and the earlier Anglian literature was copied in the West Saxon dialect, now commonly referred to as "Old English," or "Anglo-Saxon." As a language West Saxon was very different from modern English. It was burdened with grammatical gender, with declensions, conjugations, tenses, and case-endings almost equal in extent to those found in Latin. The word "stone," for example, had six forms (singular: *stān, stānes, stāne;* plural: *stānas, stāna, stānum*) representing five cases (nominative, genitive, dative, accusative, instrumental). Pronouns and verbs likewise possessed complicated inflectional systems.   In addition, the four great dialects of the Old English period (Northumbrian, Mercian, West Saxon, Kentish) differed among themselves in grammar, pronunciation, and vocabulary. The first writing was in runes (*q.v.*), which were displaced later by the Roman alphabet used by the Christian missionaries. Specimens of Old English have survived from as early as the eighth century, but most of the existing manuscripts are in West Saxon of the tenth and eleventh centuries.   Though a few Latin and fewer Celtic words were added to the vocabulary in Old English times, most of the words were Teutonic, consisting of words used by the Angles and Saxons, augmented by the introduction of Danish and Norse words as the result of later invasions.

The changes which have made modern English look like a different language from Old English are the result of the operation of certain natural tendencies in language development, such as the progressive simplification of the grammar; and the accidents of history, such as the Norman Conquest and the growth of London as a cultural center.   The greatest change took place in the earlier part of the period known as Middle English (*ca.* 1100-*ca.*1500) or a little earlier.   The leveling of inflections and other simplifying forces, already under way in late Old English times, were accelerated by the results of the Norman Conquest (*q.v.*), which dethroned English as the literary language, in favor of the French language spoken by the newcomers (see ANGLO-FRENCH and ANGLO-NORMAN).   Left to the everyday use of the subjugated native elements of the population, English changed rapidly in the direction of Modern English, as is shown in manuscripts written about 1200, when English was again coming into literary use.   By late Middle English times (fourteenth century) the process of simplification had gone so far that in Chaucer's time almost all the old inflections either were lost or were weakened to a final -*e*, often unpronounced.   The introduction of French words in the Middle English period proved a powerful source of enrichment to the English vocabulary. By this time, too, many Danish words, acquired much earlier, appear. In the fourteenth and fifteenth centuries a significant step toward the development of a standardized, uniform language came with the new prominence given the London dialect (largely East Midland), which thus became the basis for modern English. This development came chiefly from the growing importance of London commercially and politically, the influence of the writings of Chaucer and his followers, the adoption of English instead of French in the courts and schools (fourteenth century), and the employment of this dialect by Caxton, the first English printer (late fifteenth century).

Modern English (*ca.*1500 on) has been marked by an enormous expansion in vocabulary, the new words being drawn from many sources, chiefly Latin and French. Since French is itself based upon Latin, English has acquired many doublets, such as "strict" and "straight," permitting further developments in shades of meaning. An examination of a dictionary will show the vast preponderance of foreign words over native English words, though the latter include the more frequently used words of everyday intercourse, such as "man," "wife," "child," "go," "hold," "day," "bed," "sorrow," "give." The stylistic effect of English prose writing is greatly affected by the nature of the vocabulary used, particularly as between native English words and those derived from Latin, either directly or through French. The native words in general give an effect of simplicity, strength, and sincerity, while the Latin or Romance words impart smoothness and make possible fine distinctions in meaning. Modern English has also drawn freely upon many other sources for new words. Greek, for example, has been resorted to for scientific terms, new words being formed from Greek root-meanings, Greek prefixes, suffixes, etc. In grammar, the simplification process has been retarded in modern times by such conservative forces as grammars, dictionaries, printers, and school teachers. Likewise spelling and pronunciation have become fixed in somewhat chaotic and archaic forms by the influence of the same standardizing tendencies. See ANGLO-SAXON, MIDDLE ENGLISH, OLD ENGLISH (ENGLISH) DIALECTS, and the "Outline of Literary History," *passim*. (References: O. F. Emerson,

*History of the English Language;* Otto Jespersen, *Growth and Structure of the English Language;* G. H. McKnight, *Modern English in the Making;* C. N. Greenough and G. L. Kittredge, *Words and Their Ways in English Speech;* A. C. Baugh, *A History of the English Language.*)

**English Literature, Periods of:** The division of a nation's literary history into periods offers a convenient method for studying authors and movements, as well as the literature itself, in their proper perspectives. Hence most literary histories and anthologies are arranged by periods. In the case of English literature, there are almost as many arrangements as there are books on the subject. This lack of uniformity arises chiefly from two facts. In the first place, periods merge into one another because the supplanting of one literary attitude by another is a gradual process. Thus the earlier romanticists are contemporary with the later neo-classicists, just as the neo-classical attitude existed in the very heyday of Elizabethan romanticism. Dates given in any scheme of literary periods, therefore, must be regarded as approximate and suggestive only, even when they reflect some very definite fact, as 1660 (the Restoration of the Stuarts) and 1798 (the publication of *Lyrical Ballads*). In the second place, the names of periods may be chosen on very different principles. One plan is to name a period from its greatest or its most representative author: Age of Chaucer, Age of Spenser, etc. Another is to coin a descriptive adjective from the name of the ruler: Elizabethan Period, Jacobean Period, Victorian Period. Or pure chronology or names of centuries may be preferred: Fifteenth-Century Literature, Eighteenth-Century Literature, etc. Or descriptive titles designed to indicate prevailing critical or philosophical attitudes, or dominant fashions or "schools" of literature may be used: Neo-classicism, Romanticism, Age of Reason. Logically, some single principle should control in any given scheme, but such consistency is not always found. The table below gives the scheme used in this book, alternate titles being freely employed. Where the name of a period is followed by a page reference, a descriptive account may be found in this handbook, and additional descriptive data on all the periods are given in their proper places in the "Outline of Literary History" elsewhere in this book (pp. 469–579).

PERIODS OF ENGLISH LITERATURE

428–1066   Old English.   Anglo-Saxon Period (pp. 23, 291).

1066–1350   Early Middle English (p. 253).   Norman-French, Anglo-Norman.

1350–1500   Late Middle English (p. 253).
   1350–1400   Age of Chaucer.
   1400–1500   End of Middle Ages.   Fifteenth-Century Literature.

1500–1660   Renaissance (p. 363).
   1500–1558   Early Tudor Period.   Early Renaissance.
   1558–1600   Elizabethan Period.   Age of Spenser.
   1600–1625   Late Elizabethan and Jacobean Period.   Age of Jonson.
   1625–1660   Puritan and Cavalier Period.   Age of Milton.

1660–1798   Neo-Classicism (p. 273).   Eighteenth-Century Literature.
   1660–1700   Restoration Period.   Age of Dryden.
   1700–1750   Triumph of Neo-Classicism.   Age of Pope.   Age of Reason.
   1750–1798   Neo-Classicism and Advance of Romanticism.   Age of Johnson and Burns.

1798–1900   Romanticism (p. 379).   Nineteenth-Century Literature.
   1798–1832   Triumph of Romanticism.   Age of Wordsworth.
   1832–1870   Early Victorian Period (p. 458).   Age of Tennyson.
   1870–1900   Late Victorian Period (p. 458).   Advance of Realism.

1900–1930   Triumph of Realism.   Early Twentieth-Century Literature.

***Enjambement:*** A device used by poets to escape the monotonous, hobby-horse rhythm of the regular couplet or of blank verse by running the sense and grammatic structure past the second line of a couplet. *Enjambement* occurs with the presence of the "run-on" line and offers contrast to the "end-stopped" line. The first and second lines below, carried over to the second and third for completion, are illustrations of *enjambement:*

Or if Sion hill<br>
Delight thee more, and Siloa's brook, that flow'd<br>
Fast by the oracle of God.

—Milton

**Enthymeme:** A syllogism informally stated and omitting one of the two premises—either the major or the minor. The omitted premise is to be understood. Example: "Children should be seen and not heard. Be quiet, John." Here the obvious minor premise—that John is a child—is left to the ingenuity of the reader.

**Envoy (envoi):** A conventionalized stanza appearing at the close of certain poems; particularly associated with the French *ballade* form. The envoy (1) is usually addressed to a prince, a judge, a patron, or other person of importance; (2) repeats the refrain line used throughout the ballade; (3) consists normally of four lines (though not necessarily so limited); (4) usually employs the *bcbc* rime-scheme. See BALLADE.

**Epic:** A long narrative poem presenting characters of high position in a series of adventures which form an organic whole through their relation to a central figure of heroic proportions and through their development of episodes important to the development of a nation or race. The first epics took shape from the scattered work of various unknown poets. Through accretion these early episodes were gradually molded into a unified whole and an ordered sequence. The classical epic, as influenced largely by Virgil, developed certain devices which to a varying extent have been respected by all poets since. Some of these characteristic devices were: the beginning *in medias res*, the invocation of the muse, and the statement of the epic purpose. Other conventions include descriptions of warfare and battles and the use of the supernatural. The speech of the characters is distinctly formal, epic catalogues and descriptions are brought in (these often marked by considerable concrete detail), the epic simile is common, and the whole story is presented in dignified and majestic language. A few of the more prominent folk epics are: The *Iliad* and the *Odyssey* (attributed to Homer), the Saxon *Beowulf*, the East Indian *Mahabharata*, the Spanish *Cid*, the Finnish *Kalevala*, the French *Song of Roland*, and the German *Nibelungenlied*. Some of the best known art epics (those which are distinctly the work of a single writer) are: the *Aeneid* of Virgil, the *Divine Comedy* of Dante, the *Jerusalem*

*Delivered* of Tasso, the *Faerie Queene* of Spenser, and *Paradise Lost* of Milton. An instance of a contemporary epic poem is Alfred Noyes' *Drake*. Between the classical and folk epic of the ancient past and the modern epic of the sixteenth century and later there is a great mass of literature verging on the epic in form and purpose though not answering strictly to the conventional epic form. These poems are variously referred to as epic, metrical, or medieval romances. See MEDIEVAL ROMANCE. (References: W. M. Dixon, *English Epic and Heroic Poetry;* John Clark, *A History of Epic Poetry;* Gilbert Murray, *The Rise of the Greek Epic;* W. P. Ker, *Epic and Romance;* C. M. Gayley and B. P. Kurtz, *Methods and Materials of Literary Criticism.*)

**Epic Formula:** See EPIC.

**Epic Simile:** An elaborated comparison. This type differs from an ordinary simile (*q.v.*) in that it is more involved, more ornate, and is a conscious imitation of the Homeric manner. The secondary object or picture is developed into an independent esthetic object, an image which for the moment excludes the primary object with which it is compared. The following from *Paradise Lost* may serve as an example:

> Angel Forms, who lay entranced
> Thick as autumnal leaves that strow the brooks
> In Vallombrosa, where the Etrurian shades
> High over-arched embower; or scattered sedge
> Afloat, when with fierce winds Orion armed
> Hath vexed the Red-Sea coast, whose waves o'erthrew
> Busiris and his Memphian chivalry,
> While with perfidious hatred they pursued
> The sojourners of Goshen, who beheld
> From the safe shore their floating carcases
> And broken chariot-wheels.
>
> —Milton

**Epicurean:** A piece of literature may be said to be "epicurean" if it exhibits a mood or spirit of surrender to the search for pleasure, especially such sensuous pleasures as eating and drinking. The usage arose through a misunderstanding of what

Epicurus, a Greek philosopher, meant by "pleasure" when he advocated the doctrine that man's legitimate aim was the pursuit of pleasure. Of course, "epicurean" may be applied to an author himself.

**Epigram:** A pointed saying; hence an epigrammatic style is concise, pointed, often antithetical, as "Man proposes but God disposes." This rhetorical use of the word is derived from certain qualities of a type of poem known as an epigram. Originally (in ancient Greece) an epigram meant an inscription, especially an epitaph. Then it came to mean "a very short poem summing up as though in a memorial inscription what it is desired to make permanently memorable in a single action or situation" (Mackail). Hence the epigram was characterized by compression, pointedness, clarity, balance, and polish. Examples of the ancient epigram may be found in the Greek Anthology and in the work of the Roman poet Martial (A.D. 40–104), whose work supplied the models for Ben Jonson, the greatest writer of epigrams in the English Renaissance. Martial had used the epigram for various themes and purposes: eulogy, friendship, compliment, epitaphs, philosophic reflection, *jeux d'esprit*, and (especially) satire, particularly against sham and hypocrisy. Although numerous "epigrams" were written by sixteenth-century English writers, notably John Heywood, they did not conform closely to the classical type, reflecting rather various forms of medieval humor and satire. With the realistic revolt against Elizabethan romanticism soon before 1600, the classical epigram was cultivated, chiefly as a vehicle for satire. Many collections were published between 1596 and 1616, including the famous one of Sir John Harington (1615). All these reflected the current idea that an epigram was a pointed satire. Jonson undertook to restore the wider classical use of the word and he wrote not only satirical epigrams but epistles, verses of compliment, epitaphs, reflective verses, etc. Of later English poets Walter Savage Landor (1775–1864) is perhaps the most accomplished writer of epigrams modeled on the Greek. Typically, an epigram is a short poem consisting of two parts, an introduction stating the occasion or setting the tone, and a conclusion which sharply and tersely, often with the effect of surprise, gives the main point. The first epigram in Jonson's collection may be quoted as an example:

*To the Reader*
Pray thee take care, that tak'st my Book in hand,
To read it well; that is, to understand.

(Reference: T. K. Whipple, *Martial and the English Epigram*.)

**Epilogue:** A concluding statement; an appendix to a composition. Sometimes used in the sense of a peroration to a speech, but more generally applied to the final remarks of an actor addressed to the audience at the close of the play. Opposed to "prologue," a speech used to introduce the play. Puck, in *A Midsummer Night's Dream*, recites an epilogue which is characteristic of Renaissance plays in that it bespeaks the good will of the audience and courteous treatment by critics. As the use of epilogues became more general, poets of reputation were often paid to contribute epilogues to plays much as prefaces written by prominent authors are now sometimes paid for by publishers. Epilogues were an indispensable part of all major dramatic efforts in the late seventeenth century and throughout the eighteenth century, disappearing from general use about the middle of the nineteenth. They are now rarely employed.

**Episode:** An incident presented as one continuous action. Though having a unity within itself, the episode in any composition is usually accompanied by other episodes so woven together according to the conscious artistic purpose of the writer as to create a story, drama, or novel. Originally, in Greek drama, an "episode" referred to that part of a tragedy which was presented between two choruses. More narrowly the term is sometimes used to characterize an incident injected into a piece of fiction simply to illuminate character or to create background where it bears no definite relation to the plot and in no way advances the action.

**Episodic Structure:** A critical term applied to writing which consists of little more than a series of incidents. Simple narrative as opposed to narrative with plot. The episodes succeed each other, in this type of writing, with no very logical arrangement (except perhaps that of chronology) and without complication or a close interrelationship. Travel books naturally fall into episodic structure. The term is applied also to long narratives which may contain complicated plots, like the Italian "romantic epic" (*q.v.*), if the action is made leisurely by the use of numerous episodes employed for the purpose of developing character or plot.

**Epistle:** Theoretically an epistle is any letter, but in practice the term is limited to formal compositions written by an individual or a group to a distant individual or group. The most familiar use of the term, of course, is to characterize certain of the books of the New Testament. The epistle differs from the common letter in that it is a conscious literary form rather than a spontaneous, chatty, private composition. Ordinarily the epistle is associated with the scriptural writing of the past, but this is by no means a necessary restriction since the term may be used to indicate formal letters having to do with public matters and with philosophy as well as with religious problems.

**Epitaph:** Inscription used to mark burial places. Commemorative verses or lines appearing on tombs or written as if intended for such use. Since the days of early Egyptian records epitaphs have had a long and interesting history, and while they have changed somewhat as to purpose and form, they show less development than most literary types. The information usually incorporated in such memorials includes the name of the deceased, the dates of birth and death, age, profession (if a dignified one), together with some pious motto or invocation. Many prominent writers—notably Johnson, Milton, and Pope—have left epitaphs which they wrote in tribute to the dead. Early epitaphs were usually serious and dignified—since they chiefly appeared on the tombs of the great—but more recently they have, either consciously or unconsciously, taken on humorous qualities. Certainly one of the most famous inscriptions is that marking Shakespeare's burial place:

> Good frend, for Jesus sake forbeare
> To digg the dust encloased here;
> Bleste be ye man y$^t$ spares thes stones,
> And curst be he y$^t$ moves my bones,—

But this is as much a curse as an epitaph. "O rare Ben Jonson" and "*Exit* Burbage" are two examples of simple and effective epitaphs. A famous French inscription is from Père Lachaise in Paris:

> Ci-gît ma femme: ah! que c'est bien
> Pour son repos, et pour le mien!

The epitaph "On the Countess Dowager of Pembroke," formerly attributed to Ben Jonson though now credited to William Browne, deserves quotation:

> Underneath this sable hearse
> Lies the subject of all verse:
> Sidney's sister, Pembroke's mother.
> Death, ere thou hast slain another,
> Fair and learned and good as she,
> Time shall throw a dart at thee.

**Epithalamium (Epithalamion):** A bridal song; a song or poem written to celebrate a wedding. Many ancient poets (the Greek Pindar, Sappho, and Theocritus and the Roman Catullus) as well as modern poets (like the French Ronsard and the English Spenser) have cultivated the form. Perhaps Spenser's *Epithalamion* (1595), written to celebrate his own marriage, is the finest of the English marriage hymns. The successive stanzas in this poem treat such topics as: invocation to the muses to help praise his bride; bride is awakened by music; decking of the bridal path with flowers; nymphs adorn the bride; the assembling of the guests; description of the beauty of the bride, physical and spiritual; the bride at the altar; the marriage-feast; welcoming the night; asking the blessing of Diana and Juno and the stars.

**Epithet:** Strictly an adjective or adjective phrase used to point out a characteristic of a person or thing, as Goldsmith's "noisy mansions" (for schoolhouses), but sometimes applied to a noun or noun phrase used for a similar purpose, as Shakespeare's "The trumpet of the dawn" (for the cock). Many considerations enter into the success of an epithet, such as its aptness (indeed, "epithet" is actually used sometimes rather loosely to mean any apt phrase), its freshness, its pictorial quality, its connotative value (what it suggests rather than says), its musical value, etc. In literature remarkable epithets are very often figurative, as Keats' "snarling trumpets" and Milton's "laboring clouds."

The so-called "Homeric epithet," often a compound adjective, as "all-seeing" Jove, "swift-footed" Achilles, "blue-eyed" Athena, "rosy-fingered" dawn, depends upon aptness combined with familiarity rather than upon freshness or variety. It is almost a part of a name. Since epithets often play a prominent part in the calling-of-names which characterizes invective (*q.v.*) or personal satire, some persons have the mistaken notion that an epithet is always uncomplimentary. A "transferred epithet" is an adjective used to limit grammatically a noun which it does not logically modify, though the relation is so close that the meaning is left clear, as Shakespeare's "dusty death," or Milton's "blind mouths." This subtly suggestive device, often involving the "pathetic fallacy" (*q.v.*), is used effectively by the poets. The following phrases contain examples of epithets: glimmering landscape, murmuring brook, dazzling immortality, pure-eyed Faith, silver answer, prostituted muse, dark-skirted wilderness, circumambient foam, care-charmer sleep, sweet silent thought, meek-eyed peace.

**Epitome:** A summary or abridgment. A condensed statement of the content of a book. A "miniature representation" of a subject. Thus Magna Charta has been called the "epitome" of the rights of Englishmen, and Ruskin referred to St. Mark's as an "epitome" of the changes of Venetian architecture through a period of nine centuries.

**Epode:** One of the three stanza forms employed in the Pindaric ode. See Ode.

**Erotic Literature:** Amorous writing. The classification of literature as erotic is based on the subject matter—love—rather than the literary form employed. Consequently erotic literature embraces almost any form of writing—the lyric, the drama, short story, novel, even epigrams and elegies, the lyric proving perhaps the most popular vehicle. The lines which distinguish erotic literature from any writing based on the love theme are hard to draw. The classification is broad enough to include the mildly sentimental writing of an Ella Wheeler Wilcox on the one hand and actual pornography on the other, although no one thinks to call a simple love story—*Romeo and Juliet*, for instance—erotic. The presentation of love must be more physical than that in Shakespeare's play, must approach the fleshly quality of the same writer's *Venus and Adonis*, before one thinks to place it within the category of eroticism.

Classical writers of love literature included Sappho and Anacreon from the Greek and Catullus from the Latin; the Middle Ages spoke through François Villon; modern French is represented by Musset, Hugo, and Gautier; modern English by Swinburne, Rossetti, and William Morris. In American literature Walt Whitman is somewhat typical of the erotic spirit.

**Esperanto:** An artificial speech constructed from roots common to the chief European languages and designed for universal use. Esperanto was devised by Dr. L. L. Zamenhof, a Russian, and took its name from Zamenhof's pseudonym, "Dr. Esperanto," used in signing his first pamphlet on the subject in 1887. The account in *The Encyclopædia Britannica* summarizing the principles which should govern any truly universal language states that such a speech "should be international, easy for all, euphonious, phonetic, flexible, regular, adaptable, and must be tested by long continued practical use on a large scale," requirements which, the Esperantists argue, their language has met. Certain qualities of the language may here be pointed out: the grammar is so simple as to be clear after a few minutes' study, the spelling is strictly phonetic, the language is euphonious and adaptable, and pronunciation is simple since the accent always falls on the penult. Since Zamenhof's beginning in 1887, Esperanto has grown rapidly in popularity. A number of European broadcasting stations now give regular Esperanto programs; some four thousand books, including the Bible, have been translated; over one hundred magazines appear regularly, the *British Esperantist* and *La Revuo* being among the best known of the monthlies. Some of the titles of Shakespeare's plays, as translated, are interesting: *Hamleto* (Hamlet), *Rego*

*Lear* (King Lear), and *Songo de Someromeza Nokto* (Midsummer Night's Dream).

**Essay:** A moderately brief prose discussion of a restricted topic. Because of the wide application of the term, no satisfactory definition can be arrived at (one book on the essay spends forty-three pages on "What Is an Essay?"). Nor can a wholly acceptable "classification" of essay types be made. One treatment (Bryan and Crane) lists moralizing, critical, character, anecdotal, letter, and narrative essays as classes of the periodical essay alone. Other terms used in attempted classifications include: aphoristic, descriptive, reflective, biographical, historical, didactic, editorial, whimsical, psychological, outdoor, nature, cosmical, critical. One useful division can be made: formal and informal essays. The informal essay, sometimes called the "true" essay, includes moderately brief aphoristic essays like Bacon's, periodical essays like Addison's, and personal essays like Lamb's. Qualities which make an essay "informal" include: the personal element (self-revelation, individual tastes and experiences, confidential manner), humor, graceful style, rambling structure, unconventionality or novelty of theme, freshness of form, freedom from stiffness and affectation, incomplete or tentative treatment of topic. The points of view and wide range of themes in the informal essay may be suggested by citing a few typical titles: "On the Enjoyment of Unpleasant Places" (Stevenson), "A Cure for Fits in Married Ladies" (Steele), "A Chapter on Ears" (Lamb), "A Dissertation on Roast Pig" (Lamb), "Getting Up on Cold Mornings" (Hunt), "On Going a Journey" (Hazlitt—advocating the solitary hike), "Every Man's Natural Desire to Be Somebody Else" (Crothers). Qualities of the "formal" essay include: sober seriousness of purpose, dignity, logical organization, length. The term may include both short discussions, expository or argumentative, such as the serious magazine article and longer treatises, like the chapters in Carlyle's *Heroes and Hero-Worship*. However, a sharp distinction between even formal and informal essays can not be maintained at all times. In the following sketch the informal essay will be given chief consideration, since it lies entirely within the realm of "pure literature."

*Montaigne: Beginnings.*—When the French philosopher Montaigne retired from active life to devote himself to study and reflection (the "contemplative" life), he followed the fashion of the times in his practice of collecting pithy sayings—maxims, aphorisms, adages, apothegms, proverbs—along with anecdotes and quotations from his readings in the classics. A collection of such wise sayings upon a single topic was known in France as a *leçon morale*. After a time Montaigne developed the habit of recording also the results of a searching self-analysis and became attracted by the idea that he was himself representative of man in general. He published his first collection of such writings in 1580 under the title *Essais*—the first use of the word for short prose discussions. The word means "attempts," and by the use of it Montaigne meant to indicate that his discussions were tentative or incomplete as compared with ordinary formal philosophical writings. By adding the personal element to the aphoristic *leçon morale* Montaigne created the modern "essay." "Myself," he said, "am the groundwork of my book." The second edition (1588) gave even greater emphasis to the personal element. Mainly philosophical and ethical, the essays cover a wide range of topics: "Of Idleness," "Of Liars," "Of Ready and Slow Speech," "Of Smells and Odors," "Of Cannibals," "Of Sleeping," "Upon Some Verses of Vergil," etc.

*The Essay in England: Bacon and the Seventeenth Century.*— When the youthful Francis Bacon published in 1597 his first collection of aphoristic essays, he borrowed his title, *Essays*, from Montaigne's book—and became the first English "essayist." As a matter of fact Bacon's essays, which he referred to as "dispersed meditations," are less indebted to Montaigne than to earlier collections of "sentences" or wise sayings and to the wisdom literature of the Greeks and Romans, Bacon himself citing especially Seneca's *Epistles to Lucilius* as ancient examples of the type. The ten essays first published were short and consisted chiefly of a collection of maxims on a given subject. The book was very popular, and revised, enlarged editions were issued in 1612 and 1625. The later essays are longer, sometimes more personal, and are developed by a wealth of illustration, quotation, and figures of speech. In fact, Bacon's style achieved a compactness, clarity, imaginative richness, phrasal power, and sentence-rhythm which have made his essays an enduring part of the world's literature. The "aphoristic" quality of his style is seen in such typical quotations as these: "The errors of young men are the ruin of business," and "He that hath a wife and children hath given hostages to fortune." In attitude and tone Bacon's essays are highly practical and utilitarian rather than ethically idealistic. Like the Renaissance "courtesy books" (*q.v.*) they had for their chief purpose the giving of useful advice to those who wished to get on in practical life, especially as men of affairs.

After Bacon the seventeenth century contributed little to the development of the informal essay, the influence of Bacon and Montaigne dominating such essays as were produced. Owen Felltham's *Resolves* (1620) shows the application of Bacon's method to religious topics. Sir William Cornwallis' *Essays* (1600) reflects the method of Montaigne. More worthy essayists appeared after the Restoration. Sir William Temple, the statesman, and Abraham Cowley, the poet, wrote Montaigne-like personal essays while living in retirement, Cowley's being particularly happy efforts. Though the informal essay, strictly defined, received little attention in this century, there was much prose writing closely related to the informal and formal essay. The chapters of Sir Thomas Browne's *Religio Medici* (1642) in their style and in their tendency toward self-revelation and moralizing are suggestive of the informal essay, as are the miscellaneous sketches in Ben Jonson's *Timber, or Discoveries Made upon Men and Matter* (1641). Dryden's famous *Essay on Dramatic Poesy* (1668) is an example of a critical essay in conventional dialogue form. The numerous prefaces and books on literary criticism from the late sixteenth and early seventeenth centuries are also forerunners of the later critical essay. Milton's great *Areopagitica*, in form an argumentative address, is a masterly example of what might now be called a formal essay. Not unrelated to essay writing, too, are such long prose treatises as Robert Burton's *Anatomy of Melancholy* (1621), Locke's *Essay on the Human Understanding* (1690), and even Izaak Walton's famous *Compleat Angler* (1653). The letter or formal epistle as a vehicle for writing which was much like the informal essay appeared in James Howell's *Familiar Letters*

(1645–1655). The seventeenth century also saw the development in English of the "character" (*q.v.*), a brief character sketch of a quality or type-personality destined to become popular and exert an appreciable influence upon the periodical essay of the eighteenth century, partly, to be sure, through the work of a French writer of characters, La Bruyère, who had combined the character with the essay. The epigram (*q.v.*), as written by Ben Jonson, in its depiction of moral and social types sometimes became a sort of prose counterpart of the character and may have influenced essay writers.

*The Periodical Essay: Eighteenth Century.*—The second great step in the history of the informal essay came with the creation by Steele and Addison in the early years of the eighteenth century of the periodical essay, a new art-form which achieved great popularity and attracted the genius of the best writers of the time. In 1691 there had appeared with Dunton's *Athenian Gazette* a new type of periodical, small in format and designed to entertain as well as instruct. A feature of Daniel Defoe's *A Weekly Review of Affairs in France* (1704) had been a department called "Advice from the Scandalous Club," gossipy in character. From this germ Richard Steele developed the new essay in his *Tatler* (1709–1711). The purpose of the papers was "to recommend truth, innocence, honor, virtue, as the chief ornaments of life." Joseph Addison soon joined Steele and the two later launched the frankly informal daily *Spectator* (1711–1712; 1714). The new essay was affected not only by its periodical form, which prescribed the length, but by the general spirit of the times. Renaissance individualism was giving way to a centering of interest in society, and the moral reaction from the excesses of the Restoration period made timely the effort of the essayists to reform the manners of the age, refine its tastes, and provide topics for discussion at the popular coffee houses of London.

As compared with earlier essays, the periodical essay is briefer, less aphoristic, less intimate and introspective, less individualistic, less "learned," and is more informal in style and tone, making more use of humor and satire, and embracing a wider range of topics. The appeal is to the middle classes as well as to the cultivated few, but the city reader seems always to have been in the authors' minds. Addison referred to two types of *Spectator* papers: "serious essays" on such well-worn topics as death, marriage, education, and friendship; and "occasional papers," dealing with the "folly, extravagance, and caprice of the present age." The latter class especially aided in fixing as a tradition of the informal essay that delightful informality, whimsicality, humor, and grace which appear in scores of essays on such topics as women's fashions, duelling, witchcraft, coffee houses, and family portraits. The type developed much conventional machinery such as fictitious characters, clubs, visions, and imaginary correspondents.

The popularity of the form led to many imitations of the *Tatler* and *Spectator*, such as the *Re-Tatler*, the *Female Tatler*, the *Whisperer*, and men like Swift, Pope, and Berkeley contributed essays to some of them. The novelist Fielding incorporated essays in his *Tom Jones*. Later in the century Dr. Samuel Johnson (in the *Rambler*, 1750–1752, and the *Idler* papers, 1758–1760), Lord Chesterfield, Horace Walpole, and Oliver Goldsmith appeared as accomplished informal essayists. Some of Goldsmith's *Letters from a Citizen of the World* (1760–1761) are noted examples of the form. After Goldsmith the essay declined as a literary form, though pleasant specimens of the form were written by Henry Mackenzie and Richard Cumberland.

*The Personal Essay: Nineteenth Century.*—A great revival of interest in the writing of both formal and informal essays accompanied the triumph of the romantic movement and the founding of new types of magazines in the first quarter of the nineteenth century, and brought about new forms and fashions. The informal type responded to the romantic impulses of the time. The production of the "personal" essay, too, was stimulated greatly by the development of a new type of periodical: *Blackwood's Magazine* (1817) and the *London Magazine* (1820), which provided a market for the essays of Lamb, Hazlitt, Hunt, De Quincey, and others. Lamb's *Essays of Elia* (begun in 1820) exhibited an intimate style, an autobiographical interest, a light and easy humor and sentiment, an urbanity and unerring literary taste which have made Lamb one of the favorite essayists of all time. Even the novelists took up essay writing (Dickens, *Sketches by Boz*, 1836; Thackeray, *Roundabout Papers*, 1860–

1863). Though they followed in many respects their eighteenth-century predecessors, this group of nineteenth-century essayists accomplished a great change in the essay form. Freed from the space restrictions of the *Tatler* type and encouraged by a reading public eager for "original" work, these writers modified the Addisonian essay by making it more personal, longer, and more varied in theme, and by freeing it from the stereotyped features of the earlier form. Late in the century a worthy successor to Lamb appeared in Robert Louis Stevenson, for whose whimsical humor, nimble imagination, accomplished style, and buoyant personality, the personal essay formed an ideal medium of expression (*Virginibus Puerisque*, 1881; *Memories and Portraits*, 1887). More recent writers of the informal essay in England are A. C. Benson, G. K. Chesterton, and E. V. Lucas.

*The Formal Essay: Nineteenth Century.*—The formal essay of the early nineteenth century was largely the result of the appearance of the critical magazine, especially the *Edinburgh Review* (1802), the *Quarterly Review* (1809), and the *Westminster Review* (1824). Book reviews in the form of long critical essays were written by Francis Jeffrey, T. B. Macaulay, Thomas De Quincey, Sir Walter Scott, Thomas Carlyle, and later by George Eliot, Matthew Arnold, and many others. The manner of the formal essay appears also in the works of many other prose writers of the century. The separate chapters in the books of such men as Thomas Carlyle, John Ruskin, Walter Pater, Charles Kingsley, Leslie Stephen, Walter Bagehot, T. H. Huxley, Matthew Arnold, and Cardinal Newman are essay-like treatments of phases of the historical, biographical, scientific, educational, religious, and ethical topics concerned.

*The Essay in America.*—Though there is some reflection of essay literature in such early American writers as Cotton Mather, Jonathan Edwards, Benjamin Franklin, Thomas Jefferson, Alexander Hamilton, and such "itinerant" Americans as Tom Paine and J. H. St. John de Crèvecoeur, the first really great literary essayist in America is Washington Irving, whose *Sketch-Book* (1820) contains essays of the Addisonian type. Some of H. D. Thoreau's works (e.g., *Walden*) exhibited characteristics of the informal essay, and Oliver Wendell Holmes in *The Autocrat of the Breakfast Table* (1857) was a successful writer of informal, humorous essays. Ralph Waldo Emerson, reminiscent of Bacon in his aphoristic style, fired with transcendental idealism, became perhaps the best known of all American essayists. James Russell Lowell (*Among My Books*, 1870, 1876) is another notable writer of essays, as is Edgar Allan Poe, who produced important critical essays. Later able essayists, formal or informal, include G. W. Curtis, C. D. Warner, W. D. Howells, Mark Twain, and John Burroughs. More recent names are those of Agnes Repplier, S. M. Crothers, Katherine Fullerton Gerould, Dallas Lore Sharp, Henry Van Dyke, William Beebe, and Christopher Morley.

*Summary.*—In attempting to sum up the "evolution" of the essay as a form one must again note the distinction between the formal and the informal essay. The formal essay, instead of crystallizing into a set literary type, has tended to become diversified in form, spirit, and length, according to the theme and serious purpose of its author. At one extreme it is represented by the brief, serious magazine article and at the other by scientific or philosophical treatises which are books rather than essays. The technique of the formal essay is now practically identical with that of all factual or theoretical prose writing in which literary effect is secondary to serious purpose. Its tradition has doubtless tended to add clarity to English prose style by its insistence upon unity, structure, and perspicacity.

The informal essay, on the other hand, beginning in aphoristic and moralistic writing, modified by the injection of the personal element, broadened and lightened by a free treatment of human manners, modified and partly controlled in style and length by the limitations of periodical publication, has developed into a recognizable literary genre, the first purpose of which is to entertain, and the manner of which is sprightly, light, novel, or humorous. As such the form has aided in giving something of a Gallic grace to other forms of prose composition, notably letter-writing. (References: Hugh Walker, *English Essays and Essayists;* W. F. Bryan and R. S. Crane, *The English Familiar Essay;* Walter Graham, *English Literary Periodicals;* R. M. Alden, ed., *Essays, English and American.*)

**Etiquette Books (Renaissance):** See COURTESY BOOKS.

**Eulogy:** Composition oral or written, praising the character or life of a person.

**Euphemism:** A figure of speech in which an indirect statement is substituted for a direct one in an effort to avoid bluntness. With the advance of realism in recent years strained euphemisms are seldom found in literature, since authors now generally realize that such expressions are taken by discriminating readers as evidences of a tendency to be insincere or even sentimental. Small-town journalistic style, however, still abounds with such locutions as "passed on" for "died," etc. Euphemistic terms have been much used by many writers in an effort to mention a disagreeable idea in an agreeable manner.

**Euphony:** A quality of good style which demands that one should select combinations of words which sound pleasant to the ear. Harsh, grating, cacophonous sounds violate euphony and make for unpleasantness in reading. Careful writers avoid such pitfalls as the juxtaposition of harsh consonants, a series of un-accented syllables, unconscious riming or repetition of similar sounds, jerky rhythm, and excessive alliteration.

**Euphuism:** An affected style of speech and writing which flourished late in the sixteenth century in England, especially in court circles. It took its name from *Euphues* (1579) by John Lyly, who developed the style partly in an effort to refine English prose style and partly in an effort to attract, through novelty and lightness, the interest of the feminine readers whom he professed to write for. The chief characteristics of euphuism are: balanced construction, often antithetical and combined with alliteration; excessive use of the rhetorical question; a heaping up of similes, illustrations, and examples, especially those drawn from mythology and "unnatural natural history" about the fabulous habits and qualities of animals and plants. Following are some typical passages from *Euphues:* "Be sober but not too sullen; be valiant but not too venturous"; "For as the finest ruby staineth the color of the rest that be in place, or as the sun dimmeth the moon, so this gallant girl more fair than fortunate and yet more fortunate than faithful, etc."; "Do we not commonly see that in painted pots is hidden the deadliest poison?

that in the greenest grass is the greatest serpent? in the clearest water the ugliest toad?" "The filthy sow when she is sick eateth the sea-crab and is immediately recured: the tortoise having tasted the viper sucketh *Organum* and is quickly revived; the bear ready to pine eateth up ants and is recovered; the dog having surfeited . . . eateth grass and procureth remedy, etc."; "Being incensed against the one as most pernicious and enflamed with the other as most precious."

Lyly did not invent euphuism; rather he combined and popularized elements which others had developed. The Renaissance had been greatly interested in perfecting vernacular style (Italian, French, Spanish, English) in connection with the theory that modern languages were capable of being used for great literature. Important forerunners of Lyly in England were Lord Berners, in his translation of Froissart's *Chronicle* (1523, 1525); Sir Thomas North's translation (1557) of *The Dial of Princes* by Guevara (whose Spanish itself was highly colored); and George Pettie in his *A Pettie Palace of Pettie his Pleasure* (1576). One of Pettie's sentences, for example, reads: "Nay, there was never bloody tiger that did so terribly tear the little lamb, as this tyrant did furiously fare with the fair Philomela."

The chief vogue of euphuism was in the 1580's, though it was employed much later. The court ladies cultivated it for social conversation, and such writers as Robert Greene and Thomas Lodge used it in their novels (as *Menaphon* and *Rosalynde*). Sir Philip Sidney reacted against it and was followed by many others. Shakespeare both employed it and ridiculed it in *Love's Labour's Lost*. Though the extravagance and artificiality of euphuism make it seem ludicrous to a modern reader, it is to be remembered that it actually played a powerful and beneficial rôle in the development of English prose. It established the idea that prose (formerly heavy and Latinized) might be written with imagination and fancy, while its emphasis on short clauses and sentences and on balanced construction aided in imparting clearness to prose style. These virtues of clearness and lightness and pleasant ornamentation remained as a permanent contribution after a better taste had eliminated the vices of extravagant artificiality. (Reference: R. W. Bond, ed., *The Complete Works of John Lyly*, Vol. I, pp. 119 ff.)

**Exciting Force:** In a drama the force which starts the conflict of opposing interests and sets in motion the rising action of the play. Example: the witches' prophecy to Macbeth, which stirs him to schemes for making himself king. See DRAMATIC STRUCTURE.

*Exemplum:* A moralized tale. Just as modern preachers often make use of "illustrations," so medieval preachers made extensive use of tales, anecdotes, and incidents, both historical and legendary, to point morals or illustrate definite doctrines. Often highly artificial and to a modern reader incredible, these "examples" seem to have appealed very strongly to medieval congregations, because of their concreteness, their narrative and human interest, as well as their moral implications. Collections of *exempla*, classified according to subject, were prepared for the use of preachers. An important book of the sort was Jacques de Vitry's *Exempla* (early thirteenth century). At times sermons degenerated into mere series of anecdotes, sometimes even humorous in character. Dante in thirteenth-century Italy and Wycliffe in fourteenth-century England protested against this tendency, and Wycliffe as an element in his reform program omitted *exempla* from his own sermons.

The influence of *exempla* and example-books on medieval literature was very great, as may be illustrated from several of Chaucer's poems. The *Nun's Priest's Tale*, for example, itself cast into sermon form, uses *exempla*, as when Chanticleer tells Pertelot anecdotes to prove that dreams have a meaning. The *Pardoner's Tale* is itself an *exemplum* to show how Avarice leads to an evil end. (Reference: A. J. Mosher, *The Exemplum in the Early . . . Literature of England*.)

**Expletive:** An interjection to lend emphasis to a sentence or, in verse especially, the use of a superfluous word (some form of the verb "to do," for example) to make for rhythm. Profanity is, of course, another form of expletive use. Careless speech is full of superfluous words which are expletive in nature. A common colloquial expletive is "you see" added frequently to a statement, as "I went home, you see, at ten o'clock."

**Exposition:** That one of the four chief types of composition (see also ARGUMENTATION, DESCRIPTION, and NARRATION) the purpose of which is to explain the nature of an object or idea. Exposition may exist apart from the forms mentioned above (as in a handbook on the operation of an automobile engine), but usually two or more of the types are blended, description helping out exposition, or argument being mingled with explanation. The purpose of exposition is always the same: to make clear to the reader the subject under discussion. The following are some of the methods, used singly or in combination, most frequently employed to gain the desired clearness: analysis (a division of the object or idea into its parts), amplification, definition, classification, contrast and comparison with other objects in or without its class, example and illustration, and a recital of the history and development of the object or idea. For "exposition" as a part of a drama, see DRAMATIC STRUCTURE.

**Expressionism:** A literary manner marked by an effort to present an intellectual abstraction of nature, to give emphasis to some quality inherent in the object, rather than by a desire to present normal external aspects of nature. Expressionism, a phase of post-impressionism, is another literary manner borrowed from the art of painting after its influence had carried over into sculpture, music, the drama, etc. Unlike realism (*q.v.*), expressionism does not have for its object a faithful portrayal of an object or mood so much as an abstraction of that object or mood. Unlike impressionism (*q.v.*), which manifests considerable faithfulness to actual appearances even while translating the object through the personal mood of the artist, expressionism translates these appearances intellectually. That is, the expressionist presents actuality as modified by his personality *plus* an intellectual conception. The result is often, to photographic eyes, mere distortion. But this distortion springs from a desire to emphasize some inherent quality or proportion obvious to the artist though not necessarily even perceptible to a second observer. The expressionists sought to throw off all restraints and conventions in order to express such intellectual, moral, or ideal values as they saw in the object presented. In the theatre, designers have sought to work hand in hand with the dramatist and have given us settings composed of planes and angles and stairs and walls—three-dimensional settings—which would awaken in the audience moods and ideas presumably in harmony with the expressionistic idea of the dramatist. The intent or emotion underlying a play is thus symbolically reflected in the lines and lighting and planes of the setting itself. In literature some of the writers who have adopted the expressionistic manner are Maxwell Bodenheim, T. S. Eliot, Lola Ridge, and James Joyce.

Perhaps the whole matter of realism, naturalism, expressionism, etc., will be clearer if the terms applied to these literary manners are schematically arranged in a graded scale (taken not too seriously). If we start with the object itself, we pass to

1. Photography—which presumably approaches the actual as closely as any form of art can.
2. Naturalism (*q.v.*)—which employs more details than the following manners of writing and perhaps less selection.
3. Realism (*q.v.*)—which selects more rigorously than naturalism the details necessary to accomplish its somewhat stern purpose.
4. Impressionism (*q.v.*)—which portrays, but portrays chiefly those details which reflect the personal mood of the artist at the moment of composition.
5. Expressionism—which portrays an object but views it subjectively, as modified or distorted by the highly individual and intellectual conception of the author.
6. Dadaism (*q.v.*), surrealism—chaos.

**Extravaganza:** A fantastic, extravagant, or irregular composition. It is most commonly applied to dramatic compositions such as those of J. R. Planché, the creator of the dramatic extravaganza. Planché himself defined it as a "whimsical treatment of a poetical subject as distinguished from the broad caricature of a tragedy or serious opera, which was correctly described as burlesque." The subject was often a fairy tale. The presentation was elaborate, and included dancing and music. An example is Planché's *Sleeping Beauty* (acted 1840). A later use of "extravaganza," still current, is to designate any extraordinarily spectacular theatrical production. The term extravaganza is also applied to fantastic musical compositions, especially musical caricatures. In literature the term is occasionally used to characterize such rollicking or unrestrained work as Butler's *Hudibras*, a caricature of the Puritans.

**Fable:** A brief tale, either in prose or verse, told to point a moral. The characters are most frequently animals, but they need not be so restricted since people and inanimate objects as well are sometimes the central figures. The subject matter of fables has to do with supernatural and unusual incidents and often draws its origin from folklore sources. By far the most famous fables are those accredited to Aesop, a Greek slave living about 600 B.C.; but almost equally popular are those of La Fontaine, a Frenchman writing in the seventeenth century, because of their distinctive humor and wit, their wisdom and sprightly satire. Other important fabulists are Gay (England), Lessing (Germany), Krylov (Russia). "Fable" is also used to characterize any story once believed but which has since turned out to be untrue. The word is sometimes employed to designate a summary of the plot of a dramatic poem.

*Fabliau:* A humorous tale popular in medieval French literature. The *fabliaux* gained their wide diffusion largely through the popularity of the *jongleur* (*q.v.*), who spread the *fabliaux* widely throughout France. The conventional form was eight-syllable verse. These *fabliaux* consisted of stories of various types, but one point was uppermost—their humorous, sly satire on human beings. Themes frequently used in these stories, which were often risqué, dealt familiarly with the clergy, ridiculed womanhood, and were pitched in a key which made them readily and boisterously understandable to the uneducated. The form was also present in English literature of the Middle English period, Chaucer especially leaving us examples of *fabliaux*. The term should not be confused with "fable" (*q.v.*).

**Fairy Tale:** A story relating mysterious pranks and adventures of supernatural spirits who manifested themselves in the form of diminutive human beings. These spirits possessed certain qualities which are constantly drawn upon for tales of their adventures: supernatural wisdom and foresight, a mischievous temperament, the power to regulate the affairs of man for good or evil, the capacity to change themselves into any shape at any time. Fairy tales as such—though they had existed in varying forms before—became popular toward the close of the seventeenth century. Almost every nation has its own fairy literature, though the folklore element embodied in fairy tales prompts the growth of related tales among different nations. Some of the great source-collections are the *Pentamerone* of Basilio (Italian), the *Contes de ma Mère l'Oye* of Perrault (French), the *Cabinet des Fées* (French), and those of the Grimm brothers in German and of Keightley and Croker in English. Hans Christian Andersen, of Denmark, is probably the most famous writer of original fairy tales.

**Falling Action:** The second "half" or resolution of a dramatic plot. It follows the climax, beginning often with a tragic force, exhibits the failing fortunes of the hero (in tragedy) and the successful efforts of the counterplayers, and culminates in the catastrophe. See DRAMATIC STRUCTURE.

**Familiar Essay:** A term applied to the more personal, intimate type of informal essay. It deals lightly, often humorously, with personal experiences, opinions, and prejudices, stressing especially the unusual or novel in attitude and having to do with the varied aspects of everyday life. Goldsmith, Lamb, and Stevenson were particularly successful in the form. The type is found nowadays, not only in the books of such essayists as E. V. Lucas, but in such modern American magazines as the *Atlantic Monthly* ("The Contributors' Club") and *Harper's Magazine* ("The Lion's Mouth"). See ESSAY.

**Fancy:** See IMAGINATION AND FANCY.

**Fantastic Poets:** A term applied by Milton to the school of "metaphysical" poets (see METAPHYSICAL VERSE).

**Fantasy:** Though sometimes used as an equivalent of "fancy" and even of "imagination" (see IMAGINATION AND FANCY), "fantasy" more commonly is used to suggest a groundless or delusive invention. This is especially true of the adjective "fantastic," which may even mean "capricious." A "fantastic" plot, for example, can not hope to be convincing.

**Farce:** The word developed from Late Latin *farsus*, connected with a verb meaning "to stuff." Thus an expansion or amplification in the church liturgy was called a *farse*. Later, in France, *farce* meant any sort of extemporaneous addition in a play, especially comic jokes or "gags," the clownish actors speaking "more than was set down" for them. In the late seventeenth century "farce" was used in England to mean any short humorous play, as distinguished from regular five-act comedy. The development in these plays of certain elements of "low comedy" (*q.v.*) is responsible for the usual modern meaning of "farce": a dramatic piece intended to excite laughter and depending less on plot and character than on exaggerated, improbable situations, the humor arising from gross incongruities, coarse wit, or horseplay. Farce merges into comedy, and the same play (e.g., Shakespeare's *The Taming of the Shrew*) may be called by some a farce, by others a comedy. *Life Below Stairs* (1759), with the production of which Garrick was connected, has been termed the "best farce" of the eighteenth century. See FARCE-COMEDY.

**Farce-Comedy:** A term sometimes applied to comedies which rely for their interest chiefly on farcical devices (see FARCE, LOW COMEDY), but which contain some truly comic elements which elevate them above most farce. Shakespeare's *The Taming of the Shrew* and *The Merry Wives of Windsor* are called farce-comedies by some authorities. One writer distinguishes between the farce-comedy of Aristophanes (loose structure, variety of appeal, operatic quality) and that of Plautus (careful structure, intricate intrigue, broad humor). (Reference: R. M. Smith, ed., *Types of Farce-Comedy*.)

**Feature Article:** A journalistic essay on some matter of timely interest. Distinct from a news "story" which chronicles an event of the day, the feature article is both more human in interest and somewhat less hurried in preparation. A news dispatch might, for instance, tell of an earthquake in Timbuktu. The enterprising newspaper will print the news details and then for several days fill many columns with feature articles on such subjects as *Life in Timbuktu* (illustrated with photographs—genuine or artificial); *Quaint Folklore of Timbuktu* (after some feature writer has perhaps found his way to the library); *Early Recollections of Timbuktu* by some octogenerian once a resident of the town, etc. These timely essays indirectly related to the day's news are feature articles, though, by extension, the term is also used to signify any human-interest story whether of timely moment or not.

**Feminine Ending:** An extra-metrical syllable, bearing no stress, added to the end of a line in iambic or anapestic meter. This variation gives a sense of movement and an irregularity to the meter which make for grace and lightness. The form is perhaps most commonly used in blank verse. The second line below carries an illustration:

> O! I could play the woman with mine eyes
> And braggart with my tongue. But gentle heav*ens,*
> Cut short all intermission.
>
> —Shakespeare

**Feminine Rime (double rime):** A rime of two syllables, one stressed and one unstressed, as *waken* and *forsaken, audition* and *rendition.* In Chaucer, the feminine rime was very common because of the frequent recurrence of the final *-e* in Middle English. The term "feminine" is a courtesy—either to the form or to womanhood—since it is employed to connote the lightness and grace which result from the use of this type of rime.

> Above the pines the moon was slowly *drifting,*
> The river sang below;
> The dim Sierras, far beyond, *uplifting*
> Their minarets of snow.
>
> —Bret Harte

**Feudalism:** The system of social and political organization that prevailed in Western Europe during a large part of the medieval period. It developed from the anarchy which followed the fall of Charlemagne's empire in the ninth century. In feudal theory every landholder was merely the tenant of some greater landlord. Thus, the barons or powerful prelates were the tenants of the king; the lesser lords, knights, and churchmen were tenants of the barons and prelates; while the serfs or "villeins" were tenants of the lesser nobles. In practice—as the whole system was based upon force—the relations were more complicated: even kings sometimes owed allegiance to a great churchman or baron. As rent the various groups paid to their immediate superiors "service," which might consist of visible property or of military aid.   Socially, there were two sharply defined classes: the workers (villeins or free renters; serfs or bondmen); and the "prayers and fighters" (knights, upper clergy, lords).   Feudalism broke down in the fifteenth century.   The ideals of chivalry (see CHIVALRY IN ENGLISH LITERATURE) grew out of feudalism and powerfully affected the character of much medieval and even Renaissance literature, notably the romances and romantic epics.   The feudal social order is brilliantly pictured in Chaucer's *Canterbury Tales* and its evils sharply set forth in the *Vision of Piers the Plowman* (fourteenth century).

**Fiction:** Narrative writing drawn from the imagination or fancy of the author rather than from historical fact.   The term is most frequently associated with novels and short stories, though the drama and narrative poetry also furnish numerous instances of fiction.   Fables, parables, fairy tales, folklore, and dramas also include fictional qualities.   The chief function of fiction is to entertain, though it often serves subordinately to instruct.   Some authors—Winston Churchill is an example—weave fictional episodes about historical epochs and settings to give us what is often called "historical fiction."   Since fiction is a manner rather than a type of literature, one interested in any of the particular forms which fiction assumes should turn to such items as NOVEL, SHORT STORY, FABLE, DRAMA, etc., for more detailed presentation of the history and structure of these types.   In recent years there has been a great vogue even for fictional biography.

**Figurative Language:** Writing embodying one or more of the various figures of speech.   The most common figures of speech are: antithesis, apostrophe, climax, hyperbole, irony, metaphor, metonymy, personification, simile, synecdoche (each being explained in its proper place in this handbook).   Figurative language is intentional departure from the normal, "regular" language to gain strength and freshness of expression, to create a picture quality and a poetic effect.   These two lines from William Vaughn Moody will serve as illustration:

> Lewd as the palsied lips of hags
> The petals in the moon did shake.

Some of the figures of speech are: metaphor in *lewd lips* and *petals in the moon* and simile in *lewd as the lips of hags*. See IMAGERY.

**Filidh** (pl. *fili*): See IRISH LITERATURE, POET LAUREATE.

**Final Suspense, Moment of:** A dramatic term used to indicate the ray of hope sometimes appearing just before the catastrophe of a tragedy. Thus Macbeth's continued faith that he cannot be hurt by any man born of woman keeps the reader or spectator in some suspense as to the apparently inevitable tragic ending. See DRAMATIC STRUCTURE.

**Fin de siècle:** "End of the century," a phrase often applied to the last ten years of the nineteenth century. The eighteen-nineties were a transitional period, one in which writers and artists were consciously abandoning old ideas and conventions and attempting to discover and set up new techniques and artistic objectives. One writer (Holbrook Jackson) has noted three main characteristics of the decade in art and literature: decadence (*q.v.*), exemplified in Oscar Wilde and Aubrey Beardsley; realism (*q.v.*) or "sense of fact," represented by Gissing, Shaw, and George Moore, with their reaction against the sentimental; and radical or revolutionary social aspirations, marked by numerous new "movements" (including the "new woman," who dared ride a bicycle and seek political suffrage) and by a general sense of emancipation. (See Holbrook Jackson, *The Eighteen-Nineties.*) The phrase may also be applied to other end-of-age or end-of-century periods, as the seventeen-nineties (French Revolution, romanticism), the fifteen-nineties (transition from Elizabethan to Jacobean characteristics), and the fourteen-nineties (Renaissance, discovery of America).

**Fleshly School of Poetry, The:** The title of a critical essay published in the *Contemporary Review*, October, 1871. The article was signed "Thomas Maitland" (a pseudonym); actually it was written by Robert W. Buchanan. The critic took to task the poets Swinburne, Morris, and Rossetti, though most of the article is couched as a review of Rossetti's poems and Rossetti himself draws most of the fire. Buchanan accused the three of being in league to praise each other's work and refers to them as the "Mutual Admiration School." The following passage will make clear the general tone and trend of Buchanan's criticism:

The fleshly gentlemen have bound themselves by solemn league and covenant to extol fleshliness as the distinct and supreme end of poetic and pictorial art, to aver that poetic expression is greater than poetic thought, and by inference that the body is greater than the soul, and sound superior to sense; and that the poet, properly to develop his poetic faculty, must be an intellectual hermaphrodite. . . .

Rossetti replied to this denunciation by an attack called "The Stealthy School of Criticism" which was published in *The Athenaeum* (December 16, 1871).

**Folio:** See BOOK SIZES.

**Folk Drama:** In its stricter and older sense, as usually employed by folklorists, the term means dramatic activities of the folk—the unsophisticated treatment of folk themes by the folk themselves, particularly activities connected with popular festivals and religious rites (for the development of ancient Greek drama from such forms, see DRAMA). For a treatment of medieval folk drama of this sort, the student may consult the first volume of Sir Edmund Chambers's *Mediaeval Stage* and the same writer's *The English Folk-Play*, in which such forms as the sword dance, the St. George play, the mummers' play are described. The medieval religious drama, though sophisticated in the sense of being based upon Scriptural materials and a religion with a fully developed written theology, is by some folklorists regarded as a form of folk drama, and the "folk" character of such twentieth-century plays as Marc Connelly's *Green Pastures* is commonly recognized. The religious drama of the Middle Ages (see MEDIEVAL DRAMA), however, is treated by historians of the drama as a special form, not as "folk drama." Another sense in which the term "folk drama" is being increasingly employed, especially in America, includes plays which, while written by sophisticated and consciously artistic playwrights, reflect the customs, language, attitudes, and environmental difficulties of the folk. These plays are commonly performed, not by the folk themselves, but by amateur or professional actors. They tend to be realistic, close to the soil, and sympathetically human. The plays of J. M. Synge, Lady Gregory, and other authors of the Celtic Renaissance (*q.v.*) and the American plays by Paul Green and others published in the several volumes of *Carolina Folk-Plays* are examples. The latter reflect especially the life of the Negro and the Southern "mountain folk."

**Folk Epic:** See ART EPIC, EPIC.

**Folklore:** A term first used by W. J. Thoms in the middle of the nineteenth century as a substitute for "popular antiquities." The existence of varied conceptions of the term makes definition difficult. The one adopted by the Folklore Society of London about 1890 is: "The comparison and identification of the survivals of archaic beliefs, customs, and traditions in modern ages." A book on folklore published by an American scholar in 1930 affirms that folklore "limits itself to a study of the unrecorded traditions of the people as they appear in popular fiction, custom and belief, magic and ritual." The same writer (Krappe) regards it as the function of folklore to reconstruct the "spiritual history of man" from a study of the ways and sayings of the folk as contrasted with sophisticated thinkers and writers. Although concerned primarily with the psychology of early man or with that of the less cultured classes of society, some of the forms of folklore (e.g., superstitions and proverbial sayings) belong also to the life of modern man, literate as well as illiterate, and may therefore be transmitted by written record as well as by word of mouth. Folklore includes myths, legends, stories, riddles, proverbs, nursery rimes, charms, spells, omens, superstitions of all sorts, popular ballads, cowboy songs, plant lore, animal lore, and customs dealing with marriage, death, and amusements. The relations of folklore to sophisticated literature are important, but not always easy to trace. A folk tale may be retold by an author writing for a highly cultivated audience, and later in a changed form again be taken over by the folk. Folk customs are associated with the development of dramatic activity, because of the custom of performing plays at folk festivals.

Literature is full of elements taken over from folklore, and some knowledge of the formulas and conventions of folklore is often an aid to the understanding of great literature. The acceptance of the rather childish love-test in *King Lear* may rest upon the fact that the motif was an already familiar one in folklore. The effects of such works as Coleridge's *Christabel* or Keats' *Eve of St. Agnes* depend upon the recognition of popular superstitions, while some familiarity with fairy lore is necessary if one is to catch in full the charm of James Stephens' *The Crock of Gold*. The fine medieval romance of *Sir Gawain and the Green Knight*, written for a cultivated audience, centers round the folk-formula of the challenging of a mortal by a supernatural being to a beheading contest: the binding force of the covenant between Gawain and the Green Knight is explained by primitive attitudes rather than by rational rules of conduct. Shakespeare's *Hamlet* is a retelling of an old popular tale of the "exile-and-return" formula.

The study of folklore in America, particularly that of the cowboy, the mountaineer, and the Negro has received increasing attention in America in the twentieth century. (References: G. L. Gomme, *Handbook of Folklore;* Sir James G. Frazer, *The Golden Bough;* J. A. MacCulloch, *The Childhood of Fiction;* C. S. Hartland, *The Science of Fairy Tales;* A. H. Krappe, *Science of Folklore.*)

**Foot:** A measure or unit of rhythm consisting of a definite pattern. The four most common patterns are the iambus (◡—), trochee (—◡), anapest (◡◡—), and dactyl (—◡◡), which are mentioned in their proper places in this handbook.

**Forgeries, Literary:** See LITERARY FORGERIES.

**"Fourteeners":** A verse form consisting of fourteen syllables arranged in iambic feet. George Chapman, for instance, has a translation of the *Iliad* in this meter, but in recent years the form has fallen into disuse.

**"Frame-story":** A story within a narrative setting or "frame," a story within a story. This is a convention frequently used in classical and modern writing. Perhaps the best known examples are found in the *Arabian Nights*, the *Decameron*, and the *Canterbury Tales*. Chaucer, for example, introduced in his Prologue a group of people making a pilgrimage. Here we are told something of each of his characters, how they meet at the Tabard Inn, and how they proceed on their journey. This general setting may be thought of as the "frame"; the stories which the various pilgrims tell along the way are stories within the general framework, or "frame-stories."

**Free Verse:** Often called *vers libre* and *polyrhythmic verse*. It is to be distinguished from conventional verse chiefly by its irregular metrical pattern, its use of cadence rather than uniform metrical feet. Even though free verse does not follow the regular rhythm of the usual poetry, it has great possibilities for subtle effects; in fact this freedom to secure a variety of rhythmical effects instead of one is the chief justification for the existence of the form. Free verse lives in greater rhythmical units than conventional verse. In conventional verse the unit is the foot, or, perhaps, the line; in free verse the unit is the stanza or strophe.

The recent enthusiasm for *vers libre* may make us forget the honorable history of the form and think of it as a twentieth-century contribution. To do this, however, is to forget the fact that Hebrew verse (like much Oriental poetry) is based on large rhythmical units and that our familiar *Psalms* and *Song of Solomon* are as definitely free verse as anything Carl Sandburg has written. Nor is the form new to European literature: France has practised it for many years; Heinrich Heine used it in his *The North Sea;* W. E. Henley and Matthew Arnold practised it in England; Walt Whitman shocked America with it before 1860. Stephen Crane employed it before Amy Lowell. It is idle to talk of the superiority of one form over another since both are simply different manifestations of poetic mood and temper. What is important is that the extreme experimentation with free verse in the second and third decades of the twentieth century left its impress on the history of poetry in that it has done much to free poetry from certain formal conventions which might, conceivably, have mechanized it beyond all spontaneity and life. (References: Amy Lowell, *Tendencies in Modern American Poetry;* Louis Untermeyer, *American Poetry Since 1900;* and J. L. Lowes, *Convention and Revolt in Poetry.*)

**French Forms:** (Sometimes referred to as the "fixed" poetic forms.) A name given to certain definitely prescribed verse patterns which originated in France largely during the time of the troubadours. The more usual French forms are: ballade, chant royal, pantoum, rondeau, rondel, roundel, sestina, triolet, and villanelle. These are all explained in their proper places in this handbook. (Reference: Helen Louise Cohen, *Lyric Forms from France*.)

**Frontier Literature:** Up to 1890, when the free lands in America had all been pretty generally claimed, the dominant influence in American history (as Professor Turner in his *Significance of the Frontier in American History* has shown) was the frontier, its settlement, its adventures, its economics, its politics and its religion. It is not strange, then, that American literature reflected this characteristic of our life. "Optimism, self-confidence, belief in man's control over his environment, are," says Miss Lucy Hazard in her *Frontier in American Literature*,[1] "the keynotes in the glad forward song of the pioneers. . . . With the disappearance of free land disappeared the rosy illusion upon which characteristic American optimism was based. Naturalism, product of the disillusioned Old World, for the first time flourished in the soil of the New." And so, from the time of the landing of the Pilgrims in New England and of Raleigh in North Carolina, American literature has been much occupied with the activities and spirit of a pioneering people. These activities and this spirit, growing, changing, fading, have largely given the tone and color and thought to the early chronicles and histories of New England and Virginia; to the fanatic, as well as the sane, religionists of American Puritanism; to the work of such writers as John Winthrop and Captain John Smith, Jonathan Edwards and David Crockett; to the romanticizing of the Indian; to the accounts of the settlement of New York and of North Dakota; to the reports of the Far West brought by such writers as Mark Twain, Bret Harte, and Joaquin Miller; to the poetry of Thoreau, the philosophy of Emerson, and the fiction of Frank Norris. From Hector St. John Crèvecoeur to Willa Cather, American literature has been largely the record of our struggles, defeats, and conquests on the frontier.

[1] Published by Thomas Y. Crowell Company. Reprinted by permission of the publishers.

**Fundamental Image:** The central or controlling conception around which a description is written. When an author is attempting to describe some fairly complicated object or scene, a frequently used device is to select some important aspect or feature of the object and shape the details about that object. This reduction of the complex whole to one main feature or unifying principle simplifies and focuses the description in such a way as to make for clearness. This central device is sometimes called the "fundamental image." The famous description of the battle of Waterloo, in which Victor Hugo employed the outline of the letter A as illustrative of the position of the various armies, is a notable example of the clarifying value of the fundamental image.

**Gaelic Movement:** The movement begun late in the nineteenth century, especially as embodied in the Gaelic League, founded by Douglas Hyde in 1893, which aimed at the preservation of the Gaelic language. This native Celtic speech had been gradually giving way to English since the seventeenth century and had not been permitted in the new schools established in the middle of the nineteenth century. The Gaelic Movement attempted to foster the production of a new native Irish literature in Gaelic. Hyde himself wrote plays in Gaelic. Though the movement attracted wide attention and some controversy, it has not been notably successful in stopping the advance of English as a spoken language in Ireland, and on the literary side has been overshadowed by the Irish Literary Movement, which encouraged the use of English in creating a new Irish literature exploiting Irish materials. See CELTIC RENAISSANCE.

**Gallicism:** A word or phrase or idiom characteristic of the French language, or a custom or turn of thought suggestive of the French people. Thus when an Englishman uses the phrase "reason for existence" or "stroke of policy," he is probably imitating the French idiomatic phrases *raison d'être* and *coup d'état*.

**Gasconade:** Since the natives of Gascony (in France) were considered inveterate boasters, "gasconade" came to be used to mean bravado or boastful talk. Vainglorious fiction may be called "gasconade."

*Genre:* A group or classification. In its literary sense *genre* is employed to indicate a style, or medium, or manner of writing. Critically, the term might be used to state: "Mr. Blank, in his last work, uses a *genre* not adapted to his purpose," meaning that Mr. Blank's style or literary medium is poorly chosen for the particular purpose he is trying to accomplish. In another sense *genre* is employed to distinguish subject matter dealing with commonplace themes in a realistic manner from that presenting romantic themes in an idealistic manner. With this latter meaning in mind the term might be used to state: "Mr. Blank, in his last work, gives us a *genre* study," implying that Mr. Blank's writing is realistic and simple rather than fanciful or idealized. The term is also used in the sense of "literary type." The picaresque novel, for instance, may be said to be a *genre* popular in the eighteenth century. Neo-classic criticism stressed the need of following the "rules" governing the composition of various *genres*, e.g., the epic.

**Genteel Comedy:** A term employed by Addison to characterize such early eighteenth-century comedy as Cibber's *The Careless Husband.* This comedy was a sort of continuation of the Restoration comedy of manners, adapted to the polite, genteel manners of the age of Anne. Compared with Restoration comedy, the moral tone was higher, the motives of the characters more artificial, the wit less brilliant, and the general atmosphere somewhat sentimentalized.

**Georgian:** Pertaining to the reigns of the four Georges (1714–1830). The romantic poets from Wordsworth to Keats have been called "Georgians" in this sense. A group of minor poets including Thomas Lovell Beddoes, W. M. Praed, and Thomas Hood are sometimes styled the "second Georgian school," as opposed to the earlier group. They are looked upon as representing a transition from the romantic to the Victorian poets. From 1911 to 1922 there appeared four anthologies of modern verse entitled *Georgian Poetry,* "Georgian" here referring to the reign of George V, who came to the throne in 1910. These volumes, according to their editor, E. H. Marsh, reflect a belief that English poetry was "once again putting on new strength and beauty" and beginning a new "Georgian" period. W. W. Gibson, Rupert Brooke, and John Masefield are representative of the poets included.

**Gest:** An old word occasionally found in English, especially in literary titles from the medieval period, meaning a tale of war or adventure, as the *Gest Historiale of the Destruction of Troy* (fourteenth century). This use of the word is probably borrowed from the more common word in Old French, *geste*, as in the *chanson de geste* (*q.v*). The corresponding Latin word appears in a somewhat similar sense in the title of the famous collection of stories written in Latin about 1250, the *Gesta Romanorum*, "deeds of the Romans."

**Ghost-writer:** One who does journalistic writing which is published under the name of another. Business men, artists, athletes—in fact almost anyone who is much in the public eye but who is also either illiterate or uninterested in writing—often allow their names to be attached to articles and stories relating to their special fields and written by journalists employed for the purpose. Ghost-writing is more frequently employed in the preparation of newspaper and magazine articles than in the writing of books.

**Gift-books:** Literary collections, published under sentimental titles, intended primarily for souvenir gifts or keepsakes. Originating in Europe, they became popular in America early in the nineteenth century with the development of sentimentalism. Gift-books were literary miscellanies containing collections of work from different writers and avowedly aimed at the "refined" reader of "elegant" taste rather than the reader of intellectual quality.

**Gleeman:** A musical entertainer among the Anglo-Saxons. Gleemen were usually traveling professionals who recited poetry (especially stories) composed by others, though some of them were original poets. They were sometimes attached to kings' courts, but occupied a less dignified and permanent position than the scop (*q.v.*). In the main, the "scop" composed and the "gleeman" sang or recited the scop's compositions, to the accompaniment of the harp or other instrument. Some writers, however, both medieval and modern, use the term loosely for any kind of medieval composer or reciter.

**Gloss:** An explanation. A hard word in a text might be explained by a marginal or interlinear word or phrase, usually in a more familiar language. Thus Greek manuscripts were "glossed" by Latin copyists and readers who gave the Latin word or phrase equivalent to the difficult one in Greek. Similar bilingual glosses were inserted in medieval manuscripts by scribes who would explain Latin words by native, vernacular words. Some of the earliest examples of written Irish, for example, are found in the margins and between the lines of Latin manuscripts written in the early Middle Ages. Later the word came to have a broader use as in E. K.'s "Gloss" to Spenser's *Shepheardes Calender* (1579), which undertakes not only to explain the author's purpose and to comment on the degree of his success, but also to supply "notes" explaining difficult words and phrases and giving miscellaneous "learned" comments. The marginal "gloss" which Coleridge supplied in 1817 for his early *Rime of the Ancient Mariner* is little more than a summary of the story, slightly colored by the poet's effort to clarify the meaning.

The word is sometimes used in a bad sense, as when to "gloss" a passage means to misinterpret it and "to gloss over" is used in the sense of "explain away" or excuse. "Glossaries" developed from the habit of collecting glosses into lists.

**Gnomic:** Aphoristic, moralistic, sententious. The "Gnomic Poets" of ancient Greece (sixth century B.C.) arranged their wise sayings in series of maxims; hence the term *gnomic* was applied to all poetry which dealt in a sententious way with ethical questions, such as the "wisdom" poetry of the Bible, the Latin *sententiae*, the Saemundian *Edda*, and the gnomic verses in Old English. Although more properly applied to a style of poetry, as to some of the verse of Francis Quarles, prose style such as characterizes Bacon's early essays is also called gnomic when marked by the use of aphorisms. (Reference: Blanche C. Williams, *Gnomic Poetry in Old English*.)

**Gongorism:** A highly affected style taking its name from Gongóra, a Spanish poet (1561–1627), whose writings exhibited in a high degree the various qualities characteristic of the stylistic extravagances of the time, such as the introduction of new words (neologisms), innovations in grammar, bombast, puns, paradoxes, conceits, and obscurity. It reflects both cultism (affected language) and conceptism (strained figures, obscure references). It has some of the qualities of euphuism (*q.v.*), but is perhaps more closely akin to the style of the English metaphysical poets, especially Crashaw. See MARINISM, CONCEIT. (Reference: E. K. Kane, *Gongorism and the Golden Age.*)

**Gothic:** Though the Goths were a single Germanic tribe of ancient and early medieval times, the meaning of Gothic was broadened to signify Teutonic or Germanic and, later, "medieval" in general. In architecture, Gothic, though it may mean any style not classic, is more specifically applied to the style which succeeded the Romanesque in Western Europe, flourishing from the twelfth to the sixteenth centuries. It is marked by the pointed arch and vault, a tendency to vertical effects (suggesting aspiration), stained windows (mystery), slender spires, flying buttresses, intricate traceries, and especially by wealth and variety of detail and flexibility of spirit. Applied to literature the term was used by the eighteenth-century neo-classicists as synonymous with "barbaric" to indicate anything which offended their classic tastes. Addison said that both in architecture and literature those who were unable to achieve the classic graces of simplicity and dignity and unity resorted to the use of foreign ornaments, "all the extravagances of an irregular fancy." The romanticists of the next generation, however, looked with favor upon the "Gothic"; to them it suggested whatever was medieval, natural, primitive, wild, free, authentic, "romantic." Indeed, they praised such writers as Shakespeare and Spenser because of their "Gothic" elements —variety, richness, mystery, aspiration. (Reference: Kenneth Clark, *The Gothic Revival.*)

**Gothic Romance:** A form of novel in which magic, mystery, and chivalry are the chief characteristics. Horrors abound: one may expect a suit of armor suddenly to come to life, while ghosts, clanking chains, and charnel houses impart an uncanny atmosphere of terror. Although anticipations of the Gothic romance appear in Smollett (esp. in *Ferdinand, Count Fathom,* 1753), Horace Walpole was the real originator, his famous *Castle of Otranto* (1764) being the first. Its setting is in a medieval castle (hence the term "Gothic") which has long underground passages, trap-doors, dark stairways, and mysterious rooms whose doors slam unexpectedly. William Beckford's *Vathek, an Arabian Tale* (1786) added the element of Oriental luxury and magnificence to the species. Mrs. Anne Radcliffe's five romances (1789–1797), especially *The Mysteries of Udolpho,* added to the popularity of the form. Her emphasis upon setting and story rather than upon character-delineation became conventional, as did the types of characters she employed. Succeeding writers who produced Gothic romances include: Matthew ("Monk") Lewis, William Godwin, and Mary Wollstonecraft Shelley, whose *Frankenstein* is a striking performance in the tradition. The form spread to practically every European literature, being especially popular in Germany. In America the type was cultivated early by Charles Brockden Brown. The Gothic novels are not only of interest in themselves but have exerted a significant influence upon other forms. This influence made itself felt in the poetry of the Romantic period, as in Coleridge's *Christabel* and *Kubla Khan,* Wordsworth's *Guilt and Sorrow,* Byron's *Giaour,* and Keats' *Eve of St. Agnes.* Some of the romances were dramatized, and some dramas not based on romances, like Byron's *Manfred* and Morton's *Speed the Plough,* have Gothic elements. The novels of Scott, Charlotte Brontë, and others, as well as the mystery and horror type of short story exploited by Poe and his successors, contain materials and devices traceable to the Gothic novel. (References: Edith Birkhead, *The Tale of Terror;* Eino Railo, *The Haunted Castle.*)

**Grand Style, The:** See CRITICISM, HISTORICAL SKETCH.

**"Graveyard School":** A phrase sometimes used in designating the group of eighteenth-century poets who wrote long, gloomy poems on death and immortality. The "graveyard" poetry was related to early stages of the English romantic movement, reflecting the tendency to cultivate melancholy for its own sake and to react against the fastidious "niceness" of the Augustans, who took care to avoid the "shadow of the grave" and the "mystery of the future." The graveyard poets, far from shrinking from these themes, tried to get the atmosphere of "pleasing gloom" by realistic efforts to call up not only the horrors of death but the very "odor of the charnel house." An early exemplar or forerunner of the school was Thomas Parnell, whose *Night-Piece on Death* (1721) not only anticipates some of the sentiment of Gray's famous *Elegy Written in a Country Churchyard* (1751)—the most famous poem produced by the group—but whose "long palls, drawn hearses, cover'd steeds, and plumes of black" show an approach to the phraseology of Robert Blair's *The Grave* (1743), one of the most typical poems of the movement, and of the *Night-Thoughts* (1742) of Edward Young, an influential writer of melancholy verse. These last two writers, says W. L. Phelps, reflect "the joy of gloom, the fondness for bathing one's temples in the dank night air and the musical delight of the screech owl's shriek." (*Beginnings of the English Romantic Movement*, 1893, p. 100.) In American literature the poetry of the graveyard school finds a belated representative in William Cullen Bryant's famous *Thanatopsis* (1817), the theme and verse of which were influenced by Blair's *The Grave* and the poems of Henry Kirke White. (Reference: Amy L. Reed, *The Background of Gray's Elegy: A Study in the Taste for Melancholy Poetry, 1700–1751*.)

**Great Awakening, The:** See AWAKENING, THE GREAT.

**Grub Street:** Because struggling writers and literary "hacks" lived in Grub Street in London (now Milton Street), the phrase "Grub Street," since the eighteenth century, has meant either the "tribe" of poor writers living there or the qualities which characterized such authors. Grub Street poets were bitterly attacked by Pope, and "Grub Street" has been used contemptuously by Doctor Johnson, Byron, and others to suggest "literary trash."

**Harlequinade:** A play in which a "harlequin" or buffoon stars. See COMMEDIA DELL' ARTE, PANTOMIME.

**Hartford Wits:** A group of Connecticut writers, many of whom were graduates of Yale, active about the period of the American Revolution. The three most prominent were Joel Barlow, Timothy Dwight, and John Trumbull; some others in the group were Richard Alsop, Theodore Dwight, and Lemuel Hopkins. Naturally conservative in politics and philosophy, these men were, as well, conservative in their literary models, following Addison and Pope, the two literary gods of their century. Some of the best-known works of these writers are Trumbull's *McFingal*, Dwight's *Conquest of Canaan* (an epic poem of eleven books mingling Christian and Revolutionary history), and Barlow's *Columbiad*, planned as another American epic, a ten-book recitation of the glories of the future America as revealed to Columbus in prison.

**Hebraism:** The attitude toward life which subordinates all other ideals to those of conduct, obedience, and ethical purpose. It is opposed to the Hellenistic conception of life which subordinates everything to the intellectual. The two terms, *Hebraism* and *Hellenism*, have each taken on a special and limited significance—neither of which is fully fair to all the facets of the genius of the two peoples—as the result of critical discussion long centering about the question of conduct and wisdom in living. In modern literature the most notable discussion of the two conflicting ideals is found in the fourth chapter of Matthew Arnold's *Culture and Anarchy*. The following quotations in explanation of the terms are cited from Arnold:

We may regard this energy driving at practice, this paramount sense of the obligation of duty, self-control, and work, this earnestness in going manfully with the best light we have, as one force. And we may regard the intelligence driving at those ideas which are, after all, the basis of right practice, the ardent sense for all the new and changing combinations of them which man's development brings with it, the indomitable impulse to know and adjust them perfectly, as another force. And these two forces we may regard as in some sense rivals,—rivals not by the necessity of their own nature, but as exhibited in man and his history,—and rivals dividing the empire of the world between them. And to give these forces names from the two races of men who have supplied the most signal and splendid manifestations of them, we may call them respectively the forces of Hebraism and Hellenism.

Hebraism and Hellenism,—between these points of influence moves our world. . . . The final aim of both Hellenism and Hebraism, as of all great spiritual disciplines, is no doubt the same: man's perfection of salvation. . . . The governing idea of Hellenism is *spontaneity of consciousness:* that of Hebraism, *strictness of conscience.*

**Hedge Club:** See Transcendental Club, Transcendentalism.

**Hellenism:** See Hebraism.

**Heptameter:** A line of verse consisting of seven feet. See Scansion.

**Hero or Heroine:** The central character (masculine or feminine) in fictional writing, the person of chief interest. As a critical term in literary terminology, the hero or heroine of a narrative is determined not by the superiority of the moral qualities of one character over another but by the structural relationship of the character to the plot. The most important character *structurally* is the hero or heroine; he may be a rogue, an escaped convict, or worse.

**Heroic Couplet:** Iambic pentameter lines rimed in pairs. The favorite meter of Chaucer—*The Legend of Good Women* is an instance—this verse form did not come into its greatest popularity, however, until the middle of the seventeenth century (with Waller and Denham); after which time it was for several years the dominant mold for the poetic drama. The distinction of having made first use of the heroic couplet in dramatic composition is variously given to Orrery's *Henry V*, in which it was used throughout, and Etherege's *The Comical Revenge*, in which it was employed for most passages of dramatic action. Both of these plays date from 1664. D'Avenant had as early as 1656 made some use of the heroic couplet in his *Siege of Rhodes*. It was with Dryden, however, that the form became best known, Dryden using it in such plays as *Tyrannick Love, Almanzor and Almahide,* and *Aureng-Zebe.* Some other seventeenth-century dramatists who adopted the couplet now that it was the accepted form were: Sedley, Settle, Otway, Lee. With Pope the heroic couplet became so important and fixed a form—for various purposes—that its influence dominated English verse for many years and was not broken down until the romanticists dispelled the tradition in their demand for a new freedom.   An example of the heroic couplet:

> But when to mischief mortals bend their will,
> How soon they find fit instruments of ill!
> —Pope

**Heroic Drama:** A type of tragedy and tragi-comedy that developed in England during the Restoration period.   It was characterized by excessive spectacle, violent emotional conflicts in the main characters, extravagant bombastic dialogue, and more or less epic personages as chief characters.   The heroic play usually had its setting in some distant land such as Mexico, Morocco, or India.   Its hero rivals Achilles in warlike deeds and easily surpasses him in love.   This hero is constantly torn between his passion for some lady (more than likely a captive princess or the daughter of his greatest enemy) and his honor or duty to his country.   If he is able to satisfy both the demands of love and duty, the play ends happily for hero and heroine and unhappily for the villain and villainess.   The heroine is always a paragon of virtue and honor, often torn between her loyalty to her villain-father and her love for the hero.   The villain is usually a tyrant and usurper with an overweening passion for power or else with a base love for some beautiful and virtuous lady.   The villainess is the dark, violently passionate rival of the heroine.   The hero's rival in love is sometimes the villain and sometimes the hero's best friend.   All are unreal, all speak in hyperbole, all rant and rage.   Since the "heroic couplet" (q.v.) developed at the same time as did the heroic drama, the writers of heroic plays commonly, though not always, wrote in heroic couplets.   The action of the play was grand, often revolving around the conquest of some empire.   The scenery used in producing the heroic play was elaborate.

The influences that combined to produce the heroic drama were the romantic plays of the Jacobeans, especially those of Beaumont and Fletcher; the development of opera (q.v.) in England; and the French court romances by de Scudéry and La Calprenède, some of which were brought to England by the court of Charles II. Though elements of the heroic play appear in Davenant's *Siege of Rhodes* (1656), the Earl of Orrery perhaps wrote the first full-fledged heroic drama, *The General* (1662). Dryden, however, is the greatest exponent of the type, his *Conquest of Granada* typifying all that is best and all that is worst in the species. Elkanah Settle, Nahum Tate, Nathaniel Lee, Sir Robert Howard, John Crowne, and Thomas Otway are other playwrights who cultivated the heroic drama. Although the faults of the type were recognized early, the most brilliant attack being the satirical play of George Villiers, Duke of Buckingham (and others), *The Rehearsal* (1671), the plays flourished until about 1680, and the extravagances that characterized them affected eighteenth-century tragedy and perhaps have lingered on to show themselves at their worst in some forms of twentieth-century American moving pictures. (References: Allardyce Nicoll, *Restoration Drama;* L. N. Chase, *The English Heroic Play;* B. J. Pendlebury, *Dryden's Heroic Plays.*)

**Heroic Verse:** Poetry composed of iambic pentameter feet and rimed in line-pairs. Also called "heroic couplets" (*q.v.*).

**Hexameter:** A line of six metrical feet. As a classical verse form in Latin or Greek poetry, in which languages the hexameter was the conventional medium for epic and didactic verse, the term was definitely restricted to a set pattern: six feet, the first four of which were dactyls or spondees, the fifth almost always a dactyl (though sometimes a spondee in which case the verse is called spondaic), the sixth a spondee or trochee. True hexameters are scarce in English poetry because of the rarity of actual spondees in our language. However, poets writing in English, notably Longfellow in *Evangeline*, have variously modified the classical form to adapt it to the exigencies of our language and have left us hexameters much less strictly patterned than the classical. See ALEXANDRINE.

**Hiatus:** A pause or break between two vowel sounds not separated by a consonant. It is the opposite of *elision* (*q.v.*), which prompts the sliding over of one of the vowels, whereas a hiatus occurs only when in a break between two words the final vowel of the first and the initial vowel of the second are each carefully enunciated. In logic *hiatus* signifies the omission of one of the logical steps in the process of reasoning.

**High Comedy:** Pure or serious comedy, as contrasted with "low comedy" (*q.v.*). High comedy rests upon an appeal to the intellect and arouses "thoughtful" laughter by exhibiting the inconsistencies and incongruities of human nature and by displaying the follies of social manners. The purpose is not consciously didactic or ethical, though serious purpose is often implicit in the satire which is not infrequently present in high comedy. Thoughtful amusement is aimed at. Emotion, especially sentimentality, is avoided. If a man makes himself ridiculous by his vanity or ineffective by his stupid conduct or blind adherence to tradition, high comedy laughs at him. Some ability to perceive promptly the incongruity exhibited is demanded of the audience, so that high comedy has been said to be written for the few. As George Meredith suggests in his essay on *The Idea of Comedy* (a classic pronouncement on the nature of high comedy), care must be taken that the laughter provoked be not derisive, but intellectual. Laughing at an exhibition of poverty, for example, since it ridicules our unfortunate nature instead of our conventional life, is not truly comic. "But when poverty becomes ridiculous" by attempting "to make its rags conceal the bareness in a forlorn effort at decency," or foolishly tries to rival the ostentation of the rich, it becomes a fit theme for comic presentation. Although high comedy actually offers plenty of superficial laughs which the average playgoer or reader can perceive, its higher enjoyment demands a certain intellectual acumen and poise and philosophic detachment. "Life is a comedy to him who thinks." But the term "high comedy" is used in various senses. In neo-classic times a criterion was its appeal to and reflection of the "higher" social class and its observance of decorum, as illustrated in Etherege and Congreve. In a broader sense it is applied to some of Shakespeare's plays, like *As You Like It*, and to modern "comedies" of G. B. Shaw. Professor B. V. Crawford's discussion of the meaning of the term (*Philological Quarterly*, Vol. VIII, 1929) may be consulted. See COMEDY, COMEDY OF MANNERS, COMEDY OF HUMOURS, REALISTIC COMEDY.

197

**Historical Fiction:** See FICTION, HISTORICAL NOVEL.

**Historical Novel:** A novel, the characters, setting, and action of which are drawn from the records of a locality, a nation, or a people. The use of history in fiction is, in one sense, almost as old as fiction itself, but the historical novel, as such, did not, of course, come into being until well into the eighteenth century. Cross, in his *Development of the English Novel*, cites Miss Sophia Lee's *Recess*, the first volume of which appeared in 1783, as marking the new interest in history as a background for fiction. The *Recess* is a story of the time of Queen Elizabeth which includes among its characters many of the courtiers and which boasts as its heroine a fictitious daughter of Mary Queen of Scots. Some of the most illustrious writers of historical romances are Sir Walter Scott, James Fenimore Cooper, Bulwer-Lytton, Charles Reade, and Lew Wallace. See NOVEL.

**History Play:** See CHRONICLE PLAY.

**Holy Grail:** The cup from which Christ is said to have drunk at the Last Supper and which was used to catch his blood at the Crucifixion. It became the center of a tradition of Christian mysticism and eventually was linked with Arthurian romance as an object of search on the part of Arthur's knights. The grail as it appears in early Arthurian literature (Chrétien's *Perceval*) is perhaps of pagan origin, some sort of magic object not now to be traced with assurance. In the poems of Robert de Boron (*ca.*1200) it appears as a mystic symbol and is connected with Christian tradition (having been brought to England by Joseph of Arimathea). In the Vulgate Romances (see VULGATE), two great cycles are devoted to the grail, the first or "History" dealing with the Joseph tradition, the second or "Quest" dealing with the search for it by Arthurian knights. Perceval, the first hero of the quest, because he was not a pure knight, and Lancelot, because he was disqualified by his love for Guinevere, gave place to Galahad, the wholly pure knight, conceived as Lancelot's son and Perceval's kinsman. The pious quest for the grail, no less than the sinful love of Lancelot and Guinevere, helped bring about the eventual downfall of the

Round Table fellowship.  See ARTHURIAN LEGEND.  (Reference: W. M. Jaffray, *King Arthur and the Holy Grail*.)

**Homeric Epithet:** See EPITHET.

**Homeric Simile:** See SIMILE.

**Hornbook:** A kind of primer common in England from the sixteenth to the eighteenth centuries.  On a sheet of vellum or paper were printed the alphabet, combinations of consonants and vowels commonly used in making up syllables, the Lord's Prayer, and a list of Roman numerals.  The sheet was mounted on wood and covered (for protection) by transparent horn (hence "hornbook").  Its most famous use in literature is in *The Gull's Hornbook* by Thomas Dekker, an amusing and satirical "primer" of instructions for the young dandy of early seventeenth-century London.  The "hornbook" here supplies a framework for a social satire.

**Hudibrastic Verse:** The octosyllabic couplet as adapted by Samuel Butler in his satiric poem, *Hudibras*.  In this long poem, published in three parts between 1663 and 1678, Butler satirized the Puritans of England.  *Hudibras* was conspicuous for its humor, its burlesque elements, its mock-heroic form, and its wealth of satiric epigram.  The meter is iambic tetrameter riming in couplets, *aa—bb*, etc.  The term is now used to characterize any verse following the general Butler manner.

**Humanism:** Broadly, this term suggests any attitude which tends to exalt the human element or stress the importance of human interests, as opposed to the supernatural, divine elements —or as opposed to the grosser, animal elements.  So a student of human affairs may be called a "humanist," and the study of man as man, i.e., of the human race rather than of individual human beings, has been called humanism.  In a more specific and important sense, humanism suggests a devotion to those studies supposed to promote most effectively human culture— in particular, those dealing with the life, thought, language, and literature of ancient Greece and Rome.  In literary history, indeed, the most important use of the term is to designate the revival of classical culture which accompanied the Renaissance. This use of the term is justified not only by the fact that the

Renaissance humanists found in the classics a justification for their tendency to exalt human nature and build a new and highly idealistic gospel of progress upon it, but also by the fact that they found it necessary to break sharply with medieval attitudes which had subordinated one aspect of human nature by exalting the supernatural and divine. The Renaissance humanists agreed with the ancients in asserting the dignity of man and the importance of the present life, as against such medieval thinkers as looked upon the present life as chiefly useful as a preparation for a future life.

Renaissance humanism developed first in the fourteenth and fifteenth centuries in Italy and was marked by a passion for rediscovering and studying ancient literature. It spread to other Continental countries and finally to England, where a series of efforts to develop humanistic activities culminated successfully late in the fifteenth century with the introduction of the study of Greek at Oxford (see OXFORD REFORMERS). Early humanists in England applied themselves first to a mastering of the Greek as well as the Latin language and then to applying their new methods to theology, statecraft, education, and finally to criticism and literature. Unlike some Continental humanists the English group, though they reacted against medieval asceticism and scholasticism and sharply attacked current abuses in the Church, retained their full faith in Christianity. Indeed, they entered enthusiastically upon a program of human development based upon the assumption that the best of classical culture could be fused with Christianity—a faith which accounts in part for what at first seem to be incongruous mixtures of paganism and Christianity in much Renaissance literature, notably the poetry of Spenser and Milton. The zealous efforts of such men as Dean John Colet and Erasmus to reform church conditions and theology through education and an appeal to reason were checked by the success of the more vigorous and radical Lutheran movement. The "modern" character of this humanism may be indicated by recalling a few of its political and educational doctrines: political institutions are of human, not divine, origin and exist for human good, the monarch's "duties" being of greater concern than his "rights"; war is unchristian and inhumane and should be resorted to only when approved by the people themselves; the highest human happiness can come only through the virtuous life, which in turn can best be achieved through the control of reason, buttressed by education; women should be educated; nature should be employed as an educational tool; physical education is of the utmost importance; schoolmasters should be learned and gentle.

A later phase of humanistic activity was its interest in literary criticism, through which it affected powerfully the practice of Renaissance authors. The validity of critical ideas drawn from Aristotle and Horace was asserted and the production of a vernacular literature which imitated the classics was advocated. Though this led to some unfortunate and unsuccessful efforts to restrict the English vocabulary and to repress native verse forms in favor of classical words and forms, in general humanistic criticism exerted a wholesome effect upon literature by lending it dignity (as in the epic and tragedy) and grace (as in the Jonsonian lyric) and by stressing restraint and form. Its influence was especially great in the drama, where, though writers like Shakespeare rejected the three unities, it aided in establishing unified structure. The texture of Renaissance literature, too, was greatly enriched by the humanistically inspired familiarity with the incidents, characters, motives, and imagery of classical mythology, history, and literature. Sidney's *Defence of Poesie*, a humanistic document, is generally taken as the starting-point in English criticism, and the establishment of the classical attitude (see CLASSICISM) through the influence of Jonson and (later) Dryden and Pope and others was itself a fruit of Renaissance humanism. In fact, a tracing of the effects of humanism upon the literature of the seventeenth and eighteenth centuries would largely coincide with the history of classicism and neoclassicism. One of the phases of the reaction against romanticism in the nineteenth century was a revival of humanism, as exemplified in Matthew Arnold. See HUMANISM, THE NEW.

**Humanism, The New:** A philosophico-critical movement called "the new humanism" took place in the 1920's under the inspiration of the American scholars Irving Babbitt and Paul Elmer More. It flourished especially in America, and represents, in part, a reaction against certain forms of realism (*q.v.*)

and naturalism (*q.v.*) which seemed to the new humanists to overstress, with disastrous potential consequences, the "lower" or "animal" elements in human nature. It protested against the "half-baked philosophies and psychologies of our professedly scientific time." The many writers who have been called new humanists have not been in complete agreement on all points— even on what constitutes humanism—so that obviously no complete, definite, and universally applicable codification of the tenets of the new humanists can be made. The following imperfect résumé, based upon passages in *American Criticism*, by Norman Foerster, a spokesman of the group, may be useful in suggesting the general attitude of the new humanists. The prime problem is the achieving of human perfection. Humanism assumes (1) that assumptions are unavoidable, (2) that the essential quality of experience is not natural but ethical, (3) that there is a sharp dualism between man and nature, and (4) that man's will is free. On these premises the following doctrines are based: (1) an adequate human standard demands the cultivation of every part of human nature; (2) but these parts must be cultivated harmoniously and discriminatingly, not impulsively and uncritically; (3) the scale of values so implied consists of the normally or typically human—is concerned with the universal and permanent rather than with the temporary code of a conventional society; (4) the nearest approach toward such a standard is found in the great ages of the past, especially of Greece, but humanism draws also upon Christianity, Oriental philosophy, and such modern writers as Shakespeare, Milton, and Goethe; (5) unlike romanticism, humanism is faithful to the Hellenic doctrine of reason, applied to the whole of human experience, even the extra-scientific; (6) it departs from the narrowly "scientific" method by supplementing the reason with the intuitive and imaginative; (7) the ultimate ethical principle is that of restraint or control, whereby humanism avoids the anarchy of the "self-expression" cult, yet recognizes the necessity of freedom, defined as "liberation from outer constraints and subjection to inner law"; (8) though this center is the reality which gives rise to religion, humanism declines to accept a formal theology, holding that the value of intuition must be tested by the intellect.

The aesthetic growing out of this philosophy is in the main that of classicism. The critical method derived from it, while making use of the results of historical scholarship, will not allow the historical method to obscure or thwart the more important immediate task of seeking to determine actual literary values. For this purpose the critic must submit himself sympathetically to the author's intent and must dispassionately consider the beauty in a book or poem, judged both quantitatively and qualitatively. In line with these ideas, some of the new humanists have advocated a radical change in the methods of graduate study in language and literature. (References: N. Foerster, *Humanism and America* and *Toward Standards;* I. Babbitt, *Rousseau and Romanticism;* L. J. A. Mercier, *The Challenge of Humanism;* R. Shafer, *Paul Elmer More and American Criticism.*)

**Humanitarian Novel, The:** See SOCIOLOGICAL NOVEL.

**Humor:** See WIT AND HUMOR.

**Humours:** In the old theory of physiology the four chief liquids of the human body, blood, phlegm, yellow bile, and black bile, were known as "humours." They were closely allied with the four elements, air (cold), fire (hot), water (moist), and earth (dry). Thus the blood was hot and moist, the yellow bile hot and dry, phlegm cold and moist, black bile cold and dry. Both physical diseases and mental and moral dispositions ("temperaments") were caused by the condition of the humours. Disease resulted from the dominance of some element within a single humour, or from a lack of balance or proportion among the humours themselves. The humours gave off vapours which ascended to the brain. An individual's personal characteristics, physical, mental, and moral, were explained by his "temperament" or the state of his humours. The perfect temperament resulted when no one humour dominated. The sanguine man has a dominance of blood, is beneficent, joyful, amorous. The choleric man is easily angered, impatient, obstinate, vengeful. The phlegmatic man is dull, pale, cowardly. The melancholic man is gluttonous, backward, unenterprising, thoughtful, sentimental, affected. A disordered state of the humours produced, further, more exaggerated characteristics. These facts explain how the word humour in Elizabethan times came to mean "disposition," then "mood," or "characteristic peculiarity," later specialized to "folly," or "affectation." By 1600 it was common to use humour as a means of classifying characters. The influence on Elizabethan literature of the doctrines based on "humours" was very great, and familiarity with them is a great aid in understanding such characters as Horatio, Hamlet, and Jacques in Shakespeare. Many passages often taken as figurative may have had a literal meaning to the Elizabethans, as "my liver melts." See COMEDY OF HUMOURS.

**Hymn:** A lyric poem expressing religious emotion and generally intended to be sung by a chorus. Church and theological doctrine, pious feeling, and religious aspiration characterize the ideas of these lyrics, though originally the term referred to almost any song of praise whether of gods or famous men. The early Greek and Latin Christian churches developed many famous hymn writers, and the importance of hymns during the Dark and Middle Ages can hardly be exaggerated since they gave to the great mass of people a new verse form as well as a means of emotional expression. The twelfth and thirteenth centuries saw the greatest development of Latin hymns (*Dies Irae*, etc.). The wide use of hymns during these centuries helped to destroy certain literary conventions of the past and exerted an important influence on the versification of English and German poetry as well as that of the romance languages. Some famous hymn writers of England were Wesley, Cowper, Watts, Toplady, Newman; of America, Whittier and Holmes. For a concise and careful statement regarding this form see the article on hymns in the *Encyclopædia Britannica*.

**Hyperbole:** A figure of speech based on exaggeration. Used not too frequently, hyperbole is an effective device for securing attention, giving emphasis, or creating a poetic effect. It consists of such exaggerations as "rivers of blood," "millions of ships," "as the sands of the sea."

**Iambus (iamb):** A metrical foot consisting of an unaccented syllable and an accented ($\smile$ —). The most common metrical measure in English verse. A line from Marlowe will serve as an illustration:

$$\text{Cŏme līve} \mid \text{wĭth mē} \mid \text{ănd bē} \mid \text{mý lŏve}$$

**Ictus:** Accent; that stress which is given certain syllables in the reading of poetry. Thus in an iambic foot ($\smile$—) we may say that the ictus (or accent) is on the second syllable. In modern usage the unaccented syllable is called the *thesis*, the accented syllable the *arsis* (*q.v.*). Thus we would be right in saying that the *ictus* of an iambic foot falls on the second syllable and that the second syllable is, therefore, the *arsis*.

**Idiom:** A use of words, a grammatic construction peculiar to a given language, an expression which cannot be translated literally into a second language. "To carry out" may be taken as an example. Literally it means, of course, to carry something out (of a room perhaps), but idiomatically it means to see that something is done, as "to carry out a command." Idioms in a language usually arise from a peculiarity which is syntactical or structural or from the veiling of a meaning in a metaphor (as in the above instance).

**Idyl:** Not so clearly a definite poetic *form* or *type* (like the sonnet, for instance) as a general descriptive term which may be applied to one or another of the poetic forms which happen to be short and to possess marked descriptive, narrative, and pastoral qualities. In this popular sense, Whittier's *Maud Muller* might be called an idyl. Pastoral and descriptive elements must be insisted upon as the first requisites of the idyl, though it is true that this pastoral element is usually presented in a conscious, *literary* manner. The point of view of the idyl is that of a civilized and artificial society glancing from a drawing-room window over green meadows and gamboling sheep. Historically the term goes back to the "idyls" of Theocritus, who wrote short pieces depicting the simple, rustic life in Sicily to please the civilized Alexandrians.

**Imagery:** The use of figurative language for poetic or rhetorical effect. The apt use of images or figurative language is one of the first essentials of poetry; it is, one might argue, a quality without which no poetry can be written. It is the very heart of poetic and rhetorical effectiveness, since figurative language is the natural flowering of an imaginative mind and without imagination poetry cannot breathe. Facts can be recited in a city directory or in a handbook such as this, but not until facts are interpreted and given reality through imaginative thought, through the language of imagery, do they take on vividness and reality. An algebraic formula carries truth with it; deft use of figurative language carries a feeling, a convincing, capturing emotion with it. It makes the receptive reader *feel* a truth. Apt imagery gives: a vividness to presentation, color and warmth for facts and ideas, a suggestion of the concrete and specific (as opposed to the general); a pleasant sense of coöperation, since the reader must read with something of the same imaginative effort with which the poet creates. The artist making use of imagery must, however, avoid two extremes: his imagery must not be trite, or it will fail of its purpose for very staleness; and it must not be too subtle or it will turn into a "conceit" (*q.v.*) and likewise fail of its purpose because of its very remoteness from the experience of the reader. The value of imagery will be clear if one compares the effects of the italicized parts of the following sentences:

(1) When the flotilla approached the harbor it found *sixty-nine ships already at the anchorage.*

(2) When the flotilla approached the harbor it found *the anchorage white with enemy sails.*

The first is fact; the second expresses the idea figuratively. See FIGURATIVE LANGUAGE.

**Imagination and Fancy:** The theories of poetry advanced by the "romantic" critics of the early nineteenth century (Wordsworth, Coleridge, and others) led to many efforts to distinguish between "imagination" and "fancy," terms which had formerly been used as virtually synonymous. The word "imagination" itself, according to one student (Bray), already had passed through three stages of meaning in England. In Renaissance times it was opposed to reason and regarded as the "means by which poetical and religious conceptions could be attained and appreciated." Thus Bacon cited it as the one of the three faculties of the rational soul: "history has reference to the memory, poetry to the imagination, and philosophy to the reason"; and Shakespeare says the poet is "of imagination all compact." In the neo-classic period it was the faculty by which "images" were called up, especially visual images (see Addison's *The Pleasures of the Imagination*), and was related to the process by which "imitation of nature" might take place. Because of its tendency to transcend the testimony of the senses, the poet who might draw upon imagination must subject it to the check of reason, which should determine its form of presentation. Later in the eighteenth century the imagination, opposed to reason, was conceived as so vivid an imaging process that it affected the passions and formed "a world of beauty of its own," a poetical illusion which served not to affect conduct but to produce immediate pleasure.

The romantic critics, however, conceived the imagination as a blending and unifying of the powers of the mind which enabled the poet to see inner relationships, such as the identity of truth and beauty. So Wordsworth says that poets

> Have each his own peculiar faculty,
> Heaven's gift, a sense that fits him to perceive
> Objects unseen before  . . .
> An insight that in some sort he possesses,  . . .
> Proceeding from a source of untaught things.

This new conception of "imagination" necessitated a distinction between it and fancy. Coleridge (*Biographia Literaria*) especially stressed, though he never fully explained, the difference. He called imagination the "shaping and modifying" power, fancy the "aggregative and associative" power. The former "struggles to idealize and to unify," while the latter is merely "a mode of memory emancipated from the order of time and space." To illustrate the distinction Coleridge remarked that Milton had a highly imaginative mind, Cowley a very fanciful one. Leslie Stephen (1879) stated the distinction briefly, "fancy deals with the superficial resemblances, and imagination with the deeper truths that underlie them." (References: S. T. Coleridge, *Biographia Literaria;* Leigh Hunt, *Imagination and Fancy;* J. W. Bray, *A History of English Critical Terms.*)

**Imaginative Element in Literature:** See IMAGERY, EMO-
TIONAL ELEMENT IN LITERATURE, ROMANTICISM, IMAGINATION
AND FANCY.

**Imagists:** The name applied to a group of poets who rose to
prominence in America about 1912–1914. Their name came
from the French title, *Des Imagistes*, given to the first anthology
of their work (1914); this, in turn, having been borrowed from a
critical term which had been applied to some few French precursors of the movement. The most conspicuous figures of
the imagist movement were "H.D.," Robert Frost, John Gould
Fletcher, Amy Lowell, and Carl Sandburg, although no one of
these was so narrow as to confine his work only to imagist writing. In other words, imagism was a spirit of revolt against
conventionalities of the time rather than a goal set up as in
itself a permanently lasting objective. The best volume speaking critically for the group is Amy Lowell's *Tendencies in Modern
American Poetry* (1917); the major objectives of the movement,
as suggested in this volume, were: (1) to use the language of
common speech, but to employ always the exact word—not the
nearly-exact; (2) to avoid all cliché expressions; (3) to create
new rhythms as the expressions of a new mood—and not to copy
old rhythms which merely echo old moods; (4) to allow absolute
freedom in the choice of subject, since the imagists believed
passionately in the artistic value of modern life; (5) to present
an image (that is to be concrete, firm, definite in their pictures—
harsh in outline); (6) to strive always for concentration which,
they were convinced, was the very essence of poetry; (7) to
suggest rather than to offer complete statements.

**Imitation:** A critical term applied to a process of artistic production. Aristotle at the beginning of his *Poetics* said that all
the arts are modes of imitation; his idea has been interpreted
thus: a work of art is "an idealized representation of human life
—of character, emotion, action—under forms manifest to sense."
A poet, therefore, in employing "imitation" is not copying some
concrete thing, such as a landscape, or imitating (in the modern
sense) some other writer; he is rather reproducing or representing a conception of his mind, built up in part from the store of
sense images he has acquired through experience or observation.

When Aristotle declared that Art imitates Nature, he thought of Nature as the creative principle of the universe; Aristotelian imitation is thus "creating according to a true idea" and not mere mimicry. But Aristotle was misunderstood and misinterpreted. The imitation of Nature came to be regarded frequently as a realistic portrayal of life, a reproduction of natural objects and actions, rather than as an idealistic representation. Moreover, admiration of the success with which the great writers of antiquity had followed Nature bred both a practice and a theory of following in their footsteps. Renaissance and neo-classic critics accepted imitation in this secondary sense of copying illustrious models in the various types of poetry. The neo-classic writers of England did not believe that imitation should replace genius; an adherence to classical models was considered a safe method of avoiding literary vices and attaining virtues. Imitation of this un-Aristotelian character had several varieties: writing in the spirit of the masters and using merely their general principles; borrowing from the ancients with the necessity of accommodating the material to the poet's own age and even improving on the original; the collection and use of special "beauties," in thought and expression, from the works of the best poets; the exercise of paraphrase and free translation. Imitation as a copying of other writers was discussed and employed in all degrees of dependence, from the most dignified to the most servile. With the Romantic movement "imitation" passed out of favor. See PLAGIARISM. (References: S. H. Butcher, *Aristotle's Theory of Poetry and Fine Art;* H. O. White, *Plagiarism and Imitation During the English Renaissance.*)

**Impression:** See EDITION.

**Impressionism:** A highly personal manner of writing in which the author presents characters or scenes or moods as they appear to his individual temperament rather than as they are in actuality. The term is one borrowed from painting. About the middle of the nineteenth century the French painters Manet and Monet—leaders of the impressionists—together with such others as Cézanne, Renoir, and Pissarro, revolted from the conventional and academic conceptions of painting and held that it was more important to retain the impressions an object makes on the artist than meticulously to present the appearance of that object by precise detail and careful, realistic finish. Their especial concern was with the use of light on their canvases. They suggested the chief features of an object with a few strokes; they were more interested in atmosphere than in perspective or outline. "Instead of painting a tree," says Lewis Mumford, the impressionist "painted the effect of a tree." The movement had its counterpart in literature, writers accepting the same conviction that the personal attitudes and moods of the writer were legitimate elements in depicting character or setting or action. Briefly, the literary impressionist holds that the expression of such elements as these through the fleeting impression of a moment is more significant artistically than a photographic presentation of cold fact. The object of the impressionist, then, is not to present his material as it is to the realist but as it is *seen* or *felt* to be by himself in a single passing moment. See EXPRESSIONISM.

**Impropriety:** See SOLECISM.

**Incident:** See EPISODE.

**Incremental Repetition:** A form of iteration found frequently in the ballad (*q.v.*). To quote Miss Louise Pound: "By incremental repetition is meant the ballad repetition not in the refrain way but structurally or for emphasis by which successive stanzas reveal a situation or advance the interest by successive changes of a single phrase or line. A stanza repeats a preceding one with variation but adds something to advance the story."[1] A common form which this sort of repetition takes is the question and answer, the answer repeating in large part the phrasing in the question itself. Some students of ballad structure believe that this repetition is the result of the old ballad's being sung as an accompaniment to the dance, and grew out of the recurrence of certain movements and rhythms of the dance. Two stanzas from *Child Waters* will serve as illustration of incremental repetition:

---

[1] From Louise Pound's *Poetic Origins and the Ballad*. By permission of The Macmillan Company.

> There were four and twenty ladies
> Were playing at the ball,
> And Ellen, was the fairest lady,
> Must bring his steed to the stall.
>
> There were four and twenty ladies
> Was a playing at the chess,
> And Ellen, she was the fairest lady,
> Must bring his horse to grass.

**Incunabulum:** A term applied to any book printed in the last part of the fifteenth century (before 1501). Since the first printed books resembled in size, form, and appearance the medieval manuscript, which had been developed to a high degree of artistic perfection, incunabula are commonly large and ornate. As examples of early printing incunabula are prized by modern collectors. From an historical and literary point of view they are interesting as reflecting the intellectual and literary interests of the late fifteenth century. The number of existing incunabula is large, including about 360 printed in England. Among famous English incunabula are Caxton's edition of Chaucer's *Canterbury Tales* and the immortal *Le Morte d'Arthur* of Malory. Modern libraries containing important collections of incunabula are the Bodleian at Oxford, the Cambridge University Library, the John Rylands Library in Manchester, the British Museum in London, the Bibliothèque Nationale in Paris, the Library of Congress in Washington, the Henry Huntington Library in San Marino, California, the Newberry Library in Chicago, and the Pierpont Morgan Library in New York. There are over 6,500 separate editions of European incunabula in America alone. (References: Margaret B. Stillwell, *Incunabula and Americana* and references under PRINTING.)

**Induction:** An old word for *introduction*. This term was sometimes used in the sixteenth century to denote a framework introduction (see FRAME-STORY). Thus Sackville's "Induction" to a portion of *The Mirror for Magistrates* tells how the poet was led by Sorrow into a region of Hell where dwelt the shades of the historical figures whose tragic lives are the subject of the *Mirror*. In the book proper each "shade" relates his own sad tale; the "induction" supplies the framework much as the famous "Prologue" supplies the framework for the stories making up Chaucer's *Canterbury Tales*. In *The Taming of the Shrew* Shakespeare employs an induction in which a drunken tinker is persuaded that he is a lord, for whose amusement is performed a play—the play is *The Taming of the Shrew* itself.

**Industrial Revolution:** A term used to characterize the social-political-economic struggle which characterized life in England for a hundred years or more but which was most intensified in the last quarter of the eighteenth and first quarter of the nineteenth centuries. Invention, scientific discovery, changing economic, political, and social ideas and ideals all contributed to the furore that was England during these years. By 1760 blast furnaces had begun to promote the manufacture of iron; the textile industry grew by leaps and bounds with the invention of the spinning jenny and the power loom (1785). The number of English looms increased in less than two decades from three thousand to one hundred thousand. James Watt made even greater strides possible through his perfection of the steam engine. Roads, canals, and railroads increased transportation facilities. Agriculture was all but deserted; by 1826 not a third of the former population was left on the farms. Hundreds of thousands of men wandered through the country, many dying, impoverished and diseased. The sweat shop was born; the master craftsman found his trade taken from him by the machine. Home work gave way to factory work. Industry and commerce flourished in cities which grew rapidly. The villages were all but deserted. A middle-class capitalistic group developed almost overnight, and progressed at the expense of men, women, and children whom they overworked in their mills. All England turned her attention to making money. (Reference: J. R. Green, *Short History of the English People*, pp. 837-846.)

Such industrial changes as these are related to literature since the writers of the period definitely concerned themselves with these contemporary problems. The bewilderment which came with the new industry called for explanation, understanding, and attempts at solution. Crabbe in such pieces as *The Village* and

*The Borough* set forth pictures of the conditions; Charles Kingsley in such novels as *Yeast* and *Alton Locke* and Mrs. Gaskell in *Mary Barton, a Tale of Manchester Life*, presented the struggles and unfairness of the times in fiction.   Dickens turned his attention to the relief of the poor.   Ruskin and Carlyle sought to point the way to reform; Arnold in his *Essays* condemned a Philistine England which measured her greatness by her wealth and her numbers.   Mill (*Principles of Political Economy*), Bentham (*Radical Reform*), Robert Owen (*New View of Society*), and Malthus (*Principles of Political Economy*) wrestled with the problems of the time from the point of view of the social sciences. One stanza from Thomas Hood's *Song of the Shirt* (1843) will show the sympathetic attitude with which literature regarded the injustices of the Industrial Revolution:

> Work—work—work!
>   My labor never flags;
> And what are its wages?   A bed of straw,
>   A crust of bread—and rags.
> That shattered roof—and this naked floor—
>   A table—a broken chair—
> And a wall so blank, my shadow I thank
>   For sometimes falling there!

**Informal Essay:** As distinguished from the formal essay, the informal essay is less obviously serious in purpose, usually shorter, freer of structure, easier of style, and is written to please and entertain rather than to instruct.   See ESSAY.

**Inkhornists:** See PURIST, and CRITICISM, HISTORICAL SKETCH.

**Inns of Court:** The four voluntary, unchartered societies or legal guilds in London which have the privilege of admitting persons to the bar.   They take their names from the buildings they occupy—the Inner Temple, the Middle Temple, Lincoln's Inn, and Gray's Inn, buildings which they have occupied since the fourteenth century.   Though the origin of these societies is lost in the medieval inns of law, it is clear that in late medieval times they became great law schools and so continued for centuries: today they are little more than lawyers' clubs, though they do exert considerable influence in guarding admissions to the bar. The Inns of Court were educational institutions and cultural centers in the sixteenth and seventeenth centuries. Their libraries as well as their spirit of fellowship fostered literary interests. Regular drama as well as masques and interludes was nurtured by the Inns. Shakespeare's *Comedy of Errors* was acted before the fellows of Gray's Inn during the Christmas season of 1594. The Inns, like the universities, saw much playwriting and amateur acting on the part of "gentlemen" who would scorn connection with the early public theatres. Many English authors have received their education, in whole or in part, in the Inns of Court. Chaucer may have belonged to one; Sir Thomas More was a Lincoln's Inn product; George Gascoigne and Francis Bacon were admitted to law practice from Gray's Inn; Thomas Shadwell and Nicholas Rowe were members of the Inner Temple, etc. Charles Dickens was living in one of the old buildings of Lincoln's Inn when he published *The Pickwick Papers*. A vivid description of life in the Inns appears in Thackeray's *Pendennis*. (Reference: A. Wigfall Green, *The Inns of Court and the Early English Drama*.)

**Innuendo:** A hint or indirect suggestion, often with sinister connotation.

**Interlude:** A farcical dramatic production which developed early in the sixteenth century in England and which played an important part in the secularization of the drama and in the development of realistic comedy. The word may mean a play brief enough to be presented in the interval of a dramatic performance, entertainment, or feast (e. g., Medwall's *Fulgens and Lucres*, ca.1497), or it may mean a play or dialogue between two persons. Some interludes imitate French farce and do not exhibit symbolic technique and didactic purpose, while others appear to have developed from the "morality play" (*q.v.*), and still others from the Latin school drama: the two latter types are likely to be moralistic. Professor Tucker Brooke has stressed the aristocratic character of the interlude and says that the interlude was understood in Tudor times to mean a short play exhibited by professionals at the meals of the great and on other occasions where, later, masques would have been fashionable. The essential qualities are brevity and wit. Some writers, however, (like F. E. Schelling) regard such an episode as that of the sheep-stealing Mak in the Towneley *Second Shepherd's Play* as an interlude. The chief developer of the interlude was John Heywood, the first English dramatist, so far as known, to recognize that a play might be justified on the single test of ability to amuse. Heywood's interludes were produced in the 1520's and 1530's, the most famous being *The Four P's* (the Palmer, the Pardoner, the Pothecary, and the Pedlar, who engage in a sort of lying contest managed as a satire against women), and *The Merry Play of John John the Husband, Tyb His Wife, and Sir John the Priest* (in which the priest and Tyb hoodwink the husband). Homely details and realistic treatment are significant features. (References: Tucker Brooke, *The Tudor Drama;* E. K. Chambers, *Mediaeval Stage*, Vol. II; A. W. Reed, *Early Tudor Drama*.)

**Internal Rime:** See RIME, LEONINE RIME.

**Intrigue Comedy:** See COMEDY OF SITUATION.

**Introduction:** The opening sentences or paragraphs of a piece of writing. All literary combinations have been said to have three parts: beginning, middle, end. On this basis the introduction is the beginning to the beginning. Sometimes the term is applied to an essay printed at the beginning of a book—much like a preface—to explain the author's chief ideas, purposes, hopes, and disillusions regarding the book he has written. Such introductions today are often little more than advertisements for the book which a hopeful publisher is willing to pay some recognized author to write. See INDUCTION, PROLEGOMENON.

**Invective:** Harsh, abusive language directed against a person or cause. Vituperative writing. The *Letters* of Junius and the open letter written by Stevenson in defence of Father Damien have qualities of invective. See Hugh Kingsmill, *An Anthology of Invective and Abuse.*

**Invention:** Originality in thought, style, diction, imagery, or plot. In this present-day sense the term implies creative power of an independent sort. But the use of the term by early English critics often is colored by an older meaning of the term and by the implications of the theory of imitation (*q.v.*), and the student will do well to remember that Renaissance and neo-classic critics in their use of the term may have in mind the older idea of the "discovery" of literary material as something to be "imitated" or represented. In Latin rhetoric *inventio* meant the "finding" of material and was applied, for example, to an orator's "working up" of his case before making a speech. According to the Aristotelian doctrine of imitation an author did not create his materials "out of nothing"; he found them in Nature. A critic writing under the control of these classical conceptions could not think of invention in its narrower, modern sense. Yet the idea of originality, of using "new" devices, and of avoiding the trite expression appears in the use of the term in England as early as Renaissance times. As the term was used somewhat loosely for several centuries, it is not possible to give a single definition which will explain all the passages in which the term appears in writings of the sixteenth, seventeenth, and eighteenth centuries.

**Inversion:** The placing of a sentence element out of its normal position either to gain emphasis or to secure a so-called "poetic effect." Inversion used with restraint and care is an effective rhetorical device, but used too frequently or so grotesquely as to distort the language, it will immediately work ruin with a style and result in artificiality. A simple illustration is the command the small boy gives his dog: "Rover, go home," a command generally considered more efficient than "Go home, Rover," which is, perhaps, the more natural. Probably the most offensive common use of inversion is the placing of the adjective after the noun in such expressions as "home beautiful," etc.

The device is often happily employed in poetry. Where the writer of prose might say: "I saw a vision of a damsel with a dulcimer" Coleridge writes:

> A damsel with a dulcimer
> In a vision once I saw.

**Invocation:** An address to a deity for aid. In classical literature convention demanded an opening address to the muses, an invocation bespeaking their assistance in the writing. Epics, particularly, were likely to begin in this way. Milton, in *Paradise Lost*, accepts the tradition, but instead of invoking one of the muses of poetry addresses the

> Heavenly Muse, that, on the secret top
> Of Oreb, or of Sinai, didst inspire
> That shepherd who first taught the chosen seed
> In the beginning how the heavens and earth
> Rose out of Chaos:  .  .  .

***Ipse dixit:*** Any dogmatic statement. Literally the Latin means: "He himself has said." Hence the term is used to characterize any edict or brief statement emphatically uttered.

**Irish Literary Movement, Irish Literary Revival, Irish Renaissance:** Variant terms for the movement which encouraged the production of Anglo-Irish Literature. See CELTIC RENAISSANCE.

**Irish Literature:** The early literature of Ireland is of particular interest because it is greater in bulk, earlier in date, and more striking in character than any other preserved vernacular Western European literature, and because it has furnished a storehouse of literary materials for later writers, especially those of the early Romantic period and of the Celtic Renaissance. It is possible, too, that it supplies a clue to the obscure origins of Arthurian romance. The development of this extensive native literature, as well as the remarkable flourishing of Latin learning in Ireland in the early Middle Ages, is due in part to the fact that the Teutonic invasions which destroyed Roman power in the fifth century failed to reach Ireland, which became a refuge for European scholars and for several centuries the chief center of Christian culture in Western Europe. The Irish clerics, too, seemed to be unusually tolerant of native pagan culture and therefore aided in preserving a great mass of native, often primitive, legendary and literary tradition of great interest to the student of folklore and literary origins.

Although much poetry in Irish was doubtless written in very early times, definite metrical forms employing alliteration and rime having been developed as early as the seventh century, the great bulk of early Irish literature is in prose. In fact, the early Irish epics are distinguished from most other early epic literature by their employment of prose instead of verse (though the Irish prose epics frequently include poetic paraphrases or commentaries, "rhetorics," scattered throughout the text). The basic stories of the chief epic cycle reflect a state of culture prevailing about the time of Christ. Verbally preserved from generation to generation for centuries, they seem to have been written down as early as the seventh and eighth centuries. These early copies of the old stories were largely destroyed and scattered as a result of the Norse invasion (eighth and ninth centuries), the stories being imperfectly recovered and again recorded in manuscripts by the patriotic antiquarians of the tenth and later centuries. Two large manuscripts of the twelfth century containing these retellings of ancient story are still in existence, the *Book of the Dun Cow* (before 1106) and the *Book of Lenster* (before 1160).

The early saga literature is divided into three great cycles: the "mythological," based on early Celtic myths and historical legends concerning population groups or "invasions"; the Ulster Cycle, or "Red Branch," of which Cuchullin is the central heroic figure; and the Fenian Cycle, concerned with the exploits of Finn mac Cool and his famous companions. The Ulster Cycle was more aristocratic than the Fenian and is therefore preserved in greater volume in the early manuscripts. The chief story is the *Táin bó Cualnge*, "The Cattle Raid of Cooley," the greatest of the early Irish epics. Other important stories of this cycle are *The Feast of Bricriu* (containing a beheading game like that in *Sir Gawain and the Green Knight*), *The Wooing of Etaine* (a fairy mistress story), and *The Exile of the Sons of Usnech* (the famous Deirdre story). The Fenian stories, perhaps later in origin than the Ulster tales, have shown greater vitality in oral tradition, many of them still being current among the Gaelic peasants of Ireland and Scotland. They were utilized by the famous James Macpherson in the eighteenth century (see LITERARY FORGERIES).

Early Irish professional poets (*fili*) or story-tellers were ranked partly by the extent of their repertory of tales, the highest class being able to recite no less than 350 separate stories. These stories were divided into numerous classes or types, such as cattle raids, wooings, battles, deaths, elopements, feasts, exiles, destructions, slaughters, adventures, voyages, visions, etc.

In addition to the romantic or saga literature there has been preserved (partly in Latin) a vast amount of historical, legal, and religious literature, the latter including a great many saints' lives (romantically told), as well as hymns, martyrologies, and one of the earliest examples of medieval biographical writing, Adamnan's *Vita Sancti Columbae*, "The Life of Saint Columba" (before A.D. 700).

The traditional literary technique of the native Irish writers was much altered after the spread of English power and culture in Ireland in the seventeenth century, and the decline in the employment of the Irish language since that time has been accompanied by a lowering and lessening of literary activity. For "revivals" of Gaelic literature and culture see CELTIC RENAISSANCE, CELTIC REVIVAL, GAELIC MOVEMENT. (References: E. C. Quiggen, *Encyc. Brit.*, 14th ed., Vol. XII; D. Hyde, *Literary History of Ireland*.)

**Irony:** A figure of speech in which the actual intent is expressed in words which carry the opposite meaning. Irony is likely to be confused with sarcasm but it differs from sarcasm in that it is usually lighter, less harsh in its wording though in effect probably more cutting because of its indirectness. It bears, too, a close relationship to *Innuendo* (*q.v.*). The ability to recognize irony is one of the surest tests of intelligence and sophistication. Its presence is marked by a sort of grim humor, an "unemotional detachment" on the part of the writer, a coolness in expression at a time when the writer's emotions are really heated. Characteristically it speaks words of praise to imply blame and words of blame to imply praise, though its inherent critical quality makes the first type much more common than the second. The great effectiveness of irony as a literary device is the impression it gives of great restraint. The writer of irony has his tongue in his cheek; for this reason irony is more easily detected in speech than in writing since the voice can, through its intonation, so easily warn the listener of a double significance. One of the most famous ironic remarks in literature is Job's "No doubt but ye are the people, and wisdom shall die with you." Antony's insistence, in his oration over the dead Caesar, that "Brutus is an honorable man" bears the same ironic imprint. Goldsmith, Jane Austen, Thackeray—these authors have in one novel or another made frequent use of this form; but Jonathan Swift is the arch-ironist; his *Modest Proposal* for saving a starving Ireland, by suggesting that the Irish sell their babies to the English landlords, is perhaps the most sustained ironic writing in our literature. See DRAMATIC IRONY. (Reference: F. McD. C. Turner, *The Element of Irony in English Literature*.)

**Issue:** See EDITION.

**Italian Sonnet:** See SONNET.

**Jacobean:** An adjective derived from *Jacobus* (Latin for "James"). Whatever is characteristic of the reign of James I (1603–1625) or whatever took place in it may be called Jacobean. Early Jacobean literature is in reality a flowering of Elizabethan literature, while later Jacobean literature shows the new attitudes characteristic of Caroline (*q.v.*) literature. Shakespeare's later work as well as most of Bacon's and Jonson's and Donne's falls in Jacobean times. See pp. 490–495.

**Jargon:** Confused speech, resulting particularly from the mingling of several languages or dialects. The term is also used to refer to any strange language which sounds uncouth to us; in this sense outlandish speech. Sometimes jargon means simply nonsense or gibberish. Jargon, like cant, also signifies the special language of a group or profession, as the legal jargon, pedagogic jargon, thieves' jargon, etc. (Reference: Arthur Quiller-Couch's essay on jargon in *On the Art of Writing*.)

**Jest-books:** A name applied to collections of humorous, witty, or satirical anecdotes and jokes which had some vogue in England and Germany and other European countries in the sixteenth and succeeding centuries. The "jests" in these miscellanies owe something to the Latin *facetia*, something to the medieval *fabliau* (*q.v.*) and *exemplum* (*q.v.*), and borrow also from the epigram (*q.v.*), the proverb (*q.v.*), and adage (*q.v.*). They are usually short and often end with a "moral." Coarseness, ribaldry, realism, satire, and cynicism often characterize the witty turns. The material in the jest-books probably is similar in character to the stock-in-trade of the medieval minstrels, the printing press making possible the dissemination of such matter in book form. Women, friars, cuckolds, Welshmen, courtiers, tradesmen, foreigners, military officers, doctors, students, travelers, and many other classes are butts of the wit or victims of practical jokes. The earliest English jest-book is *A Hundred Merry Tales* (*ca.*1526). Another famous one was *The Gests of Skoggan* (*ca.*1565), which illustrates a tendency of jest-books to be "biographical" in making the jokes cluster about a single man. Thus the *Merie Tales of Master Skelton* was partly responsible for the poor reputation of John Skelton after his death. So there were in the seventeenth and eighteenth centuries jest-books on Ben Jonson. One famous court jester, Archie Armstrong (under James I and Charles I), published his own jest-book, *A Banquet of Jests and Merry Tales* (1630). It is divided into "Court Jests," "Camp Jests," "College Jests," "City Jests," and "Country Jests." (Reference: W. C. Hazlitt, *Shakespeare Jest-Books*, Series 1, 2, 3.)

**Jesuits:** Members of the Society of Jesus, a Catholic religious order founded by Saint Ignatius Loyola in 1534 for the purpose of serving the Church in the troublous times of the Reformation movement. In contrast with the ascetic ideals of the medieval Catholic orders, the Jesuits were conceived as a band of spiritual soldiers living under strict military discipline who were expected to engage actively in affairs. The discipline was strict, the individual having no rights as such but existing only for the purpose of serving the Order. The members were bound by personal vows of poverty, chastity, and obedience. The "general" lived in Rome and was subject to the Pope. The Jesuits became famous as schoolmasters and made effective efforts to raise the educational as well as spiritual standards of the clergy. Their activities as missionaries are well known; the letters of Jesuit missionaries in America give important pictures of early life in the colonies. Although political activities were technically forbidden, the objectives of the order actually led the Jesuits into political intrigue and it is this fact that has led to the unfavorable presentation of the Jesuits in such fiction as Kingsley's *Westward Ho*. (For a *favorable* view of the Jesuits of about the same period, late sixteenth century, see R. H. Benson, *Come Rack! Come Rope*, 1912.) Jesuits figure in the fiction of Alexandre Dumas (as in *Olympe de Clèves*, 1852) and are presented unfavorably in the Swedish romance of Zacharias Topelius, *The King's Ring*, 1901. English poetry has been enriched by the poetic work of a few Jesuit poets, notably Robert Southwell (1561–1595), whose *Saint Peter's Complaint* and his more brilliant short poems such as *The Burning Babe*, anticipate both the seriousness of Milton and the "conceits" of Donne.

**Jeu d'esprit:** A witty playing with words, a clever sally. Much of Thomas Hood's verse, for example, may be said to be marked by a happy *jeu d'esprit*.

**Jig:** A non-literary farcical dramatic performance, the words being sung to the accompaniment of dancing. It was popular on the Elizabethan stage, often being used as an afterpiece. "He's for a jig, or a tale of bawdry," Hamlet says of Polonius. See DROLL. (Reference: C. R. Baskervill, *The Elizabethan Jig*.)

**Johnson's Circle:** See LITERARY CLUB.

**Jongleur:** A French term for a professional musical entertainer of medieval times, analogous to the Anglo-Saxon gleeman (*q.v.*) and the later minstrel (*q.v.*). Though primarily one who sang or recited the lyrics, ballads, and stories of such original poets as the *troubadour* (*q.v.*) and the *trouvère* (*q.v.*), the *jongleur* sometimes composed and sometimes supplied non-musical forms of entertainment, such as juggling and tumbling. The dissemination of literary forms and materials from nation to nation in the Middle Ages is due partly to the activities of the *jongleur* and the minstrel.

**Kailyard School:** A name given to a group of Scottish writers whose work dealt idealistically with ordinary people in modern village life in Scotland. Dialect was an important element in their writing. J. M. Barrie and "Ian Maclaren" are two of the best known members of the "school," which was popular toward the close of the nineteenth century. "Kailyard" is a Scottish term for a cabbage garden.

**Katharsis:** SEE CATHARSIS.

**Kenning:** A stereotyped figurative phrase used in Old English and other Germanic tongues as a synonym for a simple noun. Kennings are often picturesque metaphorical compounds. Specimen kennings from *Beowulf* are "the bent-necked wood," "the ringed prow," "the foamy-necked," "the sea-wood," and the "sea-farer," for *ship;* "the swan-road" and "the whale-road" for the *sea;* the "leavings of the file" for the *sword;* the "twilight-spoiler" for the *dragon;* the "storm of swords" for *battle;* and "peace-bringer among nations" for the *queen.*

**King's English, The:** Correct English, as in the phrase "he murders the King's English." The "Queen's English" is sometimes used with the same meaning.

**Knickerbocker School:** A name given to an important group who happened to be writing in and about New York during the first quarter of the nineteenth century. The name "Knickerbocker," taken from the name of an early Dutch family settling in the region, was made famous by Washington Irving in his *Knickerbocker History of New York.* Journalism, editorship, the frontier, poetry, novels, songs, and, in the case of Bryant at least, translation from the classics, were the sorts of things which claimed the attention of these writers. The term "school" is, for them, a misnomer, since they consciously held few tenets in common and worked to no deliberate purpose as a group. Their association was one of geography and chance rather than of close organization. At the turn into the nineteenth century New York was forging ahead of Boston as a center of activity and of population, a fact which meant that naturally the city was becoming more important as a literary center. The more illustrious members of the school were: Washington Irving (*Salmagundi* papers, written in collaboration with others, *Knickerbocker's History of New York*, *Sketch Book*, *Tales of a Traveller*, etc.), James Fenimore Cooper (*The Spy*, *The Pioneers*, *The Pilot*, *Last of the Mohicans*, *Pathfinder*,

*Deerslayer*, etc.), William Cullen Bryant (*Poems*, and translation of Homer), Joseph Rodman Drake (*The Culprit Fay*), Fitzgreene Halleck (*Marco Bozzaris*), John Howard Payne (*Home Sweet Home*), Samuel Woodworth (*The Old Oaken Bucket*), George P. Morris (*Woodman, Spare That Tree*).

**Koran:** A Moslem collection of scriptural writings. The text was "revealed" to Mohammed from time to time over a period of years, and, after many changes and much editing, took shape in an official transcription after Mohammed's death (A.D. 632). The book is the sacred scripture of millions of followers, and presents—in addition to matters of theology—moral teaching, liturgical directions, and advice as to religious conduct and ceremonials. The speaker is usually God.

*Lai:* See LAY.

**Lake School:** A name used to characterize Coleridge, Wordsworth, and Southey—three poets who at the beginning of the nineteenth century were living among the lakes of Cumberland. The name "lakers" is credited to the *Edinburgh Review*, which for several years adopted a very contemptuous attitude toward the poets. There was, properly, no "school" in the sense of the three all working for common objectives, but it is true that Coleridge and Wordsworth had certain convictions in common. In general they stood for a return to the simple life of nature. See ROMANTICISM.

**Lament:** A poem expressing some great grief, a "complaint." *Deor's Lament*, an early Anglo-Saxon poem, for instance, presents the plaintive regret of the scop at his changed status after a rival had usurped his place in the esteem of a patron. The separate "tragedies" in such collections as the sixteenth-century *Mirror for Magistrates*, in which the ghosts of dead worthies tell the stories of their fall from fortune, were called "laments" in Renaissance times, an example being Sackville's "Lament" of the Duke of Buckingham. See COMPLAINT.

**Lampoon:** Writing which ridicules and satirizes the character or personal appearance of a person in a bitter, scurrilous manner. Lampoons were written in either verse or prose. Lampooning became a dangerous sport and fell into disuse with the development of the libel laws. Such counterparts as lampoons have in modern life are perhaps best found in the so-called "comic valentine." See EPIGRAM.

**Laureate:** See POET LAUREATE.

**Lay (*lai*):** A song or short narrative poem. The word has been applied to several different poetic forms in French and English literature. The earliest existing French *lais* were composed in the twelfth century and were professedly based upon earlier songs or verse-tales sung by Breton minstrels on themes drawn from Celtic legend; hence the term "Breton lay." Though some of the early French *lais* were lyric, most of them were narrative, like those of Marie de France, who wrote at the court of the English King Henry II about A.D. 1175. A few of Marie's *lais* are related to Arthurian romance, the *Lay of Lanval*, for example, in which Arthur and Gawain appear. The prevailing verse-form of the early French *lais* was the eight-syllabled line riming in couplets. Later French *lais*, such as those of the Renaissance, developed more complicated metrical forms.

The word "lay" was applied to English poems written in the fourteenth century in imitation of the French "Breton *lais*." Though a few of them follow the short couplet form, more use the popular "tail-rime stanza" (*q.v.*). Any short narrative poem similar to the French *lai* might be called a "Breton lay" by the English poets. Actually themes from various sources were employed, classical, Oriental, Celtic, etc. Some of the best-known English "Breton lays" are the *Lay of Launfal, Sir Orfeo, Sir Gowther*, and Chaucer's *Franklin's Tale*.

Since the sixteenth century, "lay" has been used by English writers as synonymous with "song." In the early nineteenth century, "lay" sometimes meant a short historical ballad, as Scott's *Lay of the Last Minstrel* and Macaulay's *Lays of Ancient Rome*. *Lais* as used by François Villon for the title of the poems now known as *Petit Testament* (1456) is a different word, corresponding to modern French *legs*, "bequest."

**Legend:** A narrative or tradition handed down from the past. A legend is distinguished from a myth in that the legend has more of historical truth and perhaps less of the supernatural. Legends often indicate the lore of a people, and, in this way, serve as at least a partial expression of the racial or national spirit. *Saints' legends* are narratives of the lives of the early church heroes. Loosely a legend is any brief explanatory comment accompanying paintings, maps, etc.

**Leonine Rime:** A particular form of internal rime (see RIME) characterized by the riming of the syllable preceding the cæsura with the last syllable of the line. Ordinarily Leonine rime is restricted to pentameters and hexameters, but less rigidly the term is applied to verses such as the "Stabat Mater" of the Church. The expression is said to be derived from the name of a writer of the Middle Ages, Leoninus, canon of St. Victor in Paris, who wrote elegiac lines containing this variety of internal rime. An example of Leonine rime is italicized in the following:

> Ex rex Ed*vardus*, debacchans ut Leo*pardus*.

Also called *internal rime*.

**Letter-press:** Used to distinguish the reading matter, or the "text," of a book from the illustrative matter. This use of the term may have derived from the fact that, in the older processes of printing, the letter-press printed directly from type instead of from the plates, woodcuts, or blocks used for illustrations. The term is also employed to refer to the typography of a work, or to printing in a general sense.

**Letters:** A general name sometimes given to literature (see *belles lettres*). More specifically, of course, the classification refers to notes and epistles exchanged between acquaintances, friends, or commercial firms. A great body of informal literature is preserved through collections of actual letters. The correspondence of such figures as Lord Byron, Jane and Thomas Carlyle, Lord Chesterfield, Charles Dickens, Edward Fitz-Gerald, William Hazlitt, Charles Lamb, Mary Wortley Montagu, Sydney Smith, and Robert Louis Stevenson—to mention a few of the great letter writers—constitutes one of the pleasantest of byways in the whole realm of literature. Letters, in this sense, are distinguished from "epistles" in that they present personal and natural relationships among friends, whereas epistles are more usually formal documents prepared with a view to their being read by some public.  See EPISTLE.

**Lexicography:** The art of making dictionaries or "lexicons." The most ancient dictionary extant is said to be a Greek lexicon called *Homeric Words*, prepared by Apollonius the Sophist in the reign of Augustus (27 B.C.–A.D. 14).  The technique of making lexicons and dictionaries developed slowly from the mere explanation of hard words by simpler ones in the same language to the preparation of elaborate lists, alphabetically arranged, with derivations, pronunciation, spellings, and illustrative quotations, and meanings, either in the same or other languages.  For English lexicography, see DICTIONARIES, ENGLISH.

**Lexicon:** An old word for dictionary, now used only for dictionaries of such languages as Greek or Hebrew.

**Libretto:** The text or book, containing the story, tale, or plot of an opera or of any long musical composition—a cantata, for instance.  It is the diminutive form of the Italian *libro*, a book.

**Light Opera:** A form of opera (*q.v.*) which lacks the dignity and seriousness of grand opera and usually stresses sentiment rather than passion.  It is unlike comic opera in that no spoken dialogue is commonly employed.  An example is M. W. Balfe's *The Bohemian Girl* (1843).

**Limerick:** A jingle, a particularly popular type of "nonsense-verse."  Its composition follows a rather definite pattern: five anapestic lines of which the first, second, and fifth, consisting of three feet, rime; and the third and fourth lines, consisting of two feet, rime.  Sometimes a limerick is written in four lines, but when so composed, its third line bears an internal rime and might easily be considered two lines.

The origin of the limerick is not definitely known, but Langford Reed, in his *The Complete Limerick Book*, advances the theory that it is an old French form of verse brought back to

227

Limerick, Ireland, by the returning veterans of the Irish Brigade (about 1700). Legend has it also that this type of verse was frequently sung at parties by each individual in turn, each verse being followed by the choric refrain "Will you come up to Limerick?" Though originally a kind of epigrammatic song, passed around orally, limericks increased the range of their subject matter to encompass every possible theme, nothing being sacred to their doubtful humor. They were chiefly concerned, however, with the manners, morals, and peculiarities of people. Their first recorded appearance in print was in 1821, when Loane's *History of Sixteen Wonderful Old Women* was published, but they reached the peak of their vogue when Edward Lear published his *Book of Nonsense* in 1846. The following, taken from Lear's volume, illustrates the accepted limerick form:

> There was an old Man of the Dee,
> Who was sadly annoyed by a Flea;
> When he said, "I will scratch it!"
> They gave him a hatchet
> Which grieved that Old Man of the Dee.

**Litany:** A ritualistic form of supplication commonly used in the Catholic Church. A solemn prayer. The form is sometimes adopted by writers for original poetic expression.

**Literal:** Accurate to the letter, without embellishment. Thus, in the first sense, the word is used, as in a "literal translation," to signify accuracy and thoroughness in presenting the exact meaning of the original—a translation which is according to the usual meaning of the words and allows no freedom of expression or imagination to the translator. Quite different from "paraphrase" (*q.v.*). In the second sense, the term is frequently used to distinguish language which is matter of fact and concrete from language which is given to much use of figures of speech. Literal language is the opposite of figurative (*q.v.*).

**Literary Ballad:** See ART BALLAD.

**Literary Club, The (Doctor Johnson's Circle):** A club formed in London in 1764 at the suggestion of Sir Joshua Reynolds, famous painter, and with the coöperation of the famous Dr. Samuel Johnson. Among the seven other charter members were Edmund Burke and Oliver Goldsmith. Famous men admitted to membership during Johnson's lifetime included Bishop Percy (ballad collector), David Garrick (actor), Edward Gibbon (historian), Adam Smith (economist), and James Boswell (Johnson's biographer). At first the members met at a weekly supper, and later at a fortnightly dinner during Parliament. At these meetings there was much free and spirited discussion of books and writers, classic and contemporary, Doctor Johnson frequently dominating the conversation. Johnson became a sort of literary dictator and the Club itself was a formidable power: whole editions of a book were sold off in one day by its sanction. Though commonly thought of only in connection with late eighteenth-century literature, the Club has continued in existence, its later membership including fifteen prime ministers and such authors as Scott, Macaulay, Hallam, and Tennyson.

**Literary Forgeries:** The plagiarist tries to get the world to accept as his own what someone else has written. The literary forger, on the contrary, tries to make the world accept as the genuine writing of another what he has himself composed. His motive may be to supply authority for some religious or political doctrine or scheme, or it may be to cater to some prevailing literary demand (as when spurious "ballads" were composed in the eighteenth century in response to the romantic interest in old ballads), or it may be, as Bacon would say, "for the love of the lie itself." Literary forgeries seem to be numerous in all countries and in all ages. A book of nearly 300 pages by J. A. Farrer gives accounts of many famous literary forgeries, yet, as Andrew Lang says, several additional volumes would be needed to make the account of known forgeries complete. It is possible here to call attention to but a few cases. The Greek statesman, Solon, inserted forged verses in the revered *Iliad* to further his political purposes. St. Thomas Aquinas is said to have introduced the doctrine of the infallibility of the Pope through reliance upon forged passages in the writings of some of the fathers of the Greek Church.

A forged "diary" of a supposed soldier in the Trojan War, Dares the Phrygian, actually composed by some Roman about the fourth century after Christ, had the effect of turning the sympathy of European peoples from the Greeks to the Trojans and of supplying an account of the war which for over a thousand years was accepted as more "authentic" than Homer's. In addition it supplied the kernel for what developed into one of the most famous love stories of all time, that of Troilus and Cressida. A famous Italian scholar, Carlo Sigonio, about 1582 composed what pretended to be the lost *Consolatio* of Cicero. The imitation was so clever and the genuineness of the document so effectively argued by Sigonio himself that although there was always some doubt, it was not till 200 years later that the facts were discovered.

In English literary history an example is afforded by the tragic story of Thomas Chatterton (1752–1770), the "boy poet," who wrote "faked" poems and prose pieces supposed to have been written by a fifteenth-century priest. Although Chatterton was but twelve years old when he began his forgeries, his imitation of medieval English was so clever and his actual poetic gifts were so high that his efforts attracted wide attention before his suicide at the age of eighteen. About the same time came another famous case of an effort to supply the current romantic interest in the medieval and the primitive with supposedly ancient pieces of literature, James Macpherson's "Ossianic" poems (1760–1765). Macpherson seems to have made some use of genuine Celtic tradition but in the main to have composed the epic *Fingal* himself, which he claimed had been written in the third century by Ossian, son of Fingal. Macpherson's public was sharply divided between those who accepted this "discovery" as genuine and those who, like Doctor Johnson, denounced him as an impostor. The episode is referred to as the "Ossianic Controversy."

Just as it is not easy for editors and publishers to detect all plagiarized writing presented to them, so it is difficult for them to avoid being exploited by literary forgers, who sometimes mix the authentic and the spurious so cleverly that not only the editors and publishers, but the general public and the professional critics are deceived. And this is as true of the twentieth century as of the eighteenth.  See PLAGIARISM.  (Reference: J. A. Farrer, *Literary Forgeries*.)

**Literary Magazines:** A selected bibliography of literary journals in Great Britain and the United States which have been most influential in the development of the literature of the two countries follows.

A Selected List of Some Representative American Literary Magazines
(Arranged in the order of their founding)

| | | | |
|---|---|---|---|
| 1803–1811 | Monthly Anthology | 1870–1932 | Outlook |
| 1815– | North American Review | 1880–1929 | Dial (Reorganized) |
| | | 1881–1930 | Century Magazine |
| 1821– | Saturday Evening Post | 1883– | Ladies' Home Journal |
| | | 1883– | Overland Monthly (Reorganized) |
| 1824–1826 | United States Literary Gazette | 1886– | Cosmopolitan |
| 1830–1898 | Godey's Lady's Book | 1886– | Forum |
| 1831–1835 | New England Magazine | 1886– | Scribner's Magazine |
| | | 1889–1929 | Munsey's |
| 1833–1865 | Knickerbocker | 1889– | Poet Lore |
| 1834–1864 | Southern Literary Messenger | 1890– | Review of Reviews |
| | | 1892– | Sewanee Review |
| 1837–1859 | United States Democratic Review | 1892– | Yale Review |
| | | 1893–1924 | McClure's |
| 1840–1844 | Dial | 1895–1933 | Bookman |
| 1841–1858 | Graham's | 1899–1929 | Everybody's |
| 1842–1857 | Southern Quarterly Review | 1906–1919 | Bellman |
| | | 1906– | American |
| 1844–1907 | Eclectic Magazine | 1912– | Poetry |
| 1844– | Living Age | 1914– | New Republic |
| 1850– | Harper's Magazine | 1916– | Theatre Arts Magazine |
| 1853–1870 | Putnam's | | |
| 1857–1916 | Harper's Weekly | 1920–1924 | Freeman |
| 1857– | Atlantic Monthly | 1921–1925 | Reviewer |
| 1865– | Catholic World | 1924– | American Mercury |
| 1865– | Nation | 1924– | Saturday Review of Literature |
| 1866–1878 | Galaxy | | |
| 1868–1875 | Overland Monthly | 1925– | Virginia Quarterly Review |
| 1870–1881 | Scribner's Monthly | | |

A Selected List of Some Representative British Literary Magazines
(Arranged in the order of their founding)

| | | | |
|---|---|---|---|
| 1731–1907 | Gentleman's Maga-zine | 1869–1916 | Academy |
| 1802–1929 | Edinburgh Review | 1870–1882 | Fraser's |
| 1809– | Quarterly Review | 1877– | Nineteenth Century and After |
| 1817– | Blackwood's Maga-zine | 1890– | Review of Reviews (London) |
| 1824–1914 | Westminster Review | 1891– | Bookman |
| 1828–1921 | Athenaeum | 1891– | Strand Magazine |
| 1828– | Spectator | 1893– | Canadian Magazine |
| 1836– | Dublin Review | 1894–1897 | Yellow Book |
| 1845–1886 | British Quarterly Re-view | 1902– | London Times Liter-ary Supplement |
| 1853– | London Quarterly Re-view | 1907–1931 | Nation |
| 1855– | Saturday Review | 1912– | Poetry Review |
| 1860– | Cornhill Magazine | 1913– | New Statesman |
| 1865–1901 | Argosy | 1914–1919 | Egoist |
| 1865– | Fortnightly Review | 1919– | London Mercury |
| 1866– | Contemporary Review | 1923– | Adelphi |

**Literary Periods:** See ENGLISH LITERATURE, PERIODS OF; AMERICAN LITERATURE, PERIODS OF; and "Outline of Literary History."

**Litotes:** A figure of speech which makes an affirmation by stating the fact in the negative or by saying the opposite of what one means, as "Oh, no; he is not a wise man" to carry the meaning that actually he is very wise. Sometimes, too, litotes is used as the opposite of hyperbole (*q.v.*) implying simply an understatement such as is characteristic, for instance, of Oriental speech: "My house is a very poor one, but I hope you will partake of its hospitality" even though the house may be palatial in its arrangements. See IRONY.

*Litterateur:* A literary man, one who occupies himself with the writing or criticism or appreciation of literature. To most Americans the term carries with it a certain sense of smug complacency, and one should—remembering an episode in Owen

Wister's *Virginian*—be careful to smile when applying the term in person directly to a friend.

**Little Theatre Movement:** A term applied to a succession of definite efforts to encourage the writing and production of significant plays, as opposed to the more highly commercialized productions designed primarily for long runs and box-office success. The movement was originated by André Antoine in Paris in 1887 for the purpose of trying out certain dramatic experiments in a methodical way. There gathered about Antoine, himself a gifted actor, a group of young authors, whose plays he produced at the *Théâtre Libre* before a select audience of season ticket holders. His attempts to advance the cause of good drama included also the introduction of notable foreign plays by such writers as Tolstoy, Ibsen, Hauptmann, Björnson, Strindberg, and Turgenev. Though Antoine achieved only a limited success, his experiment aided in the development of certain French dramatists (Henri Lavedan, Paul Hervieu, Jules Lemaître, and E. Brieux) and influenced the founding of two other French "little theatres": Lugné-Poë's *Théâtre de l'Œuvre* (1893) and Jacques Copeau's *Vieux Colombier* (1914). Likewise in Germany there was established in 1889 the *Freie Bühne*. It was followed by a rapid development of native talent: Hauptmann, Max Halbe, Otto Erich Hartlehen, and others.

In England the movement had its beginning in the opening of the Independent Theatre (1891) under the management of Jacob Grein. Shaw, Jones, Pinero, Barrie, Galsworthy, and Barker were to some degree products of the movement in England. In Ireland the Little Theatre (1899) made attempts to encourage new Irish writers and the use of Irish themes. William Boyle, Lennox Robinson, J. M. Synge, Lady Gregory, and William Butler Yeats wrote for the Abbey players (see CELTIC RENAISSANCE). The beginning of the little theatre movement in America came in 1906 and 1907 when three groups were organized in Chicago: The New Theatre, the Robertson Players, and the Hull House Theatre, the latter being especially vigorous. In 1911–1912 came additional establishments: The Little Theatre of Maurice Brown (Chicago), Mrs. Lyman Gale's Toy Theatre (Boston), and the Festival Players of the Henry Street

Settlement, the Provincetown Players, and the Washington Square Players (New York). During the following two decades little theatres spread rapidly in America. The American institutions have been less professional than the European and have become important factors in the evolution of a characteristically American drama and theatrical art. Certain American universities have played or are playing a prominent part in fostering the movement. (References: Kenneth Macgowan, *Footlights Across America;* Sheldon Cheney, *The Art Theatre;* Lady Augusta Gregory, *Our Irish Theatre;* Constance d'Arcy Mackaye, *The Little Theatre in the United States;* Alexander Dean, *Little Theatre Organization and Management.*)

**Liturgical Drama:** A term sometimes applied to the early phase of medieval religious drama when the mystery plays were performed as a part or an extension of the liturgical service of the church. In their earliest form they were in Latin, and were operatic in character, the lines being chanted or sung rather than spoken. The name "liturgical drama" is also sometimes used for the mystery plays developed from the liturgy. See MYSTERY PLAY, MEDIEVAL DRAMA.

**Local Color, Literature of:** Writing which capitalizes the speech, dress, mannerisms, habits of thought, and topography peculiar to a certain region. Of course all fiction has a locale, but local color writing exists primarily for the portrayal it presents of the people and life of a geographical setting. About 1880 this interest became dominant in American literature; what was called a "local color movement" developed. The various sectional divisions of America were "discovered." Bret Harte, Mark Twain, and Joaquin Miller wrote of the West; George Washington Cable, Lafcadio Hearn, Mary Noailles Murfree, and Joel Chandler Harris spoke for the South; Sarah Orne Jewett and Mary E. Wilkins Freeman interpreted New England. See REGIONAL LITERATURE. (References: J. L. Allen, *Critic* 8:13, and Lucy L. Hazard, *The Frontier in American Literature.*)

**Locution:** A manner of expression or phrasing; a peculiarity of idiom in speech or writing; a mannerism. The term frequently implies an indirect, roundabout manner of expression.

One might, for example, refer to the "psychological locutions" which often characterize the style of James Joyce.

**Lollards:** The name applied to the followers of John Wycliffe, who inspired a popular religious reform movement in England late in the fourteenth century. Lollardism sprang from the clash of two ideals—that of worldly aims, upheld by the rulers in church and state, and that of the self-sacrificing religion, separated from worldly interests, upheld by the humbler elements among the clergy and the laity. Wycliffe himself died in 1384 after sponsoring and aiding in the translation of parts of the Bible into English; but the movement continued to gain strength. In 1395 the Lollards presented a petition to Parliament demanding reform in the church. Though King Richard opposed the petition strongly and it was not successful, its terms are important as early expressions of the attitude which triumphed with the Reformation movement in the sixteenth century. It denounced the riches of the clergy, asked that war be declared unchristian, and expressed disbelief in such important Catholic doctrines and practices as transubstantiation, image-worship, and pilgrimages. Though suppressed early in the fifteenth century Lollardism lived on secretly and later flared up in time to furnish a strong native impetus to the Lutheran Reformation in England early in the sixteenth century. This survival of Lollardism helps explain the fact that the English Reformation movement in its early stages was a popular movement rather than a scholarly one. Many Lollards were burned as heretics. Early Lollardism is reflected in *Piers Plowman's Creed* (popular attitude). Chaucer's country parson, so sympathetically described in the *Prologue* to the *Canterbury Tales*, was accused by the Host of being a "Loller." Lollardist attitudes find late expression in many of the pamphlets of the Reformation controversy.

**Loose Sentence:** A sentence grammatically complete at some point (or points) before the end; the opposite of a periodic sentence. A simple loose sentence consists of an independent clause followed by a dependent clause. Most of the complex sentences we use are loose (the term implies no fault in structure), the periodic sentence being usually reserved for emphatic statements and to secure variety. The constant use of the periodic sentence would impose too great a strain on the reader's attention. Loose sentences, however, which are composed of too many dependent clauses, become "stringy."

**Low Comedy:** The opposite of "high comedy" (*q.v.*), low comedy has been called "elemental comedy," in that it is totally lacking in seriousness of purpose or subtlety of manner, having no intellectual appeal. Some typical features of low comedy are: quarreling, fighting, noisy singing, boisterous conduct in general, boasting, burlesque, trickery, buffoonery, clownishness, drunkenness, coarse jesting, servants' chatter (when unrelated to the serious action), scolding, shrewishness, etc. In English dramatic history low comedy appears first as an incidental expansion of the action, often originated by the actors themselves, who speak "more than is set down for them." Thus in medieval religious drama Noah's wife exhibits stubbornness and has to be taken into the ark by force and under loud protest, or Pilate or Herod engage in uncalled-for ranting. In the morality plays the elements of low comedy became much more pronounced, and the antics of the Vice and other boisterous horse-play were introduced to lend life to the plays. In Elizabethan drama such elements persisted, in spite of their violation of the law of decorum, because they were demanded by the public; but playwrights like Shakespeare frequently made them serve serious dramatic purposes (such as relief, marking passage of time, echoing main action). A few of the many examples of low comedy in Shakespeare are: the porter scene in *Macbeth*, Launcelot Gobbo and old Gobbo in *The Merchant of Venice*, the Audrey-William love-making scene in *As You Like It*, and the Trinculo-Stephano-Caliban scene in *The Tempest*. The famous Falstaff scenes in *King Henry the Fourth* are examples of how Shakespeare could lift low comedy into pure comedy by stressing the human and character elements and by infusing an intellectual content into what might otherwise be mere buffoonery. Low comedy is not a recognized special type of play, as is the comedy of humours, for example, but may be found either alone or combined with various sorts of both comedy and tragedy. See COMEDY, FARCE, VAUDEVILLE. (Reference:

Ora E. Winslow, *Low Comedy as a Structural Element in English Drama from the Beginning to 1642*.)

**Lyric:** A brief subjective poem strongly marked by imagination, melody, and emotion, and creating for the reader a single, unified impression. The early Greeks distinguished between lyric and choric poetry by terming that poetry "lyric" which was the expression of the emotion of a single singer accompanied by a lyre, and "choric" those verses which were the expression of a group and were sung by a chorus. This distinction has now quite disappeared, though the conception of the lyric as the individual and personal emotion of the poet still holds and is, perhaps, the chief basis for discriminating between the lyric and other poetic forms. No longer primarily designed to be sung to an accompaniment, the lyric nevertheless is essentially melodic since the melody may be secured by a variety of rhythm patterns and may be expressed either in rimed or unrimed verses. Subjectivity, too, is an important element of a form which is the personal expression of personal emotion imaginatively phrased. It partakes, in certain high examples, of the quality of ecstasy. With a record of existence for thousands of years in every literature of the world, the lyric has naturally been different things to different people at different times. Strict definition is impossible. After devoting a full volume to the record and forms of the lyric, Ernest Rhys recognizes frankly the freedom and mobility of the type as a means of poetic expression, but speaks of it ideally as "a carol or love-song in three passages: first, the theme; then an access of emotion, a pensive variation, or an enlargement of the theme; and lastly, the recoil, or the fulfilment, of the melody."

The history of the lyric in English literature starts almost with the beginnings of our literature. In that earliest epic, *Beowulf*, certain passages clearly have lyric qualities. *Deor's Lament* we may call essentially lyrical in purpose. Later the introduction of Latin hymns and the Norman conquest brought in French and Italian elements. By about 1280 we have in the famous "*Sumer is icumen in*" what would pass the strictest critic today as a lyrical expression. By 1310 a manuscript collection of poems was made which, in addition to Southern

European forms, presented some forty English lyrics. Before 1400 Chaucer had written a fair body of lyrics, particularly those modeled on French forms. The troubadour of France had done his work well and had so awakened interest in lyrical forms as to make them common to the various European literatures. Later, Petrarch made current the sonnet. Thomas Wyatt and the Earl of Surrey popularized in England these Italian lyrical forms, particularly the sonnet, and by the time Tottel's *Miscellany* appeared (1557) the body of English lyrics was notably large and creditable. In Elizabethan England the lyric burst into full bloom at the touch of such poets as Sidney, Spenser, Daniel, and Shakespeare. Songs, madrigals, airs, became the very stuff of poetry. Jonson and Herrick carried the tradition further. To seventeenth-century England Cowley introduced the Pindaric ode (a lyric form), and later Dryden adopted the form. The romantic revival brought English literature some of its noblest poetry in the odes of Gray, Collins, Wordsworth, and Coleridge. Burns raised the lyric to new power. Coleridge and Wordsworth made it the vehicle of romanticism. Scott, Byron, Shelley, and Keats molded the form to new perfection. Bryant, Emerson, Whittier, Longfellow, and Poe gave it expression in a new land. Victorian poets spoke through it most frequently. Tennyson, Browning, Rossetti, William Morris, Swinburne— England's greatest poets of the period—were also some of our greatest lyricists. And in twentieth-century England and America the lyric—in its various types—is still the most frequently used poetic expression.

The lyric is perhaps the most broadly inclusive of all the various types of verse. In a sense it could be argued, perhaps, to be not so much a form as a manner of writing. Subjectivity, imagination, melody, emotion—these qualities have been fairly persistently adhered to by the poets. But as the lyric spirit has flourished, the manner has been confined in various ways with the result that we have, within the lyric type, numerous sub-classifications. The lyric is a genus with many species. Hymns, sonnets, songs, ballads, odes, elegies, *vers de société*, the whole host of French forms, ballads, rondel, rondeau—all these are varieties of lyrical expression classified according to differing qualities of form and subject matter and mood. (References

for study of the lyric: critical, Ernest Rhys, *Lyric Poetry;* and
E. B. Reed, *English Lyric Poetry from Its Origins to the Present
Time;* collections of English lyrics, Palgrave's *Golden Treasury*
and *The Oxford Book of English Verse.*)

**Lyrical Drama:** A term used for a dramatic poem (see
DRAMATIC POETRY) in which the form of drama is used to
express lyric themes (author's own emotions or ideas of life)
instead of relying upon a story as the basis of the action.

*Mabinogion:* A term applied to a collection of old Welsh tales
translated by Lady Charlotte Guest from the *Red Book of
Hergest,* a Welsh manuscript written in the thirteenth or fourteenth century containing tales written centuries earlier.  Only
four of these tales, *Pwyll, Prince of Dyved; Branwen, Daughter
of Llyr; Manawyddan, Son of Llyr;* and *Math, Son of Mathonwy*
(the so-called "four branches"), are in the strictest sense of the
word included in the term *mabinogion.*  Although some modern
authors follow Lady Charlotte Guest in explaining this word as
meaning "a collection of tales for the young," later authorities
explain *mabinogion* as the plural of *mabinogi,* "a collection of
tales every young poet should know," a *mabinog* being a sort of
literary apprentice, a young man receiving instruction from a
qualified bard.  For a classification of the contents of the
*Mabinogion* and for the possible relation of the tales to Arthurian
romances, see WELSH LITERATURE.

**Macaronic Verse:** A type of humorous verse which mingles
two or more languages.  More especially it refers to poems
incorporating modern words (given Latin or Greek endings) with
Latin or Greek.  The origin of this pleasing sort of nonsense
is credited to a Benedictine monk, Teofilo Folengo (1491–1544),
who wrote a mock heroic called *Liber Macaronicus.*  Verse of the
sort was soon written in France and other European countries;
the best example in English is said to be the *Polemo-Middinia*
credited to William Drummond of Hawthornden.  The following, by "E.C.B.," will be a self-explanatory example to anyone
who knows his Latin (or his Mother Goose):

> Cane carmen SIXPENCE, pera plena rye,
> De multis atris avibus coctis in a pie:

Simul hæc apert'est, cantat cmnis grex,
Nonne permirabile, quod vidit ille rex?
Dimidium rex esus, misit ad reginam
Quod reliquit illa, sending back catinum.
Rex fuit in aerario, multo nummo tumens;
In culina Domina, bread and mel consumens;
Ancell' in horticulo, hanging out the clothes,
Quum descendens cornix rapuit her nose.

**Madrigal:** A short lyric usually dealing with love or pastoral topics, and suitable for musical setting.  Formally, the madrigal consists of six to thirteen lines based on three rimes.  An example is "Take, O, take those lips away" from Shakespeare's *Measure for Measure*.

**Magazines:** See LITERARY MAGAZINES.

***Magnum opus:*** A great work, a masterpiece.  Formerly the term was used in all seriousness, but nowadays it often carries with it a suggestion of irony or sarcasm.

**Malapropism:** An inappropriateness of speech resulting from the use of one word for another which has some similarity to it.  The term is derived from a character, Mrs. Malaprop, in Sheridan's *The Rivals*, who was constantly giving vent to such expressions as the following: "as headstrong as an allegory on the banks of the Nile," "a progeny of learning," "illiterate him, I say, quite from your memory."

**Malediction:** A curse.  The opposite of benediction since it invokes evil rather than good.  The famous "Cursed be he that moves my bones" used as an epitaph for Shakespeare is an example.

**Manners, Comedy of:** See COMEDY OF MANNERS.

**Manuscript, Medieval:** As the precursor of the modern printed book and as the medium through which both classical and medieval literatures were preserved for modern times, the medieval manuscript has much interest.  The art of manuscript-making was highly developed; the finer existing "illuminated" manuscripts and early printed books modeled on them show an artistry perhaps superior to that of the best examples of modern book-making. The Gutenberg Bible (1456), for example, has been called the finest printed book in existence. As no mechanical means such as printing existed for multiplying copies, each manuscript required for its manufacture an infinite amount of skilled labor. Parchment was first employed, the finest kind being vellum (made from calf-skin), though paper was employed in the later Middle Ages. The actual writing was done chiefly in the monasteries, first by ordinary monks and later by professional scribes. The process of making the book included (1) the copying of the text by the scribe on separate sheets, (2) the inspection by the corrector, (3) the insertion of the capital letters and rubrics and other colored decorative matter by the rubricator and illuminator, (4) the binding by a binder who arranged the sheets (usually by folding a group of four sheets once to make a "quire" of eight leaves of sixteen pages) and completed the binding by the use of wooden boards, leather, and velvet. The result was a substantial "manuscript," in form much like a modern book of large size but far sturdier in construction. The illuminator did his work with great care. Favorite colors were gold and red and blue, though green and purple and yellow were frequently employed. In spite of losses by fire, war, robbery, and neglect, thousands of medieval manuscripts are still in existence and are carefully preserved in numerous public and private libraries. Early printed books (see INCUNABULUM) were modeled on the manuscript. In England, many medieval manuscripts, perhaps containing literature now lost, are thought to have been destroyed as a result of the suppression of the monasteries during the Protestant Reformation. (References: Falconer Madan, *Books in Manuscript;* B. L. Ullman, *Ancient Writing and its Influence;* G. H. Putnam, *Books and their Makers during the Middle Ages;* J. A. Herbert, *Illuminated Manuscripts.*)

**Marinism:** An affected poetic style practised by the Italian poet G. Marini[1] (1569–1625) and his followers. It is the manifestation in Italy of a general tendency toward a strained, flamboyant, or shocking style which accompanied the later

[1]Or Marino.

phases of the Renaissance in Western Europe, in some respects analogous to the baroque in art. Marini expressed this aspect of his creed thus:

> Astonishment's the poet's aim and aid:
> Who cannot startle best had stick to trade.
> (Fletcher's translation)

A typical conceit of Marini is his calling stars "blazing half-dimes of the celestial mint." Another aspect of Marinism was its "effeminate voluptuousness," stressed by Professor Fletcher. Though it is not probable that Marini's influence affected Donne, some other English "metaphysical" poets were influenced; e.g., Lord Herbert of Cherbury, Thomas Stanley, Sir Edward Sherburne, and Richard Crashaw. (On this point the works of the Italian scholar Mario Praz may be consulted.) See EUPHUISM, CONCEIT, GONGORISM, METAPHYSICAL VERSE, BAROQUE. (Reference: J. B. Fletcher, *Literature of the Italian Renaissance*, Chap. XXI.)

**Marprelate Controversy:** In the 1580's the Puritan opposition to the bishops of the established church in England, whose power was greatly strengthened by state support, expressed itself in outspoken pamphlets. Some of the authors of these Puritan tracts were severely punished—one ultimately executed—and in 1585 the censorship over such publications was made more rigid by a provision limiting printing rights to London and the two universities. In defiance of these regulations the Puritan party began issuing, in 1588, a series of violent attacks on the episcopacy, printed surreptitiously and signed by the pen-name "Martin Marprelate." The attacks were answered with corresponding scurrility by the conservatives, including apparently John Lyly as well as Thomas Nash. The authorship of the Marprelate pamphlets has never been definitely established, but whoever the author was or whoever the authors were, they and their opponents supplied interesting examples of spirited prose satires. (Reference: J. Dover Wilson, *Camb. Hist. of Eng. Lit.*, Vol. III, Ch. xvii.)

**Masculine Rime:** See RIME, FEMININE RIME.

**Masked Comedy:** See COMMEDIA DELL' ARTE.

**Masque:** In England as well as in other European countries there existed in medieval times (partly at least as survivals or adaptations of ancient pagan seasonal ceremonies) species of games or spectacles characterized by a procession of masked figures. In these "disguisings" or "mummings," which were usually of a popular or folk character, a procession of masquers would go through the streets, enter house after house, silently dance, play at dice with the citizens or with each other, and pass on. Adopted by the aristocracy, these games, modified by characteristics borrowed from civic pageants, chivalric customs, sword-dances, and the religious drama, developed into elaborate and costly spectacles, which themselves evolved into the magnificent entertainments known as masques. Because of this gradual evolution of the form and the scanty character of the records it is impossible to say with assurance just when the "masque" actually came into existence. The famous Epiphany spectacle of 1512, given by and participated in by Henry VIII, is sometimes referred to as the first English masque.

The chief development of the masque came, however, in the latter part of Elizabeth's reign and, especially, in the reigns of James I and Charles I. In the first third of the seventeenth century the masque reached its climax under such poets as Daniel, Beaumont, Middleton, Ben Jonson, and others. The greatest development was due to the poetic and dramatic genius of Jonson, poet laureate, and Inigo Jones, famous court architect and deviser of stage machinery. The "essential" masque, as distinguished from the "literary" masque (e.g., *Comus*), has been described by the Rev. Ronald Bayne as "the appeal of the moment to the eye and the ear, the blaze of colour and light, the mist of perfume, the succession of rapidly changing scenes and tableaux crowded with wonderful and beautiful figures. All the gods of Olympus, all the monsters of Tartarus, all the heroes of history, all the ladies of romance, the fauns, the satyrs, the fairies, the witches—all these were presented to the eye, while every kind of musical instrument charmed the ear, and eye and ear together were delighted by an elaboration of dance and measured motion which has never been known since."[1]

[1] From *Cambridge History of English Literature* (American edition), Vol. VI, p. 371. Reprinted by permission of The Macmillan Company.

Masques became increasingly expensive of production, almost unbelievable amounts being expended in costumes, scenery, properties, and for professional musicians, dancers, actors, etc. In the masque proper, which was the arrival and set dancing of masked figures, the actors were amateurs drawn from courtly society itself—princes and princesses, even queens and kings, taking part. With the development by Jonson of the antimasque (*q.v.*), the dramatic and literary qualities increased. Mythological and pastoral elements were emphasized, Jonson maintaining (against Daniel and Jones) that the masque should be based upon some poetic idea and the action should be significant as well as spectacular, so that Milton's *Comus* (1634), one of the best known of all masques, represents a legitimate development of what was originally little but spectacle. The masque commonly was a feature of some celebration, such as a wedding or coronation, and served as a formal preliminary entertainment to a court ball, and was frequently employed at the entertainments in the Inns of Court (*q.v.*). Masques exerted much influence upon the poetry and drama of the Renaissance. Spenser, for example, incorporates masque-like episodes in his *Faerie Queene* (e.g., the procession of the Seven Deadly Sins in Book I, Canto iv, and the masque of Cupid in III, xii). The effect upon the popular drama itself was probably great, since some dramatists wrote for both the court and the London stage, and the latter gradually took on refinements imitated from courtly performances. Peele's *Arraignment of Paris* is a pastoral play much like a masque. Many of Shakespeare's plays show the influence; the betrothal masque in *The Tempest* is an example. *As You Like It* has been called a mere "series of tableaux and groupings," masque-like in the lack of serious action, in the prominence of music, and in the spectacular appearance of Hymen as a *deus ex machina* at the end. The glorious era of the masque ended with the triumph of the Puritan Revolution (1642). See ANTIMASQUE. (References: Enid Welsford: *The Court Masque;* A. W. Green, *The Inns of Court and Early English Drama;* Mary Sullivan, *Court Masques of James I.*)

**Maxim:** A short, concise statement, usually drawn from experience and inculcating some practical advice; an adage.

"When in doubt, win the trick," a saying of Hoyle's, is an example of a maxim in bridge. See APHORISM, PROVERB.

**Medieval Drama:** A general term used to include all forms of drama in the Middle Ages, though the religious drama and its allied forms are usually meant by the phrase. The medieval religious drama was an outgrowth of the liturgical services of the church. As early as the tenth century, perhaps in Northern France, tropes (*q.v.*) or musical elaborations of the church services, particularly of the Easter Mass, developed into true drama when the Latin lines telling the story of the Resurrection, instead of being sung antiphonally by the two parts of the choir, were sung or spoken by priests who impersonated the two angels and the three Marys in the scene at the tomb of Christ.

Such dramatic tropes later became detached from the liturgical service, and medieval drama was born. That such performances appeared early in England is shown by the existence of the famous *Concordia Regularis* (*ca.*975), a complete set of instructions (stage directions) supplied to the Benedictine monks by the Bishop of Winchester. This record is earlier than any similar record from the Continent. The conscious dramatic intent is shown in the first few lines of the *Concordia*: "While the third lesson is being chanted, let four brethren vest themselves. Let one of these, vested in an alb, enter as though to take part in the service, and let him approach the sepulchre without attracting attention and sit there quietly with a palm in his hand . . . and let them all . . . stepping delicately as those who seek something, approach the sepulchre" (Chambers's translation). Dramatic tropes developed around the Christmas and Easter services.

This use of the dramatic method for the purpose of making vivid religious rites and instruction must have struck a responsive chord in the medieval audience, and it was not long till further important developments, the stages of which cannot now be exactly traced, took place. The performances were transferred from the church to the outdoors; Latin gave way to native language everyone could understand; and eventually the performances became secularized when the town authorities, utilizing the trade guilds as dramatic companies, took charge of the production of the plays. Eventually great cycles of Scriptural plays developed in which the whole plan of salvation was dramatically set forth (see MYSTERY PLAY). Plays employing the same technique as the Scriptural plays but based upon the lives of saints, especially miracles performed by saints including the Virgin Mary ("Miracle Plays," or "Saints' Plays"), also developed about A.D. 1100, though they seem not to have been numerous in England. Much later (*ca.*1400) the Morality Play (dramatization of a moral allegory) became popular and with the somewhat similar play known as Interlude became an immediate precursor of Elizabethan drama. There was also a considerable body of folk drama in the late Middle Ages, performed out of doors on such festival days as Hock Tuesday—Robin Hood plays, Sword-dance Plays, Mummings and Disguisings. Perhaps also there were plays based on medieval romances. But as these forms were often non-literary, the existing records make it difficult to estimate their extent or the exact nature of their influence upon subsequent dramatic tradition.

The cyclic drama ("Mystery Plays") and the Moralities doubtless played an important part in supplying entertainment and instruction in the later Middle Ages, becoming so secularized as to bring on the disapproval of the church. The development of secular elements, especially the stressing of comic features such as the shrewish behavior of Noah's wife or the addition of comic scenes not demanded by the serious action, such as the sheep-stealing episode in the Towneley *Second Shepherd's Play*, led definitely toward Elizabethan comedy. Though it is difficult to analyze the full influence exerted by medieval drama upon later drama, it is certain, as Professor Schelling remarks, that "on the upgrowth of the literatures of modern Europe the old sacred drama exercised no small or inappreciable effect," and that in England "it was in the ruins and débris of the miracle play and morality that Elizabethan drama struck its deepest roots."[1] Professor Nicoll, too, observes, "There is freshness of fancy here, a free treatment of the material, a rich fund of humour, and at times a true sense of the profound and

[1] F. E. Schelling, *Elizabethan Drama*, Houghton Mifflin Company, Vol. I, 1908, p. 1. Reprinted by permission of and arrangement with the publishers.

tragic. If with the mysteries we are but on the border of drama proper, we can see clearly the various traditions which later were brought to culmination in the time of Queen Elizabeth."[1] For the method of performance of the medieval religious drama see MYSTERY PLAY. See DRAMA, MIRACLE PLAY, LITURGICAL DRAMA, TROPE, MORALITY PLAY, FOLK DRAMA, INTERLUDE. (For an interpretation from the literary point of view see Katherine Lee Bates, *The English Religious Drama*. For later scholarly treatments and for collections of plays, see Tucker Brooke, *Tudor Drama;* C. G. Child, ed., *Early English Plays;* A. W. Pollard, *English Miracle Plays;* E. K. Chambers, *The Mediaeval Stage*, 2 vols.; Karl Young, *The Drama of the Medieval Church*, 2 vols.)

**Medieval Manuscript:** See MANUSCRIPT, MEDIEVAL.

**Medieval Romance:** For the application of the word "romance" to this type of narrative, see ROMANCE. A useful definition by Dorothy Everett (*Essays and Studies*, 1929) may be quoted: "Medieval romances are stories of adventure in which the chief parts are played by knights, famous kings, or distressed ladies, acting most often under the impulse of love, religious faith, or, in many, the mere desire for adventure." Though the origin of the medieval romance can not be traced with confidence, it appears in Old French literature of the twelfth century as a form which supplants in popularity the older *chanson de geste (q.v.)*, an epic form. In distinguishing the romance from the epic one may note that the epic reflects an heroic age whereas the romance reflects a chivalric age; the epic has weight and solidity, whereas the romance exhibits mystery and fantasy; the epic does not stress rank or social distinctions, important in the romance; the tragic seriousness of the epic is not matched in the lighter-hearted romance; the heroic figures of the epic are more consistently conceived than the heroes of romance; where the epic hero aims at high achievement, the hero of romance is usually satisfied with more or less aimless adventure; the epic observes narrative unity, whereas the structure of the romance is loose; love is absent or

[1]Allardyce Nicoll, *British Drama*, Thomas Y. Crowell Company, 1925, p. 29. Reprinted by permission of the publishers.

of minor interest in the epic, whereas it is supreme in the romances; epic fighting is serious and well motivated, whereas fighting in the romances is spontaneous; the epic uses the dramatic method of having the characters speak for themselves, whereas the reader of a romance is kept conscious of a narrator. The romances became extremely popular in Western European countries, occupying a place comparable with that of the novel in modern literature. The earliest romances were in verse (hence the term "metrical romances"), but prose was also employed later. The materials for the early French romances were drawn chiefly from the Charlemagne material or *chansons de geste* ("Matter of France"), ancient history and literature ("Matter of Rome the Great"), and Celtic lore, especially Arthurian material ("Matter of Britain").

Romances, most of them based upon French originals, were being produced in English as early as the thirteenth century. They flourished in the fourteenth century, and continued to be produced in the fifteenth and sixteenth centuries, though the disfavor which they met at the hands of Renaissance humanists caused them to lose standing, and Renaissance versions as well as versions appearing in seventeenth- and eighteenth-century "chap-books" are frequently degenerate forms, written to appeal chiefly to the middle and lower social classes. Middle English romances may be grouped on the basis of their subject-matter. The "Matter of England" includes stories based upon Germanic (including English) tradition and embraces *King Horn* (*ca.*1225), *Richard Lionheart* (before 1300), *Beves of Hampton* (*ca.*1300), *Havelok the Dane* (*ca.*1300), *Guy of Warwick* (*ca.*1300), and *Athelstan* (*ca.*1350). The "Matter of France" includes stories of Charlemagne and William of Orange, drawn from the *chansons de geste* (*q.v.*). Important romances of the group are *Sir Ferumbras* (*ca.*1375), *Otuel* (*ca.*1300), *The Song of Roland* (late fourteenth century), and *Huon of Bordeaux* (fifteenth century). The "Matter of Antiquity" includes various legends of Alexander the Great, legends of Thebes, and legends of Troy (including Chaucer's famous *Troilus and Criseyde*). The "Matter of Britain" includes the important Arthurian literature and is represented by such classics as the fourteenth-century metrical romance, *Sir Gawain and the Green Knight* and the fifteenth-century prose *Le Morte d'Arthur* of Malory. The Arthurian romances developing about the legend of the pseudo-historical King Arthur (see ARTHURIAN LEGEND) had eventually developed into great cycles of stories in Old French literature, some of the heroes of which, such as Tristram and Lancelot, did not belong to the original legend of Arthur. They were greatly elaborated in the bulky thirteenth-century French prose romances ("Vulgate Romances") which became the chief sources for such English treatments of Arthurian themes as Malory's. A fifth group might include romances of miscellaneous origin, especially Oriental. Examples are *Amis and Amiloun* (before 1300), *Floris and Blanchefleur* (ca.1250), *Sir Isumbras* (1350–1400), and *Ipomydon* (fourteenth century).

The Middle English romances are largely in verse, a few alliterative, others in couplets or stanzaic forms borrowed from France. In comparison with French romances they usually show inferior artistry, less attention to psychological treatment (as courtly-love characteristics), less sophistication, more credulity and use of the grotesque (like Richard's eating the lion's heart), and a higher moral tone. A reader who does not wish to read them in the original Middle English texts may get an adequate notion of the character of the romances from the modernizations and summaries found in such books as Jessie L. Weston's *Chief Middle English Poets*, and George Ellis's *Specimens of Early English Metrical Romances*. See ROMANCE, ARTHURIAN LEGEND, COURTLY LOVE, MIDDLE ENGLISH. (References: J. E. Wells, *A Manual of the Writings in Middle English;* L. A. Hibbard, *Medieval Romance in England;* W. P. Ker, *Epic and Romance;* George Saintsbury, *The Flourishing of Romance;* A. B. Taylor, *An Introduction to Medieval Romance.*)

**Melodrama:** A play based on a romantic plot and developed sensationally, with little regard for convincing motivation and with a constant appeal to the emotions of the audience. The object is to keep the audience thrilled by the awakening, no matter how, of strong feelings of pity or horror or joy. Poetic justice is superficially secured, the characters (who are either very good or very bad) being rewarded or punished according to their deeds. Though typically a melodrama has a happy ending, tragedies which use much of the same technique are sometimes referred to as melodramatic. Likewise by a further extension of the term stories are sometimes said to be melodramatic in character. The "movie" and "talkie" stage abound in melodramatic technique. Originally, on the Greek stage, the entrance of an actor in a melodrama was accompanied by music; and in early nineteenth-century melodrama music was an essential element, the action being accompanied by songs and instrumental music suggested by the situations, but music is not essential in modern melodrama. T. H. Dickinson has listed the qualities of melodramas: (1) they are governed by force rather than by sentiment or emotion; (2) the story is developed by action, circumstance, and "machinery" rather than by the tracing of motives or personal revelation; (3) the characters are types; (4) within the types the characters are arranged by the most rudimentary of moral divergencies, the struggle always being between the good and the bad; (5) the action takes place on a plastic stage, with rapid changes of scene and action requiring the aid of the imagination. (*The Contemporary Drama of England*, 1920, p. 96.)

**Metaphor:** A figure of speech based on a comparison which is implied rather than directly expressed. Thus to say "He was a lion in the fight" is to use metaphor (and hackneyed metaphor at that), whereas to say "He fought like a lion" is, since the comparison is directly expressed in "like," to use simile. Most of our modern speech, which now seems prosaic enough, was once largely metaphorical. Our abstract terms are borrowed from physical objects. Natural objects and actions have passed over into abstractions because of some inherent metaphorical significance. Thus "transgression"—which today signifies a misdemeanor, an error or mistake—formerly meant "to cross a line." The metaphorical significance has been lost—is said to be "dead"—and the former figure of speech now stands simply for an abstraction. (It is thus, in fact, that abstract terms first came into language; early man was necessarily content simply to name the objects about him which he could see and feel and smell.) Metaphor, alive, fresh, spontaneous, is one of the greatest aids to poetic expression. "All flesh is grass," says

Isaiah; into the four-word metaphor he has compressed a whole lyric.

**Metaphysical Verse:** Sometimes used in the broad sense of philosophical poetry, verse dealing with the metaphysics, poetry "unified by a philosophical conception of the universe and of the rôle assigned to the human spirit in the great drama of existence" (Grierson). In this sense Lucretius and Dante wrote "metaphysical verse." Herbert Read sees it as the "emotional apprehension of thought," *felt thought,* to be contrasted with the lyric, and regards some of the poetry of Chapman and Wordsworth, as well as that of John Donne and his followers, as "metaphysical."

Commonly, however, the term is used more narrowly to designate the work of the seventeenth-century writers sometimes referred to as the "metaphysical school." They formed a school in the sense of employing similar methods and of being actuated by a spirit of revolt against the romantic conventionalism of Elizabethan love poetry. Their tendency toward psychological analysis of the emotions of love and religion, their penchant for the novel and the shocking, their use of the "conceit," and the extremes to which they sometimes carried their technique resulted frequently in obscurity, rough verse, strained imagery, repulsive realism, and violations of "good taste." These faults gave them in neo-classic times a bad reputation that still clings to them in spite of a twentieth-century revival of sympathetic interest in their work. Consequently the reader frequently will find the word *metaphysical* used in a derogatory sense.

These characteristics, however, at least as they appear in the best metaphysical verse, are now seen as logical elements in a technique which was intended to express honestly, if unconventionally, the poet's sense of the complexities and contradictions of life. The poetry is intellectual, analytical, psychological, disillusioning, bold; absorbed in thoughts of death, physical love, religious devotion. The diction itself is simple as compared with that of the Elizabethans or the neo-classicists. The imagery is drawn indifferently from the near or the remote, actual life or erudite sources, the figure itself often being elaborated with relentless ingenuity. As Grierson puts it, "the 'metaphysicals'

251

of the seventeenth century combined two things, both soon to pass away, the fantastic dialectics of medieval love poetry and the 'simple, sensuous' strain which they caught from the classics—soul and body lightly yoked and glad to run and soar together in the winged chariot of Pegasus."[1] They wrote of God and of theology, of the court and of the church, of love and of nature—often elaborately, it is true—but usually with a high regard for form and the more intricate subtleties of meter and rime. Yet the verse is often intentionally or carelessly rough. Ben Jonson thought Donne "deserved hanging" for not observing accent. The roughness may be explained in part by the dominance of thought over form, in part by the fact that ruggedness or irregularity of movement goes naturally with a sense of the seriousness and perplexity of life, with realistic method, and with the spirit of revolt.

If the results of the metaphysical manner are not always happy, if the unexpected details and surprising figures are not always integrated imaginatively and emotionally, it must be remembered that these poets were attempting a more difficult task than confronts the complacent writer of conventional verse. Their failures perhaps appear most strikingly in their fantastic "conceits"—striking turns of thought or expression, far-fetched metaphors, intolerably elaborated figures, and verbal plays.

No exact list of "metaphysical poets" can be drawn up. Donne was the acknowledged leader. Crashaw and Cowley have been called the most typically "metaphysical." Some were Protestant religious mystics, like Herbert, Vaughan, and Traherne; some Catholic, like Crashaw; some were Cavalier lyrists, like Carew and Lovelace; some were satirists, like Donne and Cleveland. Cleveland and Edward Benlowes are among the chief offenders in carrying the fantastical too far. The new recognition that has come to the metaphysicals has arisen from a realization of the seriousness of their art, an interest in their spirit of revolt, their realism, their intellectualism, and other affinities with "modern" interests, as well as from the fact that they produced some very fine poetry. T. S. Eliot and John

[1] From H. J. C. Grierson's *Metaphysical Poetry*, published by Oxford University Press. Reprinted by permission of the publishers.

Crowe Ransom are two modern poets affected by metaphysical influence. See CONCEIT, BAROQUE, MARINISM. (References: H. J. C. Grierson, *Metaphysical Lyrics and Poems of the Seventeenth Century;* T. S. Eliot, *Homage to John Dryden;* George Williamson, *The Donne Tradition;* the essays by Herbert Read in *The Criterion,* 1923, and by W. Bradford Smith in the *Sewanee Review,* 1934.)

**Meter:** A rhythm established by the regular, or almost regular, recurrence of similar accent-patterns (feet). The most commonly used meters are the iambic, trochaic, anapestic, and dactylic, with spondees and pyrrhics occurring occasionally as variations. As each of these types is discussed in its proper place, only the accent-patterns will be given here: iambus ($\smile$—), trochee (—$\smile$), anapest ($\smile\smile$—), dactyl (—$\smile\smile$), spondee (— —), pyrrhic (a two-syllable word, like "power," pronounced sometimes as one syllable).

**Metonymy:** A common figure of speech which is characterized by the substitution of a term naming an object closely associated with the word in mind for the word itself. In this way we commonly speak of the king as "the crown," an object closely associated with kingship thus being made to stand for "king." So, too, in the book of Genesis we read, "In the sweat of thy face shalt thou eat bread," a figure of speech in which "sweat" represents that with which it is closely associated, "hard labor."

**Metrical Romance:** A romantic tale in verse. The term is applied both to such medieval verse romances as *Sir Gawain and the Green Knight* and to the type of verse romances produced by Sir Walter Scott (*The Lady of the Lake, Marmion*) and Lord Byron (*Bride of Abydos, The Giaour*). The latter kind reflects the tendencies of romanticism in its freedom of technique and its preference for remote settings (the past in Scott, the Near East in Byron) as well as in its sentimental qualities. See MEDIEVAL ROMANCE.

**Middle English:** English as spoken and written in the period following the Norman Conquest and preceding the Modern English period beginning at the Renaissance. The dates most commonly given are 1100 to 1500, though both are approximate dates, as the Norman Conquest came in 1066 and some writings earlier than 1500 (e.g., Malory's *Le Morte d'Arthur*) may properly be called "modern" English. For the changes in the language which mark Middle English, see ENGLISH LANGUAGE. The phrase "Middle English" is also applied to the literary period from about 1066 to about 1500. It is often divided into two periods, Early Middle English and Late Middle English. In the Early Middle English period (1066–1350) literature written in English had to win its way against the learned literature written in Latin (theology, philosophy, lyrics, satire, and chronicles such as Geoffrey of Monmouth's famous *Historia Regum Britanniae* (*ca.*1136), and the courtly literature written in French (see ANGLO-FRENCH LITERATURE). Little record is left of any literature written in English for more than a century following the Norman Conquest, though songs and ballads doubtless flourished among the middle and lower English-speaking classes.

The earliest existing poems in Middle English, such as the *Poema Morale* (*ca.*1170), the *Ormulum* (*ca.*1200), Layamon's *Brut* (*ca.*1205), *The Owl and the Nightingale* (*ca.*1250), Thomas of Hales's *Love Rune* (*ca.*1250), *Cursor Mundi* (*ca.*1300), Rolle's *The Prick of Conscience* (*ca.*1340), *King Horn* (thirteenth century), *Beves of Hampton* (thirteenth century), *Sir Tristrem* (thirteenth century), *Floris and Blanchefleur* (thirteenth century), *Guy of Warwick* (fourteenth century), *Havelok the Dane* (fourteenth century), *Richard the Lionheart* (fourteenth century), *Amis and Amiloun* (fourteenth century), though preserving many elements of native English poetic traditions, in general betray strong French influence both in literary types (such as debates, bestiaries, fabliaux, lays, romances) and in verse form, rime and set stanzaic forms usually supplanting the alliterative verse. Before 1350, too, cyclic mystery plays (see MEDIEVAL DRAMA) were being composed in English. Late Middle English literature (1350–1500), stimulated by increasing nationalistic impulses, including the substitution of English for French and in part for Latin in courtly literature, includes not only ballads and songs and cyclic religious drama, but many romances (*Sir Gawain and the Green Knight*, late fourteenth century, being the finest) as well as such poems as *The Pearl* (fourteenth century), the *Vision of Piers Plowman* (fourteenth century), and the matchless work of Geoffrey Chaucer, the first "major" English poet.   English prose was cultivated in prose romances, voyage literature such as Mandeville's *Travels*, and the Wycliffe translation of the Bible.   Late in the period, foreshadowing the coming of modern English prose, is the classic *Le Morte d'Arthur* of Sir Thomas Malory.   For further details see "Outline of Literary History," pp. 473–481.   (References: J. J. Jusserand, *A Literary History of the English People*, Vol. I; W. H. Schofield, *English Literature from the Norman Conquest to Chaucer;* P. G. Thomas, *English Literature before Chaucer;* W. P. Ker, *English Medieval Literature;* Henry Morley, *English Writers*, Vols. III–VI; C. S. Baldwin, *Three Medieval Centuries of Literature in England;* W. W. Lawrence, *The Medieval Story;* W. J. Courthope, *A History of English Poetry*, Vol. I.)

**Mid-Victorian:** See VICTORIAN.

*Miles gloriosus:* The braggart soldier, a stock character in comedy.   The type appeared in Greek comedy, was stressed by the Roman playwrights (Terence's *Thraso* and Plautus' *Miles Gloriosus*), and adopted by Renaissance dramatists.   An early example is Ralph Roister Doister, central figure in the play named after him (the "first" English comedy).   Examples in Elizabethan drama are Captain Bobadil in Jonson's *Everyman in his Humour*, Quintiliano in Chapman's *May Day*, and Shakespeare's Sir John Falstaff (*King Henry IV*, 1, 2), Don Armado de Adriano (*Love's Labour's Lost*), Parolles (*All's Well*), and Ancient Pistol (*King Henry V*).   Although the treatments differ in different examples, the *miles gloriosus* is likely to be cowardly, parasitical, bragging, and subject to being victimized easily by practical jokers.

**Mime:** A form of popular comedy developed by the ancients (fifth century B.C. in Southern Italy).   It portrayed the events of everyday life by means of dancing, imitative gestures, and witty dialogue.   It finally degenerated into sensual displays and the performers sank to a low social level.   The Christian Church frowned upon the performances and they were largely driven from the public stage. They were kept alive, however, by wandering entertainers. In England, the exhibitions seem to have consisted generally of low forms of buffoonery. The mime aided in preserving the comic spirit in drama, its influence possibly being apparent in the medieval "mystery play" (*q.v.*) and the Renaissance interlude (*q.v.*)—perhaps also the Renaissance "dumb show" (*q.v.*) and through it the modern pantomime (*q.v.*). Many elements of modern vaudeville are in direct line of descent from the mime. The mime is not regarded as a true link between ancient classical drama and modern drama, though it perhaps did aid in keeping alive the tradition of dramatic method and of the acting profession in the so-called dark ages. (Reference: Allardyce Nicoll, *Masks, Mimes, and Pantomimes.*)

**Minnesinger:** "Singer of love," a medieval German lyric poet whose art was perhaps inspired by that of the troubadour (*q.v.*). Though the German poets reflect the love system known as "courtly love" (*q.v.*), their poetry in general is more wholesome and sincere in tone than that of the troubadours. They flourished in the twelfth and thirteenth centuries. Walther von der Vogelweide is regarded as the greatest of the class.

**Minor Plot:** See SUBPLOT.

**Minstrel:** A musical entertainer or traveling poet of the later Middle Ages who carried on the tradition of the earlier gleeman (*q.v.*) and *jongleur* (*q.v.*). Minstrels flourished especially in the late thirteenth and the fourteenth centuries and played a very prominent part in the cultural life of the time. The typical minstrel may be thought of as a gifted wandering entertainer, skilled with the harp and tabor, singing songs, reciting romances, and carrying news from town to town, castle to castle, country to country, delighting all classes of society, from kings and knights to priests and burgesses and laborers. Love lyrics, ballads, legends, and romances were so composed and disseminated.

It has been pointed out by one authority that while in the main the minstrel was a self-respecting, important figure, there were various grades of minstrels to fit the different levels of society: "Some appealed especially to the higher classes, some to the lower. Some were proud of occupying places of established dignity at court, castle, or monastery. Some reveled in a free, Bohemian life, and journeyed constantly from one place to another. Some . . . could occupy estates of their own, or found hospitals from the fortunes they amassed. Some, unkempt and tattered, sang in the market-place, the ale-house, or the kitchen of the manor, for a charitable pittance."[1] They were at once the actors and journalists and poets and orchestras of their time. The *Lay of Havelok the Dane* is a good example of the "minstrel romance." Flourishing in Chaucer's day, minstrelsy declined in the fifteenth century and tended to disappear with the increase of literacy following the introduction of printing. In their enthusiasm for "primitive" or untutored poetic genius and for medievalism in general, the poets and novelists of the romantic school, such as Beattie and Scott, imparted a somewhat idealized meaning to "minstrel" and "minstrelsy," as they did to "bard."

**Miracle Play:** Although this term is used by many authorities on English drama in a broad sense which includes the Scriptural cyclic drama (see MYSTERY PLAY), it is restricted by others to its early sense of a non-Scriptural play based upon the legend of some saint or upon a miracle performed by some saint or sacred object (such as the sacramental bread). However common miracle plays in this stricter sense may have been in medieval England, very few have been preserved. It is known that a play of St. Catherine, probably in Latin or Anglo-Norman, was performed at Dunstable about A.D. 1100. At this time miracle plays on St. Nicholas were being produced in France. A play called *Dux Moraud* (thirteenth or fourteenth century), in English, which exists in a fragmentary form, may have been a miracle play, possibly one in which the Virgin Mary supplied the *deus ex machina* (Virgin Play). Other extant English plays that either are miracle plays or plays of very similar character are the *Play of the Sacrament* (late fifteenth century) and the *Conversion of St. Paul* and *Mary Magdalene* (*ca.*1500). An interesting modern example of a miracle play is Maeterlinck's *Sister Beatrice*. See MYSTERY PLAY. (References: Tucker

---

[1] From W. H. Schofield, *English Literature from the Norman Conquest to Chaucer,* 1906, p. 17. Reprinted by permission of The Macmillan Company.

Brooke, *Tudor Drama*, Chap. i; W. Creizenach, *Camb. Hist. Eng. Lit.*, Vol. V; G. R. Coffman, *A New Theory Concerning the Origin of the Miracle Play*.)

**Miscellanies, Poetical:** The collection of poems by Wyatt, Surrey, and others published by Richard Tottel in 1557 as *Songs and Sonnets*, commonly known as *Tottel's Miscellany* (see "Courtly Makers"), set a fashion that resulted in the publication of nearly twenty poetical miscellanies within the next half-century, usually under highly figurative or alliterative titles and varying greatly in quality and kind of verse printed. Some are posthumous publications of commonplace books (*see* Commonplace Book), such as the *Paradise of Dainty Devices* of Richard Edwards (1576), a very popular collection of poems of a serious character. Some miscellanies have a specialized character, like the *Handful of Pleasant Delights* (1584), a collection of ballads. Some of the later ones, like *England's Parnassus* (1600), are collections not of complete poems but of poetical quotations. One, *The Passionate Pilgrim* (1599), was published as Shakespeare's, and does contain some of Shakespeare's verse. Frequently the miscellany was made up of poems selected from other miscellanies or from manuscript sources. Much of the verse is anonymous, some is falsely ascribed, and some indicates authorship by initials not now understandable. Much uncertainty and some intentional mystification are connected with the parts played by collectors or editors. New poems were frequently printed along with old ones, and old ones sometimes appear in variant forms. The miscellanies are important as reflecting the great poetical activity of the time, particularly of the years preceding the appearance of Spenser, Sidney, and other major figures. They reflect, too, the metrical experiments of this earlier period. The poems in *A Gorgeous Gallery of Gallant Inventions* (1578), for example, make free use of alliteration and employ a wide variety of metrical forms. Such poet-dramatists as Shakespeare borrowed lyrics from the earlier miscellanies and lived to see their own verse appear in the later ones. Aside from *Tottel's*, particularly important miscellanies are *The Phoenix Nest* (1593) and *England's Helicon* (1600). The former, assembled by "R.S.," contains poems by Sidney, Spenser, Lodge, and others.

The latter, the best of them all, is a veritable store-house of Elizabethan poetry selected from many poets, great and small.

The practice of publishing poetical miscellanies thus begun in the sixteenth century of course has continued to the present time. Professor Arthur E. Case, in his *Bibliography of English Poetical Miscellanies, 1521–1750*, lists several hundred titles of various sorts of poetical collections.

*Mise en scène:* The stage setting of a play, including the use of scenery, properties, etc., and the general arrangement of the piece. Modern drama relies far more upon *mise en scène* for its effects than did earlier drama. Indeed, the lack of scenery has been given as a partial explanation of the high literary quality of Elizabethan drama, the playwright being forced to rely upon his language for his descriptive effects; while the increased dependence upon scenery is said to be one of the reasons for the decreased attention to purely literary devices on the modern stage.

**Mixed Figures:** The mingling of one figure of speech with another immediately following with which the first is incongruous. A notable example is the sentence of Castlereagh: "And now, sir, I must embark into the feature on which this question chiefly hinges." Here, obviously, the sentence begins with a nautical figure ("embark") but closes with a mechanical figure ("hinges"). The effect is grotesque. Mixed imagery, however, is sometimes deliberately used by master writers with great effectiveness, as when, for instance, Shakespeare makes Hamlet ask if it is wise "to *take arms* against *a sea* of troubles."

**Mock Epic:** A literary form which burlesques epic poetry by treating a trivial subject in a pompous manner. It mocks the characteristics of the classical epic, particularly the invocation to a deity; the formal statement of theme; the division into books and cantos; the grandiose speeches (challenges, defiances, boastings) of the heroes; descriptions of warriors (especially their dress and equipment), battles, and games; the use of the epic or Homeric simile; and the employment of supernatural machinery (gods directing or participating in the action). When the mock poem is much shorter than a true epic some prefer to call it "mock heroic," a term also applied to poems which mock romances rather than epics. Ordinary usage, however, employs the terms interchangeably. Chaucer's *Nun's Priest's Tale* is partly mock heroic in character as is Spenser's finely wrought *Muiopotmos*, "The Fate of the Butterfly," which imitates the opening of the *Aeneid* and employs elevated style for trivial subject-matter. Swift's *Battle of the Books* is an example of a cuttingly satirical mock epic in prose. Pope's *The Rape of the Lock* is perhaps the finest mock heroic poem in English, satirizing in polished verse the trivialities of polite society in the eighteenth century. The cutting of a lady's lock by a gallant is the central act of heroic behavior, a card game is described in military terms, and such airy spirits as the sylphs hover over the scene to aid their favorite heroine. (Reference: Richmond P. Bond, *English Burlesque Poetry, 1700–1750*.)

**Mock Heroic:** See MOCK EPIC.

**Monody:** A dirge or lament in which a single mourner expresses individual grief, e.g., Arnold's *Thyrsis, A Monody*. See DIRGE, ELEGY, THRENODY.

**Monologue:** A composition, oral or written, presenting the discourse of one speaker only. A soliloquy. Any speech or narrative presented wholly by one person. Sometimes loosely used to signify merely any lengthy speech. See DRAMATIC MONOLOGUE.

**Monometer:** A line of verse consisting of only one foot. See SCANSION.

**Mood:** The tone (as "pensive," "reflective," "rollicking") which prevails in a piece of literature. See EMOTIONAL ELEMENT IN LITERATURE.

**Morality Play ("Morality"):** A kind of poetic drama which developed in the late Middle Ages (probably late fourteenth century) and which was distinguished from the religious drama proper, such as the "mystery play" (*q.v.*), by the fact that it was a dramatized allegory in which the abstract virtues and vices (like Mercy, Conscience, Perseverance, and Shame) appear in personified form, the good and the bad usually being engaged in a struggle for the soul of man. One student of the drama (A. H. Tolman) has distinguished two classes. The "full-scope" morality is one in which the theme is the saving of man's soul, and the central figure is man in the sense of humanity in general. The best-known example is *Everyman* (*ca.*1500). The "limited-scope" morality is one which deals with a single vice or moral problem or a situation applicable to a certain person. Thus Skelton's *Magnificence* has for its theme the dangers of uncontrolled expenditures and was possibly written as advice to Henry VIII. Later, pedagogical and political themes as well as theological became quite common. The limited-scope morality developed later than the full-scope and is perhaps superior dramatically because of its independence and greater concreteness and realism. Morality plays have also been classified by content or purpose, as religious (*Everyman*), doctrinal (John Bale's *King Johan*), didactic-pedagogical (*Wyt and Science*), political (Skelton's *Magnificence*), etc. By the sixteenth century some of the morality plays had admitted so much realistic, farcical material that they had begun to establish a tradition of English comedy, and doubtless contributed much to the interlude (*q.v.*). In fact, "interlude" and "morality" became more or less interchangeable in describing plays. Such comic figures as the Vice and the Devil were especially well-developed and were influential upon later comedy. Though morality themes were widely employed in Renaissance drama of the sixteenth century, the morality plays as such lost their popularity in Elizabethan times. (References: Tucker Brooke, *Tudor Drama;* W. R. Mackenzie, *The English Moralities from the Point of View of Allegory;* E. K. Chambers, *Mediaeval Stage*, Vol. II.)

*Motif* (Motive): A simple element which serves as a basis for expanded narrative; or, less strictly, a conventional situation, device, interest, or incident employed in folklore, fiction, or drama. The carrying off of a mortal queen by a fairy lover is a *motif* about which full stories were built in medieval romance. In the ballad called *The Elfin Knight* the "fairy music" motif appears when the sound of the knight's horn causes the maiden to fall in love with the unseen hero. In music and art the term is used in various other senses, as for a recurring melodic phrase, a prevailing idea or design, or a subject for detailed sculptural treatment.

**Motivation:** The justification of the action of a character in a plot by the presenting of a convincing and impelling cause for that action.   The chief difference, perhaps, between amateurish, puerile fiction and great works of imaginative power lies in this very question of motivation.   The story or drama of action is sometimes content to unfold a series of thrilling, unnatural episodes, exciting in themselves, but growing out of no inherent purpose of the author other than his desire to excite his reader. Motivated action, however, is action justified by the make-up of the character partaking in the activity.   Hamlet is slow to resolve and refuses to kill Claudius when he finds him at prayer; Othello is intensely jealous and proud—and smothers Desdemona when he thinks her unfaithful; Falstaff is more of a wit than a hero—and runs from the scene of the robbery.   All this is motivation through character.   Since the whole question of motivation springs from the author's interpretation of human character, it follows that the greater his finesse of understanding, the more subtle his presentation of human character; the closer he keeps to the truth of reality, the greater the artist he manifests himself.

**Movement:** A critical term denoting action.   Thus a play is spoken of as having, or not having, "movement," implying that the dramatic action is strong or weak, rapid or slow.   The term is also used to indicate a new development in literary activity or interest, as the "Oxford movement," the "free-verse movement."

**Mummery:** A simple dramatic performance usually presented by players masked or disguised.   A farcical presentation, a sort of pantomime.   See Masque.

**"Mummings":** See Masque.

**Muses:** Goddesses represented as presiding over song, the various departments of literature, and the liberal arts.   They were nine in number and are generally considered the daughters of

Zeus and Mnemosyne (memory). In literature, their traditional significance is that of inspiring and helping poets. In various periods of Greek history, the muses were given different names and attributes, but the conventionally accepted list and the realm of interest ascribed to each are as follows: Calliope (epic poetry), Clio (history), Erato (lyrics and love poetry), Euterpe (music), Melpomene (tragedy), Polyhymnia (sacred poetry), Terpsichore (choral dance and song), Thalia (comedy), and Urania (astronomy).

**Musical Comedy:** Closely related, especially in its earlier forms, to burlesque and vaudeville, musical comedy developed in the early twentieth century in England and America into one of the most popular of all dramatic forms. Though much use is made of music, both vocal and orchestral, the dialogue is spoken, not sung. The success of the form depends partly upon the acting, partly upon the success of the songs, and partly upon the spectacular staging. Satirical "hits" at current figures and interests are features. The comic effects are sometimes farcical (see FARCE) in character.

**Mystery Play:** A medieval religious play based upon Biblical history; a Scriptural play. Mystery plays originated in the liturgy of the Church and developed from liturgical dramas into the great cyclic plays, performed outdoors and ultimately upon movable "pageants." They were the most important forms of the medieval drama of Western Europe and flourished in England from the late Middle Ages until well into Renaissance times. They seem to have developed about three nuclei: (1) Old Testament plays treating such events as the Creation, the fallen angels, the fall of man, the death of Abel, the sacrifice of Isaac, etc., and the Prophet plays, which prepared for (2) the New Testament plays dealing with the birth of Christ—the Annunciation, the birth, the visit of the wise men, the shepherds, and the visit to the temple; and (3) the Death and Resurrection plays—entry to Jerusalem, the betrayal by Judas, trial and crucifixion, lamentation of Mary, sepulchre scenes, the resurrection, appearances to disciples, Pentecost, and sometimes the Day of Judgment. So the whole scheme of salvation was presented. They were often known as Corpus Christi plays because of the habit of performing the plays on "pageants" in connection with the Corpus Christi processional. The great "cycles" whose texts have been preserved to us are the York, the Chester, the Coventry, and the Wakefield (or "Towneley"). They differ in length and in the list of plays or scenes included as well as in literary and dramatic value, the Towneley plays being especially important in dramatic development.

After the plays left the Church and became "secularized," they were performed by trade guilds, sometimes on fixed stages or stations (the crowds moving from station to station), sometimes on movable "pageants." A writer of the sixteenth century, Archdeacon Rogers, who witnessed a late production of the Chester cycle at Whitsuntide, has left the following oft-quoted description:

> Every company had its pageant, or part, which pageants were a high scaffold with two rooms, a higher and a lower, upon four wheels. In the lower they appareled themselves, and in the higher room they played, being all open on the top, that all beholders might hear and see them. The places where they played them was in every street. They began first at the Abbey gates, and when the first pageant was played it was wheeled to the high cross before the mayor, and so to every street; and so every street had a pageant playing before them at one time, till all the pageants for the day appointed were played: and when one pageant was near ended, word was brought from street to street, that so they might come in place thereof exceeding orderly, and all the streets have their pageants afore them all at one time playing together; to see which players there was great resort, and also scaffolds and stages made in the streets in those places where they determined to play their pageants.

The word "mystery" was first applied to these plays by an eighteenth-century editor (Robert Dodsley, 1744), on the analogy of the French *mystère*, a Scriptural play; medieval writers were more likely to refer to the plays as "Corpus Christi plays," "Whitsuntide plays," "pageants," etc., and possibly as "miracle" plays, the term preferred for them by many modern authorities. See MEDIEVAL DRAMA, MIRACLE PLAY, LITURGICAL DRAMA, PAGEANT, DRAMA.

**Mystery Story (or Novel):** A loose term including stories and novels and detective fiction as well. E. T. A. Hoffman in Germany and Edgar Allan Poe are generally conceded to have crystallized the form of the mystery story though certainly the main elements existed previously in the various "Gothic romances" (*q.v.*) of Walpole, Ann Radcliffe, and Charles Brockden Brown. Structurally the chief characteristic of the mystery story is its reversal of the sequence of events: the catastrophe (the murder, for instance) is given at the opening of the novel and from the details as here presented the problem is to deduce the way in which the crime was committed, the motives for it, and, finally, to ascertain the criminal. It was this type of writing for which Poe used the term "ratiocination" and which he himself illustrated in his *Murders in the Rue Morgue*. The detective type of mystery story has a long and distinguished career as an entertainer of readers. Some of the essential qualities of stories of this type may be summarized as follows: (1) a simple and direct style; (2) an air of reality about the setting, characters, and plot; (3) an actual explanation of the crime buried in the story itself; (4) a solution which does not play a trick upon the reader by bringing in a *deus ex machina*, and (5) a unified plot, compact and containing no extraneous material. Conan Doyle is probably the chief master of the detective story form in English. (Reference: the introduction to W. H. Wright's *The Great Detective Stories*.)

**Mysticism:** Such widely varying compositions as Dante's *Divine Comedy*, William Cowper's *Olney Hymns*, William Blake's *Songs of Experience*, Wordsworth's famous "immortality" *Ode*, and the essays of Thomas Carlyle and Ralph Waldo Emerson testify to the extent to which mysticism has colored the fundamental concepts of great literature. Essentially, mysticism rests upon a faith in the possibility of the union of the soul of man with some higher and greater spirit or force, such as Nature or some conception of deity. This union is achieved through imagination or contemplation and involves the subordination of reason to intuition as a means of contact with the higher force and as a source of knowledge. Christianity, transcendental philosophy (see TRANSCENDENTALISM), and Oriental systems such as Brahminism rest upon a basis of mysticism. It has been pointed out that Oriental mysticism (like Brahminism) and occidental mysticism (like Platonism) differ in their attitude toward the natural world, including the human body. The Oriental mystic in his effort to achieve unity with the higher spirit attempts to become oblivious of the body, while the Occidental tends to regard the natural world as a symbol of, or a means of approach to, the spiritual. Thus Wordsworth through contemplation of nature feels a "sense sublime" that "rolls through all things." Mystical thinking inclines thus to lead toward pantheism. Generally speaking, English mystics can be classified according to the paths by which they attempt to gain communion with the Divine Spirit. Spenser, Shelley, Browning, Coventry Patmore, Keats, and Rossetti would gain it through love or beauty (see PLATONISM); Vaughan and Wordsworth through nature; Donne, Coleridge, Carlyle, Tennyson, and Emerson through philosophy; and many others, including Richard Rolle of Hampole, Richard Crashaw, George Herbert, Cowper, and Francis Thompson, through religion. All of these approaches were employed by William Blake (1757–1827)—perhaps the most striking example of a complete mystic in English literature. His poetry is credited with being the most symbolic and abstruse in the language. One of the finest mystical poets produced in America is William Vaughn Moody (1869–1910). (Reference: Caroline F. E. Spurgeon, *Mysticism in English Literature*.)

**Myth:** Anonymous stories having their roots in the primitive folk-beliefs of races or nations and presenting supernatural episodes as a means of interpreting natural events. English literature is shot through with references to the myths of many countries, and so familiar are such stories as that of Hercules that they are part of the cultural heritage of educated people. Myths differ from legends in that they have less of historical background and more of the supernatural; they differ from the fable in that they are less concerned with moral didacticism and are the product of a racial group rather than the creation of an individual. Every country and literature has its mythology; the best known to English readers being the Greek, Roman, and Norse. But the mythology of all groups takes shape around certain common themes; they all attempt to explain the creation, divinity, and religion, to guess at the meaning of existence and death, to account for natural phenomena, and to chronicle the adventures of racial heroes.   A good elementary introduction to classical mythology is found in C. M. Gayley's *Classic Myths in English Literature*.   A useful dictionary of classical mythology is that of Howe and Harrer.   The encyclopedic *Mythology of All Races*, 13 vols., may also be consulted.

**Narration:** That one of the four types of composition (see ARGUMENTATION, DESCRIPTION, and EXPOSITION) the purpose of which is to recount an event or a series of events.   Narration may exist, of course, entirely by itself, but it is most likely to incorporate with it considerable description.   There are two forms of narration: *simple narrative*, which is content to recite an event or events and is largely chronological in its arrangement of details—as in a newspaper account of a fire; and *narrative with plot*, which is less often chronological and more often arranged according to a preconceived artistic principle determined by the nature of the plot and the type of story intended (see PLOT).   The chief purpose of narration is to interest and entertain, though, of course, it may be used to instruct and inform.

**Narrative Essay:** An informal essay in narrative form—anecdote, incident, or allegory.   It differs from a short story not only in its simpler structure, but especially in its essay-like intent, the story being a means of developing an idea rather than being an end in itself.   Addison's *Vision of Mirzah* is an example.   See ESSAY.

**Naturalism:** A manner of literary composition distinguished by an emphasized realism and calculated to present actuality, a detached, scientific objectivity, a wide inclusiveness of details, a freedom of subject-matter, and a treatment of the natural man in any or all his strengths and weaknesses.   The "naturalist" does not shrink from the possibility that a world so written about may appear chaotic and purposeless.   Naturalism is less selective, more all-inclusive, than realism.   The realist selects according to some purpose those details which relate to his intent; the naturalist also selects, but in his desire to create a definite impression in the mind of his reader he reserves unto himself the right to go wherever he will for his material. The first distinction of naturalism, then, is its greater inclusiveness, its greater catholicity in acceptance of detail. In popular opinion naturalism is more harsh, more cruel, more concerned with sex than either realism or romanticism. This charge is not necessarily true, but where it does hold it is because of this very insistence on freedom to find its material wherever it exists in the natural world. Romance, of course, is as concerned with love as any type of writing can be; we charge naturalism with sex only because the naturalistic writer insists on his privilege of using the biological and medical as well as the social aspect of love—on using whatever material he finds ready to his pen.

Most hasty readers will probably deny that the naturalist creates; he takes, such readers say, anything which comes his way; he is a great Sargasso Sea of art. But it is not so. First of all, no artist of any type or time, because of sheer physical limitations, can include every phase, every detail of his subject. He must, then, select at least to some degree. And by what process does he admit or eliminate? By what he thinks makes up the *natural* man. He is, then, creating, but he is creating a natural character, a natural action, rather than a romantic character, an unreal action. His is the *nth* degree of realism, but it is still creation, it is still an effort to build up an impression. He will not, like his realist brother, preach a doctrine nor, like his romantic brother, tell a pretty story. In his approach to actuality—and no *art* will ever attain it—he overreaches the romantic and the realist who have set themselves other tasks.

All this freedom in choice of material, all this concern with an impression, all this struggle to attain actuality make the naturalistic artist less likely to bother to portray order in the universe. In fact his work gives first of all the impression that the world is without order, chaotic. And here again are contrasts with the realist and the romantic; the realist finds order, according to the purpose which he has at hand in his work; the romantic finds all obstacles falling away before the hero, the lover, the adventurer. The naturalistic writer is scientific, detached, impersonal; the realist is kindly even while he is stern; the romantic, like Pippa, knows in his palpitating heart that all's right with the world.

"Naturalism," says Robert Morss Lovett, "is realism disciplined by science to an agnosticism in regard to all that lies beyond the material world, and by artistic theory to the production of that world as an end in itself. It is by hypothesis disinterested, objective, impersonal as science itself."

The brothers de Goncourt in 1864 described naturalism in the following terms: "The novel of today is composed from documents, received by word of mouth or taken direct from nature, just as history is composed from written documents. Historians write narratives of the past, novelists narratives of the present."

Though it is impossible to be dogmatic as to the actual beginning of naturalism (certain naturalistic elements existed in the writing of such classics as the works of Homer, Plautus, and Juvenal), the movement is generally credited to the Goncourt brothers and to Zola in France. The latter's *L'Assommoir* is the first example of naturalism in the novel. Huysmans and Maupassant are among the early French naturalists, as are James Joyce, Theodore Dreiser, and Eugene O'Neill among the moderns writing in English. See EXPRESSIONISM.

The student will also find "naturalism" used in senses corresponding with many of the various meanings of "nature" (see below); thus, the "naturalism" of Wordsworth means this poet's philosophy about the relation of external nature to man and God. (Reference: Zola, *The Experimental Novel*.)

**Nature:** Few terms are so important to the student of literature —or so difficult—as this one. When Aristotle compared nature and art, for example, he thought of nature as the creative principle of the universe (see IMITATION). And, indeed, the term often was virtually a synonym for God or the entire cosmic order. Since conformity with nature—the resort to nature as a norm or standard for judging artistic expression—long permeated critical thinking, some knowledge of the "normative" meanings of the term is necessary to the understanding of much criticism and literature. Professor A. O. Lovejoy found as many as sixty different meanings for "nature" in its normative functions. Both neo-classicists and romanticists would "follow Nature"; but the former drew from the term ideas of order, regularity, and universality, both in "external" nature and in human nature, while the latter found in nature the justification for their enthusiasm for irregularity ("wildness") in external nature and for individualism in human nature. Other contradictory senses may be noted: the term "nature" might mean, on the one hand, human nature (typical human behavior); or, on the other hand, whatever is antithetical to human nature and man's works—what has not been "spoiled" by man.

The neo-classic view of nature as implying universal aesthetic validity led to a reverence for "rules" drawn from long-continued acceptance by human beings, such acceptance being taken as an evidence of their basis in what is universal in human nature. The rules were based upon proved models. Opposed to this was the romantic tendency to regard as "natural" the primitive, the unsophisticated, the naïve—a conception which justified the *disregard* of rules and precedents and the exaltation of the freedom of individual expression which characterizes much "romantic" literature. Among some neo-classic writers the words "reason" and "nature" were closely allied in meaning, because both were closely related to the idea of "order" (John Dennis said that nature was order in the visible world, while reason was order in the invisible realm). The distinction between nature and wit (in one of its senses) was not always clear, since both provided tests of excellence, though, properly, "wit" was specific, while nature was generic, thought of as an ultimate, as indicated in the familiar lines from Pope's *Essay on Criticism:*

> True Wit is Nature to advantage dressed,
> What oft was thought, but ne'er so well expressed.

The serious student of the literature of the Renaissance, of neo-classicism, and of romanticism may well consult the various papers of Professor Lovejoy, e.g., "Nature as an Aesthetic Norm," which appeared in *Modern Language Notes* (1927).

For the general student of literature, nature in the sense of "external nature"—the objects of the natural world such as mountains, trees, rivers, flowers, and birds—is of particular interest since it has supplied so large a part of the imaginative substance of literature, especially poetry, from the earliest times to the present day. Some survey, therefore, of the attitudes toward external nature may be useful. One writer (Shairp) lists the following different uses which poets make of external nature: (1) they express childlike delight in the open-air world; (2) they use nature as the background or setting to human action or emotion; (3) they see nature through historic coloring; (4) they make nature sympathize with their own feelings; (5) they dwell upon the infinite side of nature; (6) they give description of nature for its own sake; (7) they interpret nature with imaginative sympathy; (8) they use nature as a symbol of the spirit.

The greatest attention to nature in English literature came with the romantic movement, when the revolt against the strained conventionalities of neo-classic fashions led to much theorizing about the relation of man to external nature and the production of a vast amount of poetry putting the new theories into practice. To be sure, earlier English literature had made much use of nature. The comparatively small amount of Anglo-Saxon literature remaining reflects both a simple love of nature and a power for picturesque description—as in the "Riddles" (see RIDDLE) and such poems as the *Wife's Complaint* and the *Husband's Message*—and especially a sense of mystery and awe in the presence of nature, as in *Beowulf*. Late medieval literature—Chaucer and the romances—was apt to present nature in idyllic, conventionalized forms, a pleasant garden or "bower" on a May morning. In the Renaissance there was sometimes a genuine, subjective response to natural surroundings, as in some of Surrey's poems, though often the treatment was conventional in character, as in the pastorals and the sonnets. Shakespeare, of course, though no theorist like Wordsworth, shows a wide knowledge of nature and an unsurpassed faculty for drawing upon subjects from nature, whether conventional or fresh, to give appropriate settings and to impart an air of reality to dramatic situations and human moods—from the romantic "How sweet the moonlight sleeps upon this bank"—of the Lorenzo-Jessica love-scene to the tragic and powerfully passionate responses of the distracted Lear to the rumblings of the storm which breaks over him as a terrible echo to his growing insanity.

The eighteenth century brought the great conflict between the neo-classicists and the romantics, and nowhere were the issues sharper between the two schools than in their treatment of external nature. In their zeal to follow "correct" models, to restrain enthusiasm, and in their doctrinaire preference of city to rural life, the neo-classicists found little room for recording intimate observations of nature, though they did, of course, employ natural imagery, usually conventionalized, and use nature descriptions as settings and as a basis for philosophical reflections. For the wilder aspects of nature they expressed strong abhorrence. Winter was "the deformed wrong side of the year," while mountains were a positive blemish upon the landscape and the ocean was a dangerous, wearying waste of waters—a far cry from the passionate warmth of Byron's famous apostrophe in *Childe Harold's Pilgrimage:* "And I have loved thee, Ocean," etc. The pre-Romanticists, such as Lady Winchilsea, John Dyer, James Thomson (especially *The Seasons*, 1726–1730), were giving voice to the new enthusiasm for nature while neo-classicism was at its height, and the movement grew with Gray and Collins and Cowper and others till a little later readers were quite ready to respond to the charming presentation of the beauties of the homelier aspects of nature as sung by Robert Burns.

With Wordsworth came the climax of the nature-cult in English poetry, nature now being recognized as closely akin to man, able to minister to his spiritual needs and to reveal God to him (see *Tintern Abbey* for a classic poetic statement of the progressive phases of Wordsworth's responses to nature). Coleridge, too, gave climactic expressions to the romantic enthusiasm for the wilder, disordered aspects of nature which the neo-classicists could not brook. Observe the sharp contrast between the following passages, the first from Pope, and the second from Coleridge:

> Here hills and vales, the woodland and its plain,
> Here earth and water seem to strive again;
> Not chaos-like together crushed and bruised,
> But, as the world, harmoniously confused:
> Where order in variety we see,
> And where, though all things differ, all agree.
> Here waving groves a chequered scene display,
> And part admit, and part exclude the day;

As some coy nymph her lover's warm address
Nor quite indulges, nor can quite repress.
(*Windsor Forest*)

But oh! that deep romantic chasm which slanted
Down the green hill athwart a cedarn cover!
A savage place! as holy and enchanted
As e'er beneath a waning moon was haunted
By woman wailing for her demon lover!
(*Kubla Khan*)

The poetry of the other great romantic poets, Shelley, Keats, and Byron, is shot through with intimate, subjective presentations of nature in all its forms, from the delicate and mysterious to the grotesque and awful. This attitude was not only reflected widely in American literature (Bryant, Lowell, Whittier, Emerson, Thoreau) but persisted in much of the verse of the great Victorians, notably Tennyson. Though the realistic and naturalistic movements of post-Victorian times have reacted against a sentimental use of nature, an idealized treatment of natural phenomena, as in Joyce Kilmer's *A Tree*, is still general among modern poets. See PRIMITIVISM, NEO-CLASSICISM, ROMANTICISM. (References: J. C. Shairp, *On Poetic Interpretation of Nature;* Myra Reynolds, *Nature in English Poetry;* Christopher Hussey, *The Picturesque.*)

**Neo-Classicism:** This term (as well as "pseudo-classicism") is applied to the classicism (*q.v.*) of the Restoration and eighteenth century, partly because the movement was a "revival" of classicism, partly because its ideas were drawn largely from contemporary French attitudes and from the Roman Horace rather than directly from the Greeks. Neo-classicism represents a reaction against the imaginative and emotional enthusiasm and the sometimes disordered technique of typically "Renaissance" writing. The new spirit may be suggested, though not completely reflected, by citing the alterations made in one passage in Shakespeare's *Macbeth* by the poet Nahum Tate when he undertook to recast the play for a Restoration audience. He thought it necessary to tone down the fine but bold Renaissance imagery and diction to accord with the prevailing "neo-classic" demand for order, logic, restrained emotion, accuracy—"correctness" and "good taste." Shakespeare had made Macbeth say

> Tomorrow, and tomorrow, and tomorrow,
> Creeps in this petty pace from day to day
> To the last syllable of recorded time,
> And all our yesterdays have lighted fools
> The way to dusty death. Out, out, brief candle!
> Life's but a walking shadow, . . .

In Tate's version "last syllable" became "last moment"; "the way to dusty death" became "to the eternal night"; "brief candle" became "short candle." These changes result in expressions that are logically consistent but that rob the original passage of its strong imaginative and emotional appeal.

Quotations from two twentieth-century students of eighteenth-century literature will help to suggest more adequately the nature of neo-classicism. Professor Bernbaum says:

The neo-classic spirit dominated the age of Pope. After the political and religious unrest of the seventeenth century, the majority longed for peace, moderation, and the reign of common sense. In poetry and prose, they were tired of the fantastical, the irregular, and the hazy. They demanded correctness, and adherence to literary rules which were clear and reasonable. They loved the polite and the witty. They were chiefly interested in the urban rather than the rustic, in maturity rather than in youth, in the civilized present rather than the ruder past, in an age of Stoical rationality like the Augustan Age of Rome, rather than in an age of faith, like the medieval. In persons, in historical epochs, and in literature and art, they valued the typically human more than the individually peculiar; and they assumed that they themselves were typical. Thus in all things they tended to confuse contemporaneous conventions with permanent laws. The proper study of mankind was Man,—a dualistic creature, capable of virtue and reason, but addicted to vice and folly, and therefore requiring for his salvation much discipline. It was well that the State disciplined him by force; the Church, through prohibitions and through the terrors of eternal punishment; and Literature, through satire. Such were the views of men in other respects as different as Pope, Swift, and Addison; and, they were the most admired and influential writers of the age.[1]

[1]Ernest Bernbaum, *Guide through the Romantic Movement*, Thomas Nelson and Sons, 1930, p. 19. Reprinted by permission of the publishers.

Discussing the importance of design as an element in the theory of poetic art in the eighteenth century Professor Bredvold remarks:

> The eighteenth-century poets and readers loved the beauty of design, the beauty of the artistic whole, more than the beauty of fragments and diction, because they believed that beauty of design called into play the highest faculties of the mind.  Such qualities as proportion, harmony, graceful disposition of parts to form a satisfying unity,—these appealed not to the sensual ear, but to the intelligence that loves divine order, truth, harmony—the intelligence that is disciplined to the desire for an organized world. . . . They [eighteenth-century gentlemen] desired the world well-regulated, they desired freedom, but with order, liberty, but with subordination; this comfortable, social, not un-idealistic world is reflected in the calm beauty, the gentle dignity, the polished workmanship of eighteenth-century poetry.[1]

A few of the concrete effects of neo-classic ideals upon literature may be mentioned.  Poetic diction and imagery tended to become conventional and colorless, since details were to be subordinated to design.  The appeal to the intellect rather than to the emotions resulted in a fondness for wit and the production of much satire, both in prose and verse.  The irregular or unpleasant aspects of external nature, such as mountains, ocean, winter, were less frequently utilized than the pleasanter phases as represented in stars, flowers, or a formal garden.  A tendency to realism marks the presentation of life.  Literature exalted form—polish, clarity, brilliance.  It avoided the obscure or the mysterious.  It valued the classical critical requirements of universality and decorum.  It "imitated" (see IMITATION) the classics and cultivated classical literary forms and types, such as satire and the ode.  The earlier English authors whose works were produced in a "less cultivated" age either were ignored or were admired more for their genius than for their art.  Didactic literature flourished.  Though blank verse and the Spenserian stanza were cultivated, rimed couplets were the favorite form of verse.

Neo-classicism became somewhat suddenly dominant with the

---

[1]Louis I. Bredvold, "Introduction," *Selected Poems of Alexander Pope*, F. S. Crofts & Company, 1926, pp. xviii, xxv.  Reprinted by permission of the publishers.

return of the Stuarts to the English throne (1660), partly because of the influence of French classicism, partly because of the reaction against Puritanism, and partly by reason of a development of the classical criticism inherited from Renaissance times (Sidney, Jonson). John Dryden is the great exemplar of neo-classicism in Restoration literature (criticism, satire, odes, use of heroic couplet, etc.). The early eighteenth century, however, the "Augustan Age," when Pope, Swift, and Addison were ruling spirits in literature, is the golden age of neo-classic English literature. Although many of the attitudes and mannerisms of the neo-classicists were swept aside by the great tide of Romanticism, the movement exerted a permanently wholesome effect upon literature in its clarifying and chastening effect upon English prose style and in its establishing in English literature the importance of certain classical graces, such as recognition of order and good form, unified structure, clearness, conciseness, and restraint. Poetic technique as developed by Pope, too, has become a permanent heritage, even such romanticists as Byron having learned at his feet. Indeed, imitations of Pope's verse have been innumerable in eighteenth- and nineteenth-century English and American literature. On the danger of over-stressing the differences between the "classic" or "neo-classic" spirit and the "romantic" see remarks under ROMANTICISM in this book and the lively protest of Sir Arthur Quiller-Couch in his *Studies in Literature.* See CLASSICISM, ROMANTICISM, NATURE, ANCIENTS AND MODERNS, and the "Outline of Literary History," pp. 500–526. (References: E. Gosse, *Eighteenth Century Literature;* Oliver Elton, *A Survey of English Literature, 1730–1780,* 2 vols.; Leslie Stephen, *English Literature and Society in the Eighteenth Century;* John Dennis, *The Age of Pope;* W. J. Courthope, *History of English Poetry,* Vol. V.)

**Neologism:** A word newly introduced into a language, especially as a means of enhancing literary style. There was much conscious use of neologisms, especially from Greek and Latin sources, in Renaissance times, partly as a result of a definite critical attitude toward the enrichment of the native English vocabulary. But the practice is not confined to any one period. Too often authors employ neologisms in a somewhat "cheap" effort to give their style an atmosphere of freshness or erudition (see PEDANTRY), but the variety and flexibility and resourcefulness of the modern English vocabulary are largely the cumulative result of the successful use of neologisms. A vast number of neologisms, of course, employed by individual authors or by stylistic "schools" (see EUPHUISM, GONGORISM) have not gained permanent foothold in the vocabulary. See COINED WORDS.

**Neo-Platonism:** See PLATONISM.

**New Comedy:** See COMEDY.

**New England Renaissance:** See UNITARIANISM.

**New Humanism, The:** See HUMANISM, THE NEW.

**New Poetry, The:** A term used at different times during the period of English literary history to denote one or another of the new poetic movements as they appeared on the horizon. The introduction of continental, especially Italian, forms by Wyatt and Surrey during the Renaissance, for instance, produced a body of verse, largely experimental, which has been termed "the new poetry." See "COURTLY MAKERS." A more recent use of the term is to suggest those changes and new mannerisms which developed soon after 1912 when poetry in America became more definitely a thing of the people, when conventional verse forms gave way to imagism (see IMAGISTS) and "free verse" (*q.v.*), when diction became more colloquial, and when "poetic subjects" gave way to an effort to find poetry in commonplace, everyday objects. This "new poetry" found, in the work of such a poet as Carl Sandburg, its inspiration in industrialism. The stockyards and steel mills, the highways and wharves, all were found to have a certain beauty of their own. It found, too, an appropriate subject in modern, hardworking democracy, a flowering of the seed sown in earlier days by Walt Whitman. The poetry of Vachel Lindsay, Edgar Lee Masters, and Max Eastman expressed a blatant, noisy America. Robert Frost discovered the old beauties of rural life and gave them a new significance in his colloquial, direct language. Distrust of old attitudes and old conventions resulted in a conviction that poetry must find a new source and a new language and a new style if it was to be fresh, vigorous, and genuine; if it was to be a faithful interpreter of a new American life. It was a day of *isms:* imagism, realism, impressionism, expressionism—these were but a few of the less extreme aspects of the new poetic fervor. After a decade or more of this experimentation the radicals had pretty well worn themselves out, but not before they had left their impress most definitely on modern poetry by bringing to it a new freedom of expression, of subject, and of form. At least four books should be consulted by the student of this movement: Amy Lowell's *Tendencies in Modern American Poetry*, Louis Untermeyer's *American Poetry Since 1900*, Bruce Weirick's *From Whitman to Sandburg in American Poetry*, and J. L. Lowes's *Convention and Revolt in Poetry*.

**Nine Worthies, The:** Late medieval and early Renaissance literature reflects the widespread tradition or classification of the heroes known as the "nine worthies." Caxton lists them in his preface to Malory's *Le Morte d'Arthur* in the conventional three groups: Hector, Alexander, Julius Caesar (pre-Christian pagans); Joshua, David, Judas Maccabeus (pre-Christian Jews); Arthur, Charlemagne, Godfrey of Boulogne (Christians). They are personated in the burlesque play incorporated in Shakespeare's *Love's Labour's Lost*.

**Nobel Prize:** A large sum of money awarded annually to the person having produced during the year the most eminent piece of work in the field of idealistic literature. This award, granted through the Swedish Academy in Stockholm, was made possible by Alfred Bernhard Nobel (1833–1896), a Swedish chemist and engineer. Nobel willed the income from practically his entire estate for the establishment of such annual prizes and the endowment of research foundations, not only in the field of literature but also in physics, chemistry, medicine or physiology, and for the promotion of world peace. The amount of each prize varies with the income from the main fund, but averages about $40,000. Nationality does not enter into consideration at all in the awarding of the prizes, which was begun on December 10, 1901, the fifth anniversary of Nobel's death. A further stipulation of Nobel's will empowers the Swedish Academy, which awards the prize for literature, to withhold the grant for any one year; if no work during that year is deemed worthy of the recognition, the amount of the prize reverts to the main fund. The winners of the prize in literature have been as follows: 1901, René François Armand Sully-Prudhomme; 1902, Theodore Mommsen; 1903, Björnstjerne Björnson; 1904, equally divided between Frédéric Mistral and José Echegaray; 1905, Henryk Sienkiewicz; 1906, Giosué Carducci; 1907, Rudyard Kipling; 1908, Rudolf Eucken; 1909, Selma Lagerlöf; 1910, Paul Heyse; 1911, Maurice Maeterlinck; 1912, Gerhart Hauptmann; 1913, Rabindranath Tagore; 1915, Romain Rolland; 1916, Verner von Heidenstam; 1917, divided equally between Karl Gjellerup and Henrik Pontoppidan; 1919, Carl Spitteler; 1920, Knut Hamsun; 1921, Anatole France; 1922, Jacinto Benavente; 1923, William Butler Yeats; 1924, Vladislav St. Reymont; 1925, George Bernard Shaw; 1926, Grazia Deledda; 1927, Henri Bergson; 1928, Sigrid Undset; 1929, Thomas Mann; 1930, Sinclair Lewis; 1931, Erik Axel Karlfeldt; 1932, John Galsworthy; 1933, Ivan Bunin; 1934, Luigi Pirandello. In 1914, 1918, and 1935 no award of the literature prize was made. (Reference: Annie Russell Marble, *The Nobel Prize Winners in Literature.* 1925.)

**Nocturne:** A poetic and often sentimental composition, expressing moods supposed to be especially appropriate to evening or night time. A serenade; a song.

**Noël:** A Christmas carol or song; a poem celebrating Christmas Day or the birth of Christ. An expression of rejoicing.

*Nom de plume* **(pen name):** A fictitious name adopted by a writer for professional use or to disguise his true identity. For example, Sidney Porter assumed the pen name "O. Henry"; and Madame Amantine Lucile Aurore Dudevant, almost unknown by her real name, was famous as the French novelist, George Sand.

**Nonsense Verse:** A variety of light verse entertaining because of its strong rhythmic quality and lack of logic or consecutive development of thought. In addition to the marked rhythm, nonsense verse is often characterized by the presence of coined nonsense words ("frabjous day") a mingling of words from various languages (macaronic verse), "tongue twisters," and a calling upon the printer for unbelievably freakish arrangement of type to portray Christmas trees, pipes, men falling downstairs—anything which occurs to the fancy of the versifier. Limericks are a popular nonsense verse form. Edward Lear and Lewis Carroll have built large reputations through writing nonsense verse. See *A Nonsense Anthology* by Carolyn Wells.

**Norman Conquest:** The conquest of England by the Normans following the victory of William I in 1066 at the Battle of Senlac (Hastings) exerted directly and indirectly a considerable influence upon English literature. Indirectly it affected literature through the introduction of a new element into the national make-up: to the more phlegmatic Saxon disposition was added the fire, energy, precision, and capacity for organization of the Norman. Likewise the Conquest was not without some effect upon the English language. The substitution of French for English as the speech of the governing class permitted English, used now by the commoners only, to develop rapidly toward the simpler grammar of modern English (see ENGLISH LANGUAGE). Later, as the knowledge of both English and French became general, the English vocabulary was enriched by the borrowing of French words. The fact that the literature-producing classes of court and church circles were permeated with Norman-French culture changed the whole tone of polite writing. The Norman churchmen were active in stimulating literary activity in monastic centers, with much copying and composing of chronicles, legends, sermons, and philosophical and scientific treatises. The spread of feudalism led to the importance of chivalry in literature, as in the romances. French minstrels became the media for spreading literature. New literary types and techniques were adopted from the French. For a time this new literature was written in French (see ANGLO-FRENCH) or Latin (see ANGLO-LATIN), but after 1200 English was used in an increasing degree (see MIDDLE ENGLISH).

**Novel, The:** More recent in its development than the other great literary type-forms, the English novel may be thought of as essentially an eighteenth-century product. This does not mean, however, that it came into full bloom with any one writer or any one book in any one year; literary types are not created in this way. Without the richness of literary activity which had preceded the eighteenth century, the novel could not have matured. The narrative interest developed in the stories of Charlemagne and Arthur, the various romantic cycles, the *fabliaux;* the descriptive values and appreciation of nature found in the pastorals; the historical interest of diaries and journals; the enthusiasm for character portrayal developed in sketches and biographies; the use of suspense in tales and medieval romances—all these had to be familiar and understood before writers could evolve the novel, a form which draws certain elements from many of the literary types which preceded it.

*The Roots of the English Novel.*—But the matter is hardly as simple as this situation may suggest. Classical literature of Greece and Italy had its forms of the modern novel. In the second century B.C., Aristides wrote a series of tales of his home town, Miletus, a collection which was called *Milesiaka* but which is not known to scholars today, though Edmund Gosse ventures to say that it "was probably the beginning of the modern novel." Six centuries later Heliodorus, a Syrian, wrote *Aethiopica*—a love story at least somewhat true to life. *Daphnis and Chloe* (Greek), attributed to Longus of the third century, can be, says the same critic, "strictly called a novel." In Latin there were various contributory works of which only two will be mentioned here, the *Golden Ass* of Apuleius, a translation from the Greek, and the *Satyricon* of Petronius which presented the life and customs of the time of Nero.

But it is to the *novella* of Italy that the modern novel is most indebted both for its narrative form and for its name. The appearance of *Cento Novelle Antiche* just before the opening of the fourteenth century gave great vogue to the *novella* form. These *novelle* were stories of scandalous love, of chivalry, of mythology and morals, of the type best known to modern English readers, perhaps, through the gay stories of Boccaccio's *Decameron* (*ca.* 1348). Loose women, unscrupulous priests, rough peasants, and high-born nobles, formed the central figures of most of these tales. A few of the more famed collections of *novelle* are: Sacchetti's *Trecente Novelle*, Fiorentino's *Il Pecorone*, Masuccio's *Novellino*, and Bandello's *Novelle*.

From Spain came at least two works which influenced the development of the novel: the *Lazarillo de Tormes* (see PICARESQUE NOVEL) of 1554, and Cervantes' *Don Quixote* of 1605.

France, like Italy, was greatly given to the short tale, the *novella* form. About 1450 was written the *Quinze Joies du Mariage* (anonymous) in the manner of the Italian. Antoine de la Sale's *Cent Nouvelles Nouvelles* and Bonaventure Despériers' *Nouvelles Récréations* carried on this interest. In 1535 appeared the *Gargantua* of Rabelais, which, while not at all a novel, nevertheless has certain sustained narrative interest which warrants its inclusion in this summary. Honoré d'Urfé's *Astrée* (1610) has more definitely the qualities we demand in a novel to-day and by the middle of the seventeenth century Mlle. de Scudéry (1607–1701) was writing romantic novels which might pass muster—if interests had not changed so much—even in the twentieth century. A revolt from the romantic qualities of Scudéry called forth a realistic reaction from Scarron, who wrote *Roman Comique*. However, the author of the summary in the *Encyclopædia Britannica* reserves for Marguerite de la Vergne the honor of having created the first full-blown French novels in her *Princesse de Montpensier* and *Princesse de Clèves* written during the 1660's. "Mme. de La Fayette (de la Vergne) was," says Gosse, "the first writer of prose narrative in Europe who portrayed, as closely to nature as she could, the actual manner and conversations of well-bred people." Other French novels which were important in the development of the form, and which appeared before the English novel had fully come into its own, were: La Fontaine's *Psyché* (1669), Fénelon's *Télémaque* (1699), Le Sage's *Gil Blas* (1715, Books I–III), Marivaux's *Marianne* (1731), and Prévost's *Manon Lescaut* (1731).

English writers of the eighteenth century, then, had as a background the whole experience of continental Europe. The classical literature of Greece and Rome, the cycles of romance, pastoral literature, the picaresque tale of adventure, the interest in human character portrayed through the ana (*q.v.*)—all these elements and others held in solution the material which was eventually to crystallize into the English novel. In addition to these beginnings from Europe, the English novelists had native parallels of their own—the Arthurian materials, the *Euphues* of

Lyly (1579), the *Arcadia* of Sir Philip Sidney, the narrative interest in Lodge's *Rosalynde* (1590), the picaresque element in Nash's *Jack Wilton* (1594), the humanitarian sympathy for the slave and the narrative chronicle of Aphra Behn's *Oroonoko* (1688), the extended narrative of moral significance in John Bunyan's *Pilgrim's Progress* (1678–1684), and the character element present in the *Spectator* papers of Addison and Steele. Defoe, in *Robinson Crusoe* (1719) and *Moll Flanders* (1722), and Swift, in *Gulliver's Travels* (1726), had brought verisimilitude to adventure and to the chronicling of human life, two vital component parts of the later novel form.

*The Novel Matures.*—With these narrative qualities then already rooted in various types of English and European writing, with the actual novel flourishing in France, the ground was fertile, tilled, and seeded when Samuel Richardson, in 1740, issued his *Pamela: or Virtue Rewarded*, the single book generally conceded to be the first flowering of the novel in English literature. Richardson, a successful London printer, was seized with the idea of inculcating morality through the form of fiction. He wrote his three important novels, *Pamela* (1740), *Clarissa Harlowe* (1747–48), and *Sir Charles Grandison* (1753), chiefly in the epistolary form and with one eye full upon the ethics of the time. "The first great imaginative success of the novelist," says Wilbur Cross, "was Defoe's, who made fictitious adventure seem real; the second was Richardson's, who made equally real his men and women, and the scenes in which he placed them."

After Richardson's success with *Pamela*, followed rapidly other significant novels: Henry Fielding started his *Joseph Andrews* (1742) as a satire on the niceness of *Pamela*, but before going far he forgot his ironical intent and told a vigorous story of his own. In 1748 Smollett published *Roderick Random;* in 1749 came Fielding's greatest novel, *Tom Jones*, important for its development of plot and its realistic interpretation of English life; in 1751 both Smollett and Fielding repeated, the first with *Peregrine Pickle* and the second with *Amelia*. Defoe, Richardson, Fielding, Smollett—these men stand at the very source of the English novel. The succeeding years brought other novels and novelists, but the first real impetus to long fiction was given by these four. Sterne soon wrote *Tristram Shandy* (1760–67) and *A Sentimental Journey* (1768), neither of which perhaps can properly be called a novel, and Horace Walpole made much of the Gothic mysteries in his *Castle of Otranto* (1764). Two years later, 1766, Oliver Goldsmith wrote his idyllic story of English life, the *Vicar of Wakefield*. And then, some years later, came such important novels as Ann Radcliffe's *Mysteries of Udolpho* (1794), Jane Austen's *Sense and Sensibility* (1811), Sir Walter Scott's *Waverley* (1814), Charles Dickens' *Pickwick Papers* (1836), Charlotte Brontë's *Jane Eyre* (1847), Thackeray's *Vanity Fair* (1846), and George Eliot's *Adam Bede* (1859). While the novel underwent minor changes, and some great ones, after George Eliot, it is true that the mold was generally well set by the middle of the nineteenth century.

*The Novel in America.*—Not for fifty years after Richardson published *Pamela* were novels written in America. The colonies were too preoccupied with two responsibilities—settling a new land and practising Calvinism—to turn their attention to such frivolous matters as fiction. Indeed, for many years after this, and well into the second half of the nineteenth century, many Americans looked with disfavor upon novel reading as, at best, a waste of time and, at worst, immoral. However, before the close of the eighteenth century novels were being written in America. Sarah Wentworth Morton's *The Power of Sympathy* (1789) must stand alone here as an early example. With Charles Brockden Brown, however, America has almost her first professional literary man and certainly her first important novelist. Brown, who wrote largely in the Gothic manner, was the author of four readable tales: *Arthur Mervyn* (1799), *Ormond* (1799), *Wieland* (1798), and *Edgar Huntley* (1799), as well as others less well known. Some twenty years later James Fenimore Cooper was publishing *The Spy* (1821), *The Pioneers* (1823), *The Pilot* (1824). (With Cooper the American background assumed its first great importance in long fiction.) The Leatherstocking Series included, in addition to *The Pioneers*, already mentioned, *The Deerslayer* (1841), *The Last of the Mohicans* (1826), *The Pathfinder* (1840), and *The Prairie* (1827). By 1850, when Hawthorne's *Scarlet Letter* appeared, the American novel had come into its full powers. And, though it was many years before America became a novel-reading and novel-writing country, the American novel was, at least, launched.

*What Is a Novel?*—Enough has been said, in summarizing the development of the novel, to show that it is a growth from various roots, that it has flourished with different results in different soils, that with time it has given forth new shoots, taken on new colors, and served different purposes. In fact, since its earliest beginning, it has at no time been static. It is as though having struggled for hundreds of years to get itself born into the light of day, it were not content with its development and had persisted in further changes. But the truth of the matter is, the novel is so vigorous a literary form, so capable a vehicle of thought and art, that different writers have adapted it to their differing purposes.

Little need here be said as to the structure of the novel. Two qualities have usually been considered essential—plot and character presentation—though in late years even plot has almost been discarded by many of our acknowledged novelists. The major interest today is certainly character. But if plot be interpreted as a conflict which results in a change of fortune, then even in the extreme novel of character plot may be found to exist since, except in the most naturalistic writing, the central character of the modern novel undergoes some change or reversal in circumstance.

The novel differs from the short story chiefly in scope. Since the novelist paints on a wider canvas, he is not compelled to compress as is the teller of tales. He may include forty or fifty characters (as did Dickens or Thackeray) wheras the short story-writer must confine himself to three or four; he may interweave major plot with three or four or five minor conflicts, whereas the story-teller does well to handle one line of interest subordinate to his major plot; he is not so limited by the matter of unities, since time and place may be much more freely expanded in the greater space at his command. (See SHORT STORY.)

Two qualities of the novel, other than plot and characterization, must be cited. The novel is a form of fiction and as such it is *imaginative*. No matter how realistic the manner, how historical the material, the imaginative conceptions of the author are always woven, as woof on warp, on the background of truth to nature and truth to history and truth to life. Again, the novel is based on *human experience*. Even the romantic and idealized escapades of a Stevenson character are somehow interpretive of the natural yearnings of the human being for adventure and, as such, they are based on human experience.

The novel, then, aside from a few usual qualities such as plot, characterization, imagination, and portrayal of life, is too many-sided a form, too luxurious a growth to be fixed in this sketch, or, indeed, in any formula. We are on safer ground when we analyze the novel from other points of view.

*Novels Classified According to Purpose.*—First of all may be considered the *purpose* with which novels are written. From the subjective point of view there are possibly as many purposes prompting the writing of novels as there are authors, but it is possible to argue that objectively practically all novels issue from one of three intents: *to entertain, to present a problem or a thesis, to present an historical background.*

The first purpose—that of entertaining—is by far the most common. This type embraces all stories of adventure—such as Stevenson's *Kidnapped* or Dumas' *Three Musketeers*, such picaresque stories as Le Sage's *Gil Blas* and Thomas Nash's *Jack Wilton*, such detective stories as Conan Doyle's tales of Sherlock Holmes, such stories of mystery and the supernatural as Mary Wollstonecraft Shelley's *Frankenstein* and Horace Walpole's *The Castle of Otranto*. The second purpose, that of presenting a problem or a thesis, includes many novels of many interests: the story which is a study in character, the sociological novel, and novels of religion, ethics, and psychology. Examples of each of these may be cited by the score. For our purpose here one alone must serve for each interest: for the novel of character, Meredith's *The Ordeal of Richard Feverel;* for the sociological novel, Harriet Beecher Stowe's *Uncle Tom's Cabin;* for the novel of religious problem, Mrs. Humphrey Ward's *Robert Elsmere;* for the novel of ethical significance, George Eliot's *Silas Marner;* and for the novel of psychological interest, Conrad's *Lord Jim.* Rarely, if ever, does an author limit himself to any one of these interests; when a novel is cited as "psychological," for instance, it simply means that this element is important and uppermost, but great novels appeal because of the portrayal of the human

286

experience they present, and human experience is a strangely confused conflict of various interests, attitudes, and emotions. The third purpose, that of presenting an historical background, includes that large section of fiction which is generally called the "historical novel" (*q.v.*). Lew Wallace's *Ben Hur* will well serve as an illustration.

*Classification according to Manner.*—Novels are, from another point of view, classified according to their *manner*. The style and attitude toward life adopted by the author determine this classification. On this basis novels are spoken of as romantic, realistic, impressionistic, naturalistic, etc. As each of these manners is discussed under these heads in this Handbook, it remains for us here only to illustrate each type by one characteristic example. For the romantic novel, Kingsley's *Westward Ho!*; for the realistic, Hardy's *Return of the Native;* for the impressionistic, Crane's *Red Badge of Courage;* and for the naturalistic, Dreiser's *An American Tragedy.*

See also Gothic Romance, Historical Novel, Novel of Incident, Novel of the Soil, Picaresque Novel, Problem Novel, Psychological Novel, Romantic Novel, Sentimental Novel, Sociological Novel, Stream-of-Consciousness Novel, Mystery Story, Fiction. (References: E. A. Baker, *History of the English Novel*, 4 vols.; R. M. Lovett and H. S. Hughes, *History of the Novel in England;* Edwin Muir, *The Structure of the Novel;* Edmund Gosse and P. H. Boynton, article on "Novel" in *Encyc. Brit.*, 14th ed., Vol. XVI, for summaries and critical estimates.)

**Novel of Character:** See Novel.

**Novel of Incident:** A critical term applied to novels in which action and more or less unrelated episodes dominate, and plot is subordinate. In this type of novel the plot structure is loose and easy; emphasis is on interest and thrilling incident rather than on characterization or sustained suspense. If one may call Defoe's *Robinson Crusoe* a novel, then it may be used to illustrate this novel of incident type. Here the episodes of the shipwreck, the meeting with Friday, the clash with visiting natives—these and other incidents follow each other chronologically but they are more or less independent of each other and each does not contribute to the suspense with which the next is read. Dumas' *Three Musketeers* is also a novel of incident, though here the plot is more developed than in Defoe's story.

**Novel of Sensibility:** See SENTIMENTAL NOVEL.

**Novel of the Soil, The:** A phase of realistic writing presenting the life of a group of characters living in some remote rural section and struggling against their environment. The novel of the soil has been particularly vigorous in American literature of the last two or three decades. It is closely related to the "sociological novel" (*q.v.*). An early forerunner, though hardly a real novel of the soil, was E. W. Howe's *Story of a Country Town* (1883). Some authentic examples are Ellen Glasgow's *Barren Ground*, Edna Ferber's *So Big*, O. E. Rölvaag's *Giants in the Earth*, and Elizabeth Madox Roberts' *Time of Man*. Miss Glasgow shows her chief character, a young woman, struggling against the backwardness of a Virginia farm; Edna Ferber presents the domestic tragedy of the second generation in a line of sturdy farming forbears; O. E. Rölvaag shows the bitter reality of early settlers in the Dakotas fighting against storm and drought and hunger; Miss Roberts illustrates the life of the tenant farmer on a squalid and barren Kentucky hillside. In these realistic novels the plot conflict is usually ready made—the individual against his environment, against a fate which speaks through hardship and struggle characteristic of the region presented. But this is not to say that the novel is without artistry or purpose; there is still plenty of opportunity for craftsmanship and genius and thought. Miss Roberts, for instance, writes of her Kentucky tenants with a deep feeling for the poetry of life; Miss Glasgow subtly inculcates an economic doctrine for her South to follow; Rölvaag presents the essentially heroic aspects of pioneer manhood. In England, Thomas Hardy has done most with this type of fiction.

**Novelette:** A short novel. Short stories usually contain six, eight, or ten thousand words, novelettes perhaps thirty or forty thousand, and the novel from thirty or forty thousand to two or three hundred thousand.

*Novella:* A tale or short story. The term is particularly applied to the early tales of Italian and French writers—such as the *Decameron* of Boccaccio and the *Heptameron* of Marguerite of Valois. The form is of especial interest to students of English literature for two reasons: (1) many of these early *novelle* were used by English writers as sources for their own work, and (2) it was from this form that the later *novel* developed.

*Obiter dicta:* Things said "by the way"; incidental remarks: opposed to statements based upon calculated, deliberate judgment. Though legal in origin, the term is sometimes used in literary association, as in speaking of one author's *obiter dicta* being weightier and wiser than another's serious, labored expressions. Augustine Birrell published two series of informal essays, largely comment on literary topics, under the title *Obiter Dicta.*

**Objective Element in Literature:** See SUBJECTIVE ELEMENT.

**Occasional Verse:** Poetry written to grace or commemorate a social or historical event. The term includes *vers de société* (*q.v.*) but is more comprehensive than "society verse" since it also includes writing of more serious and more dignified purpose. Lowell's Harvard Commemoration Ode is, in that it was written for a particular event, occasional verse, though by no stretch of the imagination could it be called *vers de société.* Wordsworth wrote much occasional verse; e.g., *On My First View of the Matterhorn.*

**Octameter:** A line of verse consisting of eight feet. See SCANSION.

**Octave:** An eight-line stanza. The chief use of the term, however, is to denote the first eight-verse division of the Italian sonnet as separate from the last six-verse division, the sestet. In the strict sonnet usage the octave rimes *abbaabba*, serves to state a generalization later applied or resolved in the sestet, and comes to such a complete close at the end of the eighth line as to be marked by a full stop.

**Ode:** "Any strain of enthusiastic and exalted lyrical verse, directed to a fixed purpose, and dealing progressively with one dignified theme." (Gosse.) The term connotes certain qualities both of manner and form. In manner, the ode is an elaborate lyric, expressed in language dignified and sincere and definitely imaginative and intellectual in tone. In form the ode is much more complicated than most of the lyric types. Perhaps the essential distinction of form is the division into strophes: the strophe, antistrophe, and epode. Originally a Greek form used in dramatic poetry, the ode was then choral in quality. Accompanied by music, the chorus of singers moved up one side during the strophe, down the other during the antistrophe, and stood in place during the epode. In a general way this movement emphasized the rise and fall of emotional power. Alden (*Introduction to Poetry*) recognizes three types of odes: the Pindaric (regular), the homostrophic, and the irregular type. The Pindaric ode is characterized by the three-strophe division, the strophe and the antistrophe alike in form, the epode different from the other two. The metrics and verse lengths may vary within any one strophe of the ode, but when the movement is repeated the metrical scheme for corresponding divisions should be similar though accompanied by new rimes. It is not essential that strophe, antistrophe, and epode alternate regularly since the epode may be used at the end or inconsistently between the strophe and the antistrophe (*Ode to Liberty*, Collins). The second ode-form, the homostrophic, consists of only one stanza type, and that type may be almost infinitely varied within its pattern (*Ode to France*, Coleridge). The third form of the ode, the irregular, is credited to the poet Cowley, who seems to have thought he was writing Pindaric odes. Like the second type considered, freedom within the strophe is the characteristic earmark of this form. But here the strophes are rules unto themselves and all pretense at stanza pattern may be discarded. The length of the lines may vary, the number of lines in each strophe may vary widely, the rime pattern need not be carried over from stanza to stanza, and the metrical movement will quicken and slacken with the mood of the poet and the emotional intensity. Much more flexible than the two other forms considered, the irregular ode affords greatest freedom of expression to the poet and, consequently, greatest license (*Intimations of Immortality*, Wordsworth). For an authentic brief account of the ode see article by E. Gosse in the *Encyclopædia Britannica*. For a more specialized study see Robert Shafer's *The English Ode to 1660*.

**Old Comedy:** See COMEDY.

**Old English:** The earliest phase of the English language (*ca.* 450–1066). In the earlier part of the period (before the influence of Christianity) were composed many English poems reflecting the life of the pagan Germanic tribes both on the Continent and in Britain. Some of the best known which have survived are the great epic *Beowulf* (*ca.*700) and such fine lyrics as *The Seafarer*, *Widsith*, and *Deor's Lament*. Early Christian literature included Caedmon's *Song*, Biblical paraphrases such as Genesis, Exodus, Daniel, Judith, religious narratives such as the *Crist*, *Elene*, *Andreas*, and the allegorical *Phoenix* (a translation from Latin). Literature first flourished in Northumbria, but in the reign of Alfred the Great (871–901) West Saxon became the literary dialect. Under Alfred, much Latin literature was translated into English prose, such as Pope Gregory's *Pastoral Care*, Boëthius' *Consolation of Philosophy*, and Bede's *Ecclesiastical History;* and the great *Anglo-Saxon Chronicle* was revised and expanded. A second prose revival took place under Aelfric and Wulfstan (tenth and eleventh centuries). Late examples of Anglo-Saxon verse are the *Battle of Maldon* and the *Battle of Brunanburh*, heroic poems. The Norman Conquest (1066) put an end to serious literary work in the English language for over a century. See ANGLO-SAXON, ENGLISH LANGUAGE. (References: Henry Morley, *English Writers*, Vols. I–II; S. A. Brooke, *English Literature from the Beginning to the Norman Conquest;* P. G. Thomas, *English Literature before Chaucer;* J. J. Jusserand, *A Literary History of the English People*, Vol. I; W. P. Ker, *English Medieval Literature; Camb. Hist. Eng. Lit.*, Vol. I; Cook and Tinker, *Translations from Old English Prose* and *Translations from Old English Poetry;* E. E. Wardale, *Chapters in Old English Literature*.)

**One-Act Play:** A form of drama which has been attracting an increasing amount of attention since about 1890. Before that date one-act plays had been used chiefly on vaudeville programs and as curtain-raisers on the "legitimate" stage. About that time especial attention to the one-act play came with the "Little Theatre Movement" (*q.v.*) and the practice of relying upon a group of such short plays for a single evening's entertainment. The fact that the form was adopted by playwrights of high ability (J. M. Barrie, A. W. Pinero, Gerhart Hauptmann, G. B. Shaw) furthered its development. A widening circle of authors has produced one-act plays in the twentieth century, both in England and America, including John Masefield, Lord Dunsany, John Galsworthy, A. A. Milne, Percy MacKaye, Booth Tarkington, Eugene O'Neill, Paul Green, and a host of less well-known writers for American "little theatres." America has played and is playing a leading part in the development of the form. The technique of the one-act play is highly flexible, the most important demand being for unity of effect, with consequent vigor of dialogue, stressing of character, and economy of narrative materials. Its relation to the "regular" or longer drama has often been likened to that of the short story to the novel. (References: Percival Wilde, *The Craftsmanship of the One-Act Play;* Helen Louise Cohen, *One-Act Plays by Modern Authors.*)

**Onomatopoeia:** The use of words which in their pronunciation suggest their meaning. Some onomatopoeic words are "hiss," "slam," "buzz," "whirr," "sizzle." However, onomatopoeia in the hands of a poet becomes a much more subtle device than simply the use of such words when, in an effort to suit sound to sense, he creates verses which themselves carry their meaning in their sounds. A notable example is quoted from *The Princess* by Tennyson:

> The moan of doves in immemorial elms,
> And murmuring of innumerable bees.

**Opera:** Though the primary interest in opera is musical, the fact that it is a dramatic form which has exerted a considerable influence upon English stage history and has employed important literary themes gives it an interest to the student of literature. Only its connection with English drama will be noticed here. Opera is musical drama in the sense that the dialogue instead of being spoken is sung, to the accompaniment of instrumental music, now always an orchestra. A play in which incidental music is stressed may be called "operatic," but is not true opera if the dialogue is spoken. Greek drama contained dialogue sung to the accompaniment of the lyre or flute and is therefore a precursor, in fact somewhat of a model, for modern opera, which developed in Italy about 1600 as a result of amateur efforts to recapture the quality of the musical effects of Greek tragedy by means of musical recitation instrumentally accompanied. The form was at first a monody, as in Jacopo Peri's *Euridice* (1600), the first public production in the new style. From these beginnings developed the important form now known as grand opera. Italian opera reached England soon after 1700, but before this date certain definite advances in the direction of opera had taken place on the English stage. To some degree an outgrowth of the Renaissance masque (*q.v.*), Sir William Davenant's *Siege of Rhodes* (1656) is a precursor of the English opera, since it was "a musical entertainment . . . written in rime and designed on the lines of Italian opera to be sung in recitative and aria" (Allardyce Nicoll). The attention to scenery as well as the songs and orchestral accompaniment were suggestive of later English opera. During the Restoration period operatic versions of some of Shakespeare's plays (*The Tempest, Macbeth*) were called "dramatic operas," but the dialogue was spoken, not sung. About 1689 Henry Purcell and Nahum Tate brought out *Dido and Aeneas*, in which the dialogue was in recitative. Early in the eighteenth century Italian operas were "translated" and sung by English singers, as *Arsinoë, Queen of Cypress* (Drury Lane, 1705), and *Camilla* (1705–1707). Later "bilingual" operas appeared, in which Italian singers sang part of the dialogue in Italian while English singers sang the rest in English. The first completely Italian opera sung in Italian was *Almahide* (1710), which established the success of the form in England. About this time George Frederick Handel came to England. He produced *Rinaldo* in 1711, and exerted a powerful influence for many years thereafter. From the first the efforts to employ Italian singers and opera met with much disfavor, as evidenced by Addison's satire and by the famous burlesque opera by John Gay, *The Beggar's Opera* (1728). The success of opera and various forms of burlesque opera at this time probably had much to do with the decay of "legitimate" drama and the growth of the tendency toward lyrical and spectacular elements on the English stage in the eighteenth and nineteenth centuries. See BALLAD-OPERA. (Reference: Grove, *Dictionary of Music and Musicians*.)

**Opéra bouffe:** A French term for a very light form of "comic opera" (*q.v.*) developed from vaudeville music and said to be the ancestor of the comic operas of Gilbert and Sullivan.

**Operetta:** See COMIC OPERA.

**Oration:** A formal speech intended to inspire to some action. Carefully prepared and delivered in an impassioned manner, the oration carries its greatest power in the emotional appeal it makes. Although a major cultural interest in classical days and even up to a few decades ago, the oration has lost its popular appeal and is now but rarely heard in legislative halls, the court room, the church.

**Ossianic Controversy:** See LITERARY FORGERIES.

**Otiose:** A term used in literary criticism to characterize a style which is verbose, redundant, pleonastic. Literally it implies *leisure* and, in the special sense here employed, it designates idle, useless, inefficient writing, the use of language which is so very much at leisure that it performs no useful function.

**Ottava rima:** A stanza pattern consisting of eight iambic pentameter lines riming *abababcc*. Boccaccio is credited with originating this pattern, which was much used by Tasso and Ariosto. Some of the English poets making important use of *ottava rima* are Spenser, Milton, Keats, and Byron. The illustration is from *Don Juan*:

> But words are things, and a small drop of ink
>   Falling like dew, upon a thought, produces
> That which makes thousands, perhaps millions, think;
>   'Tis strange, the shortest letter which man uses
> Instead of speech, may form a lasting link
>   Of ages; to what straits old Time reduces
> Frail man, when paper—even a rag like this,
> Survives himself, his tomb, and all that's his!

294

**Oxford Movement:** Also known as "Tractarian Movement" and "Anglo-Catholic Revival." During the first third of the nineteenth century the English Church had become somewhat lax in urging the ancient doctrines, in enforcing discipline, in carrying out ritual, and in keeping up the church edifices. In 1833 a movement for reform got under way at Oxford following a sermon on "national apostasy" by John Keble. The leader was John Henry (later Cardinal) Newman, who wrote the first of the ninety papers (*Tracts for the Times*, 1833–1841) in which the ideas of the group were advocated. Other leaders were R. H. Froude, Isaac Williams, Hugh James Rose (a Cambridge man), and E. B. Pusey. The reformers aimed primarily at combating liberalism and skepticism and restoring to the Church and to church worship the dignity, beauty, purity, and zeal of earlier times. They hoped also to protect the Church from the encroachment of the State, as threatened by the Whig Reform Bill of 1832 and other measures looking toward reducing the revenues of the Church and curbing its authority.

To provide a solid foundation for their reforms, the sponsors of the movement undertook to prove the divine origin of the Church and the historical continuity connecting the early church with the Church of England. This led them to an espousal of certain doctrines regarded by some as purely Roman Catholic, and after the publication of Newman's final tract in 1841 a storm of criticism arose, as a result of which Newman lost his position at Oxford, became a layman, and finally (1845) joined the Roman Catholic Church, later becoming a Cardinal. When Charles Kingsley attacked his sincerity, Newman replied with the famous *Apologia pro Vita Sua* (1864), a full statement of his spiritual and mental history, the candor and beauty and force of which won for Newman the high regard which his personality and literary art have enabled him to retain ever since. Indeed, Newman is regarded as one of the masters of English prose style, as exhibited especially in his lectures on university education. He is likewise the author of one of the best loved hymns, "Lead, Kindly Light," written while on his way to England from Italy in 1833 and while he was brooding over his "mission" in connection with the needed reforms. Though some of Newman's followers also became Catholics, the main movement, led now by Pusey, continued, though in its later stages it became less controversial and theoretical and more practical, furthering the establishment of guilds, improvement of church music, revival of the ritual, building and beautifying of church buildings. Besides stimulating the work of one of the finest of English prose writers, the movement attracted the attention of various literary men, Carlyle heaping disdain upon it, Arnold attacking it, etc. Also the sponsors of the movement wrote a number of propagandist novels, like Newman's *Loss and Gain* and Charlotte M. Yonge's *The Heir of Redclyffe*. The Episcopal Church in the United States reflects much of the reform doctrine of the Tractarians. (References: R. W. Church, *The Oxford Movement;* Newman, *Apologia pro Vita Sua.*)

**Oxford Reformers:** A term applied to a group of humanist scholars whose associations began at Oxford University in early Renaissance times, particularly the three close friends John Colet, Sir Thomas More, and the great Dutch scholar Erasmus. Though Erasmus, who had come to Oxford to study Greek and who spent part of his life in England, was the most famous member of the group and More the best loved, Colet seems to have been the real leader. The group was zealously interested in effecting certain reforms in Church and State based upon current humanist ideas. Moral training and moral reform were to be accomplished through rational rather than emotional processes. Reason should dominate. Humanity should be uplifted through education and the consequent improvement of individual character. The church should be reformed from within by purging it of corrupt practices and by improving the standards, moral and educational, of the clergy. The group advocated the historical method in the study of the Bible, opposed medieval scholasticism and asceticism, and strongly advocated education as a means of improving religion, private character, and political institutions. Their activities can be merely hinted at here. More recorded his dream of a perfect human society and government in his immortal *Utopia* (1516); Colet when dean of St. Paul's founded with his own funds the famous St. Paul's school for boys, where new methods of instruction were developed and where sons of the common folk might be admitted; Erasmus outlined his ideals of state in his *Institutes of a Perfect Prince*. Keenly interested in purging the church of the evils which Luther a few years later rebelled against, the Oxford Reformers were unwilling to follow either Luther or Henry VIII in breaking with Rome, and died good Catholics, though disappointed idealists. (Reference: Frederic Seebohm: *The Oxford Reformers*.)

**Oxymoron:** Etymologically, "pointedly foolish"; a rhetorical antithesis bringing together two contradictory terms. Such a contrast makes for sharp emphasis. Examples are: "cheerful pessimist," "wise fool," "sad joy."

**Pæan:** A song of praise or joy. Originally the term was restricted to odes sung by a Greek chorus in honor of Apollo; later the term was broadened to include praise sung to other deities of antiquity. In modern times, the word has come to mean simply any song of joy. Homer indicates, too, that pæans were frequently sung on military occasions: before an attack, after a victory, when a fleet set sail, etc.

**Pageant:** Used in three senses: (1) a scaffold or stage on which dramas were performed in the Middle Ages; (2) plays performed on such stages; (3) modern dramatic spectacles designed to celebrate some historical event, often of local interest. The medieval pageant, constructed on wheels for processional use, as in celebrating Corpus Christi day, was designed for the use of a particular guild for the production of a particular play and usually reflected this special purpose. Thus the pageant of the fishermen, designed to present the play of Noah, would be constructed and painted to represent the Ark. For a contemporary description of the medieval pageant and its use, see p. 264. Though the modern pageant is an outgrowth of a very ancient tradition which includes primitive religious festivals, Roman "triumphs," etc., its recent remarkable development in England and especially in America makes it essentially a twentieth-century spectacle. It is usually understood to mean an outdoor exhibition consisting of several scenes presented with recitation (prologues, etc.), usually with dialogue, with historically appropriate costumes, sometimes with musical features, the whole being designed to commemorate some event which appeals to the emotional loyalties of the populace. Sometimes the pageant is processional, with a series of "floats," uniformed marchers, mounted officials, etc., while it is sometimes presented in an outdoor theatre of some sort, such as an athletic stadium. The true pageant is thought of as an outdoor exhibition, closely connected with the folk-drama movement. (References: Esther Willard Bates, *Pageants and Pageantry;* Robert Withington, *English Pageantry: An Historical Outline,* 2 vols.)

**Palimpsest:** A writing surface, whether of vellum, papyrus, or other material, which has been used twice or more for manuscript purposes. Before the invention of paper, the scarcity of writing material made such substances very valuable and the vellum surfaces were often scraped or rubbed or the papyrus surfaces washed. With material so used a second time it frequently happened that the earlier script either was not completely erased or that, with age, it showed through the new. In this way many documents of very early periods have been preserved for posterity. In one instance, for example, a Syriac text of St. Chrysostom of perhaps the tenth century was found to be superimposed on a sixth-century grammatical work in Latin, which again had covered some fifth-century Latin records.

**Palindrome:** See ANAGRAM.

**Palinode:** A piece of writing recanting or retracting a previous writing, particularly such a recanting in verse form of an earlier ode.

**Panegyric:** A formal written or oral composition lauding a person. In Roman literature panegyrics were usually presented in praise of a living person though in Greek literature they were more likely to be reserved for praise of the dead. This was a popular form of oratory among fulsome speakers who resorted to this sort of composition in praise of living emperors. Two famous panegyrics are those of Gorgias, the *Olympiacus*, and of Pliny the Younger delivered when he became consul, a speech praising Trajan. The term is now often used with a derogatory connotation.

**Pantheism:** A philosophic-religious attitude which finds the spirit of God manifest in all things and which holds that whereas all things speak the glory of God it is equally true that the glory of God is made up of all things. Finite objects are at once both God and the manifestation of God. Pantheism is an intuitive, transcendental conviction in the unity of all (the "Over-soul" of Emerson). The term is impossible of exact, formal definition since it is so personal a conviction as to be differently interpreted by different philosophers and religionists, but for its literary significance it is clearly enough described as an ardent faith in Nature as the revelation of deity. The word was first used in 1705 by the deist John Toland who called himself a pantheist, (from *pan* meaning "all" and *theos* meaning "deity"). The pantheistic attitude, however, is much older than the eighteenth century, since it pervades the primitive thought of Egypt and India, was common in Greece long before the time of Christ, was taken up by the Neo-platonists of the Middle Ages, and has played an important part in Christian and Hebraic doctrine. Spinoza is, from the philosophic point of view, the great spokesman of pantheism, as Goethe is, perhaps, the great poet of the idea. In literature pantheism finds frequent and almost constant expression. Wordsworth in England, Emerson in America, may be selected from many as giving typical expression to the pantheistic conception. The following, from Wordsworth's *Lines Composed a Few Miles above Tintern Abbey* is, perhaps, as classic an expression of the idea as is found in modern literature:

> A sense sublime
> Of something far more deeply interfused,
> Whose dwelling is the light of setting suns,
> And the round ocean and the living air
> And the blue sky, and in the mind of man,—
> A motion and a spirit, that impels
> All thinking things, all objects of all thoughts,
> And rolls through all things.

**Pantomime:** In its broad sense the term means silent acting; the form of dramatic activity in which silent motion, gesture, facial expression, and costume are relied upon to express emotional or narrative situations. The war dances of primitive society are thus pantomimic. Partly pantomimic was the Roman "mime" (*q.v.*) and completely so the English "dumb show" (*q.v.*). In English stage history, "pantomime" usually means the spectacular dramatic form which flourished from the early years of the eighteenth century. Though "pantomime proper" (no speaking) is said to have been introduced by a dancing master in 1702 at the Drury Lane Theatre, the usual form of pantomime, as sponsored at Lincoln's Inn Fields theatre by John Rich some years later, was somewhat more varied: "In the first place, there was usually a serious legendary story told by means of dancing and songs—in fact, a short opera. . . . In these plots moved the figures of the *commedia dell' arte*, burlesquing in silent movement the action of the more serious tale. All of this was laid upon a background of the most spectacular description, with the lavish use of 'machinery' and countless changes of scene to please the ravished spectators."[1] The pantomime flourished throughout the eighteenth century and, along with other related forms, till near the close of the nineteenth century, its popularity frequently diverting the activities of great actors (as David Garrick) from serious drama and affecting unfavorably the tradition of "legitimate" drama through its tendency to lower the public taste. (References: A. Nicoll, *A History of Early Eighteenth-Century Drama;* A. E. Wilson, *King Panto, the Story of Pantomime.*)

**Pantoum:** Usually considered as one of the sophisticated French verse forms though, as a matter of fact, the pantoum was taken over from the Malaysian by Victor Hugo and other French poets. This primitive origin is evident in the monotonous repetition of lines, a monotony possibly derived from the rhythmic beating of the Oriental tom-tom. The pantoum may consist of an indefinite number of stanzas, but in any case the second and fourth verses of one stanza must reappear as the first and third lines of the following stanza. The stanzas are quatrains, the rime scheme being monotonously *abab, abab.*

**Parable:** An illustrative story answering a question or pointing a moral or lesson. A true parable, however, is much more than an anecdote since, impliedly at least, detail for detail in the parable is parallel with the situation which calls forth the parable for

---

[1]Allardyce Nicoll, *British Drama*, Thomas Y. Crowell Company, 1925, p. 270. Reprinted by permission of the publishers.

illustration. Parables are, in this sense, allegories (see ALLE-GORY). Naturally in Christian countries the most famous parables are those told by Christ, such for instance as the parable of the sower.

**Paradox:** A statement which while seemingly contradictory or absurd may actually be well-founded or true. Paradox is a rhetorical device used to attract attention, to secure emphasis. Bentley's statement that there are "none so credulous as infidels" is an illustration. Paradox is a common element in epigrammatic writing, as the work of G. K. Chesterton, for instance, will give evidence.

**Parallelism:** A structural arrangement of parts of a sentence, sentences, paragraphs, and larger units of composition by which one element of equal importance with another is equally developed and similarly phrased. The principle of parallelism simply dictates that coördinate ideas should have coördinate presentation. Within a sentence, for instance, where several elements of equal importance are to be expressed, if one element is cast in a relative clause the others should be expressed in relative clauses, etc. Contrariwise, of course, the principle of parallelism demands that unequal elements should *not* be expressed in similar constructions. Practiced writers are not likely to attempt, for example, the comparison of positive and negative statements, of inverted and uninverted constructions, of dependent and independent clauses. And, for an example of simple parallelism, the sentence immediately above may serve.

**Paraphrase:** A restatement of an idea in such a way as to retain the meaning while changing the diction and form. A paraphrase is usually an amplification of the original for the purpose of clearness, though the term is also used for any rather general restatement of an expression or passage. Thus one might speak of a paraphrase from the French meaning a loose statement of the idea rather than an exact translation or of a paraphrase of a poem indicating a prose explanation of a difficult passage of verse.

**Parenthesis:** An explanatory remark thrown into the body of a statement and frequently separated from it by ( ). However, any comment which is an interruption of the immediate purpose is spoken of as a parenthesis whether it be a word, phrase, clause, sentence, or paragraph. Commas and dashes are substituted for the parenthesis marks when the interruption is not so abrupt as to demand the ( ). Brackets [ ] are used for parenthetical material more foreign to the subject of the sentence than parentheses will control and also to enclose material injected into a statement by some editorial hand. The tendency among modern writers seems to be toward a decreased use of parentheses.

**Parnassus:** The name of a mountain in Greece famed as the haunt of Apollo and the Muses. The word has also been used as a title for a collection or anthology of poems or poetical extracts, e.g., *England's Parnassus* (1600).

**Parody:** A composition burlesquing or imitating another, usually serious, piece of work. It is designed to ridicule in nonsensical fashion, or to criticize by brilliant treatment, an original piece of work or its author. When the parody is directed against an author or his style, it is likely to fall simply into barbed witticisms, often venting personal antagonisms of the parodist against the one parodied. When the subject matter of the original composition is parodied, however, it may prove to be a valuable indirect criticism or it may even imply a flattering tribute to the original writer. Often a parody is more powerful in its influence on affairs of current importance—politics, for instance—than an original composition. The parody is in literature what the caricature and the cartoon are in art. Known to have been used as a potent means of satire and ridicule even so far back as Aristophanes, parody has made a definite place for itself in literature and has become a popular type of literary composition (see BURLESQUE). Among the many anthologies of parodies may be mentioned Carolyn Wells, *A Parody Anthology;* Louis Untermeyer, *Collected Parodies.*

**Paronomasia:** An old term for a pun or play on words.

*Pastiche:* A French word for a parody or literary imitation. Perhaps for humorous or satirical purposes, perhaps as a mere literary exercise or *jeu d'esprit*, perhaps in all seriousness (as in some closet dramas), a writer imitates the style or technique of some recognized writer or work. Amy Lowell's *A Critical Fable* (1922) might be called a *pastiche*, since it is written in the manner of James Russell Lowell's *A Fable for Critics*. In art, a picture is called a *pastiche* when it manages to catch something of a master's peculiar style. In music, *pastiche* is applied to a medley or assembly of various pieces into a single work. The term is infrequently used in English.

**Pastoral:** A poem treating of shepherds and rustic life. In classical literature the pastoral held a definite position as a conventional poetic form, the poet (Virgil is an example) writing of his friends and acquaintances as though they were poetic shepherds moving through rural scenes. The form is artificial and unnatural—the "shepherds" of the pastoral often speaking in courtly language and appearing in dress more appropriate to the drawing room than to rocky hills and swampy meadows. In this connection G. P. Marsh noted that "pastoral poetry affects the manner or matter of rustic life, not for accurate description, but as a purely artistic device for conveying the interests and emotions of the poet himself, of the society not rural in which he lives." Between 1550 and 1750 this conventionalized pastoral was much written in England under the influence of the classical revival. In modern use the term is often loosely construed to mean any poem of rural people and setting (Untermeyer, for instance, speaks of Robert Frost as a "pastoral" poet). Since this classification is based on subject matter and manner rather than on form, we often use the term in association with other poetic types; we thus have pastoral lyrics, elegies, dramas, or even pastoral epics. Milton's *Lycidas*, Shelley's *Adonais*, and Arnold's *Thyrsis* are examples of English pastorals, as is Spenser's *Shepheardes Calender*. For a study of the form see W. W. Greg's *Pastoral Poetry and Pastoral Drama*. See ECLOGUE, PASTORAL DRAMA, PASTORAL ELEGY.

**Pastoral Drama:** The "pastoral" (*q.v.*) conventions so popular at times in poetry (as the eclogue, *q.v.*) and in the pastoral romance are reflected also in a form of drama occasionally cultivated by English dramatists. Whether the pastoral drama originated in simple dramatic eclogues (as Greg thinks) or is more closely related to such fifteenth-century mythological plays as Politian's *Orfeo*, it is certain that the type developed in Italy in the sixteenth century and was affected by the pastoral romance. Tasso's *Aminta* and Guarini's *Il Pastor Fido* (1590) were models for English Renaissance pastoral plays, as cultivated by Samuel Daniel, John Fletcher, and Ben Jonson. The best is Fletcher's *The Faithful Shepherdess* (acted 1608–1609). Some of Shakespeare's romantic comedies, such as *As You Like It*, are strongly affected by the pastoral influences and are sometimes called pastoral plays. The eighteenth-century stage saw some translations and imitations of Italian pastoral drama, and pastoral conventions were utilized along with the mythological in the more spectacular forms of dramatic activity which flourished in the eighteenth and nineteenth centuries. (References: W. W. Greg, *Pastoral Poetry and Pastoral Drama;* Jeanette Marks, *English Pastoral Drama.*)

**Pastoral Elegy:** A poem employing conventional pastoral imagery, written in dignified, serious language, and taking as its theme the expression of grief at the loss of a friend or important person. The form represents a combining of the pastoral eclogue and the elegy. The conventional divisions, as evidenced in Milton's *Lycidas*, are: the invocation of the muse, an expression of the grief felt in the loss of a friend, a procession of mourners, a digression (on the church), and, finally, a consolation in which the poet submits gracefully to the inevitable and declares his conviction that, after all, everything has turned out for the best. Other conventions often present include: appearance of the poet as shepherd, praise of the dead "shepherd," the "pathetic fallacy" (*q.v.*), flower symbolism, invective against death, reversal of the ordinary processes of nature as result of the death, bewilderment caused by grief, declaration of belief in some form of immortality, use of a refrain and of the rhetorical question. Moschus' lament for Bion (third century B.C.), the November eclogue of Spenser's *Shepheardes Calender*, and Shelley's *Adonais* are examples of the form. See ECLOGUE, ELEGY, PASTORAL.

**Pastoral Romance:** A prose narrative, usually long and complicated in plot, in which the characters bear pastoral names and in which pastoral conventions dominate. It often contains interspersed songs. Though the Greek *Daphnis and Chloë* of Longus (third century) is classed as a pastoral romance, the form was reborn in the Renaissance with Boccaccio's *Ameto* (1342). Montemayor's *Diana Enamorada* (1552) is an important Spanish pastoral romance. Typical English examples are Sir Philip Sidney's *Arcadia* (1590) and Thomas Lodge's *Rosalynde* (1590)—the source for Shakespeare's *As You Like It*. See ECLOGUE, PASTORAL, and PASTORAL DRAMA.

*Pastourelle:* A medieval type of dialogue poem in which a shepherdess is wooed by a man of higher social rank. In the Latin *pastoralia* a scholar does the courting; in the French and English, a poet. The body of the poem is the dialogue in which the case is argued. Sometimes the suit is successful, but often a father or brother happens along and ends the wooing. In the English forms the poet asks permission to accompany the maid to the fields; she refuses and threatens to call her mother. The *pastourelle* possibly developed from popular wooing-games and wooing-songs, though one of Theocritus' idylls (no. 27) is much like the medieval *pastourelle*. The form seems to have influenced the pastoral dialogue-lyrics of the Elizabethans and may have figured in the development of early romantic drama in England. (Reference: William Powell Jones, *The Pastourelle*.)

**Patent Theatres:** The removal of the ban against theatrical performances in England in 1660 resulted in much rival activity among groups seeking to operate playhouses. Before August, three independent companies were established at three old theatres, the Red Bull, the Cockpit, and Salisbury Court. At this time Sir William Davenant and Thomas Killigrew secured from Charles II a "patent" granting them the privilege of censorship of plays and the right to organize two companies and erect two theatres which should have a monopoly. Though opposed by the jealous master of the revels, Sir Henry Herbert, and by some of the independent managers, Davenant and Killigrew succeeded in enforcing their rights. Davenant's company, the "Duke of York's Company," occupied in 1661 a new theatre in Lincoln's Inn Fields and later one at Dorset Garden. Killigrew's company, the "King's Company," erected the Theatre Royal, the first of a famous succession of houses on this spot, all known as Drury Lane since 1663. The theatres used by these two favored companies are known as "patent" theatres. The companies united in 1682, but in 1695 Betterton led a rebellious group of actors to a second theatre in Lincoln's Inn Fields. After a generation of confusion, Parliament passed a licensing act in 1737, reaffirming the patent rights and establishing the monopoly of Drury Lane and Covent Garden (erected 1732). Despite strenuous efforts of rival managers to encroach upon the privileges of the patentees, this act remained in force until 1843, when it was repealed and the patents revoked. Among the managers of Drury Lane after Killigrew are Cibber, Garrick, and Sheridan; of Covent Garden, John Rich (the builder), the elder Colman, and John P. Kemble. See PRIVATE THEATRES. (Reference: A. Nicoll, *Hist. of Restoration Drama*, Appendix A.)

**Pathetic Fallacy:** A phrase coined by Ruskin to denote that tendency of poets and writers of impassioned prose to credit nature with the emotions of human beings. In a larger sense the pathetic fallacy is any false emotionalism in writing resulting in a too impassioned description of nature. It is the carrying over to inanimate objects of the moods and passions of a human being. This crediting of nature with human qualities is a constant device of poets. A frequently occurring expression of the imagination, it becomes a fault when it is overdone to the point of absurdity, in which case it approaches the "conceit" (*q.v.*). A passage from Ruskin (*Modern Painters*, Vol. 3, Part IV, Chap. xii) in which he discusses the pathetic fallacy is quoted:

> They rowed her in across the rolling foam—
> The cruel, crawling foam.

The foam is not cruel, neither does it crawl. The state of mind which attributes to it these characters of a living creature is one in which the reason is unhinged by grief. All violent feelings have the same effect. They produce in us a falseness in all our impressions of external things, which I would generally characterize as the "pathetic fallacy."

**Patriotic Lyric:** See LYRIC.

**Pedantry:** A display of learning for its own sake. The term is often used in critical reproach of an author's style when that style is marked by a superfluity of quotations, foreign phrases, allusions, etc. Holofernes in Shakespeare's *Love's Labour's Lost* can hardly open his lips without giving expression to pedantry:

Most barbarous intimation! yet a kind of insinuation, as it were, *in via*, in way, of explication; *facere*, as it were, replication, or, rather, *ostentare*, to show, as it were, his inclination,—after his undressed, unpolished, uneducated, unpruned, untrained, or rather, unlettered, or, ratherest, unconfirmed fashion,—to insert again my *haud credo* for a deer.

**Pegasus:** The winged horse of Grecian fable said to have sprung from Medusa's body at her death. Pegasus is associated with the inspiration of poetry (though in modern times in a somewhat jocular vein) because he is supposed by one blow of his hoof to have caused Hippocrene, the inspiring fountain of the Muses, to flow from Mount Helicon. As a symbol of poetic inspiration poets have sometimes invoked the aid of Pegasus instead of the Muses.

**Pelagianism:** See CALVINISM.

**Pentameter:** A line of verse consisting of five feet. See SCANSION.

**Periodic Sentence:** A sentence not grammatically complete before the end; the opposite of a "loose sentence" (*q.v.*). The characteristic of a periodic sentence is that its construction is such as constantly to throw the mind forward to the idea which will complete the meaning. The periodic sentence is effective when it is desired to arouse interest and curiosity, to hold an idea in suspense before its final revelation is made. Periodicity is accomplished by the use of parallel phrases or clauses at the opening; by the use of dependent clauses preceding the independent clause, and by the use of such correlatives as *neither . . . nor, not only . . . but also*, and *both . . . and*. "Because it was raining, I went into the house" is an example of a periodic sentence composed of a dependent clause preceding the independent clause.

**Periods of English and American Literary History:** See ENGLISH LITERATURE, AMERICAN LITERATURE, and "Outline of Literary History," *passim.*

**Peripety:** An obsolete word formerly employed by critics to mean a sudden reverse of fortune occurring in the progress of a narrative or dramatic plot.

**Periphrasis:** An indirect, abstract, roundabout method of stating ideas; the application to writing or speech of the old conviction that "the longest way 'round is the shortest way home." Used with restraint and with deliberate intent periphrasis may be a successful rhetorical device, but the danger is that it will be overdone and will result in mere Polonius-like verbosity. Fowler cites as an objectionable use of periphrasis (for "No news is good news") the periphrastic circumlocution "The absence of intelligence is an indication of satisfactory developments." Authors frequently use the form to secure humorous effects; for example, Shenstone refers to pins as "the cure of rents and separations dire, and chasms enormous."

**Peroration:** The conclusion of an oration or discourse in which the discussion is summed up, and the speaker endeavors to enforce his arguments by a pointed and rhetorical appeal to the emotions of his audience; a recapitulation of the major points of any speech.

**Persiflage:** Light, inconsequential chatter, written or spoken. The gay, satirical banter of columnists is an example; a trifling, flippant manner of dealing with any theme or subject matter.

**Personal Essay:** See ESSAY.

**Personification:** A figure of speech which endows animals, ideas, abstractions, and inanimate objects with human form, character, or sensibilities; the representing of imaginary creatures or things as having human personalities, intelligence, and emotions; an impersonation in drama of one character or person, whether real or fictitious, by another person. Keats's personification of the Grecian urn as the

> Sylvan historian, who canst thus express
> A flowery tale more sweetly than our rhyme:

is an obvious personification as are his earlier references to the urn as an "unravished bride of quietness" and as a "foster-child of silence and slow time."

**Persuasion:** That one of the major types of composition the purpose of which is to convince of the wisdom of a certain line of action. Persuasion is really a phase of argumentation and resembles it in that its purpose is to establish the truth or falsity of a proposition, but is somewhat distinct from it in that it is calculated to arouse to some action. Persuasion may draw on the other types of composition—argumentation, description, exposition, and narration—for support, and in fact does incorporate within itself elements of each. Its chief reason for consideration as a separate type is simply that it uses these forms to a specific goal—that of arousing action through the conviction it carries to the reader or hearer. The most common form of persuasion is the oration (*q.v.*), and the most effective form is that which combines the appeal to the intellect with an appeal to the emotions.

**Philippic:** In modern usage, any speech or harangue bitterly invective in character; a discourse filled with denunciations and accusations. The term comes from the twelve orations of Demosthenes in which he berated Philip II of Macedon as an enemy of Greece.

**Philistinism:** The worship of material and mechanical prosperity, the disregard of culture, beauty, and spiritual things. The term was made popular by Matthew Arnold's use of it in his essay, *Sweetness and Light*, which appeared as the first chapter of *Culture and Anarchy*. In this paper Arnold writes:

If it were not for this purging effect wrought upon our minds by culture, the whole world, the future as well as the present, would inevitably belong to the Philistines. The people who believe most that our greatness and welfare are proved by our being very rich, and who most give their lives and thoughts to becoming rich, are just the very people whom we call Philistines. Culture says: "Consider these people, then, their way of life, their habits, their manners, the very tones of their voices; look at them attentively; observe the literature they read, the things which give them pleasure, the words which come forth out of their mouths, the thoughts which make the furniture of their minds; would any amount of wealth be worth having with the condition that one was to become just like these people by having it?"

**Philology:** In its general sense philology means the scientific study of both language and literature. Thus there are "philological" clubs and journals of "philology" devoted to linguistic and literary research. The late Professor A. S. Cook even went so far as to say: "The ideal philologist is at once antiquary, palaeographer, grammarian, lexicologist, expounder, critic, historian of literature, and, above all, lover of humanity." "Philology" is also sometimes used in a narrower sense to mean the scientific study of language. A "philologist" in this sense is a specialist in linguistics, and courses in "philology" are linguistic courses, such as the study of Anglo-Saxon or Hebrew as distinguished from courses in literature. There is a tendency to discard this use of the word in favor of "linguistics."

**Picaresque Novel, The:** A chronicle, usually autobiographical, presenting the life story of a rascal of low degree engaged in menial tasks and making his living more through his wits than his industry. Episodic in nature, the picaresque novel is, in the usual sense of the term, structureless. It presents little more than a series of thrilling incidents impossible to conceive as happening in one life. The *picaro*, or central figure, through the nature of his various pranks and predicaments and by virtue of his associations with people of varying degree, affords the author an opportunity for satire on the social classes. Romantic in the sense of being a story of adventure, the picaresque novel nevertheless is strongly marked by realistic methods in its faithfulness to petty detail, its utter frankness of expression, and its drawing of incidents from low life.

From earliest times, of course, the rogue has been a favorite character in story and picture. As far back as the *Satyricon*, Petronius at the court of Nero recognized the possibilities of the type. In the Middle Ages the *fables* continued the manner though it transferred roguery from man to animals. Reynard is a typical picaroon. He lives by his wits; gets into trouble and out of it, but always interests the reader. It was not until the sixteenth century that this rogue literature crystallized and became a definite type. A novel called *La Vida de Lazarillo de Tormes y de sus fortunas y adversidades*, probably dating from 1554, brought this about. So popular did this work become and through so many different editions did it pass, that it was one of the most-read books of the century. Cervantes took up the manner. And before long French imitators sprang up. Of all the French novels Le Sage's *Gil Blas* (1715) was by far the most popular. So definitely was the type fixed as a Spanish form that the French writers—Le Sage among them—gave their characters Spanish names, placed their episodes in Spain, and paid the early Spanish writers the compliment of borrowing extensively the incidents used in their books.

It was inevitable, with all this enthusiasm, that the type should undergo modifications. Feminine characters assumed the rôle of the picaroon. In one prominent novel a nun figured as the central character. Episodes became more and more scandalous in the effort to attract more and more readers. Moralists appeared who avowed their intention of pointing out the evils of the rogue's life by presenting especially revolting and villainous incidents.

The English, as well, adopted the picaresque manner. In 1594 appeared *The Unfortunate Traveller: or, The Life of Jack Wilton* by Thomas Nash—the first important picaresque novel in the language. With Daniel Defoe in the eighteenth century the type became really important in English literature. His *Moll Flanders* presents the life record of a female picaroon. Fielding in *Jonathan Wild* and Smollett in *Ferdinand, Count Fathom*, lent dignity to the type through the importance of their literary reputation.

There are, perhaps, seven chief qualities distinguishing the picaresque novel. (1) First of all, it chronicles a part or the whole of the life of a rogue. It is likely to be done in the first person—as autobiography—but this is by no means essential. (2) The chief figure is drawn from a low social level and is of "loose" character, according to conventional standards. The occupation of this central figure, should he tolerate employment at all, is menial in nature. (3) The novel presents little plot. Rather is it a series of episodes only slightly connected. (4) There is little character interest. Progress and development of character do not take place.  The central figure starts as a *pi-caro* and ends as a *picaro*, manifesting the same aptitudes and qualities throughout.  When change occurs, as it sometimes does, it is external change brought about by the man's falling heir to a fortune or by his marrying a rich widow.  Internal character development is not a quality of the picaresque novel. (5) The method is realistic.  While the story may be romantic in itself, it is presented with a plainness of language, a freedom in vocabulary, and a vividness of detail such as the realist only is permitted.  (6) Satire is a prominent element.  Thrown with people from every class and often from different parts of the world, the *picaro* serves them intimately in one lowly capacity or another and learns all their foibles and frailties.  The pic-aresque novel may in this way be made to satirize both social castes and national or racial peculiarities.  (7) The hero of the picaresque novel usually stops just short of being an actual criminal.  The line between crime and petty rascality is a hazy one, but somehow the *picaro* always manages to draw it.  Care-free, unmoral perhaps, he avoids actual crime and turns from one peccadillo to disappear down the dust of the road in search of another.  (Reference: F. W. Chandler, *The Literature of Roguery*.)

**Pindaric Ode:** See ODE.

**Plagiarism:** Literary theft.  A writer who steals the plot of some obscure, forgotten story and uses it as new in a story of his own is a plagiarist.  Plagiarism is more noticeable when it in-volves a stealing of language than when substance only is bor-rowed.  From flagrant exhibitions of stealing both thought and language plagiarism shades off into less serious things such as unconscious borrowing, borrowing of minor elements, and mere imitation.  In fact, the critical doctrine of imitation (*q.v.*), as understood in Renaissance times, often led to what would nowa-days be called plagiarism.  Thus, Spenser's free borrowings from other romantic epics in composing his *Faerie Queene* were by him regarded as virtues, since he was "following" a predeces-sor in the same type of writing.  A modern dramatist could not with impunity borrow plots from other dramas and from old stories in the way in which Shakespeare did.  With plagiarism compare literary forgeries (*q.v.*), its converse, where an author pretends that another has written what he has actually written himself. See GHOST-WRITER.

**Plaint:** Verse expressing grief or tribulation; a chant of lamentation; a lament (*q.v.*); an expression of sorrow. See COMPLAINT.

**Platonism:** The idealistic philosophical doctrines of Plato, because of their concern with the higher aspirations of the human spirit, their tendency to exalt mind over matter, their mystical and optimistic grappling with the great problems of the universe and of man's relation to the great cosmic forces, and their highly imaginative elements, have appealed strongly to certain English authors, particularly the poets of the Renaissance and of the Romantic period. Plato himself declined to "codify" his philosophical views and perhaps altered them much during his own life. He left expressions of them in his great "dialogues" or conversations, in which various great Greeks (such as Socrates, Alcibiades, and Aristophanes) are made to discuss philosophical problems, particularly those involving problems of the universe and man's relation to it, the nature of love and beauty, the constitution of the human soul, the relation of beauty to virtue, etc. Unlike Aristotelian philosophy, which tends to be systematic, formal, scientific, logical, and critical, and which occupies itself chiefly with the visible universe, the natural world, and mankind, Platonism is flexible, interested in the unseen world, and concerned with man's possibilities and destinies. It has been called an "intellectual vision" rather than a cold, philosophical system. Plato founded his famous "Academy" in 380 B.C., where for a third of a century he taught students attracted from far and near (including Aristotle himself). Later leaders of the Academy and other followers now known as "Neo-platonists" modified and expanded Plato's teachings and it is difficult even now to distinguish the purely Platonic elements from elements added by later "Platonists." Among the "Neo-platonists" there were two groups of especial importance. (1) The Alexandrian school. This group, especially Plotinus (third century), stressed the mystical elements and amalgamated them with many ideas drawn from other sources. Their Neo-platonism

313

was in fact a sort of religion, which, though itself supplanted by Christianity, supplied medieval Christian thinkers (including Boëthius and St. Augustine) with many ideas. (2) The Neo-platonists of the Italian Renaissance. Under the leadership of Marsilio Ficino (1433–1499), who led the Platonic Academy at Florence and who translated and explained Plato, a highly complex and mystical system developed, one of the aims of which was the fusing of Platonic philosophy and Christian doctrine. It was this particular kind of Neo-platonism which kindled the imagination of such Renaissance poets as Sidney and Spenser.

Important Platonic doctrines found in English literature include:

1. The doctrine of ideas (or "forms"). True reality is found not in the realm of sense but in the higher, spiritual realm of the ideal and the universal. Here exist the "ideas" or images or patterns of which material objects are but transitory symbols or expressions.

2. The doctrine of recollection. This implies the preëxistence and immortality of the soul, which passes through a series of incarnations. Most of what the soul has seen and learned in "heaven" it forgets when imprisoned in the body of clay but it has some power of "recalling" ideas and images. Hence human knowledge.

3. The doctrine of love. There are two kinds of love and beauty, a lower and a higher. The soul or lover of beauty in its quest for perfect beauty ascends from the sensual gradually, through a process of idealization, to the spiritual, and thereby develops all the virtues both of thought and of action. Beauty and virtue become identified.

An interesting exposition of the Neo-platonic doctrines of love may be read in the fourth book of Castiglione's *The Book of the Courtier*. Representative English poems embodying Platonic ideas include: Spenser's *Hymn in Honor of Beauty*, Shelley's *Hymn to Intellectual Beauty*, and Wordsworth's *Ode on the Intimations of Immortality from Recollections of Early Childhood*. (References: P. E. More, *The Religion of Plato*; A. E. Taylor, *Platonism and Its Influence*; Dean W. R. Inge, *The Platonic Tradition in English Religious Thought*; J. S. Harrison, *Platonism in English Poetry of the Sixteenth and Seventeenth Centuries*.)

**Pléiade:** A term originally applied to an ancient group of seven authors (named after the constellation of the Pleiades), and to several later groups, the most important of which for the student of English literature is the group of critics and poets which flourished in France in the second half of the sixteenth century. The leading figures were Ronsard, Du Bellay, and (later) Desportes. The poetic manifesto of the "school" is Du Bellay's *Défense et Illustration de la Langue Française* (1549). It shows an interest in developing a new vernacular literature following the types cultivated by classical writers. The popular and the medieval were to be avoided, except that certain medieval courtly pieces were to be rewritten. The native language was to be enriched by coining words, by borrowing from the Greek and Latin, and by restoring to use lost native words, so that a literary language might be produced which would make possible the creation of a new French literature comparable with classical literature. The high function of the poet and of poetry was stressed. The influence of the group was a constructive and important one upon Elizabethan poets, notably Spenser, and the more or less mythical "Areopagus" (*q.v.*) has been regarded as an English counterpart of the *Pléiade*, since Sidney and his group were enthusiastically engaged in the effort to refine the English language and to create a new national literature based upon humanistic ideals.

**Pleonasm:** The superfluous use of words. Pleonasm may consist of needless repetition, or of the addition of unnecessary words in an effort to express an idea completely, or of a combination of the two. For example, in the sentence, "He walked the entire distance to the station on foot," the last two words are pleonastic. Although pleonasm is a violation of correct grammatical usage, it is employed occasionally to add emphasis, and in such instances its use may be considered legitimate. See TAUTOLOGY.

**Plot:** A planned series of interrelated actions progressing, because of the interplay of one force upon another, through a struggle of opposing forces to a climax and a *dénouement*. However, such abstract terms as the above mean little; it is perhaps more helpful to describe plot than to define it with generalities. The incidents which are part of a plot, are, it has been said, (1) *planned;* they are preconceived by the author; they spring from his conscious thought; they are not simply taken over from life. No matter how realistic an author may be, he must arrange and select his incidents according to a plot purpose since life itself only rarely, if ever, unfolds according to the plans of a fiction plot.   Plot is, too, (2) a *series of actions* moving from a beginning through a logically related sequence to a logical and natural outcome.   One incident—an afternoon's cruise—does not make a plot, no matter how interesting the afternoon may have been. Several incidents—if the story is one of action—are essential. There must at least be a beginning, a middle, and an end in the interplay of the opposing forces and, most frequently, this means three or more episodes.   And these incidents grow one upon another; incident two following by a causal relationship from incident one, and incident three following, by this same relationship, from two.   The difference between a simple narrative and a story of plot is the difference between a calendar and a knitted scarf.   In the calendar the pages follow one another logically, but in the scarf the texture is the result of weaving one thread over and under another.   In a story with closely knit plot the removal of one incident would bring the whole structure down upon one's head much as though he had removed an important prop from the scaffolding for a building.   In a story of mere unrelated incidents, the removal of one incident would leave, simply, a gap.   (3) This interrelationship of action is the result, as has been said, of the *interplay of one force upon another.* Without conflict, without opposition, plot *per se* does not exist. We must have a Claudius flouting a Hamlet, an Iago making jealous an Othello, if we are to have plot.   These forces may be physical (or external), or they may be spiritual (or internal); but physical or spiritual they must afford an opposition.   And this opposition it is, which knits one incident to another, which dictates the causal relationship, which develops the struggle.   This struggle between the forces, moreover, comes to a head in some one incident—the *climax (q.v.)*—which forms the turning-point of the story and which usually marks the point of greatest suspense.   In this climactic episode the rising action comes to a termination, the falling action begins; and as a result of this incident some *dénouement* or *catastrophe* is bound to follow.

Plot is, in this sense, an artificial rather than a natural ordering of events. Its function is to simplify life. It would be possible, though most tedious, to recite in a James Joyce-like manner *all* incidents, *all* events, *all* thoughts which pass through the minds of one or more characters during a period of, say, a week. And somewhere in this recital might be buried a story. But the demands of plot stipulate that the author *select* from this welter of event and reflection those items which have a certain unity, which point to a certain end, which have a common inter-relationship, which represent not more than two or three threads of interest and activity. Plot brings order out of life; it selects only one or two emotions out of a dozen, one or two conflicts out of hundreds, only two or three people out of thousands, and a half-dozen episodes from possible millions. In this sense it focuses life.

And it focuses with one principal idea in mind—character. The most effective incidents are those which spring naturally from the given characters, the most effective plot presents struggle such as would engage these given characters, and the most effective emotion for the plot to present is that inherent in the quality of the given characters. The function of plot, from this point of view, is to translate character into action.

The use of a *deus ex machina* (*q.v.*) to solve a complication is now pretty generally condemned as a weakness in plot structure since it is so generally conceded that plot action should spring from the innate quality of the characters participant in the action. But *fate*, since it may be interpreted as working through character, is, with the development of the realistic method, still very popular. The one great weakness good writers of fiction avoid is the use of incident and episode which are extraneous to the essential purposes of the plot pattern. Plot, it need hardly be added, is an element common to various forms of fiction: the novel, the short story, the drama being the types of writing most frequently making use of the interest which springs from the suspense which plots develop.

**Poem:** A composition characterized by the presence of imagination, emotion, truth (significant meaning), sense impressions, and a dignified and concrete language; expressed rhythmically and with an orderly arrangement of parts and possessing within itself a unity; the whole written with the dominant purpose of giving aesthetic or emotional pleasure. A formal and final definition of poetry is, of course, impossible; it means different things to different people at different times. See POETRY.

**Poet Laureate:** In medieval universities there arose the custom of crowning with laurel a student who was admitted to an academic degree, such as the bachelor of arts. Later the phrase *poet laureate* was used as a special degree conferred by a university as a recognition of skill in Latin grammar and versification. There also existed in the late Middle Ages the custom of bestowing a crown of laurel on a poet for distinctive work, Petrarch being so honored in 1341. Independent of these customs and usages was the ancient practice of kings and chieftains, both in educated and barbarous nations, of maintaining "court poets," persons attached to the prince's household and maintained for the purpose of celebrating the virtues of the royal family or singing the praises of military exploits. Court poets of this type included the *scop* among Anglo-Saxon peoples, the *skald* among the Scandinavian, the *filidh* among the Irish, and the higher ranks of *bards* among the Welsh. An example of a court poet in classical antiquity is Theocritus (third century B.C.), who served as such both at the court of Ptolemy Philadelphus in Alexandria and the Tyrant Hiero in Syracuse. The modern office of Poet Laureate in England resulted from the application of the academic term *poet laureate* to the traditional court poet.

The present official laureateship was established in the seventeenth century, though there were interesting anticipations earlier. Henri d'Avranches, for example, was an official *versificator regis* for Henry III and received an annual grant of wine as part of his stipend. Later, at the courts of Henry VII and Henry VIII, an academic *poet laureate* named Bernardus Andreas of Toulouse (a blind poet) was officially recognized as a Poet Laureate, wrote Latin odes for his masters, and received a pension. The tradition was not carried on after the poet's death. The first officially appointed Poet Laureate was John Dryden, though Spenser, Daniel, Drayton, Ben Jonson, and William Davenant are often included in the list, the latter two with strong justification. Spenser, Daniel, and Drayton were court poets of the same sort Chaucer was and were in no sense poets laureate. Jonson, however, received a pension, a grant of wine, and was an official (though not exclusive) writer of masques for James I and Charles I. Moreover, his contemporaries called him "the Poet Laureate" and he was ambitious to be so known. After Jonson's death in 1637 Davenant was hailed as Jonson's successor and at the Restoration (1660) he was informally recognized even at court as Jonson's successor as Poet Laureate, though he seems not to have received any official designation as such during his lifetime. Upon Davenant's death, however, Dryden received (1670) an official appointment to the office, the warrant mentioning the office as "void by the death of Sir William Davenant." Davenant thereby received a sort of *ex post facto* official recognition and actually was informally recognized during his life, but Dryden was the first whose official appointment is recorded. After the Revolution Dryden was displaced, and in 1689 Thomas Shadwell was appointed Poet Laureate. Successive laureates were: Nahum Tate (1692–1715), Nicholas Rowe (1715–1718), Laurence Eusden (1718–1730), Colley Cibber (1730–1757), William Whitehead (1757–1785), Thomas Warton (1785–1790), Henry James Pye (1790–1813), Robert Southey (1813–1843), William Wordsworth (1843–1850), Alfred Tennyson (1850–1892), Alfred Austin (1896–1913), Robert Bridges (1913–1930). In 1930 John Masefield was made Poet Laureate.

The early, primary duty of the laureate was to render professional service to the royal family and the court. The practice of composing odes in celebration of royal birthdays, New Year's, and other occasions developed in the seventeenth century and became obligatory upon the laureate in the eighteenth century. Each year such an ode was sung at a formal court reception held to wish the king a happy new year. This custom lapsed during the illness of George III and was abolished in Southey's time. Sometimes the laureate has served as a "poet-defender" of the king in personal and political as well as national disputes (for example, Dryden). Later the more appropriate custom of expecting a poem in times of national stress or strong patriotic feeling developed, though since Southey the writing of verse for special occasions has not been obligatory. Two of the best-known "laureate" poems are Tennyson's "Ode" written to be sung at the funeral of the Duke of Wellington and the same writer's *Charge of the Light Brigade.*

The servile or perfunctory character of the laureate's duties often prevented the appointment of the best living poets, though since Wordsworth's time the appointment has been regarded as a recognition of poetic distinction. Gray, Scott, and Samuel Rogers declined appointments as poet laureate. Gray actually asserted that a poet accepting the post was certain to be humiliated either by having his poor verses advertised or by incurring the active enmity of jealous versifiers. Until recent times the custom of satirizing the Poet Laureate was almost as traditional as the annual gift of a butt of wine; it grew out of the character of some of the appointees and their perfunctory duties. Cibber, who was much jibed at for his servile flattery, admitted to Pope that he wrote "more to be fed than to be famous." (Reference: E. K. Broadus, *The Laureateship.*)

**Poetic** (noun): A system or body of theory concerning the nature of poetry. The principles and rules of poetic composition. The term is used in two forms, "poetic" and "poetics," both referring to the body of principles promulgated or exemplified by a poet or critic. The classic example, of course, is Aristotle's *Poetics* and the first paragraph of that work indicates that it is Aristotle's purpose to treat of "poetry in itself and of its various kinds, noting the essential quality of each; to inquire into the structure of the plot as requisite to a good poem; into the number and nature of the parts of which a poem is composed; and similarly into whatever else falls within the same inquiry."

**Poetic Diction:** Words chosen for a supposedly inherent poetic quality. Styles change in diction as in clothes, and we condemn poetic words of a past age even as we make new ones in the present. A modern poet would scorn to use such words as "ere," "whilst," "beauteous," "eke," "e'en" on the basis that they are *clichés* from which all the poetry was worn by the hard use given by the Victorians, but at the same time they will create a vocabulary of their own, consisting of such words as "brick-yard," "slut," "cuspidor." See further, ROMANTIC CRITICISM, ROMANTICISM, NEO-CLASSICISM.

**Poetic Drama:** A term properly restricted to poetic plays written to be acted. It is thus distinguished from "dramatic poetry" (*q.v.*) and "closet drama" (*q.v.*), although some writers treat "poetic drama" as synonymous with "dramatic poetry," and some use "poetic drama" to designate "closet drama."

**Poetic Justice:** Loosely, that ideal judgment which rewards virtue and punishes vice among the characters of a narrative.

The use of "poetic" in the term, however, does not so much imply that the phrase is restricted to poetry as that it is based on a philosophic system of "poetic." The eighteenth century particularly interested itself in the question. (See Clarence C. Green, *The Neo-Classic Theory of Tragedy in England during the Eighteenth Century*, Chap. VI.) Dennis and Addison were the proponents of the two points of view. C. C. Green, to focus this eighteenth-century quarrel, quotes each as follows:

I conceive that every Tragedy ought to be a very solemn Lecture, inculcating a particular Providence, and showing it plainly protecting the good, and chastizing the bad, or at least the violent: and that if it is otherwise, it is either an empty amusement, or a scandalous and pernicious Libel upon the government of the world.

—Dennis

The *English* Writers of Tragedy are possessed with a Notion, that when they represent a virtuous or innocent Person in Distress, they ought not to leave him till they have delivered him out of his Troubles, or made him triumph over his Enemies. This Error they have been led into by a ridiculous Doctrine in Modern Criticism, that they are obliged to an equal Distribution of Rewards and Punishments, and an impartial Execution of Poetical Justice.

—Addison

Aristotle announced that "the mere spectacle of a virtuous man brought from prosperity to adversity moves neither pity nor fear; it merely shocks us." And here is, really, the heart of the whole question. Suffering as an end in itself is intolerable dramatically. Hamlet dead with poison, Desdemona smothered, Juliet buried alive—all these placed before us on the stage unmotivated, unexplained, constitute not tragedy but sheer pain. Such scenes would be exhibitions of fate over which the characters have had no control and for which they were in no sense responsible; they would be, had not Shakespeare been the artist he was, mere *accidents* and as such would have no claim to poetic justice. But, in a higher, a more spiritual, a more *dramatic* sense, poetic justice may be said to have been attained since, as Shakespeare *wrote* the plays, the actions moved logically, thoughtfully, consistently to some such catastrophes as those which awaited these three tragic characters. Poetic justice, then, in this higher sense, is something greater than the mere rewarding of virtue and the punishment of vice; *it is the logical and motivated outcome of the given conditions and terms of the tragic plan as presented in the earlier acts of the drama even though, from a worldly sense, virtue meets with disaster and vice seems temporarily rewarded.* With catastrophes less fatal than those which visited Hamlet and Desdemona, tragedy would be in danger of becoming comedy; drama, in its purest sense, would disappear. For the reader of poetic tragedy, the beauty of sorrow, the catharsis which comes with the spectacle of the mysteries of life, are greater values than the knowledge that Claudius had perhaps been exiled and Iago hanged, or that Hamlet had been married to Ophelia and Othello had lived to look upon Desdemona's wrinkled cheek. In its modern sense, then, poetic justice may be considered as fulfilled when the outcome, however fatal to virtue, however it may reward vice, is the logical and necessary result of the action and principles of the major characters as they have been presented by the dramatist.

**Poetic License:** The privilege, sometimes claimed by poets, of departing from normal order, diction, rime, or pronunciation in order that their verse may meet the requirements of their metrical pattern. The best poets rarely resort to the excuse of poetic license since they take enough care with their writing to avoid such distortions. Readers of poetry should not be too hasty in setting down as "license" an irregularity—such as the use of an archaic word or the departure from normal word order —which may have been deliberately planned by the poet to establish a desired poetic effect. If one applies the strict demands of prose to poetry, of course most poetic expression will, from such a point of view, consist of poetic license. The decision is largely relative. Prose, for instance, would state boldly: "Kubla Khan decreed that a stately palace be built in Xanadu." Coleridge, however, has it that

> In Xanadu did Kubla Khan
> A stately pleasure-dome decree:

The Coleridge form includes (1) inversion of order (since "in Xanadu" precedes the subject and predicate), (2) the expletive use of "did" for the simple past tense form "decreed," and (3) a coined expression, "pleasure-dome," for "palace" or "pavilion." The reader who has no poetry in his soul will condemn such methods as nonsense and hail it all as poetic license. Yet all that is distorted is the normal *prose* form; as poetry the lines are readily acceptable to the tolerant reader of verse. And, after all, the poet uses his "license" as a poet only when it is necessary to distort diction or grammar for the sake of form.

**Poetical Miscellanies:** See MISCELLANIES, POETICAL.

**Poetry:** The origin of poetic expression is concealed in the dim past of man. No literary historian will presume to point out the earliest beginnings of poetry, though it is conceded on all sides that the first conscious literary expression took the form of primitive verse. The fact that verse is inherently emotional and that man, under emotional stress, breaks naturally into rhythmic expression establishes this point. Further evidence pointing to the same inference comes from early tribal ceremonials; races which have no written literature nevertheless employ poetic and rhythmic forms in their tribal ceremonies. In fact, it is evident that the first poetry was associated with the other arts of music and the dance. When a tribe or a people experienced any great event, a war, a migration, a flood, it seemed natural to chronicle and preserve these episodes in dance and song. Until recent years it had been frequently assumed that the earliest poetry was communal in origin, was the work not of one conscious literary artist, but rather of a group working together to commemorate some event. (See BALLAD.) The point is now made, by some literary historians, that it is absurd to imagine a group doing as a whole what any single member of that group could not do as an individual. (Reference: Gummere, *The Beginnings of Poetry*.)

323

The stream of poetry of interest to students of English and American literature finds its source in the pagan epic and lyric poems written probably in the sixth and seventh centuries and in Christian poems, Biblical paraphrases, the legends and lyrics of the seventh and eighth centuries. Of this early period *Beowulf* is now the chief extant poem. The student interested in tracing the chronological development of English and American verse will find the major trends summarized for him in the "Outline of Literary History" in this volume. The major purpose of this item must be an effort to explain the nature of poetry, the distinctions between poetry and prose, rather than an historical summary of the poetry of England and America. This book, however, will attempt no new definition of poetry. It will content itself with listing a number of statements regarding the quality of poetry, not in the belief that by so doing it is defining poetry, but with the purpose of showing just how far apart—as well as how close together—we all are in the matter, and just how unreasonable it is that we should try to fix on any one characterization of the subject. Here, then, are fifteen worthy statements on the nature of poetry:

Poetry is the imaginative expression of strong feeling, usually rhythmical . . . the spontaneous overflow of powerful feelings recollected in tranquillity.

—William Wordsworth

The proper and immediate object of Science is the acquirement or communication of truth; the proper and immediate object of Poetry is the communication of pleasure . . . I wish our clever young poets would remember my homely definitions of prose and poetry; that is, *prose:* words in their best order; *poetry:* the best words in the best order.

—Samuel Taylor Coleridge

I would define, in brief, the poetry of words as the rhythmical creation of beauty.

—Edgar Allan Poe

Poetry . . . a criticism of life under the conditions fixed for such a criticism by the laws of poetic truth and beauty.

—Matthew Arnold

Poetry is the utterance of a passion for truth, beauty, and power, embodying and illustrating its conceptions by imagination and fancy, and modulating its language on the principle of variety in uniformity.

—Leigh Hunt

By poetry we mean the art of employing words in such a manner as to produce an illusion of the imagination, the art of doing by means of words what the painter does by means of colors.

—Macaulay

Absolute poetry is the concrete and artistic expression of the human mind in emotional and rhythmical language.

—Theodore Watts-Dunton

Poetry, therefore, we will call musical Thought.

—Carlyle

Poetry is rhythmical, imaginative language expressing the invention, taste, thought, passion, and insight of the human soul.

—E. C. Stedman

. . . imaginative metrical discourse; . . . the art of representing human experiences, insofar as they are of lasting or universal interest, in metrical language, usually with chief reference to the emotions and by means of the imagination.

—Raymond Macdonald Alden

By poetry I mean the art of producing pleasure by the just expression of imaginative thought and feeling in metrical language.

—W. J. Courthope

Poetry is the record of the best and happiest moments of the best and happiest minds.

—Shelley

. . . the presentment, in musical form, to the imagination, of noble grounds for the noble emotions.

—Ruskin

If I read a book and it makes my whole body so cold no fire can ever warm me, I know that it is poetry. If I feel physically as if the top of my head were taken off, I know that it is poetry.

—Emily Dickinson

Poetry is language that tells us, through a more or less emotional reaction, something that cannot be said. All poetry, great or small, does this.

—Edwin Arlington Robinson

Reading over any such list of statements, brings us, time and again, certain words, certain qualities, certain ideas: *emotion, imagination, idea* (or *thought*), *truth* (or *meaning*), *sentiment, passion, power, sense impression, interpretation* ("criticism of life"), *beauty, dignity, rhythm, freshness of expression, orderly arrangement, concreteness, pleasure.* And a further consideration of these words and phrases shows that they fall rather naturally into three classifications and point the way to three qualities common to all poetry: (1) It has a particular *content*, (2) it has a more or less particular *form*, and (3) it has a particular *effect*.

This three-fold aspect of poetry it is which makes the term so impossible of acceptable definition. Poets, critics, readers are of varying natures and prejudices. To some content is all important; to others form is the *sine qua non;* and to others all is to be judged by effect. A Carlyle will emphasize thought, a Poe beauty, a Matthew Arnold interpretation.

We shall do well, then, to limit our discussion of the nature of poetry to a consideration of these three qualities: *content, form,* and *effect*.

*The Content of Poetry.*—Poetry is definitely emotional. It presents the emotions of the poet as they are aroused by some scene of beauty, some experience, some attachment. For this reason it is often rich in sentiment and passion. Almost any lyric of Robert Burns is an instance of this emotional, passionate element. (See EMOTIONAL ELEMENT IN LITERATURE.) The content of poetry is, equally, imaginative. The poet, as someone has said, does not speak the accurate language of science, does not, for example, refer to water as $H_2O$ but rather as "rippling," a "mirror," or "blue," seeing, as he does, not so much the elements which compose the water as the effect which the water creates in his imaginative mind. It is this emotional, imaginative quality which Shakespeare had in mind in *A Midsummer Night's Dream:*

> The lunatic, the lover and the poet
> Are of imagination all compact:
> One sees more devils than vast hell can hold,
> That is the madman: the lover, all as frantic,
> Sees Helen's beauty in a brow of Egypt:

The poet's eye, in a fine frenzy rolling,
Doth glance from heaven to earth, from earth to heaven;
And as imagination bodies forth
The forms of things unknown, the poet's pen
Turns them to shapes and gives to airy nothing
A local habitation and a name.
Such tricks hath strong imagination,
That, if it would but apprehend some joy,
It comprehends some bringer of that joy;
Or in the night, imagining some fear,
How easy is a bush supposed a bear!

Again, our series of statements concerning the nature of poetry emphasizes the elements of truth, thought, idea, meaning. Poetry must have, then, some significance: it must somehow contribute to the store of human knowledge and experience. This is what Matthew Arnold meant when he wrote of it as a "criticism of life"; what Watts-Dunton meant when he called it an "artistic expression of the human mind"; what Carlyle meant by "musical Thought," and Stedman by his statement that poetry gives an "insight of the human soul." This insistence on the presence of truth and meaning was, no doubt, in the mind of Edwin Arlington Robinson when he said that poetry tries to tell us "something that cannot be said." The existence of an idea, a significance, a meaning distinguishes poetry from doggerel and from light or occasional verse. Perhaps here the student should be cautioned against thinking that because poetry is concerned with truth and meaning, it is necessarily didactic. Far from it. Great didactic poetry does exist, but poetry certainly is not great because it is didactic. A further help to an understanding of what constitutes real poetry is found in the word "*power.*" In the words of Leigh Hunt, poetry is a "passion for truth, beauty, and power." To Wordsworth it meant "strong feeling," to Alden "lasting or universal interest," to Ruskin "noble grounds for noble emotions." And Emily Dickinson's test was that real poetry left her whole body so cold no fire could ever warm her. All these requisites indicate the need for sincerity, for honesty of emotion, for depth of passion and feeling, for, in short, power. There is plenty of room in verse for frivolity, light humor, the tongue-in-cheek

327

attitude, but great poetry, absolute poetry, will tolerate none of these insincerities.

A further keyword, in this effort to understand the content of poetry, is *beauty*. All poets will agree to this element although by no means will all poets agree as to what is beautiful. To Shelley beauty meant the song of the skylark; Carl Sandburg finds it in a brickyard. But beauty, of some degree, must be present. If it is a new, strange beauty of some familiar object so much the better. The poet, like the artist and the musician, is different from most other people because of his sensitivity to beauty in all its various forms; he is, in short, a poet chiefly because of this sensitivity, this passion. "Poetry," says Shelley, "turns all things to loveliness; it exalts the beauty of that which is most beautiful, and it adds beauty to that which is most deformed; . . . its secret alchemy turns to potable gold the poisonous waters which flow from death through life; it strips the veil of familiarity from the world, and lays bare the naked and sleeping beauty, which is the spirit of its forms."

And lastly, perhaps implied in the foregoing, poetry must be dignified. In poetic composition life is on parade; grand, magnificent, and marching with a fanfare. Poetry lives forever in Carcassonne. Enough has been said, then, to show that the content of poetry is marked by certain characteristics, that it is, most frequently: *emotional, imaginative*, compact with *thought*, marked by the presence of *power, beauty*, and *dignity*.

*The Form of Poetry.*—The second element with which we are concerned in this discussion of the nature of poetry is *form*. If poetry may be set off from other writing by its *content*, the distinction of *form* is much more clear-cut. While it is true that in some forms of writing ("polyphonic prose" for example) poetry borders closely upon the form of prose and prose upon the form of verse, for most cases this distinction of form is serviceable enough. The first characteristic of poetry, from the point of view of form, is the presence of *rhythm*. Of course all good prose has a more or less conscious rhythm, but the rhythm of poetry is marked by a degree of regularity far surpassing that of prose. (See PROSE RHYTHM.) In fact one of the chief rewards of reading poetry is the satisfaction which comes from finding "variety in uniformity," a shifting of rhythms which, nevertheless, constantly return to the forms of a pattern. (See RHYTHM.) The ear recognizes the existence of recurring accents at stated intervals and recognizes, too, variations from these rhythm patterns. Whatever the pattern, iambic pentameter, dactylic dimeter, or any one of the many possible combinations, there is a regularity of rise and fall in accent which is more uniform than in prose. Frequently, of course, *rime* (*q.v.*) affords an obvious difference by which one may distinguish the form of poetry from prose. Another key-word is *arrangement, order.* The demands of the verse pattern—the combination of rhythm and rime— often exact a "poetic" arrangement of the phrases and clauses. Inversion is more justified in poetry than in prose; syncope is more common. The poet is granted a license (though modern poets hesitate to avail themselves of it) in sequence and syntax which is denied the prose-writer. Since most poetry is relatively short it is likely to be characterized by compactness of thought and expression, to possess an intense unity, to be carefully arranged in climactic order. The distinction between poetry and prose on these points is not so much the presence of these qualities as the degree to which they are respected. A vital element of all great poetry is its *concreteness.* Here, again, the form is different from that of most prose. Prose is satisfied, usually, to state a fact baldly and in general or abstract terms. Poetry insists on the specific, the concrete. The point may be made more obvious by quoting the following lines by Shakespeare:

> Our revels now are ended. These our actors,
> As I foretold you, were all spirits, and
> Are melted into air, into thin air:
> And, like the baseless fabric of this vision,
> The cloud-capp'd towers, the gorgeous palaces,
> The solemn temples, the great globe itself,
> Yea, all which it inherit, shall dissolve,
> And, like this insubstantial pageant faded,
> Leave not a rack behind. We are such stuff
> As dreams are made on; and our little life
> Is rounded with a sleep.

Here almost every line presents a concrete image or shows a picture-quality. The lines are alive with specific language. In a passage on the imagination Shakespeare has himself written imaginatively. What does it all mean? Prose would express the idea simply and bluntly; it might, indeed, be content with the first five words of the passage. And here is one of the qualities of verse which makes so many people pretend to dislike it. "Why can't poets say exactly what they mean?" people who like to call themselves "practical" ask. The answer is, of course, that they do say what they mean; it is no fault of theirs if subtlety of expression, beauty of imagery, and music of words fall on deaf ears.

One more distinction between the form of poetry and the form of prose must be cited—*language*. In addition to this concreteness, this imagery already mentioned, the very language of poetry usually differs from that of prose. To Milton the language of poetry was "simple, sensuous, and impassioned." Since the function of poetry is to present concretely the images of the poet, it is the responsibility of the poet to select language which succeeds in making his images concrete. The specific word, the word rich in connotative value, the word carrying implications of sound and color and action—these are the especial stock of the true poet. Modern poetry (see FREE VERSE) has thrown overboard, lock, stock, and barrel, the special vocabulary which was once thought of as the special language of poetry, the *thees* and *thous* and *e'ers*. The language of the poet is more rich in the figures of speech, in metonomy, synecdoche, and metaphor, than is the language of the prose-writer. And so we find that the *form* of poetry, as well as the *content*, serves to distinguish poetry from prose.

*The Effect or Purpose of Poetry.*—There remains only one further distinction to make—that based on *effect*. Prose is, of course, written with a hundred purposes in the minds of authors. It may be to please, as in fiction; or it may be to instruct, as in this reference book, in a geography, a history, or a volume of philosophy. Again, prose is used to convince, to persuade to a line of action: to explain and to expound, to describe a scene or to narrate an action. All of these purposes may be blended together, any combination of them may exist together, or any one of them may stand almost alone. But with poetry, the chief, the ultimate purpose must be *to please*. The various senses of sight and sound and color may be appealed to, the various emotions of love and fear and appreciation of beauty may be called forth by the poet, but *whatever the immediate appeal, the ultimate effect of poetry is that of giving pleasure.*

With the advance of the years from the dim past wherein poetry found its origin, the art of poetic composition has undergone a long process of refinement. From its general or racial interest it has become intensely individualistic; from the ceremonial recounting of tribal and group movements it has become the vehicle for drama, for history, for personal emotion. It is, however, still common today to classify poetry into three great type-divisions; the *epic*, the *dramatic*, and the *lyric*.

*Forms and Types of Poetry.*—The three types just mentioned are, in turn, broken up into further classifications. With the development of conscious artistry, numerous set patterns such as the *sonnet*, the *ode*, the *elegy* have evolved. Further subdivisions have been made on the basis of mood and purpose, such as the *pastoral*, and *satiric* and *didactic* poetry. All of these types and manners are discussed in their proper position in this handbook, and the terms connected with them are included in the list that follows the definition of VERSIFICATION on pp. 457–458. (References: Raymond M. Alden, *An Introduction to Poetry* and *English Verse: Specimens Illustrating its Principles and History;* Max Eastman, *The Enjoyment of Poetry;* Francis B. Gummere, *The Beginnings of Poetry;* John Livingston Lowes, *Convention and Revolt in Poetry;* Bliss Perry, *A Study of Poetry;* Louis Untermeyer, *Modern American Poetry* and *Modern British Poetry.*)

**Point of View:** A principle in composition demanding that a writer presenting a scene or a character maintain a consistent outlook toward the objects of which he writes. When it is necessary for the author to change his point of view this principle dictates that the writer shall in some way make the reader aware that the change is taking place. The rule is one intended simply to make for consistency and clearness. Only confusion would result from a description of a mountain, for instance, which presents first what is seen from the top of the mountain, then from the foot, and which confuses items of interest on the east and west with those on the north and south. A logical and discriminating use of point of view is, in short, nothing more than a device to secure unity.

In fiction-writing the term is used in a somewhat special sense. The author may adopt one of several "points of view." He may, if he finds his story best presented by his doing so, choose to tell the story as one present within the action, from the point of view of one in the story. Or, again, he may write of the events as one from without, before whom the events of the story simply unfolded themselves, in which case the point of view is that of a witness to the story. Or, once more, he may write omnisciently, as one who knows what is happening in Timbuktu, in Patagonia, in New York City; who knows what is going on in the minds of all of his people, and who sees motives as well as moods and characters at work. This, and it is a very common narrative method, is sometimes called the *omniscient point of view.*

**"Polyphonic Prose":** According to Amy Lowell, who made considerable use of the form, not really prose at all, but verse. She defined the term as follows: "'Polyphonic' means—many voiced—and the form is so called because it makes use of all the 'voices' of poetry, namely: metre, *vers libre*, assonance, alliteration, rhyme, and return." Printed as prose, this form, when read aloud as Miss Lowell suggested, reveals fleeting glimpses of the various poetic practices.

**Popular Ballad:** See BALLAD.

**Portmanteau Words:** Words concocted by accident or for deliberate humorous effect by telescoping two words into one, as the making of "squarson" (attributed to Bishop Wilberforce) from "squire" and "parson." "Portmanteau words" was a name given by Lewis Carroll to this type of fabrication, a type which he himself used in *Through the Looking Glass.* An example of Carroll's manner occurs in his famous *Jabberwocky* poem where, for instance, he made "slithy" of "lithe" and "slimy." In his *History of the Snark* Carroll explained the system by which such words were made: "For instance, take the two words 'fuming' and 'furious.' Make up your mind that you will say both words, but leave it unsettled which you will say first. Now open your mouth and speak. If your thoughts incline ever so little towards 'fuming' you will say 'fuming-furious'; if they turn by even a hair's breadth towards 'furious,' you will say 'furious-fuming'; but if you have that rarest of gifts, a perfectly balanced mind, you will say 'frumious.'"

**Posy (Posie):** Sometimes used in the sense of "a collection of flowers" to indicate an anthology. The term also signifies a motto, usually in verse, inscribed on a ring. When the "mouse-trap" play begins and the prologue has been spoken Hamlet asks Ophelia: "Is this a prologue, or the posy of a ring?"

**Pot-boiler:** A slang term given to a book or an article written solely for the income derived from it. It is writing which will "keep the pot boiling" and thus supply sustenance, presumably, for more worthy work.

**Poulter's Measure:** A metrical pattern, now rarely used, consisting of a couplet composed of a first line in iambic hexameter and a second line in iambic heptameter. The term is said to have originated from a custom of the London poulterers of giving the customer twelve eggs to the dozen in the first dozen bought, and fourteen in the second dozen. Wyatt and Surrey, Sidney, Nicholas Grimald, and Arthur Brooke are some of the poets who have used this form. Poulter's measure exists today in a modified form; it is a four-line stanza composed of iambic trimeter verses for the first, second, and fourth lines, and an iambic tetrameter for the third. The opening lines of Arthur Brooke's *Romeus and Juliet* afford an example of poulter's measure:

> There is beyond the Alps, a town of ancient fame,
> Whose bright renown yet shineth clear, Verona men it name;
> Built in a happy time, built on a fertile soil,
> Maintainéd by the heavenly fates, and by the townish toil.

**Preamble:** An introductory portion of a written document. In formal sets of "resolutions" there is usually a "preamble" which sets forth the occasion for the resolutions. This preamble is introduced by one or more statements beginning with "Whereas" and is followed by the resolutions proper, each article of which is introduced by the word "Therefore."

**Preciosity:** A critical term sometimes applied to writing which is consciously "pretty," labored or affected in style, fastidious in diction.

**Preface:** A short introductory statement printed at the beginning of a book or article—and separate from it—in which the author states his purpose in writing, makes necessary acknowledgments of assistance, points out difficulties and uncertainties in connection with the writing of the book, and, in general, informs the reader of such facts as he thinks pertinent to a reading of the text.   Some writers, notably Dryden and Shaw, have written "prefaces" which were really extended essays.

**Prelude:** A short poem, introductory in character, prefixed to a long poem or to a section of a long poem.   Lowell's *The Vision of Sir Launfal* contains preludes of the latter sort.   Rarely, as in the case of Wordsworth's famous *Prelude*, a poem so entitled may itself be lengthy.

**Pre-Raphaelitism:** The Pre-Raphaelite movement, a phase of romanticism, originated with the establishment in 1848 of the Pre-Raphaelite brotherhood by Dante Gabriel Rossetti, Holman Hunt, John Everett Millais, and other artists as a protest against the conventional methods of painting then in use.   The Pre-Raphaelites wished to regain the spirit of simple devotion and adherence to nature which they found in Italian religious art before Raphael.   Ruskin asserted that Pre-Raphaelitism had but one principle, that of absolute uncompromising truth in all that it did, truth attained by elaborating everything, down to the most minute detail, from nature and from nature only. This meant the rejection of all conventions designed to heighten effects artificially.   Several of the group were both artists and poets, and the effect of the cult was therefore felt in English literature.   Rossetti was the most influential. His *Blessed Damozel*, published in 1850 in one of the four issues of *The Germ*, the organ of the group, is a religious narrative with pictorial qualities. In general, the characteristics of Pre-Raphaelite poetry are: pictorial elements, symbolism, sensuousness, tendency to metrical experimentation, attention to minute detail, and an interest in the medieval and the supernatural. By certain critics, who deemed sensuousness the dominant characteristic of their poetry, the Pre-Raphaelites were styled the "fleshly school" (*q.v.*). The chief literary products of the movement were Rossetti's translation of Dante, his sonnets, and his ballad-like verse; Christina Rossetti's lyrics; and the poems of William Morris, such as *The Earthly Paradise* and *The Defense of Guinevere*. Morris' practical application of medieval craftsmanship to business effected a great change in public taste in home decoration. (Reference: P. H. Bate, *The English Pre-Raphaelite Painters*.)

**Primitivism:** The doctrine that primitive man, because he has remained closer to nature and has been less subject to the corrupt influences of society, was nobler and more nearly perfect than is civilized man. The idea flourished in eighteenth-century England and France and was an important element in the creed of the "sentimentalists" of the romantic movement. Though it is perhaps not possible to trace all the forces which aided in the development and promulgation of the primitivistic doctrine, a few may be suggested. The rationalistic philosopher, the third Earl of Shaftesbury (*fl. ca.* 1710), in his effort to show that God had revealed himself completely in Nature—and that Nature was therefore perfect—reasoned that primitive peoples were close to God and therefore essentially moral. Man is by nature prone to do good: his evil comes from self-imposed limitations of his freedom. Romantic accounts of savage peoples by writers of travel literature added impetus to the movement, as did also the linguistic researches into the origin of language by such men as Lord Monboddo (*The Origin of Language*, 1773–1792), and the effort of various scholars to find the reason for Homer's greatness in his assumed primitive surroundings. Tremendous impetus from France was given the movement by the writings of Rousseau, whose slogan of "Return to Nature" was based upon his belief that man was potentially perfect and that his faults were due to the vicious effect of the type of society he had developed, one which tended progressively to restrict the freedom and hence lessen the moral goodness of man.

One of the most interesting phases of the primitivistic movement in English literature was its doctrine that the best poetry should be natural or instinctive, not cultivated. There was therefore a feverish search not only for a perfect primitive man but for a perfect "untutored" poet. Among the many savages brought by the primitivists to England in their search for the perfect natural man the enthusiasts searched for evidence of poetic genius. The "inspired peasant" was sought for, too, among the unlettered population of Great Britain, and many such "geniuses" were fêted by high society till their fame wore out: Henry Jones, the poetical bricklayer; James Woodhouse, the poetical shoemaker; and Ann Yearsley, the poetical milkwoman of Bristol, who signed her poems "Lactilla" and was sponsored by the "bluestockings" (*q.v.*). Gray's *The Bard* (1757) and James Beattie's *The Minstrel* (1771–1774) reflect the doctrine of primitive poetic genius, and no lover of English poetry can forget the "some mute inglorious Milton" of Gray's famous *Elegy*. For a time the forged "Ossian" poems of James Macpherson (see LITERARY FORGERIES) seemed an answer to the romantic prayer for the discovery in Britain of the work of some primitive epic poet. When, finally, Robert Burns appeared, the doctrine of the peasant poet seemed proved, and the Scotch bard was received with extravagant enthusiasm, especially in Edinburgh.

Of course, all England did not go primitivistic. The craze was ironically attacked by such conservatives as Doctor Johnson and Edmund Burke. The "noble savage" idea produced the idealized American Indian, as in Cooper's novels, and American life was exploited as ideal because primitive, as in Crèvecoeur's *Letters from an American Farmer* and G. Imlay's novel of pioneer life, *The Emigrants*. (For the later reaction against these idealized treatments of the Indian and the pioneer see Francis Parkman's *The Oregon Trail* and Hamlin Garland's *Main Travelled Roads* or his *A Son of the Middle Border*.) It has been seriously asserted that the enthusiastic reception of Benjamin Franklin in Paris was partly attributable to the interest in Americans stirred by the primitivists. (References: Lois Whitney,

*Primitivism and the Idea of Progress*, esp. the "Foreword" by Arthur O. Lovejoy; C. B. Tinker, *Nature's Simple Plan;* H. N. Fairchild, *The Noble Savage.*)

**Printing, Introduction into American Colonies:** Although the Spaniards had brought printing presses to Mexico and elsewhere much earlier, the real beginning of printing in America dates from 1639, when, according to Governor Winthrop's *Diary,* a printing house was begun by Stephen Daye. In reality, Daye was the printer, not the proprietor. The first thing printed was the freeman's oath, the next an almanac, and the next the famous "Bay Psalm Book" (1640), the earliest surviving American book. William Bradford was printing in Philadelphia as early as 1683. Later he moved to New York and became the government printer. The introduction of printing into Virginia was opposed by Governor Berkeley and a printing establishment was suppressed in 1682, though printing was reintroduced not long thereafter. (References: F. W. Hamilton, *A Brief History of Printing in America;* Isaiah Thomas, *History of Printing in America,* 2 vols.; Milton Waldman, *Americana;* John T. Winterich, *Early American Books and Printing.*)

**Printing, Introduction into England:** The debt which literature owes to the art of printing is so great that every reader of books should acquaint himself with its history. The development of printing in the fifteenth century was not only encouraged by the new intellectual curiosity of Renaissance times but itself supplied a powerful stimulus to the revival of learning and the literature which followed in its wake. The first generation or so of printers busied themselves chiefly with the reproduction of the great works of the past, medieval and classical, and with ecclesiastical documents. By the first decade of the sixteenth century printers were beginning to be of service to contemporary writers by supplying them with a vastly enlarged potential audience, and the glorious harvest in literature produced by the Renaissance could hardly have been possible without the aid of the printing press. Relations between printers and writers became increasingly close, and it was a publisher (Richard Tottel) rather than a professional man of letters who supplied the great impetus to creative poetic work in England by publishing a large collection of manuscript poems of Wyatt and Surrey and others just before the beginning of Elizabeth's reign (*Tottel's Miscellany*, 1557). By making literature salable, the printers helped create the professional man of letters. The circumstances surrounding the invention and development of printing in Western Europe (the Chinese and Japanese had practised a simple form of printing centuries before) are so lost in obscurity that it is impossible now to assign the invention to any country or person or exact date. Although there seems to have been some sort of forerunner of the printed book in Holland, it is fairly certain that the most important development of the art took place in Mainz, Germany, during the forties and fifties of the fifteenth century. The earliest existing book which can be dated is an "Indulgence" (Mainz, 1454); the most famous existing early book is the so-called Gutenberg Bible (Mainz, 1456). On the authority of fifteenth-century writers, John Gutenberg of Mainz is commonly given credit for the invention.

From Mainz the art spread to Italy, France, Holland, and other countries, reaching England in 1476, when William Caxton set up his famous press at Westminster. Caxton had learned printing on the Continent, and at Bruges, probably in 1475, had brought out the first book printed in English, the *Recuyell of the Histories of Troy*. The first printed books in England were perhaps pamphlets, some of them in Latin, but the first dated English book printed in England was Caxton's *Dictes or Sayings of the Philosophers* (1477). Before his death Caxton had printed about a hundred separate books. He did much to direct the public taste in reading. He specialized in translations, poetry, and romances, two of his most important books being his edition of Chaucer's *Canterbury Tales* (1483) and his publication of Malory's *Le Morte d'Arthur* (1485). Other early presses in England include one at Oxford (1478) and one at St. Albans (1479), both devoted chiefly to learned works. Caxton himself was succeeded by his assistant, Wynken de Worde, a printer without literary talent but important because he published, during his long career, about 800 books, some of them of literary interest. An important contemporary was Richard Pynson (*fl.*1490–1530). (References: H. G. Aldis, *History of Printing;* H. R. Plomer, *A Short History of English Printing;* W. Blades, *The Biography and*

*Typography of William Caxton*, 2 vols.; C. J. Sawyer, *English Books, 1475–1900;* J. E. Oswald, *History of Printing.*)

**Private Theatres:** This term seems to have arisen about 1596, when the Blackfriars theatre was so described by its sponsors who were seeking privileges not granted to the "public" theatres. The name is misleading, since the "private" theatres, though they charged a higher admission fee and attracted in general a higher class of spectators than did their "public" rivals, were open to all classes. They did differ from the public theatres in that they were indoor institutions, artificially lighted, smaller, and rectangular in shape. As the private theatre was connected in its origin with companies of child actors, so in its maturity it was used chiefly (not exclusively) by the companies of child actors. The Elizabethan private theatres were the Blackfriars, Paul's School, the Cockpit (or Phoenix), and Salisbury Court, the latter two being known also as "court theatres." Shakespeare's company in the early seventeenth century controlled both the Blackfriars, the chief private theatre, and the Globe, the chief public theatre. The private theatres, being indoor institutions of a somewhat aristocratic character, became of increasing importance in the seventeenth century, when the Court was fostering elaborate exhibitions (see MASQUE) and encouraging drama with spectacular features, and it is from them rather than from the public theatres that the elaborate playhouses of the Restoration and later times are directly descended. See PUBLIC THEATRES. (References: A. H. Thorndike, *Shakespeare's Theatre;* J. Q. Adams, *Shakespearean Playhouses.*)

**Problem Novel:** A name given to that type of prose fiction which derives its chief interest from working out, through characters and incidents, some central problem. In a loose sense almost every novel or plot presents a problem since the opposition of forces which make for plot-conflict also should arouse some interest in the reader as to "how this is to turn out." However, the term is usually more restricted than this. It is sometimes carelessly applied to those novels which are written for a deliberate purpose, a thesis, which are better called "propaganda novels" since they present a brief for or against one class

339

of people, one type of living, one activity of civilization. Since human character is the subject surest to interest readers and since humankind is constantly confronted by problems of life and conduct, it follows that the problem novel—when it is thought of as a story *with* a purpose rather than *for* a purpose— is fairly common. In this sense *The Scarlet Letter* may be thought of as a problem novel: "How can a young woman settling in a new Puritan community and convicted of adultery work out her own salvation against the smugness of the life about her?" Some of the more common problems introduced into fiction of this sort are: "How shall one choose between honor and love, between patriotic duty and love, between honorable poverty and dishonorable wealth, between one's profession or art and love, between individuality of life and life for the common good of humanity?" An interesting instance of the problem in a short story is Frank R. Stockton's *The Lady or the Tiger?*—a story in which the author deliberately refuses to answer his own question, leaving the reader to work out his solution according to his convictions of the strength or frailty of womankind.

**Problem Play:** Like its analogue in non-dramatic fiction, the "problem novel" (*q.v.*), this term is used both in a broad sense to cover all serious drama in which problems of human life are presented as such, e.g., Shakespeare's *King Lear*, and in a more specialized sense to designate the modern "drama of ideas," as exemplified in the plays of Ibsen, Shaw, Galsworthy, and many others. (References: T. H. Dickinson, *An Outline of Contemporary Drama*; Ramsden Balmforth, *The Problem-Play and its Influence on Modern Thought and Life*; W. W. Lawrence, *Shakespeare's Problem Comedies*.)

**Proem:** A brief introduction, a preface or preamble.

**Prolegomenon:** A foreword or preface. The heading *prolegomena* may be given to the introductory section of a book containing observations on the subject of the book itself.

**Prolepsis:** An anticipating; the type of anachronism in which an event is pictured as taking place before it could have done so, the treating of a future event as if past. Rhetorically, the word may be applied to a preliminary statement or summary which is to be followed by a detailed treatment. In argumentation "prolepsis" may mean the device of anticipating and answering an opponent's argument before the opponent has an opportunity to introduce it, thus detracting from its effectiveness if later employed.

**Prologue:** A preface or introduction most frequently associated with drama and especially common in England in the plays of the Restoration and the eighteenth century. In the plays of ancient Greece a speaker announced, before the beginning of the play proper, such salient facts as were necessary for the audience to know to understand the play itself. In Latin drama the same custom prevailed, Plautus having left some of the most matured prologues in dramatic literature. European dramatists in both France and England followed the classical tradition, from the time of the miracle and mystery plays (which may be said to have used prologues of a *moral* nature) well into modern times. Prologues were frequently written by the author of a play and delivered by one of the chief actors; it was, however, in the eighteenth century, common practice for writers of established reputations, such as Pope, Doctor Johnson, and Garrick, to write prologues for the plays of their friends and acquaintances. Sometimes, as in the play within the play in *Hamlet*, the actor who spoke the prologue was himself called "the prologue." The first part of Shakespeare's *King Henry IV* opens with an explanatory speech, not formally a prologue, which serves the function of a real prologue. Part two of the same play opens with a prologue called an "induction." See INDUCTION and EPILOGUE.

**Propaganda Novel:** See PROBLEM NOVEL.

**Proscenium:** Properly used, the term now designates that part of the stage in a modern theatre which lies between the orchestra and the curtain. In the ancient theatre the proscenium extended from the orchestra to the background, and the term is not infrequently used, even nowadays, merely as a synonym for the stage itself.

341

**Prose:** "All forms of careful literary expression which are not metrically versified" writes Edmund Gosse in his article in the *Encyclopædia Britannica*. The definition deserves some elaboration. "Careful" is included to indicate that any collection of words thrown together, any setting down of haphazard conversation, for instance, is not to be considered prose. Prose is "literary expression" in that it must be a conscious, cultivated writing, not merely a bringing together of vocabularies, a listing of ideas, a catalogue of objects. And, while prose is like verse in that good prose has a rhythm, it is unlike verse in that this rhythm is not to be scanned by any metrical pattern. But a clear line between prose and poetry is difficult to draw. Is bad verse prose? Is rhythmical prose verse? Is Miss Lowell's "polyphonic prose" verse, or prose, or something between the two? It is easier, perhaps, to list some of the qualities of prose: (1) it is without sustained metrical regularity, (2) it has some logical, grammatical order and its ideas are connectedly stated rather than merely listed, (3) it is characterized by the virtues of style though the style will vary, naturally, from writer to writer, (4) it will secure variety of expression through diction and through sentence structure.

Prose, interestingly enough, has in all literatures developed more slowly than verse. English prose is conceded to find its origin in the work of Alfred, whose *Handbook* (887) is cited by Edmund Gosse as "probably the earliest specimen of finished English prose." Other names significant in the development of English prose are Thomas Usk, John Wycliffe, Malory, Caxton, Roger Ascham, Holinshed, Lyly, Raleigh, Donne, Jeremy Taylor, Milton, Dryden, and Addison. For many centuries English prose had to compete with Latin for recognition, and for many more years Latin forms and syntax modeled the style. The single book which did most to mold English prose style was obviously the Bible and, more particularly, the King James version of the Bible. See following definition and "Outline of Literary History," *passim*. (References: G. P. Krapp, *Modern English* and *The Rise of English Literary Prose*.)

**Prose Rhythm:** The recurrence of accent and emphasis at regular or, much more usually, irregular intervals which gives to the best prose a pleasurable rise and fall of movement. Prose rhythm is distinguished from the rhythm of verse in that it never for long falls into a recognizable meter, for if it does, of course, it becomes verse rather than prose. Rhythm in prose is essentially a quality of style, the superior stylist using a more rhythmical expression than the jerky staccato of a beginner, avoiding, as he does, the sing-song monotony of regularity and making every effort to secure a constant *flow* of accent, always changing yet always harmonizing with the thought and sense he is expressing. In emotional passages the author may trust rhythm more deliberately than in his more pedestrian moments since rhythm is itself so definitely and naturally the voice of passion.

The greater freedom of prose rhythm, as compared with the rhythm of verse, springs from its wider choice in the placing of accents. There is no necessity to force a line to a certain metrical pattern. The normal accent of words, of course, first determines the rhythmic emphasis. But this is augmented by the secondary accents (in such words as ob''-ser-va'-tion and el''-e-men'-ta-ry) and increased again by the tendency of the reader to emphasize certain words importantly placed or rendered significant because of their meaning. A brief passage from the writing of Walter Pater, an author whose work is among the most rhythmic writings in English, is selected at random and accented according to the ear of at least one reader:

"To such a tremulous wisp constantly reforming itself on the stream, to a single sharp impression, with a sense in it, a relic more or less fleeting, of such moments gone by, what is real in our life fines itself down."

A rhythmic analysis of the sentence shows an almost consistent use of anapests and iambs—a preponderant tendency toward the use of one or two (or sometimes three) unaccented syllables followed by an accented one. But, granting that Pater is exceptional, that the accents indicated are perhaps arbitrary, and that some other reader will record the emphasis differently, the fact will remain that the passage is definitely rhythmical. (References: G. P. Krapp, *The Rise of English*

*Literary Prose;* George Saintsbury, *A History of English Prose Rhythm.*)

**Prosody:** The theory and principles of versification, particularly as they refer to rhythm and accent. For list of separate terms in prosody defined in this book, see VERSIFICATION.

**Protagonist:** The chief character in a play or story. When the plot involves conflict, the chief opponent or rival of the protagonist is called an antagonist. If the main plot centers about the career of a hero who overcomes a "villain" who tries to thwart his efforts, the hero would be called the protagonist, the villain the antagonist. If, however, the main interest lies in the career of a villain, whose plans are defeated by the appearance of a successful hero, the villain would be called the protagonist and the hero the antagonist. In Shakespeare's *Hamlet*, Hamlet is himself the protagonist, as his fortunes are the chief interest in the play. King Claudius and Laertes are his antagonists. The sentence "The protagonists of Christopher Marlowe's tragedies are usually of the super-personality type" illustrates a usual use of the word. In a looser sense "protagonist" is sometimes used in the sense of champion or chief advocate of a cause or movement, as when Bryan is referred to as the protagonist of the free-silver movement in 1896.

**Prototype:** A first form or original instance of a thing, or model or pattern for later forms or examples. Thus the "periodical" essay of the eighteenth century as written by Addison or Steele may be referred to as the prototype of the modern familiar essay as written by Lamb or Stevenson, the later form being developed from the earlier. Or the "Vice" of the morality plays may be regarded as the prototype of the clown of Elizabethan drama.

**Proverb:** A sentence or phrase which briefly and strikingly expresses some recognized truth or shrewd observation about practical life and which has been preserved by oral tradition, though it may be preserved and transmitted in written literature as well. It commonly originates with the folk. So far as form goes, proverbs may owe their appeal to the use of a metaphor ("Still waters run deep"); antithesis ("Man proposes, God disposes"); a play on words ("Forewarned, forearmed"); rime

("A friend in need is a friend indeed"); or such devices as alliteration or parallel structure. Some are epigrammatic. Since the true proverb is old, its language is sometimes archaic. Words or meanings or idioms or grammatical constructions not now common may be used. A misunderstanding of the original meaning may result. Thus in "Time and tide wait for no man" *tide* is probably the old word for "season." "Feed a cold, starve a fever," which seems to be medical advice of questionable value, becomes sensible if it means "If you feed a cold, you'll have a fever to starve." The range of interest of the proverb is, of course, wide: the weather, remedies for illness, legal shifts, superstitions, agriculture, efficiency in practical life, satire on other races or on rival countries or localities, etc. Proverbs pass freely from language to language. Those with a long "literary" history, though popular in origin, are sometimes called "learned proverbs." For a careful study of the proverb by an American scholar see Archer Taylor, *The Proverb*. G. L. Apperson's *English Proverbs* and G. W. Smith's *The Oxford Dictionary of English Proverbs* are collections in dictionary form. See APHORISM.

**Provincialism:** See COLLOQUIALISM.

**Psalm:** A lyrical composition of praise. Most frequently, of course, the term is applied to the sacred and devout lyrics in the Book of Psalms ascribed to David.

**Pseudo-Classicism:** See NEO-CLASSICISM.

**Pseudonym:** A fictitious name sometimes assumed by writers and others. See NOM DE PLUME.

**Pseudo-Shakespearean Plays:** The list of plays attributed to Shakespeare at one time or another but not accepted as his by the best authorities. There are about as many plays in this list as in the "true" list. Because of Shakespeare's reputation, some non-Shakespearean plays, such as *Locrine*, were printed during Shakespeare's lifetime with his initials or name on the title page; others, such as *The Birth of Merlin*, were so printed after Shakespeare's death. Another group, including *Mucedorus*, consists of plays labeled as Shakespeare's in the copies of them found in the library of Charles II. Many others, including *Sir Thomas More* (the manuscript copy of which is thought by some experts to be partly in Shakespeare's handwriting) and *Arden of Feversham*, have been assigned to Shakespeare by editors, booksellers, or critics chiefly on the basis of their literary or technical qualities. The First Folio (1623) contains plays assembled by Shakespeare's fellow actors, Heming and Condell, who, it would seem, were in position to know the facts. But they may have been forced to omit some genuine plays because of ownership difficulties (they omit, for example, *Pericles*, now regarded as largely Shakespeare's). Further, they included some plays, such as *Henry VIII*, *Titus Andronicus*, and the Henry VI plays, which there are grounds for regarding as partly non-Shakespearean. The custom of collaboration— the writing of a single play by two or more playwrights—may have left the 1623 editors in doubt as to the inclusion of plays of which Shakespeare was a reviser or part author. A collection of pseudo-Shakespearean plays has been printed by Tucker Brooke in his *Shakespeare Apocrypha*. Some of the plays dubiously assigned to Shakespeare, such as *Cardenio*, have not survived.

**Psychological Novel, The:** Prose fiction which places more than the usual amount of emphasis on characterization, and on the motives, circumstances, and internal action which springs from, and develops, external action. The psychological novel is not content to state what happens but goes on to explain the *why* and the *wherefore* of this action. In this type of writing character and characterization are more than usually important. Of course in one sense the psychological story is as old as the first drama or tale or ballad which accounted for external action by recounting qualities of character of the hero. Chaucer's *Troilus and Criseyde* is a psychological novel in verse. *Hamlet* is a psychological drama; but, in somewhat lesser degree, so are most of Shakespeare's better plays. The psychological novel is, as one critic has said, an interpretation of "the invisible life." As such it is more likely to be related to the realistic novel than to the romantic. The term was first importantly applied to a group of novelists in the middle of the nineteenth century, a group of which Mrs. Gaskell, George Eliot, and George Meredith were perhaps the chief writers. Mrs. Gaskell, writing about the middle of the nineteenth century, stated that "all deeds however hidden and long passed by have their external consequences"—thus giving expression to an attitude long realized and felt if not always deliberately expressed. Thackeray and Dickens, too, were interested enough in motives and details to be classified, in a looser sense, as writers of the psychological novel. Hardy and Conrad, to advance our chronicle to later years, also wrote psychologically. But it is in the twentieth century, with the advance of psychology as a science, that the term has come into most popular use. Freudianism particularly gave impetus to the type; for some years it appeared that there was no deity but Freud and that James Joyce was to be his prophet. In this stricter, more modern sense, the term *psychological novel* is now applied to such writings as Joyce's *Ulysses* and Dreiser's *An American Tragedy*. See NOVEL, STREAM-OF-CONSCIOUSNESS NOVEL.

**Public Theatres:** The English playhouse developed in Elizabethan times as a natural accompaniment of the increased interest in the drama. In earlier times plays had been produced on "pageants" (see PAGEANT) and in indoor rooms such as guild halls and the halls of great houses, schools, and inns of court. The demand for larger places resulted in the use of innyards, which were square or rectangular courts enclosed by the inner porches or balconies of the inn building. In one end would be erected a temporary stage connected with rooms of the inn. The spectators might stand in the open court ("groundlings") or get seats on the surrounding balconies. Meantime the need for a place for bear- or bull-baiting spectacles and acrobatic performances had been met in the development of a sort of ring or amphitheatre. Out of the physical features of the inn-yard (surrounding galleries or boxes, open central space or pit, stage extending into pit) and the bear garden (circular form of building) the plan of the first public theatre was evolved. The front stage was open to the sky, the rear stage covered by a ceiling. Above this ceiling was a room for the machinery needed in lowering persons and objects to the stage below, or raising them from it. There was an "inner" stage at the rear, provided with a curtain and connected with a balcony above, also curtained. The rear stage was used chiefly for special settings such as a forest or bedroom, while the bare outer stage was used for street scenes, battles, and the like. The scenery and the costumes of the actors were largely conventional and symbolic, though certainly very realistic at times.

The first public theatre in London was the Theatre, built in 1576 by James Burbage in Shoreditch. It was followed in 1577 by the Curtain in the same neighborhood. About ten years later Henslowe built the Rose on the Bankside, and in this locality appeared also the Swan (1594). In 1599 the Theatre was torn down and re-erected on the Bankside as the Globe, the most important one of the public theatres. The Globe was used and controlled by the company to which Shakespeare belonged. Henslowe built the Fortune in 1600, the Red Bull appeared soon after in St. John's Street, and the Hope in 1614 near the Rose and the new Globe. For distinction between "public" and "private" theatres see PRIVATE THEATRES. (References: A. H. Thorndike, *Shakespeare's Theatre;* J. Q. Adams, *Shakespearean Playhouses.*)

**Pun:** A play on words based on the similarity of sound between two words with different meanings. An example is Thomas Hood's: "They went and told the sexton and the sexton tolled the bell."

**Purist:** One who habitually stresses, or overstresses, correctness or "purity" in language, particularly in minor or "fine" points of grammar, diction, pronunciation, and rhetorical style. The term is commonly used in a spirit of deprecation or mild reproach, because the extreme purist is felt not only to have lost his sense of proportion in his zeal for preserving fine distinctions but also frequently to exhibit ignorance of the actual laws of language, since he is prone to regard language as a static thing instead of a developing instrument of communication. An example is perhaps the insistence upon certain subjunctive forms of the English verb in constructions where the subjunctive mood would be demanded by formal grammar based upon the rules of Latin grammar but where actual English usage has substituted the indicative for the subjunctive, as in the sentence "if it *be* a good thing, let us approve it" where "if it *is* a good thing, let us approve it" has become established as more common and equally good English. The purist, too, is likely to ignore the existence of different levels of speech and to insist upon the use of "bookish" English on all occasions, ignoring the fact that an English style which would be eminently appropriate at a White House audience might be highly injudicious and inappropriate in a lumber camp or on the sporting pages of a newspaper. It must be remembered, however, that it is difficult to draw the line between the "purist" and the person who takes a commendable interest in achieving that accuracy and precision in language which are regarded as an important social grace and which lend dignity to his personality. The distinction is often one of degree only or of manner, and after all the purist has a more wholesome attitude toward the problem than does the careless person who is satisfied in his use of slovenly English.

A related though quite different use of the word is seen in its application to a person who feels that the "purity" of a language can be preserved only by the exclusion of foreign words and of words not used by the best stylists. Thus the so-called Ciceronians of the Renaissance, a group of Latin stylists who would not use any Latin word that could not be found in Cicero's writings, have been called "purists," as have the English scholars of the sixteenth century and later who insisted upon a "pure" English diction "unmixed and unmangled with borrowing of other tongues." The famous schoolmasters Sir John Cheke and Roger Ascham and the rhetorician Thomas Wilson were leaders in this movement. In the main they were not absolute purists, however, since they recognized that English might legitimately be enriched by the use of some foreign words; but they opposed strongly the pedantic tendency of the time which threatened to make literary English a mere Latin *patois*. The struggle between these "purists" and their "inkhorn" opponents is sometimes referred to as the "purist-improver" controversy.

Later movements toward purism included: the unsuccessful effort in the seventeenth century to establish (on the model of the French Academy) a British Academy to regulate language; eighteenth-century efforts at standardization through the establishment of some definite linguistic authority (opposed by Doctor Johnson); Wordsworth's attempt to employ in his poems only simple words drawn from actual speech; and later efforts to stress the Anglo-Saxon elements in the vocabulary and to check the importation of foreign words (noteworthy is Edna St. Vincent Millay's attempt to write a long poem, *The King's Henchman*, employing only words of Anglo-Saxon derivation). Some good doubtless has resulted from efforts to preserve the strong and picturesque elements of native English speech and to check foolish or unnecessary adoption of foreign words; yet it seems clear that the English language will continue to enrich its resources in the future as it has done in the past by appropriating needed words wherever it finds them. (Reference: G. P. Krapp, *Modern English*.)

**Puritanism:** A religious-political movement which developed in England about the middle of the sixteenth century and later spread its influence most importantly into the New England colonies in America. While politically it died with the return of Charles the Second to London in 1660, Puritanism left its impress and many of its attitudes on the habits and thought of the people, especially of America today. As a term, "Puritan" was, in Elizabeth's reign, applied to those who wished to "purify" the Church of England. The name was at first one of derision. The spirit which prompted the reforms of Puritanism was an outgrowth of Calvinism which had spread from Geneva to England.

In principle the Puritans objected to certain forms of the established Church. They objected, for instance, to the wearing of the surplice, and to government by the prelates, and they demanded the right to partake of the communion in a sitting posture. The Millenary Petitions (1603) of the Puritans requested a reform of the church courts, a doing away with "superstitious" customs, a discarding of the use of apocryphal books of the Bible, a serious observance of Sunday, and various ecclesiastical reforms. While at first Puritanism in England was not directly affiliated with Presbyterianism, it later on allied itself, largely for political reasons, very definitely with the Presbyterian movement. Thomas Cartwright, the first important spokesman of Puritanism, hated most emphatically the Church of England; "his bigotry," writes John Richard Green, "was that of a medieval inquisitor. The relics of the old ritual, the cross in baptism, the surplice, the giving of a ring in marriage, were to him not merely distasteful, as they were to the Puritans at large, they were idolatrous and the mark of the beast."

The conception of the Puritans popularly held today, however, is very unfair to the general tone and temper of the early sponsors of the movement. These early English Puritans were not long-faced reformers, not teetotalers, not haters of art and music. They were often, later on, patrons of art and lovers of music, fencing, and dancing. They were intelligent, self-controlled, plainly dressed citizens who held to simplicity and to democratic principles. But it is true that under the persecution of Charles and the double-dealing of Laud they were harried into bitterness. To quote Green again,

Humour, the faculty which above all corrects exaggerations and extravagance, died away before the new stress and strain of existence. The absolute devotion of the Puritan to a Supreme Will tended more and more to rob him of all sense of measure and proportion in common matters. Little things became great things in the glare of religious zeal; and the godly man learnt to shrink from a surplice, or a mince-pie at Christmas, as he shrank from impurity of a lie. Life became hard, rigid, colourless, as it became intense. The play, the geniality, the delight of the Elizabethan age were exchanged for a measured sobriety, seriousness, and self-restraint. But the self-restraint and sobriety which marked the Calvinist limited itself wholly to his outer life. In his inner soul sense, reason, judgment, were too often overborne by the terrible reality of invisible things.

The history of the rise and fall of Puritanism in England is too much involved with religious, political, and social attitudes for even a simple presentation here. All that can be said is that, as we look back from this period of time, Puritanism seems a natural enough aftermath of the Renaissance, the Reformation, the establishment of the Church of England, and the growth of Presbyterianism. Through all of these great movements one somehow sees steadily emerging the right of the individual to political and religious independence. The reading of the Bible had become general. The Catholic Church had lost its pristine power in England, but there were still thousands of Catholics who wanted their old power restored. The people were always suspicious that their rulers, a James I or a Charles I, might swing back to the faith of Spain and Italy. Political power for the commoners lay with Presbyterianism, a religious movement based on the political control of presbyters drawn from the people. Catholicism and even the Church of England were far too reminiscent of autocracy and of divine right to rule. Whitgift and Laud wished to stamp out Puritanism; James I had promised that if necessary he would "harry the Puritans out of the land." Charles I and Laud fought popular rights and suppressed Parliament. The Church of England took little note of the handwriting on the wall. Milton at this time wrote his famous digression in *Lycidas* to condemn the Church and the clergy: "Blind mouths! that scarce themselves know how to hold a sheephook." From 1642 to 1646 civil war was waged in England, a civil war from which rose to power a new Puritan leader, Oliver Cromwell. In 1649 Charles was beheaded. The Puritan Commonwealth was established. And then, on May 25, 1660, Charles II landed at Dover.

So far we have noted the trend of Puritanism only in England. But to America Puritanism was almost of more moment, since to the dissatisfaction with political life in England and the consequent emigration to the colonies, American life, and thought, and literature may almost be said to owe their origins. Some of the "Brownists," a group of Puritans who had left England for seclusion in Holland, came to America in the *Mayflower*. They wished to set up a new theocracy in which the Puritan ideas of religion and government were to go hand in hand. "I shall call that my country where I may most glorify God and enjoy the presence of my dearest friends," said young Winthrop. In one year as many as three thousand disgruntled rebels left England for the Colonies; in ten years there were twenty thousand English in America. And many of these newcomers were men of education, of intelligence, of family position and culture. And those at least who settled in and around Massachusetts were bent on forming a new government, a theocracy, with God and Christ at the head, and with their own chosen rulers to interpret God's will for them. What now seems, as we look back at it all, a gesture toward conservatism, a threat against freedom of speech, and art, and individualism, was, it should be remembered, at that time essentially a radical movement. If in the twentieth century the Puritan attitude seems pretty strait-laced, we should recall that its exponents were rebels against religious and governmental intolerance at home.

No great change, no political and religious upheaval such as the development of Puritanism, can be isolated from the literature of the time. In England, the epoch has given a name to a period of literature, the so-called "Cavalier-Puritan Period." From the writers of this mood in England two great names emerge to tower over all others of the century, John Bunyan and John Milton.

In America, a dozen or two writers have attained a sort of immortality in American literature largely because they happened to stand at the source of the stream. Such theologians as John Cotton, Thomas Hooker, John Eliot, Cotton Mather; such historians as William Bradford, John Winthrop, Thomas Hutchinson, and Samuel Sewall; and such poets as Nathaniel Ward, Anne Bradstreet, and Michael Wigglesworth derive a fictitious importance from their historical position. But whatever their importance to literature may be, the early divines left clear-cut their imprint on American life. *The Bay Psalm Book* (1640) became almost the book of a people. In America the difficulties of settlement, the sordidness of life during the early years in a new land, the religious fervor of most of the settlers—these gave a dim color to Colonial life which is not yet completely erased and which still gives tone to our literature and criticism. See CALVINISM.

**"Purple Patch":** A piece of "fine writing." Now and then authors in a strongly emotional passage will give free play to most of the stylistic tricks in their bag. They will write prose which is intensely colorful, more than usually rhythmic, marked by an involved parallelism, full of imagery and figures of speech, characterized by a poetic diction, etc. When there is an unusual piling up of these devices in such a way as to evidence a self-conscious literary effort, the section is spoken of as a "purple patch"—a colorful, stylistic passage standing out from the writing around it.

**Pyrrhic:** A foot of two unaccented syllables (⌣⌣); the opposite of spondee (＿＿). Common in classical poetry, the pyrrhic is unusual in English versification and is not accepted as a foot at all by some prosodists since it contains no accented syllable. Fowler states that the English pyrrhic is represented chiefly by double anacrusis (*q.v.*), as *O my* in

$$\breve{O} \; m\breve{y} \; | \; \overline{Mari} \; | \; \overline{on's \; \breve{a}} \; | \; \overline{bonn\breve{y}} \; | \; \overline{lass}.$$

**Quadrivium:** See SEVEN ARTS.

**Quantity:** The duration and intensity (stress) employed in pronouncing a syllable. Thus we have long and short syllables, accented and unaccented syllables, the "quantity" of long or accented syllables being "greater" than that of short or unaccented syllables. In classic poetry the long syllables were, for purposes of meter, counted as the equal of two short syllables in *quantity*. English versification is generally said to be based on *accent* rather than on *quantity*, since the differences in the languages prevented the use of the classical system in English versification; but even so quantity is obviously present in our poetry. To realize just how significant quantity is we need only consider the difference in stress between two such one-syllable words as "ton" and "town," or between "ten" and "strange." As one-syllable words any one of the four might appear either accented or unaccented in a line of verse, but it certainly would not be possible to argue that they were, even if all were given stressed positions, of equal quantity. It would appear, then, that even with a metrical system based on accent (*q.v.*) quantity still remains a definite influence. Certainly all accented syllables are not of equal quantity any more than all unaccented syllables are.

Quantity is an important element in verse-style since the poet with a keen appreciation of quantitative values has just so much more range, so many more delicate rhythmic values, at his command. As the grace note in music gives to that art especial charm and variation, so a deft distinction as to the quantity of syllables gives to poetry a more graceful beauty than a mere alternation of monotonous accented and unaccented syllables could ever do. Furthermore, the skillful poet may vary his possibilities for different effects of quantity by making use of the emphasis inherent in mere grammatical structure, in positions carrying stress because of their rhetorical importance, and in extra pauses arising from forms of punctuation. See STRESS, ACCENT.

**Quarterly Review, The:** See EDINBURGH REVIEW.

**Quarto:** See BOOK SIZES.

**Quatorzain:** A poem of fourteen lines. The term, however, is not now specifically applied to the sonnet (though of course the sonnet is a fourteen-line form) but is reserved for poems which do not otherwise conform to one or another of the sonnet patterns.

**Quatrain:** A stanza consisting of four verses. In its narrow meaning, the term is restricted to a complete poem consisting of four lines only, but in its broader sense it signifies any one of many four-verse stanza forms. The possible rime schemes within the stanza vary from an unrimed quatrain to almost any arrangement of one-rime, two-rime, or three-rime lines. Perhaps the most common form is the *abab* sequence; other popular rime-patterns are *aabb; abba; aaba; abcb.* A quatrain of this last pattern is quoted from Robert Burns:

> Ye flowery banks o' bonnie Doon
> How can ye blume sae fair?
> How can ye chant, ye little birds,
> And I sae fu' o' care?

**Quibble:** A pun or play upon words, especially a verbal device for evading the point at issue, as when debaters engage in quibbles over the interpretation of a question or term.

**Quip:** A retort or sarcastic jest; hence any witty saying, especially a pun or quibble.

**Ratiocination:** Reasoning which proceeds from the general to the specific; syllogistic or deductive reasoning. A term made popular by Poe, who wrote several "ratiocinative" tales such as *The Murders in the Rue Morgue*, *The Gold Bug*, and *The Purloined Letter*, tales characterized by deductive reasoning. The introductory paragraphs of *Murders in the Rue Morgue* manifest Poe's high respect for the type of mind which works in this way. The same writer's deciphering of the code in *The Gold Bug* may be cited as a specific example of this type of reasoning. In general, then, ratiocination, as a literary or critical term, signifies a type of writing which solves, through deductive reasoning, some sort of enigma. More particularly is it applied to fiction of the detective story type.

**Rationalism:** This term embraces related "systems" of thought (philosophical, scientific, religious) which rest upon the authority of reason rather than sense-perceptions, revelation, or traditional authority. In England the rationalist attitude, especially in the eighteenth century, profoundly affected religion and literature. The early humanists (see OXFORD REFORMERS) had insisted upon the control of reason, but their teachings had little effect upon prevailing religious thought until reinforced by the scientific thinking of the seventeenth century (Newton), although as early as 1624 Lord Herbert of Cherbury had drawn up certain general principles which he thought all existing religious factions could accept. By the end of the century the theologians were generally agreed that the most vital religious doctrines were deducible from reason or "nature." The more conservative ones ("supernatural rationalists") insisted also upon the importance of revelation in addition, while the more radical "deists" (see DEISM) rejected revelation. The former group included Newton himself and the great philosopher John Locke. The "natural religion" arising from rationalism stressed reason as a guide and good conduct as an effect. Its three propositions were: (1) there is an omnipotent God, (2) he demands virtuous living in obedience to his will, (3) there is a future life where the good will be rewarded and the wicked punished. This creed was accepted both by radicals and conservatives. The stressing of reason made rationalism an ally of neo-classicism, while the stressing of the potential power and good in human nature, as by Shaftesbury, led toward romanticism. For notices of some of the effects of rationalism upon literature, see DEISM, PRIMITIVISM, ROMANTICISM, SENTIMENTALISM, NEO-CLASSICISM, HUMANISM. See also CALVINISM, PURITANISM, and MYSTICISM for opposing attitudes. (References: Leslie Stephen, *History of Thought in the Eighteenth Century;* Alfred W. Benn, *A History of English Rationalism in the Nineteenth Century;* J. H. Randall, *The Making of the Modern Mind.*)

**Rationalize:** A verb which in recent years has crept into literary criticism to indicate a rather specious form of *ex parte* reasoning. Today an author is said "to rationalize" when, once having accepted a position, a belief, through some intuitive process or through some prejudice, he tries to justify his stand by some process of the mind. That is, writing is said to "rationalize" when the author reasons insincerely and with intellectual sophistry to justify a position prompted by his emotions rather than by his reason.

**Realism:** A manner and method of literary composition by which the author makes a definite effort to present actuality, as he perceives it, untouched by idealism or romantic coloring. Usually realism is considered simply as a manner of writing, a manner relying very largely on the use of infinite detail, honestly and truthfully interpreting life, and as free as possible from subjective writing and prejudices. It has been called the "truthful treatment of material" by one realist. Its purpose, William Dean Howells has said, is "to widen the bounds of sympathy" through the faithfulness to the conditions of human existence which it presents. It is opposed to romance, which is concerned with the bizarre and heroic in that it is "simple, natural, and honest." Realism is, to quote Howells again, "robust enough to front the every day world and catch the charm of its work-worn, care-worn, brave, kindly face." It is definitely the effort to see, feel, and think straight about life, and is more concerned with natural, everyday happenings than with the unusual and strange. Action and incident are subordinated to people and motives from which they act. Tennyson spoke of *Clarissa Harlowe* as a "still" book, and, as contrasted with the romantic, the realistic novel is, certainly, "still." One further quality of realism should be emphasized: it presents the *individual* rather than the *type* character; it should be interested in George Babbitt who may be a "realtor" rather than in George Babbitt as a representative of all realtors. As a corollary to this, it follows almost necessarily that realism should be psychological in its approach to character.

But beyond this it may almost be argued that realism consists of a particular *content* as well as of a particular method. It is, of course, true that one may write of a sunrise either realistically or romantically; but, largely as a result of an extreme to which many writers have gone, we have learned to expect the realist to present his sun rising over a squalid tenement district crowded with anaemic children, and to expect the romanticist to present *his* sun as lighting up an emerald lake from which gray mists drift slowly into wooded uplands. There is, then, some argument in support of the contention that the realist selects only certain types of material. But this selection need not, certainly, present only the sordid. All one need grant the realist is license to go farther afield for his details than the pleasant meadow in which the romantic picks daisies. The realist must be privileged to select *according to his purpose*, and this is all he asks. Certain it is that with the realist fate plays a major rôle in the action of his characters. The supreme interest in character, as the spring from which human action flows, means that to the realist action is subordinate to mental state. It is true, too, that the realist in the catholicity of the detail he uses resorts frequently to details which create sense impressions, details which play on the reader's sense of smell and taste, of hearing, seeing, and feeling.

As no new literary movement or method is ever made overnight of whole cloth, so no one can hail a single author as the father of realism. It has been a manner familiar to the literature of all people ever since the time when authors were first made with different temperaments and attitudes toward life. English realism, in its more rigorous aspects, and in its relation to the novel (with which we most frequently associate it), became prominent with such writers as Defoe (*Robinson Crusoe* and *Moll Flanders*), Samuel Richardson (*Clarissa Harlowe*), Henry Fielding (*Joseph Andrews* and *Tom Jones*), Tobias Smollett, Laurence Sterne, Jane Austen, Charlotte Brontë,

Anthony Trollope, William Makepeace Thackeray. For efforts to distinguish "realism" from other manners of writing see ROMANTICISM, NATURALISM, IMPRESSIONISM, and, particularly, EXPRESSIONISM.

**Realistic Comedy:** Any comedy employing the methods of realism (*q.v.*), but particularly the comedy developed by Jonson, Chapman, Middleton, and other Elizabethan and Jacobean dramatists. It is opposed to the romantic comedy; in fact it appeared more or less as a protest against the "romantic comedy" (*q.v.*) of the Elizabethans. It reflects the general reaction in the late 1590's against Elizabethan romanticism and extravagance as well as an effort to produce an English comedy after the manner of classical comedy. This realistic comedy deals with London life, is strongly satirical and sometimes cynical in tone, is interested in both individuals and types of character, and rests upon an observation of contemporary life. The appeal is intellectual and the tone coarse. This comedy is sometimes treated as "comedy of manners" (*q.v.*), various subclasses being distinguishable in Jacobean plays (see F. E. Schelling, *Elizabethan Drama*). It became especially popular in the reign of James I. The "comedy of humours" (*q.v.*) was a special form representing the first stage of the development of important realistic comedy. Jonson's *The Alchemist* and Middleton's *A Trick to Catch the Old One* are typical Jacobean realistic comedies. Though in the main Shakespeare represents the tradition of romantic comedy, it is to be noted that the comic subplot of the *King Henry IV* plays and some others is realistic in technique. The Restoration comedy of manners, though chiefly a new growth, owes something to this earlier form, and one Restoration dramatist (Shadwell) actually wrote comedy of the Jonsonian type.

**Realistic Novel:** See NOVEL, REALISM.

**Rebuttal:** A term borrowed from debating procedure and signifying a rejoinder or reply to an argument; particularly it is a final summing up of answers to the arguments of the opposition.

**Redaction:** A revision or editing of a manuscript. The purpose of redaction is to express appropriately writing inappropriately phrased or stated in a wrong form. Sometimes, too, the term implies simply a digest of a longer piece of work, or a new version or edition of an older piece of writing. Malory's *Le Morte d'Arthur* is a "redaction" of many of the Arthurian stories.

***Reductio ad absurdum:*** A "reducing to absurdity" to show the falsity of an argument or position. As a method of argument or persuasion this is a process which carries to its extreme, but logical, conclusion some general statement. One might say, for instance, that the more sleep one takes the more healthy one is, and then, by the logical *reductio ad absurdum* process someone would be sure to point out that, on such a premise, he who has sleeping sickness and sleeps for a month on end is really in the best of health.

**Redundant:** Writing which is characterized by the use of superfluous words. As a critical term "redundant" is applied to a literary style marked by verbiage, an excess of repetition, pleonastic expression. (See PLEONASM, TAUTOLOGY.) The use of repetition and pleonasm may, on occasion, be justified by a desire to secure emphasis, but redundancy differs from these rhetorical devices in that it is usually applied to the superfluous, the unjustified repetition which springs from carelessness or ignorance. Old Polonius is made the doddering old man he is largely through the redundancies of his expression:

> Madam, I swear I use no art at all.
> That he is mad, 'tis true; 'tis true 'tis pity;
> And pity 'tis 'tis true; a foolish figure;
> But farewell it, for I will use no art.
> Mad let us grant him, then; and now remains
> That we find out the cause of this effect,
> Or rather say, the cause of this defect,
> For this effect defective comes by cause;
> Thus it remains, and the remainder thus.

**Reform Bill of 1832:** Much of the keen interest in problems of democracy and social justice which has been shown in increasing degree by English and American writers of the last hundred years is traceable to the agitation which preceded and followed this important liberal enactment of the English Parliament. It was proposed in 1830 and passed in 1832 with the support of King William IV and the Whig Party under Earl Grey over the strong opposition of Wellington. The measure denied Parliamentary representation to 56 "rotten" boroughs, provided representation for 156 new communities, and extended the voting power so as to include large numbers of the upper and middle classes before denied the ballot, though it did not give the franchise to the laborers. It was but the beginning of a series of reform measures which followed during the next decade, including the suppression of slavery in the British colonies (1833); the curbing of commercial monopoly; a lessening of pauperism; a liberalization of the marriage laws; and great expansion and extension of public educational facilities. These events stimulated the idealism of most of the great authors of the time, some of whom were active agitators for reform, and consequently affected profoundly the spirit and body of Victorian literature. Carlyle and Ruskin in their lectures and essays, Dickens, Disraeli, Mrs. Gaskell, Kingsley, and George Eliot in their novels, and Hood, Tennyson, and Mrs. Browning in their poems reflect the new aspirations aroused by these humanitarian movements and the subsequent efforts for further reforms in social, political, and educational realism. See INDUSTRIAL REVOLUTION, CHARTISM.

**Reformation:** In addition to the powerful general or indirect effect upon literature which the profound changes in life and thought attendant upon the Protestant Reformation in England (early sixteenth century) produced—changes which colored and conditioned the work of Spenser and Milton and Bunyan and scores of other writers—there were certain immediate connections of the movement with literature which may be noted. On its more "learned" side the Reformation is represented in literature by the sermons and disputations of William Tyndale, Thomas Cranmer, and Hugh Latimer, as well as by the English Book of Common Prayer and the series of English Bibles which culminated in the famous King James version. However, the English Reformation was essentially a popular movement and was accompanied by a flood of popular works: sermons and controversial tracts which played their part in the development of English prose style; reprints of suppressed Lollard tracts of the pre-Reformation period; translations and imitations of German Protestant pieces, such as "dialogues"; satirical verse of much intrinsic interest, like Simon Fish's *Supplication for Beggars* (*ca.*1529); and the controversial plays of John Bale. In Scotland there appeared a mass of Reformation literature, including Sir David Lyndsay's satirical morality play, *A Pleasant Satire of the Three Estates*, and the vigorous politico-religious prose of John Knox. (Reference: J. P. Whitney, *Camb. Hist. Eng. Lit.*, Vol. III, Chap. ii.)

**Reformed Comedy:** See SENTIMENTAL COMEDY.

**Refrain:** A group of words forming a phrase or sentence and consisting of one or more lines repeated at intervals in the poem, usually at the end of a stanza. Historically it is likely that the popularity of the refrain developed from the old ballad, the stanza of which was recited by a single speaker while the whole group joined in the refrain. But there is another reason for the persistence of the refrain in poetry; like rime and rhythm, the refrain affords the ear the pleasure which comes from the recognition of the recurrence of sound. Rime and rhythm in that they more frequently recur mark off small units of time; the refrain in that it less frequently recurs sets off and finishes larger units of time.

Refrains are of various types. First and most regular is the use of the same line at the close of each stanza (as is common in the ballad). Another, less regular form, is that in which the refrain line (or lines) recurs somewhat erratically throughout the stanzas—sometimes in one place, sometimes in another. Again a refrain may be used with a slight variation in wording at each recurrence, though here it approaches the repetend (*q.v.*). Still another variety of the refrain is the use of some rather meaningless phrase which, by its mere repetition at the close of stanzas presenting different ideas and different moods, seems to take on a different significance upon each appearance— as in Poe's "Nevermore" and William Morris's "Two red roses across the moon." Poets, in their exuberance, have made so much of the refrain, have wrought so many variations in form and manner, as to have greatly enriched English verse.

**Regional Literature:** Writing which is indigenous to a geographical section, which presents the habits and speech and manners, as well as the geography, history, folklore, and setting of a fairly large section of country. Thus we might speak of the literature from the Southern states, the writing of Harris, Cable, Page and others, as regional; or again we might say that literature in New England at the opening of the nineteenth century was largely regional. In a very real sense Thomas Hardy in his portrayal of life in Wessex wrote regional novels. Regionalism, then, is likely to be opposed to the "universal" in that the life portrayed definitely grows out of an actual locale. To select two writers from the same locality, Virginia, Thomas Nelson Page may be cited as a regional author; Edgar Allan Poe as a "universal." The term may be used in the same sense as "local color literature" (*q.v.*), but strictly speaking writing of local color presents an even more specific area than does regional writing.

**Relief Scene:** See DRAMATIC STRUCTURE.

**Religious Drama:** See MEDIEVAL DRAMA, MYSTERY PLAY, MIRACLE PLAY, MORALITY PLAY.

**Relique:** An old spelling for "relic," something which survives. The famous use of the term in literature is in the title of Bishop Percy's printed collection of old ballads: *Reliques of Ancient Poetry* (1765).

**Renaissance:** This word, meaning "rebirth," is commonly applied to the movement or period which marks the transition from the medieval to the modern world in Western Europe. Although special students of the movement may be inclined to trace the impulse back to the earlier renaissance of the twelfth and thirteenth centuries and to date the full realization or effects of Renaissance forces as late as the eighteenth century, in the usual sense of the word Renaissance suggests especially the fourteenth, fifteenth, sixteenth, and early seventeenth centuries, the dates differing for different countries (the English Renaissance, for example, being a full century behind the Italian Renaissance in its flowering). The break from medievalism was gradual, some "Renaissance" attitudes going back into the heart of the medieval period and some "medieval" traits persisting well into or even through the Renaissance. Yet the fact that a break *was* effected is the essential thing about the Renaissance, and the change when completed was so radical a one that "medieval" on the one hand and "Renaissance" or "modern" on the other imply a sharp contrast.

It is perhaps best to regard the Renaissance as the result of a new emphasis upon and a new combination of tendencies and attitudes already existing, stimulated by a series of historical events. Regarding the central feature as "an outgrowing, a freeing from ties that have proved to be bonds," Professor Randall notes that "we have to do with new forces arising within an old order, with stresses and strains, with unstable attempts to effect some kind of adjustment between traditional allegiances and modern appeal."[1] So it was an age of compromise, a chief aspect of which was a noble but difficult and confusing endeavor to harmonize a newly interpreted Christian tradition with an ardently admired and in part a newly discovered tradition of pagan classical culture.

The new humanistic learning (see HUMANISM) which resulted from the rediscovery of classical literature is not infrequently taken as the beginning and the heart of the Renaissance on its conscious, intellectual side, since it was to the treasures of classical culture and to the authority of classical writers that the man of the Renaissance turned for inspiration. Here the break with medievalism was unescapable. In medieval society, man's interests as an individual were subordinated to his function as an element in a social unit (see FEUDALISM); in medieval theology man's relation to the world about him was largely reduced to a problem of adapting or avoiding the circumstances of earthly life in an effort to prepare his soul for a future life.

---

[1] J. H. Randall, *The Making of the Modern Mind*, Houghton Mifflin Company, 1926, p. 111. Reprinted by permission of and by arrangement with the publishers.

But the Renaissance man had caught from his glimpses of classical culture a vision of human life quite at odds with these attitudes. The hellenistic spirit (see HEBRAISM) had taught him that man, far from being a groveling worm, was a glorious creature, capable of infinite individual development in the direction of perfection, and set in a world it was his not to despise but to interrogate and explore and enjoy. And the full realization of his capacities as an individual rested upon a balanced development of mind and body.

The individualism implied in this view of life exerted a strong influence upon English Renaissance life and literature, as did many other facts and forces; such as: the Protestant Reformation, itself in part an aspect of the Renaissance in Germany; the introduction of printing (see PRINTING, INTRODUCTION INTO ENGLAND), leading to a commercial market for literature; the great economic and political changes leading to the rise of democracy, the spirit of nationalism, an ambitious commercialism, opportunities for individuals to rise above their birth economically and politically; the revitalized university life; the courtly encouragement of literature; the new geography (discovery of America); the new astronomy (Copernicus, Galileo); the English Bible.

The period from Caxton to Milton cannot, of course, be viewed in a single cross section. There were enthusiasms and reactions and clashing cross-currents of thought as decade succeeded decade. The early and often imperfectly disciplined manifestations of the Renaissance in England culminated in the latter part of Elizabeth's reign, and even before the accession of James (1603) there were evidences of disillusionment and reaction. The succession of favorite literary forms records the change. The artificial and extravagant idealism of such conventional forms as the pastorals and the sonnet-sequences (borrowed from Italian and French Renaissance literature) began to yield by the end of the century to the protest of Donne and the classicism of Jonson and to give place to satire and realism. Decadence soon appeared in the drama, and the melancholy mood which characterizes so much of the literature of the early seventeenth century, both Puritan and Cavalier, began to permeate all forms of literary expression, whether

Spenserian allegory, metaphysical verse, philosophical prose, or Cavalier lyric.

Special treatment of Renaissance English literature appears in the *Cambridge History of English Literature*, Vols. III–VI; F. E. Schelling, *English Literature in the Lifetime of Shakespeare;* J. M. Berdan, *Early Tudor Poetry.* (References: T. Seccomb and J. W. Allen, *The Age of Shakespeare*, 2 vols.; J. J. Jusserand, *A Literary History of the English People*, Vol. II; Henry Morley, *English Writers*, Vols. VII–XI; Lewis Einstein, *The Italian Renaissance in England* and *Tudor Ideals;* W. J. Courthope, *A History of English Poetry*, Vols. II–IV.) Some detailed facts may be found also in the "Outline of Literary History," pp. 481–500. See HUMANISM, PLATONISM, REFORMATION, ELIZABETHAN DRAMA—and other topics there noted.

**Repartee:** A quick, ingenious response or rejoinder; a retort aptly twisted; conversation made up of brilliant witticisms, or, more loosely, any clever reply; also anyone's facility and aptness in such ready wit. The term is borrowed from fencing terminology. Sydney Smith and Charles Lamb are two figures important in literature famous for their command of repartee. An instance of repartee may be cited from an Oxford account of the meeting of "Beau" Nash and John Wesley. According to this tradition the two met on a narrow pavement. Nash was brusque. "I never make way for a fool," he said insolently. "Don't you? I always do," responded Wesley, stepping to one side.

**Repetend:** A poetical device marked by a repetition or partial repetition of a word, phrase, or clause more or less frequently throughout a stanza or poem. Repetend differs from refrain (*q.v.*) in that the refrain usually appears at predetermined places within the poem whereas the chief poetic merit of the repetend is the element of pleasant surprise it is supposed to bring to the reader through its irregular appearance. A further difference from the refrain lies in the fact that the repetend only partially repeats whereas the refrain usually repeats in its entirety a whole line or combination of lines. Both Coleridge and Poe make frequent use of the repetend. An example from Poe's *Ulalume* is quoted, with some of the repetends italicized:

> The skies *they were* ashen *and* sober:
> *The leaves they were* crisped *and sere*—
> *The leaves they were* withering *and sere;*
> *It was* night in the lonesome October
> Of my most immemorial year;
> *It was* hard *by the* dim lake *of Auber,*
> *In the* misty mid region *of Weir*—
> *It was* down *by the* dank tarn *of Auber,*
> *In the* ghoul-haunted woodland *of Weir.*

**Repetition:** A rhetorical device reiterating a word or phrase, or rewording the same idea, to secure emphasis. Repetition used carelessly (see Tautology, Pleonasm) is unpleasantly noticeable. Employed by deliberate design, it adds force and clarity to a statement. Particularly effective in persuasion, repetition is a favorite form with orators. The use of the repetend or refrain in verse, uses essentially based on repetition, makes this rhetorical method more obvious than is usual in prose. One of the most notable examples is, of course, Poe's *The Bells*.

**Requiem:** A chant embodying a prayer for the repose of the dead; a dirge (*q.v.*); a solemn mass beginning as in *Requiem aeternam dona eis, Domine* ("Give eternal rest to them, O Lord"). The following lines are an example from Matthew Arnold's *Requiescat:*

> Strew on her roses, roses
> And never a spray of yew!
> In quiet she reposes;
> Ah, would that I did too!

**Resolution:** See Plot, Falling Action, Dramatic Structure.

**Restoration:** The restoration of the Stuarts in the person of Charles II in 1660 has given a name to the short period of literary history embracing the latter part of the seventeenth century. The fashionable literature of the time reflects the reaction against Puritanism, the receptiveness to French influence, and the dominance of the "classical" point of view in criticism and original compositions. The revival of the drama, under new influences and theories, is an especially interesting feature of the Restoration period. For further details see "Outline of Literary History" (pp. 500–507) and such other terms in this handbook as NEO-CLASSICISM, CLASSICISM, HEROIC PLAYS, COMEDY OF MANNERS, ESSAY, CHARACTER, SATIRE. (References: *Camb. Hist. of Eng. Lit.*, Vol. VIII; R. Garnett, *The Age of Dryden;* E. Gosse, *A History of Eighteenth-Century Literature;* Allardyce Nicoll, *History of Restoration Drama.*)

**Restraint:** A critical term applied to writing which holds in decent check the emotional elements of a given situation. Great literature, fiction and poetry especially, makes frequent use of the "emotional element" (*q.v.*), but distinguishes itself from tawdry writing in that the emotional qualities of the situation are held somewhat in reserve. Psychologically it is true that mankind attributes greater strength and force of character to the person who gives the impression of holding something back than to the person who pours forth all his feelings and sensibilities. In fact, it is largely this very matter of restraint in emotional situations which marks off the work of great artists from that of mere scribes. It is restraint which so often surcharges a Shakespeare line with feeling. In the last scene of *King Lear,* for instance, when the old king comes to the end of his tether, deserted by his courtiers and his daughters, with the dead Cordelia in his arms, everything, even life itself, falling away from him, he says to Kent, "Pray you, undo this button," and somehow the reader is more moved by the crowding emotions of Lear than he could possibly be had Shakespeare given a thousand words of detailed effects. That is restraint.

**Revenge Tragedy:** A form of tragedy made popular on the Elizabethan stage by Thomas Kyd, whose *Spanish Tragedy* is an early example of the type. It is largely Senecan in its inspiration and technique. The theme is the revenge of a father for a son or *vice versa*, the revenge being directed by the ghost of the murdered man, as in *Hamlet.* Other traits often found in the revenge tragedies include the hesitation of the hero, the use of either real or pretended insanity, suicide, intrigue, an able scheming villain, philosophic soliloquies, and the sensational use of horrors (murders on the stage, exhibition of dead bodies, etc.). Examples of the type are Shakespeare's (?) *Titus Andronicus*, Marston's *Antonio's Revenge*, Shakespeare's *Hamlet*, *Hoffman* (author not known), and Tourneur's *Atheist's Tragedy*. See SENECAN TRAGEDY, TRAGEDY OF BLOOD.

**Revue:** A light musical entertainment without connected plot and consisting of a variety of songs, dances, choruses, and skits. Satiric comment on contemporary personalities and events forms a characteristic element as does the effort to impress by a spectacular display of magnificence in setting and scenery.

**Rhetoric:** The body of principles and theory having to do with the presentation of facts and ideas in clear, convincing, and attractive language. Rhetoric as an art has had a long and honorable career in the curricula of ancient and modern schools. Along with grammar and logic it made up the basic "trivium" of medieval academic study. Before this, such ancients as Aristotle, who wrote a "rhetoric" about 320 B.C.; Quintilian, whose *De Institutione Oratoria* (about A.D. 90) long served as the background for study even in the more modern days of Oxford and Cambridge; Longinus, who wrote an *Art of Rhetoric* (about A.D. 260), and Aphthonius (about A.D. 380) gave the subject a code and organization which have persisted throughout the centuries. The actual founder of rhetoric is said to be Corax of Syracuse, who in the fifth century B.C. stipulated certain fundamental principles for public argument and laid down five divisions for a speech: proem, narrative, argument, remarks, and peroration or conclusion. For a period the sophists emphasized the importance of rhetoric for its own sake—deftness, skill, and cleverness in performance being rated above even soundness and truth of argument.

In general it may be pointed out that to the ancients the aim of rhetoric was to give effectiveness to public speech, to oratory. According to the Aristotelian conception *rhetoric* was a manner of effectively organizing material for the presentation of truth, for an appeal to the intellect through speech, and was distinct from *poetic*, a manner of composition presenting ideas emotionally and imaginatively. At one time the sophists and others so exalted rhetoric that it threatened to become little more than a system of public discussion whereby, rightly or wrongly, by fair means or foul, a point was carried. It was, as Isocrates once noted, "the art of making great matters small, and small things great." This tendency has given to modern ears the suggestion of oratorical emptiness which we so often associate with the word "rhetorical."

In England the Renaissance brought little that was new to rhetoric though such books as Sir Thomas Wilson's *The Arte of Rhetorique* (1553) did much to popularize the best practice of the early classical writers on the subject. In modern education rhetoric as a subject by itself has largely disappeared though, of course, it still is respected as a phase of study in "English" courses and persists in debating and oratorical contests. The great number of rhetorical terms included in this handbook shows, perhaps as clearly as any other testimony, the basic importance of rhetorical principles in their relation to literature.

**Rhetorical Question:** A question propounded for its rhetorical effect and not requiring a reply or intended to induce a reply. The rhetorical question is most used in persuasion and in oratory, the principle supporting the use of the rhetorical question being that since its answer is obvious and usually the only one possible, a deeper impression will be made on the hearer by raising the question than by the speaker's making a direct statement. The too frequent use of this device imparts a tone of artificiality and insincerity to discourse.

> Was it for this you took such constant care
> The bodkin, comb, and essence to prepare?
> For this your locks in paper durance bound?
> For this with tort'ring irons wreath'd around?
> For this with fillets strain'd your tender head,
> And bravely bore the double loads of lead?
> Gods! shall the ravisher display your hair,
> While the fops envy, and the ladies stare?
>
> —Pope

**Rhythm:** The sense of movement accompanying the rise and fall of emphasis, which exists more or less loosely in all good prose and more or less rigidly in all good verse. Most beginners in the study of literature look upon rhythm as something artificial, something unnatural which somehow the poet and the prose writer superimpose upon natural expression. Of course this is not true. Man, in periods of great emotional stress, naturally expresses himself in language which is highly rhythmical. The point, then, is that rhythm is natural and inherent. The savage expresses his emotions through elemental rhythms of the drum; quick and short for one mood; slow and long for another. Prose recognizes this almost as much as verse, but in prose the rise and fall of emphasis and accent are less regular than in verse, since in verse the rhythmic forms succeed each other so regularly as to make it possible for us to measure the rhythm with meter (*q.v.*) and to divide it into feet. See PROSE RHYTHM, QUANTITY, METER, FOOT.

**Rhythmical Prose:** See PROSE RHYTHM.

**Riddle:** The modern riddle has its more dignified ancestor in the riddles of medieval literature. Based on Latin prototypes, riddles became an important "type" of the vernacular literatures of Western Europe, including Anglo-Saxon. The riddles of Aldhelm (seventh century), though written in Latin, are English in tone, and the Exeter Book (eleventh century) contains an interesting collection of nearly a hundred riddles in Old English. They are of unknown authorship (formerly ascribed to Cynewulf). The interpretation of the riddles is sometimes obvious, sometimes obscure; but the descriptive power of the poetry is often high, and the imagery is fresh and picturesque. The new moon is a young viking sailing the skies; the falcon wears the bloom of trees upon her breast; the swan is a wandering spirit wearing a "noiseless robe." The swan, the falcon, the helmet, the horn, the hen, the onion, beer, the Bible manuscript, the storm-spirit, and many other objects connected with war, seamanship, nature, religion, and everyday life, describe themselves by descriptive epithet, characteristic act, apt metaphor, and end with a "Tell me what I'm called." These riddles contain some of the best existing evidence of the use of external nature in the period and have been termed the most secular of all existing Old English literature.

**Rime:** Similarity or identity of sound existing between accented syllables occupying corresponding positions within two or more lines of verse. The correspondence of sound is based on the *vowels* of the accented syllables, which must, for a perfect rime, be preceded by different consonants. That is, "fan" and "ran" constitute perfect rimes because the vowel sounds are identical and the preceding consonants ("f" and "r") are different. Rime, in that it is based on this correspondence of sounds, is related to *assonance* (*q.v.*) and *alliteration* (*q.v.*), but is unlike these two forms both in construction and in the fact that it is commonly used at stipulated intervals, whereas assonance and alliteration are pretty likely to range freely through various positions.

Rime is more than a mere ornament or device of versification. It performs certain valuable functions. To begin with, it affords pleasure through the sense impression it makes. The ear of the reader recognizes a sound already echoing in his consciousness and the accord the two similar sounds set up is likely, if the poet has deftly rimed, to bring the reader a real, sensuous gratification. Again, the recurrence of rime at regular intervals serves to emphasize the meter of the stanza, an emphasis which combines time with sound impressions to the greater gratification of the reader since it piles up sense impressions. Rime further serves to unify and distinguish divisions of the poem since it is likely that the rime sounds followed in one stanza—the Spenserian for instance—will be changed when the next stanza is started. This principle at once gives unity to the one stanza and marks it off as separate from the next, affording a sense of movement and progress to the poem as a whole. The fact that these qualities as well as others reside in rime will be immediately granted when we recall how commonly folklore and the play of children—to take only two instances—resort to rime to make memorizing easy.

The types of rime are classified according to two schemes: (1) as to the position of the rimed syllables in the line, and (2) as to the number of syllables in which the identity of sound occurs.

On the basis of the position of the rime, we have:

1. *End rime*, much the most common type, which occurs at the end of the verse.

2. *Internal rime* (sometimes called *leonine* rime), which occurs at some place after the beginning and before the closing syllables.

3. *Beginning rime*, which occurs in the first syllable (or syllables) of the verse.

On the basis of the number of syllables presenting similarity of sound, we have:

1. *Masculine rime*, where the correspondence of sound is restricted to the final accented syllable as "fan" and "ran." This type of rime is generally more forceful, more vigorous than those below.

2. *Feminine rime*, where the correspondence of sound lies in *two* consecutive syllables, as in "lighting" and "fighting." This is sometimes called *double rime*. Feminine rime is used for lightness and delicacy in movement.

3. *Triple rime*, where the correspondence of sound lies in *three* consecutive syllables, as in "glorious" and "victorious." Triple rime has been used for serious work—such as Thomas Hood's *Bridge of Sighs*—but much more frequently it is reserved for humorous, satirical verse, for the sort of use Byron makes of it in his satiric poems.

While at one time or another most poets have been responsible for poor rimes, have violated consciously one or another of the riming customs, still these conventions persist. Some of them may be mentioned here:

1. Syllables which are spelled differently but which have the same pronunciation (such as "rite" and "right") do not make acceptable rimes.

2. A true rime is based on the correspondence of sound in *accented* syllables as opposed to unaccented syllables. "Stating" and "mating" thus make a good rime, and for the same reason, "rating" and "forming" make a bad rime since the correspondence is between unaccented syllables.

3. For a true rime all syllables *following* the accented syllable must rime, as is the case, for instance, with "fascinate" and "deracinate." According to this rule "fascinate" and "deracinating" would not be true rime because of the difference between the last syllables.

4. It is well to avoid repetition of the same vowel sounds in different rimes which occur near each other. For instance "stone" and "bone" are good rimes as are also "home" and "tome" but a quatrain composed of those four rimes would usually be condemned as weak because of the repetition of the long *o* throughout. Of course, like all rules, this may be violated when there is a special reason for doing so.

5. Conversely to 4 above, it should be noted that there should not be too great a separation between rime-sounds since such separation will result in a loss of effect. A rime occurring in the first line and the sixth line, for instance, is rather a strain on the reader's attention.

6. It is permissible, when not done too frequently, to allow a rime to fall on an unaccented syllable. There is a certain variety coming from the riming of "free" and "prosperity," for instance, which justifies its use occasionally.

Rime and the importance it enjoys in modern versification are comparatively modern developments. The ancient Greek and Latin poetry was not rimed; the earliest verse we have (*Beowulf* is an example) was not based on rime. Historians of the subject generally credit the development of rime to ceremonials within the Catholic Church and suggest that the priests made use of rime as a device to aid the worshippers in their singing and memorizing of the ritualistic procedure. *Dies Irae* is an example of one of the earliest rimed songs of the Church. A good discussion of rime may be found in Chap. VI of R. M. Alden's *Introduction to Poetry*.

**Rime Royal:** A seven-line iambic pentameter stanza riming *ababbcc*. The name has been said to derive from the fact that the form was first used by James I, but since Chaucer and other predecessors of James had used rime royal extensively it must be attributed to James, if at all, as an honor in recognition of the fact that a king wrote verse at all rather than that he originated the pattern. Chaucer used rime royal in the *Parlement of Foules*, the *Man of Law's Tale*, the *Clerk's Tale*, and in *Troilus and Criseyde*, and found the form adapted to his best descriptive, narrative, and reflective manners. Some other poets who have written in rime royal are Lydgate, Hoccleve, Dunbar, Skelton, Wyatt, Shakespeare, and Morris. In recent times the poet who has used it with most success has perhaps been John Masefield, who wrote both *The Widow in the Bye Street* and *Dauber* in rime royal. As an example, the last stanza of Shakespeare's *Rape of Lucrece* is quoted:

> When they had sworn to this advised doom,
> They did conclude to bear dead Lucrece thence;
> To show her bleeding body thorough Rome,

And so to publish Tarquin's foul offence:
Which being done with speedy diligence,
   The Romans plausibly did give consent
   To Tarquin's everlasting banishment.

**Rime-scheme:** The pattern, or sequence, in which the rime
sounds occur in a stanza or poem. Rime-schemes, for the
purpose of analysis, are usually presented by the assignment to
each similar sound in a stanza of the same letter of the alphabet.
Thus, the pattern of the Spenserian stanza (*q.v.*) is *ababbcbcc*.
An example of another rime pattern follows:

| | |
|---|---|
| The time I've lost in wooing, | *a* |
| In watching and pursuing | *a* |
| The light that lies | *b* |
| In woman's eyes, | *b* |
| Has been my heart's undoing. | *a* |
| Tho' wisdom oft has sought me, | *c* |
| I scorned the lore she brought me, | *c* |
| My only books | *d* |
| Were woman's looks, | *d* |
| And folly's all they've taught me. | *c* |

—Thomas Moore

Here *wooing, pursuing, undoing* all have the same rime and are
arbitrarily marked with the symbol *a; lies, eyes* are alike and
assigned the symbol *b; sought me, brought me, taught me* are all
alike and given the symbol *c; books* and *looks* are alike and are
set down as symbol *d*. Thus finally the rime-scheme of the
stanza is *aabbaccddc*. For a survey of conventional rime-schemes
in English stanzaic verse see R. M. Alden's *English Verse*.

**Rising Action:** The part of a dramatic plot which has to do
with the complication of the action. It begins with the exciting
force, gains in interest and power as the opposing groups come
into conflict (the hero usually being in the ascendency), and
proceeds to the climax or turning point. See DRAMATIC STRUC-
TURE, SHORT STORY.

**Rococo:** In the history of European architecture the "rococo"
period follows the baroque and precedes the neo-classic, embracing in time most of the eighteenth century. The style

arose in France, flourished on the Continent, but made little headway in England. It was marked by a wealth of decorative detail suggestive of grace, intimacy, playfulness. The fashion spread to furniture. It avoided the grandiose, the serious, the "logical" effects. As the style was often regarded in England as a decadent phase of the Renaissance or baroque styles, the term "rococo" has been frequently employed in a derogatory sense to suggest the overdecorative or "impudently audacious," and is not infrequently confused with the baroque (also unfavorably interpreted). An example of the older use of the term in English is found in Swinburne's use of it as the title of one of his love lyrics—one in which the lover implores his three-day mistress not to forget their ardent but brief love. An example of the more discriminating use of the term is found in Professor Friedrich Brie's phrase the "rococo epic," as applied to such pieces as Pope's *Rape of the Lock* and Gay's *Fan*, in which the small luxuries of life, particularly of fashionable women, are prominent sources of interest. See BAROQUE.

**Rodomontade:** Ostentatious bragging or blustering. Falstaff's famous description of his bold fight with the highwaymen is an example of rodomontade, as is his boastful, "There live not three good men unhanged in England, and one of them is fat and grows old. . . ."

**Romance:** This word was first used for Old French as a language *derived* from Latin or "Roman" to distinguish it from Latin itself (this meaning has now been extended so that any of the languages derived from Latin, such as Spanish or Italian, is called a Romance language). Later "romance" was applied to any work written in French, and as stories of knights and their deeds were the dominant form of Old French literature, the word "romance" was narrowed to mean such stories. It has also been noted that the first Old French romances were translated from Latin and this fact may have helped to fix the name "romance" upon them. For a further account of these early romances, see MEDIEVAL ROMANCE. Special modern uses of the word "romance" may be noted from the account in the New English Dictionary: "romantic fiction"; "an extravagant fiction"; "a fictitious narrative in prose of which the scene and incidents are very remote from those of ordinary life, especially of the class prevalent in the sixteenth and seventeenth centuries, in which the story is overlaid with digressions." In Renaissance criticism the "romantic epic" (*q.v.*) was called simply "romance." See Novel, Romantic Novel, Romanticism, Medieval Romance, Metrical Romance, Arthurian Legend.

**Romances of Chivalry:** See Chivalric Romance.

**Romanesque:** A term sometimes used to characterize writing which is fanciful or fabulous. It is more rarely used simply to denote the presence of a romance quality in a work.

**Romantic Comedy:** A comedy in which serious love is the chief concern and source of interest, especially the type of comedy developed on the early Elizabethan stage by such writers as Robert Greene and Shakespeare. Greene's *James the Fourth* represents the romantic comedy as Shakespeare found it and is supposed to have influenced Shakespeare in his *Two Gentlemen of Verona*. A few years later Shakespeare perfected and glorified the type in such great plays as *The Merchant of Venice* and *As You Like It*. Characteristics commonly found include: love as chief motive; much out-of-door action; an idealized heroine (who usually masks as a man); love subjected to great difficulties; poetic justice often violated; balancing of characters; easy reconciliations; happy ending. Italian stories were often employed for the plots. Shakespeare's last group of plays, the tragi-comedies or "serene romances" (such as *Winter's Tale* and *Cymbeline*), are in some sense a modification of the earlier romantic comedy.

**Romantic Criticism:** A term sometimes used for the body of critical ideas which developed late in the eighteenth and early in the nineteenth century as a part of the triumph of romanticism (*q.v.*) over neo-classicism (*q.v.*). It accompanied and to some extent guided and justified the revolt against the "classical" attitudes of the eighteenth century, and was inspired in part by the necessity of "answering" such conservative critics as Francis Jeffrey, Sydney Smith, and William Gifford. The "artificial" character of Pope's poetic imagery was attacked by W. L. Bowles, who in turn was "answered" by Lord Byron and others. New theories about the genius of Shakespeare were espoused by Coleridge and others: instead of being regarded as a "wild, irregular genius," who succeeded in spite of his violation of the "laws" of dramatic composition, his art was studied on the assumption that it succeeded because it followed the laws of its own organism, which were more authentic than manmade "formal" rules. This view harmonized with the new critical ideas as to the nature of the poetic imagination (see IMAGINATION and FANCY). The romantic criticism of Shakespeare thus led to the view that Shakespeare, like Nature, was infallible. "If we do not understand him, it is our fault or the fault of copyists or typographers" (Coleridge). Much extravagant Shakespeare "idolatry" followed in the wake of this attitude. One other aspect of romantic criticism may be mentioned—Wordsworth's famous theory of poetry as calling for simple themes drawn from humble life expressed in the language of ordinary life—a sharp reaction from the conventions of neo-classic poetry. Other romantic critics were Shelley, De Quincey, Lamb, Hazlitt, and Hunt. See ROMANTICISM, CRITICISM, HISTORICAL SKETCH, and references there listed.

**Romantic Epic:** A type of long narrative poem developed by Italian Renaissance poets (late fifteenth and sixteenth centuries) by combining the materials and something of the method of the "medieval romance" (*q.v.*) with the manner and technique of the classical epic (see EPIC). Such poets as Pulci, Boiardo, and Ariosto produced romantic epics which were like medieval romances in their stressing of the love element, in their complicated and loose structure, in the multiplicity of characters and episodes, and in freedom of verse form. Yet they were like the Virgilian epic in their use of a formal invocation, statement of theme, set speeches, formal descriptions, use of epic similes, supernatural machinery, division into books, etc. Later, Tasso (*Jerusalem Delivered*, 1581) infused a strong tone of moral instruction and religious propaganda into the type. The method of allegory (*q.v.*) was also employed in the Italian romantic epics. The literary critics of the time were divided in their attitudes toward the new type of epic, the conservatives strongly opposing it because of its departure from classical standards. The form proved generally popular with readers, however, and when Edmund Spenser came to write his ambitious English epic, he actually modeled his poem largely upon the romantic epics of Ariosto (*Orlando Furioso,* 1516) and Tasso. Thus the *Faerie Queene,* epic in its high patriotic purpose and in much of its technique, romantic in its chivalric atmosphere and Arthurian setting, became, by following the general method of Ariosto and Tasso, the great example in English literature of a romantic epic.

**Romantic Novel:** A type of novel marked by strong interest in action and presenting episodes often based on love, adventure, and combat. The term "romantic" owes its origin to the early type of story embraced by the *romance* (*q.v.*) of medieval times, but with the march of time other elements have been added. The *fabliau* (*q.v.*) and the *novella* (*q.v.*) particularly have contributed qualities. "A romance," in its modern meaning, signifies that type of novel which is more concerned with action than with character, which is more properly fictional than legendary since it is woven so largely from the imagination of the author, which is read more as a means of escape from existence than of familiarity with the actualities of life. The writers of modern romance are too numerous to mention: Sir Walter Scott's name must be allowed to represent the long list of romancers in English and American literature. See NOVEL.

**Romantic Tragedy:** Non-classical tragedy. The term is used for such modern tragedy as does not conform to the traditions or aims of "classical" tragedy. It differs from the latter in its greater freedom of technique, its wider scope of theme and treatment, its greater emphasis on character (as compared with emphasis on plot), its looser structure, its freer employment of imagination, its greater variety of style, and its easy readiness to admit humorous and even grotesque elements. Elizabethan tragedy is largely romantic, e.g., Shakespeare's. See CLASSICAL TRAGEDY, TRAGEDY, CRITICISM, HISTORICAL SKETCH, and references under these topics.

**Romanticism:** A movement of the eighteenth and nineteenth centuries which marked the reaction in literature, philosophy, art, religion, and politics from the neo-classicism and formal orthodoxy of the preceding period. Romanticism arose so gradually and exhibited so many phases that a satisfactory definition is hardly possible. The aspect most stressed in France is reflected in Victor Hugo's phrase "liberalism in literature," meaning especially the freeing of the artist and writer from the restraints and rules of the classicists and suggesting that phase of individualism marked by the encouragement of revolutionary political ideas. The poet Heine noted the chief aspect of German romanticism in calling it the revival of medievalism in art, letters, and life. A late nineteenth-century English critic, Walter Pater, thought the addition of strangeness to beauty (the neo-classicists having insisted upon order in beauty) constituted the romantic temper. An American transcendentalist, Dr. F. H. Hedge, thought the essence of romanticism was aspiration, having its origin in wonder and mystery. An interesting schematic explanation by an American scholar (Neilson) calls romanticism the predominance of imagination over reason (classicism) and over the sense of fact (realism), a formula which recalls Hazlitt's statement (1816) that the "classic" beauty of a Greek temple resided chiefly in its actual form and its obvious connotations, while the "romantic" beauty of a Gothic building or ruin arose from associated ideas which the imagination was stimulated to conjure up. The term is used in many senses, a favorite recent one being that which sees in the romantic mood a psychological desire to escape from unpleasant realities.

Perhaps more useful to the student than definitions will be a list of romantic characteristics or "earmarks," though, as Professor Bernbaum has remarked, romanticism was not a clearly conceived system, but a somewhat confused growth. Among the aspects of the "romantic" movement in England may be listed: sentimentalism; primitivism; love of external nature; sympathetic interest in the past, especially the medieval (see GOTHIC); mysticism; individualism; romantic criticism; and a reaction against whatever characterized neo-classicism. Among the specific characteristics embraced by these general attitudes are: the abandonment of the heroic couplet and the ode in favor of blank verse, the sonnet, the Spenserian stanza, and many experimental verse forms; the dropping of the conventional "poetic" imagery in favor of fresher and bolder figures; the idealization of rural life (Goldsmith); enthusiasm for the wild, irregular, or grotesque in nature and art; unrestrained imagination; enthusiasm for the uncivilized or "natural"; interest in human rights (Burns, Byron); sympathy with animal life (Cowper); sentimental melancholy (Gray); emotional psychology in fiction (Richardson); collection and imitation of popular ballads (Percy, Scott); interest in ancient Celtic and Scandinavian mythology and literature (see CELTIC REVIVAL); renewed interest in Spenser, Shakespeare, and Milton. Typical literary forms of the romantic writers include the lyric (*q.v.*), especially the love lyric, the reflective lyric, the nature lyric (see NATURE), and the lyric of morbid melancholy (see GRAVE-YARD SCHOOL); the "sentimental novel" (*q.v.*); the "metrical romance" (*q.v.*); "sentimental comedy" (*q.v.*); the ballad (*q.v.*); the "problem novel" (*q.v.*); the "historical novel" (*q.v.*); the "Gothic romance" (*q.v.*); the sonnet (*q.v.*); and the critical essay (see ROMANTIC CRITICISM).

Although the romantic movement in English literature had its beginnings or anticipations in the earlier eighteenth century (Shaftesbury, Thomson, Dyer, Lady Winchilsea), it was not till the middle of the century that it became prominent and self-conscious (Blair, Akenside, Joseph and Thomas Warton, Gray, Richardson, Sterne, Walpole, Goldsmith, and somewhat later Cowper, Burns, and Blake), while its complete triumph was reserved for the early years of the nineteenth century (Wordsworth, Coleridge, Scott, Southey, Byron, Shelley, Keats). A little later in the nineteenth century came the great romantic period in American literature (Bryant, Emerson, Lowell, Thoreau, Whittier, Hawthorne, Melville). (For additional details of the movement see "Outline of Literary History" from the years 1700 on, pp. 507 ff.)

The middle of the nineteenth century witnessed the substitution of a soberer mood than prevailed earlier in the century, and although the late nineteenth century and the early twentieth century, both in England and America, have been marked by a sharp reaction against the romantic, especially the sentimental, spirit in literature, it is to be remembered that Victorian literature was largely romantic and that the vitality of romanticism is evidenced by the great volume of romantic writing still being produced in the twentieth century. Nor must it be forgotten that the modern mind and modern society owe very much to the upheaval in thought which accompanied romantic thinking and writing, sponsoring as they did revolutionary and idealistic theories of individual freedom and personal rights as well as significant speculations concerning man's relation to the universe about him.

By way of caution it may be said that such descriptions of romanticism as this one probably overstress the distinction between romanticism and classicism or neo-classicism, and cannot hope to resolve that confusion over what "romantic" means which Professor Lovejoy asserts has "for a century been the scandal" of literary history and criticism. As early as 1824 an effort to discover what the authorities meant by the term proved disappointing, and the succeeding century has increased the number of divergent, often contradictory, senses in which the term is employed. Some writers, like Professor Walter Raleigh and Sir Arthur Quiller-Couch, have even urged the desirability of abandoning the terms "romantic" and "classic," pointing out that their use adds to the critical confusion and tends to distort the facts of literary history and divert attention away from the natural processes of literary composition. Several have noted that Homer's *Odyssey*, for example, is cited by some as the very essence of the romantic, by others as a true exemplar of classicism. Professor Lovejoy, noting that the "romantic" movement has meant different things in different countries and that even in a single country "romantic" is often used in conflicting senses, proposes that the term be employed in the plural only, as a recognition of the various "romanticisms." Even if the term "romantic" were always employed in the same sense and its characteristics could be safely and comprehensively enumerated, it would still be true that one could not use a single characteristic, like the love of wild scenery or the use of blank verse, as a "key" for classifying as romantic any single poem or poet. Professor R. D. Havens showed some years ago (in an article in the *Publications of the Modern Language Association* for 1912) that many "romantic" characteristics existed in the age of

Pope, when neo-classicism was dominant. Special students of eighteenth-century literature are inclined to give less stress than formerly to the opposing "schools" of neo-classicism and romanticism. Yet the distinction as suggested by the qualities listed above does exist as applied to the great mass of eighteenth- and nineteenth-century literature, and the student will do well to get some grasp of the more important implications of the terms in question. Between the neat couplets of Pope and the dreamy cadences of *Kubla Khan* there is a great gulf fixed, and the difference in the poetic fashions is conveniently indicated by "neo-classic" and "romantic."

For the difficulties of definition see the address of A. O. Lovejoy in the *Publications of the Modern Language Association* for 1924 and the paper of Paul Kaufman in *Modern Language Notes* for 1925. For an interesting sketch of the development of the word "romantic," see Logan Pearsall Smith's chapter on "Four Romantic Words," in his *Words and Idioms*. See NEO-CLASSICISM, CLASSICISM, NATURE, PRIMITIVISM, GOTHIC, SENTIMENTALISM, REALISM, NATURALISM, ROMANTIC CRITICISM, and "Outline of Literary History," pp. 526–559. Professor Ernest Bernbaum's *Guide Through the Romantic Movement* is a useful treatment of the English movement. Among the older books giving detailed accounts may be mentioned (the first two treat of European romanticism, the rest of English): C. E. Vaughan, *The Romantic Revolt;* T. S. Omond, *The Romantic Triumph;* C. H. Herford, *The Age of Wordsworth;* W. L. Phelps, *The Beginnings of the Romantic Movement;* H. A. Beers, *A History of English Romanticism*, 2 vols.; Oliver Elton, *Survey of English Literature*, 1730–1780, 2 vols. and 1780–1830, 2 vols.; W. J. Courthope, *A History of English Poetry*, Vols. V–VI.

**Romany:** The language of the gypsies. It is a corrupted form of the Indian branch of the Indo-Iranian languages, blended with many words and phrases from various European languages and spoken in many dialects. A gypsy; or a descriptive way of designating anything pertaining to the gypsies. Romany ways and manners have been much written about by George Borrow.

**Rondeau:** A set French verse pattern, artificial but very popular with many English poets. Generally used for light and fanciful expression. The rondeau pattern consists character-istically of fifteen lines, the ninth and fifteenth being short lines —a refrain. Only two rimes (exclusive of the refrain) are allowed, the rime-scheme running aabba aabc aabbac. The *c*-rime here represents the refrain, a group of words, usually the first half of the line, selected from the opening verse. The form divides itself into three stanzas with the refrain at the end of the second and third stanzas. The verses most frequently consist of eight syllables.

**Rondel:** A French verse form, a variant of the rondeau, to which it is related historically. It consists of fourteen or thirteen lines (depending on whether the two-line refrain is kept at the close or simply one line). The rime-scheme most usual is *ab*baab*ab*abbaa*b* (the italicized rimes here representing verses used as a refrain and repeated in their entirety). As in the other French forms repetition of rime-words is not allowed. The rondel differs from the rondeau in two chief respects: the number of lines, and the use of complete (rather than partial) lines for the refrain.

**Roundel:** A variation of the French rondeau pattern, generally attributed to Swinburne who wrote "A Century of Roundels" and gave the form its popularity. The roundel is characterized by its eleven-line form and the presence, in the fourth and ninth lines, of a refrain taken, as in the rondeau, from the first part of the first line. The rime-scheme (using *c* to indicate the refrain) is aba*c*bababa*c*.

**Roundelay:** A modification of the rondel (*q.v.*), a French lyric verse form. The roundelay is a simple poem or song of about fourteen lines in which part of one line frequently recurs as a refrain. The term may also mean the musical setting of a rondeau so that it may be sung or chanted as an accompaniment for a folk-dance.

**Rune:** A character in a sort of alphabet developed about the second or third century by the Germanic tribes in Europe. The runic characters perhaps were based largely upon the letters of the Greek or Roman alphabets, simplified so as to be suitable for carving upon tablets of wood. A *boc* (modern "book") was a runic tablet of "beech" wood. Later, runes were carved upon stones, drinking horns, weapons, and ornaments. In very early times "rune" developed the special meaning of a character or sign or written formula which had magical power. Runes were used for charms, healing formulas, incantations, etc. The Norse god Odin is said to have been driven to insanity by the power of a rune sent to him by a certain maiden who was declining his love. Likewise, a "rune" came to mean any secret means of communication. Thus the Anglo-Saxon poet Cynewulf signed some of his poems by placing in runic characters in these poems a sequence of words the first letters of which spelled his name. Runic writing was very common in Anglo-Saxon England until gradually crowded out by the Latin alphabet used by the Christian missionaries. "Rune" may also mean a Finnish poem and (less accurately) an old Scandinavian poem. Emerson even used the word in the sense of "any song, poem, or verse."

**Run-on Lines:** The carrying over of sense and grammatic structure from one verse to a succeeding one for completion. The opposite of end-stopped lines. See ENJAMBEMENT.

**Saga:** In its strictest sense, applied to Icelandic or other Scandinavian stories of the medieval period recording the legendary and historical accounts of heroic adventure, especially of members of certain important families. The earlier Icelandic sagas, like the early Irish epics and romances, were in prose. There were also "mythological" sagas. Less strictly, the term came to be used for an historical legend developed by oral tradition till it was popularly accepted as true—a form lying between authentic history and intentional fiction. This meaning is not confined to Scandinavian pieces, and indeed the commonest meaning nowadays for saga is a narrative having the characteristics of the Icelandic sagas; hence any traditional tale of heroic achievement or extraordinary or marvelous adventure. Perhaps the best example of the true saga is that of Grettir the Strong, suggestive of the story of Beowulf. Others are included in the famous *Heimskringla*, from which Longfellow drew material for his *Saga of King Olaf.* John Galsworthy has used the term happily in the title of his great story of the Forsytes, a series of novels called *The Forsyte Saga*.

**Saint's Play:** See MIRACLE PLAY.

**Sapphic:** A stanzaic pattern deriving its name from the Greek poetess, Sappho, who wrote love lyrics of great beauty about 600 B.C. The pattern consists of three verses of eleven syllables each (——|——|——ᵕ|——ᵕ|——ᵕ) and a fourth verse of five syllables (——ᵕᵕ|——ᵕ). The pattern has been frequently tried in English, but the demand for three spondees in each stanza results too often in distortion. Swinburne is generally conceded to have been the most successful modern writer of sapphics. A stanza from Swinburne is quoted:

> Then to | me so | lying a | wake a | vision
> Came with | out sleep | over the | seas and | touched me,
> Softly | touched mine | eyelids and | lips; and | I too,
>     Full of the | vision, (etc.)

**Sarcasm:** See IRONY.

**"Satanic School":** A phrase used by Southey in the "Preface" to his *Vision of Judgment* (1821) to designate the members of the literary group made up of Byron, Shelley, Hunt, and their associates, whose irregular lives and radical ideas—defiantly flaunted in their writings—suggested the term. They were not infrequently contrasted with the "pious" group of the Lake School (*q.v.*)—Wordsworth, Coleridge, and Southey. By a natural extension in the use of the term writers of more recent times who have attacked conventional moral standards sometimes have been spoken of as belonging to the "Satanic School" of literature.

**Satire:** A literary manner which blends a critical attitude with humor and wit to the end that human institutions may be improved. The true satirist is conscious of the frailty of institutions of man's devising and attempts through laughter not so much to tear them down as to inspire a remodeling. If the critic simply abuses he is writing invective; if he is personal and splenetic he is writing sarcasm; if he is sad and morose over the state of society he is writing irony or mere gloom. As a rule modern satire spares the individual and follows Addison's self-imposed rule: to "pass over a single foe to charge whole armies."

Satire existed in early classical literature of Greece and Rome. It is only necessary to name Aristophanes, Juvenal, Horace, Martial, and Petronius to recall the rich vein which ran at that time. Through the Middle Ages the manner persisted in the *fabliau* (*q.v.*) and beast-epic (*q.v.*). In Spain the "picaresque novel" (*q.v.*) developed a strong element of satire to lend it interest; in France Molière and Le Sage proved themselves capable of handling the manner deftly and somewhat later Voltaire established himself as the arch-satirist of literature. In England, from the time of Gascoigne (*Steel Glass*—1576) and Lodge (*Fig for Momus*—1595) writers condemned the vices and follies of the age (Hall, Nash, Donne, Jonson) in verse and prose. By the time of Charles I, however, interest in satire had declined, only to revive with the struggle between Cavaliers and Puritans. At the hands of Dryden the heroic couplet, already the favorite form with most English satirists, developed into the finest satire of English literature. The eighteenth century in England became a period of satire; poetry, drama, essays, criticism, all took on the satirical manner at the hands of such men as Dryden, Swift, Addison, Steele, Pope and Fielding,—a golden age of satire, which, great as are such later satirists as Byron and Thackeray, marks off the period as that in English literature most definitely satirical.

Early American satire naturally followed English in style. Before the Revolution, American satire dealt chiefly with the political struggle. Of the "Hartford Wits" (*q.v.*) Trumbull produced *McFingal*, a Hudibrastic satire on Tories. Freneau (*The British Prison Ship*) wrote the strongest and most original Revolutionary satire. Shortly after the Revolution, the *Anarchiad* (verse), by Trumbull, Barlow, Humphreys, and Hopkins, and *Modern Chivalry* (fiction) by Breckenridge, attacked domestic political difficulties and the crudities of our frontier. Irving's good-humored satire in the *Sketchbook* and *Knickerbocker Papers*, Holmes' society verse, Lowell's dialect poems (*Biglow Papers*), and Mark Twain's prose represent the general trend of American satire up to the twentieth century. In the new century, both in England and America, the satirical spirit is displayed to a marked degree by such writers as Shaw, Bennett, Galsworthy, O'Neill, and Lewis. (References: Hugh Walker, *English Satire and Satirists;* R. M. Alden, *The Rise of Formal Satire in England.*)

**Satiric Poetry:** Verses treating their subject with irony or ridicule. (See SATIRE above.) The term is a loose one, since it characterizes method of treatment rather than content or form. Thus we may have a satiric epic (Pope's *Dunciad*) or a satiric lyric (Stephen Crane's *War Is Kind*). Perhaps the greatest masters of satire in English poetry are Dryden, Pope, and Byron. In America, Lowell with his *Biglow Papers* and *Fable for Critics* holds first place although both Emily Dickinson and Stephen Crane have written fine ironic verses.

**Saturday Club:** A club of literary and scientific people in and around Cambridge and Boston, the members of which came together chiefly for social intercourse and good conversation. There were no by-laws. Some of the more famous members were: Emerson, Longfellow, Agassiz, Pierce, and Holmes; among the frequent visitors were Hawthorne, Motley, and Sumner. Holmes paid tribute to the organization in verse (*At the Saturday Club*) and Dr. E. W. Emerson wrote an official history of the Club.

**Scald:** See SKALD.

**Scansion:** The dividing of verse into feet by indicating accents and counting syllables to determine the meter of a poem. Scansion is a means of studying the mechanical elements by which the poet has established his rhythmical effects. The meter, once the scanning has been performed, is named according to the type and number of feet employed in a verse. The major types of meter, explained elsewhere, are iambus (◡—), trochee (—◡), anapest (◡◡—), dactyl (—◡◡), spondee (— —), and pyrrhic (◡◡). A verse of one foot (of any type) is called *monometer;* of two feet, *dimeter;* of three feet, *trimeter;* of four feet, *tetrameter;* of five feet, *pentameter;* of six feet, *hexameter;*

of seven feet, *heptameter;* of eight feet, *octameter.* Thus a verse consisting of two trochaic feet is called *trochaic dimeter;* of five iambic feet, *iambic pentameter;* of six dactylic feet, *dactylic hexameter,* and so on.

Applied to a single stanza of *The Eve of St. Agnes,* a scanning would show (if we are pretty mechanical and are content to resort to sing song for the sake of emphasis and clearness) the following accents and divisions into feet:

And still | she slept | an az | ure-lid | ded sleep |   *Iambics pentate*
In blanch | ed lin | en, smooth | and lav | endered, |
While he | from forth | the clos | et brought | a heap |
Of can | died ap | ple, quince, | and plum, | and gourd; |
With jel | lies sooth | er than | the cream | y curd, |
And lu | cent syr | ops, tinct | with cin | namon; |
*trochee* Manna | and dates, | in ar | gosy | transferred |
From Fez; | and spic | ed dain | ties, ev | ery one |
From silk | en Sam | ar cand | to ce | dared Leb | a non. |   *alexand*

Such a mechanical marking of accents and dividing into feet discloses that the meter of the stanza is predominantly composed of one unaccented syllable followed by an accented syllable, and this we have called above the *iambic foot.* We next discover that characteristically there are five of these feet to the line, and a five-foot line we have called *pentameter.* We are now, as the result of our scanning, prepared to state that the meter of *The Eve of St. Agnes* is *iambic pentameter.* As the stanza is scanned above, there are only two obvious exceptions to this pattern: (1) the first foot of the seventh verse consists of an accented syllable preceding an unaccented (and is thus a *trochee*) and, (2) the ninth verse consists of six iambic feet instead of five (and is thus an *hexameter* or an *Alexandrine*). So, finally, we have found that our stanza consists of eight iambic pentameter verses with a ninth verse which is an Alexandrine—a pattern called the *Spenserian stanza (q.v.).* For a more complete discussion of *scansion* see George Saintsbury's *Manual of English Prosody* (1930).

**Scenario:** A working synopsis of a story plot arranged according to the particular needs of the moving-picture industry. A summary of a story told in picturizing words.

**Scenes** (of a Drama): The division of the act of a drama into scenes is less logical or scientifically systematic even than the division of the play itself into acts (*q.v.*). This is partly due to the lack of agreement as to what should constitute a scene. Sometimes the entrances and exits of important personages determine the beginning and ending of scenes, as in French drama. In some plays a scene is a logical unit in the development of the action. Many English dramatists regard the clearing of the stage as the sign of a change of scene. Some authorities, however, think that not all stage-clearances or entrances and exits really indicate a new scene. Thus Sir Edmund Chambers (*Elizabethan Stage*) uses scene as "a continuous section of action in an unchanged locality." Theoretically, a well-managed scene should have a structure comparable with that of a play itself, with the five logical parts (see DRAMATIC STRUCTURE). The plays of Shakespeare, of course, do not conform to this requirement, though some of the scenes can be analyzed successfully on this basis. The most important principle in scene-construction, perhaps, is that of climactic arrangement. Scenes have been loosely classified on such varying principles as length, structural function, internal technique, external background. Thus there may be long scenes and short scenes; transitional scenes, expository scenes, development scenes, climactic scenes, relief scenes, and the like; messenger scenes, monologue scenes, dialogue scenes, *ensemble* scenes; forest scenes, battle scenes, balcony scenes, street scenes, garden or orchard scenes, court scenes, banquet-hall scenes, and chamber scenes. (References: see under DRAMATIC STRUCTURE.)

**Scholasticism:** The name is said to have come from the title *doctor scholasticus* applied to a teacher in the religious "schools" established in the ninth and tenth centuries. Although such doctors were supposed to teach the "seven arts" (*q.v.*), they became chiefly professors of logic. As developed a century or so later, scholasticism became a complicated system which relied upon logical methods in an effort to reconcile the tenets of Christianity with the demands of reason, "an application of reason to theology, not in order to revise the creed or to explore for new truth, but to systematize and prove existing traditional beliefs."[1]  The logical method of Aristotle was employed.  It has been said that no problem was so difficult that the Schoolmen would not confidently attempt to solve it by syllogistic reasoning.  "The ordinary method of discussion  .  .  .  was to state general subjects, which are then resolved into subordinate topics, and the ramification is carried forward until it is considered complete.  Under each head, questions are proposed, each question being pluralized by analysis, and its branches separately handled.  First, the grounds negative of the thesis are set down in order, including passages from Augustine, Aristotle, and other authors.  Then follow the grounds in the affirmative, and, in the last place, the writer sums up, answering the objections and reconciling seeming contradictions."[2]  Such speculative problems as the relations to one another of the persons of the Holy Trinity, the nature and attributes of God, and the relation of the finite to the infinite were so treated.

Scholastic reasoning as applied by different men led to diverging views.  The "first era" of scholasticism (twelfth century) marked the break from the freer reasoning of the earlier ("patristic") theologians, and includes Abelard, Bernard of Clairvaux, and Anselm, "father of scholasticism."  The second era (thirteenth century) was the flourishing period, marked by the dominance of Aristotelian influence, and includes the two great Schoolmen Thomas Aquinas and Duns Scotus, heads of opposing groups known as "Thomists" and "Scotists."  The third era (especially fifteenth century) marked the decline of scholasticism, when, though its methods were perfected, it became largely occupied with trivialities.  This lost vitality made it an easy victim to the fresh and vigorous intellectualism of the Renaissance, and scholasticism had lost its dominance by the early sixteenth century.  Indeed, the great Erasmus, typical of Renaissance humanism, at first an adherent of scholastic method, is said to have been persuaded to forsake it by the

---

[1]George P. Fisher, *History of Christian Doctrine*, Charles Scribner's Sons, 1908, p. 213.  Reprinted by permission of the publishers.

[2]Fisher, *op. cit.*, p. 215.

English bishop, John Colet. Scholasticism employed the deductive method of reasoning, and its overthrow prepared the way for the inductive method, advocated by Francis Bacon, which has led to the achievements of modern science. The positive effect of scholastic thinking upon all medieval literature and thinking was incalculable in extent, and its insistence upon rigid, accurate reasoning has had a wholesome effect upon succeeding thought and writing, while the indirect influence upon philosophy and literature of its overthrow has been even more pronounced. (References: George Park Fisher, *History of Christian Doctrine;* H. O. Taylor, *The Medieval Mind;* E. Gilson, *Thomism.*)

**Scholiast:** One who wrote *scholia* or marginal comments explaining the grammar or meaning of passages in medieval manuscripts, particularly copies of Greek and Latin texts.

**School Drama:** See ACADEMIC DRAMA.

**School of Sensibility:** See SENSIBILITY.

**School of Spenser:** A name given to a group of seventeenth-century poets who showed the influence of Edmund Spenser. The chief poets of the school were Giles and Phineas Fletcher, William Browne, George Wither, William Drummond of Hawthornden, Sir John Davies, and the Scottish Sir William Alexander. The school is marked by such characteristics as sensuousness, melody, personifications, pictorial quality, interest in narrative, medievalism (especially in use of allegory), archaisms, modified or genuine Spenserian stanza, pastoralism, moral earnestness. The art and outlook of the school led in the direction of Milton, whom they influenced. They thus form a link between Spenser and Milton, the two great Puritan poets of the English Renaissance.

**Schoolmen:** Medieval philosophers who followed the method of scholasticism (*q.v.*) in their "disputations." Called "hair-splitters" by Francis Bacon.

**Scop:** A sort of Anglo-Saxon court poet. Though the scop perhaps traveled about from court to court like the gleeman (*q.v.*), he occupied a position of importance and permanence in the king's retinue comparable to that of the Welsh bard (see WELSH LITERATURE) and the Irish *filidh* (see IRISH LITERATURE). He was a composer as well as a reciter, and his themes were drawn chiefly from the heroic traditions of the early Germanic peoples, though later he employed Biblical themes, and he no doubt was expected in general to eulogize the family which employed him. He has been called a precursor of the modern poet laureate.

**Scottish Literature:** Though the main stream of the literature of Scotland is rightly regarded as a part of English literary history, the fact of political independence in early times and the use of the Scots language or Scottish dialect of English by many writers warrants some special notice of Scottish literature. John Barbour's *Bruce* (1375), a sort of Scottish national epic (in twenty books), is often taken as the beginning of Scottish literature. In the fifteenth and sixteenth centuries there flourished a school of "Scottish Chaucerians," Robert Henryson (*Testament of Cresseid*), William Dunbar (*Thrissil and the Rois*, *Golden Targe*), Gavin Douglas (trans. of *Aeneid*), and James I (?) (*The King's Quair*). Somewhat later came Sir David Lyndsay (*Satire of the Three Estates*, an ambitious morality play said to have been acted in 1540). Early Scotland is noted, too, for her popular ballads, some of which probably belong to the fifteenth and sixteenth centuries, though most of the existing ones seem to have been composed a century or more later. The controversial prose, on religious and historical or political topics, of the famous John Knox (sixteenth century) aided a tendency toward the use of English by Scottish writers. Among the poets Alexander Montgomerie (*ca.*1545-*ca.*1610) is sometimes called the last of the native Scottish "makers." By the seventeenth century the Scots dialect as a literary vehicle was rare.

A migration of Scottish professional and business men to London in the early eighteenth century makes increasingly difficult a separation of Scottish and English literature. In poetry the works of James Thomson (*The Seasons*) and Robert Blair (*The Grave*) are noteworthy monuments in English literary history, as are such prose pieces as Adam Smith's *Wealth of Nations* and David Hume's *Inquiry Concerning the Human Understanding*. At the very end of the century appeared the immortal Robert Burns, whose use of native dialect (following a tradition set by Allan Ramsay and others) found an immediate response among the romantically inclined literary circles of Edinburgh.

Though much conscious feeling for native tradition appears in some nineteenth-century Scottish writers (like Sir Walter Scott) and though the native dialects have been employed by such writers of "regional" literature as J. M. Barrie (see KAIL-YARD SCHOOL), in general literary men of Scottish birth (e.g., Carlyle, Stevenson) have been regarded, since 1800, as "English." One notable achievement in English literary history was the establishment in Scotland in the early nineteenth century of literary and critical magazines, e.g., *The Edinburgh Review* (1802). (References: J. H. Millar, *Literary History of Scotland;* T. F. Henderson, *Scottish Vernacular Literature;* Agnes M. MacKenzie, *An Historical Survey of Scottish Literature to 1714.*)

**Scriptural Drama:** See MYSTERY PLAY.

**Senecan Tragedy:** The Latin tragedies attributed to the Stoic philosopher Seneca (first century). They were modeled largely upon the Greek tragedies of Euripides (but written to be recited rather than acted) and exerted a great influence upon Renaissance playwrights, who thought them intended for actual performance. In general the plays (about ten in number) are marked by: (1) conventional five-act division; (2) the use of a Chorus (for comment rather than participation in the action) and such stock characters as a ghost, a cruel tyrant, the faithful male servant, and the female confidante; (3) the presentation of much of the action (especially the horrors) through long narrative reports recited by messengers as a substitute for stage-action; (4) the employment of sensational themes drawn from Greek mythology, involving much use of "blood and lust" material connected with unnatural crimes (adultery, incest, infanticide, etc.) and often motivated by revenge and leading to retribution; (5) a highly rhetorical style marked by hyperbolic expressions, detailed descriptions, exaggerated comparisons, aphorisms, epigrams, and the sharp line-for-line dialogue known as stichomythia (*q.v.*); (6) lack of careful character delineation but much use of introspection and soliloquy.

Renaissance humanism stimulated interest in the Senecan tragedies and they were translated and imitated in early academic and court drama in Italy, France, and England. The "first" English tragedy, Sackville and Norton's *Gorboduc* (acted 1562), was an imitation of Seneca as were such later Inns-of-Court plays as *Jocasta* (acted 1566), *Tancred and Gismunda* (acted 1568), and *The Misfortunes of Arthur* (1588), some of which were influenced by Italian Senecan plays rather than by the Latin plays themselves. After 1588 two groups of English Senecan tragedies are to be distinguished. The Countess of Pembroke and playwrights under her influence produced "true" Senecan plays modeled upon the French Senecan tragedies of Robert Garnier. In this group are Kyd's translation of Garnier's *Cornélie*, Daniel's *The Tragedy of Cleopatra* and his *Philotas* (1603), and Fulke Greville's original plays based on Senecan models, e.g., *Mustapha*.

The second and far more important group begins with the plays produced by Marlowe and Kyd for the popular stage. These plays combined native English tragic tradition with a modified Senecan technique and led directly toward the typical Elizabethan tragedy. Kyd's *Spanish Tragedy*, for example, though reflecting such Senecan traits as sensationalism, bombastic rhetoric, the use of the Chorus and the ghost, departed from the Senecan method in that it placed the murders and horrors upon the stage, in response to popular Elizabethan taste and in defiance of Horace's dictum that good taste demanded leaving such matters for off-stage action. The fashion so inaugurated led to a long line of Elizabethan tragedies, the greatest of which is perhaps Shakespeare's *Hamlet*. The importance of the Latin Senecan plays in the evolution of English tragedy is very great. In Professor Thorndike's words, they called attention to drama "not as an exposition of events or as an allegory of life, but as a field for the study of human emotion. Their brilliant if bombastic rhetoric aroused enthusiasm for the drama as literature and poetry; and their reflective and aphoristic style encouraged an effort to elevate tragedy above its too familiar converse with comedy into the realm of austere philosophy." See REVENGE TRAGEDY, TRAGEDY OF BLOOD. (References: J. W. Cunliffe, *Influence of Seneca on Elizabethan Tragedy;* F. L. Lucas, *Seneca and Elizabethan Tragedy;* A. H. Thorndike, *Tragedy;* J. M. Manly's introductory essay in F. J. Miller's *The Tragedies of Seneca, trans. into English Verse.*)

**Sense Element in Literature:** See SENSUOUS.

**Sensibility:** A term used to indicate emotionalism as opposed to rationalism; a reliance upon the feelings as guides to truth and conduct as opposed to reason and law as regulations both in human and metaphysical relations. It is connected with such eighteenth-century attitudes as primitivism (*q.v.*), sentimentalism (*q.v.*), the nature movement (See NATURE), and other aspects of romanticism. Joseph Warton in *The Enthusiast* (1744) reflects many of the attitudes of the "School of Sensibility": "on the one hand, he expressed the contempt for cities, formal gardens, conventional society, business, law-courts, and Augustan style; on the other, the love of the simple life, solitude, mountains, stormy oceans, instinctively noble savages, untutored poets who 'warbled wildly,' and tragedies of terror" (Bernbaum). (References: E. Bernbaum, *The Drama of Sensibility* and *Guide Through the Romantic Movement.*)

**Sensuous:** A critical term characterizing writing which plays fully upon the various *senses* of the reader. The term is not to be confused with "sensual" which is now generally used in an unfavorable sense and implies writing which is fleshly or carnal, in which the author displays the voluptuous and abandons his work to the presentation of a single sense impression. "Sensuous," then, denotes writing that makes a restrained use of the various senses; "sensual" denotes writing that approaches unrestrained abandonment to one sense—the passion of physical love. Through the careful use of pictures and images which appeal to the senses, such a use as Keats makes in *The Eve of St. Agnes,* writing may be said to be made sensuous, a quality which Milton stipulated as characterizing good poetry in his famous estimate of poetry as "simple, sensuous, and passionate."

**Sentence:** A rhetorical term formerly in use in the sense of apothegm or maxim (Lat. *sententia*), usually applied to quoted "wise sayings." In old writings, too, the student may come upon the use of "sentence" for *sense, gist,* or *theme,* as when Chanticleer in Chaucer's *Nun's Priest's Tale* tells Pertelot (trickily) that the "sentence" of the Latin phrase is such and such. In modern grammatical usage, of course, "sentence" is restricted to a group of words having a subject and predicate and expressing a complete thought.

**Sentimental Comedy:** Just as the "comedy of manners" (*q.v.*) reflected in its immorality the reaction of the Restoration from the severity of the Puritan code of the Commonwealth period, so the comedy which displaced it, known as "sentimental comedy," or "reformed comedy," sprang up in the early years of the eighteenth century in response to a growing reaction against the tone of Restoration plays. Signs of this reaction appeared soon after the dethronement of James II (1688) and found influential expression in Jeremy Collier's famous *Short View of the Immorality and Profaneness of the English Stage* (1698), which charged that plays as a whole "rewarded debauchery," "ridiculed virtue and learning," and were "disserviceable to probity and religion." Although Colley Cibber's *Love's Last Shift* (1696) shows transitional anticipations of the new reformed comedy, Richard Steele is generally regarded as the founder of the type. His *The Funeral* (1701), *The Lying Lover* (1703), and *The Tender Husband* (1705) reflect the development of the form, while his *The Conscious Lovers* (1722) is the classic example of the fully developed type.

Through the violence of its reaction sentimental comedy became a very weak thing dramatically, lacking humor, reality, spice, and lightness of touch. The characters were either so good or so bad that they became mere caricatures, and plots were violently handled so that virtue should triumph. The dramatists resorted shamelessly to sentimental emotion in their effort to interest and move the spectators. The hero in *The Conscious Lovers* ("conscious" in the sense of "conscientious") is perfectly moral; he has no bad habits; he is indifferent to "sordid lucre"; he is good to inferiors from principle, even thanking servants for paid services; he is guided by a sense of honor and is superior to all ordinary passions. His conversations with the heroine Indiana, whom he loves but who agrees with him that he must marry Lucinda to please his parents, are veritable travesties upon the art of love-making. Where the comedy of manners of the preceding age had sacrificed moral tone in its effort to amuse, the sentimental comedy sacrificed dramatic reality in its effort to instruct through an appeal to the heart. The domestic trials of middle-class couples are usually portrayed: their "private woes" are exhibited with much emotional stress intended to arouse the spectator's pity and suspense in advance of the approaching melodramatic happy ending.

This comedy held the boards on the English stage for more than a half century. Hugh Kelley's *False Delicacy* (1768), first acted shortly before the appearance of Goldsmith's *Good Natured Man* (brought out in protest against sentimental comedies), and Richard Cumberland's *The West Indian* (1771) illustrate the complete development of the type. Though weakened by the attacks and dramatic performances of Goldsmith and Sheridan, who revived in a somewhat chastened form the old comedy of manners, plays of the sentimental type lived on till after the middle of the nineteenth century, though no longer dominant. The domestic tragedy of a sentimental sort developed by Nicholas Rowe (1674–1718) and George Lillo (1693–1739) shows much the same characteristics as the comedy with which it coëxisted. Both forms are based upon the same fundamentals as those of melodrama (*q.v.*). (References: E. Bernbaum, *The Drama of Sensibility;* A. Nicoll, *History of Early Eighteenth Century Drama.*)

**Sentimental Novel:** The sentimentalism (*q.v.*) of the eighteenth century was reflected not only in the "sentimental comedy" (*q.v.*) and in the "domestic tragedy" (*q.v.*), but in the early novels as well. Richardson's *Pamela, or Virtue Rewarded* (1740) was the beginning of the vogue, and although the rival realistic novel sprang up in protest (e.g., Fielding's *Tom Jones*) the sentimental novel (also called "novel of sensibility") continued popular for many years. One of the best of the type is Goldsmith's *The Vicar of Wakefield* (1766) and one of the most extravagant is Henry Mackenzie's *Man of Feeling* (1771). Laurence Sterne's *Tristram Shandy* (1760–1767) is another example of the type. See NOVEL, SENTIMENTALISM.

**Sentimentalism:** The term is used in two senses important in the study of literature: (1) an overindulgence in emotion, especially the conscious effort to induce emotion in order to analyze or enjoy it; also the failure to restrain or evaluate emotion through the exercise of the judgment; (2) an optimistic overemphasis of the goodness of humanity ("sensibility"), representing in part a rationalistic reaction against orthodox Calvinistic theology, which regarded human nature as depraved. It is connected with the development of primitivism (*q.v.*). In the first sense given above sentimentalism is found in melodrama (*q.v.*), in the fainting heroines of sentimental fiction, in the melancholic verse of the "Graveyard School" (*q.v.*), in humanitarian literature, and in such modern phenomena as moving pictures and legal and political oratory. In the second sense it appears in "sentimental comedy" (*q.v.*), sentimental fiction, and primitivistic poetry. Both types of sentimentality figured largely in the literature of the romantic movement. Writers reflecting eighteenth-century sentimentalism include Richard Steele (*The Conscious Lovers*); Joseph Warton (*The Enthusiast*); the poems of William Collins and Thomas Gray; Laurence Sterne (*A Sentimental Journey*); Oliver Goldsmith (*The Deserted Village*); Henry Mackenzie (*The Man of Feeling*). The neo-classicists themselves, though opposed fundamentally to sentimentalism, sometimes exhibit it, as when Addison avers that he resorts to Westminster Abbey for the purpose of enjoying the emotions called up by the sombre surroundings. See EMOTIONAL ELEMENT IN LITERATURE, PRIMITIVISM, SENSIBILITY.

**Sentimentality:** See SENTIMENTALISM.

**Septenary:** A seven-stress verse often employed in medieval and Renaissance poetry. See FOURTEENERS.

**Septuagint:** A Greek version of the Old Testament begun in the third century before Christ. It is still in use in the Greek Church and is the version from which New Testament writers quote. It takes its name from an old but discredited story that it was prepared by seventy-two Jewish scholars at the request of Ptolemy Philadelphus (284-247 B.C.).

**Serenade:** A sentimental composition, written as though intended to be sung out of doors at night under a lady's window and in praise of a loved one. Bayard Taylor's *Bedouin Song*, the last stanza of which is quoted, is a serenade which once was very popular:

> My steps are nightly driven,
>   By the fever in my breast
> To hear from thy lattice breathed
>   The word that shall give me rest.
> Open the door of thy heart,
>   And open thy chamber door,
> And my kisses shall teach thy lips
>   The love that shall fade no more
>     *Till the sun grows cold,*
>     *And the stars are old,*
>   *And the leaves of the Judgment Book unfold!*

**Sestet:** The second, six-verse division of a sonnet. Following the eight-verse division (see OCTAVE) the sestet usually makes specific a general statement which has been presented in the octave or indicates the personal emotion of the author in a situation which the octave has developed. The most authentic rime-scheme is the *cdecde* (following the *abbaabba* of the octave), but sonneteers have tried so many rearrangements of the sonnet rime pattern as to make almost any sequence now acceptable.

**Sestina:** The most difficult and complex of the various French lyrical forms. The sestina is a poem consisting of six six-line stanzas and a three-line envoy. It makes no use of the refrain. This form is usually unrimed, the effect of rime being taken over by a fixed pattern of end-words which demands that these end-words in each stanza be the same, though arranged in a different sequence each time. If we take 1-2-3-4-5-6 to represent the end-words of the first stanza, then the first line of the second stanza must end with 6 (the last end-word used in the preceding stanza), the second with 1, the third with 5, the fourth with 2, the fifth with 4, the sixth with 3—and so to the next stanza. The order of the first three stanzas, for instance, would be: 1-2-3-4-5-6; 6-1-5-2-4-3; 3-6-4-1-2-5. The conclusion, or envoy, of three lines must use as end-words 5-3-1, these being the final end-words, in the same sequence, of the sixth stanza. But the poet must exercise even greater ingenuity than all this since buried in each line of the envoy must appear the other three end-words, 2-4-6. Thus so highly artificial a pattern affords a form which, for most poets, can never prove anything more than a poetic exercise.

**Setting:** The physical, and sometimes spiritual, background against which the action of a narrative (novel, drama, short story, etc.) takes place. The elements which go to make up a setting are: (1) the actual geographical location, its topography, scenery, and such physical arrangements as the location of the windows and doors in a room; (2) the occupations and daily manner of living of the characters; (3) the time or period in which the action takes place, e.g., epoch in history, season of the year, etc.; (4) the general environment of the characters, e.g., religious, mental, moral, social, and emotional conditions through which the people in the narrative move. From one point of view most fiction can be broken up into four elements: *setting, incident* (or *plot*), *characterization*, and—added at Poe's insistence—*effect*. (Each of these terms is explained in its proper place.) When setting dominates, or when a piece of fiction is written largely to present the manners and customs of a locality, the writing is often called a story of local color (*q.v.*).

**Seven Arts, The:** The seven subjects studied in the medieval university. The three studies pursued during the four-year course leading to the A.B. degree were known as the Trivium. They were grammar (Latin), logic, and rhetoric (especially public speaking). The four branches followed in the three-year course leading to the M.A. degree were arithmetic, music, geometry, astronomy. These were called the Quadrivium.

**Seven Deadly Sins, The:** The seven cardinal sins which, according to medieval theology, entailed spiritual death and could be atoned for only by perfect penitence: pride, envy, wrath, sloth, avarice, gluttony, and lust. Dante treats all seven as arising from imperfect love—pride, envy, and wrath resulting from perverted love; sloth from defective love; avarice, gluttony, and lust from excessive love. Pride was the most heinous of the sins, because it led to treachery and disloyalty, as in the case of Satan. Innumerable didactic and theological works on the seven deadly sins appeared in the Middle Ages and thousands of sermons were based upon them. The conception of the seven deadly sins was so widespread that it permeated the literature of medieval and Renaissance times, its influence appearing not only in the ideas implicit in many literary works but often controlling the very structure, as in the "visions" built around a framework of the seven sins. A few examples of the idea in English literature are: Chaucer's "Parson's Tale" in the *Canterbury Tales; The Vision of Piers the Plowman*, Gower's *Confessio Amantis*, and Spenser's *Faerie Queene* (Book 1, Canto iv).

The seven sins were matched by seven cardinal virtues: faith, hope, and love (theological and Biblical); and prudence, justice, fortitude, and temperance (adapted from the four cardinal virtues of the Greeks). Seven was, of course, a mystic number, and there were also "the seven arts" (*q.v.*), "the seven ages of the world," "the seven blessings of heaven," "the seven gifts of the Holy Spirit," "the seven joys of Mary in Heaven," "the seven sacraments," "the seven heresies," "the seven points to be asked a dying man," etc.

**Shakespeare, Editors and Editions of:** About half of Shakespeare's plays were printed separately during his lifetime in quarto editions, presumably without the author's consent in most cases. Shakespeare was a shareholder in the company which acted his plays, and companies owning acting rights often objected to efforts to sell their plays to the public in printed form while the plays were in their current repertoire. Though there may have been an imperfect effort in 1619, three years after the dramatist's death, to get together a collection of Shakespeare's plays (involving the false dating of certain quartos), the first edition is the famous First Folio (1623) prepared by Shakespeare's friends, the actors John Heminge and Henry Condell. For several reasons the texts of the plays in the First Folio vary greatly in accuracy. Some of them follow quarto texts closely, others vary both in length and readings, and there are a good many mistakes—e.g., the printing of one word for another word similar in sound or spelling—so that in many passages we cannot be sure what Shakespeare wrote. There is also reason for thinking that the folio both omits plays which Shakespeare wrote, at least in part (as *Pericles*), and includes some which he probably had little to do with (see PSEUDO-SHAKESPEAREAN PLAYS). This situation has created a series of problems which have greatly concerned later editors and critics eager to find out as nearly as possible just what Shakespeare wrote. The Second Folio appeared in 1632 and a third in 1663, the third being reissued in 1664 with *Pericles* and six "spurious" plays added. The fourth folio was printed in 1684. These late folios were only slightly edited.

The first real editor of Shakespeare was Nicholas Rowe, Poet Laureate. In his editions (1709 and 1714) Rowe made some corrections in the text, modernized the punctuation and spelling, supplied lists of characters and made act- and scene-divisions for most of the plays (this had been partly done in the folios), and added stage directions. In 1725 Alexander Pope undertook to make an "authoritative" edition. In fact, however, he did much mischievous tampering with Rowe's text. He "corrected" the meter, emended (by guess largely) difficult passages, placed "degrading" passages at the foot of the page, and placed marks of approval on what he thought to be fine passages. He omitted the seven plays not in the First Folio. Pope's work was followed by a careful edition by Lewis Theobald (1733), who had before exposed some of Pope's pretences and mistakes and made some ingenious emendations. In retaliation Pope made him the chief dunce in the revised edition of his *Dunciad*. In 1744 Sir Thomas Hanmer printed an elegant edition, which followed Pope. William Warburton's edition (1747) was of little value, but in 1765 appeared the famous edition of Samuel Johnson, whose "Preface" and notes have high critical value.

Edward Capell (1768) made the first serious effort to prepare a scientific text based on all the early editions, including quartos. In 1773 appeared the Johnson-Steevens "variorum edition" (*q.v.*); this reappeared in 1785 with revisions by Isaac Reed. In 1790 was printed an edition by the important scholar Edward Malone, whose still more extensive "third variorum" edition, published after Malone's death by James Boswell (the younger), came in 1820. Many editions appeared after 1800, only a few of which can be mentioned here. Charles Knight's editions (1838–1844) relied entirely on the First Folio for the texts. John Payne Collier's edition (1844) used the quartos rather slavishly. Collier's desire to provide authority for some of his guesses led him later to forge corrections in an old folio copy. An edition by the German scholar Delius appeared in 1854, and in 1865 was completed the handsome edition of J. O. Halliwell-Phillips, a scholar whose knowledge of Elizabethan life and literature proved valuable. In 1857 came an excellent edition by Alexander Dyce. The first important American edition, by Richard Grant White, was completed in 1860. The widely used "Cambridge Shakespeare" appeared first from 1863 to 1866 edited by W. G. Clark, J. Glover, and W. A. Wright, and in a revised edition in 1891–1893. This Cambridge edition, done with great care and good judgment, is the "standard" modern text, though the excellent one-volume editions of W. J. Craig (Oxford Shakespeare) and of W. A. Neilson (Students' Cambridge) are widely used. More than half of the plays have been edited separately in the *New Variorum Shakespeare* (beginning in 1871), by Henry Howard Furness (father and son), which undertakes to give a complete abstract of all earlier efforts to establish a text and of all important Shakespearean criticism. When available this edition is always consulted by serious students. (References: T. R. Lounsbury, *The Text of Shakespeare;* A. Nicoll, *The Editors of Shakespeare from the First Folio to Malone.*)

**Shakespearean Plays, Pseudo-:** See PSEUDO-SHAKESPEAREAN PLAYS.

**Short Story, The:** Stories, in one form or another, have existed throughout all ages. Egyptian papyri, dating from 3000 or 4000 B.C., reveal how the sons of Cheops regaled their father with narrative; later Scheherezade saved her own head and those of other fair Oriental ladies by her ability to interest Sultan Schariar in her fictional style. Some three hundred years before the birth of Christ, we had such Old Testament stories as those of Jonah and of Ruth. Christ spoke in parables. The Greeks and Romans left us episodes and incidents in their early classics. In medieval days this same enthusiasm manifested itself in fables and epics concerning beasts. In England, about 1250, some two hundred well-known tales were collected in the *Gesta Romanorum*. In the middle of the fourteenth century Boccaccio brought together a hundred tales told by lords and ladies in exile, tales read perhaps more frequently for their naughtinesses than from a sincere effort to understand the really great influence they have manifested on modern literature. About the same time Chaucer made his collection of *The Canterbury Tales*. Again, in the fifteenth century, there is the famous *Le Morte d'Arthur* of Malory, a series of long narratives reciting the exploits of ancient knighthood. Somewhat later came the novel, a final tribute to man's love of narrative, and a factor contributing to short-story development inasmuch as so many of the early novels were so loose in structure as to be made up essentially of many a tale, many a brief narrative. The eighteenth century, too, saw the rise of the essay which in its early forms (as well as its later ones) frequently derived its readability from such episodes and sketches as Addison rounds out in the *Sir Roger de Coverley* papers or *The Vision of Mirzah*. After Addison came Washington Irving, Sir Walter Scott, Jane Austen, Nathaniel Hawthorne, Edgar Allan Poe, Mérimée and Balzac, Gautier and Musset, and E. T. A. Hoffman. With these writers the short story as a conventionalized form had matured.

In view of this long development and slow growth it seems foolish to try to name any one man as the founder of the short-story type. A form which comes to us from prehistoric times and was known in both the Orient and the Occident, which drew its first breath from oral tradition, and which, finally, ran its course through the drama, the essay, and the novel, has no origin other than the inherent creative spirit of man seeking narrative expression.

But this is not the same thing as saying that there has been no change in the conception of the story as a literary form. Most of the earliest stories we have, those from China, Egypt, Greece, Arabia, from medieval and modern Europe, are simple narrative, plotless, have little emphasis on characterization, have little definite unity or compression. They interest us for what they say rather than for their way of saying it.

Early in the nineteenth century, Hawthorne and Poe in America, Mérimée and Balzac in France, and E. T. A. Hoffman in Germany, along with others, gradually formulated the short story more or less as we know it. Critics, then, began to proclaim what they called the "technique" of the form. For years every one—at least every writer of handbooks pointing the way to story-writing—knew just what a story was. Prescriptions for success were jotted down by countless doctors of composition. And then, at the beginning of the twentieth century, the advent of realism and naturalism taught us that the short story is a bigger thing than any one prescription and that there are countless ways to present a story. How is one to reconcile Katherine Mansfield with Rudyard Kipling, Sherwood Anderson with Edgar Allan Poe? And all are writers of stories. The pendulum has swung from the formless, free methods of the early raconteur over to the rigid, restricted formulae of the textbooks, and then, of late, back again to freedom from technique and form restrictions.

And this is as it should be. Any art for which a definite formula may be written is a dead art. Growth and change are as essential indications of life in an art-form as in human life itself. When the time comes that the short story must be written in a certain manner on certain subjects with a certain technique, then the short story will pass out as a form and something new will take its place.

But as yet this has not happened. The interests and attitudes of the story are carried in various directions. We have stories of problem (perhaps Stockton's *The Lady or the Tiger?* is a good example); stories of local color (Harte's *Outcasts of Poker Flat*); stories of atmosphere (Maupassant's *Moonlight*); of imagination (Poe's *Ligeia*); of the mind's working (James' *The Real Thing*); of emotions and moods (Maupassant's *Happiness*); of mystery (O'Brien's *What Was It?*); of character (Stevenson's *Dr. Jekyll and Mr. Hyde*); of effect (Poe's *Masque of the Red Death*); and stories of action (London's *Love of Life*).

With this range of interests we have also a range in manner. Each of the above types may be varied by difference of treatment. Bret Harte, Robert Louis Stevenson, Rudyard Kipling, for instance, may write of their people romantically; Hamlin Garland, Thomas Hardy, Katherine Mansfield may see their characters realistically; Theodore Dreiser, Aldous Huxley, Emile Zola may develop one phase or another of naturalism. Or, again, the writer may see life as comedy or tragedy. Only the editors of the wood-pulp magazines, the teachers of short-cut commercial courses, and some college professors try to mold the short story into rigidly prescribed forms and attitudes.

*The Short Story Distinguished from Other Literary Forms.*—If it is not easy, then, to state exactly what makes a short story, we may approach it from the other side: what a short story is not. First of all it is not a *simple tale*, an account of a fishing trip. Such an account, most likely, will lack any progressive complication, any sequence of events other than the chronological. Of course fishing trips may be *made* into short stories, but that is just the point: they must be *made* by the artist; the events are not likely to unfold themselves naturally in short-story form. And this gives us our first clue to what a story is: it is a form of art and is, therefore, *artificial*. It is a constructed form; it rarely if ever occurs in nature by itself. Even the realist will admit this.

The short story is not, again, a *simple incident*. An incident, an episode, an anecdote—these present only one event and are, of themselves, without complication and without dramatic appeal. Short stories have been made of anecdotes and incidents—O. Henry did it frequently—but each time he created for them additional fittings and trappings which increased suspense and added dramatic effect and complication. And so, perhaps, we find in this negative attitude another positive quality: the short story, through some means or another, achieves suspense and dramatic effect through complication.

Nor is the short story a *sketch*. The sketch is little more than mere description. Action is subordinated to picture. Through Kipling's *City of Dreadful Night* moves one man, who does little more than walk among the sleeping villagers, watch the scene from the top of a minaret, and return to his home. In Poe's *Landor's Cottage* we have landscape description and almost no action. Setting, while an element in most stories, is not important enough in itself to constitute a real short story. Action, and action with some sort of a progressive development and outcome, is, then, essential to that form of writing which by common consent we call a short story. Psychology has taught us that this action, however, need not always be external. The internal and mental struggle of a Hamlet may be, often is, much more fascinating than purely external happenings.

Again, the short story is not a *novel*. The essential distinction between the two forms rests upon their difference in length. It is not that five thousand or ten thousand words are sacred limits of the story or that sixty thousand or eighty thousand are demanded for the novel, but, rather, that the greater space available to the novelist allows him to accomplish different results from what the writer of the short story, in much less space, can hope to secure. For this reason the story-teller must compress. Where the novelist may present ten characters rather thoroughly, the story-teller will be content with one or two; where the novelist may take the span of a human life to chronicle, the story-teller will be content with one phase of that life; where the novelist will show his central character in various crises of his life, the story-teller will stop with the presentation of one such crisis. The demand that any piece of writing should have a beginning, middle, and end is almost as well recognized today as it was when Aristotle gave expression to it. The novelist, ranging through a whole human life or a whole period, may select a larger unit to present in his greater space; the short-story writer, because of the restriction placed upon him by the form he has chosen to use, must content himself with a lesser unit, a smaller aspect of that life. Thomas Hardy, in his novel *The Return of the Native*, shows us several years of the life of Clem Yeobright; in *The Three Strangers*, a short story, the same author presents only what happened in an hour or so on one stormy night in one room of a small English cottage. And such is the method of the short story.

The short story differs, too, from the *drama*. The dramatist is restricted by the very nature of his medium to dialogue. Practically all that he wants the audience to know must be told by one or another of his characters. He is bound, too, by other restrictions: his story must be essentially dramatic; his stage imposes certain restrictions of place and time upon him; his characters are watched carefully by his audience and must constantly be accounted for in one way or another. The short story, like the drama, uses dialogue, but it may as well use various other means. The author is free to speak in his own right whenever he wishes; events may freely be moved from New York to Chicago, from London to Sydney. Time may be passed over, a dozen years in a sentence. Yet, like the drama, the story must progress toward some definite end, some outcome. Like the drama, too, it will ordinarily reach this end by passing through a climax. In the story, as well, there are at least two opposing forces; and though these forces may be either external or internal it is their interplay which pretty largely molds the rising action. And, in one final aspect, the short story approaches the drama in method: the action, the conflict, are dictated by the characters portrayed. That is to say only this: any given bit of action should be motivated in characterization. Hamlet should act as Hamlet would and Laertes should act as Laertes would. And both drama and short story move most convincingly when their action springs from the interplay of two or more characters upon each other.

*Characteristic Qualities of the Short Story.*—In this effort to distinguish the short story from certain other forms of fiction, we have hit upon some few qualities which characterize the story as a form. From our discussion of it in relation to the simple tale we discovered that the story is an art form and demands both selection and arrangement of incidents and materials; we learned, too, that it differs from simple incident in that it has suspense; from the sketch in that it has action with progressive development and a dénouement; from the novel in that, because of its brevity, it can hope to present adequately only one crisis, one small unit of life; and from the drama in that its material may be presented in a variety of ways since the story development is not restricted to dialogue as a means.

These characteristic qualities make it possible for us to attempt a more succinct description of the form. A definition we avoid since, with a form as fluid as the short story, once we try to confine the term to certain set rules our reading discloses one example after another which demands that exceptions be made.

409

But we may say that characteristically the short story is an imaginative narrative consisting of a series of incidents drawn from one situation and creating upon the reader a singleness of effect. We may say further that these incidents are so arranged as to show the action progressing through a climax to a dénouement as the result of the interplay of opposing forces upon each other, this interplay springing from qualities of character inherent and natural to the participants.

*The Form of the Short Story Analyzed.*—Mindful of what has been said regarding the impossibility of drawing up specifications which every short story must meet, we may still seek to find some common points of relationship between one story and another. Structurally, for instance, it is true that most short stories of plot break up into five divisions or steps. These are:

1. The situation
2. The generating circumstance
3. The rising action
4. The climax
5. The dénouement

These divisions most often follow in this order, but it is not essential that they do so. The detective story is likely to play havoc with such a schematic plan, to start with what appears the dénouement and work back toward the original situation. But, as a rule, some such division as this is possible.

1. *The situation.*—This serves as the preliminary introduction giving the reader the information necessary to an intelligent reading of the story. The situation may be that of setting, giving us the geographical and physical background for the events. (See SETTING.) In a story of character, the author may well start with one or another of his leading people. Again, the story may plunge immediately into some essential bit of action which grips our interest and, at the same time, imparts facts we need to know. Or, as in some of Kipling's stories, the situation may consist of a preliminary discussion of some abstract truth, the author writing a little introductory essay which his story will perhaps support, perhaps deny.

2. *The generating circumstance.*—This term used by teachers of the short-story form is applied to that incident in the story

which first piques the reader's curiosity, first starts his interest in the events. It is that episode or fact which brings on the rising action. "Initial impulse" and "exciting force" (*q.v.*) are terms sometimes substituted for "generating circumstance."

3. *The rising action.*—This division includes all the incidents which follow the generating circumstance and precede the climactic scene. It is characterized by one or more episodes each brought on as the result of previous events, each closely tied to its neighbor by the cause-and-effect principle, and all pointing assuredly toward some approaching solution.

4. *The climax.*—With the climax the action and interest of a story reach that fine balancing point from which, the reader feels confident, the action will take one turn or another. It is that scene which holds for the reader the highest interest or the greatest emotional intensity. The story, he knows, will immediately swing one way or the other: the hero will be rescued or killed; Jack will win Jill or lose her. (See CLIMAX.)

5. *The dénouement.*—This step brings the solution of the complication. The hero *was* rescued, we find, and, most likely, Jack *did* win his Jill. (See DÉNOUEMENT.)

Since the reader intent on ascertaining what goes into a short story will find an analysis through these five divisions most useful, it seems fair to apply them briefly to such a well-known story as Poe's *Fall of the House of Usher*. The *situation*, in this story, may be said to extend to that point where the "I" first meets with Usher. It includes, then, such items as the traveler's approach to the house, the gloomy appearance of the Usher mansion, the forebodings which disconcerted the traveler, a brief statement of the previous relations between Usher and the narrator, the crossing of the causeway, the silent meeting with the physician, and, finally, the description of the interior room. At this point the reader has been given the essential details of the situation: he knows *where* and *when* and something of the *how* though he does not yet know the *what* or the *why*. Suspense has been aroused even in the sketching in of the situation. The *generating circumstance*—that initial incident which piques one's curiosity to read further—the reader finds in the character-description given to Usher, his "excessive nervous agitation,"

411

his "morbid acuteness of the senses," and his sense of fear. The events presented in the *rising action* include the information given us that Usher's sister is hopelessly ill with a mysterious malady, her appearance now and then in the story, her confinement to her bed, Usher's weird paintings, the death of Lady Madeline and her burial in the vault. The *climax* is reached with the night when both Usher and the narrator of the story are aroused by strange sounds. In an effort to quiet his own nerves and those of Usher, the narrator reads from the "Mad Trist." The passage forebodes some mysterious event. "What is to happen? What of Madeline?" the reader asks. And, for a *dénouement*, Madeline enters in her bloody garments; the narrator flees; the mighty walls of the house of Usher "rushed asunder." (For further study of the short story—for the history of the form —see Henry Seidel Canby's *The Short Story in English* and Fred Lewis Patee's *The Development of the American Short Story;* for the technique see Esenwein and Chambers' *The Art of the Short Story* and Blanche Colton Williams' *A Handbook of Story Writing.*)

**Sibilants (Sigmatism):** The letters *s*, *z*, and such related combinations of letters as *sh* and *zh* are called *sibilants*. They are mentioned here because of their relation to *assonance* (*q.v.*) and because a too great profusion of sibilant sounds constitutes a fault which good writers avoid. On the other hand, for certain effects they have been much used in poetry. Poe, in the *Valley of Unrest*, has twenty-seven lines each with its sibilants, the whole somehow planned to give an effect of unease:

> Now each visitor shall confess
> The sad valley's restlessness.
> Nothing there is motionless—
> Nothing save the airs that brood
> Over the magic solitude.

Tennyson tried to avoid the too frequent use of sibilants and is credited with calling his efforts to rid his verse of them "kicking the geese out of the boat."

**Sigmatism:** See SIBILANTS.

**Signature** (in printing): See BOOK SIZES.

**Simile:** A figure of speech in which a similarity between two objects is directly expressed, as in Milton's

> *A dungeon horrible*, on all sides round,
> *As one great furnace flamed;*

Here the comparison between the dungeon (Hell) and the great furnace is directly expressed in the *as* which labels the comparison a simile. Most similes are introduced by *as* or *like*. In the illustration above, the similarity between Hell (the dungeon) and the furnace is based on the great heat of the two. So it is generally with this figure of speech: the comparison of two things essentially unlike, on the basis of a resemblance in one aspect, forms a simile. It is, however, no simile to say, "My house is like your house," although, of course, comparison does exist. See EPIC, SIMILE, METAPHOR.

**Sincerity:** A term often used in critical estimates of an author's style, a term expressing the degree to which honesty of thought is wedded to honesty of style. Sincerity demands that a writer should not display his bag of literary tricks to no honest purpose. Sincerity objects particularly to ornateness for its own sake; it is suspicious of the "purple patch" (*q.v.*) and a too great use of the "pathetic fallacy" (*q.v.*); it avoids sentimentality. It does not demand that all writing be didactic or moral or serious, but it does demand that all writing be exactly what it would seem. Sincerity knows that literature is an interpretation of life and it insists that the interpretation be honestly, not falsely, rendered. Hazlitt made use of the term when he wrote that "the beauty of Milton's sonnets is their sincerity."

**Situation:** A technical term used in the discussion of plot to denote (1) a given group of circumstances in which a character finds himself, or (2) the given conditions under which a story opens before the action of the plot proper actually begins. Thus, to use *Hamlet* for illustration, the question might be asked, in the first sense, what the proper line of action was for Hamlet when he found himself in the "situation" brought about by the fact that Laertes had challenged him to a duel. In the second, and more technical sense, the "situation" consists of those events which had taken place before the play opens: the murder

413

of Hamlet's father, the incestuous acts of his mother, the general down-at-the-heel condition of the state. In its primary relation to plot, then, the "situation" is the group of circumstances in which the character or characters find themselves at the beginning of the dramatic action. See SHORT STORY.

**Skald (Scald):** An ancient Scandinavian poet, especially of the Viking period, corresponding roughly with the Anglo-Saxon scop (*q.v.*).

**Skeltonic Verse ("Skeltonics" or "Skeltoniads"):** A rollicking form of verse employed by the English poet John Skelton (*ca.*1460–1529) consisting of short lines rimed in groups of varying length, intentionally designed to give the effects of unconventionality and lack of dignity which Skelton felt to be a fitting vehicle for his "poetry of revolt." Skeltonic verse is felt, especially by a modern reader, to be closely akin to doggerel (*q.v.*). Something of its spirit and characteristics, though not its full variety, may be found in the following brief passage from *The Tunnynge of Elynoure Rummynge:*

> But to make up my tale,
> She brueth noppy ale,
> And maketh thereof sale
> To travellers, to tinkers,
> To sweaters, to swinkers,
> And all good ale-drinkers,
> That will nothing spare
> But dryncke till they stare
> And bring themselves bare,
> With now away the mare
> And let us slay Care,
> As wise as an hare.

Much of Skelton's poetry is satirical, and Skelton himself was at outs with the humanists of his day. In his desire to shock, to be novel, and to write in a verse form as defiant as was his satire, he plays with this peculiar verse form in a fashion that was apparently intentionally irritating to his more formal and orthodox contemporaries. No doubt the conditions attending upon an age of transition had much to do with Skelton's experimentation, but Professor Berdan has pointed out that Skeltonic verse has its analogues in French (the *fratrasie*) and in Italian (the *frottola*) and that it derives from a form of medieval Latin verse which was associated with the unruly side of university life and which was particularly distasteful to Skelton's humanistic, learned contemporaries. That Skelton deliberately chose the form and developed it for his own particular purposes is evident from the fact that he sometimes, as in his autobiographical and apologetic *Garland of Laurel*, used the conventional rime royal. For a lively description of the effects of Skeltonic verse, see Saintsbury's *History of English Prosody*. For a more recent study of its origin and nature see J. M. Berdan's *Early Tudor Poetry*.

**Sketch:** A brief composition simply composed and usually most unified in that it presents a single scene, a single character, a single incident. Its simplicity means that it lacks developed plot or any very great characterization. Originally used in the sense of an artist's sketch as preliminary groundwork for more developed work, it is now often employed for a finished product of simple proportions, as a *character sketch*, a *vaudeville sketch*, a *descriptive sketch*, etc. See SHORT STORY.

**Slang:** A vernacular speech, not accepted as literary though much used in conversation and colloquial expression. Some authorities suggest that the term is derived from the Norwegian *sleng* in *slengja kjeften*—to sling the jaw—and the idea is expressive enough to make one wish to accept it. The purpose behind the origin of all slang is that of stating an idea vividly, though sometimes the expressions themselves are not obvious enough to reveal how this purpose is accomplished. The aptness of slang is usually based on its humor, its exaggeration, its onomatopoeic effect, or on a combination of these qualities. Frequently, too, slang develops as a short cut, an abbreviated form of expression. And there are, as well, the special terms developing in professions or trades, in sports, in localities, and among groups possessing any common interest.

Collections of slang date from the sixteenth century, but there are plenty of instances to show that slang expressions developed much earlier than this. François Villon, for instance, introduced much rogue's *argot* in his verses of the fifteenth century.

Slang terms ultimately pass in one of three directions: (1) they die out and are lost unless their vividness is such that (2) they continue as slang over a long period and (3) they frequently become accepted good usage. "Twenty-three" in the sense of "go away" is an instance of the first; "cove" meaning "a man" is an instance of the second; and "banter" in the sense of "ridicule" is an example of the third. A good one-volume reference on this subject is *Slang, Today and Yesterday* by Eric Partridge.

**Society Verse:** See VERS DE SOCIÉTÉ and OCCASIONAL VERSE.

**Sociological Novel, The:** Prose fiction deriving its major interest, background, and problem from conditions of society among which the characters move. Although more importantly, perhaps, a development of recent years, the sociological novel is by no means of contemporary origin. A good argument could be made for Defoe's *Journal of the Plague Year* (1722) as a prototype of the form, but inasmuch as almost all novels have somehow grown out of contemporary life it is largely a question of degree which will determine whether a novel is to be termed "sociological" or something else. The Industrial Revolution (*q.v.*) in England focused attention on the condition of the laborer and his family and resulted in such novels as Kingsley's *Yeast* and Mrs. Gaskell's *Mary Barton*. Zola, in France, wrote realistically of the society about him; later, Israel Zangwill's *Children of the Ghetto* carried on the interest. A special use of the sociological novel has been made recently in America in the various novels setting forth the conditions and social status of the Negroes—such books as Walter White's *Flight*. Two contemporary novels of the sociological type are, in England, Galsworthy's *Forsyte Saga* and, in America, Sinclair Lewis's *Babbitt*. The sociological novel is, then, a form of the problem novel; it presents a thesis, quietly as in the *Forsyte Saga*, or raucously as in *Babbitt*. See PROBLEM NOVEL, NOVEL OF THE SOIL.

**Sock:** The low-heeled slipper conventionally worn by the comic actor on the ancient stage, hence (figuratively) comedy itself. See BUSKIN.

**Socratic:** The "Socratic method" in argument or explanation is the use of the question-and-answer formula employed by

Socrates in Plato's *Dialogues*. Socrates would feign ignorance of the subject under discussion and then proceed to develop his point by the question-and-answer device. The method of assuming ignorance for the sake of taking advantage of an opponent in debate is known as "Socratic irony." This pretense of ignorance on the part of Socrates, who was really regarded as the most intellectual of the group, was referred to as his "irony" by his companions. It has been suggested that Socratic irony originated in Socrates' sense of humor and his dislike of pretentiousness and is not to be regarded as a mere dialectic trick.

**Solecism:** A violation of grammatical structure or idiom in speech or writing. "He don't" and "between you and I" are solecisms. Loosely any error in diction or grammar or propriety is called a solecism. Strictly interpreted, however, the term "solecism" is reserved for errors in grammar and idiom and is distinguished from "impropriety," which is employed to indicate the false use of one part of speech for another (as "to suicide" for "to commit suicide"), and from "barbarism," which is used to indicate words coined from analogies falsely made with other words in good standing (as "preventative" for "preventive").

**Soliloquy:** A speech of a character in a play or other composition delivered while the speaker is alone (*solus*) and calculated to inform the audience or reader of what is passing in the character's mind or to give information concerning other participants in the action which it is essential for the reader to know. Hamlet's famous soliloquy, "To be, or not to be," is the most obvious example.

**Solution:** A term sometimes employed in place of catastrophe or dénouement to indicate the outcome of a piece of fiction. It is used in the sense that a "solution" is presented for the complication which was developed in the plot.

**Song:** A lyric poem adapted to musical expression. Song lyrics are usually short, simple, sensuous, emotional—perhaps the most spontaneous lyric form. Since civilized and barbaric man has always sought emotional outlet through songs, either communal or individual, the record of the form extends back into the dim past. Songs have been of every type and subject; no satisfactory classification for the various types can be devised. There have been, for instance, a variety of working-songs, dance-songs, love-songs, war-songs, play-songs, drinking-songs, and songs for festivals, church gatherings, and political meetings, as well as a host of others. Perhaps the period in English literature richest in songs was the Elizabethan, when Shakespeare gave us such song poems as *Who is Sylvia?* and Jonson the famous *Drink to Me Only with Thine Eyes*.

**Sonnet:** A lyric poem of fourteen lines, highly arbitrary in form, and following one or another of several set rime conventions. Critics of the sonnet have recognized varying classifications, but to all essential purposes two types only need be discussed if the student will understand that each of these two, in turn, has undergone various modifications by experimenters. The two characteristic sonnet types are the Italian (Petrarchan) and the English (Shakespearean). The first, the Italian form, is distinguished by its bipartite division into the octave and the sestet: the octave consisting of a first division of eight lines riming *abba abba* and the sestet, or second division, consisting of six lines riming *cde cde*. On this twofold division of the Italian sonnet Gayley notes: "The octave bears the burden; a doubt, a problem, a reflection, a query, an historical statement, a cry of indignation or desire, a vision of the ideal. The sestet eases the load, resolves the problem or doubt, answers the query, solaces the yearning, realizes the vision." Again it might be said that the octave presents the narrative, states the proposition or raises a question; the sestet drives home the narrative by making an abstract comment, applies the proposition, or solves the problem. So much for the strict interpretation of the Italian form; as a matter of fact English poets have varied these items greatly. The octave and sestet division is not always kept; the rime scheme is often varied, but within limits—no Italian sonnet properly allowing more than five rimes. Iambic pentameter is essentially the meter, but here again certain poets have experimented with hexameter and other meters.

The English (Shakespearean) sonnet, on the other hand, is so different from the Italian (though it grew from that form) as to permit of a separate classification. Instead of the octave and sestet divisions, this sonnet type characteristically embodies four divisions: three quatrains (each with a rime pattern of its own) and a rimed couplet. Thus the typical rime scheme for the English sonnet is *abab cdcd efef gg*. The couplet at the end is usually a commentary on the foregoing, an epigrammatic close.

Certain qualities common to the sonnet as a type should be noted. Its definite restrictions as to form make it a challenge to the artistry of the poet and call for all the technical skill at the poet's command. The more or less set rime patterns occurring regularly within the short space of fourteen lines afford a pleasant piquancy to the ear of the reader, and create truly musical effects. The rigidity of the form precludes a too great economy or too great prodigality of words. Emphasis is placed on exactness and perfection of expression. The brevity of the form favors concentrated expression of idea or passion.

The sonnet as a form developed in Italy probably in the thirteenth century. Petrarch, in the fourteenth century, raised the sonnet to its greatest Italian perfection and so gave it, for English readers, his own name. The form was introduced into England by Thomas Wyatt, who translated Petrarchan sonnets and left over thirty examples of his own in English. Surrey, an associate, shares with Wyatt the credit for introducing the form to England and is important as an early modifier of the Italian form. Gradually the Italian sonnet pattern (which had proved somewhat too rigid for English poets) was modified and since Shakespeare attained greatest fame for poems of this modified type his name has often been given to the English form. Among the most famous sonneteers in England have been Shakespeare, Milton, Wordsworth, and Rossetti. Longfellow is generally credited with writing some of the best sonnets in America. With the interest in this poetic form, certain poets following the example of Petrarch have written a series of sonnets linked one to the other and dealing with some unified subject. Such series are called "sonnet sequences." Some of the most famous sonnet sequences in English literature are those by Shakespeare (154 in the group), Sidney's *Astrophel and Stella*, Spenser's *Amoretti*, Rossetti's *House of Life*, and Mrs. Browning's *Sonnets from the Portuguese*. William Ellery Leonard, an American poet, has published in *Two Lives* a sonnet sequence almost sure to take high rank in American literature. For further study of the sonnet as a type see C. Tomlinson, *The Sonnet, its Origin, Structure, and Place in Poetry.*

**Sonnet Sequence:** See SONNET.

**Spasmodic School:** A phrase applied by W. E. Aytoun in 1854 to a group of English poets who wrote in the 1840's and 1850's. The spirit of the verse (influenced by Shelley and Byron) reflected discontent and unrest, while its style was marked by jerkiness and forced or strained emphasis. In his poem "America" (1855) Sydney Dobell in addressing "Columbia" alludes to the typical early English progenitor of Americans as "thy satchelled ancestor." Belonging to the group, besides Dobell, were Alexander Smith, P. J. Bailey, George Gilfillan, and other minor writers. The general "spasmodic" tendency is said also to appear in the early verse of Robert Browning and Elizabeth Barrett Browning, and in Tennyson's *Maud.*

**Spenserian Stanza:** A stanzaic pattern consisting of nine verses, the first eight being iambic pentameter, the ninth an iambic hexameter. The rime-scheme is *ababbcbcc.* (See SCANSION.) The form derives its name from Edmund Spenser, who created the pattern for his *Faerie Queene*, from which the first stanza of Canto I is cited as an example:

> A Gentle Knight was pricking on the plaine,
> Y-cladd in mightie armes and silver shielde,
> Wherein old dints of deepe wounds did remaine,
> The cruell markes of many' a bloudy fielde;
> Yet armes till that time did he never wield:
> His angry steede did chide his foming bitt,
> As much disdayning to the curbe to yield:
> Full jolly knight he seemd, and faire did sitt,
> As one for knightly giusts and fierce encounters fitt.

This stanzaic form is notable for two qualities: the method of "tying-in" the three rimes promotes unity of effect and tightness of thought; the Alexandrine at the close adds dignity to the sweep of the form and, at the same time, affords an opportunity for summary and epigrammatic expression which permits the line to knit up the thought of the whole stanza. Other poets than Spenser have made notable use of the form. Burns used the Spenserian pattern in *The Cotter's Saturday Night*, Shelley in *The Revolt of Islam* and in *Adonais;* Keats used it in *The Eve of St. Agnes*, and Byron in *Childe Harold*.

**Spondee:** A foot composed of two accented syllables ($\_\_$ $\_\_$). The form is rare in English verse, since most of our polysyllabic words carry a primary accent. Spondees in our poetry are usually composed of two monosyllabic words as *all joy!* Poe in writing of the subject found only three or four instances (one of which was *football*) in English where real spondees occurred in a single word. Untermeyer finds a longer list (really compounds composed of monosyllabic words) and cites *heartbreak, childhood, bright-eyed, bookcase, wineglass,* and *Mayday*. In Milton's line:

> Silence, ye troubled waves, and thou deep, peace!

"deep, peace" presents a perfect spondaic foot.

**Stanza:** A division of a poem composed, usually, according to a single pattern. However, the division into stanzas is sometimes made according to *thought* as well as form, in which case the stanza is a unit not unlike a paragraph of prose. "Strophe" is another term used for stanza, but one should avoid "verse" in this sense, since verse is properly reserved to indicate a single line of poetry. Some of the more common stanzaic forms are couplet, tercet, quatrain, rime royal, *ottava rima*, and the Spenserian stanza, all of which are discussed in their proper place.

**Stave:** A stanza, particularly of a poem intended to be sung.

**Stichomythia:** A form of repartee developed in classical drama and often employed by Elizabethan writers, especially in plays which imitated the Senecan tragedies. It is a sort of line-for-line "verbal fencing match" in which the principals in the dialogue retort sharply to each other in lines which echo the opponent's words and figures of speech. Antithesis is freely used. The thought is often sententious. A few lines quoted from

Hamlet's interview with his mother in the scene where Polonius is killed will serve as an instance of stichomythia:

*Hamlet:* Now, mother, what's the matter?
*Queen:* Hamlet, thou hast thy father much offended.
*Hamlet:* Mother, you have my father much offended.
*Queen:* Come, come, you answer with an idle tongue.
*Hamlet:* Go, go, you question with a wicked tongue.

A more sustained example is found in the interview between King Richard and Queen Elizabeth in *King Richard III* (IV, iv, 343 ff.).

**Stock Characters:** Conventional character types belonging by custom to given forms of literature. Thus a boisterous character known as the Vice came to be expected in a morality play. The Elizabethan revenge tragedy, "tragedy of blood," commonly employed, among other stock characters, a high-thinking vengeance-seeking hero (Hamlet), the ghost of a murdered father or son, and a scheming murderer-villain (Claudius). In Elizabethan dramatic tradition in general one may expect such stock figures as a disguised romantic heroine (Portia), a melancholy man (Jacques), a loquacious old counsellor (Polonius), a female servant-confidante (Nerissa), a court fool (Feste), a witty clownish servant (Launcelot Gobbo). In fairy tales the cruel stepmother and prince charming are examples. In the sentimental novel one expects a fainting heroine. So every type of fictional literature—novels, romances, detective tales, moving pictures, the various kinds of comedies and tragedies, metrical romances—tends to develop stock characters whose conventional nature a reader does well to recognize so that he can distinguish between the individual, personal characteristics of a given character and the conventional traits drawn from the tradition of the stock character represented. See further under various types of literature, such as COMEDY OF HUMOURS, PICARESQUE NOVEL.

**Storm and Stress:** See STURM UND DRANG.

**Stream–of–Consciousness Novel, The:** A variety of the psychological novel (*q.v.*) which is chiefly concerned with chronicling the mind and thought of the central character as that person passes through a series of experiences—happenings which may to the outside world sometimes seem very trivial but which, to the central figure of the story, assume a physical and spiritual import most vital. The chief interest of this form of writing is internal, is in the consciousness—on the part of the central figure—of those external forces which play upon him. In this type of realism the mind of the character becomes the stage on which most of the action occurs; we see the plot development not so much in activity as in the effect of the activity upon the central character. This stream-of-consciousness type is largely a twentieth-century development and is attributable to the influence of the so-called "new psychology." Writers who have performed in this realm are James Joyce, Dorothy Richardson, Virginia Woolf, Ernest Hemingway, Sherwood Anderson, and Elizabeth Madox Roberts.

Characteristics of the stream-of-consciousness novel, other than the major ones mentioned above, may be summarized as follows: (1) trivial incidents are often thought to be more revelatory of character and action than major incidents; (2) mental reactions are as legitimate material for the novel as physical and external action; (3) the narrative is often buried in a great mass of detail; (4) and this detail may seem jerky, disconnected, and irrelevant to the reader until he finds that such unity as the details have lies only in the mental furniture of the major character; (5) the reflective nature of the detail, chaotic as it may appear at first, has a sort of underlying rhythm or pattern which causes the consciousness of the central figure to return time and again to the same or similar mental state. As the mind in its meanderings constantly returns to starting points, progresses in cycles, so, in these novels, does the reflective detail presented recur to points already emphasized; (6) the minor characters are likely to be very minor indeed. Whereas Thackeray or Dickens felt called upon in his last chapter to dispose of all his people, writers of this psychological novel feel free to bring in people as they are met and as they relate to the central figure, and then, as in real life, to allow them to disappear from the reader's awareness; (7) this novel of mental adventure, as it might be called, is built up on analysis, and the moods, emotions, and mental states of the central character form the subject of the analysis.

**Stress:** The emphasis given a syllable or word in rhythmic writing. See ACCENT, ARSIS, ICTUS, SCANSION.

**Strophe:** A stanza. In the Pindaric ode (see ODE) the strophe signifies particularly the first stanza, and every subsequent third stanza—i.e., the fourth, seventh, etc.

**Structure:** The planned framework of a piece of literature. Though such external matters as kind of language used (French or English, prose or verse, or kind of verse, or type of sentence) are sometimes referred to as "structural" features, the term usually is applied to the general plan or outline. Thus the scheme of topics (as revealed in a topical outline) determines the structure of a formal essay. The logical division of the action of a drama (see DRAMATIC STRUCTURE) and also the mechanical division into acts and scenes are matters of structure. In a narrative the plot itself is the structural element. Groups of stories may be set in a larger structural plan (see FRAMED STORY) such as the pilgrimage in Chaucer's *Canterbury Tales*. The structure of an Italian sonnet (*q.v.*) suggests first its division into octave and sestet, and more minutely the internal plan of each of these two parts. A Pindaric ode (see ODE) follows a special structural plan which determines not only the development of the theme but the sequence of stanzaic forms. Often the author advertises his structure as a means of securing clearness (as in some college textbooks), while at other times the artistic purpose of the author leads him to conceal his structure (as in narratives) or subordinate it altogether (as in some informal essays).

***Sturm und Drang*** (Storm and Stress): The name given a literary movement important in Germany during the last quarter of the eighteenth century. The movement derives its name from the title of a drama, *Sturm und Drang* (1776) by Klinger, although Goethe's *Götz von Berlichingen* was probably the most significant single literary production of the group. Goethe's *Werthers Leiden* (a novel) reflects the *Sturm und Drang* attitude as does Schiller's *Die Räuber* (1781). The real founder and pioneer of the movement was Herder (1744–1803). Other leaders were Lenz, Wagner, and Müller. The drama was much used as a medium of expression and the dramatists themselves were greatly influenced by the power of Shakespeare and the freedom of the English playwright from classical standards. In essence the *Sturm und Drang* movement was a revolt from classical conventions and, particularly, an expression of dissatisfaction with the tenets of French classicism. The writing was imbued with a strong nationalistic and folk element, was characterized by fervor and enthusiasm, a restless turbulency of spirit, the portrayal of great passion, a reliance upon emotional experiences and spiritual struggles and was intensely personal. The writers were more interested in character than in plot or in literary form.

**Style:** The arrangement of words in a manner which at once best expresses the individuality of the author and the idea and intent in his mind. The best style, for any given purpose, is that which most nearly approximates a perfect adaptation of one's language to one's ideas. In a perfect world, it is perhaps true that each speaker or writer would find expression in words which would exactly present the idea in his mind and would carry with them the exact personality of the author; but this side of paradise all that authors can do is to labor to achieve that end as closely as human limitations will permit.

Style, then, is a combination of two elements: the idea to be expressed, and the individuality of the author. It is, as Lowell said, "the establishment of a perfect mutual understanding between the worker and his material." From this point of view it is impossible to change the diction or to alter the phrasing of a statement and thus to say exactly the same thing; for what the reader receives from a statement is not alone what is said, but also certain connotations which affect his consciousness from the manner in which the statement is made. And from this it follows that, just as no two personalities are alike, no two styles are actually alike.

There are, in fact, many "styles." The critic is fond of categories and fixes a label to a Milton, a Lyly, a Pope; gives a name to a style and calls it ornamental, forceful, poetic, or what-not, in the conviction perhaps that he has described the style of a writer when all he has done has been to place him in a group with many others who have written ornate or forceful or poetic

425

prose. A mere recital of some of these categories may, however, be suggestive of the infinite range of manners the one word *style* covers. We speak, for instance, of journalistic, scientific, or literary styles; we call the manners of other writers abstract or concrete, rhythmic or pedestrian, sincere or artificial, dignified or comic, original or imitative, dull or vivid, as though each of these was somehow a final category of its own. But, if we are actually to estimate a style, we need more delicate tests than these; we need terms which will be so final in their sensitiveness as ultimately to distinguish the work of each writer from that of all other writers, since, as has been said, in the last analysis no two styles are exactly comparable.

A study of styles for the purpose of analysis will include, in addition to the infinity of personal detail suggested above, such general qualities as: diction, sentence structure and variety, imagery, rhythm, coherence, emphasis, arrangement of ideas, etc. (J. T. Middleton Murry's *The Problem of Style* is an interesting short discussion from which to begin a study of style. See also H. E. Read's *English Prose Style*.)

**Subjective Element in Literature:** A term frequently used in criticism to denote writing which is expressive in an intensely personal manner of the inner convictions, beliefs, dreams, or ideals of the author. Subjective writing is, of course, opposed to objective writing, which is impersonal, concrete, and concerned largely with narrative, analysis, or description of externalities. One might, for instance, speak of the subjective element in Shakespeare's sonnets and of the objective qualities of *The Rape of Lucrece;* the first tells of Shakespeare's reflective spirit; the second retells an old Roman story. The individuality of an author is more likely to find its best expression in his subjective work.

**Subplot:** A subordinate or minor complication running through a piece of fiction. This secondary plot interest, if skillfully handled, has a direct relationship to the main plot, contributing to it in interest and in complication and struggle. (See PLOT.) Some writers—particularly English and American authors—have carried the intricacies and surprises of plot relationships so far as to create not only one, but sometimes three or four—or more—subplots. The characteristic difference, it has been observed, between the fiction of France, Italy—the romance countries in general—and the fiction of the Anglo-Saxons is that the romance authors are generally satisfied with simple, unified plot relationships, whereas northern writers are more given to an intricate series of subplots supporting and complicating the major plot. There are said to be seventy-five characters in Dickens' *Our Mutual Friend* and sixty in Thackeray's *Vanity Fair*. (Bliss Perry.) When so many people are introduced into a work of fiction it is obvious that their relationship to the chief characters of the main plot must shade off into very subordinate subplots. As instances of subplots in Shakespeare may be cited from *Hamlet* the Laertes-Hamlet struggle (as subordinate to the Claudius-Hamlet major plot), and from *The Merchant of Venice* the love interest of the Jessica-Lorenzo story (as subordinate to the Portia-Bassanio plot). It may be observed that writers use subplots of at least two different degrees: first, those which are directly related to, and which give impetus and action to, the main plot; and second, those which are more or less extraneous to the chief plot interest and which are introduced frankly as a secondary story to give zest and emphasis, or relief, to the main plot.

**Supernatural Element in Literature:** Writing concerned with man's attempt to explain the mysteries of existence. Wonder is one of the emotions (see EMOTIONAL ELEMENT) which most constantly moves man, and literature, recognizing this, makes two uses of the supernatural: (1) as an interpreter of life it naturally speculates largely as to the meaning of these mysteries, and (2) since man is so readily interested in the strange and mysterious, it very often makes use of the supernatural simply as a means of securing the reader's attention. Of the first type are all books on religion, occult philosophy, and all essays, poems, etc., which make guesses at existence. In this sense, Wordsworth's *Ode on the Intimations of Immortality* is based on the supernatural. Of the second type are all mystery stories and poems touched with the quality of strangeness—such writing, for instance, as Coleridge's *Christabel*. It is readily seen, then, that the supernatural is one of the major elements of

English, or, for that matter, of world literature.   See MYSTICISM, EPIC.

**"Sweetness and Light":** A phrase given great popularity by Matthew Arnold, who used it as the title for the first chapter of *Culture and Anarchy* (1869).   Arnold did not create the term but borrowed it from Swift's *The Battle of the Books*, where Swift, in recounting the apologue of the Spider and the Bee, summarized the argument relating to the superiority of ancient over modern authors (see ANCIENTS AND MODERNS, QUARREL OF) in these words: "Instead of dirt and poison we have rather chose to fill our hives with honey and wax, thus furnishing mankind with the two noblest of things, which are sweetness and light." These two "noblest of things," as Arnold uses the term, are *beauty* and *intelligence*—and it is to these two qualities that "sweetness and light" refers.

**Syllabus:** An outline or abstract containing the major heads of a book, a course of lectures, an argument, program of study. A digest of the chief "points" of a larger work.

**Syllogism:** A formula for presenting an argument logically. The syllogism affords a method of demonstrating the logic of an argument through analysis.   It consists of three divisions, a major premise, a minor premise, and a conclusion.

> *Major premise:* All public libraries should serve the people.
> *Minor premise:* This is a public library.
> *Conclusion:* Therefore this library should serve the people.

There are, it is to be noticed, three terms as well as three divisions to the syllogism.   In the major premise "should serve the people" is the "major term"; in the minor premise "this (library)" is the "minor term"; and the term appearing in both the major and the minor premise, "public library," is called the "middle term."

**Symbolism:** In its general sense, simply the use of imagery and fancy in writing.   The tendency of symbolism is to seize upon some aspect of an object and to dignify it with imaginative, fantastic, esoteric qualities, that it may represent some philosophic, religious, spiritual, or social abstraction. When symbolism is employed for any of these purposes it tends to build up a ritualistic, mystic literature which is not clear to an outsider without a key to the special significances and imagined correspondences. Symbolistic literature is likely to be vague, abstract, mystical; to strike the outsider as full of fantasy and fancy. Perhaps the writing of Maurice Maeterlinck represents this aspect as well as any that might be cited.

In a second, and more narrow, sense, *symbolism* is the name given a literary movement in France and Belgium which developed during the 1880's. The *symbolists*, as the adherents were called, were chiefly poets, and their effort was to translate impressions of the senses through sound and rhythm in their writing. As a protest against the starkness of realism, they sought to conceal outlines rather than to delineate them, and against the concreteness of the earlier form they raised the banner of abstraction. In brief it was their purpose to *suggest* rather than to sketch in the details of a scene or an emotion. And here they lost themselves—at least so far as the uninitiated were concerned—in the vaguenesses mentioned above as so often accompanying a private, esoteric symbolism. Verlaine gave the symbolists a motto which bespeaks their purpose: "*Pas de couleur, rien que la nuance*" ("no color, nothing but the lightest of shading").

The symbolists in some of their doctrines were related to the Pre-Raphaelite movement (see PRE-RAPHAELITISM) in England and were the precursors of the "free verse" (*q.v.*) and imagist poets (see IMAGISTS) of recent decades. Some of the leaders among the symbolists were Rimbaud, Mallarmé, Verlaine, Verhaeren, de Regnier, Rémy de Gourmont, Claudel, and, in prose especially, J. K. Huysmans. (Reference: Arthur Symons, *The Symbolist Movement.*)

**Symposium**: A Greek word meaning "a drinking together" or banquet. As such convivial meetings were characterized by free conversation, the word later came to mean discussion by different persons of a single topic, or a collection of speeches or essays on a given subject. One of Plato's best known "dialogues" is *The Symposium* and later literary uses of the word are much under its influence, as is G. Lowes Dickinson's *A Modern Symposium*.

**Symposium Club:** See TRANSCENDENTAL CLUB, TRANSCENDENTALISM.

**Syncope:** A cutting short of words through the omission of a letter or a syllable. Syncope is distinguished from elision in that it is usually confined to omissions of letters (usually vowels) within the word, whereas elision usually runs two words together by the omission of a final or initial letter. *Ev'ry* for *every* is an example of syncope. Naturally the greatest use for this omission of sounds is in verse where a desired metrical effect is sought. However, syncope has taken place frequently in English simply to shorten words, as *pacificist* has become *pacifist*.

**Synecdoche:** A form of metaphor which in mentioning a part signifies the whole. In order to be clear, a good synecdoche must be based on an *important* part of the whole and not a minor part and, usually, the part selected to stand for the whole must be the part most directly associated with the subject under discussion. Thus under the first restriction we say *motor* for automobile (rather than *tire*), and under the second we speak of infantry on the march as *foot* rather than as *hands* just as we use *hands* rather than *foot* for men who are at work at manual labor.

**Synonyms:** Words in the same language with the same or similar meanings. Rarely in English are two words exact synonyms although it may happen that in a single sentence any one of two or three words may serve the desired purpose. Conventional usage has given most of our words certain associations and connotations, certain idiomatic connections, which make impossible a free substituting of one for another. As one commentator has pointed out *humble* and *lowly* may appear synonymous, but no one yet has ever signed a letter "your *lowly* servant." The presence of so many romance words in English has enriched the language by offering choice between old English and romance forms—*help* and *assist* for example.

**Synopsis:** A summary, a résumé of the main points of a composition or argument so made as to show the relationship of each part to the whole. An abstract. A synopsis is usually more connected than an outline since it is likely to be given in complete sentences.

**Tail-rime Romance:** A term applied to metrical romances employing the tail-rime stanza (*q.v.*), especially the large group of romances, including *Amis and Amiloun*, *Athelston*, *Horn Child* (and some twenty others) which employed a tail-rime stanza of twelve lines made up of four groups or parts, each with a short "tail" line, such as aa*b* aa*b* cc*b* dd*b*. It has recently been shown (Trounce, *Medium Aevum*, Vols. I–III) that there existed a "school" of minstrels writing tail-rime romances in East Anglia in the fourteenth century.

**Tail-rime Stanza:** A stanza of verse containing among longer lines two or more short lines which rime with each other and serve as "tails" to the divisions or parts of the stanza. The form developed in medieval times and is known in French as *rime couée*. A modern example is found in Charles Lamb's *Hester* (*Golden Treasury*, No. 276).

**Tale:** A simple narrative without complicated plot. Formerly no very real distinction was made between the *tale* and the *short story;* the two terms were used interchangeably. Tale, however, has always been a more general term than short story since the latter has been reserved for narrative following a fairly technical routine and the former has been loosely used to denote any short narrative.

**Taste:** A basis for critical judgment of a piece of literature founded upon a personal aesthetic appreciation rather than upon logical laws or established standards of criticism. In any matter of art, taste is reliable only when it springs from a general background of culture, from familiarity with the history and character of the form judged, from a sensitivity to the author's moods and emotions, and an awareness of the relationship which normally exists between form and content. In this sense taste may be said to be balance, proportion. In another sense good taste springs from an ability to place oneself in the mood and intent of the writer through a sympathetic understanding of his creative purpose. These things are emphasized as qualities of taste since too often careless readers think they have expressed an opinion of a work when they say they "like it" or "don't like it." No one has a right to make a statement of this sort in the belief that he has advanced a critical judgment or that he is giving expression to his own *taste* in literary matters, since taste is not mere expression of a verdict; it is an intelligent verdict for which the critic can advance reasons from his cultural background, from his familiarity with form and method, from his sensitivity, from his sense of balance and proportion. The right to judge requires as a prerequisite a knowledge of the thing to be judged, and this knowledge comes only as the result of serious effort and thoughtful study. As few people would be absurd enough to buy an automobile upon the recommendation of a Hottentot who had never seen one, so no one should take the opinion of a person that a book is "good" or "bad" unless he has reason to believe that the utterance is supported by a discriminating and intelligent cultural background. Taste, then, is personal opinion growing out of an intelligently intimate experience in the field in which judgment is to be passed.

**Tautology:** The use of superfluous, repetitious words. "He wrote an autobiography of his life" might much better be stated "He wrote an autobiography."

**Tercet:** A stanza of three lines, a triplet, in which each line ends with the same rime. The term is also used to denote either one of the two three-line groups forming the sestet of the Italian sonnet. A tercet of the type first mentioned is quoted from Herrick:

> Whenas in silks my Julia goes,
> Then, then, methinks, how sweetly flows
> That liquefaction of her clothes.

***Terza rima:*** A three-line stanza form borrowed from the Italian poets. The rime scheme is *aba, bcb, cdc, ded,* etc. In other words, one rime-sound is used for the first and third line of each stanza and a new rime introduced for the second line, this new rime, in turn, being used for the first and third lines of the subsequent stanza. Usually the meter is iambic pentameter, but in the illustration quoted (from Browning's *The Statue and the Bust*) the meter is iambic tetrameter:

There's a palace in Florence, the world knows well,   *a*
And a statue watches it from the square,   *b*
And this story of both do our townsmen tell.   *a*

Ages ago, a lady there,   *b*
At the farthest window facing the East   *c*
Asked, "Who rides by with the royal air?"   *b*

**Testament:** As a literary form the term has two rather distinct meanings. It may be a literary "last will and testament" or it may be a piece of literature which "bears witness to" or "makes a covenant with" in the Biblical sense. The former sort of "testament" originated with the Romans of the decadent period and was developed by the French in the late medieval and early Renaissance periods. It was especially popular in the fifteenth century and was often characterized by humor, ribaldry, and satire, as in the half-serious, half-ribald *Grand Testament* and *Petit Testament* of François Villon, perhaps the greatest examples of this type. In the popular literature of the first half of the sixteenth century in England there were many wills and testaments of the humorous and satiric sort, such as *Jyl of Breyntford's Testament, Colin Blowbol's Testament,* and Humphrey Powell's popular *Wyll of the Devil* (*ca*.1550). Some literary testaments, however, were more serious; for example, the *Testament of Cresseid* by the Scotch poet Robert Henryson (1430–1506), a continuation of Chaucer's *Troilus and Criseyde* in which Cressida is pictured as thoroughly degraded in character and suffering from leprosy. In her poverty-stricken last days she bequeaths her scant belongings to her fellow-sufferers. Another serious testament is the love complaint "The Testament of the Hawthorne" in *Tottel's Miscellany* (1557).

The second type of testament, that which "bears witness to," was also developed in the late medieval period. Its best representative in English is perhaps *The Testament of Love* by Thomas Usk (?), written about 1384. This is a long prose treatise in which Divine Love appears in a rôle similar to that of Philosophy in Boëthius' *Consolation of Philosophy*, to which it is

433

somewhat akin. A notable modern representative of this type is Robert Bridges' *The Testament of Beauty* (1929).

**Tetrameter:** A line of verse consisting of four feet. See SCANSION.

**Theatres, English:** See PUBLIC THEATRES, PRIVATE THEATRES, PATENT THEATRES.

**Thesis:** An attitude or position on a problem taken by a writer or speaker with the purpose of proving or supporting it. The term is also used for the paper which is written to support the thesis. That is, *thesis* is used both for the problem to be established and for the essay which, presumably, establishes it. In college and university circles the word has the special connotation of a paper expounding some special problem and written as a requirement for a bachelor's or master's degree. See DISSERTATION. For *thesis* as a term in prosody, see ICTUS.

**Threnody:** A song of death, a dirge, a lamentation.

**Title:** The title given a piece of writing usually accomplishes certain ends; it is brief (rarely is a modern title longer than four or five words); it catches the eye and piques the interest; it suggests more than it states; and it is specific rather than general. An analysis of the titles of novels, plays, short stories, etc., discloses certain ways by which the ends mentioned above are secured. The most common title types have been classified as follows:

Titles which give the gist of the story (*The Mark of the Beast*)
Titles which derive from the setting (*The City of Dreadful Night*)
Titles which are drawn from the name of a character (*Markheim*)
Titles which combine character and setting (*The Outcasts of Poker Flat*)
Titles drawn from the central object in a story (*The Great Stone Face*)
Titles based on some reference to literature (*Gift of the Magi*)

**Toleration Controversy:** A phrase sometimes used to designate the struggle in seventeenth-century New England over religious toleration. The early Puritan leaders, such as John Cotton, who were educated men—not ignorant bigots—were led by their firm faith in Calvinistic theology (see CALVINISM) to a logical position which forced them to oppose the toleration of non-Calvinistic views. They held that the Scriptures con-tained all truth; that the Puritan theologians had searched the Scriptures till they had found the truth; that, therefore, all who differed had *not* found the truth and should not be tolerated in the religious community. Hence there was stern opposition to such groups as the Quakers, the adherents of the Church of Eng-land, and later the Baptists.

But there were among the Puritans themselves occasional dis-senters from this view, chief of whom was Roger Williams, a liberal-minded Oxford-trained Welshman who had come to Massachusetts about 1630 and been banished a few years later because of his radical views (he objected to the taking of the land from the Indians and to forcing non-Christians to take oath). In 1636 he established the colony of Rhode Island, where he tolerated all sects—even non-Christians. From 1644 to 1652 he engaged in a pamphlet war with John Cotton which is the "toler-ation controversy" proper. Cotton had published an answer to an argument written by an English prisoner protesting against persecution for sake of conscience. In 1644 (the very year in which Williams' friend Milton published his liberal *Areopagitica*) Williams published (in London) a reply to Cotton under the title *The Bloudy Tenent of Persecution for Cause of Conscience*, in which he espoused the doctrine of intellectual freedom. Cotton replied with his *The Bloudy Tenent Washed and Made White in the Bloud of the Lambe* (1647), to which Wil-liams retorted with his *The Bloody Tenent Yet More Bloody*, etc. (1652).

The general controversy over toleration continued throughout the century, with the liberal elements gaining ground following the reaction against the Salem Witchcraft (1692). From 1637 to about 1680 the anti-tolerationists were generally able to en-force conformity in Massachusetts. Especially severe was the government under John Endicott and John Norton in the 1650's and 1660's, as evidenced by the case against Mrs. Anne Hutchin-son and the brutally severe treatment of Quakers and Baptists. The *Cambridge Platform* (1648, 1651), providing that the power of the state be used to enforce religious conformity, gave the anti-tolerationists a powerful weapon. Representative of this group in early literature is Nathaniel Ward's picturesquely writ-

435

ten *Simple Cobbler of Aggawam* (1647), while Peter Folger's later *A Looking Glass for the Times* is a versified plea for toleration. See PURITANISM.

**Tone (Tone Color):** A term sometimes used in criticism to denote the mood or "pitch" of a piece of writing. Good writers not only blend "sound and sense," but they are also careful to blend color and sense. The emotions of human beings find their outlet in such expressions of feeling as tapping a table with one's finger, humming to one's self, stamping one's feet, applauding, and, if we are not so very restrained or happen to be present at a football game or a political caucus, in shouting aloud. We naturally, then, find a relationship between our moods and the noises we make. In the same way, too, there is a close relationship between emotions and colors. We associate green with envy, yellow with jealousy, red with passion and anger. And so on.

Now the literary artist knows all this well. He resorts to short, staccato sentences to show action and excited emotions; he uses slow, ponderous sentences to express slow movement and dejection. And in the field of color he strikes off the various moods with appropriate adjectives and adverbs; his nouns carry connotations expressive of gayety, serenity, pathos. And writing which so blends one or another of the emotions into the very texture of the writing itself has, it is said, *tone* or *color*.

**Tract:** A pamphlet, usually an argumentative document on some religious or political topic, often distributed free for propaganda purposes. For a classic example of the use of the term, see OXFORD MOVEMENT.

**Tractarian Movement:** See OXFORD MOVEMENT.

**Tradition:** A body of beliefs, customs, sayings, or skills handed down from age to age or from generation to generation. Thus ballads and folk literature in general as well as superstitions and popular proverbs are passed on by oral tradition. A set idea may be called a tradition, like the idea which prevailed throughout the Middle Ages that Homer's account of the Trojan War was to be discredited in favor of certain forged accounts claiming to be written by participants in the war. The "tradition" of pastoral literature means the underlying conceptions and technique of pastoral literature carried down, with modifications, from Theocritus (third century B.C.) to Pope. A "traditional" element in literature suggests something which the author has inherited from the past rather than something of his own invention.

**Tragedy:** This dramatic form has such a long and varied history that it is impossible to frame a flawless definition. The starting-point is Aristotle's famous statement (given below), which can not be regarded as complete or universally applicable. A useful approach is that of Professor Thorndike, who, after noting that subsequent dramatic history has shown that some of Aristotle's requirements, such as the "unities" (*q.v.*), can not be held essential to tragedy, summarizes those elements in Aristotle's definition which may be regarded as still valid: "Tragedy is a form of drama exciting the emotions of pity and fear. Its action should be single and complete, presenting a reversal of fortune, involving persons renowned and of superior attainments, and it should be written in poetry embellished with every kind of artistic expression." By an analysis of later tragedy, especially Shakespearean, Professor Thorndike then notes the elements which must be added to the Aristotelian: "The action of a tragedy should represent a conflict of wills, or of will with circumstance, or will with itself, and should therefore be based on the characters of the persons involved. A typical tragedy is concerned with a great personality engaged in a struggle that ends disastrously."[1] Yet it must be remembered that not *all* of these elements are to be found in *all* tragedies. Ibsen, for example, has written tragedies in prose rather than in verse, dealing with bourgeois rather than aristocratic figures. Aristotle's famous dictum as to the effects of the tragic action upon the spectator—the purging of the emotional nature (see CATHARSIS), has not met with universal favor, since it seems to overstress the moral and psychological effects of a play.

English tragedy begins in Elizabethan times. To its develop-

[1]Ashley H. Thorndike, *Tragedy*, Houghton, Mifflin and Company, pp. 8, 9. Reprinted by permission of and by arrangement with the publishers.

ment medieval drama doubtless contributed something: the high seriousness of the themes in the mystery plays and the moralities, especially the stressing of the element of conflict in the latter, must have had some effect. Yet the chief influence, so far as dramatic tradition and theory are concerned, was classical: the tragedies of Seneca and the *Poetics* of Aristotle. In 1559 came the first translation of a Senecan tragedy, and in 1562 was acted Sackville and Norton's *Gorboduc*, the "first regular English tragedy," a rather wooden play which Sidney praised, though regretting its failure to observe the unities of time and place. The strict classical conception of tragedy, however, was not destined to dominate the Elizabethan stage, in spite of its stout advocacy by Ben Jonson.

The high achievements of Shakespeare represent the triumph of the romantic tragedy (*q.v.*) that resulted from the popular revolt against classical restrictions. Where the classicists, as Allardyce Nicoll notes, insisted upon the unities, avoided "tragicomedy" (*q.v.*), and stressed Senecan declamation and a scrupulous observance of the laws of "decorum" (*q.v.*), the "progressives" ignored the unities, followed medieval tradition in mixing sadness and mirth, and strove at any cost to satisfy the spectators with vigorous action and gripping spectacle. The different kinds of theatres, audiences, and sponsors further contributed to the somewhat heterogeneous character of Elizabethan tragedy. Cultured gentlemen of the Inns of Court (*q.v.*) fostered and produced drama; plays at schools and universities flourished (see ACADEMIC DRAMA); companies of child actors performed at court and in "private theatres" (*q.v.*); while professional companies traveled about the country, performed at times at court, and served as stock companies in the great "public theatres" (*q.v.*), patronized at first chiefly by the lower social classes. Shakespeare himself was powerfully influenced not only by early examples of the "revenge tragedy" (*q.v.*) and of the "chronicle play" (*q.v.*), but by the great blank-verse tragedies of character and personality written by Marlowe. Out of such elements the master playwright eventually evolved a type of tragedy which, in such plays as *Hamlet, King Lear,* and *Macbeth,* became the pattern for the greatest achievements of the English stage.

While our attention is focused upon the greatest period of

English tragedy, it may be well to note that tragedy as few other forms of literature (a Hardy novel is perhaps comparable) raises questions of supreme difficulty and of absorbing interest to the student of literature. If we reject Aristotle's theory of catharsis as the chief justification of tragedy and admit that tragedy is written and acted and read and observed primarily because of the pleasure it begets, then how are we to explain the pleasure derived from the tragic action? Is it sadistic and base? Is the tragic stage but a weakened version of the gladiatorial arena? Is tragedy a "luxury of sorrow"? Do we enjoy it because it enables us to play with fire—without being burnt? Or do we like one tragedy because it exemplifies our notions of "poetic justice" (*q.v.*), and enjoy being puzzled over the failure of another tragedy to conform in the same way to our feeling of how human affairs should be carried on? Do we enjoy tragedy because it feeds a cynic mood in which we like to think of life as a vain and futile thing, "full of sound and fury, signifying nothing"? Or is it for mere enjoyment of emotional experience, artificially excited, "to banquet, not to purge" the emotions, that we expose ourselves to the painful sights of the tragic stage? Or do we find in tragedy (to quote the words of Mr. Lucas) "a representation of human unhappiness which pleases us notwithstanding, by the truth with which it is seen and the skill with which it is communicated"? Does our perennial interest in man attract us to a tragedy which exhibits, though it does not solve, great problems of man's relation to external circumstance and to destiny? Do we see in *Macbeth* a masterly embodiment of a specific question: can a man attain to satisfaction of soul through seeking to achieve an ambition by wrong means? If so, does the drama supply a clear answer? Is it fair to an author to look for a "moral" in his tragedy? Are we fascinated by the mystery of human suffering which the disillusioned Gloucester in *King Lear* would resolve with his "As flies to wantoun boys are we to the gods; They kill us for their sport"? Is Hamlet's doubt itself a symbol of the secret of tragedy—the presentation in such a way as to excite the emotions and stimulate the mind of a problem of life that is, after all, quite baffling?

In considering these and similar questions raised by an effort to interpret the great Shakespearean tragedies, we must bear in mind that Shakespeare was in part working under the influence of prevailing Renaissance conceptions of tragedy, which strongly emphasized the moral element—itself partly due to the inherited medieval idea of what a "tragedy" was. To Chaucer "tragedy" did not mean a play but a narrative of a person of high rank who, through ill fortune or through his own vice or error, had fallen from high estate to low. The "tragedies" of the *Monk's Tale*, of Lydgate's *Fall of Princes*, and of the famous Renaissance collection known as *The Mirror for Magistrates* are of this sort. The transition from this medieval conception of "tragedy" to the dominant Renaissance view has been summarized thus by one writer (Miss Campbell): "Tragedy started to picture the fall of princes. It came to seek an explanation that could justify the ways of God to men. It came to seek the justice which must inhere in such falls if there was a God of justice in his heaven. And it found that justice in the error or the folly which caused men to bring down evil on themselves. And gradually it came to find in men's passions the cause of their errors and their folly, and therefore the cause of the evil which they bring upon themselves. Thus fortune is not to be dissociated from cause in the change from happiness to unhappiness."[1]

It is not possible here to trace in any detail the story of the decline of English tragedy after Shakespeare. It suffered from the decadent tendencies of the early seventeenth century, was revived in an altered and weakened form under neo-classical influences, and reappeared as literary or "closet drama" (*q.v.*) in the nineteenth century. Although the late nineteenth century witnessed some revival, partly under the influence of Ibsen, the general tendency toward the breakdown of the old distinction between tragedy and comedy in favor of such forms as the *drame* (*q.v.*) or problem play has operated against traditional tragedy.

A representative list of English writers of tragedy before 1800 might include: Thomas Kyd, Christopher Marlowe, George Peele, William Shakespeare, Ben Jonson, Thomas Heywood, George Chapman, John Marston, Thomas Middleton, John

---

[1]From L. B. Campbell, *Shakespeare's Tragic Heroes, Slaves of Passion*, p. 22. Cambridge University Press. Reprinted by permission of The Macmillan Company.

Webster, Francis Beaumont and John Fletcher, Philip Massinger, James Shirley, John Ford; John Dryden, Nathaniel Lee, Thomas Otway; Nicholas Rowe, John Home, Richard Cumberland, George Lillo, and Edward Moore. See COMEDY, DRAMA, and other items there listed. (References: A. H. Thorndike, *Tragedy*; F. L. Lucas, *Tragedy in Relation to Aristotle's Poetics*; Allardyce Nicoll, *The Theory of Drama*; L. B. Campbell, *Shakespeare's Tragic Heroes*; Lane Cooper, *Aristotle on the Art of Poetry*; A. C. Bradley, *Shakespearean Tragedy*; Bonamy Dobrée, *Restoration Tragedy, 1660–1720*; C. C. Green, *The Neo-Classic Theory of Tragedy*; C. E. Vaughan, *Types of Tragic Drama*; W. M. Dixon, *Tragedy*.)

**Tragedy of Blood:** An intensified form of the revenge tragedy popular on the Elizabethan stage. It works out the theme of revenge and retribution (borrowed from Seneca) through murder, assassination, mutilation, and downright carnage. The horrors which in the Latin Senecan plays had been merely described were placed upon the stage to satisfy the craving for morbid excitement displayed by an Elizabethan audience brought up on bear-baiting spectacles and public executions (hangings, mutilations, burnings). Besides including such revenge plays as Kyd's *Spanish Tragedy*, Shakespeare's (?) *Titus Andronicus*, and Shakespeare's *Hamlet*, the tragedy of blood led to such later "horror" tragedies as Webster's *The Duchess of Malfi* and *The White Devil*. See REVENGE TRAGEDY, SENECAN TRAGEDY.

**Tragic Force:** The event or force which starts the falling action in a tragedy. It is either a separate event following closely upon the climax or is identified with the climax itself. The escape of Fleance is the tragic force in *Macbeth*, marking as it does the beginning of Macbeth's misfortunes and leading to the overthrow of the hero in the resulting catastrophe. See DRAMATIC STRUCTURE.

**Tragic Irony:** That form of "dramatic irony" (*q.v.*) in which a character in a tragedy uses words which mean one thing to him and another to those better acquainted with his real situation, especially when he is about to become a victim of Fate. Othello's allusion to the villain who is about to deceive him as "honest Iago" is an example.

**Tragi-comedy:** A play which employs a plot suitable to tragedy but which ends happily like a comedy. The action, serious in theme and subject matter and sometimes in tone also, seems to be leading to a tragic catastrophe until an unexpected turn in events, often in the form of a *deus ex machina* (*q.v.*), brings about the happy dénouement. In this sense Shakespeare's *The Merchant of Venice* is a tragi-comedy, though it is also a "romantic comedy" (*q.v*). If the "trick" about the shedding of blood were omitted and Shylock allowed to "have his bond," the play might easily be made into a tragedy; conversely Shakespeare's *King Lear*, a pure tragedy, was made into a comedy by Nahum Tate for the Restoration stage. In English dramatic history the term "tragi-comedy" is usually employed to designate the particular kind of play developed by Beaumont and Fletcher about 1610, a type of which *Philaster* is perhaps most typical. Fletcher's own definition may be quoted: "A tragi-comedy is not so called in respect of mirth and killing, but in respect it wants deaths, which is enough to make it no tragedy, yet brings some near it, which is enough to make it no comedy, which must be a representation of familiar people, with such kind of trouble as no life be questioned; so that a god is as lawful in this (tragi-comedy) as in a tragedy, and mean people as in a comedy" (from "To the Reader," *The Faithful Shepherdess*). Some of the characteristics are: improbable plot; unnatural situations; actors of high social class, usually of the nobility; love as the central interest, pure love and gross love often being contrasted; highly complicated plot; rapid action; contrast of deep villainy and exalted virtue; saving of hero and heroine in the nick of time; penitent villain (as Iachimo in *Cymbeline*); disguises; surprises; jealousy; treachery; intrigue; enveloping action of war or rebellion. Shakespeare's *Cymbeline* and *The Winter's Tale* are examples of the *genre*. Fletcher's *The Faithful Shepherdess* is a pastoral tragi-comedy. Later seventeenth-century tragi-comedies are Massinger's *The Prisoner*, Davenant's *Fair Favorite*, Shadwell's *Royal Shepherdess*, and Dryden's

*Secret Love* and *Love Triumphant*. Such plays as these tended to approach the "heroic drama" (*q.v.*). The type practically disappeared in the early eighteenth century, though the name is still sometimes employed, Henry Arthur Jones having called his *Galilean's Victory* (1907) a "tragi-comedy of religious life in England." (References: F. H. Ristine, *English Tragicomedy;* F. E. Schelling, *Elizabethan Drama*, Vol. II, Chap. xvii; Allardyce Nicoll, *The Theory of Drama*, Chap. IV.)

**Transcendental Club:** An informal organization of leading transcendentalists living in or near Boston. The group came together for their first formal meeting, September 19, 1836, at the home of George Ripley. Their chief interests were the new developments in theology, philosophy, and literature, and the purpose of their coming together was simply to discuss the "new thought" of the day. The movement was closely associated with the growth of the Unitarian spirit in New England. The leading members of the Club were such figures as Ralph Waldo Emerson, Convers Francis, Frederick Henry Hedge, Amos Bronson Alcott, George Ripley, Margaret Fuller, Nathaniel Hawthorne, Henry D. Thoreau, and William Ellery Channing. See TRANSCENDENTALISM.

**Transcendentalism:** A reliance on the intuition and the conscience, a form of idealism; a philosophical romanticism reaching America a generation or two after it developed in Europe. Transcendentalism, though based on doctrines of ancient and modern European philosophers (particularly Kant) and sponsored in America chiefly by Emerson after he had absorbed it from Carlyle, Coleridge, Goethe, and others, took on especial significance in the United States, where it so largely dominated the New England authors as to become a literary movement as well as a philosophic conception. The movement gained its impetus in America from meetings of a small group which came together to discuss the "new thought" of the time. While holding different opinions about many things, the group seemed in general harmony in their conviction that within the nature of man there was a something which transcended human experience—an intuitive and personal revelation of what

443

constituted right and wrong. Variously called the Symposium Club and the Hedge Club, the group was soon known as the Transcendental Club (*q.v.*) because of the ideas advanced by its members.

As the "movement" developed, it sponsored two important activities: the publication of *The Dial* (*q.v.*) from 1840–1844 and Brook Farm (*q.v.*). Some of the various doctrines which one or another of the American transcendentalists promulgated and which have somehow been accepted as "transcendental" may be restated here. They believed in living close to nature (Thoreau) and taught the dignity of manual labor (Thoreau). They strongly felt the need of intellectual companionships and interests (Brook Farm) and placed great emphasis on the importance of spiritual living. Man's relationship to God was a personal matter and was to be established directly by the individual himself (Unitarianism) rather than through the intermediation of the ritualistic church. They held firmly that man was divine in his own right, an opinion opposed to the doctrines held by the Puritan Calvinists in New England, and they urged strongly the essential divinity of man and one great brotherhood. Self-trust and self-reliance were to be practised at all times and on all occasions, since to trust self was really to trust the voice of God speaking intuitively within us (Emerson). The transcendentalists felt called upon to resist the "vulgar prosperity of the barbarian"; believed firmly in a democracy, and insisted on an intense individualism. Some of the extremists in their number went so far as to evolve a system of dietetics and to rule out coffee, wine, and tobacco—all on the basis that the body was the temple of the soul and that for the tenant's sake it was well to keep the dwelling undefiled. And most of the transcendentalists were by nature reformers, though Emerson—the most vocal interpreter of the group—refused to go so far in this direction as, for instance, Bronson Alcott. Emerson's position here is that it is man's responsibility to be "a brave and upright man, who must find or cut a straight path to everything excellent in the earth, and not only go honorably himself, but make it easier for all who follow him to go in honor and with benefit." In this way most of the reforms were attempts to awaken and regenerate the human spirit rather than to prescribe particular and concrete movements which were to be fostered. The transcendentalists were, for instance, among the early advocates of the enfranchisement of women.

Among the most famous of the transcendental leaders, in addition to Emerson, Thoreau, and Alcott already mentioned, were Margaret Fuller, George Ripley, F. H. Hedge, James Freeman Clark, Elizabeth Peabody, Theodore Parker, Jones Very, and W. H. Channing. But the arch-advocates in literature of most that the transcendentalists stood for were Emerson and Thoreau; and the two documents which most definitely give literary expression of their views were Emerson's *Nature* (1836) and Thoreau's *Walden* (1854). (References: O. B. Frothingham, *Transcendentalism in New England;* Lindsay Swift, *Brook Farm.*)

**Transferred Epithet:** See EPITHET.

**Transition:** The passing from one subject or division of a composition to another. A good prose style makes clear all such transition points and yet avoids such bold and obvious terms as are pedantic or puerile. Transitions occur, of course, between clauses, sentences, paragraphs, divisions, and chapters, and they are made smooth by the careful use (1) of such connective words as *again, too, further, then, first, secondly,* etc.; (2) of phrases and terms which show the relationships between two ideas, as *for this reason, it therefore follows, consequently,* etc.; (3) of terms which call attention to contrasts such as *on the contrary, however,* and *on the other hand.* Between paragraphs and larger divisions of thought the transitions are further aided by the inclusion of summary sentences marking the close of one idea and introductory sentences pointing toward the discussion of a new subject. Natural and easy transitions are among the subtle qualities of a good prose style which, when present, go unnoticed, but which, when absent, call down condemnation upon the author for his failure to make his writing clear and coherent.

**Travesty:** Writing which by its incongruity of style or treatment ridicules a subject inherently noble or dignified. The derivation

445

of the word, from *trans* (over or across) and *vestire* (to clothe or dress) clearly suggests the meaning of presenting a subject in a dress intended for another type of subject. Travesty may be thought of as the opposite of the "mock epic" (*q.v.*) since the latter treats a frivolous subject seriously and the travesty usually presents a serious subject frivolously. *Don Quixote* is, in a very real sense, a travesty on the medieval romance. See BURLESQUE.

**"Tribe of Ben":** A contemporary nickname for the young poets and dramatists of the seventeenth century who acknowledged "rare Ben Jonson" as their master. The boasted chief of the "tribe" was Robert Herrick, and the group included the Cavalier Lyrists (*q.v.*) and other of the younger poets and dramatists of Jacobean times. Jonson's influence upon his followers was in the direction of classical polish and sense of form, study and imitation of classical writers and literary types (as the ode, the epigram, satire), and classical ideals of criticism. The attitude represented a revolt from the Puritanism and Italian romanticism represented in Spenser. The poets strove to make the lyric graceful and in general the group followed the creed: "Live merrily and write good verses."

**Trilogy:** A literary composition, more usually a novel or a play, written in three parts, each of which is in itself a complete unit. Shakespeare's *King Henry VI* is an example. The trilogy usually is written against a large background which may be historical, philosophical, or social in its interests.

**Trimeter:** A line of verse consisting of three feet. See SCANSION.

**Triolet:** One of the simpler French verse forms. It consists of eight lines, the first two being repeated as the last two lines and the first recurring also as the fourth line. There are only two rimes, and their arrangement is: *abaaabab*. (Italics indicate repetition of whole lines.) Certain skillful poets, notably Austin Dobson, have contrived to add piquancy to the form by giving a different meaning to the refrain lines from that which they carried at the opening of the poem. Example:

446

## A KISS[1]

Rose kissed me today.
　　Will she kiss me tomorrow?
Let it be as it may,
Rose kissed me today.
But the pleasure gives way
　　To a savor of sorrow;—
Rose kissed me today,—
　　*Will* she kiss me tomorrow?
　　　　　　　—Austin Dobson

**Triple Rime:** See RIME.

**Trite Expression:** A *cliché* (*q.v.*).

**Trivium:** See SEVEN ARTS.

**Trochee:** A two-syllabled poetic measure consisting of an accented and an unaccented syllable, as in the word *happy*. Trochaics are generally unpopular with poets for sustained writing since they so soon degenerate into hobby-horse rhythm, a fact which makes them, perversely, popular with children and undeveloped minds. The ease and frequency with which Longfellow's *Hiawatha* has been parodied ("Sweet trochaic milk and water") bears evidence to this quality of the trochaic measure. On the other hand, for short songs and lyrics the trochee has been very popular. It is often used as the meter of the supernatural as in Shakespeare's

Double, double, toil and trouble,
Fire burn and cauldron bubble.

**Trope:** In rhetoric a trope is a figure of speech involving a "turn" or change of sense—the use of a word in a sense other than its proper or literal one; in this sense figures of comparison (see METAPHOR, SIMILE) as well as ironical expressions are "tropes" or figures of speech.

Another use of the word is important to students of the origin of medieval drama. As early as the eighth or ninth centuries,

---

[1] Printed with the courteous permission of Mr. Alban Dobson, representing the executors, and of the Oxford University Press.

certain musical additions to the Gregorian antiphons in the liturgy of the Catholic Church were permitted as pleasurable elaborations of the service. At first they were merely prolongations of the melody on a vowel sound, giving rise to *jubila*, the manuscript notation for a *jubilum* being known as a *neuma*, which looked somewhat like shorthand notes. Later, words were added to old *jubila* and new compositions of both words and music added, the texts of which were called "tropes." These tropes, or "amplifications of the liturgical texts," were sometimes in prose, sometimes in verse; sometimes purely musical, sometimes requiring dialogue, presented antiphonally by the two parts of the choir. From this dialogue form of the trope developed the liturgical drama. See MEDIEVAL DRAMA. (Reference: W. H. Frere, *Winchester Troper*.)

**Troubadour:** A name given to the aristocratic lyric poets of Provence (Southern France) in the twelfth and thirteenth centuries. The name is derived from a word meaning "to find," suggesting that the troubadour was regarded as an inventor and experimenter in poetic technique. Troubadours were essentially lyric poets, occupied with themes of love and chivalry. The conventional themes arose from the social conditions, the troubadour usually addressing his verse to a married lady, whose patronage he courted. Troubadour poetry figured importantly in the development of "courtly love" (*q.v.*), and influenced the *trouvère* (*q.v.*) of Northern France. The earliest troubadour of record is William, Count of Poitiers (1071–1127), other famous troubadours being Bernard de Ventadour, Arnaut de Mareuil, Bertran de Born, and Arnaut Daniel. Some of the forms invented by the troubadours are: the *canso* (love song), *ballata* (dance song), *tenso* (dialogue), *pastorela* (pastoral wooing song), and the *alba* (dawn song). Much use was made of rime, and varied stanzaic forms were developed, including the *sestina* (*q.v.*) used later by Dante and others. The sonnet form itself probably developed from troubadour stanzaic inventions. The poetry was intended to be sung, sometimes by the troubadour himself, sometimes by an assistant or apprentice or professional entertainer, as the *jongleur*. (Reference: H. J. Chaytor, *The Troubadours*.)

448

*Trouvère:* A term applied to a group or school of poets who flourished in Northern France in the twelfth and thirteenth centuries. The *trouvères* were much influenced by the art of the troubadour (*q.v.*) of Southern France, and concerned themselves largely with lyrics of love, though they produced also *chansons de geste* and chivalric romances. Indeed, to the activity of one of them, the famous Chrétien de Troyes (twelfth century), we owe some of the earliest and best of the Arthurian romances. See ARTHURIAN LEGEND.

**Truncation:** See CATALEXIS.

*Ubi sunt* **Formula:** A convention much used in verse, especially in the French forms, which asks "where are" (*ubi sunt*) these things, and these, and these, the poetic impression on the reader being largely effected by the emphasis the formula places on the transitory qualities of life. The most famous example in English is probably Dante Gabriel Rossetti's *The Ballad of Dead Ladies*, a poetic translation of François Villon's famous ballade:

> But where are the snows of yester-year?

In Justin McCarthy's poem, *I Wonder in What Isle of Bliss*, successive stanzas close with "Where are the Gods of Yesterday?" "Where are the Dreams of Yesterday?" "Where are the Girls of Yesterday?" "Where are the Snows of Yesterday?" In Edmund Gosse's *The Ballad of Dead Cities*, the three stanzas begin with "Where are the Cities of the plain?" "Where now is Karnak, that great fane . . . ?" "And where is white Shushan, again . . . ?" Each of the stanzas in this poem closes with "Where are the cities of old time?" These examples illustrate the tendency to place the *ubi sunt* query in the opening line of a stanza or to use it as a refrain or repetend.

*Ultima Thule:* The farthest possible place. Used often in the sense of a remote goal, an ideal and mysterious country. To the ancients *Thule* was one of the northern lands of Europe, most likely one of the Shetland Islands, although Iceland and Norway have been suggested. From the Latin reference to the region as the *ultima* (farthest) *Thule*, the expression has taken on the literary significance given it above.

**Unitarianism:** The creed of a sect coming into importance in America about 1820, a sect which discarded the earlier faith in the existence of a Trinity and held for the unity of God, accepting Christ as divine in the same sense that man is, but not as a member of a divine Trinity. In its more evolved form this new Unitarianism stood for "the fatherhood of God, the brotherhood of man, the leadership of Jesus, salvation by character, and the progress of mankind onward and upward forever."

All this, of course, was quite different from the attitude of early American Calvinists; from the point of view presented, for instance, by the characters in such a book as Hawthorne's *Scarlet Letter*. This early Unitarianism in America was so closely allied with the general cultural awakening in the first quarter of the nineteenth century (the so-called "New England Renaissance") and was so closely affiliated with the development of American transcendentalism that the term has almost taken on the significance of a literary movement even as it most positively stood for an intellectual movement. Though Unitarianism was by no means restricted to the United States, its most famous sponsor in America was William Ellery Channing, and the sermon Channing preached on *Unitarian Christianity* in Baltimore (1819) stands as the most important single utterance of this new doctrine. Religious and spiritual in essence, the movement nevertheless took on strong intellectual, social, and cultural significances. Throughout New England one old Calvinistic church after another adopted the new doctrine and made itself a center for the new thought and the new culture. The freedom from traditional doctrine it brought made possible and natural, for instance, the easy and quick acceptance of New England transcendentalism which followed so closely in its wake.

**Unities:** The principles of dramatic structure involving *action*, *time*, and *place*. The most important unity and the only one enjoined by Aristotle is that of action. He called a tragedy "an imitation of an action that is complete, and whole, and of a certain magnitude"; a whole should have beginning, middle, and end, with a causal relationship in the different parts of the play. Inevitability and concentration result from adherence to the unity of action. This unity, Aristotle warned, was not necessarily obtained simply by making one man the subject. Later critics declared that a sub-plot tends to destroy the unity of any serious play and that tragic and comic elements should not be mixed. Thus the legitimacy of tragi-comedy (*q.v.*) was for a long time a matter of dispute; Sidney opposed it and Doctor Johnson vindicated it.

The unity of time was developed from Aristotle's simple and undogmatic statement concerning tragic usage: "Tragedy endeavors, as far as possible, to confine itself to a single revolution of the sun, or but slightly to exceed this limit." The Italian critics of the sixteenth century formulated the doctrine that the action should be limited to one day; many French and English critics of the seventeenth and eighteenth centuries accepted this unity, and many dramatists used it. There were different interpretations of the unity of time—some favored the natural day of twenty-four hours, others the artificial day of twelve hours, and others the several hours that correspond to the actual time of theatrical representation.

The unity of place, limiting the action to one place, was the last to emerge and was not mentioned by Aristotle. It followed, quite naturally, the requirement of limiting the action to a particular time; as the Renaissance critics of Italy developed their theories of verisimilitude, of making the action of a play approximate that of stage representation, the unity of place completed the trilogy. Some critics were content to have the action confined merely to the same town or city. The unity of place was closely allied to that of time in the theory and practice of neo-classic writers.

The dramatic unities have had a long and extremely complicated history. For more than two centuries in England the three unities were denounced and defended and (as in Dryden's *Essay of Dramatic Poesy*) debated. When neo-classicism gave way to Romanticism, they lost their importance.

Many great English plays violate all three unities. Unity of action, however, is commonly recognized as an important requirement in serious drama, and Shakespeare's greatest tragedies, such as *Hamlet* and *Othello*, show the effects of unification. In two plays, the *Comedy of Errors* and *The Tempest*, Shakespeare observed all three of the unities. The theory of the unities has been, in truth, a matter of more concern to critics than dramatists. Yet the concentration and strength that result from efforts at attaining unity of action, time, and place may be regarded as dramatic virtues.

Modern dramatists are less interested in traditional formulae than in the unity of impression, the singleness of emotional effect, which is related to the unity of action. Moreover, in recent years effective experiments with the minor unities of time and place have been made in stage and screen plays. See Criticism, Historical Sketch.

**Universality:** A critical term frequently employed to indicate the presence in a piece of writing of an appeal to all readers of all time. When writing presents the great human emotions common to all peoples of all civilizations—jealousy, love, pride, courage, etc.—it may be said to have "universality." Of all qualities which make for universality in literature, the successful portrayal of human character is the most important.

**University Wits:** A name used for certain young University men who came to London in the late 1580's and undertook careers as professional men of letters. They played an extremely important part in the development of the great literature, especially the drama, that characterized the latter part of Elizabeth's reign. The most important one was Christopher Marlowe. Others included are Robert Greene, George Peele, Thomas Lodge, Thomas Nash, and Thomas Kyd. Some authorities include John Lyly, though Lyly was an older man and perhaps not personally associated with the others. They lived irregular lives, Greene and Marlowe being particularly known as Bohemians. Their literary work, while uneven in quality, much of it being hack work, was varied and influential, especially in the field of drama. They were largely instrumental in freeing tragedy from the artificial restrictions imposed by classical authority, and their cultivation of blank verse, especially the "mighty line" of Marlowe, paved the way for Shakespeare's masterful use of this form. They devised or developed types of plays later perfected by Shakespeare: the revenge tragedy or "tragedy of blood" (Kyd), the tragedy built around a great personality (Marlowe), romantic comedy (Greene and Peele), chronicle history (Marlowe and others), and the "court comedy" (Lyly). Lodge and Greene cultivated the pastoral romance and Nash wrote the first picaresque novel in English. The group was especially active between 1585 and 1595. The personal and literary interests of these "wits" sometimes made them rivals or enemies of one another.

**Usage:** The standard which sets the speech of a people. Good usage is established by the forms of language used by educated people and by intelligent writers, but this does not mean at all that usage is *fixed*. It is, in fact, constantly shifting, old forms becoming obsolescent and obsolete, new forms entering by way of slang, passing through the colloquial stage, and sometimes finally arriving at recognition as "good usage." Dictionaries and grammars properly *follow* usage rather than *set* it, though, of course, both do much toward standardization and stabilization.

**Utopia:** A word meaning "no where" coined by Thomas More to represent the seat of his ideal republic as pictured in his *Utopia* (1516). The idea of presenting plans for ideal commonwealths has interested many philosophers and writers. Plato's *Republic* of course is the best known. Some others are Campanella's *Civitas Solis* (1623), Bacon's *New Atlantis* (1627), Harrington's *Oceana* (1656), Samuel Butler's *Erewhon* (1872), Bellamy's *Looking Backward* (1888), William Morris' *News from Nowhere* (1890), and H. G. Wells' *A Modern Utopia* (1905).

***Vade mecum:*** An article which one keeps constantly with him. By association the term has come to mean any book much used, as a *handbook*, a *thesaurus*.

**Vapours** (see HUMOURS): A word commonly used in eighteenth-century literature to account for the eccentric action of people. Vapours were exhalations which were presumably given off by the stomach or other organs of the body and rose to the head causing depression, melancholy, hysteria, etc. As early as 1541 Sir Thomas Elyot wrote that "of humours some are more grosse and cold, some are subtyl and hot and are called vapours."

453

Heroines of eighteenth-century fiction were particularly subject to attacks of this malady. Young, in 1728, gave us these lines:

> Sometimes, thro' pride the sexes change their airs;
> My lord has vapours, and my lady swears.

**Variety:** A quality of style, whether in prose or verse, which demands that the author avoid monotonous expression of his ideas. There are various ways in which this variety of expression is secured. Perhaps the easiest and most effective lies in varying the structure and type of sentences used. This is accomplished by the author's alternating between long, or fairly long, sentences and short sentences, by shifting from compound and complex sentences to simple, and by substituting, probably only rarely to be sure, an exclamatory or interrogative sentence for the more usual declarative statement.

There are other devices which the good writer uses unconsciously in his effort to avoid monotony. He will shift, in long discourse, from narration to description, an anecdote will be introduced into an argument, a description into a story. He will illustrate a statement by reference to a personal experience or to an allusion in history or literature. His plain, matter-of-fact discourse will be relieved here and there by poetic imagery; he will call upon one of the figures of speech to make his language vivid. His diction will vary with his mood, his purpose, his characters. The serious will be relieved by the comic and discussion of abstractions will sometimes become concrete. He will not be content to play on one emotion for long but will seek rather complete freedom from emotional tensity—what has been called "tragic relief"—by a scene of comic import, or he will, at least, vary the emotion he presents. If he is writing indirect discourse primarily, he will stop to introduce a bit of dialogue. The author who knows his art is like the expert organist before his console—he has an infinite number of possibilities before him.

**Variorum Edition:** An edition of an author's work presenting complete variant readings of the possible texts and full notes of critical comments and interpretation passed upon the text by major writers. The term is an abbreviation of the Latin phrase *cum notis variorum* ("with notes of various persons"). In the field of English literature, the most conspicuous success in this type of editing is that of the "New Variorum Shakespeare" edited by Furness. See SHAKESPEARE, EDITORS AND EDITIONS.

**Vaudeville:** An entertainment consisting of successive performances of unrelated songs, dances, dramatic sketches, acrobatic feats, juggling, pantomime, puppet-shows, and varied "stunts." The word is derived from *Vau-de-Vire*, a village in Normandy, where a famous composer of lively, satirical songs lived in the eighteenth century. From these songs, modified later by pantomime, developed the "variety" shows now known as vaudeville. The elements of vaudeville are, of course, old (see LOW COMEDY, BURLESQUE, FARCE), but the modern vaudeville type or variety show developed in the eighteenth and nineteenth centuries. Under the direction of John Rich these shows became very popular in eighteenth-century England and continued so through the nineteenth century. The name vaudeville seems to have become finally attached to the variety show as a result of its development in America, especially in the early years of the twentieth century, when vaudeville actors were organized into "circuits" by B. F. Keith and others and when elaborate theatres were devoted to their use. The popularity of vaudeville decreased after the advent of the talking moving pictures.

**Verisimilitude:** The appearance or semblance of truth and actuality. The term has been used in criticism to indicate the degree to which a writer faithfully presents the truth. In his *Life of Swift*, Scott writes: "Swift possessed the art of verisimilitude." The word was a favorite one with Poe who, however, used it in the special sense of presenting details, howsoever far-fetched, in such a way as to give them the *semblance* of truth. In *The Facts in the Case of M. Valdemar*, for instance, Poe gives way to the wildest kind of romancing, but the items are so marshalled as to sweep the reader into at least a momentary acceptance of them, and the story may, therefore, be said to respect Poe's own demands for verisimilitude.

***Vers de société:*** Brief lyrical verse written in genial, sportive mood and sophisticated both in subject and treatment.

Sometimes called "light verse." Characteristics are polish, *savoir faire*, grace, and ease of expression. Usually presents aspects of conventional social relationships. Epigrammatic. Locker-Lampson in a much-quoted introduction to his collection of *vers de société* states: "Occasional Verse should be short, graceful, refined, and fanciful, not seldom distinguished by chastened sentiment, and often playful. The tone should not be pitched high; it should be terse and idiomatic, and rather in the conversational key. The rhythm should be crisp and sparkling, the rhyme frequent and never forced, while the entire poem should be marked by tasteful moderation, high finish and completeness." Though perhaps gaining in favor in recent centuries, light verse was popular in Greek and Latin classical literature. The seventeenth and eighteenth centuries in England, too, saw a high development of the type. For study see the prefaces to the two collections of *vers de société:* Locker-Lampson, *Lyra Elegantiarum* and Carolyn Wells, *Vers de Société Anthology.*

**Vers libre:** See FREE VERSE.

**Verse:** Is used in two senses: (1) as a unit of poetry, in which case it has the same significance as *line;* and (2) as a name given generally to metrical composition. In the second sense, verse is simply a generic term applied to rhythmical and, most frequently, metrical and rimed composition, in which case it implies little as to the merit of the composition, the term *poetry* or *poem* being reserved especially to indicate verse of high merit. An inherent suggestion that verse is of a lower order than poetry lies in the fact that *verse* is used in association with such terms as *society verse, occasional verse,* etc., which, it is generally conceded, are rarely great poetry. The use of verse to indicate a *stanza,* while common, is hardly justified.

**Versification:** The art and practice of writing verse. Like *prosody* the term is an inclusive one being generally used to connote all the mechanical elements going to make up poetic composition: *accent, rhythm,* the *foot, meter, rime, stanza form, diction,* and such figurative aids as *assonance, onomatopoeia,* and *alliteration* (all of which are explained in their proper alpha-

456

betical positions).   In a narrower sense "versification" signifies simply the *structural* form of a verse or stanza such as is revealed by careful *scansion*.

See ACCENT and QUANTITY for reference to the underlying principles of English verse.

Following is a list of terms connected with versification and poetic art which may be found defined in their proper alphabetical positions in this handbook:

Acatalectic
Accent
Adonic Verse
Alcaics
Alexandrine
Alliteration
Alliterative Verse
Amphibrach
Anacreontic Poetry
Anacrusis
Anapest
Anastrophe
Anthem
Anthology
Antistrophe
Arsis
Art Ballad
Art Epic
Art Lyric
Assonance
Ballad
Ballade
Blank Verse
Blues
Broadside Ballad
Bucolic
Cadence
Cæsura
Canto
*Canzone*
Carol
Catalexis
Cavalier Lyric

Cavalier Lyrists
Chanson
*Chanson de geste*
Chant
*Chant royal*
Chantey
Chorus
Closed Couplet
Closet Drama
Common Meter
Complaint
Coronach
Couplet
Dactyl
Didactic Poetry
Dimeter
Dirge
Distich
Dithyramb
Ditty
Doggerel
Doric
Dramatic Monologue
Dramatic Poetry
Eclogue
Elegy
End-stopped Lines
*Enjambement*
Envoy
Epic
Epic Simile
Epitaph
Epithalamion

Epithet
Epode
Feminine Ending
Feminine Rime
Figurative Language
Foot
Fourteeners
Free Verse
French Forms
Heptameter
Heroic Couplet
Heroic Verse
Hexameter
Hiatus
Hudibrastic Verse
Hymn
Iambus
Ictus
Idyl
Imagery
Imagists
Incremental Repetition
Interlude
Inversion
Invocation
*Jongleur*
Lament
Lay
Leonine Rime
Libretto
Limerick
Lyric

| | | |
|---|---|---|
| Macaronic Verse | Poetic | Scansion |
| Madrigal | Poetic Diction | Serenade |
| Masque | Poetic Drama | Sestet |
| Metaphysical Verse | Poetic License | Sestina |
| Meter | Poetry | Skeltonic Verse |
| Metrical Romance | Polyphonic Prose | Song |
| Minstrel | Popular Ballad | Sonnet |
| Miscellanies, Poetical | Posy | Spenserian Stanza |
| Mock Epic | Poulter's Measure | Spondee |
| Mock Heroic | Prosody | Stanza |
| Monometer | Psalm | Stave |
| Muses | Pyrrhic | Stress |
| New Poetry, the | Quantity | Strophe |
| Nocturne | Quatorzain | Tercet |
| Nonsense Verse | Quatrain | *Terza rima* |
| Occasional Verse | Refrain | Tetrameter |
| Octameter | Repetend | Threnody |
| Octave | Requiem | Trilogy |
| Ode | Rhythm | Trimeter |
| *Ottava rima* | Rime | Triolet |
| Pæan | Rime Royal | Trochee |
| Pantoum | Rime-scheme | Trouvère |
| Pastoral | Romantic Epic | Troubadour |
| Pastoral Elegy | Rondeau | *Ubi sunt* Formula |
| *Pastourelle* | Rondel | *Vers de société* |
| Pentameter | Roundel | Verse |
| Plaint | Roundelay | Villanelle |
| Poem | Run-on Lines | Virelay |
| Poet Laureate | Sapphic | |

**Victorian:** A term used (1) to designate broadly the literature of the age of Queen Victoria (1837–1901) or its characteristic qualities and attitudes; and (2) more narrowly, to suggest a certain complacency or hypocrisy or squeamishness more or less justly assumed to be traceable to or similar to prevailing Victorian attitudes. Pride in the growing power of England, optimism born of the new science, the dominance of Puritan ideals tenaciously held by the rising middle class, and the example of a royal court scrupulous in its adherence to high standards of "decency" and respectability combined to produce a spirit of moral earnestness linked with self-satisfaction which was protested against at the time and in the generations immediately to follow as hypocritical, false, complacent, and narrow. The cautious manner in which "mid-Victorian" writers in particular were prone to treat such matters as profanity and sex has been especially responsible for the common use of the term "Victorian" or "mid-Victorian," to indicate false modesty, empty respectability, or callous complacency. Though justified in part, this use of "Victorian" rests in some degree upon exaggeration, and at best fails to take into consideration the fact that even in the heart of the Victorian period a very large part of the literature either did not exhibit such traits or set itself flatly in protest against them. As a matter of fact, Victorian literature is many-sided and complex, and reflects both romantically and realistically the great changes that were going on in life and thought. The religious and philosophical doubts and hopes raised by the new science, the social problems arising from the new industrial conditions, the conscious resort of literary men to foreign sources of inspiration, the rise of a new middle-class audience and new media of publication (the magazines) are among the forces which colored the literature of the period. Some added details concerning the Victorian period may be found by consulting such other terms in this handbook as INDUSTRIAL REVOLUTION, REFORM BILL OF 1832, OXFORD MOVEMENT, and PRE-RAPHAELITISM. See also "Outline of Literary History" (pp. 536–559). Special treatments of Victorian literature are found in the *Cambridge History of English Literature*, Vols. XII–XIV; H. Walker, *The Age of Tennyson* and *The Literature of the Victorian Era*; G. K. Chesterton, *The Victorian Age in Literature*; Oliver Elton, *A Survey of English Literature, 1830–1880*, 2 vols.; W. C. Brownell, *Victorian Prose Masters*; W. H. Hudson, *English Literature in the Nineteenth Century*; D. C. Somerville, *English Thought in the Nineteenth Century*.

**Villanelle:** A French verse form calculated, through its complexity and artificiality, to give an impression of simplicity and spontaneity. The villanelle was perhaps originally chiefly pastoral and an element of formal lightness is still uppermost since it is most frequently used for poetic expression which is idyllic, delicate, simple, and slight. In form the villanelle is characterized by nineteen lines divided into five tercets and a final four-line stanza, and the presence of only two rimes. The division of verses is, then: *aba aba aba aba aba abaa.* Line 1 is repeated entirely to form lines 6, 12, and 18, and line 3 is repeated entirely to form lines 9, 15, and 19: thus eight of the nineteen lines are refrain.

**Virelay:** A French verse form (related to *lai*) of which the number of stanzas and the number of lines to the stanza are unlimited. Each stanza is made up of an indefinite number of tercets (see TERCET) riming *aab* for the first stanza, *bbc* for the second, *ccd* for the third, etc. The virelay has never become popular among English poets, probably because of the monotony of the riming.

**Virgin Play:** See MIRACLE PLAY.

**Vulgate:** The word comes from Lat. *vulgus*, "crowd" and means "common" or commonly used. Note two chief uses: (1) the Vulgate Bible is the Latin version made by Saint Jerome in the fourth century and is the authorized Bible of the Catholic Church; (2) the "Vulgate Romances" are the versions of various cycles of Arthurian romance which were written in Old French prose (common or colloquial speech) in the thirteenth century and were the most widely used forms of these stories, forming the basis of Malory's *Le Morte d'Arthur* and other later treatments. See ARTHURIAN ROMANCE.

**Wardour-Street English:** A style strongly marked by archaisms; an insincere, artificial expression. Wardour Street, in London, is a street housing many antique dealers selling genuine and imitation antiques. Wardour-Street English is a term coined on the analogy of imitation archaisms in writing and imitation antiques in furniture, etc. It was, for instance, applied to William Morris's translation of the *Odyssey*.

**War of the Theatres:** A complicated series of quarrels among certain Elizabethan dramatists in the years 1598–1602. Ben Jonson and John Marston were the chief opponents, though many other dramatists, including Dekker certainly and Shakespeare possibly, were concerned. Among the causes of the quarrel may be mentioned the personal and professional jealousies among some of the playwrights and the keen competition among the rival theatres and their associated companies of actors. Particularly important was the struggle for supremacy between the stock companies of professionals (see PUBLIC THEATRES) and the companies of boy actors, the "Children of the Chapel" —acting at the Blackfriars—and the "Children of Paul's." The child actors were becoming very popular and were threatening to supersede the "common stages," as Shakespeare himself termed his fellows and himself in his allusion to the situation in *Hamlet* (Act II, Scene ii). The details of the affair have not been very completely recovered by modern students. Some of the plays concerned are: Jonson's *Everyman in his Humour* (1598), Marston's *Histriomastix* (1599) and *Jack Drum's Entertainment* (1600), Dekker and others' *Patient Grissel* (1600), Jonson's *Cynthia's Revels* (1601), Dekker's *Satiromastix* (1601). Shakespeare's connection with the quarrel is inferred from the statement in the university play *The Return from Parnassus* (1601–1602) that Shakespeare had bested Jonson, and from the theory that *Troilus and Cressida* reflects the "war." There is a clear allusion to the rivalry of the boy actors and the "common stages" in *Hamlet* (Act II, Scene ii). See ACADEMIC DRAMA. (References: R. A. Small, *The Stage Quarrel;* R. B. Sharpe, *The Real War of the Theatres*.)

**Welsh Literature:** Though records are scanty it is probable that there was much literary activity in Wales in the early Middle Ages (sixth to ninth centuries). In eastern and central Wales there developed the *englyn*, a form of epigrammatic verse possibly derived from Latin literature. The northern district produced the most famous of early Welsh poets, Taleissin and Aneiren (sixth century?), who sang of early Welsh warriors, including heroes traditionally associated with King Arthur. This literature is probably related to the Irish. The western "cycle" deals with very early material, such as myths of the gods. Chiefly from this Western literature come the best known stories of early Welsh authorship, those now collected in the famous *Mabinogion*. These tales were probably collected and written down in the eleventh and twelfth centuries, though the manuscripts of the *Mabinogion* date from a few centuries later. The stories in the *Mabinogion* (for meaning of the word, see MABINOGION) fall into five classes, according to Griffith. The first is the *Mabinogion* proper, or the "four branches." It includes four stories which are the written versions of spoken tales belonging to the repertory of the lower orders of Welsh bards, and which preserve primitive tradition. The titles are *Pwyll Prince of Dyved, Branwen daughter of Llir, Manawyddan son of Llir*, and *Math son of Mathonwy*. The second group includes two tales based on legendary British historical tradition: *Dream of Maxen Wledig, Llud and Llwellys*. The third class, old Arthurian folk-tales current in southwest Wales retold by eleventh- or twelfth-century writers with some admixture of other matter, partly Irish, is represented by *Kulwch and Olwen*. This story is of great interest to students of Arthurian romance as it may reflect a very early stage in the development of Arthurian stories, when magic and grotesqueness had not been displaced by chivalric manners. The fourth class consists of Arthurian stories paralleled in courtly French versions of the twelfth century (some and perhaps all based partly at least upon the French versions): *Peredur, Geraint, The Lady of the Fountain* (or *Owein*). The fifth class (imaginary, sophisticated literary tales) is represented by *The Dream of Rhonabwry*.

Under Griffith son of Cynan (1054–1137) there was a renaissance of Welsh poetry with courtly patronage—the bardic system was now flourishing. These court poets followed a traditional poetic technique, employing ancient conventions and archaic words to such an extent that a contemporary could hardly understand the verse. With the English conquest (1282) the old poetry declined, and in the fourteenth and fifteenth centuries, known as a "golden age," under the leadership of the poet David ap Gwilynn, a contemporary of Chaucer, the basis of modern Welsh poetry was laid. The language actually spoken was employed, and love and nature were exploited as poetic themes. Under the Tudors the aggressive English influence depressed native Welsh poetry, though the bards remained active till mid-seventeenth century. In the seventeenth century a new school of poets who utilized native folk materials arose and in the eighteenth century came the classical revival

under the influence of the English "Augustans" (see AUGUSTAN).
Poetry in the nineteenth century was largely religious.

The development of prose in Wales, as in England, in the
sixteenth and seventeenth centuries was fostered by the availabil-
ity of the printing press and by the vogue of controversial writings, especially those connected with the religious movements of
early Protestant times. In the late eighteenth and early nineteenth centuries the liberal movement in politics stimulated
further activity in prose, and thereafter Welsh literature, both
prose and poetry, has been inclined to follow general European
movements, as has criticism. Coincident with other phases of
the Celtic Renaissance (*q.v.*) there was a distinct revival of
literary activity in the late nineteenth and early twentieth centuries. (Reference: W. J. Griffith, *Encyc. Brit.*, 14th ed., Vol.
XXIII.)

**Whimsical:** A critical term characterizing writing which is
fanciful, odd, eccentric. Whimsy, in a sense now obsolete, was
used as "a whimsy in the head, or in the blood," implying a
sort of vertigo. Whimsical writing, then, is writing inspired by
a fantastic or fanciful mood. Lamb's essays are often "whimsical" in this sense.

**Wit and Humor:** Although neither of these words originally
was concerned with the laughable, both now find their chief uses
in this connection. At present the distinction between the two
terms, though generally recognized to exist, is difficult to draw,
although there have been numerous attempts at definition. One
great "wit" in fact made a witticism out of his observation that
any person who attempted to distinguish between "wit" and
"humor" thereby demonstrated that he himself possessed
neither wit (in the sense of superior mental powers) nor humor
(which implies a sense of proportion and self-evaluation that
would show him the difficulty of attempting a cold analysis of
so fugitive a thing as humor).

"Humor" is the American spelling of "humour" (*q.v.*),
originally a physiological term which because of its psychological
implications came to carry the meaning of "eccentric": from
this meaning developed the modern implications of the term.
"Wit," meaning originally knowledge, came in the late Middle

Ages to signify "intellect," "the seat of consciousness," the "inner" senses as contrasted with the five "outer" senses. In Renaissance times, though used in various senses, wit usually meant "wisdom" or "mental activity." An important critical use developed in the seventeenth century when the term, as applied for example to the "metaphysical" poets (see META-PHYSICAL VERSE), meant "fancy," in the sense of inspiration, originality, or creative imagination—this being the literary virtue particularly prized at the time. With the coming of neo-classicism (*q.v.*), however, the term took on new meanings to reflect new critical attitudes, and for a hundred years many philosophers (including Hobbes, Locke, and Hume) and critics (including Dryden, Addison, Pope, and Johnson) wrestled with efforts to define "wit." Hobbes asserted that fancy without judgment or reason could not constitute wit, though judgment without fancy could. Pope used the word in both of the contrasting senses of fancy and judgment. Dryden had called wit "propriety of thought and words," and Locke thought of it as an agreeable and prompt assemblage of ideas, ability to see comparisons. Hume stressed the idea that wit is that which pleases ("good taste" being the criterion). Amid the confusing variety of eighteenth-century uses of the word, this notion of wit as a social grace which gave pleasure led to its comparison with "humor," and before 1800 both words came to be associated with the laughable, though the older, serious meaning of wit did not die out, as the earlier meanings of humor (both the medical meaning of one of the four liquids of the human body and the derived meaning of "individual disposition" or "eccentricity") had done. Modern definitions of "wit" reflect both the original and the late eighteenth-century conceptions: "that quality of speech or writing which consists in the apt association of thought and expression, calculated to surprise and delight by its unexpectedness; later always with reference to the utterance of brilliant or sparkling things in an amusing way" (*New English Dictionary*).

It is for the most part agreed that "wit" is primarily intellectual—the "swift play and flash of mind," and is expressed in skillful phraseology, plays upon words, surprising contrasts, paradoxes, epigrams, comparisons, etc., while "humor" implies

WIT AND HUMOR

a sympathetic recognition of human values and deals with the foibles and incongruities of human nature, good-naturedly exhibited. A few quotations from writers who have made serious attempts to distinguish between the two terms may help further to clarify the conceptions. Humor "deals with incongruities of character and circumstance, as Wit does in those of arbitrary ideas" (Hunt). "Wit is intensive or incisive, while humor is expansive. Wit is rapid, humor is slow. Wit is sharp, humor is gentle. . . . Wit is subjective while humor is objective. . . . Wit is art, humor is nature."[1] "Humor is meant, in a literal sense, to make game of a man; that is, to dethrone him from his official dignity and hunt him like game. It is meant to remind us human beings that we have things about us as ungainly and ludicrous as the nose of the elephant or the neck of the giraffe."[2] "Wit, apart from Humor, generally speaking, is but an element for professors to sport with. In combination with Humor it runs into the richest utility, and helps to humanize the world" (Hunt). "Humor always laughs, however earnestly it feels, and sometimes chuckles; but it never sniggers" (Saintsbury).

The immortal figure of Falstaff in Shakespeare's *Henry IV*, Part I, is an example of a subtle interweaving of wit and humor. The verbal fencing, the punning, and particularly the sophistical maneuvering whereby Falstaff invariably extricates himself from difficult situations with an apparent saving of his face, rest upon his "wit." On the other hand, the easy recognition on the part of the reader not only that Falstaff is bluffing and is cutting a highly ludicrous figure but also that the old rascal is inwardly laughing at himself, that he sees clearly the incongruities of his situation and behavior and realizes that his lies will be recognized as such by the Prince, is an element of "humor." See HUMOURS, COMEDY, SATIRE. (References: Carolyn Wells, *An Outline of Humor;* Max Eastman, *The Sense of Humor;* Louis Cazamian, *Development of English Humor;* Leigh Hunt, *Wit and Humor;* Samuel S. Seward, *The Paradox*

[1] Carolyn Wells, *An Outline of Humor*, G. P. Putnam's Sons, 1923, p. 17. Reprinted by permission of the publishers.

[2] From G. K. Chesterton, *Alarms and Discursions*, Dodd, Mead & Company, p. 233. Reprinted by permission of the publishers.

465

*of the Ludicrous.*  Eastman gives a summary of the underlying theories on the nature of humor.)

**Women as Actors:** Although they appeared on the Italian and French stages during the Renaissance, women were not countenanced on the professional stage in England, where boys were specially trained to act women's parts.  There were sporadic cases of the appearance of women on the stage in England, as in the case of the French actresses in London in 1629, but they were unfavorably received.  The part of Ianthe in Davenant's *Siege of Rhodes* (1656) was played by Mrs. Coleman, and the tradition of English actresses is usually dated from this event. However, this piece was more musical and spectacular than dramatic, and Mrs. Coleman's appearance may have been regarded as justified by the custom of having women (not professional actresses) take parts in masques.  The lady may have been employed in this entertainment because of her powers as a singer.  With the sudden revival of dramatic activity in 1660, actresses became a permanent feature of the English stage. The influence of the French theatre and the lack of a supply of trained boy-actors were perhaps chiefly responsible.  Boy-actors were by no means unknown in feminine rôles on the Restoration stage, however.  Some women who early gained fame as actresses were: Mrs. Barry, Mrs. Betterton, Mrs. Bracegirdle (seventeenth century); and Mrs. Susannah Cibber, Mrs. Prichard, and Mrs. Siddons (eighteenth century).

OUTLINE OF LITERARY HISTORY
ENGLISH AND AMERICAN

# OUTLINE OF LITERARY HISTORY
# ENGLISH AND AMERICAN

*Explanatory Note.*—The authors have prepared this outline in the belief that a tabular display of the chief external facts in the history of English and American literature, arranged by periods, will be of definite assistance to students of the literature itself, especially those who find it difficult to acquire from running accounts of literary history the "backbone" of chronology necessary to an understanding of men and movements. Beginning with the year 1600, American items appear in a separate column which runs parallel with the English. The dated items are intended to be suggestive, not comprehensive. A few "non-literary" items are included for their value either as chronological guide-posts or as indications of prevailing cultural conditions. In connection with the summaries at the beginnings of periods and subdivisions of periods, the authors expect their readers to share their own realization that the characteristics and tendencies therein listed must not be over-stressed or misinterpreted. These lists are intended to remind students of prevailing forces and fashions and changing emphases, not to set up attempted definitions of the periods. The items found, for example, under "Poetry" in the period called "Triumph of Romanticism" may not be taken separately or in an absolute sense as elements *necessarily* present in romantic, or absent in non-romantic, poetry.

*Titles* are often abbreviated or modernized to forms commonly encountered by the student. Translated titles appear in quotation marks in the early periods.

*Dates* for titles of printed books are ordinarily the dates of first publication. Dates for works written before the era of printing are dates of composition, often approximate.

*Abbreviations and Symbols*
   ?    —questionable date or statement of fact.
   *    —non-English item.
   *w*   —written.
   *a*   —acted.
   *ca.*  —about: dating is approximate.
   *fl.*   —flourishing, or flourished.
   Lat.—Latin.
   A.S.—Anglo-Saxon.

## ? B.C.–A.D. 428  Celtic and Roman Britain

? B.C.–A.D. 82    Celtic Britain.

55, 54 B.C.       Julius Caesar invades Britain.

51 B.C.      *Julius Caesar, "Commentaries" (Lat.): early conditions in Western Europe reflected.

31 B.C.–A.D. 180   *Flourishing period of Roman Empire.

*ca.*A.D. 30      *Crucifixion of Jesus Christ.

43–410      Roman-Celtic period in Britain: government Roman, population largely Celtic. No literature extant.

43      Invasion of Claudius.

82      Roman power established in Britain.

98      *Tacitus, *Germania* (Lat.): early account of Teutonic ancestors of English.

180–476      *Decline of Roman Empire.

313      *Christianity established at Rome by Constantine.

410      *Rome sacked by Alaric.
Roman legions leave Britain.

## 428–1066 Old English (Anglo-Saxon) Period

428–1066      **Teutonic Period in Britain. The "Dark Ages."** Celts crowded back by Angles, Saxons, Jutes. Saxon monarchies established in 5th and 6th centuries: Sussex, Wessex, Essex. Anglian monarchies established in 6th and 7th centuries: Northumbria (Deira, Bernicia), East Anglia, Mercia. Introduction of Christianity; gradual triumph of Christian over pagan culture. Intertribal conflicts and later (9th century) struggles with Danes. Unification of Teutonic groups in 9th century. General cultural state low. Learning and letters flourished chiefly in monasteries. Church dominant after 7th century. Old English literature first written in the Anglian dialect in Northumbria, later in the Mercian and West Saxon dialects. Earliest literature pagan in origin, reflecting Teutonic life on Continent. Later literature Christian. Whitby the "cradle" of English poetry in the North, Winchester of English prose in the South. Teutonic dialects spoken by invaders little affected by that of the conquered Celts because of continuation of hostile relations. Christian monks begin about 700 to write in the vernacular. Sentence structure influenced slightly by Latin and a few Latin words added to vocabulary. Some Danish words added in latter part of period. By time of Alfred (late 9th century) four English dialects noticeable: Northumbrian, Mercian, Kentish, West Saxon. Last named becomes standard literary dialect.

POETRY.–Alliterative in form, with complex metrical structure built around stress accent. Pagan epic and lyric poems written in 6th and 7th centuries (probably). Christian poems, Biblical paraphrases, legends, and lyrics written chiefly in 7th, 8th, and 9th centuries. *Beowulf* chief extant poem. Pagan poems show effects of Christian reworking.

PROSE.–Cultivated in 9th, 10th, and 11th centuries: chronicles, sermons, laws, leech-books, lives, and Christian legends —much of this literature being translations from Latin.

DRAMA.–Liturgical drama begins on Continent (*ca.*900). Established in England before 1000.

|  |  |
|---|---|
| 428 | Germanic tribes begin invasion of Britain. |
| 449 | Traditional date (from Gildas and Bede) for Germanic invasion of Britain under Hengist and Horsa. |
| *ca.*450–*ca.*700 | Probable period of composition of Old English poems (chiefly pagan) reflecting Continental life: *Beowulf*, epic; *Waldhere*, fragmentary epic of Theodoric saga; *Finnsburg*, fragmentary, related to *Beowulf* background; *Widsith*, lyric, adventures of a wandering poet; *Deor's Lament*, lyric account of poet's troubles; *The Wanderer*, reflective poem on cruelty of fate; *The Seafarer*, reflective, descriptive lyric on sailor's lot in life; *The Wife's Complaint, The Husband's Message:* love poems notable for romantic treatment of nature; *Charms*, miscellaneous incantations reflecting early superstitions, ceremonies, and remedies; formulistic. |
| *ca.*500–*ca.*700 | *Christian culture flourishes in Ireland after being almost obliterated on Continent by Teutonic invasion; activity of Irish missionaries in Scotland, Iceland, France, Germany, Switzerland, and Italy aids in rechristianizing Western Europe. |
| 509 | *Closing of Athenian philosophical schools (founded by Plato). |
| *ca.*524 | *Boëthius, "Consolation of Philosophy" (Lat.): one of greatest books of early Middle Ages; translated into English, successively, by King Alfred, Chaucer, and Queen Elizabeth. |
| 563 | St. Columba (Irish monk) establishes monastery at Iona, thus preparing for spread of Celtic Christianity in Scotland and Northern England. |
| 570–632 | *Mohammed. |
| 590–604 | *Pope Gregory the Great: temporal power of papacy, Gregorian Calendar, Gregorian music. |
| 597 | Saint Augustine (the missionary) places Roman Christianity on firm basis in Southern England. |
| 600–700 | Establishment of powerful Anglo-Saxon kingdoms. |

| | |
|---|---|
| *ca.*600–*ca.*800 | \*Irish saga literature assumes written form. |
| *ca.*633 | \*The Koran. |
| 650?–709 | Aldhelm: famous scholar of Canterbury school—Latin works survive; English poems (probably ballads) lost. |
| 664 | Synod of Whitby: triumph of Roman over Celtic Christianity in Britain. |
| *ca.*670 | Caedmon, *Hymns*, etc.: first English poet known by name. |
| *ca.*690 | Adamnan, *Life of St. Columba* (Lat.): "first authentic manifestation of the biographical impulse in Britain." |
| *ca.*700 | "School of Caedmon" *fl.*: Genesis, Exodus, Daniel—Biblical paraphrases; Judith, apocryphal. |
| | *Beowulf* composed in present form: great Anglo-Saxon epic. |
| 731 | Bede (Bæda), The Venerable, "Ecclesiastical History" (Lat.): important source-book; first history of English people. |

## 750

| | |
|---|---|
| *ca.*750–*ca.*800 | Flourishing period of Christian poetry in Northumbria (preserved in later West Saxon versions). |
| | Cynewulf and his "school": *Crist*, narrative; *Elene*, saint's legend; *Juliana*, saint's legend (dialogue form); *Fates of the Apostles*, saints' legends; *Andreas*, saint's legend (voyage tale); *The Phoenix*, myth interpreted as Christian allegory, notable for conscious poetic art, esp. nature descriptions. |
| 787 | First Danish invasion. |
| | \*Charlemagne orders schools established in abbeys. |
| *ca.*800 | Nennius (a Welshman), "History of the Britons" (Lat.): first mention of Arthur. |
| 800–814 | \*Reign of Charlemagne: renaissance of learning and literature. |
| 827–1017 | Anglo-Saxon kings (Egbert to Edmund Ironside). |

## 850

| | |
|---|---|
| *ca.*850 | Danish conquest of England. |
| 871–901 | Reign of Alfred the Great: Danes repulsed; Wessex leadership in literature; Alfred both author and patron of literature, esp. prose translations; Alfred's translations of Pope Gregory's *Pastoral Care*, Boëthius, Orosius, Bede; *Anglo-Saxon Chronicle* revised and continued to 892; West Saxon *Martyrology;* sermons; saints' lives. |

| | |
|---|---|
| *ca.*875–900 | *Probable beginnings of medieval drama.  Dramatization of liturgy.  First known text an Easter trope, *Quem Quaeritis,* from Swiss monastery of St. Gall. |
| 878 | Peace of Wedmore; partial Danish evacuation. |
| 893 | Asser, *Life of Alfred the Great:* "first life-record of a layman." |
| 901–1066 | Later Old English Period.  *Chronicle* continued; poetry, sermons, Biblical translations and paraphrases, saints' lives, lyrics. |
| *ca.*937 | *Battle of Brunanburh:* heroic poem. |
| 950–1000 | Monastic revival under Dunstan, Aethelwold, and Aelfric. |
| *ca.*950 | *Junius* MS written: contains Caedmon poems. |
| 971 | *Blickling Homilies:* colloquial tendencies. |
| *ca.*975 | St. Ethelwold's *Concordia Regularis,* directions for acting a trope at Winchester: earliest evidence of dramatic activity in England. |
| 979–1016 | Second period of Danish invasions. |
| *ca.*991 | *Battle of Maldon:* heroic poem. |

## 1000

| | |
|---|---|
| 1000–1200 | Transition period, English to Norman French.  Decline of A.S. heroic verse; reduced literary activity in English; medieval English lyrics possibly developing; germs of English romances possibly existing in tales and ballads. |
| *ca.*1000 | A.S. *Gospels* written. |
| | Aelfric, *Sermons:* Aelfric comparable to Bede and Alfred in influence upon Old English culture. |
| | *Beowulf* MS written. |
| 1000–1025 | The *Exeter Book:* A.S. MS containing Cynewulf poems. |
| *ca.*1000–1100 | *Vercelli Book:* A.S. MS containing *Andreas,* etc. |
| | *Probable period of full development of Christmas and Easter cycles of plays in Western Europe. |
| 1017–1042 | Danish kings (Canute to Hardicanute). |
| 1042–1066 | Saxon kings restored (Edward the Confessor to Harold II). |

## 1066–1350  Early Middle English Period

| | |
|---|---|
| **1066–1350** | **Anglo-Norman and Early Middle English Period.** Latin used for learned works, French for courtly literature, English chiefly for popular works.  Transition from Old English |

to Modern English taking place: loss of inflections, adoption of French words. Use of English increasing in 13th and 14th centuries. French influence (both from central France and from Normandy) dominant, adding grace, humor, and chivalric ideals to English culture and literature. Cultural internationalism. Feudalism established in England. Age of chivalry. Establishment of Parliament. Advance of democracy. Rise of Oxford and Cambridge universities. Scholasticism strong. Church a dominant force in society, government, literature. Survival of older attitudes revealed in reverence for favorite classical writers and in popularity of saints' legends. Allegorical method a favorite literary device. Romances, lyrics, religious legends, didactic treatises, sermons, "debates," satires, chronicles, fables, bestiaries, tales, "lays," popular ballads.

POETRY.–Native alliterative verse lives on, though largely supplanted in cultural circles by French rimed forms, often stanzaic. Influence of French poetry strong, as shown in lyrics, lays, romances, and religious verse. Popular ballads also probably produced.

PROSE.–Religious and historical chiefly. Some narrative.

DRAMA.–Religious drama ("mystery" plays and "miracle" plays) develops, first under supervision of clergy, later of towns and of trade-guilds.

| | |
|---|---|
| 1066 | Battle of Senlac (Hastings). Norman conquest. |
| 1066–1154 | Norman kings (William I to Stephen). |
| 1079 | *Abélard born. Died 1142. French ecclesiastical philosopher. Lover of Héloïse. |
| 1086 | *Domesday Book:* important Engilsh census. |
| 1087–1100 | William II: centralization of kingdom. |
| 1096–1099 | The First Crusade: the crusades exerted some influence upon Western European literature by stimulating the imagination, widening mental horizons, and by making Oriental culture available. |

## 1100

| | |
|---|---|
| 1100–1200 | *French literature dominating Western Europe. |
| 1100–1135 | Reign of Henry I ("Beauclerc"). |
| ca.1100–1250 | *Icelandic sagas written: *Grettirsaga, Volsungsaga,* etc. |
| ca.1100 | "Play of St. Catherine" (*a.* at Dunstable): first recorded "miracle" or saint's play in England. |
| | *Earlier tales in Welsh *Mabinogion* (*w*). |

*"The Book of the Dun Cow": earliest existing MS containing early Irish romantic literature.

*Great period of French poetry begins, lyric in South (Provence), narrative in North. *Chanson de Roland:* French epic. Count William of Poitiers (Provençal lyricist), "the first modern poet."

ca.1125–1300    Latin chronicles *fl.*

ca.1125    Henry of Huntingdon and William of Malmesbury: chronicles.

1135–1154    Reign of Stephen.

ca.1136    Geoffrey of Monmouth, "History of the Kings of Britain" (Lat. chronicle). Stresses Arthur as national hero and monarch: first elaborate, romantic account of Arthurian court; a source for many later writers.

ca.1140    Eadmer, *Life of Anselm:* human element in biography.

# 1150

1150–1200    *Influential French poets flourishing: Wace, Chrétien de Troyes, Marie de France, Thomas, Benoît de Ste. More, etc. Romance themes, courtly ideals.

ca.1150    *The *Nibelungenlied:* great epic poem treating early Germanic history.

1154–1399    Plantagenet kings (Henry II to Richard II).

1154–1189    Reign of Henry II: his court a center of literature and learning—historians, philosophers, theologians, poets. French and Latin chiefly employed.

1154    End of entries in *A.S. Chronicle* (Peterborough).

ca.1155    *Wace, *Brut* (French): earliest mention of Arthur's Round Table.

ca.1160    *Benoît de Ste. More, *Roman de Troie:* contains first romantic treatment of Troilus and Cressida.

ca.1170    *Poema Morale:* didactic verse.

1172    First English effort to conquer Ireland.

ca.1185–1190    *Giraldus Cambrensis, "Itinerary": description of Wales.

1187    *Saracens capture Jerusalem.

1189–1199    Reign of Richard I ("The Lion-hearted").

ca.1190    Nigel Wireker, *Speculum stultorum* (Lat.), "The Fool's Looking-glass": ecclesiastical and educational satire in elegiac verse.

1199–1216    Reign of John.

## 1200

| | |
|---|---|
| 1200–1300 | *Gothic architecture *fl.* |
| *ca.*1200–1250 | *King Horn, Beves of Hampton* (earliest form): English metrical romances using English themes. |
| *ca.*1200–1225 | *The Vulgate Romances (expansion of Arthurian romance material in French prose). |
| | *Walther von der Vogelweide *fl.* (German lyric poet). |
| *ca.*1200 | Walter Map *fl.:* court satirist, reputed author of Arthurian prose romances. |
| | Orm, *Ormulum:* Scriptural poem; early, though detached, effort to spell English words systematically. |
| | *Robert de Boron: trilogy of Arthurian poems (French): connects Grail story with Christian legend. |
| *ca.*1205 | Layamon, *Brut:* includes famous account of Arthur's Round Table; native (Anglo-Saxon) tendencies in language and style. |
| 1215 | *Magna Charta.* |
| 1216–1272 | Reign of Henry III. |
| *ca.*1225 | *St. Thomas Aquinas born.   Died 1274.   One of the greatest of medieval "scholastic" teachers and writers.   Founder of "Thomists." |
| *ca.*1230, *ca.*1270 | *Roman de la Rose* by Guillaume de Lorris and Jean de Meun: great allegorical poem (French); influenced Chaucer. |

## 1250

| | |
|---|---|
| *ca.*1250–1300 | Satiric spirit prominent in literature. |
| | *Sir Tristrem, Floris and Blanchefleur* (romances). |
| *ca.*1250 | Nicholas of Guilford, *The Owl and the Nightingale:* "debate." The "Cuckoo Song" (*Sumer is Icumen in*): lyric beginnings in Middle English. |
| | *Gesta Romanorum:* collection of tales. |
| 1258 | Henry III uses English as well as French in proclamation. |
| 1265 | *Dante born.   Died 1321. |
| 1272–1307 | Reign of Edward I. |
| 1287 | *Guido della Colonna, "History of Troy" (Lat.): widely read medieval version of Trojan war. |
| *ca.*1294 | *Dante, *Vita Nuova.* |

## 1300

| | |
|---|---|
| 1300–1400 | Leveling of inflections. Growth of English language in subtlety and power, as it is increasingly used for learned works. Decay of dialectal forms in English progressing. East Midland dialect (descended from Mercian) becomes standard literary English. English displaces French in speech of upper classes, and in schools and law pleadings. Mystery plays now in hands of guilds: more actors, more spectators, outdoor stages, comic elements, "cyclic" development (York plays probably oldest existing cycle). |
| ca.1300–1321 | *Dante's later works: *Il Convito* (begun *ca.*1300), *De Vulgari Eloquentia* (*ca.*1305, criticism), *Divina Commedia* (*ca.*1307–1321). |
| ca.1300–1350 | *Guy of Warwick, Havelok the Dane, Richard Lionheart, Amis and Amiloun:* romances. |
| ca.1300 | *Marco Polo, "Travels." |
| | *Cursor Mundi:* didactic, religious verse intended to compete with worldly romances. |
| 1304 | *Petrarch born. Died 1374. Great influence upon English poetry of Renaissance, esp. sonnet sequences. |
| 1306 | *Bruce crowned in Scotland. |
| 1307–1327 | Reign of Edward II. |
| 1311 | Feast of Corpus Christi established, leading to popularization of cyclic plays at this summer festival and perhaps to use of movable stages or "pageants." |
| 1313 | *Boccaccio born. Died 1375: important source-influence on Chaucer and many Renaissance authors; author of world-famous tales. |
| 1314 | Battle of Bannockburn. |
| ca.1325 | *Giotto (Ital. painter) and Jan van Eyck (Flemish painter) *fl.* |
| 1327–1377 | Reign of Edward III. |
| 1328? | Chester cycle of plays composed. |
| 1337–1453 | The Hundred Years' War. |
| ca.1340 | Geoffrey Chaucer born. Died 1400. |
| | Rolle, *The Prick of Conscience.* |
| 1342 | *Boccaccio, *Ameto:* "first pastoral romance." |
| 1346 | Battle of Crécy. |

477

| 1348–1350 | The Black Death. |
| 1349 | Order of the Garter established. |

## 1350–1500  Late Middle English

**1350–1400**  **Age of Chaucer.** Italy supplanting France in literary leadership. Petrarch and Boccaccio *fl.* Humanism in Italy. Some humanistic activity in England. Intellectual unrest. Religious dissatisfaction. Lollardism. Growing nationalistic spirit following military successes against France. Reestablishment of English language. Decline in use of Latin and French for literature. Romances, popular ballads, cyclic plays flourishing. English vocabulary expanding through adoption of French and Latin words. Dominance of East Midland (London) dialect.

POETRY.–Courtly poetry of Chaucer, largely under Italian and French influences. Revival of alliterative verse. Popular ballads, metrical romances, dream allegories, satire.

PROSE.–Wycliffe's English sermons and Biblical translations show some reaction against flowery, Latinized prose style. *Mandeville's Travels* an influential prose monument.

DRAMA.–Cyclic plays flourishing.

**1350–1400**  *Sir Eglamour, Morte Arthure, Sir Gawayne and the Green Knight, Athelstan, William of Palerne, Sir Ferumbras, Sir Isumbras,* and other romances.

*ca.*1350  \*Petrarch, eclogues (Lat.), printed 1504. "Sonnets to Laura" partly written.

\*Boccaccio, *Decameron.*

1356 (?)  "Sir John Mandeville," *Voyage and Travels.*

*ca.*1360  *The Pearl:* religious poem, dream framework.

1362  English language used in court pleadings and in opening Parliament.

*ca.*1362 *et. seq.*  *Piers Plowman:* dream allegory, alliterative verse, protests against social abuses.

*ca.*1370  Chaucer, *The Book of the Duchess:* French influence, love vision, elegy.

*ca.*1375  Barbour, *Bruce:* Scottish romantic history.

"Paternoster" and "Creed" plays (*a*): forerunners of morality plays.

1377–1399  Richard II.

*ca.*1379  Chaucer, *House of Fame:* allegory.

478

| | |
|---|---|
| *ca.*1380 | Wycliffe and others, translation of Bible into English. |
| 1381 | Wat Tyler's rebellion. |
| *ca.*1383 | Chaucer, *Troilus and Criseyde:* verse-romance; courtly love; "first psychological novel in English."<br>Usk (?) *The Testament of Love.* |
| *ca.*1385 | English replaces French as language of the schools.<br>Chaucer, *Legend of Good Women.* |
| *ca.*1387 | Chaucer, "Prologue" to *Canterbury Tales* (tales themselves written some earlier, some later.) |
| 1390–1392 | Gower, *Confessio Amantis:* court-of-love allegory. |
| 1399–1461 | House of Lancaster (Henry IV to Henry VI). |
| 1399–1413 | Reign of Henry IV. |
| 1400 | Death of Chaucer. |

## 1400

| | |
|---|---|
| **1400–1500** | **End of Middle Ages.** Wars of the Roses, resulting in checking of democratic movement. Comparative dearth of literature in England. "Chaucerian" school of poets flourishes in Scotland. Romances, ballads, religious drama persist. Italian Renaissance accompanied in England by some humanistic activity. Introduction of printing. Discovery of America. Language changing.<br>Poetry.–Weak, lacking vitality and metrical skill. Chaucer imitated. Metrical romances continue. Popular ballads flourish.<br>Prose.–Important development late in century—Malory, Caxton. Prose romances.<br>Drama.–Cyclic plays flourishing. Beginning of morality plays. Folk drama. Romantic drama possibly performed at out-of-doors festivals. |
| 1400–1450 | Later romances in prose and verse: *Lancelot of the Lake, Four Sons of Aymon, Squire of Low Degree, Huon of Bordeaux, Sir Triamour, Godfrey of Boulogne,* etc.<br>*Brunelleschi (Ital. architect) and Vittorino de Feltre (Ital. educator) *fl.* |
| 1400–1425 | Wakefield cycle of plays (MS, *ca.*1450).<br>*The Pride of Life* (fragmentary): earliest extant morality play. |
| 1400 | *Froissart, *Chronicles.* |
| *ca.*1412 | Hoccleve, *The Regiment of Princes* (*w*): courtesy book. |

479

| | |
|---|---|
| 1413–1422 | Reign of Henry V: further progress of English in replacing French among guilds and in other similar everyday business. |
| 1415 | Battle of Agincourt. |
| *ca.*1415 | Lydgate, *Troy Book*. |
| 1422–1507 | The *Paston Letters:* family correspondence reflecting social conditions. |
| 1422–1461 | Reign of Henry VI. |
| *ca.*1425 | Humanists active under patronage of Humphrey, Duke of Gloucester: Lydgate, Pecock, etc. English students attend Italian universities. Manuscripts collected. Translations made. |
| | *Castle of Perseverance:* first complete morality play. |
| 1440 | Galfridus Grammaticus, *Promptorium Parvulorum:* English-Latin word-list, beginning of English lexicography. |

## 1450

| | |
|---|---|
| 1450 | Jack Cade's rebellion. |
| *ca.*1450 | "Tiptoft" School of humanists active. |
| | *Gutenberg press: beginning of modern printing. |
| | Beginning of Lowland Scotch as northern literary dialect. |
| *ca.*1450–1525 | Scottish poets of Chaucerian school: Henryson, Dunbar Douglas, and probably King James I of Scotland. |
| | *Italian Renaissance at its height: scholars, theologians, teachers, philosophers, painters, poets. |
| *ca.*1450–1490 | *Platonic Academy at Florence flourishing under Lorenzo the Magnificent: Ficino, Poliziano, Pico della Mirandola, etc. |
| 1453 | *Fall of Constantinople: end of Eastern Empire. |
| 1455–1485 | Wars of the Roses: depressing effect on literary activity. |
| 1456 | *The Gutenberg Bible. |
| 1458–1464 | *Pope Pius II (Æneas Sylvius Piccolomini): great humanist. |
| *ca.*1460 | John Skelton born. Died 1529. |
| 1461–1485 | House of York (Edward IV to Richard III). |
| 1461–1483 | Reign of Edward IV. |
| 1469 | Sir Thomas Malory completes composition of *Le Morte d'Arthur* (pub. 1485). |
| 1474 | *Ariosto born. Died 1532. |
| *ca.*1474 | Caxton prints (at Bruges) the *Recuyell of the Histories of Troy:* first book printed in English. |

| | |
|---|---|
| 1475–1500 | Renewal of French influence. Italian influence continues. Transition to Renaissance. Printing of books begins in England. Humanistic activity renewed. *Romantic epics written in Italy. |
| *ca.*1477 | Caxton's press set up at Westminster: first printing press in England. *Dictes and Sayings of the Philosophers,* the first dated book (1477) printed in England. |
| 1478 | Sir Thomas More born. Died 1538. |
| 1483 | Reign of Edward V. |
| 1483–1485 | Reign of Richard III. |
| 1485–1603 | House of Tudor (Henry VII to Elizabeth). |
| 1485–1509 | Reign of Henry VII. |
| 1485 | Caxton publishes Malory's *Le Morte d'Arthur:* great prose compilation of Arthurian lore; important source-book for later English poets. |
| *ca.*1490 | *Sannazzaro, *Arcadia:* Italian pastoral romance. *Rabelais born. Died 1553. |
| 1490–1520 | "Oxford Reformers" (Linacre, Grocyn, Colet, Erasmus, More) active: classical scholarship, Biblical and literary criticism, humanistic education. |
| 1491 | Greek taught at Oxford. |
| 1492 | *Discovery of America by Columbus. |
| *ca.*1497 | Medwall, *Fulgens and Lucres* (a): interlude. |
| 1498 | *Savonarola executed. |
| 1499 | Erasmus in England. |

## 1500–1660    The Renaissance[1]

| | |
|---|---|
| 1500–1557 | **The Early Tudors.**   Renaissance ideals supplanting those of Middle Ages. Humanism. Individualism. The Reformation. Explorations. Commercial expansion. Rise of the middle classes. New theories of statecraft, education, Biblical criticism, literature. Printing presses active. Experimental period in literature: native forms modified and supplemented by Italian and French influences (esp. on courtly and sophisticated literature), and by German (esp. on religious and popular pieces). |
| | POETRY.–Medieval and Renaissance manners mingle in Skelton. Court poets under Henry VIII, esp. Wyatt and Surrey, introduce the "new poetry" from Italy, notably the |

---

[1] See RENAISSANCE, p. 363.

sonnet and blank verse. Cultivation of "classical" satire under Italian influence, by Wyatt and others. Satire, humanistic or medieval, also present in moralities, interludes, and poems of Barclay and Skelton. Popular satire fostered by Reformation controversy. Robin Hood ballads.

PROSE.—Most serious writing still in Latin, but movement for development of English furthered by work of Lord Berners and Sir Thomas Elyot and by the English Prayer-Book. Religious pamphlets. First efforts at biographical writing in English.

DRAMA.—Cyclic plays and moralities in vogue. Interludes develop. "School dramas" written and acted in schools and universities. Folk plays and possibly romantic drama performed at festivals on holidays. Acting by strolling players, guilds, and students in inn-yards, halls, and on improvised stages and "pageants." Comic and realistic tendencies noticeable, esp. in interludes.

| | |
|---|---|
| 1500–1550 | *Artists flourishing: Dürer, Holbein (German), Leonardo da Vinci, Michael Angelo, Raphael, Titian, Correggio (Ital.). |
| | ROMANCES.—*Valentine and Orson*, Lord Berners' *Arthur of Little Britain, Huon of Bordeaux*, etc. |
| ca.1500 | *Everyman:* important morality play. |
| 1503 (?) | Sir Thomas Wyatt born. Died 1542. |
| ca.1508 | Skelton, *Philip Sparrow:* society verse. |
| 1509–1547 | Reign of Henry VIII. |
| 1509 | Barclay, *Ship of Fools:* social satire; German influence. |
| | Hawes, *Pastime of Pleasure:* allegorical romance; didactic. |
| 1510 | Acting of Terence's comedies an established practice at Oxford and Cambridge. |
| ca.1511 | *Erasmus, "The Praise of Folly" (Lat.), social satire. |
| 1515 | Roger Ascham born. Died 1568. |
| 1516 | More, *Utopia* (Lat.): social satire; ideal commonwealth. |
| 1516 (?) | *Ariosto, *Orlando Furioso:* influential Ital. romantic epic. |
| | Skelton, *Magnificence:* morality play, political satire. |
| | Henry Howard, Earl of Surrey born. Died 1547. |
| 1517 | *Luther posts his theses in Wittenberg; leads to Protestant Revolution, 1520 *et seq.* |
| 1518 | Linacre founds Royal College of Physicians. |

| | |
|---|---|
| 1519 | Rastell, *The Four Elements* (*w. ca.*1512): first published interlude. Advocates adequacy of English for literary purposes. |
| | *Cortez conquers Mexico. |
| 1520–1530 | Latin plays (both original and translated from classics) acted in grammar schools. |
| *ca.*1520 | Skelton's poetical satires, personal, political, ecclesiastical (*Colin Clout, Why Come Ye Not to Court*, etc.). |
| 1523 | Lord Berners' trans. of Froissart's *Chronicles:* prose style striking. |
| 1523 | *Ronsard born. Died 1585. |

## 1525

| | |
|---|---|
| 1525 | Tyndale, *New Testament:* printed at Worms; first printed English translation of any part of Bible; influenced phraseology of later versions. |
| 1528 | *Castiglione, *The Courtier:* Italian "courtesy book." |
| 1529 | Simon Fish, *Supplication for Beggars:* typical Reformation pamphlet of "popular" sort. |
| | Fall of Wolsey. |
| 1530–1535 | *Marot (French poet) *fl.:* influenced Spenser. |
| *ca.*1530–1540 | Heywood's "Interludes": realistic farce; approach to comedy. |
| *ca.*1530 | The "New Poetry" movement under way; Italian influence. |
| 1531 | Elyot, *The Book of the Governour:* influential educational treatise of "courtesy book" type; English prose employed and defended. |
| 1532 | *Machiavelli, *The Prince* (*w.* 1513). |
| 1533 | Separation of English church from Rome. |
| | John Leland made "King's Antiquary." |
| | *Rabelais, *Pantagruel.* |
| 1534 | Act of Supremacy: Henry VIII head of Church of England. |
| | *Loyola founds Society of Jesus ("Jesuits"). |
| 1535 | Suppression of monasteries under way: loss of precious manuscripts; redistribution of land; changed social conditions. |
| | Execution of More. |
| | Coverdale's first complete English Bible. |
| | *Rabelais, *Gargantua.* |

| | |
|---|---|
| 1536 | Execution of Tyndale. |
| | *Calvin, *Institutes of Christian Religion* (Lat.): foundation of "Calvinism." |
| 1538 | Sir Thomas Elyot, *Dictionarie*. |
| 1540 | English Bible (the "Great Bible") set up in churches. |
| 1542 | Death of Wyatt. |
| | Hall's *Chronicle*. |
| 1542 (?) | George Gascoigne born. Died 1577. |
| 1543 | *Death of Copernicus. |
| 1545 | Ascham, *Toxophilus*. |
| | *Council of Trent. |
| 1547–1553 | Reign of Edward VI. |
| 1547 | Execution of Surrey. |
| 1548–1552 | *Book of Common Prayer:* important influence on prose style. |
| 1549 | *Du Bellay, *Defense et Illustration de la Langue Française:* poetic platform of the *Pléiade*. |

## 1550

| | |
|---|---|
| 1550–1575 | *The *Pléiade* group of French poets *fl.* (Du Bellay, Ronsard, etc.): influenced Elizabethan poets. |
| 1552 | Lyndsay, *Satyre of the Three Estaits:* Scotch satire; morality play. |
| | *Ronsard, *Amours:* influential French sonnets. |
| ca.1552 | Edmund Spenser born. Died 1599. |
| | Sir Walter Raleigh born. Died 1618. |
| | Udall, *Ralph Roister Doister* (w): first "regular" English comedy. |
| 1553–1558 | Reign of Mary. |
| 1553 | Wilson, *Arte of Rhetorique*. |
| 1554 | Sir Philip Sidney born. Died 1586. |
| | *Bandello, *Novelle* (Ital. tales): source-book for English dramatists. |
| ca.1554 | *La Vida de Lazarillo de Tormes:* influential Spanish picaresque tale. |
| ca.1555 | Roper, *Life of Sir Thomas More* (w): important effort at biographical writing in English. |
| | Cavendish, *Life of Cardinal Wolsey* (w): significant early English biographical writing. |

1557     *Songs and Sonnets* ("Tottel's Miscellany"): a collection of the "new poetry," which paves the way for Elizabethan poetic activity.

Surrey's trans. of two books of the *Aeneid* in blank verse.

North's trans. of Guevara's *Dial of Princes*.

Stationers' Company incorporated.

## 1558

1558–1599     **Elizabethan Period proper.** Growth of nationalism: commerce, colonization efforts, gold-hunting, struggle with Spain; English prestige increasing. Protestant-Catholic controversies. Beginnings of Puritan movement. The stricter humanism giving ground to native traditions, as in versification and dramatic structure. Much interest in literary criticism. Foreign influences important: Italian, French, Spanish. Many translations, esp. from the classics and from Italian. One of greatest periods in English literary history. Flourishing of Sidney, Spenser, Marlowe, Shakespeare; appearance of Bacon, Jonson, Donne, and many important dramatists. Culmination of struggle between those who would "improve" English language by coinages and borrowings from foreign languages (Elyot, Pettie, Nash) and the "purists" (Ascham, Wilson, Puttenham) in a "compromise" attitude reached in last decade of the century.

POETRY.–Continued cultivation of the "new poetry," stressing songs, pastorals, and sonnets. Much experimenting. Native verse traditions, as use of accent, and contemporary forms borrowed from the Continent, as rimed stanzas, triumph over effort to apply classical forms, as the hexameter, to English verse. Influence of French *Pléiade* writers visible in critical attitudes, metrical forms, phraseology, sentiment, themes. Later in period (*ca.*1585–1595) the development of verse, esp. blank verse, fostered by its use in drama. Poetical "miscellanies" popular. Verse-chronicles, epics, and epigrams also written. Satire of both medieval type (framework, allegory, against classes) and classical type (didactic, heroic couplet, against individuals) cultivated.

PROSE.–Used in translations, sermons, fiction, criticism, and controversial pamphlets. Euphuism, though over-decorative, adds color and clarity to English prose style. Further development in Sidney's "Arcadian" prose, in Hooker's discourses, and in Bacon's epigrammatic essays. Bizarre, stylistic effects cultivated by Nash. In general, prose style heavy, involved, and affected by Latinisms. Growing interest in fiction appears in translations and imitations of

Italian *novelle*, Italian and Spanish pastoral romances, and Spanish picaresque or rogue stories.

DRAMA.–Rapid development of modern drama from such early plays as *Ralph Roister Doister, Gorboduc*, and *Cambises* to the highest achievements in both comedy and tragedy under Shakespeare and his contemporaries. Cyclic and morality plays still occasionally performed. Professional theatres built. Great stock companies with able actors develop.

| | |
|---|---|
| 1558–1575 | Period of experiment and preparation. Age of Gascoigne. Translations numerous, classics often translated into English through French versions. Much interest in lyrics. |
| 1558–1603 | Reign of Elizabeth. |
| 1558 | John Knox, *First Blast of the Trumpet against the Monstrous Regiment of Women:* attack on women rulers. |
| 1559 | Elizabethan Prayer-book. |
| | *The Mirror for Magistrates:* collection of medieval "tragedies"; source for many historical dramas. |
| | *Amyot, Plutarch's *Lives* translated into French: basis of North's English version of Plutarch. |
| | *Minturno, *De Poeta:* Ital. critical work. |
| 1559 (?) | George Chapman born. Died 1634. |
| ca.1560 | *Gammer Gurton's Needle* (w): comedy, a university play. |
| 1561 | Hoby's translation of Castiglione's *The Courtier.* |
| | Francis Bacon born. Died 1626. |
| | *Scaliger, *Poetics:* influential Italian critical work. |
| 1562 | Sackville and Norton, *Gorboduc* (a): first English tragedy. |
| | Samuel Daniel born. Died 1618. |
| 1563 | Foxe, *Book of Martyrs:* stories of Protestant martyrs; influential anti-Catholic document (Lat. original, 1559). |
| | Sackville's "Induction" (to portion of *Mirror for Magistrates*). |
| | Michael Drayton born. Died 1631. |
| ca.1563 | Sir Humphrey Gilbert, *Queen Elizabeth's Academy:* scheme for liberalizing education of the gentleman; a "courtesy-book." |
| 1564 | Preston, *Cambises* (a): tragedy in bombastic style. |
| | Christopher Marlowe born. Died 1593. |
| | William Shakespeare born. Died 1616. |
| | *Galileo born. Died 1642. |
| 1565–1567 | Golding's translation of Ovid's *Metamorphoses.* |

| | |
|---|---|
| 1566 | Gascoigne's *Supposes* (a) and *Jocasta* (a). |
| 1566–1567 | Painter, *Palace of Pleasure:* collection of prose tales; reflects popularity of Italian *novelle* (plots borrowed by Elizabethan dramatists). |
| 1567 | Turbervile, *Epitaphs, Epigrams, Songes, and Sonets.* |
| 1570 | Ascham, *Schoolmaster:* humanistic pedagogy and criticism. |
| 1572 | *Massacre of St. Bartholomew.* Founding of Society of Antiquaries. |
| 1573 | John Donne born.   Died 1631. Ben Jonson born.   Died 1637. |

## 1575

| | |
|---|---|
| 1575–1590 | Activity of Shakespeare's predecessors and early contemporaries—Kyd, Lyly, Marlowe, Peele, Greene, Nash.   Court comedies, melodramatic tragedies, chronicle history plays popular.   Interest in literary criticism.   Puritan attack on poetry.   Patriotic poems.   Translations.   Spenser's early work.   Early pastoral and euphuistic romances. |
| 1575 | Gascoigne, *The Posies:* Poems with first English treatise on versification appended. Mystery plays still being acted at Chester. |
| 1576–1580 | Spenser's early poetry (w). |
| 1576 | *Paradise of Dainty Devices:* popular poetical miscellany. The Theatre (first London playhouse) built. Gascoigne, *The Steel Glass:* blank verse satire combining native (medieval) and classical types. George Pettie, *A Pettie Palace of Pettie his Pleasure.* |
| 1578 | Holinshed, *Chronicles:* important source for patriotic chronicle plays on London stage. Drake circumnavigates globe. *A Gorgeous Gallery of Gallant Inventions:* poetical miscellany. |
| 1579 | Lyly, *Euphues, the Anatomy of Wit:* promoted popularity of "euphuistic" style in English. Spenser, *The Shepheardes Calender* (pub. anonymously): conventional pastoral "eclogues." Gosson, *School of Abuse:* attack on poetry and the stage. North, trans. of Plutarch's *Lives:* source book for English dramatists. John Fletcher born.   Died 1625. |

| | |
|---|---|
| 1580–1600 | Elizabethan "novels" popular: Lyly, Greene, Lodge, Sidney, Nash, Deloney. Pastoral poetry popular. |
| 1580 | *Montaigne, *Essays:* beginning of modern "personal" essay. |
| *ca.*1580 | Lyly, *Alexander and Campaspe* (a): court comedy. |
| 1581 | *Tasso, *Jerusalem Delivered:* Ital. romantic epic. |
| *ca.*1581 | Peele, *Arraignment of Paris* (a): masque. |
| | Sidney, *Defence of Poesie* (w) (pub. 1595): first great critical essay in English. |
| 1582–1600 | Hakluyt publishes various collections of "voyages"— Renaissance and medieval, notably *Principal Navigations* (1st ed. 1589). |
| 1582 | Camden, *Britannia* (Lat.): topographical, antiquarian. |
| | Stanyhurst, trans. of Virgil's *Æneid* (i-iv) in quantitative verse. |
| 1583 | P. Stubbs, *Anatomie of Abuses.* |
| 1584 | Scot, *Discovery of Witchcraft:* exposé of witchcraft and magic. |
| | *Handful of Pleasant Delights:* ballad miscellany. |
| 1585 | Raleigh fails in effort to colonize Virginia. |
| | *Guarini, *Pastor Fido* (a): Ital. pastoral drama. |
| 1586 | Kyd, *The Spanish Tragedy* (a): important revenge tragedy. |
| | Warner, *Albion's England.* |
| | Death of Sidney. |
| 1586 (?) | Shakespeare comes to London. |
| 1587 | Marlowe, *Tamburlaine* (a): tragedy of romantic personality ("super-hero"); strong use of dramatic blank verse. |
| | Execution of Mary Queen of Scots. |
| 1588–1589 | "Martin Marprelate" papers: first sustained prose satire in English; Puritan attacks on episcopacy. |
| 1588 | Defeat of Spanish Armada. |
| *ca.*1588 | Marlowe, *Doctor Faustus* (a). |
| 1589 | Greene, *Menaphon:* pastoral romance. |
| | Puttenham (?), *The Arte of English Poesie.* |

## 1590

| | |
|---|---|
| 1590–1600 | Greatly increased literary activity, richest decade of Elizabethan literature; great activity in poetry, flourishing of lyrics, pastorals, sonnets, dramatic poetry, serious verse (historical, didactic, patriotic), classical verse-satire; rapid |

development of drama of all types; realistic tendencies beginning to challenge romantic; classical spirit rising. Prose fiction continues: pastoral romance, picaresque novel.

| | |
|---|---|
| 1590 | Lodge, *Rosalynde:* pastoral romance; source for Shakespeare. |
| | Sidney, *Arcadia* (*w. ca.*1581): pastoral romance; distinctive prose. |
| | Spenser, *Faerie Queene*, Books I–III: allegorical romantic epic. |
| *ca.*1590 | Greene, *James IV* (*a*)*:* influential romantic comedy. |
| | Shakespeare begins career as playwright. |
| 1591–1596 | Flourishing period of sonnet cycles: Sidney, Daniel, Drayton, Lodge, Spenser, and others. |
| 1591 | Spenser, *Complaints:* includes *Mother Hubberds Tale* (satirical beast fable in heroic couplets), and other poems. |
| | Harrington, trans. of Ariosto's *Orlando Furioso.* |
| | Sidney, *Astrophel and Stella:* sonnet sequence. |
| | Robert Herrick born.   Died 1674. |
| 1593 | Shakespeare, *Venus and Adonis:* mythological love poem. |
| | *Phoenix Nest:* poetical miscellany. |
| | Death of Marlowe. |
| | Izaak Walton born.   Died 1683. |
| | George Herbert born.   Died 1633. |
| 1594 | Hooker, *Ecclesiastical Polity*, Books I–IV: eloquent statement of conservative Anglican theology and political attitudes. |
| | Shakespeare, *Rape of Lucrece.* |
| | Nash, *The Unfortunate Traveler:* picaresque romance. |
| 1595 | Shakespeare, *Richard III* (*a*). |
| | Spenser, *Amoretti:* sonnet-sequence; *Epithalamion.* |
| | Sidney, *Defence of Poesie* (*w. ca.*1581). |
| | Daniel, *Civil Wars:* historical poetry. |
| | Lodge, *A Fig for Momus:* satire. |
| | Donne's poetry of revolt and classical satires circulating in manuscript. |
| 1596 | Raleigh, *Discovery of Guiana* (*w*) (pub. 1606). |
| | Shakespeare, *Romeo and Juliet* (*a*), *Midsummer Night's Dream* (*a*). |
| | Spenser, *Faerie Queene*, Books IV–VI. |
| 1597–1599 | Shakespeare's Falstaff plays (*a*): *Henry IV*, 1, 2; *Henry V*; *Merry Wives of Windsor.* |

| | |
|---|---|
| 1597 | Shakespeare, *Merchant of Venice* (a). |
| | Drayton, *Heroical Epistles.* |
| | Bacon, *Essays* (1st ed.): beginning of English essay, aphoristic. |
| | Hall, *Virgidemiarum:* "classical" verse satire. |
| | King James (of Scotland), *Demonology:* answers Scot (see p. 488), defends reality of witchcraft. |
| 1598 | Shakespeare, *Julius Caesar* (a). |
| | Meres, *Palladis Tamia,* "Wit's Treasury": praises Shakespeare as playwright; important contemporary evidence of Shakespeare's reputation. |
| | Ben Jonson begins career as playwright—*Everyman in His Humour* (a): "comedy of humours." |
| | Marston, *The Scourge of Villainy:* malicious satire. |
| | Chapman, translation of *Iliad* (seven books in "fourteeners"). |
| | Globe theatre built: used by Shakespeare's company. |
| *ca.*1598 | Deloney, *The Gentle Craft:* bourgeois fiction. |
| 1599 | Shakespeare's "joyous comedies": *Much Ado about Nothing; As You Like It; Twelfth Night.* |
| | *The Passionate Pilgrim:* miscellany containing some of Shakespeare's poems. |
| | Death of Spenser. |

## 1600

| ENGLISH | AMERICAN |
|---|---|
| **1600–1625 Late Elizabethan and Jacobean Period.** Literary careers of following writers *closed* by 1600: Ascham, Udall, Gascoigne, Sackville, Sidney, Spenser, Kyd, Greene, Marlowe, Lyly, Nash, Peele, Hooker. *Active* in 1600: Breton, Campion, Daniel, Dekker, Drayton, Florio, Jonson, Lodge, Raleigh, Sylvester, Shakespeare, Bacon, Donne, Joseph Hall, Marston, Middleton, T. Heywood. Appeared *after* 1600: Beaumont, John Fletcher, W. Browne, Wither, Quarles, Overbury, Massinger, Webster, Ford, Shir- | **1600–1625 Period of first successful colonizing of America.** Royalists in South, Puritans in New England. Efforts of colonists centered in conquering new territory and establishing social order and stable governments. Writing is imitative of English and done partly by temporary residents of America. Consists chiefly of travel and personal records, diaries, historical and descriptive accounts, sermons, and a few examples of crude verse. Purpose of writing frequently is stimulation of interest in further colonization. Some |

ENGLISH

ley. The quarter-century marked by widening of breach between Puritans and Cavaliers, growth of classicism, realism, cynicism, formality and restraint, with reaction from earlier Elizabethan extravagance and imaginative enthusiasm, and tendency toward sober intellectuality and controlled emotion. Witchcraft still generally credited.

POETRY.–Affected by revolt of Donne (ca.1595) against conventionalized love-poetry and by his metaphysical tendencies; by Jonson's classicism, esp. in sense of form, in restraint, use of satire, imitation of classical writers; and by a school of admirers and imitators of Spenser, who cultivated, weakly, Spenserian versification, imagery, diction, allegory, and heralded Milton in epic use of Biblical material. Formal satire, epigram, "classical" lyrics (as odes), and devotional verse tend to replace sonnets and pastorals as favorite forms.

PROSE.–Style becoming clarified through cultivation of English diction and through partial emancipation from complex Latinized sentence-structure. King James translation of Bible exhibits simplicity without loss of imaginative quality. Prose forms practised: essay, criticism, "characters," sermons, prose epigrams, travel literature, philosophical and religious treatises, popular moral tales, popular versions of medieval romances.

AMERICAN

reflection of the spirit of the new country is present, however.

491

DRAMA.–Reaches highest level ever attained by English playwrights. Dominant forms: tragedies, realistic comedies, romantic "tragi-comedies." Chief figures: Shakespeare, Jonson, Beaumont and Fletcher, Chapman, Middleton, Massinger, Webster. Spectacular elements encouraged by the Court. Masques flourish.

1600–1625 Artists flourishing: Inigo Jones (Eng. architect); *Rubens, Van Dyck (Flemish painters).

1600 *England's Helicon:* great poetical miscellany.

*Peri, *Euridice* (Ital.): beginning of Italian opera.

1601 Failure of Essex rebellion.

1602–1603 Shakespeare, the "bitter comedies": *Troilus and Cressida, All's Well That Ends Well, Measure for Measure* (a).

1602 Shakespeare, *Hamlet* (a).

Campion, *Observations in the Art of English Poesie;* attacks use of rime.

Founding of the Bodleian Library (Oxford).

*ca.*1602 Daniel, *Defence of Ryme.*

1603–1649 The Stuarts.

1603–1625 Reign of James I—union of English and Scottish crowns.

1603 T. Heywood, *A Woman Killed with Kindness* (a): domestic tragedy.

Jonson, *Sejanus* (a): classical tragedy.

492

| ENGLISH | AMERICAN |
|---|---|
| Florio, translation of Montaigne. | |
| 1604 Shakespeare, *Othello* (*a*). | 1604 *French found Port Royal in Nova Scotia. |
| 1605 Bacon, *Advancement of Learning:* sweeping outline of knowledge. | |
| Gunpowder Plot. | |
| *Cervantes, *Don Quixote*, Part I: chivalry burlesqued. | |
| Sir Thomas Browne born. Died 1682. | |
| 1606 Shakespeare, *Macbeth* (*a*), *King Lear:* tragedies of character. | 1606 Plymouth and London companies formed for colonization projects. |
| Jonson, *Volpone* (*a*): comedy. | |
| Sir William Davenant born. Died 1668. | Roger Williams born. Died 1683. |
| *Corneille born. Died 1684. | |
| 1607 Bacon made Solicitor-General. | 1607 Settlement at Jamestown, Va. |
| Shakespeare, *Antony and Cleopatra* (*a*). | |
| Beaumont and Fletcher, *Knight of the Burning Pestle* (*a*): burlesques heroic drama. | |
| 1608 John Milton born. Died 1674. | 1608 *Champlain founds Quebec. |
| Joseph Hall, *Characters of Virtues and Vices*. | Capt. John Smith,[1] *True Relation:* early experiences in Virginia. |
| 1609 Shakespeare, *Sonnets* (*w*. earlier): addressed chiefly to a male friend. | 1609 Champlain discovers Lake Champlain. |
| Beaumont and Fletcher, *Philaster* (*a*): typical tragi-comedy. | Henry Hudson explores Hudson River. |
| Dekker, *Gull's Hornbook:* prose satire on London gallants. | |

[1]A few writers, such as Smith, Strachey, and Sandys—not Americans, strictly speaking—are listed in the "American" column because of their significance in relation to early American literary activity.

*Life of Sir Thomas Bodley* (*w*) (pub. 1647): "oldest prose autobiography in English."

*Galileo active with telescope.

## 1610

1610 Jonson, *Alchemist* (*a*): realistic comedy.

1610 Lord Delaware becomes governor of Virginia.

Strachey, *True Repertory*.

1610-1611 Shakespeare, the "serene romances" or tragi-comedies: *Cymbeline, Winter's Tale, Tempest* (*a*).

1611 King James or "authorized" translation of the Bible: one of the greatest of literary achievements.

*ca.*1611 Shakespeare returns to Stratford.

1612 Bacon, *Essays* (2nd ed.).

1612 Capt. John Smith, *A Map of Virginia*.

Donne, First and Second *Anniversaries*.

Samuel Butler born. Died 1680.

1613 *Purchas His Pilgrimage:* travel literature.

Wither, *Abuses Stript and Whipt*.

1614 Overbury, *Characters*.

Raleigh, *History of the World*.

Webster, *Duchess of Malfi* (*a*): tragedy.

*Lope de Vega *fl.*

1615 Harrington, *Epigrams*.

1616 Death of Shakespeare and of *Cervantes.

1616 Capt. John Smith, *A Description of New England*.

| ENGLISH | AMERICAN |
|---|---|
| Chapman, *Odyssey* translated in heroic couplets. | |
| 1618–1648 *The Thirty Years' War, Protestants against Catholics. | |
| 1618 Raleigh executed. | |
| Bacon made Lord Chancellor. | |
| Harvey discovers circulation of the blood. | |
| Abraham Cowley born. Died 1667. | |
| 1619 Drayton, *Collected Poems:* reflects types and fashions in poetry, 1590–1619. | 1619 First American legislative assembly, at Jamestown. |
| | Negro slavery introduced into Virginia. |

## 1620

| | |
|---|---|
| 1620 Bacon, *Novum Organum* (Lat.): expounds inductive method. | 1620 Pilgrims land at Plymouth. |
| | *Mayflower Compact* (w). |
| 1621 Burton, *Anatomy of Melancholy:* influential prose treatise, wide in range of subject; style marked by "conceits." | |
| 1622 *Molière (French dramatist) born. Died 1673. | 1622 George Sandys completes poetical translation of Ovid's *Metamorphoses* (English author writing in America). |
| Donne, *Sermon on Judges xx. 15* (other sermons published in 1623, 1624, 1625, 1626, 1627, and later). | "Mourt's Relation" by Bradford and others: journal. |
| 1623 First Folio edition of Shakespeare's *Plays:* edited by Heming and Condell, fellow-actors in Shakespeare's company. | |
| | 1624 Capt. John Smith, *General History of Virginia.* |
| | Edward Winslow, *Good News out of New England.* |

# 1625

**1625–1660 Puritan and Cavalier Period. Age of Milton.** Great Puritan emigration to escape tyranny of Charles I and Archbishop Laud. Puritan rebellion results in establishment of the Commonwealth. Freshness of Elizabethan romanticism gives way in literature to melancholy and religious intensity. Effects of new scientific thought beginning to be felt. General unrest reflected in conflicting ideals and varying forms in literature. Witchcraft still believed in by most Englishmen: churchmen, philosophers, physicians. Painters *Velasquez (Span.) and *Rembrandt (Dutch) flourishing.

POETRY.–Influence of Donne and Jonson on metaphysical poets and Cavalier lyrists. Neoclassicism advancing. Early poems of Milton. Much weak religious verse.

PROSE.–Controversial, philosophical, and scientific writing heralds rise of modern prose style. Writers of distinctive prose: Milton, Sir Thomas Browne, Izaak Walton, Jeremy Taylor, Thomas Fuller, Thomas Hobbes. Walton's serious efforts advance the art and status of prose biography. Translations of French heroic romances influence fiction.

DRAMA.–Decadence hastened by corrupt court and by passing of great playwrights. Elaborate masques performed at courtly

**1625–1660 Colonization continuing.** Great period of migration from England to Bermuda, East Indies, and America. Rise of Puritan oligarchy in Massachusetts. Toleration questions vital: Merrymount episode, Roger Williams, Baptists, Mrs. Anne Hutchinson, the Friends (Quakers). Writing mainly utilitarian, controversial, historical. Anne Bradstreet's verse the nearest approach to pure literature. Crude verse epitaphs and "psalms" written. English models followed. Much superstition, as belief in witchcraft and demonic character of Indians.

496

| ENGLISH | AMERICAN |
|---|---|

entertainments (Jonson the chief writer). Shirley and Ford the leading active playwrights for London stage. Theatres closed in 1642, but dramatic performances continue more or less openly.

1625–1649 Reign of Charles I.

1625 Bacon, *Essays*, final edition.

1626 Death of Bacon.

1627 Bacon, *New Atlantis* (Lat.): fragmentary "utopia."

Drayton, *Ballad of Agincourt.*

1628 John Bunyan born. Died 1688.

1629 Ford, *The Broken Heart* (a): decadent tragedy.

Milton, *Ode on the Nativity* (w). Unsuccessful appearance of French actresses on English stage.

1625 Morrell, *Nova Anglia.*

1626 Minuit founds New Amsterdam.

1627 Thomas Morton sets up Maypole at Merrymount: reflects opposition to Puritans.

## 1630

1630–1649 Winthrop, *History of New England* (w).

1630–1647 Bradford, *History of the Plymouth Plantation* (w).

1630 Milton, *On Shakespeare* (w): sonnet.

*Malherbe (1555–1628), *Works:* Renaissance French forerunner of classicism.

1631 Deaths of Drayton and Donne.

John Dryden born. Died 1700.

1632 Second Folio edition of Shakespeare.

1633 Herbert, *The Temple:* metaphysical lyrics.

1630 Massachusetts Bay colony established at Salem by non-Separatist dissenters.

1632 Thomas Hooker, *The Soul's Preparation.*

| ENGLISH | AMERICAN |
|---|---|
| Donne, *Poems* (first collected edition). | |
| Phineas Fletcher, *The Purple Island:* allegory of human body. | |
| 1633(?) Milton's *L'Allegro* and *Il Penseroso* written. | |
| Samuel Pepys born. Died 1703. | |
| 1634 Milton, *Comus* (a): masque. | 1634 Maryland settled by English. |
| Davenant, *The Temple of Love:* French Platonic love. | Connecticut Valley settled. |
| 1635 Quarles, *Emblems.* | 1635 Roger Williams decides Massachusetts belongs to Indians and is banished. |
| *French Academy incorporated. | |
| 1636 *Corneille, *The Cid:* tragicomedy. | 1636 Roger Williams founds Providence; all sects tolerated. |
| | Harvard College founded. |
| 1637 Death of Jonson. | 1637 Pequot War. |
| *Descartes, *Discours sur la Méthode:* rationalistic philosophy. | Thomas Morton, *New English Canaan:* anti-Puritan. |
| 1638 Milton, *Lycidas:* pastoral elegy. | |
| 1639 *Racine (French dramatist) born. Died 1699. | 1639 Baptist Church in America founded by Williams. |
| | First printing press in America set up at Cambridge. |
| | Increase Mather born. Died 1723. |

## 1640

| | |
|---|---|
| 1640 Jonson, *Timber, or Discoveries Made upon Men and Matter.* | 1640 *Bay Psalm Book:* first book printed in America. |
| Izaak Walton, *Life of Donne:* first "artistic" and "professional" biography. | |

ENGLISH

AMERICAN

1641 Shepard, *The Sincere Convert.*

1642 Fuller, *Holy State.*

Denham, *Cooper's Hill:* heroic couplets.

Sir Thomas Browne, *Religio Medici:* philosophical reflections; prose notable.

Sir Isaac Newton born. Died 1727.

Theatres closed. Civil War.

1643–1715 *Louis XIV King of France.

1643–1647 Height of religious toleration controversy between John Cotton and Roger Williams.

1644 Milton, *Areopagitica:* noble plea for freedom of press.

Milton, *Tractate on Education* and divorce pamphlets.

1644 Roger Williams, *Bloody Tenent of Persecution:* advocates toleration.

Roger Williams visits Milton; teaches him Dutch.

1645 Howell, *Familiar Letters.*

Waller, *Poems:* development of "closed" heroic couplet.

Founding of Philosophical Society.

1646 Vaughan, *Poems:* mystical verse.

1647 Nathaniel Ward, *Simple Cobbler of Aggawam:* crude picturesque writing; satirizes women; opposes toleration.

1648 Herrick, *Hesperides* (including "Noble Numbers"): graceful lyrics and pious verse.

1649 Epidemic of "witch-finding."

Execution of Charles I.

Lovelace, *Lucasta:* Cavalier verse.

499

# 1650

| ENGLISH | AMERICAN |
|---|---|
| | 1650–1728 Flourishing of the "Mather Dynasty." |
| 1650 Davenant, *Gondibert:* fragmentary epic, French influence. | 1650 Anne Bradstreet, *The Tenth Muse, Lately Sprung up in America:* simple religious and nature poems by America's earliest woman poet. |
| Taylor, *Holy Living:* notable prose. | |
| ca.1650 Many French romances and novels translated into English. | Cavaliers migrating to Virginia. |
| 1651 Milton, *Defence of the English People* (Lat.): defends execution of Charles I. | 1651 *Cambridge Platform* passed by General Court; reflects prevailing intolerance in Massachusetts under Endicott and Norton. |
| Hobbes, *Leviathan:* defense of monarchy. | |
| 1652 "Quaker" Movement culminating. | 1652 "Half-Way Covenant": lowers requirements for church membership in Massachusetts. |
| Milton becomes blind. | |
| 1653 Walton, *The Compleat Angler.* | |
| 1654 Boyle, *Parthenissa:* imitates French romance. | 1654 Capt. Edward Johnson, *Wonder-Working Providence.* |
| 1656 Cowley, *Poems, Davideis, Pindaric Odes.* | 1656 Hammond, *Leah and Rachel,* or *the Two Fruitful Sisters, Virginia and Maryland.* |
| Davenant, *Siege of Rhodes* (a): dramatic spectacle related to masque, opera, heroic comedy. | Quakers arrive in Massachusetts (four executed by 1661). |
| 1658 Dryden, *Stanzas on the Death of Cromwell.* | |
| 1659 *Molière, *Les Précieuses ridicules:* great comedy of manners. | 1659 John Eliot, *The Christian Commonwealth.* |

## 1660–1798 Neo-Classicism[1]

| | |
|---|---|
| **1660–1700 Restoration Period.** Reaction against Puritanism. Lax morals in fashionable society. Renaissance individualism and | **1660–1700 Struggle between Puritan oligarchy and liberal elements in New England.** Persecution of Baptists, Quakers, |

---

[1]See NEO-CLASSICISM, p. 273.

ENGLISH

enthusiasm replaced by conservatism, moderation, conformity. Increased interest in scientific investigation and philosophical thought. Reassertion politically of doctrine of divine right. Rise of Whigs (liberals) and Tories (conservatives). Neoclassicism becoming dominant in literature. French influences strong. Exaltation of form, polish, critical spirit. Milton's and Bunyan's masterpieces appear, seemingly out of harmony with prevailing spirit. Rationalistic thought becoming important.

POETRY.–Dominated by neoclassic traits. The ode a favorite form. Preëminence of heroic couplet. Poetry shows intellectual vigor, wit, polish; employed largely for didactic or satirical purposes (political, personal, critical, religious). Emotion and "high imagination" lacking. Milton's epic poetry produced early in period represents a late flowering of Renaissance genius and Puritan mood.

PROSE.–A favored form because of factual, realistic tendencies of the times. Criticism, scientific and philosophical treatises, essays, journals, biographies, histories, allegory. Dryden's style influential in creating "modern" prose: brief, well-ordered sentences; precision, clearness, lack of ostentatious decoration.

DRAMA. –Theatres re-opened. Patent theatres established. Influence of Jonson and of Beaumont and Fletcher important; French influence dominant: cur-

AMERICAN

witches. Writing mostly occasional, personal, didactic, controversial. Pure literature lacking.

tain, scenery, music, women as actors. Flourishing of heroic drama in couplets (Dryden, *Indian Emperor*); prose comedy of manners (Etherege, *The Man of Mode*); "Elizabethan" tragedies (Otway, *Venice Preserved*); Shakespeare rewritten and "corrected." Ideals of "honor," realism, witty dialogue (in comedy of manners), and (later) tendency to burlesque.

1660–1714 Stuarts restored (Charles II to Anne).

1660–1685 Reign of Charles II.

1660–1688 Many books on both sides of witchcraft controversy.

1660–1669 Pepys's *Diary* (w) (pub. 1825): intimate self-revelation; informative Restoration document.

1660 Dryden, *Astraea Redux:* welcomes Charles II.

*ca.*1660 Daniel Defoe born. Died 1731.

1662 Fuller, *Worthies of England:* patriotic biography; easy style.

The Royal Society founded as reorganization of the Philosophical Society.

1663 Butler, *Hudibras,* Part I: rollicking satire on Puritan groups in mock epic style; tetrameter couplets.

Drury Lane Theatre (first called Theatre Royal) built.

Dryden proposes an "academy" to "regulate" English language.

1660–1700 Verse elegies popular.

1662 Wigglesworth, *Day of Doom:* "rimed sermon" defending Calvinistic doctrines.

1663 Eliot translates Bible into Indian language.

Cotton Mather born. Died 1728.

ENGLISH

AMERICAN

1664 Dryden and Howard, *The Indian Queen* (a): heroic play.

1665 Dryden, *The Indian Emperor:* heroic play.

Head, *The English Rogue:* realistic tale of roguery.

1665 Baptist Church established in Boston.

1666 Bunyan, *Grace Abounding:* autobiography.

*Molière, *Le Misanthrope:* satiric play.

1666 George Alsop, *A Character of the Province of Maryland:* descriptive medley of verse and prose.

1667 Jonathan Swift born. Died 1745.

Sprat, *History of the Royal Society.*

Milton, *Paradise Lost.*

*Molière, *Tartuffe.*

*Racine, *Andromaque:* classical tragedy.

1668 Sprat, *Life of Cowley:* starts tradition of "discreet" biography.

*La Fontaine, *Fables.*

Dryden, *Essay of Dramatic Poesy:* critical prose—dialogue form; unities and rime in tragedies defended.

## 1670

1670 Dryden, *Conquest of Granada* (a).

*Pascal, *Thoughts.*

Dryden made Poet Laureate.

1670 Denton, *Brief Description of New York.*

Mason, *Pequot War* (w) (pub. 1736).

1671 Milton, *Paradise Regained* (epic) and *Samson Agonistes* (tragedy).

1671 Eliot, *Progress of the Gospel Among the Indians in New England.*

Villiers (Buckingham) and others, *The Rehearsal* (a): burlesque satire on Dryden and heroic plays.

1672 Joseph Addison born. Died 1719.

Sir Richard Steele born. Died 1729.

1673 *Death of Molière.

1674 Wycherley, *The Plain-Dealer* (a): comedy of manners.

*Boileau, *L'Art Poétique:* neoclassical criticism.

Death of Milton.

1676 Etherege, *The Man of Mode:* comedy of manners; introduces the "fop."

1678 Bunyan, *Pilgrim's Progress,* Part I: "most successful prose allegory in literature."

Dryden, *All for Love:* Antony and Cleopatra story in blank-verse tragedy.

Popish Plot.

1679 Cessation of censorship of press. Rise of Whig and Tory parties.

1672 Eliot, *The Logick Primer:* "for the use of praying Indians."

1673 Increase Mather, *Woe to Drunkards.*

1674–1729 Samuel Sewall, *Diary* (w): an American counterpart of Pepys.

1677 Urian Oakes, *Elegy on Thomas Shepard:* perhaps the first verse to be printed in America (excepting *Bay Psalm Book*).

Peter Folger, *Looking-Glass for the Times:* homely verse advocating religious toleration.

504

# 1680

ENGLISH

AMERICAN

1680–1700 The Mathers at height of power in New England.

1680 *The Burwell Papers* (w).

1681 Dryden, *Absalom and Achitophel:* verse satire, personal, political.

1682 Otway, *Venice Preserved:* "best romantic tragedy of the Restoration."

Dryden, *MacFlecknoe:* literary satire.

1682 Penn settles Pennsylvania.

La Salle explores Mississippi.

Mary Rowlandson, *Narrative of the Captivity* (w): life among the Indians.

1683 Increase Mather, *Discourse Concerning Comets.*

1684 Increase Mather, *Illustrious Providences.*

1685–1688 Reign of James II.

1685–1688 Catholic-Protestant conflict.

1685 Cotton Mather, *Memorable Providences.*

1687 Sir Isaac Newton, *Principia* (Lat.): announces law of gravitation.

Dryden, *The Hind and the Panther:* pro-Catholic satire in form of verse fable.

1687 Church of England worship established in Boston.

1688 The "Bloodless Revolution": Parliament regains power.

Death of Bunyan.

Alexander Pope born. Died 1744.

Mrs. Behn, *Oroonoko:* precursor of modern novel.

*La Bruyère, *Characters:* influence on periodical essay.

1689–1702 Reign of William and Mary.

1689 The Toleration Act: establishing freedom of worship.

Samuel Richardson born. Died 1761.

## 1690

1690–1699 "Ancient and Modern" controversy ("Battle of the Books").

1690 Locke, *Essay Concerning the Human Understanding:* influential philosophical treatise.

1691 Dunton, *Athenian Gazette:* new magazine designed to entertain as well as instruct.

1691 (or earlier) *New England Primer.*

1692 Sir William Temple, *Essays.*

1692 Salem Witchcraft executions.

Increased power of Parliament.

1692–1702 Reaction from Salem Witchcraft breaks power of conservative clergy. Harvard somewhat liberalized.

1693 William and Mary College founded.

Cotton Mather, *Wonders of the Invisible World:* defends witchcraft executions.

1694 Wotton, *Reflections upon Ancient and Modern Learning:* defends "moderns."

*Voltaire (French philosopher and man of letters) born. Died 1778.

1696 Toland, *Christianity not Mysterious:* deistic.

ENGLISH

1697 Dryden, *Alexander's Feast:* ode on power of music.

1698 Congreve, *Love for Love.*

Jeremy Collier, *Short View of the Immorality and Profaneness of the English Stage.*

AMERICAN

1699 Jonathan Dickinson, *God's Protecting Providence:* description of shipwreck off Florida coast.

## 1700

**1700–1750  Triumph of Neo-Classicism. Age of Pope.** The "Augustans." English prestige in Europe increasing. Power of Parliament strengthened under first German kings (House of Hanover). Bitter struggle between Whigs and Tories. Little interest in real democracy. Critical spirit strong. "Classical" ideals of taste, polish, "common sense," reason (drawn from ancients, from France, and from Age of Dryden, and modified by current philosophical and scientific activities) more important than emotion and imagination. Deism advancing. Germs of later romanticism present but subordinated to common view that external nature and earlier life and literature were rough and uncouth in comparison with courtly or city life. Literature, still under "patronage" system, is realistic, satirical, "moral," correct, governed by definite rules and formulas, affected strongly by politics and intrigue.

POETRY.–Heroic couplet chief form. Diction and imagery conventionalized. Metrical regularity. Epigrammatic qual-

**1700–1750  Decline of Calvinistic Puritanism. Age of Jonathan Edwards.** Early career of Franklin. Religious revivals stressing emotional experiences. Doctrinal controversies rife. Conservative attitude prevalent. Increasing laxity in morals. Decline in power of clergy, esp. after 1720. Scientific spirit advancing. Rise of newspapers. Almanacs flourish. Literature imitative in character and not great in amount.

POETRY.–No important verse produced. Neo-classic poets of England the models. Heroic couplet used.

507

ity strong. Cut-and-dried epithets. Didactic spirit. The
verse essay (Pope). Much verse
satire, personal, social, political
(Pope). The mock epic and
society verse. Some signs of
later romantic tendencies in
primitivistic theory (Shaftesbury), response to external nature (Lady Winchilsea, Dyer),
sentimental melancholy (Parnell, Young), and variety of
verse form such as blank verse
and Spenserian stanza (Thomson). Some interest in popular
ballads (Ramsay).

PROSE.–A dominant form in
literature, responding to current
ideals of clearness, correctness,
intellectual appeal. Prose satires (Swift). Flourishing of
periodical essay (Addison,
Steele). Beginnings of modern
novel. Chief tendencies: realism (Defoe), sentimentalism
(Richardson), satire (Fielding).
Picaresque tales influenced by
Cervantes (Span.) and Le Sage
(French). Prose style shows
increasing flexibility, delicacy,
and "elegance."

DRAMA.–Sentimental comedy,
consciously but superficially
moral, replaces corrupt comedy
of manners. Heroic play not
cultivated. "Genteel comedy."
Adaptations of Racine and
Corneille. Domestic drama
(Lillo) and classical tragedies
(Addison's *Cato*). Revival of
interest in Shakespeare. Development of Shakespearean
criticism. Burlesques and pantomimes gain some popularity.
French influence.

PROSE.–Style follows English
models, more successfully than
does current poetry. Chief
forms: sermons, controversial
and didactic essays, travel accounts, newspaper stories.

DRAMA.–No native drama.

ENGLISH

AMERICAN

1700–1720 Decline of influence of the Mathers in New England church.

1700 Death of Dryden.

1700 Samuel Sewall, *The Selling of Joseph:* early anti-slavery tract.

1701 Steele, *The Christian Hero:* handbook of morals; *The Funeral:* sentimental comedy.

1701 Cotton Mather, *Death Made Easy and Happy.*

Yale University founded as conservative center.

1702 *The Daily Courant:* first daily newspaper.

Defoe, *The Shortest Way with the Dissenters:* prose satire.

1702 Cotton Mather, *Magnalia Christi Americani:* encyclopedic history of Puritan movement in New England.

Increase Mather, *Ichabod:* "the glory of the Lord departing from New England."

1702–1714 Reign of Anne.

1703 John Wesley (founder of Methodist Church) born. Died 1791.

Rowe, *The Fair Penitent:* domestic tragedy.

1703 Jonathan Edwards born. Died 1758.

1704–1711 Defoe, *Weekly Review:* periodical with tendencies toward style of the essay.

1704 Swift, *Battle of the Books (w. ca.*1697): literary satire; *Tale of a Tub:* satiric religious allegory.

Marlborough's victory at Blenheim (War of Spanish Succession).

1704 First American newspaper established, *Boston News Letter.*

Sarah K. Knight, *Journal of a Journey (w):* lively description.

1705 Steele, *The Tender Husband.*

1705 Anon., *Questions and Proposals:* scheme for strengthening power of clergy.

1706 Benjamin Franklin born. Died 1790.

1707 Henry Fielding born. Died 1754.

<table>
<tr><td>ENGLISH</td><td>AMERICAN</td></tr>
</table>

ENGLISH        AMERICAN

1708 Ebenezer Cook, *Sot-Weed Factor:* humor.

Cotton Mather, *Consequences of the Prevailing Abuse of Rum.*

1709–1711 Steele (and Addison), *The Tatler:* beginning of the periodical essay.

1709 Pope, *Pastorals.*

Rowe's edition of Shakespeare: Shakespeare "edited" for the first time.

Samuel Johnson born. Died 1784.

## 1710

1710–1713 Swift, *Journal to Stella* (w).

1710 Berkeley, *Principles of Human Knowledge.*

First complete performance of Italian opera in England (*Almahide*).

Handel comes to England.

1711 Pope, *Essay on Criticism:* "classical" critical verse essay.

Addison, Steele, etc. *The Spectator:* perfection of periodical essay.

Shaftesbury, *Characteristics of Men:* deistic and sentimental (primitivistic) philosophy; influenced "romanticism" of next generation.

1712, 1714 Pope, *Rape of the Lock:* mock heroic poem, social satire.

1712 *Rousseau born. Died 1778.

1710 Cotton Mather, *Essays to Do Good.*

John Wise, *The Churches' Quarrel Espoused:* democratic ideas.

| ENGLISH | AMERICAN |
|---|---|
| 1713 Pope, *Windsor Forest.* | 1713 Increase Mather, *A Plain Discourse Showing Who Shall and Who Shall not Enter Heaven.* |
| Addison, *Cato:* neo-classic tragedy. | |
| Lady Winchilsea, *A Nocturnal Reverie:* romantic poetry, external nature. | |
| 1714–1901 House of Hanover (George I to Victoria). | |
| 1714–1727 George I. | |
| 1714 Mandeville, *Fable of the Bees:* cynical attack on idealistic philosophy. | |
| 1715 Pope, trans. *Iliad,* i–iv. | |
| Jacobite Revolt. | |
| *Death of Louis XIV. | |
| 1716 Thomas Gray born. Died 1771. | |
| 1717 Last witchcraft trial in England. | 1717 William Penn, *Religion Professed by the Quakers.* |
| Horace Walpole born. Died 1797. | William Southeby, *An Anti-Slavery Tract.* |
| David Garrick born. Died 1779. | |
| 1719 Watts, *Psalms and Hymns.* | 1719 Establishment of *Boston Gazette* and the *American Weekly Mercury* (Phila). |
| Defoe, *Robinson Crusoe.* | |
| Death of Addison. | |

## 1720

| | |
|---|---|
| | 1720–1750 Flourishing of religious revivals. |
| 1720 "South Sea Bubble." | 1720 Wadsworth, *The Lord's Day Proved to be the Christian Sabbath.* |
| 1721 Parnell, *Night-Piece on Death.* | 1721 James Franklin establishes the *New England Courant.* |

| ENGLISH | AMERICAN |
|---|---|
| 1722 Defoe, *Journal of the Plague Year; Moll Flanders:* "female rogue" tale. | 1722 Benjamin Franklin, *Silence Do-good* papers: "Addisonian" essays. |
| Steele, *The Conscious Lovers* (a): sentimental comedy. | |
| | 1723 Charles Johnson, *General History of the Pirates.* |
| | Death of Increase Mather. |
| | Franklin arrives in Philadelphia. |
| 1724 Swift, *Drapier's Letters.* | |
| Ramsay, *The Evergreen:* collection of old Scotch poetry. | |
| *Kant born. Died 1804. | |
| | 1725–1775 Nathaniel Ames, *Astronomical Diary and Almanac.* |
| 1725 Pope's edition of Shakespeare: judges and "corrects" the dramatist. | 1725 Josiah Dwight, *Essay to Silence the Outcry . . . against Regular Singing.* |
| | *New York Gazette* estab. |
| 1726–1750 Signs of romantic attitudes appearing. | |
| 1726 Thomson, *Winter:* blank verse, romantic poety of nature. | 1726 Anon., *Hoop Petticoats Arraigned and Condemned by the Light of Nature and the Law of God.* |
| Swift, *Gulliver's Travels:* satirical allegory. | |
| Dyer, *Grongar Hill:* descriptive nature poem. | |
| 1727–1760 George II. | |
| | 1727 Byles, *Poem on Death of King George I.* |
| 1728 Pope, *Dunciad:* personal and literary satire. | 1728 First newspaper in Maryland estab. |
| Gay, *Beggar's Opera:* burlesque opera. | Death of Cotton Mather. |

Oliver Goldsmith born. Died 1774.

1729 Swift, *A Modest Proposal:* ironic social satire.

Death of Steele.

Edmund Burke born. Died 1797.

1729 Byrd, *History of the Dividing Line* (*w*): Virginia-North Carolina country described.

## 1730

1730 Methodist Society at Oxford.

Tindal, *Christianity as Old as the Creation:* the "Bible" of deism.

1731 *Gentleman's Magazine* estab.

Lillo, *The London Merchant:* bourgeois tragedy.

Death of Defoe.

William Cowper born. Died 1800.

1730 Seccomb, *Father Abbey's Will:* crude humorous verse.

Printing press set up in Charleston, S. C.

1732–1757 Franklin, *Poor Richard's Almanac.*

1732 Covent Garden Theatre built.

1732 Byles, *Sermon on the Vileness of the Body.*

Franklin opens first public library in America (Philadelphia). First newspapers in South Carolina and Rhode Island established.

First issue of Franklin's *Poor Richard's Almanac.*

George Washington born. Died 1799.

1733 Pope, *Essay on Man:* rationalistic moralizing in verse.

Theobald's edition of Shakespeare: advances scientific method of editing Shakespearean text.

1733 William Byrd, *Journal of Journey to the Land of Eden* (North Carolina) (*w*).

Georgia settled by Oglethorpe. J. P. Zenger begins publication of *New York Weekly Journal.*

513

ENGLISH

AMERICAN

1734 Edwards conducts his first great revival meetings at Northampton.

Important victory for freedom of press won by Zenger.

1735 Pope, *Epistle to Dr. Arbuthnot.*

1735 John and Charles Wesley visit America.

1736 Joseph Butler, *The Analogy of Religion:* appeal to nature for evidence of religious belief.

1736 First newspaper in Virginia.

1737 Shenstone, *Schoolmistress:* light Spenserian burlesque.

Edward Gibbon born. Died 1794.

Theatre Licensing Act: confirms monopoly of patent theatres.

1738 Johnson, *London:* verse satire.

Wesley, *Psalms and Hymns.*

Bolingbroke, *Letters on the Study of History.*

1738 Whitefield's first preaching tour in America.

1739 Beginnings of Methodist preaching in America.

## 1740

1740–1786 *Reign of Frederick the Great of Prussia.

1740 Cibber, *Apology for the Life of Colley Cibber.*

Richardson, *Pamela:* "first modern novel, epistolary, moralistic.

1741 Fielding, *Joseph Andrews:* sentimental novel satirized.

1742 Young, *Night Thoughts:* "graveyard" poetry.

1742–44 Roger North, *Lives of the Norths:* reaction against "panegyric" biography.

1740–1745 The "Great Awakening" (religious revival).

1741 Edwards, *Sinners in the Hands of An Angry God:* sermon.

ENGLISH

1743 Blair, *The Grave.*

1744 Joseph Warton, *The Enthusiast:* romantic "nature" poetry in blank verse.

Dr. Johnson, *Life of Richard Savage:* literary biography.

Death of Pope.

1745 Death of Swift.

Jacobite Rebellion.

1747 Collins, *Odes:* romantic.

1748 Thomson, *Castle of Indolence:* Spenserian stanza.

Richardson, *Clarissa Harlowe:* popular "novel of sensibility."

Smollett, *Roderick Random:* use of sea in fiction; picaresque novel.

Hume, *Inquiry Concerning Human Understanding:* rationalistic philosophy.

*Montesquieu, *L'Esprit des Lois:* political philosophy.

1749 Fielding, *Tom Jones:* satiric novel of manners; plot structure notable.

Johnson, *The Vanity of Human Wishes:* classical satire.

*Goethe born. Died 1832.

*Swedenborg, *Arcana Celesta.*

AMERICAN

1743 Thomas Jefferson born. Died 1826.

1744–1745 Pamphlets against Whitefield issued from Harvard and Yale.

1747 Stith, *First Discovery and Settlement of Virginia.*

1749 University of Pennsylvania founded.

## 1750

**1750–1798 Neo–Classicism and Advance of Romanticism.** Age of Johnson (neo-classic) and Burns (romantic). Expansion of British Empire, esp. in India and Canada. Loss of American colonies. Important interchange of French and English philosophic ideas. German romanticism influential upon English thought and literature. Scandinavian influence on romantic movement. French Revolution. French liberals aid the quickening of interest in political democracy and the growth of the "romantic" attitude in literature and life. Widening range of intellectual interests and human sympathies; rights of the poor; glory of the past; cult of the primitive; appreciation of external nature; idealization of country life; all these romantic qualities tend to shake the still dominant "classical" standards. Decline of satire with rise of sentimentality. Decline of literary patronage. Rise of Methodism. Dominance of prose. Continued scientific activity.

POETRY.–Transition from neoclassic forms toward romanticism shown in revival of interest in Spenser, Shakespeare, and Milton; in use of varied metrical forms; in cultivation of lyrics; in collection of popular ballads and composition of "art ballads"; in increased interest in "romantic" themes: the past, the poor, animals, the primitive, wild nature, etc. But prevail-

**1750–1798 Revolutionary Period. Beginnings of Nationalism.** Age of Franklin and Jefferson. Religious interest still high, with increase of influence of deism, but political problems gradually becoming dominant. Literature affected by political and philosophical thought. Literary groups form at Hartford, New York, and Philadelphia. Scientific interests.

POETRY.–Both neo-classic and romantic streams of English poetry reflected, the influence of Pope dominating, as shown in satire, heroic couplet, mock epics, but blank verse and nature poetry also used. Much patriotic verse.

ing practice in poetry and poetic criticism is to follow neo-classicism of Pope.

PROSE.–Development of the novel continues: sentimental novels (Mackenzie, Sterne), novels of manners (Goldsmith, Burney), Gothic novels (Walpole, Radcliffe, Reeves), novels of purpose (Brooke, Godwin). Novels widely read by middle class. Much travel literature (Capt. Cook) results from increased interest in voyaging in last quarter of the century. Great advance in writing of history and biography based on original research. Oratory cultivated (Burke, Pitt). Long prose treatises. Informal essays continue (Chesterfield, Walpole, Goldsmith). Much letter-writing, formal and informal (Gray, Walpole, Cowper, Chesterfield, Johnson). Prose style somewhat affected by Johnson's weighty, sonorous, periodic manner.

DRAMA.–Becoming less literary. Comedy of manners (Goldsmith, Sheridan) revived without Restoration coarseness and challenges supremacy of the still popular sentimental comedy (Cumberland). Shakespeare popular on stage. Garrick and Kemble, famous actors, flourish. General tendency is toward decline in literary drama and development of spectacular drama—burlesques, pantomimes, melodramas. Increasing number of "minor" theatres.

PROSE.–Political and philosophical writings, oratory, beginnings of the American novel. Style often rhetorical but usually vigorous.

DRAMA.–Beginning. Professional actors appear. Lessened activity during Revolutionary War, when some political plays appear. Increased popularity after the Revolution. Tragedies and comedies, imitative of English, written for native stage.

ENGLISH

1750–1798 Artists flourishing: Gainsborough and Reynolds (painters), Blake (painter and engraver), *Haydn, *Mozart (German musicians).

1750–1752 Johnson, *The Rambler:* periodical essays.

1751 Gray, *Elegy Written in a Country Churchyard:* sentimental melancholy.

*Vol. I of French *Encyclopédie.*

1752 Gregorian Calendar adopted.

1753 British Museum founded.

1754 T. Warton, *Observations on the Fairy Queen of Spenser:* romantic attitude toward early English poetry.

1755–1756 *Mallet's French history of Denmark: helped introduce Norse mythology into romantic poetry.

1755 Johnson, *Dictionary.*

1756 J. Warton, *Essay on Pope.*

Home, *Douglas:* pseudo-romantic tragedy.

1757 Gray, *The Bard* and *The Progress of Poesy:* important romantic poems; primitivistic.

William Blake born. Died 1827.

AMERICAN

1750 Edwards dismissed from Northampton pastorate.

1751 Bartram, *Observations on American Plants.*

Franklin, *Experiments and Observations in Electricity.*

1752 Franklin's discovery that lightning is electrical.

Philip Freneau born. Died 1832.

1754 Franklin's plan for union of colonies.

Edwards, *Freedom of the Will:* philosophic treatise, modified Calvinism.

1755–1772 Woolman, *Journal* (w) Pub. 1774: "Quaker" autobiography, an American classic.

1757 Edwards made President of Princeton.

Witherspoon, *Serious Inquiry into the Nature and Effects of the Stage.*

518

1758–1760 Johnson, The "Idler" papers: periodical essays.

1758 Edwards, *The Great Christian Doctrine of Original Sin Defended.*

Death of Edwards.

1759 Johnson, *Rasselas:* Oriental tale.

*Annual Register* established: annual review of "history, politics, and literature."

Robert Burns born.  Died 1796.

*Voltaire, *Candide:* philosophical novel.

1759 Winthrop, *Lectures on the Comets.*

## 1760

1760–1820 George III.

1760–1767 Sterne, *Tristram Shandy:* stresses character rather than plot.

1760–1761 Goldsmith, *Letters from a Citizen of the World:* essays.

1760 *Rousseau, *Nouvelle Héloïse.*

MacPherson publishes his Ossianic *Fragments of Ancient Poetry Collected in the Highlands of Scotland.*

1761 Churchill, *The Rosciad:* satire on actors.

1761 Otis, Speeches.

1762 Macpherson, *Fingal:* forged "Celtic epic."

Leland, *Longsword:* early historical novel.

*Rousseau, *Contrat Social:* political radicalism; *Emile:* influential novel of education.

1762 Printing press set up in Georgia.

519

**1764–1770** The Chatterton poems (*w*) (pub. 1777): literary forgery.

**1764** Walpole, *Castle of Otranto:* first important Gothic novel.

Literary Club established in London (Doctor Samuel Johnson and others).

*Winckelmann, *History of the Art of Antiquity:* new Hellenism, interest in Greek antiquities.

**1765** Percy, *Reliques of Ancient English Poetry:* famous ballad collection.

Invention of steam engine by Watt.

**1766–1770** Brooke, *The Fool of Quality:* "romantic" educational novel.

**1766** Goldsmith, *The Vicar of Wakefield:* novel of country manners.

*Lessing, *Laokoön:* criticism (art and literature).

Colman and Garrick, *The Clandestine Marriage:* comedy of manners.

**1768** Kelly, *False Delicacy* (*a*): sentimental comedy.

Goldsmith, *Good-Natured Man* (*a*): comedy of manners.

Gray, *Poems.*

Sterne, *Sentimental Journey.*

**1764** Otis, *Rights of British Colonies:* able attack on British colonial policies.

**1765** The Stamp Act.

**1766** Franklin, *Examination before the House of Commons.*

**1767–1768** Dickinson, *Letters of a Farmer in Pennsylvania.*

**1767** Godfrey, *Prince of Parthia* (*a*): tragedy, first American play to be acted.

| ENGLISH | AMERICAN |
|---|---|

Spinning machine invented.

1769–1772 *Letters of Junius.*

1769 Samuel Adams (and others), *Appeal to the World.*

## 1770

1770 Goldsmith, *Deserted Village:* idealizes rural life.

Burke, *Thoughts on the Present Discontent.*

Lord North becomes Prime Minister.

William Wordsworth born. Died 1850.

1771, 1784, and later, Franklin, *Autobiography* (w).

1771 Beattie, *The Minstrel.* Bk. I.

Smollett, *Expedition of Humphrey Clinker.*

Mackenzie, *The Man of Feeling:* typical "sentimental" novel.

Sir Walter Scott born. Died 1832.

1771 Charles Brockden Brown born. Died 1810.

1772 Samuel Taylor Coleridge born. Died 1834.

1772 Trumbull, *Progress of Dullness,* Part I: social satire.

Freneau, *Rising Glories of America.*

1773 Goldsmith, *She Stoops to Conquer:* comedy of manners revived and chastened.

Steevens' edition of Shakespeare.

Lord Monboddo, *Origin and Progress of Language:* primitivistic and "evolutionary."

Kenrich's *Dictionary:* first in which vowel sounds are marked.

1773 Phillis Wheatley (Peters), *Poems:* poetry written by a young slave girl.

First theatre in Charleston, S. C.

521

### ENGLISH

1774 T. Warton, *History of English Poetry*, Vol. I.

Chesterfield, *Letters to His Son.*

*Goethe, *Sorrows of Werther:* morbidly sentimental "auto-biographical novel."

Death of Goldsmith.

Robert Southey born.    Died 1843.

1775–1783 War with American colonies.

1775 Sheridan, *The Rivals:* comedy of manners.

Burke, *Speech on Conciliation.*

Mason, *Memoirs of the Life and Writings of Thomas Gray:* letters combined with biography.

Charles Lamb born.    Died 1834.

Walter Savage Landor born. Died 1864.

Jane Austen born.    Died 1817.

1776 Gibbon, *Decline and Fall of the Roman Empire.*

Adam Smith, *Wealth of Nations:* new science of economics.

1777 Sheridan, *School for Scandal* (a).

Burke, *Letter to the Sheriffs of Bristol.*

Capt. Cook, *A Voyage toward the South Pole and Round the World.*

### AMERICAN

1774 Jefferson, *Summary of View of Rights of British America.*

Rush, *Natural History of Medicine Among Indians of North America.*

Boston Port Bill.

First Continental Congress.

1775–1788 Patrick Henry's Speeches.

1775–1783 Revolutionary War.

1775 Trumbull, *McFingal*, Canto I: burlesque epic against Tories, Hudibrastic verse.

Mrs. Warren, *The Group:* anti-loyalist play.

Battles of Lexington and Bunker Hill.

1776–1783 Thomas Paine, *The Crisis:* patriotic essays.

1776 Paine, *Common Sense:* advocating a declaration of independence.

Brackenridge, *Battle of Bunker Hill:* blank verse drama.

Jefferson, *Declaration of Independence.*

1777 *Articles of Confederation.*

Surrender of Burgoyne.

1778 Frances Burney, *Evelina:* novel of manners.

Reeve, *The Old English Baron:* Gothic novel somewhat "toned down" (first pub. as *The Champion of Virtue*, 1777).

William Hazlitt born. Died 1830.

*Death of Rousseau and Voltaire.

1779 Cumberland, *Wheel of Fortune.*

Johnson, *Lives of the Poets:* criticism combined with biography.

Rev. John Newton and William Cowper, *Olney Hymns:* Calvinistic.

Lord Monboddo, *Ancient Metaphysics:* an evolutionary theory of man's progress.

Hume, *Natural History of Religion.*

Death of Garrick.

1778 Franklin, *Ephemera.*

Freneau, *American Independence.*

Carver, *Travels.*

Treaty with France.

1779–1785 Franklin in France.

1779 Odell, *The Conflagration:* royalist verse.

Hopkinson, *Battle of the Kegs:* patriotic satirical ballad.

Ethan Allen, *Narrative of the Captivity.*

Paul Jones' naval victories.

## 1780

*ca.*1780 Preferred by many modern scholars as date for beginning of period of "Romanticism."

1781 Macklin, *Man of the World.*

*Kant, *Critique of Pure Reason:* transcendental philosophy.

*Schiller, *Die Räuber* (a).

1782 Cowper, *Table Talk.*

1781 Surrender of Cornwallis at Yorktown.

Articles of Confederation ratified.

State constitutions framed.

1782 Crèvecoeur, *Letters from an American Farmer:* idealistic "romantic" essays on rural life.

Paine, *Letter to the Abbé Raynal.*

1783 Crabbe, *The Village:* realistic social satire.

Blair, *Rhetoric.*

Ritson, *Collection of English Songs.*

1784 Death of Samuel Johnson.

Pitt (the younger), Prime Minister.

Leigh Hunt born. Died 1859.

1785 Cowper, *The Task:* blank verse, humor, love of nature.

Thomas De Quincey born. Died 1859.

1786 Burns, *Poems.*

Beckford, *Vathek:* Oriental tale of horror.

1787 John Wesley, *Sermons.*

1788 George Gordon, Lord Byron born. Died 1824.

1783–1785 Noah Webster, *Grammatical Institute of the English Language* (speller, grammar, reader).

1783 Washington Irving born. Died 1859.

England acknowledges American independence in Treaty of Peace.

1784 Franklin, *Information for Those Who Would Remove to America.*

1785 Dwight, *Conquest of Canaan:* epic.

1786–1787 Trumbull and others, *The Anarchiad:* political satire.

1786 Freneau, *Poems.*

1787–1788 Hamilton (and others), *The Federalist.*

1787 Barlow, *Vision of Columbus:* American epic.

Tyler, *The Contrast* (a): first American comedy acted by professionals.

Constitutional Convention.

1788 Markoe, *The Times:* social satire.

Constitution ratified by eleven states.

| ENGLISH | AMERICAN |
|---|---|
| 1789 Blake, *Songs of Innocence:* mystical lyrics.<br><br>Bowles, *Fourteen Sonnets:* reaction against neo-classic conventions in poetry.<br><br>*French Revolution begins. | 1789 Mrs. Morton, *The Power of Sympathy:* early American novel.<br><br>Washington, *First Inaugural.*<br><br>James Fenimore Cooper born. Died 1851.<br><br>Federal government established. |

## 1790

| | |
|---|---|
| *ca.*1790 German influence strong, esp. on romantic literature. | |
| 1790 Burke, *Reflections on the Revolution in France:* attacks Revolutionists.<br><br>Malone's edition of Shakespeare.<br><br>*Goethe, *Faust, A Fragment.* | 1790 Death of Franklin. |
| 1791 Boswell, *Life of Johnson:* great biography achieved through combining anecdote, conversation, and letters with narrative.<br><br>Erasmus Darwin, *The Botanic Garden.*<br><br>Paine, *Rights of Man:* defense of French Revolutionists.<br><br>Wordsworth visits France. | 1791 William Bartram, *Travels through North and South Carolina:* observations of a naturalist. |
| | 1792–1806 Brackenridge, *Modern Chivalry:* satiric novel on American democracy. |
| 1792 Paine, *Age of Reason:* deistic attack on Christianity.<br><br>Wollstonecraft, *Rights of Woman.*<br><br>Percy Bysshe Shelley born. Died 1822. | |
| 1793 Wordsworth, *Descriptive Sketches.*<br><br>Godwin, *Political Justice:* "philosophic anarchy."<br><br>*Louis XVI executed.<br><br>War with France. | 1793 Barlow, *Hasty Pudding:* mock heroic.<br><br>Imlay, *Emigrants:* "tale of the West." |

1794 Blake, *Songs of Experience.*

Radcliffe, *Mysteries of Udolpho:* melodramatic but "rationalized" Gothic novel.

Godwin, *Caleb Williams:* novel on social justice.

*Fall of Robespierre.

1795 Lewis, *The Monk:* extravagant Gothic novel.

Ritson, *Robin Hood Poems.*

John Keats born. Died 1821.

Thomas Carlyle born. Died 1881.

1795–1796 *Goethe, *Wilhelm Meister.*

1796 Coleridge, *The Watchman.*
Southey, *Joan of Arc.*

Colman, *Iron Chest* (a).

Scott, *William and Helen:* ballad in German Gothic manner, trans. of Bürger's *Lenore.*

Death of Burns.

1797–1798 *The Anti-Jacobin:* journalistic political verse-satire.

1797 Wordsworth, *The Borderers* (w) (pub. 1842).

1794 Dwight, *Greenfield Hill:* poetic medley, American themes.

Mrs. Susanna Rowson, *Charlotte:* novel.

Dunlap, *Leicester:* "*The Fatal Legacy*" (a): tragedy.

William Cullen Bryant born. Died 1878.

1795 Murray, *English Grammar:* widely used school text.

1796 Washington, *Farewell Address.*

Dennie, *Lay Preacher.*

1797 C. B. Brown, *Alcuin: a Dialogue on The Rights of Women:* influenced by the Godwins.

## 1798–1900 Romanticism[1]

**1798–1832 Triumph of Romanticism. Age of Wordsworth.** Napoleonic wars. Union with Ireland. Scientific progress. Industrial revolution. Growth of cities. Advance of humanita-

**1798–1832 Early National Period. Advance of Romanticism.** Consolidation of government; territorial expansion. War with England (1812–1814). Growing controversy between New Eng-

[1] See ROMANTICISM, page 379.

rianism. Revival of individualism. Conservative neo-classic criticism persists in face of romantic, experimental spirit among creative writers. Increased recognition of emotional and imaginative elements in literature. Literature reflects conflicting and shifting attitudes of the time: radical thought (Godwin, Shelley, Byron), political conservatism (Scott, the later Wordsworth), romantic view of external nature (Wordsworth, Coleridge, Southey, Shelley, Keats, Byron), Platonism (Wordsworth, Keats), interest in the past (Scott), transcendental philosophy (Coleridge, Wordsworth), etc. Reaction against literary conventions of neo-classicism. French and German influences apparent in philosophy, criticism, and literature (Godwin, Scott, Coleridge). Some Spanish influence (Southey) and Italian (Hunt, Byron, Keats, Shelley).

POETRY.—A golden age—the second great creative period. Flourishing of the great romantic poets: Wordsworth, Cole-

land Puritanism and Southern aristocracy on question of slavery. Monroe doctrine formulated (1823). The period of birth of many of America's greatest literary figures: Poe, Whitman, Emerson, Lowell, Whittier, Hawthorne, Longfellow, Holmes, Thoreau, Motley, Parkman and others in the North, and of Kennedy and Simms in the South. Has been called the period of "New England Renaissance" because of increased impetus to learning, culture, literature, and the development of railroads, shipping, and manufacture. In literature strong romantic influences manifested through individualism, interest in nature, the man and nature relationship, and supernaturalism. Strong following for such writers as Godwin, Coleridge, Wordsworth, and Shelley. The growth of novel as important form. America's "first professional novelist" in Charles Brockden Brown. The historical romance (Cooper). The essay and sketch (Irving). Political papers and speeches. Growth of periodical literature. Philadelphia and New York (Knickerbocker School) important literary centers. Philosophic and religious thought marked by breaking down of Calvinism before Unitarianism and a growing humanitarian sympathy (abolition movement).

POETRY.—Marked by two tendencies side by side: the old classic spirit evident in the followers of Pope and the new ridge, Scott, Shelley, Keats, Byron. Poetry reflects spirit of revolt against classical manner and themes and expresses the newer romantic enthusiasms and ideals: individualism, freedom of style and theme, passion for political liberty, philosophical idealism, religious skepticism, search for beauty, interest in the strange, weird, and novel—the "renascence of wonder," sensuous and spiritual response to external nature, a new Hellenism. Variety of metrical forms: heroic couplet, blank verse, Spenserian stanza, sonnets, miscellaneous stanzaic forms both traditional and experimental. Lyrics especially successful. Dramatic poems, reflective verse, literary ballads. Decline of formal odes and verse satire.

PROSE.–Stimulated by the prevailing creative impulse and to some extent by the new magazines, both critical (*Edinburgh, Quarterly*) and literary (*Blackwoods, London*), essays (esp. the informal essays of Lamb, Hazlitt, Hunt, DeQuincey) and criticism cultivated. Philosophical treatises. Dearth of great biographies, though some lives of historical and literary figures were written (Southey's *Nelson* and *Wesley*). Romantic fiction, especially the highly developed historical novel (Scott), and the realistic novel of manners (Austen) established as forms. Some novels of low London life and some of aristocratic life.

DRAMA.–At a low level. The restriction of serious drama to

romantic outlook influenced by Gray, Collins, Southey and others. Didactic element mingled with romantic in Bryant. Satiric quality (Barlow). Patriotic poetry and love of liberty evident in ballads and lyrics. With the writing of Freneau and Bryant, and the early work of Holmes, Whittier, and Poe, American poetry begins to take on real importance.

PROSE.–Most important developments the growth of periodicals demanding short forms of writing (the tale) and the progress of the novel. Popularity of "gift books" encourages development of short fiction. Tales and sketches by Irving and Poe; beginning of short story; important novels by Brown and Cooper. Biographies, histories, and orations by such figures as Marshall, Irving, Calhoun, Clay, Webster, and Hayne.

DRAMA.–Growing interest in the theatre. William Dunlap writes the two licensed theatres, Drury Lane and Covent Garden, effective since 1737, now results in a flourishing of spectacular, quasi-dramatic forms (burletta, farce, burlesque, melodrama) in the "minor" theatres. German and other romantic influences strong. Sentimental dramas of Kotzebue popular at beginning of period. "Tragedies of passion" of Joanna Baillie, ca.1798–ca.1812, and poetic dramas of Knowles, ca.1810–1844, theatrically successful but of low literary value. Other efforts to create new poetic drama by great romantic figures of the time—Coleridge, Wordsworth, Byron, Shelley, Lamb and others—resulted usually in plays which had high literary value but were not well adapted to the stage.

1798 Wordsworth and Coleridge, *Lyrical Ballads:* the "new poetry."

Landor, *Gebir.*

Malthus, *Essay on Population.*

1799 *Memoirs of the Life and Writings of Edward Gibbon:* advances art of autobiographical writing.

sixty-five pieces, many strongly influenced by foreign dramatists. James N. Barker, John Howard Payne, Robert Montgomery Bird, and Richard Penn Smith also popular. Barker writes of American subjects, treating the Pocahontas story and witchcraft. New York begins to take precedence over Philadelphia for theatrical productions. Italian opera introduced in 1825. Edwin Forrest an important actor. Many types of drama written, but the tragedy most successful form. Chief historical significance of period perhaps the growing use of American subjects for dramatic writing.

1798 Brown, *Wieland.*

1799 Death of Washington.

Tyler, *Algerian Captive:* novel of contemporary interests.

Brown, *Ormond; Arthur Mervyn,* Part I.

## 1800

1800 Coleridge, trans. of Schiller's *Wallenstein.*

Maria Edgeworth, *Castle Rackrent:* novel of Irish life.

1800 Weems, *Life of Washington:* idealized biography.

Library of Congress founded.

ENGLISH

Wordsworth and Coleridge, *Lyrical Ballads*, 2d ed., with famous *Preface*.

Thomas Babington Macaulay born. Died 1859.

1801 Southey, *Thalaba*.

*A. W. and F. Schlegel, *Characteristics:* romantic criticism.

John Henry Newman born. Died 1890.

1802 Scott, *Minstrelsy of the Scottish Border*.

*Edinburgh Review* founded.

*Victor Hugo born. Died 1885.

1803 Jane Porter, *Thaddeus of Warsaw:* historical novel.

Campbell, *Poems*.

Bulwer-Lytton born. Died 1873.

1804 *Schiller, *Wilhelm Tell*.

Benjamin Disraeli, Earl of Beaconsfield born. Died 1881.

1805 Wordsworth, *Prelude* (*w*) (pub. 1850).

Scott, *Lay of the Last Minstrel*.

1806 Elizabeth Barrett (Browning) born. Died 1861.

John Stuart Mill born. Died 1873.

1807 Byron, *Hours of Idleness*.

C. and M. Lamb, *Tales from Shakespeare*.

Abolition of slave trade.

AMERICAN

1801 Brown, *Edgar Huntly, Clara Howard, Jane Talbot*.

1803 Wirt, *Letters of a British Spy*.

Louisiana Purchase.

Ralph Waldo Emerson born. Died 1882.

1804 J. Q. Adams, *Letters*.

Marshall, *Life of Washington*.

Nathaniel Hawthorne born. Died 1864.

1806 Noah Webster, *Compendious Dictionary of the English Language*.

William Gilmore Simms born. Died 1870.

1807 Barlow, *Columbiad*.

Irving and Paulding, *Salmagundi Papers:* imitates *Spectator* papers.

ENGLISH

*Hegel, *Phenomenology:* idealistic philosophy.

AMERICAN

Robert E. Lee born. Died 1870.

John Greenleaf Whittier born. Died 1892.

Henry Wadsworth Longfellow born. Died 1882.

1808 Hunt, *The Examiner.*

Scott, *Marmion:* metrical romance.

Lamb, *Specimens of English Dramatic Poets:* dramatic criticism.

*Goethe, *Faust,* Part I: poetic drama.

1808 Bryant, *The Embargo:* political satire.

Congress stops importation of slaves.

1809 Byron, *English Bards and Scotch Reviewers:* verse satire.

Charles Darwin born. Died 1882.

Alfred, Lord Tennyson born. Died 1892.

William E. Gladstone born. Died 1898.

First issue of *Quarterly Review.*

1809 Irving, *Knickerbocker History:* burlesque.

Edgar Allan Poe born. Died 1849.

Oliver Wendell Holmes born. Died 1894.

Abraham Lincoln born. Died 1865.

## 1810

1810 Scott, *Lady of the Lake:* metrical romance.

Porter, *Scottish Chiefs.*

Crabbe, *The Borough.*

Southey, *Curse of Kehama.*

1811 Austen, *Sense and Sensibility:* novel of manners ridiculing sentimentalism.

William Makepeace Thackeray born. Died 1863.

531

| ENGLISH | AMERICAN |
|---|---|
| | 1812–1814 War with England. |
| | 1812 American Academy of Natural Science founded. |
| 1812 Byron, *Childe Harold*, Cantos I, II. | |
| *The Grimm brothers: *Fairy Tales*. | |
| Charles Dickens born. Died 1870. | |
| Robert Browning born. Died 1889. | |
| 1813 Byron, *Bride of Abydos:* metrical romance, Oriental. | 1813 Allston, *Sylphs of the Seasons:* delicate verse. |
| Shelley, *Queen Mab*. | Massachusetts Temperance Society founded. |
| Austen, *Pride and Prejudice*. | |
| Southey made Poet Laureate. | |
| Southey, *Life of Nelson*. | |
| *Madame de Staël, *De l'Allemagne:* "romantic" interpretation of the new German literature. | |
| 1814 Scott, *Waverly:* begins vogue of romantic historical novel. | |
| Wordsworth, *Excursion*. | |
| 1815 Scott, *Guy Mannering*. | 1815 Freneau, *Poems on American Affairs*. |
| Battle of Waterloo. | *North American Review* established. |
| Anthony Trollope born. Died 1882. | |
| 1816 Coleridge, *Christabel*. | 1816 Pickering, *Vocabulary of Americanisms:* recognizes process of separation of American English from British English. |
| Byron, *Prisoner of Chillon*. | |
| Shelley, *Alastor*. | |
| Peacock, *Headlong Hall:* satire and romance. | |

ENGLISH

AMERICAN

1817 Mary Shelley, *Frankenstein:* Gothic tale of terror.

Moore, *Lalla Rookh.*

Byron, *Manfred:* dramatic poem

Coleridge, *Biographia Literaria:* romantic criticism.

Keats, *Poems.*

*Blackwood's Magazine* established.

1818 Keats, *Endymion.*

Scott, *Heart of Midlothian.*

Shelley, *Revolt of Islam.*

Austen, *Northanger Abbey* (*w. ca.*1800): satire on Gothic novels

1819 Byron, *Don Juan*, I, II: "epic-satire," typically Byronic.

Shelley, *The Cenci:* tragedy.

Mary Ann Evans ("George Eliot") born. Died 1880.

John Ruskin born. Died 1900.

Charles Kingsley born. Died 1875.

*Schopenhauer, *The World as Will and Idea:* pessimistic philosophy.

1817 Bryant, *Thanatopsis* (*w.* 1811): reflective melancholic poem; influenced by "graveyard school"; competent blank verse.

Henry David Thoreau born. Died 1862.

1818 Payne, *Brutus* (*a.* London): tragedy.

1819 Halleck, *Fanny:* Byronic social verse satire.

Drake, *The Culprit Fay:* poem of nature and fairies.

James Russell Lowell born. Died 1891.

Herman Melville born. Died 1891.

Walt Whitman born. Died 1892.

## 1820

1820–1830 George IV.

1820–1823 Lamb, *Essays of Elia.*

*ca.*1820–1846 *Balzac's tales and novels.

1820 Scott, *Ivanhoe.*

Shelley, *Prometheus Unbound.*

1820 Missouri Compromise.

Irving, *Sketch Book:* essays and tales; English recognition.

533

Keats, *Lamia . . . and other Poems:* contains the great odes.

Maturin, *Melmoth the Wanderer:* Gothic tale.

*London Magazine* established.

Herbert Spencer born. Died 1903.

1821 Scott, *Kenilworth.*

Southey, *Vision of Judgment.*

Shelley, *Adonais.*

De Quincey, *Confessions of an English Opium-Eater.*

Byron, *Cain.*

Egan, *Tom and Jerry:* forerunner of Dickens' novels of London life.

Death of Keats.

1821 Bryant, *Poems.*

Cooper, *The Spy:* novel of Revolutionary times.

1822 Byron, *Vision of Judgment:* satirical parody on Southey's poem.

Matthew Arnold born. Died 1888.

Death of Shelley.

1822 Irving, *Bracebridge Hall:* essays and sketches.

1823 Scott, *Quentin Durward.*

Carlyle, *Life of Schiller.*

1823 Cooper, *Pioneers:* first of Leatherstocking series.

The Monroe Doctrine.

Francis Parkman born. Died 1893.

1824 Landor, *Imaginary Conversations,* Vol. I.

Death of Byron.

1824 Irving, *Tales of a Traveler.*

E. Everett, *Progress of Literature in America.*

1825 Macaulay, *Essay on Milton.*

Hazlitt, *Spirit of the Age.*

Thomas Henry Huxley born. Died 1895.

1825 Halleck, *Marco Bozzaris.*

Italian opera introduced into America.

534

| ENGLISH | AMERICAN |
|---|---|
| 1826 Scott, *Woodstock.* | 1826 Cooper, *Last of the Mohicans.* |
| Disraeli, *Vivian Gray:* novel of fashionable life. | Payne, *Richelieu (a).* |
| | Woodworth, *The Old Oaken Bucket.* |
| | Clay's speeches in Congress. |
| | *The Atlantic Souvenir:* annual "gift book"; encouraged short fiction. |
| 1827 *Heine, *Songs.* | 1827 Cooper, *The Prairie.* |
| | Dana, *Poems.* |
| | Poe, *Tamerlane.* |
| | Simms, *Lyrical and Other Poems.* |
| | Mrs. Sigourney, *Poems.* |
| | Willis, *Sketches:* poems. |
| 1828-1830 Taylor, *Historic Survey of German Poetry:* reflects "romantic" interest in German literature. | |
| 1828 Catholic Emancipation Act. | 1828 Hawthorne, *Fanshaw.* |
| Dante Gabriel Rossetti born. Died 1882. | Irving, *Columbus.* |
| George Meredith born. Died 1909. | Webster, *An American Dictionary.* |
| | Hall, *The Western Souvenir:* pioneer "Western" fiction. |
| 1829 Jerrold, *Black-ey'd Susan.* | 1829 Irving, *Conquest of Granada.* |
| | Henry B. Timrod born. Died 1867. |

### 1830

| | |
|---|---|
| 1830–1837 William IV. | 1830–1838 Audubon, *Birds of America.* |
| 1830–1833 Lyell, *Principles of Geology:* stressed uniformity of processes of nature. | |

| ENGLISH | AMERICAN |
|---|---|
| 1830 Tennyson, *Poems Chiefly Lyrical.* | 1830 Webster, *Speeches.* |
| Moore, *Letters and Journals of Lord Byron.* | Worcester, *Dictionary.* |
| Scott, *Letters on Demonology and Witchcraft.* | Holmes, *Old Ironsides.* |
| | *Godey's Lady's Book* founded. |
| *Heine, *The Romantic School:* German romantic criticism. | Emily Dickinson born. Died 1886. |
| 1831 Scott, *Castle Dangerous.* | 1831 Poe, *Poems.* |
| Disraeli, *The Young Duke.* | Whittier, *Legends of New England.* |
| | Garrison founds the *Liberator.* American Anti-Slavery Society founded. |

## 1832

**1832–1870 Victorian Period.[1] Age of Tennyson.** Romantic rather than neo-classic spirit prevails, but romanticism is modified by increasing tendency to adapt literature to current social conditions, and to reflect current attitudes in science, religion, politics, philosophy. Reaction from extravagancies of earlier romanticists and tendency toward conventional attitudes. Period of liberalism in thought, so far as reflected in leading writers, but of conventionalism in conduct. "Victorian insularity" and increased internal prosperity. Foreign influences limited. Increased industrialism, development of democracy, and advances in science profoundly affect literature and foster growth of the realistic attitude. Social and philosoph-

**1832–1870 Romanticism. Age of Emerson.** First great creative period of American literature. Chief historical interest the slavery issue culminating in the Civil War. Literary activity shifts its center to Boston and Cambridge. Charleston the chief center in the South. Has been called "The Golden Age of American Literature." From the past period Irving, Cooper, Bryant still writing and new figures arise in Hawthorne, Poe, Longfellow, Whittier, Lowell, Holmes, Thoreau, Emerson, Melville, Whitman, and Simms. Deliberate effort to break away from European tradition in such writers as Poe, Emerson, Lowell, and Whitman, though European attitudes still obvious in the dominance of romanticism, the interest in sentiment, and the

[1]See VICTORIAN, p. 458.

ical problems treated in literature. Dominant strain of earnestness and optimism, often complacent and conservative. A purer romanticism is reflected in the transcendentalism of Carlyle and the medievalism of the Pre-Raphaelites. Great increase in size of reading public and in volume of creative work. Humanitarian spirit strong. Increasing interest in popular education. Thought-upheaval follows promulgation of theory of evolution. Literature reflects both the newer materialistic attitudes and the idealistic and romantic opposition to them. Satires grow more urbane.

POETRY.–Prevailingly romantic in spirit, as shown in dominance of the imaginative and emotional elements, in experimentation in verse forms, in the worship of beauty expressed in Tennyson's early work, and in the individualism of Browning. Later work of Tennyson reflects modified romanticism in increase of intellectual element and tendency to reflect and treat serious problems of society. Serious spirit of later Victorians appears in Arnold. The lyric remains a favorite form; sonnets (Mrs. Browning, Rossetti); some great elegies (Tennyson's *In Memoriam*, Arnold's *Thyrsis*). High degree of technical perfection

German thought mixed with New England transcendentalism. Gift books and annuals give way to regular periodical literature—the rise of the magazines. Literature attractive enough for some few men to build professional careers upon their writing. Technique for the novel, drama, and short story becomes more fixed. Serious criticism develops under tutelage of such critics as Margaret Fuller, Lowell, and Poe. War literature important. Patriotic lyrics from both North and South. Experimentation in literary form of Whitman. The beginnings of local color movement after the Civil War. Next to political thought molded by the war the most important intellectual concern is centered around Unitarianism and transcendentalism.

POETRY.–Prevailingly romantic in spirit as shown in dominance of imaginative and emotional elements (Poe). Moral and didactic qualities continue in Bryant, Longfellow, Whittier, Lowell, and Emerson. Antislavery verse of Whittier and Lowell answered in South by spirited verse of Timrod and Hayne. Nature common to all major poets except Poe. Other contributions are: narrative verse (Longfellow and Lowell); dialect verse (Lowell); *vers de société* and humor (Holmes). Throwing over of conventional verse forms by Whitman in effort to write "American" poetry.

537

achieved in verse. Browning develops the dramatic monologue. The Pre-Raphaelites.

PROSE.–Great activity. Informal essays (Dickens, Thackeray) less popular. Notable prose treatises and formal essays on literary, critical, artistic, philosophical, historical, political, scientific, educational, religious, social, and economic themes by such writers as Carlyle, Ruskin, Macaulay, Arnold, Newman, Kingsley, Huxley. Moral earnestness. Style varied and often highly individual: Carlyle (nervous, picturesque, emphatic), Ruskin (rich, "eloquent"), Macaulay (terse, journalistic). Formal biographies of the "authorized" type, heavy in tone, adulatory rather than detached. In fiction the short story fails to reflect the interest in the form being shown in America and France. The novel flourishes and attains position of leading literary form: romantic (esp. historical) novels continue (Bulwer-Lytton, Thackeray, Kingsley); varied types of realistic novels develop—psychological character-analysis (George Eliot), setting (E. Brontë), social satire and reform (Thackeray, Dickens, Kingsley, Trollope, Reade), politics (Disraeli, Trollope).

DRAMA.–Gradual decline of the romantic and poetic drama in spite of efforts of such literary men as Bulwer-Lytton and Browning and such dramatists and actors as Knowles and

PROSE.–The American novel comes into full being. Subjects are varied: the frontier (Cooper and Simms), the sea and adventure (Dana and Melville), moral problems (Hawthorne), propaganda (Mrs. Stowe). Continued development of magazines and periodicals calls for countless short pieces of writing and promotes the essay (Lowell) and the tale (Poe and Hawthorne). Philosophy and moral teachings of Emerson, Thoreau, and other transcendentalists. Humor takes on importance under Mark Twain, Artemus Ward, Josh Billings. Americans begin to take interest in scholarship as evidenced in the Verplanck and Hudson studies in Shakespeare, Child's work with the ballad, Duyckinck's editorial work in American literature, the science of Agassiz, and the histories of Bancroft, Prescott, and Parkman. Biography develops. American criticism influenced by doctrines of Poe, Lowell, and Emerson.

DRAMA.–Romantic tragedies most characteristic and popular type. George Henry Boker most important dramatist so far writing in America. Creative period actually begins.

Macready. Confused conditions partly traceable to the repeal (1843) of the Licensing Act of 1737. Except for Shakespearean productions (especially successful under Charles Kean in the fifties and sixties) and certain closet dramas and domestic plays, dramatic activity reflects the vogue of sentimentality, melodrama, spectacle—these forms increasing in popularity after the retirement of Macready in 1851. Influenced by French drama. No new theatres built in London between 1841 and 1866.

Popular play drawn from history, the Indians, and the American wars. Social satire and plays of local life prominent. Dramatized fiction (notably *Uncle Tom's Cabin* and *Rip Van Winkle*) is successful. Melodrama common (*Ten Nights in a Bar Room*). Some few dramatists, George Henry Boker, N. P. Willis, Epes Sargent, Charlotte Barnes Conner, and George H. Miles not only write stage successes but actually contribute to dramatic literature in America.

1832–1840 Important scientific developments; appearance of new literary figures; increasing optimism follows post-war depression.

1832 Reform Bill.

"Lewis Carroll" (C. L. Dodgson) born. Died 1898.

Death of Scott and *Goethe.

1832 Poe: five tales appear in *Philadelphia Saturday Courier*.

Bryant, *Poems* (2d ed.)

Simms, *Atalantis*.

Whittier, *Moll Pitcher*.

Irving, *The Alhambra*.

Dunlap, *History of the American Theatre*.

1833–1841 The Oxford Movement (Tractarians)

1833–1834 Carlyle, *Sartor Resartus*.

1833 Lamb, *Last Essays of Elia*.

Browning, *Pauline*.

Newman, *Tracts for the Times* (begun).

Surtees, *Jorrock's Jaunts and Jollities:* precursor of *Pickwick Papers*.

1833 Longfellow, *Outre-Mer* (first numbers).

Poe, *Manuscript Found in a Bottle*.

ENGLISH

AMERICAN

1834–1848 Sparks, *Library of American Biography.*

1834 Bulwer-Lytton, *Last Days of Pompeii.*

William Morris born. Died 1896.

Death of Coleridge and Lamb.

1835 Browning, *Paracelsus.*

Samuel Butler born. Died 1902.

Alfred Austin born. Died 1913.

1834 Bancroft, *History of the United States*, Vol. I.

Crockett, *Autobiography.*

*Southern Literary Messenger* established.

1835 Simms, *The Partisan; The Yemassee.*

Frances A. Kemble, *Journal.*

Longstreet, *Georgia Scenes:* realistic sketches of Georgia life.

"Mark Twain" born. Died 1910.

1836 Dickens, *Pickwick Papers:* humor.

Planché, *Riquet with the Tuft (a):* dramatic "extravaganza."

Marryat, *Mr. Midshipman Easy:* sea-novel.

Dickens, *Sketches by Boz.*

1836 Emerson, *Nature:* transcendental philosophy.

Holmes, *Poems.*

Irving, *Astoria:* novel of the far Northwest.

Paulding, *View of Slavery.*

Morse's invention of telegraph instrument.

Bret Harte born. Died 1902.

1837–1901 Victoria.

1837 Dickens, *Oliver Twist:* attacks Poor Laws.

Browning, *Strafford.*

Carlyle, *French Revolution.*

Lockhart, *Life of Scott.*

Algernon Charles Swinburne born. Died 1909.

1837 Hawthorne, *Twice-Told Tales:* romantic, allegorical tales of New England.

Whittier, *Poems.*

Emerson, *The American Scholar* (delivered as an address): "the American Declaration of Intellectual Independence."

Prescott, *Ferdinand and Isabella:* history.

ENGLISH

AMERICAN

John Burroughs born. Died 1921.

William Dean Howells born. Died 1920.

1838–1849 The Chartist Movement for extending the franchise.

1838 First railway train enters London.

Ocean steamships connect England and United States.

1838 Morse demonstrates telegraph apparatus before President Van Buren.

1839 Bulwer-Lytton, *Cardinal Richelieu.*

Carlyle, *Chartism.*

Ainsworth, *Jack Sheppard:* novel of crime.

Walter Pater born. Died 1894.

1839 Longfellow, *Hyperion; Voices of the Night.*

## 1840

1840–1841 Hood, *Miss Kilmansagg and her Golden Leg:* poetic satire on wealth.

1840 Browning, *Sordello.*

Dickens, *Old Curiosity Shop.*

Planché, *Sleeping Beauty* (*a*): an "extravaganza."

Thomas Hardy born. Died 1928.

1840 Cooper, *Pathfinder.*

Dana, *Two Years before the Mast.*

Poe, *Tales of the Grotesque and Arabesque:* short stories, original, influential.

Brook Farm established.

*The Dial* established (discontinued 1844): transcendentalist magazine.

1841 Browning, *Pippa Passes:* closet drama.

Carlyle, *Heroes and Hero-Worship.*

Macaulay, *Warren Hastings.*

Boucicault, *London Assurance* (*a*).

1841 Cooper, *The Deerslayer.*

Emerson, *Essays.*

Longfellow, *Ballads and Other Poems.*

1842 Browning, *Dramatic Lyrics*.

Tennyson, *Poems*.

Dickens, *American Notes:* sharp criticism of American manners.

Macaulay, *Lays of Ancient Rome*.

Newman, *Essay on Miracles*.

Burney (Madame D'Arblay), *Diary and Letters*.

1843 Carlyle, *Past and Present*.

Dickens, *Christmas Carol*.

Ruskin, *Modern Painters*, Vol. I.

Hood, *Song of the Shirt:* social satire.

Wordsworth made Poet Laureate.

Repeal of Licensing Act of 1737: end of monopoly of the "patent" theatres in London.

1844 Thackeray, *Barry Lyndon:* Irish rogue story.

Elizabeth Barrett (Browning), *Poems*.

Disraeli, *Coningsby:* political novel championing monarchy.

*Dumas, *The Three Musketeers*

Robert Bridges born. Died 1930.

1845 Dickens, *Cricket on the Hearth*.

Repeal of Corn Laws.

*Wagner, *Tannhäuser:* great literary opera.

1842 Longfellow, *Poems on Slavery*.

Griswold, *Poets and Poetry of America*.

Sidney Lanier born. Died 1881.

1843 Prescott, *Conquest of Mexico*.

Whittier, *Lays of My Home and Other Poems*.

Henry James born. Died 1916.

1844 Emerson, *Essays* (2d ser.).

Bayard Taylor, *Ximena*.

Beecher, *Lectures to Young Men*.

Margaret Fuller (Ossoli), *Woman in the Nineteenth Century*.

First private telegraph company organized by Morse and others.

1845 Lowell, *Conversations on Some of the Old Poets*.

Poe, *The Raven*.

| ENGLISH | AMERICAN |
|---|---|
| 1846 Brontë sisters, *Poems.* | 1846 Hawthorne, *Mosses from an Old Manse.* |
| Thackeray, *Vanity Fair:* novel of manners. | Holmes, *Poems.* |
| | Melville, *Typee.* |
| | Taylor, *Views Afoot.* |
| 1847 E. Brontë, *Wuthering Heights:* emphasizes setting. | 1847 Emerson, *Poems.* |
| C. Brontë, *Jane Eyre.* | Longfellow, *Evangeline.* |
| Tennyson, *The Princess.* | Prescott, *Conquest of Peru.* |
| Hunt, *Men, Women, and Books.* | Agassiz, *Introduction to Natural History.* |
| | Melville, *Omoo.* |
| 1848 Mill, *Political Economy.* | 1848 Lowell, *A Fable for Critics:* humor, satire, literary criticism in verse; *Biglow Papers:* Yankee dialect, political satire. |
| Macaulay, *History of England,* Vols. I, II. | |
| Pre-Raphaelite Brotherhood founded by Rossetti. | Bartlett, *Dictionary of American-isms.* |
| 1849 Dickens, *David Copperfield:* semi-autobiographical. | 1849 Alice and Phoebe Cary, *Poems.* |
| Thackeray, *Pendennis:* semi-autobiographical. | Irving, *Life of Goldsmith.* |
| | Whittier, *Voices of Freedom.* |
| Ruskin, *Seven Lamps of Architecture.* | Parkman, *Oregon Trail.* |
| Bulwer-Lytton, *The Caxtons:* realistic, family life. | Thoreau, *Week on the Concord and Merrimac Rivers.* |
| | Melville, *Mardi.* |
| | Ticknor, *History of Spanish Literature.* |
| | Death of Poe. |

## 1850

| | |
|---|---|
| *ca.*1850–*ca.*1875 *Dumas *fils* fl.:* important realistic drama. | |
| 1850 Mrs. Browning, *Sonnets from the Portuguese.* | 1850 Emerson, *Representative Men.* |
| Tennyson, *In Memoriam.* | Hawthorne, *Scarlet Letter:* first "great" American novel. |

| ENGLISH | AMERICAN |
|---|---|
| Hunt, *Autobiography; Table Talk.* | Irving, *Mahomet.* |
| Kingsley, *Alton Locke:* realistic novel dealing with London sweat-shops. | Whittier, *Songs of Labor.* |
| | Poe, *Poetic Principle.* |
| Death of Wordsworth. | *Harper's Magazine* established. |
| Tennyson made Poet Laureate. | |
| Robert Louis Stevenson born. Died 1894. | |

**1851** Ruskin, *Stones of Venice.* — **1851** Hawthorne, *House of Seven Gables.*

| ENGLISH | AMERICAN |
|---|---|
| Borrow, *Lavengro:* autobiographical. | Melville, *Moby Dick:* novel of whaling industry. |
| Charles Kean begins successful productions of Shakespeare. | |

**1852** Dickens, *Bleak House:* satirizes law courts. — **1852** Hawthorne, *Blithedale Romance:* "Brook Farm" novel.

| ENGLISH | AMERICAN |
|---|---|
| Thackeray, *Henry Esmond:* historical novel. | Stoddard, *Poems.* |
| Reade, *Peg Woffington.* | Mrs. Stowe, *Uncle Tom's Cabin.* |
| Newman, *The Idea of a University.* | |
| Tennyson, *Ode on the Death of the Duke of Wellington.* | |

**1853** Thackeray, *English Humorists.* — **1853** Hawthorne, *Tanglewood Tales.*

| ENGLISH | AMERICAN |
|---|---|
| Mrs. Gaskell, *Cranford:* novel of manners. | James Whitcomb Riley born. Died 1916. |
| Kingsley, *Hypatia.* | |
| Arnold, *Poems.* | |
| C. Brontë, *Villette:* semi-autobiographical. | |
| George Moore born. | |

**1854** Dickens, *Hard Times:* serious social novel. — **1854** Thoreau, *Walden:* transcendental philosophy, individualism, nature description.

| ENGLISH | AMERICAN |
|---|---|
| The Crimean War. | B. Taylor, *Poems of the Orient.* |

1855–1876 *Turgenev's novels of character and Russian life.

1855 Browning, *Men and Women.*

Tennyson, *Maud:* monologue.

Thackeray, *The Newcomes.*

Dickens, *Little Dorrit:* attacks social abuses.

Trollope, *The Warden.*

Kingsley, *Westward Ho.*

Gaskell, *North and South:* social novel.

Spencer, *Principles of Psychology,* Vol. I.

Lewes, *Life of Goethe.*

1856 Mrs. Browning, *Aurora Leigh.*

Reade, *It is Never too Late to Mend:* social novel.

Wilkie Collins, *A Terribly Strange Bed:* horror story.

James Anthony Froude, *History of England,* Vols. I, II.

Oscar Wilde born. Died 1900.

George Bernard Shaw born.

*Death of Heine.

1857 Thackeray, *The Virginians.*

Trollope, *Barchester Towers.*

Borrow, *The Romany Rye.*

Hughes, *Tom Brown's School Days.*

*Flaubert, *Madame Bovary:* influenced later English realists.

Joseph Conrad born. Died 1924.

1855 Whitman, *Leaves of Grass:* original verse form, individualism, patriotic democracy.

Longfellow, *Hiawatha.*

Irving, *Life of Washington* (begun).

Hayne, *Poems.*

Boker, *Francesca da Rimini,* tragedy (a).

Duyckinck, *Cyclopedia of American Literature.*

1856 Emerson, *English Traits.*

Curtis, *Prue and I.*

Motley, *Rise of the Dutch Republic.*

Woodrow Wilson born. Died 1924.

1857 Child, ed., *English and Scottish Ballads.*

*Atlantic Monthly* established.

Dred Scott decision.

Rose Terry (Cooke) publishes the first realistic short stories of New England life.

Holmes, *Autocrat of the Breakfast Table.*

1858–1888 *Daudet, French novels and tales, psychological, realistic.

1858 "George Eliot," *Scenes of Clerical Life.*

Carlyle, *Frederick II*, Vols. I, II.

Morris, *Defence of Guinevere.*

Brown, *Rab and his Friends:* short stories.

1859 Tennyson, *Idylls of the King.*

Dickens, *Tale of Two Cities:* historical novel.

Eliot, *Adam Bede:* psychological novel.

Meredith, *Ordeal of Richard Feverel.*

Fitzgerald, trans. *Rubaiyat of Omar Khayyam.*

Darwin, *Origin of Species.*

John Stuart Mill, *On Liberty.*

Death of Macaulay, Hunt, DeQuincey.

Alfred E. Housman born.

Arthur Conan Doyle born. Died 1930.

Francis Thompson born. Died 1907.

1858 Holmes, *Autocrat of the Breakfast Table:* personal essays, humor.

Longfellow, *Courtship of Miles Standish.*

Allibone, *Critical Dictionary of English Literature.*

Lincoln-Douglas debate.

Theodore Roosevelt born. Died 1919.

1859 Marsh, *Lectures on the English Language.*

Margaret Fuller (Ossoli), *Life Without and Life Within:* transcendental.

O'Brien, *What Was It:* mystery story.

Joseph Jefferson, *Rip Van Winkle* (a).

# 1860

| ENGLISH | AMERICAN |
|---|---|
| 1860–1863 Thackeray, *Roundabout Papers.* | |
| 1860 Eliot, *Mill on the Floss.* | 1860 Emerson, *Conduct of Life.* |
| "Owen Meredith," *Lucille.* | Hawthorne, *Marble Faun.* |
| Collins, *Woman in White:* "novel of plot." | Timrod, *Poems:* Southern poetry. |
| James Barrie born. | Stedman, *Poems.* |
| | Harte, *The Work on Red Mountain:* Western "local color" fiction. |
| | South Carolina secedes from Union. |
| 1861 Eliot, *Silas Marner.* | 1861 Holmes, *Elsie Venner.* |
| Reade, *The Cloister and the Hearth.* | Timrod, *The Cotton Boll* (w). |
| Arnold, *On Translating Homer.* | Lincoln becomes President. |
| Imprisonment for debt abolished. | Outbreak of Civil War. |
| 1862 Ruskin, *Unto This Last.* | 1862 Browne, *Artemus Ward: His Book:* humor. |
| Spencer, *First Principles:* formulates Law of Evolution. | Julia Ward Howe, *Battle Hymn of the Republic.* |
| Meredith, *Poems and Ballads.* | Battle of Shiloh; *Monitor* and *Merrimac.* |
| Maurice, *Claims of the Bible and Science.* | |
| *Turgenev, *Fathers and Sons.* | |
| *Ibsen, *Love's Comedy.* | |
| 1863 Eliot, *Romola:* historical novel. | 1863 Bryant, *Thirty Poems.* |
| Huxley, *Man's Place in Nature.* | Longfellow, *Tales of a Wayside Inn.* |
| Kingsley, *Water Babies.* | Louisa M. Alcott, *Hospital Sketches.* |
| Jean Ingelow, *Poems.* | |

547

| ENGLISH | AMERICAN |
|---|---|
| Taylor, *The Ticket-of-Leave Man:* comedy. | Beecher, *Freedom and Life.* |
| Death of Thackeray. | Whittier, *In War Time.* |
| | Emancipation Proclamation. |
| | Lincoln, *Gettysburg Address.* |

1864–1866 *Tolstoi, *War and Peace:* realistic historical novel.

1864 Browning, *Dramatis Personae.*

Tennyson, *Enoch Arden.*

Swinburne, *Atalanta in Calydon.*

Newman, *Apologia pro Vita Sua.*

Dickens, *Our Mutual Friend.*

*Taine, *History of English Literature.*

ca.1865–ca.1900 *Zola's "naturalistic" novels.

1865 Arnold, *Essays in Criticism.*

Ruskin, *Sesame and Lilies.*

"Lewis Carroll," *Alice's Adventures in Wonderland.*

Robertson, *Caste:* social problem comedy.

Rudyard Kipling born. Died 1936.

William Butler Yeats born.

1866 Arnold, *Thyrsis:* pastoral elegy.

Swinburne, *Poems and Ballads.*

Dickens, *The Signal-Man:* short story.

Ruskin, *Crown of Wild Olive.*

Kingsley, *Hereward the Wake.*

1864 Thoreau, *The Maine Woods.*

Greeley, *The American Conflict.*

Lowell, *Fireside Travels.*

Paul Elmer More born.

1865 Thoreau, *Cape Cod.*

Lowell, *Commemoration Ode.*

Whitman, *Drum Taps.*

Whittier, *National Lyrics.*

End of Civil War.

Assassination of Lincoln.

1866 Shaw, *Josh Billings: His Sayings.*

Whittier, *Snow-Bound.*

Howells, *Venetian Life.*

Atlantic cable completed.

| ENGLISH | AMERICAN |
|---|---|

*Dostoyevski, *Crime and Punishment:* powerful realistic novel.

H. G. Wells born.

**1867** Bagehot, *English Constitution.*

Freeman, *Norman Conquest,* Vol. I.

Darwin, *Plants and Animals under Domestication.*

*Karl Marx, *Das Kapital:* socialistic.

Arnold Bennett born. Died 1931.

John Galsworthy born. Died 1933.

**1867** Mark Twain, *The Celebrated Jumping Frog of Calaveras County.*

Holmes, *Guardian Angel.*

Harte, *Condensed Novels:* burlesque.

Lanier, *Tiger Lilies.*

Longfellow, translation of Dante.

Lowell, *Biglow Papers* (2d ser.).

Whittier, *Tent on the Beach.*

Sill, *The Hermitage and Other Poems.*

**1868** Browning, *The Ring and the Book.*

Collins, *The Moonstone.*

Morris, *Earthly Paradise,* Vols. I, II.

*Müller, *Chips from a German Workshop.*

**1868** Alcott, *Little Women.*

Hale, *The Man Without a Country.*

Hawthorne, *American Notebooks.*

Whittier, *Among the Hills.*

**1869** Trollope, *Phineas Finn:* political novel.

Blackmore, *Lorna Doone:* historical novel.

Ruskin, *Queen of the Air:* symbolic interpretation of Greek mythology.

Arnold, *Culture and Anarchy.*

Suez Canal opened.

**1869** Mark Twain, *The Innocents Abroad:* satire on European culture.

Aldrich, *Story of a Bad Boy.*

Transcontinental railroad completed.

Edwin Arlington Robinson born. Died 1935.

William Vaughn Moody born. Died 1910.

## 1870

ENGLISH

**1870–1900 Late Victorians. Advance of Realism.** Growth of imperialism and cosmopolitanism. Progress of scientific thought and growing receptiveness to foreign influences (e.g., Ibsen, Maupassant, Zola, Tolstoi, Turgenev, Dostoyevski, Nietzsche, Hauptmann) aid in advance of realism. Passing of the great Victorians. Decline in creative power. "Conflict" between science and religion. Increasing manifestations of melancholy and philosophic despair. The "decadents." Some revival of romanticism (Stevenson, the Celtic Renaissance). Last decade of century an important transitional period. Much experimentation. The new "renaissance." Self-conscious emancipation. "New" movements in society, art, literature. Celtic Renaissance (Yeats, Russell, Lady Gregory). New literary drama (Shaw, Pinero, Jones). New dramatic criticism (Archer, Shaw). Romantic fiction (Stevenson, Kipling, Conrad). Realism (Hardy, Gissing). Dialect fiction (Barrie, "Ian Maclaren"). Decadence (Wilde, Beardsley). Foreign authors widely read: Zola, Balzac, Flaubert, Maupassant, Sudermann, Schnitzler, Ibsen, Tolstoi, Chekhov, Gorky, Turgenev, D'Annunzio.

POETRY.–Reaction from Tennysonian tradition manifest as interest shifts to realistic prose and drama. Some experimentation in French verse forms.

AMERICAN

**1870–1900 Romance and local color dominant; literature beginning, however, to be self-conscious of nationality and to reflect a realistic attitude.** Rapid growth of America, settlement and expansion. Pioneer period about completed with an outline of American civilization pretty well established, economically, commercially, politically, if not culturally. Progress in scientific thought and the "conflict" between science and religion waged. Greater effort on part of literature to understand life and its significances. Dominant literary tendencies: sentimental and historical romance, use of local color, and the advance of realism. Growing reliance on American subjects as result of enthusiasm for local color. Beginning of naturalism. Criticism of Howells and James influential in the new realistic attitude.

POETRY.–Conventional romantic lyrics (Taylor, Stoddard, Stedman, Aldrich) characteristic of the beginning of the period. Poetry at a rather low ebb as

ENGLISH

Important new poets: Swinburne, Henley, Hardy, Stevenson, Housman, Kipling, Stephen Phillips, Moore, Yeats, Watson, Bridges. Confused trends.

PROSE.–Interest and varied activity in prose literature continues. Serious treatises and essays (Arnold, Huxley, Ruskin, Spencer, Lecky, Bagehot, Pater, Stephen) cover wide range of theme and mark development of prose style. Stevenson successfully revives the light, personal essay. Some notable biographies of the "life and letters" type. Fiction loses restraint and decorum of earlier Victorian novel: freer treatment of religion, sex, radical social theories; increasingly realistic treatment, partly influenced by French naturalism: Hardy, Meredith, Gissing. Regional novels by Barrie and first of great sea-novels by Conrad appear. Stevenson attempts revival of romantic fiction; short story, under American influence, scantily cultivated, though notable short stories by Kipling and Stevenson appear.

AMERICAN

romanticism becomes a set convention and then loses ground. New England poets drop from dominant position. Local color evident in work of such poets as Hay, Miller, and Lanier. In the nineties the published work of Emily Dickinson, Stephen Crane, Carmen and Hovey brings in a spirit of revolt and experiment.

PROSE.–The fiction of the first decades distinguished by strong interest in local color. The West represented by Bret Harte and Mark Twain; the South by Cable, Hearne, and Craddock; New England by M. E. W. Freeman and Sarah Orne Jewett. Along with these stories was strong leaning toward sentimental and moralistic novel (E. P. Roe and Augusta Evans). Growing from the enthusiasm for writing of local color came realistic movement influenced by E. W. Howe's *Story of a Country Town* and developed most definitely by Henry James, William Dean Howells, and Hamlin Garland. The novel became reputable and the short story attained perfected technique and great popularity. Particular currents in prose included the frontier interest (Harte), scientific thought (Fiske), politics, government, and economics (Henry Adams, Woodrow Wilson, Henry George), social castes (James and Howells), nature (Burroughs and Muir). In the writing of Stephen Crane naturalism gained a foothold. Realism sponsored in field of criticism by Howells and James.

## ENGLISH

DRAMA.–Decline of Shakespearean productions. Dominance of realistic plays, largely under French influence. Great influence of Ibsen in the eighties and early nineties. Literary dramas of Tennyson. Appearance of Shaw. London theatres more numerous and luxurious. Era of the actor Irving. Tendency toward breakdown of older dramatic classifications and technique as dramatists center attention upon ideas, dialogue, situation. The problem drama. Reappearance of actable literary drama in the nineties (Wilde, Pinero, Jones, Barrie, Phillips, Shaw). Beginning of the drama of Celtic Renaissance. The "Little Theatre" movement in France, Germany, England. Flourishing of the light opera of Gilbert and Sullivan.

*ca.*1870–1922 *"Anatole France" *fl.*: great French novelist, satirist, and critic.

1870 Rossetti, *Poems.*

Huxley, *Lay Sermons.*

Death of Dickens.

1871 Darwin, *Descent of Man.*

John Millington Synge born. Died 1909.

## AMERICAN

DRAMA.–Rise of commercial drama under great managers; development of "stars." Bronson Howard (*Shenandoah*), James A. Hearn (*Shore Acres*), Augustus Thomas (*Arizona*), William Gillette (*Sherlock Holmes*), Langdon Mitchell (*Vanity Fair*) among most important dramatists. Joseph Jefferson the greatest actor. Growing technical ability, great development in staging effects. Social satire, American themes characteristic. Literary drama written by Howells, James, and others.

1870 Lowell, *Among My Books* (1st ser.): essays.

Whitman, *Democratic Vistas:* prose.

Taylor, trans. Goethe's *Faust*, Part I.

Harte, *Luck of Roaring Camp:* short stories of the West.

Bryant, blank verse translation of the *Odyssey.*

1871 Burroughs, *Wake-Robin:* nature essays.

Eggleston, *Hoosier Schoolmaster:* realistic regional fiction.

Hay, *Pike County Ballads:* local "dialect" verse.

Howells, *Their Wedding Journey.*

Joaquin Miller, *Songs of the Sierras.*

Lowell, *My Study Windows:* essays.

1872 Butler, *Erewhon:* satirical "Utopia."

Hardy, *Under the Greenwood Tree.*

Eliot, *Middlemarch.*

1872 A. B. Alcott, *Concord Days.*

Mark Twain, *Roughing It.*

Warner, *Backlog Studies.*

E. P. Roe, *Barriers Burned Away.*

1873 Arnold, *Literature and Dogma.*

Pater, *Studies in the Renaissance.*

1873 Aldrich, *Marjorie Daw:* French influence (lightness of touch).

1874 Hardy, *Far from the Madding Crowd.*

L. Stephen, *Hours in a Library.*

Green, *Short History of England.*

John Stuart Mill, *Autobiography:* stresses mental development.

Disraeli, Prime Minister.

1874 Bigelow, *Life of Franklin.*

Amy Lowell born. Died 1925.

1875–1877 *Tolstoi, *Anna Karenina:* realistic novel.

1875 Arnold, *God and the Bible.*

1875 Henry James, *Roderick Hudson:* realistic fiction.

Howells, *A Foregone Conclusion.*

1876 Eliot, *Daniel Deronda.*

Morris, *Sigurd the Volsung.*

Tennyson, *Queen Mary* (a).

Trevelyan, *Life of Macaulay:* "established the two-volume life-and-letters biography."

1876 Mark Twain, *Tom Sawyer.*

Lanier, *Poems.*

Lowell, *Among My Books* (2d ser.).

Invention of telephone.

| ENGLISH | AMERICAN |
|---|---|
| 1877 Stevenson, *A Lodging for the Night:* short story. | 1877 James, *The American.* |
| | Warner, *Being a Boy.* |
| | Burroughs, *Birds and Poets.* |
| 1878 Stevenson, *An Inland Voyage:* travel sketch. | 1878 James, *Daisy Miller.* |
| Hardy, *Return of the Native.* | |
| Bagehot, *Literary Studies.* | |
| Lecky, *History of England in the Eighteenth Century.* | |
| Stanley, *Through the Dark Continent.* | |
| *Zola, *L'Assommoir:* naturalistic fiction. | |
| 1879 Meredith, *The Egoist:* "plotless" novel along lines of "high comedy." | 1879 Howells, *The Lady of the Aroostook.* |
| Spencer, *Data of Ethics.* | Cable, *Old Creole Days.* |
| Browning, *Dramatic Idylls* (1st ser.). | Stockton, *Rudder Grange.* |
| | Fiske, *Darwinism.* |
| *Ibsen, *The Doll's House.* | Burroughs, *Locusts and Wild Honey.* |
| | Henry George, *Progress and Poverty:* radical economic theory, "single tax." |

## 1880[1]

| | |
|---|---|
| 1880–1892 *De Maupassant: novels and influential short stories. | |
| 1880 George Gissing: *Workers in the Dawn.* | 1880 Longfellow, *Ultima Thule.* |
| Gladstone Prime Minister. | Joel Chandler Harris, *Uncle Remus:* a classic collection of negro dialect folk tales. |
| | Cable, *The Grandissimes.* |
| | Lew Wallace, *Ben Hur.* |
| | Lanier, *Science of English Verse.* |

[1]Names in this Outline appearing for the first time in 1880 or thereafter are entered with initials or Christian names.

| ENGLISH | AMERICAN |
|---|---|
| 1881 Stevenson, *Virginibus Puerisque:* informal essays. | 1881 James, *Portrait of a Lady.* |
| Rossetti, *Ballads and Sonnets.* | Cable, *Madame Delphine.* |
| Swinburne, *Mary Stuart.* | *Century Magazine* established. |
| Death of Carlyle. | |
| *Ibsen, *Ghosts.* | |
| *"Anatole France," *The Crime of Sylvestre Bonnard.* | |
| 1882 Swinburne, *Tristram of Lyonesse.* | 1882 Mark Twain, *The Prince and the Pauper.* |
| Stevenson, *Familiar Studies, New Arabian Nights, Treasure Island.* | Howells, *A Modern Instance.* |
| Froude, *Life of Carlyle.* | Whitman, *Specimen Days.* |
| Death of Darwin, Rossetti, Trollope. | |
| 1883 Sir James Robert Seeley, *Expansion of England:* marks rise of imperialistic movement. | 1883 Mark Twain, *Life on the Mississippi:* semi-autobiographic "epic of the Mississippi." |
| Olive Schreiner, *The Story of an African Farm:* social and religious ideas. | Riley, *The Ole Swimmin' Hole.* |
| | Edgar W. Howe, *Story of a Country Town.* |
| | Joel Chandler Harris, *Nights with Uncle Remus.* |
| 1884 Tennyson, *Becket.* | 1884 Mark Twain, *Huckleberry Finn.* |
| Henry Arthur Jones, *Saints and Sinners* (a). | Stockton, *The Lady or the Tiger?* |
| *Daudet, *Sapho.* | Sarah Orne Jewett, *A Country Doctor.* |
| | "Charles Egbert Craddock," *In the Tennessee Mountains:* dialect tales. |
| 1885 W. H. Hudson, *The Purple Land.* | 1885 Howells, *Rise of Silas Lapham:* realistic novel of New England life. |
| Sir William Gilbert and Sir Arthur Sullivan, *The Mikado* (a). | |

| ENGLISH | AMERICAN |
|---|---|
| Meredith, *Diana of the Crossways.* | Woodrow Wilson, *Congressional Government.* |
| Ruskin, *Praeterita.* | |
| Stevenson, *Child's Garden of Verses.* | |
| *Dictionary of National Biography*, Vol. I: great biographical encyclopedia. | |
| 1886 Hardy, *Mayor of Casterbridge.* | 1886 Lowell, *Democracy.* |
| Stevenson, *Doctor Jekyll and Mr. Hyde; Kidnapped.* | Howells, *Indian Summer.* |
| Tennyson, *Locksley Hall Sixty Years After.* | Henry W. Grady, *The New South.* |
| Rudyard Kipling, *Departmental Ditties.* | James, *The Bostonians.* |
| | *Scribner's Magazine* established. |
| 1887 Andrew Lang, *Myth, Ritual, and Religion.* | 1887 Thomas Nelson Page, *In Ole Virginia:* romantic short stories of the old South. |
| *Strindberg, *The Fathers:* Swedish influence on realistic novel and drama. | Francis Marion Crawford, *Saracinesca.* |
| | Mary E. Wilkins Freeman, *A Humble Romance:* New England local-color stories. |
| | Octave Thanet, *Knitters in the Sun:* short stories. |
| 1888 Rudyard Kipling, *Plain Tales from the Hills:* journalistic, romantic, local-color stories. | 1888 James, *Partial Portraits.* |
| Mrs. Humphrey Ward, *Robert Elsmere:* Oxford life, science and religion. | Lowell, *Political Essays.* |
| | Edward Bellamy, *Looking Backward:* a utopia of the future. |
| Charles Montagu Doughty, *Travels in Arabia Deserta.* | |
| Death of Arnold. | |

| ENGLISH | AMERICAN |
|---|---|
| 1889 Browning, *Asolando*. | 1889 Mark Twain, *A Connecticut Yankee at King Arthur's Court:* satire on chivalry. |
| Stevenson, *Master of Ballantrae*. | |
| Pater, *Appreciations*. | Fiske, *Beginnings of New England*. |
| James Barrie, *A Window in Thrums:* regional fiction. | |
| Death of Browning. | Theodore Roosevelt, *Winning of the West*. |
| | Bronson Howard, *Shenandoah* (a). |

## 1890

| | |
|---|---|
| 1890 William Watson, *Wordsworth's Grave*. | 1890 Holmes, *Over the Teacups*. |
| | Emily Dickinson, *Poems*. |
| Robert Bridges, *Shorter Poems*. | E. C. Bunner, *Short Sixes:* "stories to be read while the candle burns." |
| | William James, *Principles of Psychology*. |
| 1891 Hardy, *Tess of the D'Urbervilles*. | 1891 Hamlin Garland, *Main Travelled Roads:* realistic midwestern "pioneer" stories. |
| Sir Arthur Conan Doyle, *Adventures of Sherlock Holmes*. | |
| | Ambrose Bierce, *In the Midst of Life*. |
| James Barrie, *The Little Minister:* sentimental novel. | |
| | F. Hopkinson Smith, *Colonel Carter of Cartersville*. |
| George Gissing, *The New Grub Street*. | |
| | Mary E. Wilkins Freeman, *A New England Nun*. |
| Rudyard Kipling, *The Light that Failed*. | |
| | James Lane Allen, *Flute and Violin*. |
| Independent Theatre opened: beginning of "Little Theatre" movement in England. | |
| | Richard Harding Davis, *Gallagher and Other Stories*. |
| | Howells, *Criticism and Fiction*. |
| | International Copyright Act: protecting rights of foreign authors and publishers. |

| ENGLISH | AMERICAN |
|---|---|
| 1892 Rudyard Kipling, *Barrack Room Ballads*. | 1892 Thomas Nelson Page, *The Old South*. |
| William E. Henley, *Song of the Sword*. | Bronson Howard, *Aristocracy* (*a*). |
| Israel Zangwill, *Children of the Ghetto*. | *Yale Review* established. |
| Oscar Wilde, *Lady Windermere's Fan* (*a*). | |
| Death of Tennyson. | |
| 1893 W. H. Hudson, *Idle Days in Patagonia*. | |
| Francis Thompson, *Poems:* the Catholic revival. | 1893 James, *The Real Thing and Other Tales*. |
| George Bernard Shaw, *Mrs. Warren's Profession* (*w*. acted 1902). | |
| Arthur Wing Pinero, *The Second Mrs. Tanqueray* (*a*). | |
| 1894 William Butler Yeats, *Land of Heart's Desire*. | 1894 Howells, *A Traveler from Altruria*. |
| George Moore, *Esther Waters*. | Bliss Carman and Richard Hovey, *Songs from Vagabondia*. |
| Rudyard Kipling, *Jungle Book*. | Lafcadio Hearn, *Glimpses of Unfamiliar Japan*. |
| "Anthony Hope," *Prisoner of Zenda*. | |
| "Ian Maclaren," *Beside the Bonny Briar Bush:* sentimentalization of Scotch life. | |
| Death of Stevenson. | |
| 1895 Oscar Wilde, *The Importance of Being Earnest* (*a*). | 1895 Stephen Crane, *The Red Badge of Courage*. |
| H. G. Wells, *The Time Machine*. | Alice Brown, *Meadow Grass:* New England tales. |
| Joseph Conrad, *Almayer's Folly*. | F. Hopkinson Smith, *A Gentleman Vagabond and Some Others*. |
| Rudyard Kipling, *The Brushwood Boy:* psychological short story. | |

ENGLISH

1896 A. E. Housman, *A Shropshire Lad.*

James Barrie, *Sentimental Tommy.*

Hardy, *Jude the Obscure:* novel based on author's philosophy of futility.

Alfred Austin made Poet Laureate.

1897 Stephen Phillips, *Poems.*

Joseph Conrad, *The Nigger of the Narcissus.*

Rudyard Kipling, *Captains Courageous.*

1898 Hardy, *Wessex Poems.*

George Bernard Shaw, *Plays Pleasant and Unpleasant.*

Oscar Wilde, *Ballad of Reading Gaol.*

George Moore, *Evelyn Innes.*

H. G. Wells, *The War of the Worlds:* romance.

1899 Stephen Phillips, *Paolo and Francesca.*

Irish Literary Theatre founded in Dublin.

AMERICAN

1896 Stephen Crane, *Maggie: A Girl of the Streets.*

Edwin Arlington Robinson, *The Torrent and the Night Before.*

Owen Wister, *Red Men and White:* short stories of the West.

John Fox, Jr., *A Cumberland Vendetta and Other Stories.*

1897 James Lane Allen, *The Choir Invisible.*

1898 Thomas Wentworth Higginson, *Cheerful Yesterdays.*

Thomas Nelson Page, *Red Rock.*

Edward Noyes Westcott, *David Harum.*

Margaret Deland, *Old Chester Tales.*

1899 Winston Churchill, *Richard Carvel.*

Stephen Crane, *War is Kind.*

Peter Finley Dunne, *Mr. Dooley in Peace and War.*

Booth Tarkington, *Gentleman from Indiana.*

William Allen White, *The Court of Boyville:* short stories.

Edwin Markham, *The Man with the Hoe:* passionate appeal for social justice.

## 1900–1930 Triumph of Realism

### ENGLISH

**1900–1930 The period as a whole marked by two great influences—the shock brought by the War and the development of science.** The first decade (1900–1910) belongs to the "Edwardians"—Barrie, Bennett, Conrad, Kipling, Yeats and others. Prose becomes more serious than in the nineties; novelists concerned with effort to evolve a philosophy of life. The second decade (1910–1920) is given over to the Georgians, whose first interest is in realistic writing of the World War. Continental influences noted in the period 1870–1900 develop further, particularly the realism of the Russian writers. The advancement of the new science, especially Freudian psychology, promotes characterization in the novel, creates a new manner in biography, and makes poetry more esoteric. The World War brings new enthusiasms and points of view and the development of realism greatly increases range of subject matter for novelist, story writer, and poet. Galsworthy, Wells, Shaw, and others manifest strong interest in problems of society. Many women assume importance in prose fiction. The new poetic fervor noticeable particularly in the second decade with growth of Imagist movement after 1912. All these new interests and subject matters accompanied likewise by changes in technique. Plot loses ground as interest in characterization

### AMERICAN

**1900–1930 The World War the most important factor in the history and thought of this period.** The first effect of the War a unifying of the interests of the people, but this is succeeded in 1919 and later years by a feeling of frustration and disillusionment. Science develops rapidly; inventions such as the automobile and airplane intensify activity and accelerate the tempo; results reflected in literature and thought. Muckraking in the early years an important feature in magazines and books. The newspaper contributes a practically new type of writing—the "column" ("F. P. A.," Morley, Broun, Marquis). Interest in local color dominant in last two decades of nineteenth century dies out, except in the South, in the first half of this period. The Negro is suddenly discovered as a literary figure for realistic fiction and drama and poetry—the Negro himself joining white authors in writing about his race. Realism swings over to naturalism in such writers as Theodore Dreiser, Evelyn Scott, and William Faulkner. The decade from 1915 to 1925 important as bringing a revolt from past interests and manners. The "new" psychology an important element in this revolt (Floyd Dell, John Dos Passos, and Sherwood Anderson). This same revolt evident in work of poets of the Imagist group and others. In general this may be develops. Biography reflects the new psychological interest in character; Strachey especially successful in this form. Biography adopts methods of fiction (under impetus of Maurois) and fiction becomes biographic. As a whole technique and form give way to freedom of treatment and greater tolerance of content. Many literary conventions are broken down.

POETRY.–Period opens with Edwardian poets (Austin, Bridges, Watson, Kipling, Newbolt, Noyes) pretty firmly fixed in one or another tradition of the Victorians and with Ireland speaking with such new voices as those of "A. E." (Russell) and Yeats. About 1911 the realistic movement affects the poets (Masefield's *Everlasting Mercy*). Georgian poetry soon becomes experimental (Harold Monro's *Georgian Poetry* anthologies). New poets (Rupert Brooke, John Drinkwater, W. W. Gibson) revolt against the niceties of the Victorian manner. The Imagist movement (see p. 208), with Richard Aldington as chief figure, gives incentive to much experimentation; verse becomes fantastic, esoteric, metaphysical, intellectual, and, in all these aspects, largely realistic.

thought of as a time when American literature becomes cosmopolitan. The frontier development is definitely a past aspect of our life. The World War forces America to more definite international relationships than the country has known before. While bitter doubt of our civilization follows directly upon the War, the new international point of view which the country has gained serves definitely to enrich our intellectual life and to cause American writers to look at our institutions with a new understanding and a broader outlook.

POETRY.–The first decade continues the barrenness of the nineties; it is conventional and imitative of the Victorian manner. Hovey and Carman rebel (*Vagabondia* series) against the anemic niceties and *isms* of the age, and Moody writes poetry with great resentment at social and political injustices in America. The founding of *Poetry: A Magazine of Verse* (1912) by Harriet Monroe conventionally given as the focal point for a new enthusiasm which stirred the poets of America. Experimentation becomes rife; beauty sought in new places; old forms and clichés tabooed. In 1915 is published an anthology, *Some Imagist Poets*. The Imagist group, with Amy Lowell as its chief American spokesman, entrenches itself and fights back all attackers valiantly. Free verse revived. The movement wanes after a few years but not until Amy Lowell, Carl Sandburg, John Gould Fletcher, "H. D.", and others have revivified poetry, striking from it the shackles of convention, and arousing audiences of poetry readers all over America. Robert Frost and Edwin Arlington Robinson express New England life and character with vigor and simplicity; Vachel Lindsay crusades for rhythm and the reading aloud of verse, trying to bring beauty to his Middle West; Elinor Wylie and Edna St. Vincent Millay prove authentic new poets. Extremists like Pound, Kreymborg, Cummings, and Williams persist in cerebral experimentation. The period closes with American poetry greatly freshened and invigorated.

PROSE.—Very active prose interest, particularly in fiction, in the second decade. The first ten years (1900–1910) dominated by such writers as Conrad, Galsworthy, Bennett, and Wells who are realistically concerned with social problems and life. Influence of Samuel Butler's *Way of All Flesh* important particularly among such Georgian novelists as Walpole and Maugham. World War (1914–1918) single most important subject as reflected in work of writers like T. E. Lawrence, Ford Madox Ford, May Sinclair, Sylvia Thompson, and H. G. Wells. The way having been prepared by realism of the previous decades, fiction accepts the sex-psychology of Freud,

PROSE.—Of the three trends inherited from previous decades— local color, historical romance, and realism—the first two drop from importance after the first decade. The influence of Howells and James uppermost in first decade. Decorum prominent quality. Realism, however, soon flourishes and actually passes over into naturalism. Even historical romances sometimes become realistic (Boyd's *Drums*). When interest in local color remains novels give up their romantic quality and become realistic novels of the soil, as, for instance, Ellen Glasgow's *Barren Ground* and Elizabeth Madox Roberts' *Time of Man*. The novel of outdoor adventure is capitalized by such writers as

562

ENGLISH

and human character is interpreted frequently from this angle: James Joyce, Aldous Huxley, Virginia Woolf, Rebecca West. Many new feminine writers come to the front: E. M. Delafield, Sheila Kaye-Smith, G. B. Stern, Stella Benson, Margaret Kennedy, V. Sackville-West, those already mentioned above, and others. The short story grows in importance at hands of writers like Katherine Mansfield, Virginia Woolf, Thomas Burke, Aldous Huxley, and A. E. Coppard. Biography, under the influence of Lytton Strachey and *André Maurois (see p. 56), takes on new methods and new importance. Technique during the three decades gives way to the freedom resulting from realistic and naturalistic enthusiasms.

AMERICAN

Jack London. The sentimental novel of the past persists in the work of John Fox, Jr., Gene Stratton-Porter, and Harold Bell Wright. The novel and story of social problems become important. Evidence of the change which has come over prose is best observed in the contrast between such names as Edith Wharton, Booth Tarkington, Winston Churchill (earlier in the period), and Theodore Dreiser, James Branch Cabell, Sherwood Anderson, Sinclair Lewis, Ernest Hemingway (later in the period). These three decades also see numerous feminine writers assuming importance: Edith Wharton, Willa Cather, Dorothy Canfield Fisher, Zona Gale, and Julia Peterkin. DuBose Heyward, Paul Green, Roark Bradford, and others write of the Negro in a manner quite different from that of Harris, Page, and Cable of an earlier generation. Walter White, W. E. DuBois, and Benjamin Brawley write of their own Negro race. The novel becomes psychological and socialistic. The short story for a while threatens to become standardized; the first two decades are the era of the short-story handbook and formuli; rapid increase in number of low-priced magazines. From 1920 on the story frees itself from convention and becomes experimental with deep interest in character and less in plot.

DRAMA.–The period is dominated by four great dramatists: Shaw, Galsworthy, Granville-

DRAMA.–The first decade unimportant in drama. Commercial drama in control and

Barker, and Barrie. With Shaw as a leading figure, the Ibsen influence, strong in the previous period, continues to grow and drama is characteristically realistic. New technique for settings is developed—often impressionistic—and much change in stage technique. While Barrie and Dunsany maintain the romantic tradition, realism is characteristic, and as a result less emphasis is placed on plot and structure and more on subject matter related to life. The new psychology affects drama as well as novel, short story, and poetry. Galsworthy notable for his concern with social problems. Period marked by two important movements: the Celtic Renaissance (Yeats, Russell, Colum, Ervine, Synge, and Lady Gregory) focusing about the Abbey Theater in Dublin, and the development of the repertory theater in the English provinces. The end of the period closes with drama less flourishing than in its opening decade.

European models frequently imitated. Clyde Fitch, Augustus Thomas, and David Belasco the leaders of this time; David Warfield the great actor. Belasco develops realistic stage settings. Many plays, but little great art. Little Theatre movement of the second decade does much to educate audiences to possibilities of the theatre. The "art" and the "community" theatres take on importance. William Vaughn Moody (*The Great Divide*), Josephine Peabody (*The Piper*) and Percy MacKaye (*This Fine Pretty World*) introduce literary drama as distinguished from the commercial. Comedy not especially important, except in *revues* and vaudeville, but Rachel Crothers (*Expressing Willie*) is significant figure. "Folk" drama is made popular by such writers as Lulu Vollmer, Hatcher Hughes, and Paul Green and by work in universities such as is done by Professor Koch at North Carolina. The aftermath of the War brings such plays as *What Price Glory*. Realistic comedy and disillusionment. The Negro, as in other literary forms, becomes significant in the work of DuBose Heyward, Roark Bradford, and Paul Green. Sidney Howard scores successes. The major figure of American drama for the whole period, however, is Eugene O'Neill who unites poetry and romance with realism and whose experiments promise greatly to enrich American dramatic literature.

ENGLISH

1900 Laurence Binyon, *Odes*.

Joseph Conrad, *Lord Jim*.

Maurice Hewlett, *Life and Death of Richard Yea-and-Nay*.

W. H. Hudson, *Nature in Downland*.

*Edmond Rostand, *L'Aiglon*.

Death of Ruskin.

1901 James Barrie, *Quality Street*.

Rudyard Kipling, *Kim:* the philosophy of India in the adventures of a half-caste lad.

Death of Victoria.

1901–1910 Reign of Edward VII.

1902 Hilaire Belloc, *The Path to Rome*.

AMERICAN

1900 George Ade, *Fables in Slang:* a successful continuation of the American humorous tradition.

Alexander V. G. Allen, *Life and Letters of Phillips Brooks*.

Irving Bacheller, *Eben Holden*.

Stephen Crane, *Wounds in the Rain:* War stories with little plot, avoiding convention and sentiment.

Theodore Dreiser, *Sister Carrie*.

Finley Peter Dunne, *Mr. Dooley's Philosophy*.

Mary Johnston, *To Have and to Hold*.

Jack London, *The Son of the Wolf:* short stories of vigorous adventure expressing a revolt against sentimentalism.

Booth Tarkington, *Monsieur Beaucaire*.

1901 W. C. Brownell, *Victorian Prose Masters*.

Winston Churchill, *The Crisis*.

William Vaughn Moody, *Poems*.

Frank Norris, *The Octopus:* the first of a planned American trilogy based on the story of wheat.

Alice Hegan Rice, *Mrs. Wiggs of the Cabbage Patch*.

Booker T. Washington, *Up From Slavery*.

1902 Ellen Glasgow, *The Battle-Ground*.

## ENGLISH

Arnold Bennett, *Anna of the Five Towns.*

Joseph Conrad, *Youth.*

Lady Gregory, *Cuchulain of Muirthemne.*

John Masefield, *Saltwater Ballads.*

W. B. Yeats, *Cathleen ni Hoolihan.*

Death of Samuel Butler.

1903 Joseph Conrad, *Typhoon and Other Stories.*

W. H. Hudson, *Hampshire Days.*

Rudyard Kipling, *The Five Nations.*

George Bernard Shaw, *Man and Superman.*

Samuel Butler, *The Way of All Flesh.*

1904 James Barrie, *Peter Pan.*

Thomas Hardy, *The Dynasts* (first part).

Hilaire Belloc, *The Old Road.*

Joseph Conrad, *Nostromo.*

W. H. Hudson, *Green Mansions.*

Rudyard Kipling, *Traffics and Discoveries.*

May Sinclair, *The Divine Fire.*

*Anton Chekhov, *The Cherry Orchard.*

*Romain Rolland, *Jean Christophe:* "an epic of French life," publication begun 1904, finished 1912.

## AMERICAN

Bliss Perry, *A Study of Prose Fiction.*

F. Hopkinson Smith, *Fortunes of Oliver Horn.*

Stewart Edward White, *The Blazed Trail.*

Owen Wister, *The Virginian.*

Death of Bret Harte.

1903 Samuel McChord Crothers, *The Gentle Reader.*

Margaret Deland, *Dr. Lavendar's People.*

John Fox, Jr., *The Little Shepherd of Kingdom Come.*

Jack London, *The Call of the Wild.*

Frank Norris, *The Pit.*

Kate Douglas Wiggin, *Rebecca of Sunnybrook Farm.*

1904 Winston Churchill, *The Crossing.*

O. Henry, *Cabbages and Kings.*

Robert Herrick, *The Common Lot.*

James Gibbons Huneker, *Overtones.*

Jack London, *The Sea-Wolf.*

William Vaughn Moody, *The Fire-Bringer.*

Paul Elmer More, *Shelburne Essays:* an important series of critical essays continuing under this title until 1921.
Stewart Edward White, *The Silent Places.*

1905 Edward Carpenter, *Towards Democracy* (complete edition).

G. K. Chesterton, *Heretics.*

Henry Arthur Jones, *Mrs. Dane's Defence.*

John Masefield, *A Mainsail Haul.*

J. M. Synge, *Riders to the Sea:* drama important in Celtic revival.

1906 Joseph Conrad, *Mirror of the Sea.*

William De Morgan, *Joseph Vance.*

Rudyard Kipling, *Puck of Pook's Hill.*

William Watson, *Collected Poems.*

1907 Max Beerbohm, *A Book of Caricatures.*

Algernon Blackwood, *The Listener.*

Padraic Colum, *Wild Earth.*
Jerome K. Jerome, *Passing of the Third Floor Back.*

George Russell (A. E.), *Deirdre.*

J. M. Synge, *Playboy of the Western World.*

W. B. Yeats, *Deirdre.*

*Maxim Gorki, *Mother:* the proletarian in fiction.

1908 Arnold Bennett, *The Old Wives' Tale.*

G. K. Chesterton, *The Man Who Was Thursday.*

1905 Edith Wharton, *The House of Mirth.*

1906 Henry Adams, *The Education of Henry Adams* (privately printed).

O. Henry, *The Four Million.*

Upton Sinclair, *The Jungle.*

Owen Wister, *Lady Baltimore.*

Beginning of "Little Theatre" movement in America.

1907 Clyde Fitch, *The Truth.*

George Edward Woodberry, *The Appreciation of Literature.*

1908 O. Henry, *The Voice of the City.*

Robert Herrick, *Together.*

Charles Rann Kennedy, *The Servant in the House.*

| ENGLISH | AMERICAN |
|---|---|
| H. G. Wells, *New Worlds for Old; Tono-Bungay.* | |
| James Barrie, *What Every Woman Knows.* | |
| *Anatole France, *Penguin Island.* | |

| | ENGLISH | | AMERICAN |
|---|---|---|---|
| 1909 | H. Granville-Barker, *Three Plays.* | 1909 | W. C. Brownell, *American Prose Masters.* |
| | John Galsworthy, *Plays.* | | Josephine Preston Peabody, *The Piper.* |
| | Lady Gregory, *Seven Short Plays.* | | Lizette Woodworth Reese, *A Wayside Lute.* |
| | Rudyard Kipling, *Actions and Reactions.* | | Hamlin Garland, *Cavanagh, Forest Ranger.* |
| | H. G. Wells, *Ann Veronica.* | | |
| | Death of Meredith. | | James Gibbons Huneker, *Promenades of an Impressionist.* |
| | John Masefield, *The Tragedy of Nan.* | | William Vaughn Moody, *The Great Divide.* |

## 1910

| | ENGLISH | | AMERICAN |
|---|---|---|---|
| 1910 | Richard Aldington, *Images: early imagist verse.* | 1910 | Edwin Arlington Robinson, *The Town Down the River.* |
| | H. Granville-Barker, *The Madras House.* | | Edward Sheldon, *The Nigger.* |
| | Arnold Bennett, *Clayhanger.* | | Death of William Vaughn Moody. |
| | Lord Dunsany, *A Dreamer's Tales.* | | Death of Mark Twain. |
| | John Galsworthy, *Justice.* | | |
| | W. H. Hudson, *A Shepherd's Life.* | | |
| | Rudyard Kipling, *Rewards and Fairies.* | | |
| | Henry Newbolt, *Collected Poems.* | | |
| | Alfred Noyes, *Collected Poems.* | | |
| | Death of Edward VII. | | |

1910–1936 Reign of George V.

1911 Max Beerbohm, *Zuleika Dobson.*

Arnold Bennett, *Hilda Lessways.*

J. D. Beresford, *Jacob Stahl.*

G. K. Chesterton, *The Innocence of Father Brown.*

Jeffery Farnol, *The Broad Highway.*

John Galsworthy, *The Patrician.*

Edmund Gosse, *Collected Poems.*

L. P. Jacks, *Among the Idolmakers.*

Stephen Leacock, *Nonsense Novels.*

John Masefield, *The Everlasting Mercy.*

George Moore, *Hail and Farewell.*

Arthur Pinero, *Mid-Channel.*

1912 Robert Bridges, *Poetical Works.*

John Galsworthy, *The Pigeon.*

Harold Monro (ed.), *Georgian Poetry.*

Bertrand Russell, *The Problems of Philosophy.*

James Stephens, *The Crock of Gold.*

H. M. Tomlinson, *The Sea and the Jungle.*

1911 Mary Austin, *The Arrow Maker.*

David Belasco, *The Return of Peter Grimm.*

Theodore Dreiser, *Jennie Gerhardt.*

Anne Douglas Sedgwick, *Tante.*

Henry Van Dyke, *Collected Poems.*

Edith Wharton, *Ethan Frome.*

1912 Mary Austin, *A Woman of Genius.*

Bliss Carman, *Echoes from Vagabondia.*

Amy Lowell, *A Dome of Many-Colored Glass:* conventional verse and some imagist pieces.

Bliss Perry, *The American Mind.*

*Poetry: A Magazine of Verse:* edited by Harriet Monroe in Chicago, this new publication for many years served as a focal point for all movements in the "new poetry."

1913 Edmund Gosse, *Collected Essays.*

D. H. Lawrence, *Sons and Lovers.*

Compton Mackenzie, *Sinister Street.*

John Masefield, *Dauber.*

Death of Alfred Austin.

Robert Bridges made Poet Laureate.

*Marcel Proust, *A la recherche du temps perdu:* publication begun 1913 and finished 1925; a long novel notable for its searching presentation of human motives and "acute sensitivity." Stream-of-consciousness method.

1914 James Barrie, *Admirable Crichton.*

James Barrie, *Half Hours:* plays.

Cunninghame Graham, *Scottish Stories.*

May Sinclair, *The Three Sisters.*

1915 John Buchan, *Greenmantle.*

Joseph Conrad, *Victory.*

1913 Willa Cather, *O Pioneers!*

Winston Churchill, *The Inside of the Cup.*

Max Eastman, *The Enjoyment of Poetry.*

Vachel Lindsay, *General William Booth Enters into Heaven.*

Edith Wharton, *The Custom of the Country.*

1914 Robert Frost, *North of Boston:* New England settings again presented through poetry.

Vachel Lindsay, *The Congo:* Lindsay carries his theory of rhythm and sound in poetry to its greatest development.

Amy Lowell, *Sword Blades and Poppy Seeds:* Miss Lowell's first important imagist volume.

James Oppenheim, *Songs for the New Age.*

Gertrude Stein, *Tender Buttons:* example of experimentation in modern literature.

Booth Tarkington, *Penrod.*

*Des Imagistes:* an early imagist anthology.

1915 Van Wyck Brooks, *America's Coming of Age.*

ENGLISH

John Galsworthy, *The Free-lands:* social criticism.

W. Somerset Maugham, *Of Human Bondage:* a realistic novel of mental experience.

Dorothy Richardson, *Pointed Roofs.*

George Bernard Shaw, *Fanny's First Play.*

Francis Brett Young, *The Dark Tower.*

H. G. Wells, *The Research Magnificent.*

1916 Thomas Burke, *Limehouse Nights.*

W. H. Davies, *Collected Poems.*

Lord Dunsany, *Tales of Wonder.*

James Joyce, *Portrait of the Artist as a Young Man.*

George Moore, *The Brook Kerith.*

George Bernard Shaw, *Androcles and the Lion; Pygmalion.*

Hugh Walpole, *The Dark Forest.*

*Henri Barbusse, *Le Feu:* brutally realistic chronicle of the World War.

H. G. Wells, *Mr. Britling Sees It Through.*

AMERICAN

James Branch Cabell, *The Rivet in Grandfather's Neck.*

Dorothy Canfield Fisher, *The Bent Twig.*

Robert Frost, *A Boy's Will.*

James Gibbons Huneker, *Ivory Apes and Peacocks.*

Edgar Lee Masters, *Spoon River Anthology:* the American small town treated realistically and satirically in important verse.

John G. Neihardt, *The Song of Hugh Glass.*

Ernest Poole, *The Harbor.*

1916 Irvin S. Cobb, *Old Judge Priest.*

Robert Frost, *Mountain Interval.*

Amy Lowell, *Men, Women and Ghosts.*

Agnes Repplier, *Counter-Currents.*

Edwin Arlington Robinson, *The Man Against the Sky.*

Carl Sandburg, *Chicago Poems:* poetry found in the stock yards.

Alan Seeger, *Poems.*

Booth Tarkington, *Seventeen.*

Mark Twain, *The Mysterious Stranger.*

*Some Imagist Poets:* a collection of the work of several poets.

Death of Henry James.

Death of Jack London.

| ENGLISH | AMERICAN |
|---|---|
| 1917 Norman Douglas, *South Wind:* sophisticated, social novel with little plot. | 1917 Hamlin Garland, *A Son of the Middle Border.* |
| Ralph Hodgson, *Poems.* | Joseph Hergesheimer, *The Three Black Pennys.* |
| Frank Swinnerton, *Nocturne.* | Amy Lowell, *Tendencies in Modern American Poetry:* important critical statement of purposes of imagist movement. |
| | H. L. Mencken, *A Book of Prefaces.* |
| | Edna St. Vincent Millay, *Renascence.* |
| | Christopher Morley, *Songs for a Little House.* |
| | Stuart P. Sherman, *On Contemporary Literature.* |
| 1918 James Barrie, *Echoes of the War:* plays. | 1918 William Beebe, *Jungle Peace:* nature and science in the jungle. |
| Rupert Brooke, *Collected Poems.* | Willa Cather, *My Ántonia.* |
| John Drinkwater, *Abraham Lincoln.* | Max Eastman, *Colors of Life.* |
| W. H. Hudson, *Far Away and Long Ago:* autobiography of the youth of a naturalist. | Amy Lowell, *Can Grande's Castle.* |
| | Christopher Morley, *Shandygaff.* |
| D. H. Lawrence, *New Poems.* | |
| Stephen Leacock, *Frenzied Fiction.* | |
| Arthur Quiller-Couch, *Studies in Literature.* | |
| Lytton Strachey, *Eminent Victorians.* | |
| Hugh Walpole, *The Green Mirror.* | |
| H. G. Wells, *Joan and Peter, the Story of an Education.* | |

ENGLISH

AMERICAN

1919 Stella Benson, *Living Alone.*

Joseph Conrad, *The Arrow of Gold.*

Clemence Dane, *Legend.*

Havelock Ellis, *The Philosophy of Conflict.*

W. W. Jacobs, *Deep Waters.*

Sheila Kaye-Smith, *Tamarisk Town.*

W. Somerset Maugham, *The Moon and Sixpence.*

George Bernard Shaw, *Heartbreak House.*

1919 Sherwood Anderson, *Winesburg, Ohio:* psychological and realistic stories of small-town American life.

Irving Babbitt, *Rousseau and Romanticism:* provocative criticism on the romantic attitude.

John Burroughs, *Field and Study.*

James Branch Cabell, *Jurgen:* artistry and the *double entendre,* with the help of American censorship, make a popular classic.

T. A. Daly, *McAroni Ballads.*

Joseph Hergesheimer, *Java Head.*

Fannie Hurst, *Humoresque.*

Amy Lowell, *Pictures of the Floating World.*

H. L. Mencken, *The American Language.*

Eugene O'Neill, *The Moon of the Caribbees.*

Upton Sinclair, *The Brass Check.*

## 1920

1920 James Barrie, *A Kiss for Cinderella.*

Walter De la Mare, *Collected Poems.*

Katherine Mansfield, *Bliss.*

H. G. Wells, *The Outline of History:* introduces the "capsule formula" for knowledge.

*Maxim Gorki, *Recollections.*

1920 Sherwood Anderson, *Poor White.*

Floyd Dell, *Moon-Calf.*

William E. B. DuBois, *Darkwater.*

Zona Gale, *Miss Lulu Bett.*

Sinclair Lewis, *Main Street:* a study of the mores and culture of an American small town.

Eugene O'Neill, *Beyond the Horizon.*

Carl Sandburg, *Smoke and Steel.*

F. J. Turner, *The Frontier in American Literature:* an essay which has greatly influenced the modern conception of American history and literature.

Edith Wharton, *The Age of Innocence.*

Death of William Dean Howells.

1921 Walter De la Mare, *Memoirs of a Midget.*

Sheila Kaye-Smith, *Joanna Godden:* an English novel of local color and character.

Rudyard Kipling, *Verse* (Inclusive edition).

Lytton Strachey, *Queen Victoria:* the "new biography" is established.

George Moore, *Héloïse and Abélard.*

1921 Floyd Dell, *The Briary-Bush.*

John Dos Passos, *Three Soldiers:* the World War realistically presented in fiction.

Dorothy Canfield Fisher, *The Brimming Cup.*

Ben Hecht, *Erik Dorn.*

Eugene O'Neill, *The Emperor Jones.*

Edwin Arlington Robinson, *Collected Poems.*

Booth Tarkington, *Alice Adams.*

John V. A. Weaver, *In American.*

Elinor Wylie, *Nets to Catch the Wind.*

1922 John Galsworthy, *Loyalties; The Forsyte Saga:* social, economic, political study of the times through the recording of the life of an English family.

David Garnett, *Lady into Fox.*

A. E. Housman, *Last Poems.*

James Joyce, *Ulysses:* psychological, naturalistic, plotless novel.

1922 Hervey Allen, in collaboration with DuBose Heyward, *Carolina Chansons:* a volume of poems ushering in the recent poetry revival in the South.

Gamaliel Bradford, *American Portraits.*

Henry Seidel Canby, *Definitions.*

T. S. Eliot, *The Waste Land:* intellectualized experimentation in verse.

ENGLISH

Katherine Mansfield, *The Garden Party and Other Stories:* realistic stories of character.

Hugh Walpole, *The Cathedral.*

Rebecca West, *The Judge.*

Virginia Woolf, *Jacob's Room.*

W. B. Yeats, *Later Poems.*

*Arthur Schnitzler, *Casanova's Homecoming.*

1923 Hilaire Belloc, *Sonnets and Verse.*

A. E. Coppard, *The Black Dog.*

John Drinkwater, *Collected Poems.*

Havelock Ellis, *The Dance of Life.*

Thomas Hardy, *Collected Poems.*

Rose Macaulay, *Told by an Idiot.*

Katherine Mansfield, *Poems.*

A. A. Milne, *Three Plays.*

Alice Meynell, *Poems.*

T. F. Powys, *Black Bryony.*

*André Maurois, *Ariel, or the Life of Shelley:* psychological biography which reads like fiction.

AMERICAN

Sinclair Lewis, *Babbitt:* modern realism used to satirize the American business man.

Ludwig Lewisohn, *Up Stream:* American civilization weighed by a cultivated and sensitive Jewish mind.

Christopher Morley, *Where the Blue Begins.*

Kathleen Norris, *Certain People of Importance.*

T. S. Stribling, *Birthright.*

Augustus Thomas, *The Copperhead.*

1923 Thomas Boyd, *Through the Wheat.*

Gamaliel Bradford, *Damaged Souls.*

James Branch Cabell, *The High Place.*

Willa Cather, *A Lost Lady.*

Samuel McChord Crothers, *The Cheerful Giver.*

Vachel Lindsay, *Collected Poems.*

George Santayana, *Poems.*

George Sterling, *Selected Poems.*

Sara Teasdale, *Poems.*

Louis Untermeyer, *American Poetry Since 1900:* important criticism on modern American poetry.

Carl Van Vechten, *The Blind Bow-Boy.*

Elinor Wylie, *Jennifer Lorn.*

| ENGLISH | AMERICAN |
|---|---|
| 1924 Ford Madox Ford, *Some Do Not.* | 1924 George Ade, *The County Chairman.* |
| E. M. Forster, *A Passage to India.* | Sherwood Anderson, *A Story-Teller's Story:* an autobiographical record which discloses the importance of the personal element in most of Anderson's writing. |
| Margaret Kennedy, *The Constant Nymph.* | |
| John Masefield, *Sard Harker.* | |
| A. A. Milne, *When We Were Very Young.* | Thomas Beer, *Sandoval.* |
| Eden Phillpotts, *Cheat-the-Boys.* | Louis Bromfield, *The Green Bay Tree.* |
| George Bernard Shaw, *Saint Joan.* | W. C. Brownell, *The Genius of Style.* |
| G. B. Stern, *Tents of Israel.* | Edna Ferber, *So Big.* |
| Death of Joseph Conrad. | DuBose Heyward, *Skylines and Horizons.* |
| | Percy MacKaye, *This Fine Pretty World.* |
| | Lewis Mumford, *Sticks and Stones.* |
| | Laurence Stallings, *Plumes:* "war and disillusionment." |
| 1925 John Galsworthy, *Caravan: The Assembled Tales of John Galsworthy.* | 1925 Sherwood Anderson, *Dark Laughter.* |
| Aldous Huxley, *Selected Poems.* | William Beebe, *Jungle Days.* |
| Virginia Woolf, *Mrs. Dalloway.* | James Boyd, *Drums:* realistic, historical romance of the Revolution in the South. |
| | E. E. Cummings, *XLI Poems:* American poetry attains the *n*th degree of experimentation. |
| | George Philip Krapp, *The English Language in America.* |
| | H. D. (Hilda Doolittle), *Collected Poems.* |

AMERICAN

Olive Tilford Dargan, *Highland Annals.*

John Dos Passos, *Manhattan Transfer.*

Theodore Dreiser, *An American Tragedy:* American realism becomes naturalistic.

Ellen Glasgow, *Barren Ground:* "realism crosses the Potomac."

DuBose Heyward, *Porgy.*

William Ellery Leonard, *Two Lives:* autobiographical record in a poignant sonnet sequence.

Eugene O'Neill, *Desire Under the Elms.*

Death of Amy Lowell.

1926 W. W. Gibson, *Collected Poems.*

Laurence Housman, *Ironical Tales.*

Aldous Huxley, *Two or Three Graces.*

Rudyard Kipling, *Debits and Credits.*

Bertrand Russell, *Education and the Good Life.*

George Russell (A. E.), *Collected Poems.*

Llewelyn Powys, *The Verdict of Bridlegoose.*

James Stephens, *Collected Poems.*

H. G. Wells, *The World of William Clissold.*

*Emil Ludwig, *Bismarck* (translated).

*Oswald Spengler, *The Decline of the West.*

1926 Maxwell Anderson, in collaboration with Laurence Stallings, *Three American Plays:* contains *What Price Glory,* a prominent play of life during the World War.

Ellen Glasgow, *The Romantic Comedians:* the Southern tradition gently satirized.

Paul Green, *Lonesome Road.*

Lizette Woodworth Reese, *Selected Poems.*

Elizabeth Madox Roberts, *The Time of Man.*

Carl Sandburg, *Selected Poems.*

Stuart Pratt Sherman, *Critical Woodcuts.*

Ruth Suckow, *Iowa Interiors.*

Thornton Wilder, *The Cabala.*

Stark Young, *Heaven Trees.*

577

ENGLISH

1927 G. K. Chesterton, *Collected Poems.*

T. E. Lawrence, *Revolt in the Desert:* a chronicle of the Great War in the Near East.

H. M. Tomlinson, *Gallions Reach.*

*Thomas Mann, *The Magic Mountain.*

1928 Donn Byrne, *Crusade.*

W. H. Davies, *Collected Poems.*

Aldous Huxley, *Point Counter Point:* a sophisticated, social record.

Eden Phillpotts, *The Ring Fence.*

T. F. Powys, *Mr. Weston's Good Wine.*

Humbert Wolfe, *This Blind Rose.*

*Emil Ludwig, *Goethe* (translated): psychological biography.

AMERICAN

1927 Willa Cather, *Death Comes for the Archbishop.*

Paul Green, *The Field God;* and *In Abraham's Bosom:* a Pulitzer Prize play with the Negro as a dramatic figure.

Robinson Jeffers, *The Women at Point Sur.*

William Ellery Leonard, *The Locomotive God:* the new psychology applied to autobiographical writing.

John Livingston Lowes, *The Road to Xanadu.*

Edna St. Vincent Millay, *The King's Henchman.*

Vernon L. Parrington, *Main Currents in American Thought:* an interpretation of American literature from the beginnings to 1920.

Edwin Arlington Robinson, *Tristram.*

Thornton Wilder, *The Bridge of San Luis Rey.*

1928 Stephen Vincent Benét, *John Brown's Body:* revival of the long poetic narrative in American Poetry.

Norman Foerster, *The Reinterpretation of American Literature.*

Amy Lowell, *Selected Poems.*

Eugene O'Neill, *Strange Interlude.*

Julia Peterkin, *Scarlet Sister Mary.*

Ezra Pound, *Selected Poems.*

ENGLISH

*Arnold Zweig, *The Case of Sergeant Grischa*.

Death of Thomas Hardy.

1929 Richard Aldington, *Death of a Hero*.

Robert Bridges, *The Testament of Beauty*.

Philip Gibbs, *Hidden City*.

Robert Graves, *Goodbye to All That*.

John Cowper Powys, *Wolf Solent*.

J. B. Priestley, *The Good Companions*.

Rebecca West, *Harriet Hume*.

John Galsworthy, *The Modern Comedy*.

1930 John Masefield, *Collected Poems*.

W. Somerset Maugham, *Cakes and Ale*.

Edith Sitwell, *Collected Poems*.

G. B. Stern, *Mosaic*.

H. M. Tomlinson, *All Our Yesterdays*.

Hugh Walpole, *Rogue Herries:* the first of an important trilogy.

Death of Bridges.

Masefield made Poet Laureate.

AMERICAN

Edith Wharton, *The Children*.

*Dictionary of American Biography*, Vol. I of a twenty-volume set.

William Ellery Leonard, *A Son of Earth*.

1929 Marcus Cook Connelly, *Green Pastures*.

Ernest Hemingway, *Farewell to Arms*.

Joseph Wood Krutch, *The Modern Temper:* searching criticism of the contemporary mind.

Walter Lippmann, *A Preface to Morals*.

Evelyn Scott, *The Wave*.

1930 William Faulkner, *As I Lay Dying*.

Dorothy Canfield Fisher, *The Deepening Stream*.

Robert Frost, *Collected Poems*.

Elizabeth Madox Roberts, *The Great Meadow*.